Generative AI and Implications for Ethics, Security, and Data Management

Jeganathan Gomathi Sankar
BSSS Institute of Advanced Studies, India

Arokiaraj David
Al Tareeqah Management Studies, Swiss Business School, UAE

A volume in the Advances in Computational Intelligence and Robotics (ACIR) Book Series

IGI Global
Publishing Tomorrow's Research Today

Published in the United States of America by
IGI Global
Engineering Science Reference (an imprint of IGI Global)
701 E. Chocolate Avenue
Hershey PA, USA 17033
Tel: 717-533-8845
Fax: 717-533-8661
E-mail: cust@igi-global.com
Web site: http://www.igi-global.com

Library of Congress Cataloging-in-Publication Data

CIP DATA PENDING

ISBN: 9798369385579
Isbn: 9798369385586
eISBN: 9798369385593

British Cataloguing in Publication Data
A Cataloguing in Publication record for this book is available from the British Library.

For electronic access to this publication, please contact: eresources@igi-global.com.

Table of Contents

Detailed Table of Contents

The chapter serves as an intricate exploration into the domain of Generative AI, offering a comprehensive understanding of its fundamental principles, diverse methodologies, and wide-ranging applications. Beginning with a clear definition and overview, it progresses to clarify key concepts such as probability distributions and sampling while providing an overview of various generative models, including autoregressive models, variational autoencoders, and generative adversarial networks. Architectural components, training methods, and optimization techniques are thoroughly examined, alongside an in-depth analysis of challenges and considerations in model design and selection. Through real-world examples, the chapter showcases the transformative potential of Generative AI across domains such as image generation, text processing, music composition, creative arts, etc. Addressing current limitations and outlining future directions offers valuable insights into the growing landscape of Generative AI, positioning it as a catalyst for innovation and creative expression.

For nearly 50 years, artificial intelligence (AI) has been a technology and a field of study. Its advancement had been conflicting and differed after some time. Due to the development of intriguing AI applications like Alpha Go and Alpha Fold, large data sets, advancements in the internet and semiconductors, the most significant development in machine learning and deep learning occurred in the 2000s. Generative AI models have recently gained a lot of popularity. AI has become a household name thanks to massive language models like GPT (generative pre-trained transformer) and tools like Midjourney and ChatGPT. Microsoft and Google have been incorporating these models into their enterprise and search offerings as generative AI has had a significant impact on everyday life. The part dug into the potential outcomes and difficulties related to the condition of generative computer-based intelligence around then and investigated its future. Additionally, it offered recommendations for generative AI-using businesses.

In today's cybernetic world, Generative AI (Gen AI) and Natural Language Processing (NLP) made a vibrant change in the technology. Intertwine between Generative AI and NLP creates a different angle that comes to light. NLP algorithms enhanced by Generative AI not only understands the language but also generates human-like responses, opening doors to more nuanced and context-aware interactions. This chapter focuses on two specific dimensions such as language generation and multilingual capability. Large Language Models (LLMs) are considered as a foundational element or backbone for generating texts. Thereby, prompting LLM is a crucial element for generating the desired text. The main aim of this chapter is to explore importance of prompting LLM, various prompting techniques used for interacting with LLM and the frameworks available for accessing the LLM, and issues involved in prompting LLM and their challenges and future directions will also be discussed.

This study provides a comprehensive view of the state of generative AI today, touching on its uses, foundational models, obstacles, prospects, and potential future courses of action. Autoregressive models like Transformers, GANs, and Variational Autoencoders (VAEs) are the backbone of generative AI. Generated AI still has a way to go before fully realizing its potential. Problems with model interpretability, training stability, and generated content bias are all examples of such challenges. Computer scientists, psychologists, and ethicists must work together to find solutions to these problems. Generative AI does, however, offer tremendous potential. Artists, designers, and storytellers have new tools at their fingertips. Improving the robustness of models, granting greater control over generated outputs, and investigating uses in interactive storytelling and real-time content production are all potential future areas for generative AI.

The chapter examines the ethical landscape of AI, focusing on the development and deployment of Responsible AI systems. The increased deployment of systems powered by artificial intelligence technologies necessitates making work more predictable, trustworthy, and ethical. The development and deployment of such systems require the use of Responsible AI. A healthcare system, for example, is a classic system where AI is used in healthcare collaborations and decision-making. Studying the ethical landscape of AI allows us to understand the historical context and evolution of AI Ethics and the challenges and risks associated with such systems. Ethical frameworks examines the six AI assurance goals, the existing ethical frameworks and guidelines, and the core principles behind them. Future challenges and considerations for further research that emerge because of evolving concerns and potential misuse of AI systems are discussed.

Artificial intelligence (AI) and territorial intelligence (TI) are currently two key fields. AI enables the development of systems capable of performing tasks that generally require human intelligence, such as pattern recognition, classification, and prediction. Business intelligence applied to territories is at the heart of research into sustainable territorial development, as part of the paradigm of intelligent territories. So how can digital technology be used to develop territorial intelligence and help improve the digital sovereignty of regions? The study traces the many challenges posed by the application of AI and IT in real-life scenarios and identifies opportunities for combining the two fields via a hybrid approach aimed at decision-making in digital territorial management.

The intersection of cybersecurity and generative artificial intelligence (AI) has become a crucial frontier as the digital landscape changes. By examining the interaction between AI-powered attacks and defence mechanisms and concentrating on applications like anomaly detection, synthetic data generation, automated incident response, and forensics, the chapter examines the potential of generative artificial intelligence (AI) in redefining conventional cybersecurity paradigms. In order to reduce the hazards associated with deepfakes and synthetic media, the chapter discusses the examination of adversarial machine learning techniques and strategies. Along with offering guidance on incorporating AI into security operations, encouraging human-AI cooperation, and building strong AI skills, it also discusses the ethical ramifications of AI-driven security procedures. It also serves as a comprehensive guide for security professionals, researchers, and decision-makers, offering a holistic understanding of the synergies between AI and cybersecurity.

This chapter explores the burgeoning role of generative artificial intelligence (AI) in the realm of cybersecurity. As our digital world expands, so do the threats posed by malicious actors. In response, the emergence of generative AI technologies presents a promising avenue for bolstering cybersecurity defenses. This chapter examines the various applications of generative AI in fortifying digital security, including its use in threat detection, anomaly identification, and vulnerability assessment. By harnessing the power of machine learning and neural networks, generative AI systems exhibit remarkable capabilities in predicting, pre-empting, and mitigating cyber threats. Moreover, this chapter delves into the ethical considerations and potential challenges associated with deploying generative AI in cybersecurity contexts, emphasizing the importance of responsible development and deployment practices. Ultimately, this exploration highlights the pivotal role of generative AI as guardians of the digital realm, ushering in a new era of enhanced cybersecurity measures.

As the demand for efficient and scalable data storage solutions continues to rise, the integration of artificial intelligence (AI) technologies with cloud storage systems has emerged as a promising avenue for innovation. This chapter explores the intersection of AI and cloud storage, investigating how AI-driven approaches are revolutionizing traditional cloud storage practices and unlocking new opportunities for enhanced performance and functionality. Through a comprehensive review of literature and case studies, this study examines the role of AI in optimizing data management, improving security measures, and enabling intelligent data processing within cloud storage environments. Furthermore, this chapter delves into the implications of AI-driven innovation for businesses and organizations, highlighting the potential benefits of increased efficiency, cost savings, and competitive advantage.

This chapter examined the utilization of GeoAI for healthcare issues like patient demographics, socio-economic factors, health insurance coverage, and environmental conditions to enhance healthcare delivery. By analyzing population density and socio-economic data, GeoAI can optimize the placement of healthcare facilities and resources, ensuring equitable access. Environmental data, such as air and water quality, can identify regions at risk for specific health issues, guiding targeted interventions. GeoAI can address healthcare disparities by considering social determinants of health and enabling personalized treatment plans. Integrating high-quality, timely, and relevant geospatial data can allow GeoAI to facilitate accurate decision-making and resource allocation, improving patient outcomes and public health strategies. However, challenges include ensuring data privacy and security, managing technical and operational integration complexities, and requiring specialized expertise, which can be overcome with robust data governance and interdisciplinary collaboration.

Preface

Generative AI and Implications for Ethics, Security, and Data Management explores the profound impact of artificial intelligence (AI) on the landscape of modern management. This book serves as a beacon, guiding readers through the intersection of cutting-edge generative AI and visionary leadership, and offering insights into how these technologies can redefine traditional management paradigms. The potential of generative AI becomes a catalyst for organizational transformation, empowering leaders to make proactive decisions, foster innovation, and navigate the complexities of the digital age.

In this comprehensive exploration, we delve into the symbiotic relationship between generative AI and transformational management. We present real-world applications, case studies, and thought-provoking discussions aiming to provide a holistic understanding of how AI, particularly generative AI, can be integrated into leadership practices to drive transformative outcomes. By bridging the gap between generative AI and leadership, we offer a synthesis of these two domains, demonstrating how organizations have successfully implemented generative AI through tangible examples of transformative practices.

A critical aspect of this book is addressing the responsibility that comes with deploying AI. We explore ethical frameworks and considerations, providing insights into how leaders can navigate the ethical dimensions of AI-driven decision-making. Through discussions, reflections, and practical exercises, we aim to create an engaging and interactive learning experience for readers. This approach ensures that readers not only understand the concepts but also apply them in practical scenarios.

Anticipating future trends and innovations, we provide forward-looking perspectives on the evolving landscape of AI. By doing so, we add a predictive dimension to current research, helping readers stay abreast of emerging developments. Our goal is to build a knowledge base that consolidates current research while laying the groundwork for future investigations in this dynamic field.

This book is designed to support academics, post-graduate students, and researchers working in the field of AI. Additionally, it offers insights and support for those involved in research supervision, ensuring a comprehensive understanding of the intersection between AI and transformative leadership. Welcome to a captivating journey through the realms of *Generative AI and Implications for Ethics, Security, and Data Management.*

ORGANIZATION OF THE BOOK

Chapter 1: An Introduction to Generative AI: Crafting Worlds From Code

This chapter serves as an intricate exploration into the domain of Generative AI, offering a comprehensive understanding of its fundamental principles, diverse methodologies, and wide-ranging applications. Beginning with a clear definition and overview, it progresses to clarify key concepts such as probability distributions and sampling while providing an overview of various generative models, including autoregressive models, variational autoencoders, and generative adversarial networks. Architectural components, training methods, and optimization techniques are thoroughly examined, alongside an in-depth analysis of challenges and considerations in model design and selection. Through real-world examples, the chapter showcases the transformative potential of Generative AI across domains such as image generation, text processing, music composition, and creative arts. Addressing current limitations and outlining future directions offers valuable insights into the growing landscape of Generative AI, positioning it as a catalyst for innovation and creative expression.

Chapter 2: Generative AI: The Impact, Possibilities, and Difficulties

For nearly 50 years, artificial intelligence (AI) has been a technology and a field of study, advancing unevenly over time. This chapter delves into the impact, possibilities, and difficulties of generative AI, which gained popularity through applications like Alpha Go and Alpha Fold, and large language models like GPT. The chapter explores how generative AI has permeated everyday life, impacting enterprises and search functionalities by companies like Microsoft and Google. The discussion extends to future potential outcomes and challenges associated with generative AI and offers recommendations for businesses integrating these technologies.

Chapter 3: Unleashing Creativity in Natural Language: An Overview of Prompting Techniques Used in Large Language Models

Generative AI and Natural Language Processing (NLP) have significantly changed technology, enabling nuanced and context-aware interactions. This chapter focuses on language generation and multilingual capabilities enhanced by Generative AI. It explores the importance of prompting Large Language Models (LLMs), various prompting techniques, frameworks for accessing LLMs, and the associated challenges. The chapter provides insights into current issues and future directions in prompting LLMs, highlighting their potential to revolutionize human-computer interaction.

Chapter 4: Generative AI Applications, Models, Challenges, Opportunities, and Future Directions

This chapter provides a comprehensive view of the current state of generative AI, discussing its uses, foundational models, obstacles, prospects, and future directions. It covers autoregressive models like Transformers, GANs, and Variational Autoencoders (VAEs) and addresses challenges such as model interpretability, training stability, and content bias. Collaboration between computer scientists, psychologists, and ethicists is emphasized to overcome these challenges. The chapter also explores the potential of generative AI in creative fields and future improvements in model robustness and control over generated outputs.

Chapter 5: Ethical Frameworks for Use in Artificial Intelligence Systems

The chapter examines the ethical landscape of AI, focusing on the development and deployment of Responsible AI systems to ensure work is predictable, trustworthy, and ethical. It discusses the ethical frameworks and guidelines for AI, highlighting the six AI Assurance Goals. The chapter uses the example of healthcare systems to illustrate AI's role in decision-making and collaborations. Future challenges and considerations for further research on AI's ethical implications are also discussed, emphasizing the need for responsible AI development.

Chapter 6: Ethical Considerations for Generative AI in Social Science Research

This chapter addresses the ethical considerations of using generative AI in social science research, focusing on qualitative, quantitative, and mixed methods research designs. It discusses the potential for research misconduct and unethical practices with the widespread use of generative AI technologies like ChatGPT. The chapter highlights the lack of tools for journal reviewers, editors, and publishers to differentiate between human-written and AI-authored manuscripts, emphasizing the need for ethical guidelines and responsible behavior from researchers.

Chapter 7: Harmonizing Ethics with Artificial Intelligence: A Compassionate Path to Technological Advancement

This chapter highlights the critical connection between AI and ethics, emphasizing the need to align AI with human values. It provides a comprehensive understanding of AI's ethical implications through a systematic literature review. The chapter offers practical tools for AI developers to navigate ethical dimensions and promotes ethically sound practices in AI development. It explores societal concerns requiring ethical decision-making and advocates for a compassionate approach to AI development to safeguard humanity's interests.

Chapter 8: AI-Driven Territorial Intelligence: An Integrated Approach to Enhancing Digital Sovereignty

This chapter explores the intersection of AI and Territorial Intelligence (TI), focusing on sustainable territorial development and digital sovereignty. It discusses the challenges and opportunities of applying AI and IT in real-life scenarios and identifies a hybrid approach to decision-making in digital territorial management. The chapter highlights the potential of combining AI and TI to enhance regional development and improve digital sovereignty.

Chapter 9: Generative AI for Cybersecurity: An Introduction

This chapter examines the intersection of cybersecurity and generative AI, focusing on applications such as anomaly detection, synthetic data generation, automated incident response, and forensics. It discusses AI-powered attacks and defense mechanisms, adversarial machine learning techniques, and strategies to mitigate risks associated with deepfakes and synthetic media. The chapter also addresses the ethical implications of AI-driven security procedures and offers guidance for incorporating AI into security operations, emphasizing human-AI cooperation.

Chapter 10: Guardians of the Digital Realm: Generative AI's Role in Cybersecurity

This chapter explores the role of generative AI in enhancing cybersecurity. It examines applications of generative AI in threat detection, anomaly identification, and vulnerability assessment, highlighting the technology's potential to predict, preempt, and mitigate cyber threats. Ethical considerations and challenges associated with deploying generative AI in cybersecurity contexts are discussed, emphasizing the importance of responsible development and deployment practices. The chapter underscores generative AI's pivotal role in ushering in a new era of enhanced cybersecurity measures.

Chapter 11: Innovations in Cloud Storage: Leveraging Generative AI for Enhanced Data Management

This chapter explores the integration of AI technologies with cloud storage systems, investigating how AI-driven approaches revolutionize traditional cloud storage practices. It examines the role of AI in optimizing data management, improving security measures, and enabling intelligent data processing within cloud storage environments. The chapter highlights the implications of AI-driven innovation for businesses and organizations, emphasizing potential benefits such as increased efficiency, cost savings, and competitive advantage.

Chapter 12: From Data to Insights: Harnessing GeoAI for Informed Decision-Making in Healthcare

This chapter examines the utilization of GeoAI in addressing healthcare issues such as patient demographics, socio-economic factors, health insurance coverage, and environmental conditions. It explores how GeoAI can optimize the placement of healthcare facilities and resources, ensuring equitable access and guiding targeted interventions. The chapter addresses challenges such as data privacy and security, technical and operational integration complexities, and the need for specialized expertise. It advocates for robust data governance and interdisciplinary collaboration to overcome these challenges and enhance healthcare delivery.

CONCLUSION

In conclusion, this edited reference book on generative AI represents a comprehensive exploration into one of the most transformative and dynamic fields in contemporary technology. Through the collaborative efforts of distinguished scholars and industry experts from around the globe, each chapter delves into the multifaceted dimensions of generative AI, providing in-depth analyses, practical applications, and forward-looking perspectives.

Chapter by chapter, our contributors have meticulously unpacked the intricate frameworks, methodologies, and models that form the bedrock of generative AI. Beginning with a solid foundation in the fundamental principles and advancing through nuanced discussions on prompting techniques, ethical frameworks, and innovative applications, this compendium offers a well-rounded understanding of both the theoretical underpinnings and practical implications of generative AI.

The exploration of generative AI's potential across various domains, from cybersecurity to cloud storage and healthcare, underscores its far-reaching impact and versatility. As highlighted, the intersection of AI with natural language processing, territorial intelligence, and cybersecurity demonstrates the capability of AI to revolutionize industries and reshape our digital landscape. Yet, this potential is tempered by the pressing need to address ethical considerations, ensuring responsible and transparent deployment of AI technologies.

As editors, we believe this collection not only sheds light on the current state of generative AI but also paves the way for future research and innovation. The diverse perspectives and insights presented herein aim to equip researchers, practitioners, and policymakers with the knowledge needed to navigate the challenges and seize the opportunities presented by generative AI. In doing so, we aspire to contribute to the ongoing dialogue on AI's role in fostering creativity, enhancing security, and driving societal progress.

Ultimately, this book is a testament to the collaborative spirit of the AI community and its unwavering commitment to advancing knowledge and innovation. We hope it serves as a valuable resource and inspiration for all those engaged in the exciting journey of exploring and harnessing the power of generative AI.

Jeganathan Gomathi Sankar
BSSS Institute of Advanced Studies, India

Arokiaraj David
Al Tareeqah Management Studies, Swiss Business School, UAE

Acknowledgment

We extend our profound gratitude to all those who played a role in the creation of this edited book.

First and foremost, we wish to thank our contributing authors. Your insightful research and dedication to excellence have greatly enriched this volume. Your efforts are the cornerstone of this book's success.

We are also very appreciative of our reviewers. Your constructive critiques and meticulous attention to detail have significantly improved the quality of this work.

We are especially thankful to our publisher, IGI Global, for their steadfast support throughout the publication process. A special thanks to Nina Eddinger, Assistant Development Editor for IGI Global, whose expertise and guidance have been crucial.

We owe a debt of gratitude to our families and friends for their patience, understanding, and unwavering support during this endeavor. Your encouragement has been an invaluable source of strength.

Lastly, we acknowledge our readers. We hope that the insights and knowledge contained within these pages will inspire and inform your work in the field of Generative AI.

Thank you all for your contributions and support.

Chapter 1

An Introduction to Generative AI: Crafting Worlds From Code

Arokiaraj David
https://orcid.org/0000-0002-9591-2410
Al Tareeqah Management Studies, Swiss Business School, UAE

Jeganathan Gomathi Sankar
https://orcid.org/0000-0002-5077-5109
BSSS Institute of Advanced Studies, India

C. Ganeshkumar
https://orcid.org/0000-0002-0913-2849
Indian Institute Foreign Trade, India

Mohammad Kashif
https://orcid.org/0000-0002-4940-8264
Graphic Era University (Deemed), India

ABSTRACT

The chapter serves as an intricate exploration into the domain of Generative AI, offering a comprehensive understanding of its fundamental principles, diverse methodologies, and wide-ranging applications. Beginning with a clear definition and overview, it progresses to clarify key concepts such as probability distributions and sampling while providing an overview of various generative models, including autoregressive models, variational autoencoders, and generative adversarial networks. Architectural components, training methods, and optimization techniques are thoroughly examined, alongside an in-depth analysis of challenges and considerations in model design and selection. Through real-world examples, the chapter

DOI: 10.4018/979-8-3693-8557-9.ch001

showcases the transformative potential of Generative AI across domains such as image generation, text processing, music composition, creative arts, etc. Addressing current limitations and outlining future directions offers valuable insights into the growing landscape of Generative AI, positioning it as a catalyst for innovation and creative expression.

1. INTRODUCTION TO GENERATIVE AI

1.1 Overview and Definition of Generative AI

Generative Artificial Intelligence (Generative AI) represents a paradigm shift in the field of Artificial Intelligence (AI), introducing the remarkable ability for machines to autonomously produce original and meaningful content (Kenwright, 2023). Unlike traditional AI approaches that primarily handle tasks like classification and prediction, Generative AI is fundamentally about creating new data samples that closely resemble those from a given dataset. The branch of AI encompasses a diverse array of algorithms and methodologies, including but not limited to Generative Adversarial Networks (GANs), Variational Autoencoders (VAEs), and autoregressive models (Vyas & Priya, 2023). At its core, Generative AI leverages sophisticated mathematical frameworks to generate images, text, music, and other forms of content, often indistinguishable from human-created counterparts. This introductory section aims to provide readers with a comprehensive understanding of the foundational principles that underpin Generative AI, elucidating its significance and transformative potential across various domains (Jiang, 2023).

Generative AI can be defined as encompassing deep-learning models capable of producing high-quality text, images, and diverse content derived from the datasets on which they were trained. Generative AI is a machine-learning model trained to generate new data, focusing on creating content rather than predicting specific outcomes within a dataset. Essentially, a generative AI system learns to produce additional objects resembling the data it was trained on (Amankwah-Amoah et al., 2024; Chimbga, 2023).

1.2 Importance and Applications in Various Domains

Generative AI holds profound importance and boasts a plethora of applications across a diverse spectrum of domains, each showcasing its remarkable versatility and efficacy (Yu et al., 2023; Wadood, 2024). In the realm of entertainment and media, Generative AI serves as a catalyst for innovation, enabling the creation of immersive virtual environments, lifelike characters, and dynamic storytelling experiences. Additionally, it revolutionizes the creative process within art and design by offering novel tools for generating visually stunning graphics, sculptures, and digital artworks (Sipahioglu, 2024). In the field of healthcare, Generative AI plays a pivotal role in medical imaging analysis, drug discovery, and personalized treatment regimens, thereby enhancing patient care and outcomes (Saluja et al., 2024; Ravi et al., 2018; Huang et al., 2023). Financial institutions leverage Generative AI for fraud detection, risk assessment, and algorithmic trading, bolstering operational efficiency and mitigating financial risks. Moreover, in the domain of natural language processing, Generative AI facilitates the generation of coherent and contextually relevant text, thereby advancing conversational agents, language translation, and content generation platforms (Michelucci, 2019). As such, Generative AI stands at the forefront of innovation, driving transformative change and unlocking unprecedented possibilities across various sectors (David et al., 2022; Ch'ng, 2024).

2. FUNDAMENTALS OF GENERATIVE MODELS

Generative models are at the heart of Generative AI, facilitating the creation of new data samples that closely resemble those from a given dataset. In this section, we delve into the fundamental concepts that underpin generative models, providing insights into probability distributions and sampling techniques (Sudhakar et al., 2017; Madaan et al., 2021; Pratheepkumar et al., 2017). Additionally, we offer an overview of different types of generative models, including autoregressive models, variational autoencoders, and Generative Adversarial Networks (GANs), elucidating their distinctive features and applications.

2.1 Explanation of Key Concepts

2.1.1 Probability Distributions

Probability distributions form the cornerstone of generative modelling, serving as mathematical representations of the likelihood of various outcomes. In the context of Generative AI, probability distributions define the range of possible values that a generated sample can assume. Common probability distributions used in generative modelling include Gaussian (normal), Bernoulli, and categorical distributions (Ganeshkumar et al., 2022; Thummula et al., 2019). These distributions play a crucial role in generating realistic and diverse samples by capturing the underlying patterns and characteristics of the data (Latha et al., 2020).

2.1.2 Sampling Techniques

Sampling techniques are employed to generate data samples from probability distributions, enabling the creation of new instances that mimic the characteristics of the original dataset. Monte Carlo methods, such as Markov Chain Monte Carlo (MCMC) and importance sampling, are frequently utilized for sampling from complex probability distributions (Srivastava et al., 2022). Additionally, techniques like Gibbs sampling and the Metropolis-Hastings algorithm offer efficient ways to sample from high-dimensional spaces (Ganeshkumar et al., 2023). Sampling plays a pivotal role in generative modelling, allowing for the exploration of diverse data distributions and the generation of novel and realistic samples (Jeganathan et al., 2022; Sankar et al., 2023).

2.2 Overview of Different Types of Generative Models

2.2.1 Autoregressive Models

Autoregressive models are a class of generative models that predict the probability distribution of the next data point given the previous observations. These models assume a sequential dependency structure, where each data point is generated based on a conditional distribution conditioned on the preceding observations (David et al., 2023). Notable examples of autoregressive models include PixelCNN and WaveNet, which are widely used for generating images and audio signals, respectively. Autoregressive models offer flexibility and scalability, making them suitable for a wide range of generative tasks.

2.2.2 Variational Autoencoders (VAEs)

Variational Autoencoders (VAEs) are probabilistic generative models that learn to encode and decode data samples in a latent space. VAEs consist of an encoder network that maps input data to a latent space and a decoder network that reconstructs the input data from the latent representations. By optimizing a variational lower bound on the likelihood of the data, VAEs learn a continuous and structured latent space that captures the underlying data distribution (Feuerriegel et al., 2024). VAEs are widely used for tasks such as image generation, anomaly detection, and data imputation.

2.2.3 Generative Adversarial Networks (GANs)

Generative adversarial networks (GANs) are a class of generative models that learn to generate data samples by pitting two neural networks against each other in a game-theoretic framework. GANs consist of a generator network that produces fake samples and a discriminator network that distinguishes between real and fake samples. Through an adversarial training process, the generator learns to generate increasingly realistic samples that fool the discriminator while the discriminator improves its ability to distinguish between real and fake samples (Kashif et al., 2024). GANs have demonstrated remarkable success in generating high-resolution images, synthesizing realistic textures, and generating data samples across various domains. The generative models encompass a diverse range of methodologies and techniques aimed at developing new data samples that closely resemble those from a given dataset (Hacker et al., 2023). By leveraging probability distributions, sampling techniques, and advanced modelling architectures, generative models have emerged as powerful tools for creative expression, data generation, and problem-solving in numerous domains.

3. BUILDING BLOCKS OF GENERATIVE MODELS

Generative models serve as the cornerstone of Generative AI, enabling the creation of new data samples that closely resemble those from a given dataset. In this section, we delve into the building blocks of generative models, providing insights into their architecture, components, training methods, and optimization techniques, as well as challenges and considerations in model design and selection.

3.1 Architecture and Components of Common Generative Models

Generative models exhibit diverse architectural designs and components, each tailored to the specific task at hand. One common architecture is the encoder-decoder framework, utilized in VAEs. In VAEs, the encoder network maps input data to a latent space while the decoder network reconstructs the input data from the latent representations. Another prevalent architecture is the generator-discriminator framework, employed in GANs. GANs comprise a generator network that generates fake samples and a discriminator network that distinguishes between real and fake samples. Other architectures include autoregressive models, where each data point is generated sequentially based on a conditional distribution, and flow-based models, which model complex probability distributions through invertible transformations

(Brynjolfsson et al., 2023). The choice of architecture depends on factors such as the nature of the data, computational resources, and the desired output quality.

3.2 Training Methods and Optimization Techniques

Training generative models involve optimizing parameters to minimize a loss function that quantifies the discrepancy between generated samples and real data. Common training methods include Maximum Likelihood Estimation (MLE), which maximizes the likelihood of generating observed data, and adversarial training, which pits a generator against a discriminator in a minimax game. Additionally, variational inference techniques, such as variational Bayes and Expectation-Maximization (EM), are utilized in variational autoencoders to approximate intractable posterior distributions. Optimization techniques such as Stochastic Gradient Descent (SGD) and its variants, including Adam and RMSprop, are employed to update model parameters efficiently (Frey & Osborne, 2023). Furthermore, regularization methods such as weight decay and dropout are applied to prevent overfitting and improve generalization performance. The choice of training method and optimization technique depends on factors such as the model architecture, dataset size, and computational constraints.

3.3 Challenges and Considerations in Model Design and Selection

Designing and selecting appropriate generative models pose several challenges and considerations. One challenge is mode collapse, where the generator of a GAN learns to produce a limited set of samples, leading to poor sample diversity. Mode collapse can be mitigated through architectural modifications, regularization techniques, and training strategies such as curriculum learning and progressive growth. Another challenge is the evaluation of generative models, as traditional metrics such as log-likelihood and perplexity may correlate poorly with human perception. Alternative evaluation metrics, such as Fréchet Inception Distance (FID) and Inception Score (IS), have been proposed to assess the quality and diversity of generated samples (Fui-Hoon Nah et al., 2023).

Furthermore, selecting the appropriate model architecture requires balancing considerations such as expressiveness, scalability, and computational efficiency. Recent advances in deep learning, including attention mechanisms, self-attention, and transformers, have led to significant improvements in generative model performance across various domains. However, designing effective architectures requires careful consideration of factors such as model capacity, parameter sharing, and computational complexity (Alasadi & Baiz, 2023). Overall, addressing these challenges and concerns is essential for developing generative models that are robust, scalable, and capable of generating high-quality samples across diverse datasets and domains.

The building blocks of generative models encompass architectural designs, components, training methods, optimization techniques, and considerations in model design and selection. By leveraging these building blocks effectively, researchers and practitioners can develop generative models that push the boundaries of creativity, innovation, and problem-solving in artificial intelligence (Kumar et al., 2023).

4. APPLICATIONS OF GENERATIVE AI

Generative Artificial Intelligence has witnessed a surge in applications across various domains, leveraging its ability to create original and meaningful content autonomously. In this section, we explore the diverse applications of Generative AI, spanning image generation and manipulation, text generation and natural language processing, music and audio generation, as well as creative applications in art and design.

4.1 Image Generation and Manipulation

Generative AI has revolutionized the field of image generation and manipulation, enabling the creation of photorealistic images and artistic visuals. One notable application is the generation of high-resolution images using GANs. GANs have been utilized to generate realistic human faces, landscapes, and even entire scenes, showcasing their potential in creative content generation (Chen & Esmaeilzadeh, 2024). Moreover, GANs can be employed for image-to-image translation tasks, such as converting sketches into photographs or enhancing low-resolution images. Style transfer techniques, inspired by neural style transfer algorithms, enable users to apply artistic styles to pictures, creating visually stunning compositions. Furthermore, image inpainting algorithms leverage generative models to fill in missing or damaged portions of images seamlessly, with applications in photo restoration and editing.

4.2 Text Generation and Natural Language Processing

Generative AI has made significant strides in text generation and natural language processing, facilitating the creation of coherent and contextually relevant textual content. One prominent application is the generation of human-like text using Recurrent Neural Networks (RNNs) and transformers (David et al., 2022). These models can generate realistic text passages, stories, and even poetry, mimicking the style and tone of human authors (David et al., 2023). Furthermore, text summarization algorithms leverage generative models to condense lengthy documents into concise summaries, aiding in information retrieval and content analysis. Additionally, chatbots and virtual assistants powered by generative AI enable human-like conversations and interactions, enhancing customer service and user engagement across various platforms (David et al., 2022).

4.3 Music and Audio Generation

Generative AI has also made significant strides in the domain of music and audio generation, facilitating the creation of original compositions and soundscapes. One notable application is the generation of music using RNNs and GANs. These models can compose melodies, harmonies, and entire musical pieces across various genres and styles. Additionally, generative models can be employed for audio synthesis tasks, such as speech synthesis and sound effects generation. Voice cloning algorithms utilize generative models to replicate human voices, enabling personalized speech synthesis for voice assistants and audiobooks (David et al., 2022). Furthermore, audio generation techniques inspired by deep learning architectures allow the creation of realistic soundscapes and immersive auditory experiences in virtual reality and gaming applications.

4.4 Creative Applications in Art and Design

Generative AI has emerged as a powerful tool for creative expression and innovation in the fields of art and design. Artists and designers leverage generative models to generate novel visual aesthetics, explore unconventional design concepts, and push the boundaries of traditional art forms. Style transfer algorithms enable artists to apply artistic styles to photographs and videos, creating unique visual compositions (David et al., 2022). Moreover, generative design techniques facilitate the creation of complex geometries and structures with applications in architecture, fashion design, and product design. Additionally, interactive generative art installations engage audiences in immersive and participatory experiences, blurring the lines between creator and spectator. Overall, generative AI empowers artists and designers to explore new creative territories, inspire audiences, and redefine the boundaries of artistic expression.

Generative AI offers a myriad of applications across diverse domains, including image generation and manipulation, text generation and natural language processing, music and audio generation, as well as creative applications in art and design. By harnessing the power of generative models, researchers, practitioners, and artists can unlock new avenues for creativity, innovation, and expression in the digital age.

5. CHALLENGES AND FUTURE DIRECTIONS

Generative Artificial Intelligence has emerged as a transformative force, empowering machines to create content that is original and meaningful autonomously. However, despite its rapid progress and remarkable achievements, Generative AI still faces various challenges and limitations. In this section, we explore the current constraints of generative models, identify areas for improvement and ongoing research efforts, and speculate on future trends and emerging technologies that hold the potential to shape the landscape of Generative AI.

5.1 Limitations and Challenges of Current Generative Models

While generative models have demonstrated impressive capabilities, they have limitations and challenges. One significant challenge is mode collapse in GANs, where the generator produces a limited set of samples, leading to poor sample diversity. Mode collapse hampers the ability of GANs to capture the full complexity of the data distribution, resulting in generated samples that lack variability and realism. Moreover, generative models may need help with generating realistic long-range dependencies in sequences, such as in natural language generation tasks. Existing models may produce outputs that need coherence and structure, posing challenges in generating contextually relevant and grammatically correct text. Additionally, evaluating the quality and diversity of generated samples is a challenging task. Traditional metrics such as log-likelihood and perplexity may not capture the nuances of human perception accurately, necessitating the development of novel evaluation metrics that align with human judgment.

5.2 Areas for Improvement and Ongoing Research Efforts

Addressing the limitations of current generative models requires concerted research efforts in several key areas. One area of focus is improving sample diversity and reducing mode collapse in GANs. Researchers are exploring novel architectural designs, training strategies, and regularization techniques to encourage the generation of diverse and realistic samples. Techniques such as spectral normalization, feature matching, and gradient penalties have shown promise in mitigating mode collapse and improving sample quality. Moreover, enhancing the ability of generative models to capture long-range dependencies in sequences is crucial for generating coherent and contextually relevant text. Attention mechanisms, memory-augmented architectures, and transformer-based models have been proposed to address this challenge, enabling generative models to produce more structured and grammatically correct outputs. Additionally, developing robust evaluation metrics that align with human perception is essential for assessing the quality and realism of generated samples accurately. Researchers are exploring perceptual metrics, adversarial evaluation methods, and human evaluation studies to evaluate the fidelity and diversity of generative models effectively (Alasadi et al., 2023).

5.3 Future Trends and Emerging Technologies in the Field of Generative AI

Looking ahead, the field of Generative AI is poised for significant advancements and innovations. One emerging trend is the integration of Generative AI with reinforcement learning techniques. By combining generative models with reinforcement learning algorithms, researchers aim to develop agents that can generate content dynamically in interactive environments (Kenwright, 2023). This integration opens up new possibilities for applications such as interactive storytelling, content creation in video games, and personalized recommendation systems. Moreover, advancements in unsupervised and self-supervised learning paradigms are expected to enhance the robustness and generalization capabilities of generative models (Frey et al., 2023). Techniques such as contrastive learning, momentum contrast, and self-supervised pretraining enable generative models to learn rich representations from unlabeled data, improving their performance on downstream tasks. The convergence of Generative AI with other emerging technologies, such as Augmented Reality (AR) and blockchain, has the potential to revolutionize content creation, distribution, and ownership in the digital ecosystem. AR applications powered by generative models enable immersive and interactive experiences, blurring the boundaries between the physical and virtual worlds (Kenwright, 2023). Furthermore, blockchain technology facilitates secure and transparent transactions for digital assets generated by generative models, enabling creators to monetize their creations and maintain ownership rights in decentralized marketplaces.

Generative AI holds immense potential for transforming various industries and reshaping human-machine interactions. While current generative models face challenges and limitations, ongoing research efforts and future directions promise to unlock new possibilities and drive innovation in the field of Generative AI (Frey et al., 2023). By addressing these challenges and embracing emerging technologies, researchers and practitioners can harness the full potential of Generative AI to create, innovate, and inspire in the digital age.

6. CONCLUSION

Generative Artificial Intelligence (Generative AI) stands are at the forefront of innovation, offering unprecedented capabilities in autonomously creating original and meaningful content. Throughout this chapter, we have explored the foundational principles, diverse applications, challenges, and future directions of Generative AI. In this concluding section, we provide a summary of key concepts and insights gleaned from our discussion, followed by reflections on the transformative potential of Generative AI.

6.1 Summary of Key Concepts and Insights

Generative AI encompasses a diverse array of algorithms and methodologies aimed at generating new data samples that closely resemble those from a given dataset. We began by examining the fundamental concepts underlying generative models, including probability distributions, sampling techniques, and architectural designs. We then explored the applications of Generative AI across various domains, such as image generation and manipulation, text generation and natural language processing, music and audio generation, and creative applications in art and design. Generative models have demonstrated remarkable capabilities in generating photorealistic images, coherent text passages, original compositions, and immersive visual experiences, revolutionizing industries and inspiring creative expression.

Despite its successes, Generative AI faces challenges and limitations, including mode collapse in GANs, difficulty in generating long-range dependencies in sequences, and the need for robust evaluation metrics. Researchers are actively addressing these challenges through advancements in architectural design, training strategies, and evaluation methodologies. Moreover, future trends and emerging technologies such as reinforcement learning integration, unsupervised learning paradigms, and blockchain integration hold the promise of unlocking new possibilities and driving innovation in the field.

6.2 Reflections on the Transformative Potential of Generative AI

Generative AI holds immense transformative potential across various domains, revolutionizing industries, enhancing creativity, and reshaping human-machine interactions (David et al., 2023). By empowering machines to create original and meaningful content autonomously, Generative AI unlocks new avenues for innovation and expression. In the realm of entertainment and media, Generative AI enables immersive virtual experiences, lifelike character animations, and dynamic storytelling. In healthcare, it aids in medical image analysis, drug discovery, and personalized treatment regimens, improving patient care and outcomes. Financial institutions leverage Generative AI for fraud detection, risk assessment, and algorithmic trading, enhancing operational efficiency and mitigating financial risks. Moreover, in the field of natural language processing, Generative AI facilitates the generation of coherent and contextually relevant text, enabling human-like conversations and interactions.

Generative AI also fuels creativity and innovation in art and design, empowering artists and designers to explore new creative territories and push the boundaries of traditional art forms. Style transfer algorithms enable artists to apply artistic styles to photographs and videos, creating visually captivating compositions. Generative design techniques facilitate the creation of complex geometries and structures with applications in architecture, fashion design, and product design. Additionally, interactive generative art installations engage audiences in immersive and participatory experiences, fostering new forms of artistic expression.

In conclusion, Generative AI represents a paradigm shift in the capabilities of artificial intelligence, offering unprecedented opportunities for innovation, creativity, and collaboration. By harnessing the transformative potential of Generative AI, researchers, practitioners, and artists can pave the way for a future where machines and humans collaborate seamlessly to create, inspire, and shape the world around us. As we embark on this journey, let us embrace the endless possibilities of Generative AI and strive to unlock its full potential for the benefit of society and humanity as a whole.

REFERENCES

Alasadi, E. A., & Baiz, C. R. (2023). Generative AI in education and research: Opportunities, concerns, and solutions. *Journal of Chemical Education*, 100(8), 2965–2971. 10.1021/acs.jchemed.3c00323

Amankwah-Amoah, J., Abdalla, S., Mogaji, E., Elbanna, A., & Dwivedi, Y. K. (2024). The impending disruption of creative industries by generative AI: Opportunities, challenges, and research agenda. *International Journal of Information Management*, 102759. 10.1016/j.ijinfomgt.2024.102759

Brynjolfsson, E., Li, D., & Raymond, L. R. (2023). *Generative AI at work* (No. w31161). National Bureau of Economic Research.

Ch'ng, L. K. (2024). Standing on the Shoulders of Generative AI. In *Transforming Education with Generative AI: Prompt Engineering and Synthetic Content Creation* (pp. 1-21). IGI Global. 10.4018/979-8-3693-1351-0.ch001

Chen, Y., & Esmaeilzadeh, P. (2024). Generative AI in Medical Practice: In-Depth Exploration of Privacy and Security Challenges. *Journal of Medical Internet Research*, 26, e53008. 10.2196/5300838457208

Chimbga, B. (2023). Exploring the Ethical and Societal Concerns of Generative AI in Internet of Things (IoT) Environments. In *Southern African Conference for Artificial Intelligence Research* (pp. 44-56). Cham: Springer Nature Switzerland. 10.1007/978-3-031-49002-6_4

David, A., & Jeganathan, G. S., & MD Sikandar Azam, S. A. (2023, May). Internet Users Top Concerns Ensuring Data Privacy, Security, and Protection. *10th International Conference on Multidisciplinary Research and Modern Education, ISBN* (No. 978-920, pp. 5-20241).

David, A., Kumar, C. G., & Paul, P. V. (2022). Blockchain technology in the food supply chain: Empirical analysis. *International Journal of Information Systems and Supply Chain Management*, 15(3), 1–12. 10.4018/IJISSCM.290014

Feuerriegel, S., Hartmann, J., Janiesch, C., & Zschech, P. (2024). Generative ai. *Business & Information Systems Engineering*, 66(1), 111–126. 10.1007/s12599-023-00834-7

Frey, C. B., & Osborne, M. (2023). Generative AI and the future of work: A reappraisal. *The Brown Journal of World Affairs*, 30(1).

Fui-Hoon Nah, F., Zheng, R., Cai, J., Siau, K., & Chen, L. (2023). Generative AI and ChatGPT: Applications, challenges, and AI-human collaboration. *Journal of Information Technology Case and Application Research*, 25(3), 277–304. 10.1080/15228053.2023.2233814

Ganeshkumar, C., David, A., & Jebasingh, D. R. (2022). Digital transformation: artificial intelligence-based product benefits and problems of Agritech industry. In *Agri-Food 4.0* (Vol. 27, pp. 141–163). Emerald Publishing Limited. 10.1108/S1877-636120220000027010

Ganeshkumar, C., Sankar, J. G., & David, A. (2023). Adoption of Big Data Analytics: Determinants and Performances Among Food Industries. *International Journal of Business Intelligence Research*, 14(1), 1–17. 10.4018/IJBIR.317419

Hacker, P., Engel, A., & Mauer, M. (2023, June). Regulating ChatGPT and other large generative AI models. In *Proceedings of the 2023 ACM Conference on Fairness, Accountability, and Transparency* (pp. 1112-1123). 10.1145/3593013.3594067

Huang, L., Song, M., Shen, H., Hong, H., Gong, P., Deng, H. W., & Zhang, C. (2023). Deep learning methods for omics data imputation. *Biology (Basel)*, 12(10), 1313. 10.3390/biology1210131337887023

Jeganathan, G. S., David, A., & Ganesh Kumar, C. (2022). Adaptation of Blockchain technology in HRM. *Korea Review of International Studies*, 10-22.

Jiang, W., Guo, Z., & Liang, R. (2023). Using ensemble models to detect deepfake images of human faces. In *Proceedings of the 2023 International Conference on Mathematics, Intelligent Computing and Machine Learning* (pp. 31-35). 10.1145/3638264.3638272

Kashif, M., David, A., Gupta, V. P., & Alam, S. (2024). Integration of Artificial Intelligence in the Financial Sector. In *Artificial Intelligence and Machine Learning-Powered Smart Finance* (pp. 96–108). IGI Global. 10.4018/979-8-3693-3264-1.ch005

Kenwright, B. (2023). Next Generation of the Web Will Engage Your Senses: Unleashing Interactive Web-Based XR Experiences. In *Concepts, Technologies, Challenges, and the Future of Web 3* (pp. 271-288). IGI Global.

Kumar, S., Musharaf, D., Musharaf, S., & Sagar, A. K. (2023). A Comprehensive Review of the Latest Advancements in Large Generative AI Models. In *International Conference on Advanced Communication and Intelligent Systems* (pp. 90-103). Cham: Springer Nature Switzerland. 10.1007/978-3-031-45121-8_9

Latha, C. J., Sankriti, R., David, A., & Srivel, R. (2020). IoT based water purification process using ultrasonic aquatic sound waves. *Test Engineering & Management, The Mattingley Publishing Co., Inc. ISSN*, 0193-4120.

Madaan, G., Swapna, H. R., Kumar, A., Singh, A., & David, A. (2021). Enactment of sustainable technovations on healthcare sectors. *Asia Pacific Journal of Health Management*, 16(3), 184–192. 10.24083/apjhm.v16i3.989

Michelucci, U. (2019). *Advanced applied deep learning: convolutional neural networks and object detection*. Apress. 10.1007/978-1-4842-4976-5

Pratheepkumar, P., Sharmila, J. J., & Arokiaraj, D. (2017). Towards mobile opportunistic in cloud computing. *Indian Journal of Scientific Research*, 17(02), 2250–0138.

Ravi, S., David, A., & Imaduddin, M. (2018). Controlling & calibrating vehicle-related issues using RFID technology. *International Journal of Mechanical and Production Engineering Research and Development*, 8(2), 1125–1132. 10.24247/ijmperdapr2018130

Saluja, S., Kukreja, J., & Sharma, S. (Eds.). (2024). *Building Organizational Resilience with Neuroleadership*. IGI Global. 10.4018/979-8-3693-1785-3

Sankar, J. G., David, A., & Valan, P. (2023). Examining User Understanding and Perceptions of E-Commerce Data Privacy, Security, and Protection. In *Confronting Security and Privacy Challenges in Digital Marketing* (pp. 159–185). IGI Global. 10.4018/978-1-6684-8958-1.ch008

Sipahioglu, M. (2024). Empowering Teachers with Generative AI Tools and Support. In *Transforming Education with Generative AI: Prompt Engineering and Synthetic Content Creation* (pp. 214-238). IGI Global. 10.4018/979-8-3693-1351-0.ch011

Srivastava, V., Singh, A. K., David, A., & Rai, N. (2022). Modelling student employability on an academic basis: A supervised machine learning approach with R. In *Handbook of Research on Innovative Management Using AI in Industry 5.0* (pp. 179–191). IGI Global. 10.4018/978-1-7998-8497-2.ch012

Sudhakar, B. D., Kattepogu, N., & David, A. (2017). Marketing assistance and digital branding-an insight for technology up-gradation for MSME's. *International Journal of Management Studies & Research*, 5(1), 2455–1562.

Thummula, E., Yadav, R. K., & David, A. (2019). A cost-effective technique to avoid communication and computation overhead in vehicle insurance database for online record monitoring. *International Journal of Mechanical and Production Engineering Research and Development*, 9(2), 711–722.

van der Zant, T., Kouw, M., & Schomaker, L. (2013). *Generative artificial intelligence*. Springer Berlin Heidelberg.

Vyas, P. G., & Priya, S. (2023). Social Media and Gen Y at Work: The Uses and Gratifications of Technology. In *5G, Artificial Intelligence, and Next Generation Internet of Things: Digital Innovation for Green and Sustainable Economies* (pp. 123-142). IGI Global.

Wadood, A. (2024). Generative AI From Theory to Model: Unleashing the Creative Power of Artificial Intelligence. In *Deep Learning, Reinforcement Learning, and the Rise of Intelligent Systems* (pp. 77-105). IGI Global.

Yu, P., Mulli, J., Syed, Z. A. S., & Umme, L. (Eds.). (2023). *Facilitating Global Collaboration and Knowledge Sharing in Higher Education with Generative AI*. IGI Global.

Chapter 2
Generative AI
The Impact, Possibilities, and Difficulties

Amrita Baid More
Prestige Institute of Management and Research, Indore, India

ABSTRACT

For nearly 50 years, artificial intelligence (AI) has been a technology and a field of study. Its advancement had been conflicting and differed after some time. Due to the development of intriguing AI applications like Alpha Go and Alpha Fold, large data sets, advancements in the internet and semiconductors, the most significant development in machine learning and deep learning occurred in the 2000s. Generative AI models have recently gained a lot of popularity. AI has become a household name thanks to massive language models like GPT (generative pre-trained transformer) and tools like Midjourney and ChatGPT. Microsoft and Google have been incorporating these models into their enterprise and search offerings as generative AI has had a significant impact on everyday life. The part dug into the potential outcomes and difficulties related to the condition of generative computer-based intelligence around then and investigated its future. Additionally, it offered recommendations for generative AI-using businesses.

INTRODUCTION

Over more than 50 years, artificial intelligence (AI) has progressed and achieved varying degrees of success. The new progressions in AI and profound learning, powered by immense information pools and headways in innovation, have brought us captivating simulated intelligence programs like Alpha Go and Alpha Overlay. However, in recent months, AI has finally entered the mainstream thanks to the

DOI: 10.4018/979-8-3693-8557-9.ch002

introduction of transformer design in 2018 and the succeeding explosion of generative AI models like GPT.

It is democratizing content creation in creative organizations by enabling individuals and small businesses to provide first-class modernized craftsmanship, music, and composing without requiring extensive resources or dominance (Elgammal et al., 2017). By automating routine tasks, producing reports, and personalizing marketing efforts, generative AI is cutting costs and increasing productivity in the business world (Zhang et al., 2021). PC-based insight-driven levels of progress are also benefiting clinical benefits, with applications ranging from clinical imaging and diagnostics to modified treatment plans (Esteva et al., 2019).

The applications of generative simulated intelligence are numerous and exciting. Experiences in education, entertainment, and personalized customer service could all benefit from this technology. It can make extraordinarily created learning materials, make cunning storylines for games, and give changed reactions in unobtrusive aides (Johnson et al., 2022). Additionally, Wu et al. found that generative simulated intelligence offers extraordinary scales of information analysis, reproduction, and critical thinking tools. and ensures natural maintainability and logical examination. 2019).

However, the emergence of generative AI entails several significant difficulties as well as ethical concerns. Significant concerns include data bias, transparency, and the possibility of using AI-generated content for malicious or false information (Bender et al., 2021). The scene is further bewildered by the biological effects of creating massive man-made reasoning models and the need for solid regulatory frameworks to ensure careful use (Strubell et al., 2019).

Providing a comprehensive overview of how this technology is shaping our world and what lies ahead for its development and application, this chapter examines the profound impact, expansive possibilities, and complex difficulties of generative AI.

The chapter aims to:

1. Delve into the possibilities and challenges associated with the state of generative AI at that time.
2. Explore the prospects and potential developments in generative AI.
3. Offer practical suggestions for businesses on how to effectively utilize generative AI.

What is Generative AI?

Algorithms such as ChatGPT, Midjourney, Bard, DALL E, and others that are capable of generating new content such as text, images, audio, videos, code, and simulations are referred to as generational artificial intelligence (GAI). To generate original content, generative AI models make use of neural networks to recognize patterns and structures in existing data. Huge-scope models are turning out to be progressively significant in the artificial intelligence-produced content space, bringing about superior age results. As information and demonstration sizes develop, the models' ability to learn circulation turns out to be more exhaustive, bringing about a more reasonable and top-notch content age (Eloundou et al., 2023).

Generative AI (GAI) models have been around since the beginning of AI, contrary to popular belief. Secret Markov Models (Well) and Gaussian Combination Models (GMMs) were created during the 1950s and were utilized to produce consecutive information like discourse and time series. Generative Models saw critical execution enhancements with the coming of Profound Learning.

The ongoing blast of Generative man-made intelligence has its underlying foundations in the progression of Regular Language Handling (NLP), a subfield of artificial intelligence that spotlights how PCs process and dissect a lot of normal language information (Aaronson, 2024). N-gram language modelling was used in traditional sentence-making techniques to learn word distribution and find the best sequence. This display was utilized to disambiguate input and select a likely arrangement given likelihood.

However, this approach was ineffective when dealing with lengthy sentences, so Recurrent Neural Networks were developed to address this problem. The introduction of the Transformer Architecture brought about a convergence of generative AI models from various domains. A Transformer Model is a neural network that, like words in a sentence, learns context and implication by chasing associations in chronological data.

Transformer models use consideration or self-consideration, numerical procedures that recognize unpretentious ways even far-off information components in a series impact and rely upon one another, to learn setting. Transformers became the predominant backbone for numerous generative models across a variety of domains after their application in computer vision. (Maglogiannis et al., 2023)

Figure 1. A comprehensive survey of AI generated content (AIGC): A history of generative AI from GAN to ChatGPT (Yihan Cao & others, March 2023)

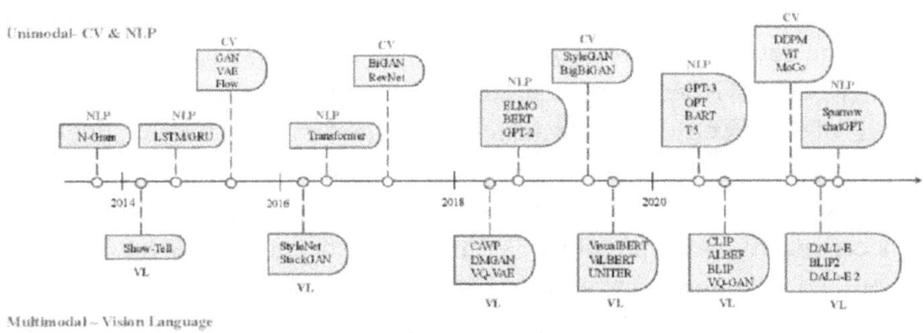

A HOLISTIC LITERATURE REVIEW ON GENERATIVE AI TOOLS, MODELS, AND THEIR EVOLUTION

Generative AI has become a transformative force in the realm of artificial intelligence, bringing unprecedented capabilities to the creation of text, images, and other forms of media. The evolution of these tools and models has been marked by significant advancements, spurred by improvements in data availability, computational power, and algorithmic innovations. This writing audit investigates the improvement of generative man-made intelligence, zeroing in on key models and apparatuses, their capabilities, and their effect on different fields.

In the early days of artificial intelligence research, simple pattern recognition and rule-based systems were the primary areas of interest. This is where the idea of generative AI originated. Beginning endeavours at generative models included essential probabilistic techniques and early brain organizations, which missing the mark on refinement and size of current methodologies (Goodfellow et al., 2014).

Generative adversarial networks (GANs) were introduced by Ian Goodfellow and his colleagues in 2014, marking a significant advancement. GANs are made up of two brain organizations—a generator and a discriminator—that are constantly prepared competitively. The discriminator validates the authenticity of the generated data, resulting in ever-improving data generation (Goodfellow et al., 2014). The establishment of various resulting progressions in generative simulated intelligence was laid out by this development.

Another period in generative PC-based knowledge started with the improvement of transformer models and the coming of significant learning. Transformers, which Vaswani et al. presented in 2017, depend on systems of self-consideration that accelerate the handling of successive information like messages—this turn of events assisted in the development of extremely refined language models.

OpenAI's GPT (Generative Pre-prepared Transformer) series provides the best illustration of the effectiveness of transformers in generative simulated intelligence. Radford et al. state that GPT-2's 2019 release demonstrated its ability to generate text that is coherent and relevant to the context. which sparked a lot of interest and concern regarding the possibility of misuse of such technology. 2019). GPT-3 further pushed the boundaries with 175 billion boundaries by delivering text that is frequently indistinguishable from text written by humans (Brown et al., 2020).

Generative AI has led to similar advancements in the visual arts. Midjourney and DALL-E have demonstrated how textual descriptions can be used by AI to create imaginative and detailed images. OpenAI's DALL-E combines computer vision and natural language processing by generating images that match text prompts using a version of the GPT-3 architecture (Ramesh et al., 2021).

Another notable tool, Midjourney, produces artistic-quality images by utilizing cutting-edge AI methods. By providing direct information sources, it empowers customers to create distinctive expressive art and democratizes the arrangement of mechanized craftsmanship. Advertising, entertainment, and design are just a few of the sectors that stand to gain greatly from these tools, which have provided completely new opportunities for creative expression.

Generative AI can be used in content creation, healthcare, and scientific research, among other areas. In satisfied creation, man-made consciousness (simulated intelligence) models like GPT-3 are used to automate the creation of articles, encourage copy, and, surprisingly, exploratory writing. As a result, these models work with new types of narration and increase efficiency (Zellers et al., 2019).

In the medical services area, generative computer-based intelligence is utilized to blend clinical pictures for preparing, upgrading demonstrative systems, and even planning new medications. GANs, for instance, have been utilized to create realistic medical images that aid in the training of machine-learning models without jeopardizing the privacy of patients (Yi et al., 2019).

Generative AI also helps scientists study things like chemistry and material science. The capacity of artificial intelligence models to foresee the properties of new mixtures and materials makes it conceivable to rapidly find them more. Deep Mind's Alpha Fold uses generative AI to accurately predict protein structures, revolutionizing structural biology (Jumper et al., 2021).

Generic computer-based intelligence raises several moral issues despite its promising applications. The chance of abuse, for example, the development of deepfakes or counterfeit news, raises security and deception issues. Additionally, the task of comprehending and easing natural tendencies in the arrangement of data is complicated by the disclosure concept of various recreated knowledge models (Drinking Binge et al., 2021).

Intellectual property and authorship are two additional issues. As simulated intelligence-produced content becomes more common, ownership and inventiveness of such works are being questioned. This is especially true in the creative industries, where the line between human creativity and machine creativity is getting blurrier by the day (Elgammal et al., 2017).

Due to ongoing research and technological advancements, the prospects for the development of generative AI in the future are exciting. Doshi-Velez and Kim (2017) say that one area of focus is making computer-based intelligence models easier to understand, making it clearer how they generate results, and making sure they are reasonable and responsible.

The creation of multimodal generative models that can seamlessly incorporate audio, text, and image data is another promising direction. According to Gao et al., this could result in AI applications that are more sophisticated and adaptable, capable of carrying out intricate tasks that call for an in-depth comprehension of multiple modalities. 2021).

In addition, the combination of generative AI with other nascent technologies like quantum registering and edge figuring may open up new possibilities and overcome the limitations of the present information-handling capacities and computational power (Biamonte et al., 2017).

Generational artificial intelligence has expanded rapidly, moving from early probabilistic models to cutting-edge profound learning and transformer-based structures. GPT-3, DALL-E, and Midjourney are just a few examples of generative AI's transformative potential in a variety of fields, including content creation, healthcare, the visual arts, and scientific research. Midjourney is one more example. However, these advancements also bring with them ethical issues and difficulties that require resolution. The future of generative AI appears to be both exciting and challenging as research continues to push the limits of what is possible. It will also open up brand-new questions and opportunities for society.

Foundation Models for AI

To circumvent the boundaries imposed by conventional prototypes like RNNs, the Transformer architecture was proposed. It is now the foundation of numerous cutting-edge models, such as GPT-3, Codex, DALL-E-2, and Gopher. Due to their parallelism and learning capabilities, pre-trained language models based on the Transformer architecture have emerged as the standard in NLP since their introduction. Autoregressive language displaying and veiled language demonstrating are the two kinds of preparing undertakings for these transformer-based pre-prepared language models. (Aaronson, 2024)

Even though it was trained on a lot of data, the AIGC might not always yield output that matches the user's intent. RLHF has been used to fine-tune models in a variety of contexts to address this issue. The improvement of processing with upgraded equipment circulated preparation, and distributed computing has added to the advancement of the establishment model. (Eloundou et al., 2023)

Unimodal and Multimodal

There are two kinds of models in AI: unimodal and multimodal. Unimodal models take guidelines and create content from a similar methodology, while multimodal models can acknowledge directions from various modalities and produce about various modalities as well.

The Generative Language Model (GLM) is one type of unimodal model. Based on the patterns and assemblies in the input information they have been trained on, these models are trained to generate human-like language. GLMs are useful for a wide assortment of NLP tasks, including translation, dialogue systems, and answering questions. GLMs can be divided into two categories: encoder-decoder models and decoder models. Another kind of unimodal model is the vision generative model. On the other hand, learning unimodal models is easier than learning multimodal ones.

Education, coding for AI-based programming systems, chatbots, and AI-based art and music production are just a few of the areas where these models can be used.

Figure 2. A History of the generative AI (Legoux, 2023)

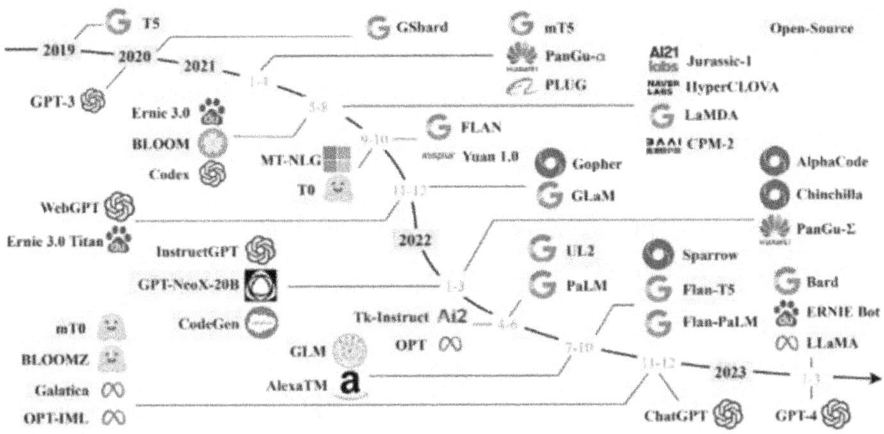

THE CURRENT STATE OF GENERATIVE AI

Due to their numerous applications and advanced capabilities, the three well-known generative AI models GPT-3, DALL-E, and Midjourney have attracted a lot of attention. For chatbots and content creation, OpenAI's GPT-3 excels in natural language processing tasks by producing human-like text. DALL-E, another headway by OpenAI, addresses significant experts in making organized and creative pictures from printed portrayals, stretching the boundaries of the visual creative mind. The AI-driven platform Midjourney lets users create one-of-a-kind, intricate artwork and focuses on producing high-quality artistic visuals. These models, which transform industries by enhancing creativity, automating content production, and offering novel solutions in a variety of domains, are an example of cutting-edge developments in generative AI.

There has been a new flood in the ubiquity of Generative computer-based intelligence with the presentation of ChatGPT. NVIDIA's CEO and founder, Jensen Huang, claims that Generative AI has ushered in a new era in AI research (Lv, 2023). Huang depicts it as the iPhone second for computer-based intelligence, as another registering stage has arisen, which can be customized utilizing human language.

Now that ChatGPT is open to the public, it has acquired 100 million users in less than two months. About ninety days after its release, Stable Dissemination by Solidness computer-based intelligence, another generative simulated intelligence device that generates images founded on text imageries, received over 30,000 stars on GitHub. A lot of individuals believe that ChatGPT can alter how companies operate.

Some of the available simulated intelligence tools and their capabilities are listed in the table below:

Table 1. Popular generative AI models and their functions

Name	Description	Function
ChatGPT	In just two months, it became well-known as one of the most prominent chatbots. OpenAI has created a language model that approximates a human-to-human dialogue. Conversations and data cycles are beneficial to it because of its insights. Moreover, ChatGPT is trained using a neural architecture of a Generative Pre-Trained Transformer.	ChatGPT operates in a manner akin to automated chat systems used on customer support websites. It may generate many different types of textual material, such as emails, postings on social media, articles, essays, and code. It's even capable of answering inquiries.
DALL- E	OpenAI's DALL-E and DALL-E 2 deep learning models are designed to produce digital pictures based on regular language inputs.	DALLE 2 may use a given description to produce unique, realistic artwork and images. It can combine concepts, traits, and styles. It may be used on pictures you upload, or ones made with DALL-E 2. It has been used to magnify well-known pieces of art, including the Mona Lisa, by adding extra background to the image.
Midjourney	Midjourney is an independent research lab situated in San Francisco that developed and hosts a generative artificial intelligence program and service called Midjourney, Inc. Midjourney uses "prompts," or natural language descriptions, to create visuals.	With the new /describe option from Midjourney, users may upload a picture and get textual instructions that try to explain it. Then, by using these prompts, AI-generated art may be used to produce unique, captivating works of art that are unmatched on the internet.
Chatsonic	It is an innovative generative AI tool that surpasses all Open AI constraints, making it the greatest substitute for ChatGPT. To produce material with the most recent information, it connects with Google Search. It can also process voice instructions and produce digital pictures.	Based on the signals it gets, Chatsonic can produce excellent text, images, and content for emails, websites, and a variety of social networking networks. You may utilize voice commands with Chatsonic in addition to textual instructions.
Jasper Chat	A new procreative method of communicating with generative AI is called Jasper Chat. With each interaction, you may improve your replies and have a conversation with AI rather than thinking in hard prompts or directions.	Jasper Chat may come up with ideas, alter text sections, respond to questions, and make original works of art like poetry or short tales. Jasper Chat is designed for business applications like social media updates and marketing and sales.

continued on following page

Table 1. Continued

Name	Description	Function
Copy.ai	Copy.ai is the newest generative AI for content marketing and sales teams. You may be able to write blog posts, sales emails, ad text, social media captions, articles, code, and more with the use of real-time data.	Text.ai helps the team with a range of sales and copywriting duties, such as creating product descriptions, ads, blogs, emails, and website text. It can create bullet points from LinkedIn profiles. With only one sentence, it may generate an entire content brief.
ChatFlash –Neuroflash AI	With this chat tool, you may ask questions and provide directions quickly. You will receive an answer and outcomes from Chatflash AI.	High-caliber artificial intelligence content is produced by Neuroflash.
GrowthBar	GrowthBar is an AI-powered SEO content creation platform with a focus on artificial intelligence.	GrowthBar uses cutting-edge algorithms to generate and improve your blog entries with artificial intelligence. Moreover, GrowthBar uses the same methodology as major SEO tools for keyword research, rank tracking, and backlink analysis.
Rytr Chat	With Rytr, an AI writing helper, you can produce excellent material quickly and for a small fraction of the price. Using cutting-edge language artificial intelligence, you can create fresh, distinctive content for nearly any vertical.	To provide Rytr managers with a more organic and conversational understanding, Rytr Chat was developed. Using only one click, you can produce content using Rytr Chat. It modifies the length, tone, or style of the text.
Easy Peasy AI Chat	Simple as pie.AI stands for Artificial Intelligence Content Generator, which helps you and your team overcome creative blocks and produce amazing, unique content ten times more quickly.	Users may quickly and simply create resumes, blog posts, emails, social media messages, and other documents using Easy Peasy AI Chat. Additionally, it can transcribe sounds, create AI images, and summarize lengthy texts.
GhostWryter .	An AI program called GhostWryter produces excellent content for marketing strategies like blog posts and SEO text. It utilizes artificial intelligence technology and is readily accessible through Google Docs with the use of an OpenAI licensing key.	Your company may benefit from the app's use of AI to generate blog entries, marketing material, and language that is optimized for search engines. With GhostWryter, creating blog articles and other marketing content is easy.
Ellie AI	Ellie AI is a platform that provides frameworks and tools to data teams so that fresh data is always beneficial to the company. It is designed for businesses of all sizes and offers information architecture components and lightweight data modelling. Ellie AI also provides an AI email assistant that can reply to emails in the manner you choose.	Ellie works only as a writing assistant when it comes to composing email responses. Ellie picks up on your writing style and lets users choose the "mood" she wants to respond in (for example, she may be witty, professional, angry, etc.). Ellie can speak several languages; thus she will automatically respond in the language that was used to write her.

continued on following page

Table 1. Continued

Name	Description	Function
Murf AI	With Murf AI, users can utilize text to create voiceovers in the studio quality for a variety of purposes, including instructional videos, podcasts, ads, and more. Select from more than 120 speech types on the website, which include options for more than 20 languages and accents.	The user interface of Murf AI is simple enough for anybody to utilize. Just upload your text, then choose a voice from the collection. The voice's pitch and pace may be changed as desired. To make your sound clip sound more professional, you may also upload it and use the voice changer.
Stockimg.AI	Stocking.AI supports the creation of art. You inform the AI during the picture generation process whether you want it to generate a book cover, logo, icon, wallpaper, or stock image, and it produces visual material that meets your requirements.	Stocking.AI is an AI image-generating platform that facilitates the creation of AI images such as posters, book covers, and logos. Some categories include stock photos, book covers, posters, wallpapers, logos, graphics, icons, and user interfaces for websites and mobile devices.
Heyday	Though it functions more like a research helper, Heyday refers to itself as an AI-powered memory aid. The software helps "resurface" material that you might need to discover after you've previously studied it by integrating with search engines, browsers, and programs like Gmail and Google Docs.	A conversational AI platform, Heyday by Hootsuite, was created to help retailers and e-commerce companies increase shopper engagement and lead generation. The main features are push alerts, programmed replies, wait time management, customizable branding, and multi-channel communication.
Adobe Sensei	Adobe Marketo Engages Sensei GenAI leverages real-time conversational experiences to facilitate communication between marketing and sales teams, accelerating time to market and increasing the number of planned meetings.	Adobe Analytics may use Adobe Sensei to automatically evaluate users and audience groups to spot important distinctions, pinpoint conversion drivers, and forecast user behavior in the future.
Amazon Bedrock	With Amazon Bedrock, a fully managed service, you may choose from a variety of FMs to find the one that best fits your use case. Major AI firms provide FMs, and Amazon makes them available via an API.	With the help of AWS tools and capabilities, you can easily customize FMs with your data in private, integrate them into your applications, and launch them using Amazon Bedrock's server-less architecture.

Public View on Artificial Intelligence

There has been a new flood in the ubiquity of Generative computer-based intelligence with the presentation of ChatGPT. NVIDIA's CEO and founder, Jensen Huang, claims that Generative AI has ushered in a new era in AI research. Huang depicts it as the iPhone second for computer-based intelligence, as another registering stage has arisen, which can be customized utilizing human language.

In less than two months, ChatGPT, which is now available to the general public, has gained 100 million users. One more Generative simulated intelligence apparatus, Stable Dissemination by Solidness computer-based intelligence, which produces pictures given text portrayals, has gotten more than 30,000 stars on GitHub somewhere around 90 days after its delivery. Many people think that ChatGPT has the potential to change the way businesses work.

Is Generative AI 'Creative' or 'Generative'?

The question of whether new creative tools like Midjourney and DALL-E are actually "creative" has sparked a debate. Prof. Chandra Sekhar of the IISc Bangalore argues that imagination remains unique to humans, as natural intelligence is challenging to replicate (Jeleel-Ojuade, 2024). He adds that the real threat is that artificial intelligence is still in its infancy. Even though AI can generate something based on the information given, it still lacks thought, and self-learning remains a distant goal for these models. A human must still provide the initial input.

Conversely, Abhinav Aggarwal, whose company Fluid AI recently published an AI-authored book, points out that even individuals considered "creative" rely on other sources before making a model. He questions why it is viewed as imaginative and generative when a human does it, yet not when AI does it. He goes on to say that AI systems will use memory-based logic ten years from now, whereas they currently use inference-based logic. An AI system is considered non-creative when it learns from data, whereas a human is considered creative when doing the same. This raises the question of whether one is regarded as less creative than the other or if the definition of creativity is ambiguous.

The need to distinguish between generative and creative AI was emphasized at the first INDIA AI Generative AI Roundtable. Although both terms are currently used interchangeably, the distinction will become more pronounced in ten years. Defining creativity in the era of ChatGPT is a challenging task.

Impact of Generative AI on Future of Jobs

Concerns about job loss have arisen as a result of the emergence of Generative AI, which raises the possibility of machines replacing human workers. (Targett, 2023) According to reports, Generative AI could affect up to 300 million jobs worldwide, with the technology having the potential to replace 25% of current work in the United States and 24% in Europe. (Johnson, 2023) Experts, however, maintain that correct innovation is the key and that human intervention is still required for the correct output (Jalan, 2023). Generative AI will not only create new job profiles and improve job efficiency, but it may also replace some jobs. (Mdaka, 2023)

Then again, assuming Generative computer-based intelligence arrives at its maximum capacity, it could prompt critical employment cutback and commotion in the work market. As per a Goldman Sachs report, roughly 66% of existing positions are vulnerable somewhat to man-made intelligence robotization, and Generative simulated intelligence could supplant dependent upon one-fourth of the ongoing responsibility (Breuer et al., 2024). However, AI has the potential to generate employment opportunities as well. By 2027, the World Economic Forum projects a 40% increase in the number of specialists in AI and machine learning, resulting in approximately 1 million new jobs across all industry sectors. (Badawy, 2023) Furthermore, jobs like information examiners, information researchers, huge information subject matter experts, and data security investigators are supposed to encounter an increment of 30-35% and 31% separately, producing an extra 2.6 million positions. (Jalan, 2023)

Lastly, brief designing is an urgent expertise that will acquire noticeable quality in the future as it assists with guaranteeing smooth, clear, and proficient human-simulated intelligence collaboration. (Musiol, 2024)

Figure 3. Fastest growing and declining jobs (World Economic Forum, Future of Jobs Report 2023)

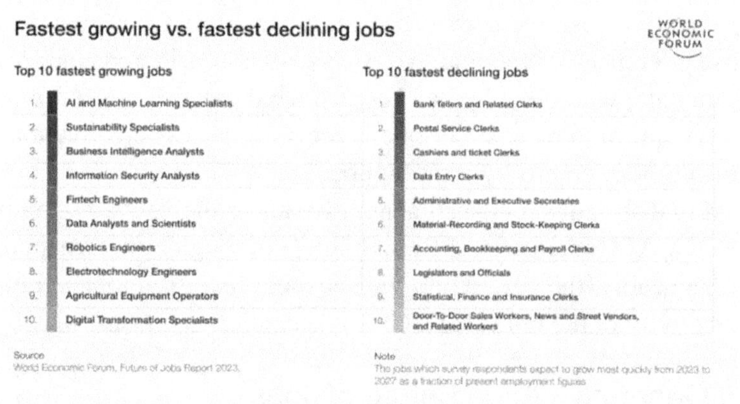

Opportunities With Generative AI

Generative artificial intelligence has turned into a distinct advantage in different ventures, offering a large number of monetary advantages like expanded efficiency, computerization, and improved dynamic capacities (Badawy, 2023). With its capability to drive development, productivity, and seriousness across areas, generative simulated intelligence is supposed to develop from USD 11.3 billion in 2023 to USD 51.8 billion by 2028, with a CAGR of 36%. Subject matter authorities agree generative man-made intelligence has vast conceivable outcomes in India, from enormous organizations making chatbots to understudies involving ChatGPT for scholarly composition.

Jaspreet Bindra says that there are five options for generative AI in India: making everyone a 10x engineer, giving more opportunities to entrepreneurs, helping service businesses, giving huge opportunities to the creative industry, and using India's abundant data. (Insights, 2024) The applications and services of the generative AI value chain represent a significant portion of the numerous opportunities. (Iliadis, 2014) Even though approximately 416,000 people are working in AI and data science, India is having trouble finding AI talent at the moment. There is as yet an interest for roughly 629,000 computer-based intelligence gifts, with an extra interest for 1,000,000 laborers in space, expected to increment dramatically before long, as per NASSCOM.

Bridging the Digital Divide Through Generative AI

Jensen Huang, CEO of NVIDIA, thinks that Generative AI has the potential to benefit nations like India and present a fantastic opportunity to bridge the social and technological divide. Generative AI has made it possible for anyone to make use of this potent technology for the benefit of themselves, their company, or their nation, whereas, in the past, only a select few people were able to program computers. The computer will write the software by itself if it communicates what they need and wants, making everyone now a computer programmer. This democratization of innovation will lift many sections of society and carry training to the individuals who don't approach it.

With the help of the Government of India's Bhashini program, generational AI can also be a useful tool for overcoming linguistic barriers in India. Harsha Mundhada of Inflexor Adventure accepts that Generative computer-based intelligence devices can assist with making content in various dialects, making India's pinnacle legal bodies more open to individuals the nation over. Generative AI tools can also be beneficial to people with disabilities, such as autism or speech disorders, who can benefit from AI technologies for life-altering experiences. (Insights, 2024)

Generative AI's Impact on Different Sectors

The monetary open doors achieved by generative artificial intelligence are immense and different. It gives businesses the ability to use data-driven understandings, increase productivity, and stimulate novelty. We can anticipate further sectoral alterations as technology advances, paving the way for a future that is more technologically advanced, personalized, and efficient. Healthcare, fintech, and education are among the significant impact sectors for Generative AI, with the edification sector already being transformed by the technology. Generative computer-based intelligence can assume the part of customized educators in the training area. Students can receive individualized classes and modules based on their aptitude. AI is replacing human tutors by providing students with individualized lesson plans. I see solicitations which are providing food towards that, be it in one-on-one expertise advancement preparing to somewhat as straightforward as familiarity upgrades," said Neethu Mariam Satisfaction, who is at present employed on another Generative computer-based intelligence start-up that spotlights on EdTech. "Not in EdTech, in medical care, it is easy to construct a question-based framework where computer-based intelligence plays the job of intermediary specialists. The majority of the applications are bringing personalization into whichever area you are applying it into," she added. (Insights, 2024)

Figure 4. The future of AI in India (Kapil, 2023)

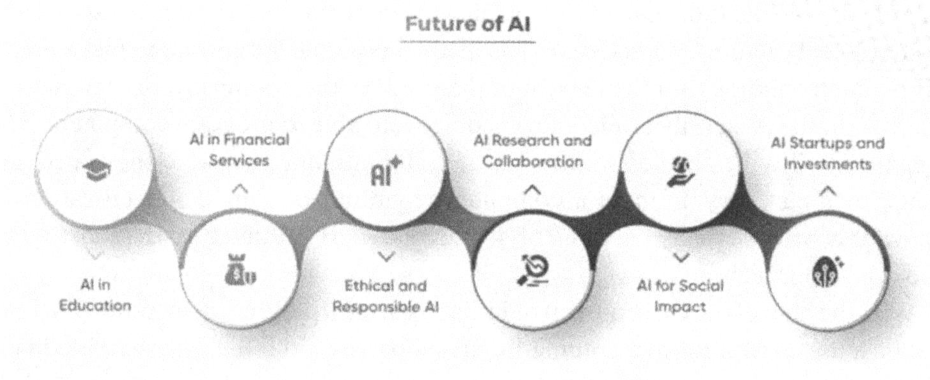

By assisting physicians in the analysis of medical data, the diagnosis of patients, and the creation of individualized treatment plans, the application of generative AI has the potential to transform the healthcare sector. As of late, scientists from Drexel College's School of Biomedical Designing, Science and Wellbeing Frameworks showed the way that Open artificial intelligence's GPT-3 program could precisely recognize beginning phases of dementia by investigating unconstrained discourse with an exactness pace of 80%. With no known solution for dementia, an early finding can give patients more choices for treatment and backing. (Ray, 2023) Currently, the patient's medical history and a series of extensive physical and neural tests are used to make the diagnosis. The table below provides a sector wise application and tools available with generative AI:

Table 2. Generative AI impact on different sectors

Sector	Applications	Tools
Agriculture	• Crop The board Generative man-made intelligence frameworks can track down examples and patterns in satellite symbolism, climate information, and soil organization to assist ranchers with choosing when and where to plant, water, and collect harvests. • Crop Enhancement - Generative man-made intelligence can likewise assist ranchers with picking the best yields and creation techniques for their necessities. • Asset The executive's Generative simulated intelligence can help ranchers in expanding water, manure, and pesticide use, supporting reasonable cultivating. • Bug control - Generative artificial intelligence can further develop bug control by surveying nuisance populaces, climate, and yield wellbeing to anticipate flare-ups and offer centered mediations. • Inventory network Streamlining - Generative man-made intelligence assists ranchers and agribusinesses with surveying huge strategic information, identifying blockages and shortcomings, and improving supply chains. • Crop Advancement - Generative simulated intelligence can help analysts and plant raisers find and foster innovative harvest types with further developed execution, harvest, and nuisance and sickness opposition. • Rancher instruction - Generative artificial intelligence could change ranchers' data accessibility and independent direction.	• Ama KrushAI • Farmer. chat • Apurva.ai • Kissan GPT jiva ag
Education	• Course Plan - Generative man-made intelligence strategies can put together schedules, example plans, and tests. Practice issues and intuitive activities can be customized to understudies' information holes, abilities, and learning strategies. • Customized Illustrations - Customized example plans assist understudies with getting the best training in light of their necessities and interests. • Content Creation for Courses - Generative computer-based intelligence can help make tests, activities, and idea clarifications. It can assist educators who with expecting to foster a great deal of stuff. AI can make new content out of existing content. • Repairing Old Learning Materials - Generative artificial intelligence can upgrade inferior quality learning materials, including authentic reports, photographs, and movies. Simulated intelligence can work on the goal of these things, making them more fascinating for youngsters adjusted to great media. • Mentoring - Understudies can interface with a virtual coach and get continuous input and direction utilizing generative computer-based intelligence. Students without in-person tutoring may benefit from it.	• NOLEJ • TutorAI • Snapxam • QANDA • tab nine
Healthcare	• Diagnosis and Screening: Generative AI enables clinicians to quickly and accurately identify and treat patients, thereby improving outcomes for patients. • Personalized Medicine: Generative AI algorithms are capable of analyzing enormous medical datasets to discover patterns, anticipate outcomes, and enhance health. These customized medication techniques can assist specialists with making more compelling treatment regimens and follow-up care. • Drug Revelation - Generative simulated intelligence calculations can break down clinical preliminaries and different information to find potential prescription targets and anticipate the best atoms. It might be possible to develop new medications more quickly and for less money. • Coming up with New Concepts for Research In healthcare, generative AI can also be used to come up with new ideas for research. • Keeping away from Clinical Mistakes - Generative man-made intelligence can consequently fix spelling issues in the documentation, which is useful for electronic remedies, and populate the framework with the applicable information.	• MedPaLM • Viz.ai • Enlitic • Merative • CloudMedX
Manufacturing	• Item, Advancement and Plan - Geniterative artificial intelligence can speed up the improvement of new plan ideas, drugs, materials, and statistical surveying, decreasing the chance to advertise. • Quality Control - Prescient artificial intelligence frameworks screen and report creation worries progressively, though generative simulated intelligence frameworks find and alarm against shortcomings.	• Autodesk • Fanuc • Birlasoft • FortiSandbox • AltexSoft

continued on following page

Table 2. Continued

Sector	Applications	Tools
Retail	• Customized Product Recommendations: Generative AI can use customer data to tailor journeys, discounts, and engaging content to specific customers by analyzing that data. • Oversee Stock Levels - Generative simulated intelligence examinations deal with information and recommend stock administration. Simulated intelligence can assist retailers with streamlining inventory networks and conveyance by dissecting verifiable information, purchaser feelings, and contest information to anticipate patterns and settle on shrewd buying and creation choices. • Screen And Enhance Costs - Generative man-made intelligence calculations can rapidly advance retail costs by examining rival costs, request examples, and market patterns. • Construct Client Care Chatbots - Generative artificial intelligence can assist clients with tackling issues with chatbots. Accordingly, it can assist retailers with further developing client care and lessen client care specialists' responsibility. • Detecting Fraudulent Behavior: Generative AI systems can deter fraudulent purchases and returns, saving businesses money and boosting customer confidence.	• Vertex AI vision • Discovery AI • Market360 • Scanunlimited • numerator
Media	• Computerized Content age: LLM can be utilized to produce content, for example, articles, blog entries, or virtual entertainment posts. This will be helpful for individuals who need to routinely make content. For instance, online entertainment powerhouses, • Assortment and work on happiness: LLMs can make an assortment of intriguing substances that take care of various crowd segments. The nature of the content will be vastly improved as simulated intelligence models gain from a lot of information. • Customized content: Simulated intelligence models can create customized content given the inclinations of individual clients • Client the executives: Generative simulated intelligence can help clients the executives, furnishing opportune reactions and commitment with a computerized crowd. Generic inquiries can be answered with ChatGPT, a type of Generative AI. Off late, there are Google Chrome expansions that permit brands and Twitter clients to introduce Talk GPT bots that answer all Tweet's • Limitation of content utilizing profound fakes: The OTT stages have expanded the need to make content in nearby/local dialects. For instance, the errand of naming and content balance for lip-synchronizing with an on-screen character can be flawlessly achieved utilizing profound phoney innovation. The innovation superimposes voice from a source to an objective face with an ideal lip-sync. Face synthesis is used to accomplish this. • Upscaling content through super-goal: Using machine learning (ML) algorithms, super-resolution is a technique for creating a second image with more pixels from an original image with fixed pixels. Super-goal works on the presentation of pictures and video. Documentaries about nature, wildlife, or even sports typically require this kind of super-resolution. • Upscaling Enhanced visualizations: The ascent popular for liveliness and VFX content has controlled vivid encounters, with dramatic development in AR and VR innovation that has Media the amusement market. For instance, man-made intelligence can help in superimposing/rendering a source face to an objective face with no sweat.	• Lately • Sprout Social • HubSpot • Copy.ai • Emplifi
Marketing	• Time and money savings: Using synthetic media to clone a voice can save time searching for occupied voice actors. To lay it out, if you have Awkwafina voicing a person in your enlivened film, you can catch her voice test and create the lines. • Reaching people in their native tongue: Using AI synthesis, you can make a malaria-themed video for David Beckham in Gujarati or a mask-wearing video for Jackie Chan in Tamil. This can set out a freedom for publicists to connect with individuals in their dialects. • Documenting individuals around - Headways in engineered media can allow us to save ourselves as well as our friends and family. You could pose inquiries to a 5-year-old you or pay attention to your grandma singing long after she's gone.	• Jasper AI • MarketMuse • Acrolinx • Semrush • Seventh Sense

Future Directions in Generative AI

The field of medical services might be changed by the utilization of generative artificial intelligence. Medical data analysis, patient diagnosis, and personalized treatment planning can all benefit greatly from this technology. (Ray, 2023) An illustration of this is the new review led by specialists from Drexel College's School of Biomedical Designing, Science and Wellbeing Frameworks, which demonstrated the way that Open man-made intelligence's GPT-3 program can precisely foresee the beginning phases of dementia by examining unconstrained discourse with a great

80% exactness rate. At this point, there is no known remedy for dementia, so early identification can offer patients more choices for help and treatment. A comprehensive review of the patient's medical history and a series of physical and neurological tests are part of the current diagnostic procedure. (Feuerriegel et al., 2023)

Challenges

Generative AI, according to experts will disrupt the FinTech industry in the coming years. According to Aveekshith Bushan, Vice President and General Manager for APJ at Aerospike, fraud in the FinTech industry has the potential to harm thousands of users. Additionally, he believes that a breach of security protocols could occur. Jaspreet Bindra, then again, recommends that the IT area, which made the innovation, will be the one that faces interruption. Bindra features how Generative simulated intelligence has been computerizing cycles and in any event, composing codes, making the worth of certain software engineers' abilities dive.

Ethics, Rights, and Intellectual Property

Although generative AI has shown great promise and success in several domains, it also comes with several special difficulties. The strength and intricacy of generative AI algorithms may give rise to moral, legal, and societal issues. While generative man-made intelligence has propelled numerous to acquire direct involvement in simulated intelligence as of late, there is as yet obscurity in information assortment, engineers of models, and predispositions being taken care of into the framework. Kazim Rizvi, the founder and director of the tech policy think tank The Dialogue, asserts that this ambiguity will not disappear despite the advancement of technology.

Generative AI's potential to amplify the dissemination of varying degrees of false information is currently a major concern. Language models can frequently create yields that aren't genuine, and this peculiarity is called fantasy. When these outputs are confident responses that can spread false information, this becomes even more problematic. Generative artificial intelligence models likewise show various types of predispositions in the outcomes delivered by them. "We don't know what kind of data it will generate and what kind of bias it will come up with since we already have made these models very biased as a result of our nature," asserts Divya Dwivedi, a tech law specialist at the Supreme Court of India. The issue of bias in AI models has long been a hotly debated topic, and generative AI models have only made these biases worse. As Prateek Sibal, Program Expert for Simulated Intelligence, Arising Tech and Web Administration at UNESCO, notes, "There is an inborn predisposition that is there when we are preparing the dataset that emerges from how people have sort of implanted their biases in the framework."

The issue of biases has been brought to light even more in recent political experiments involving leading AI platforms that generate visual imagery (Cao et al., 2023). These stages could be one-sided concerning their insight and comprehension of different countries. Midjourney, a generative AI tool, only included Western-looking leaders like Angela Merkel, Emmanuel Macron, and Donald Trump in the AI-generated image; none of the popular Asian leaders were included in the result. These showings have just fortified the conviction that these models enhance human predispositions.

How to Guarantee the Accountable Use of Generative AI?

Given the expanding use of generative AI, a comprehensive and all-encompassing framework that would guarantee ethical use of the technology to maximize its advantages and minimize its hazards is desperately needed. This framework will include ethical strategies, procedural safeguards, candor, answerability, and continuing partner alliance (Cao et al., 2023). By promoting ethical behavior, we can protect the technology, build public confidence in it, keep it safe from damage, and make sure that generative AI benefits individuals and society more broadly.

As indicated by Jaspreet Bindra, Pioneer, and MD of Tech Whisperer Ltd. "The greatest thing we should sort out is how to control this beast. The democratization of innovation is the greatest test here. Nuclear power is the closest thing I can think of to something like AI that we encountered. Nations will meet up to manage it."

Then again, individuals like Deepak Visweswaraiah, VP of Stage Designing and Site Overseeing Chief at Pegasus Frameworks, bring up that "Controlling the beast doesn't occur because of unofficial laws. It ought to be a team sweat. How can we instruct designers to consider AI ethics? To prevent misuse, the developers ought to communicate the purpose of each model and be clear about it.

Computer-based intelligence is an instrument to upgrade human capacities and further develop efficiency across different areas.

1. Develop interdisciplinary and coordinated approaches: Numerous partners are involved in the development of generative computer-based intelligence models. To ensure a comprehensive understanding of the social benefits and potential dangers of generative AI and to develop multidisciplinary approaches, encourage academics, developers, policymakers, and domain experts to collaborate.
2. Solve Moral Problems: Ethical issues and the potential misuse of generative AI must be addressed due to its intellectual capacity. Architects ought to think about the ethical ramifications of their models and effectively look to forestall any underhandedness or expected aftereffects.

3. Encourage Openness and Inclusion: People who have communication difficulties or disabilities may benefit from generative AI. Support the improvement of thorough PC-based insight frameworks that cook explicitly to the necessities of discourse-impeded people, restoratively contemplative people, and others who could profit from further developed particular apparatuses.
4. Safety and control should come first: As generative simulated intelligence generates, well-being and control estimates ought to take precedence over everything else. Administrations, organizations, and developers collaborate to establish safeguards that prevent malicious use or unforeseen effects to guarantee that technology is utilized for society's benefit.
5. Future Upgrades for the Screen: Future enhancements to deep learning replicas that don't require as much physical activity should be on your radar. To guarantee a capable and safe arrangement of generative simulated intelligence advances, it is essential to meticulously examine the consequences of these advancements, including potential risks and unobserved side effects. In business areas like India, content can go out and spread quickly," says Aveekshith Bushan." False information and biases may exist. On the other side of ChatGPT, where the result is irrelevant to the substance being examined, we have proactively observed it. What appears to be relevant and what does not will be up to the individual," he added.

Global Initiatives to Regulate AI

The capacities of computer-based intelligence innovation have involved worry for states, scientists, and individuals all over the planet. Consequently, several nations have enacted AI usage regulations.

Every one of these nations' computer-based intelligence guidelines is extraordinarily careful and has major areas of strength for the utilization and insurance of man-made intelligence. The Computer-based Intelligence Act centers on a gamble-based way to deal with and guide the utilization of man-made intelligence in both private and public areas. The simulated intelligence Bill of Privileges targets explicit use cases. While the Chinese government has not yet enacted general regulations regarding AI technology, the country recently enacted a law that governs the methods by which private businesses can utilize online algorithms for consumer marketing.

Regulation

Governments, researchers, and individuals all over the world are concerned about the use of AI technology. Consequently, usage regulations have been enacted in several nations (Kaal, 2024). The European Association's Computer-based Intelligence Act, Canada's Man-made Brainpower and Information Act (AIDA), the US's simulated intelligence Bill of Freedoms and State Drives, and China's Calculation Straightforwardness and Advancing Computer-based Intelligence Industry Improvement have been broadly examined in different gatherings.

With a clear plan for AI use and protection, each of these nations has developed comprehensive AI regulations. The AI Act's primary focus is on directing the use of AI in both the public and private segments with a risk-based strategy. The AI Bill of Rights, on the other hand, focuses on explicit use cases. Although the Chinese government has not yet presented rules on artificial intelligence innovation as a general rule, the nation has as of late ordered a regulation to direct the way that privately owned businesses use online calculations for buyer showcasing.

Table 3. AI regulation efforts across the globe

Name of the country	Description
EU	• The EU guideline puts the counteraction of damage to people up front in its draft Artificial Intelligence Act. • According to the plan, these AI tools will be categorized according to the perceived risk level, which ranges from low to high to unacceptable. • As per the proposition, these man-made intelligence devices will be characterized under their apparent gamble level, from insignificant to restricted, high and unsatisfactory. • The demonstration centers on biometric observation, spreading falsehood or prejudicial dialects. • The high-risk devices are not supposed to be prohibited yet are supposed to be exceptionally straightforward in their activities.
US	• The Biden-Harris Organization has declared new activities that will additionally advance capable American development in Computerized reasoning, taking into account individuals' privileges and well-being. • focus on individuals and networks by upgrading dependable development that serves the public greatly, offsetting it with safeguarding society, security, and the economy. • Organizations have a crucial obligation to guarantee their offered items are protected to use before they get conveyed.

continued on following page

Table 3. Continued

Name of the country	Description
China	• The Internet Organization of China, the nation's top web guard dog, as of late passed a guideline on "profound combination" innovation, which it characterizes as "innovation that utilizes profound learning, augmented reality, and other union calculations to produce text, pictures, sound, video, and virtual scenes." • It is against the law for users to use generative AI for activities that are illegal, harmful to the public interest, or endanger national security • There is no anonymity on the Chinese internet • The government wants to control what algorithms can produce • Service providers must manually or technologically audit AI-generated content and user prompts • Baidu, one of the first companies to launch a Chinese text-to-image model, already filters politically sensitive content. • The guideline restricts individuals from utilizing profound amalgamation tech to create and scatter counterfeit news • At the point when the information utilized for computer-based intelligence preparation contains individual data, innovation suppliers ought to follow the country's very own data insurance regulation. • Stages ought to likewise remind clients to look for endorsement before they adjust others' countenances and voices utilizing profound blend innovation. • On the off chance that the consequence of generative computer-based intelligence might create turmoil or misidentification among people in general, the specialist co-op ought to place a watermark in an unmistakable spot to illuminate the public that it is a work by the machine.
UK	• The UK Government distributed a White Paper named "A supportive of development way to deal with man-made intelligence guidelines" • The White Paper explains the way to deal with computer-based intelligence set out by the Public authority in its 2022 simulated intelligence Administration and Guideline Strategy Explanation • The white paper distinguishes five significant standards: ▪ The man-made intelligence frameworks ought to work in a Protected, Secure and Powerful way. ▪ Straightforwardness and Logic of associations creating and sending man-made intelligence to convey the motivation behind artificial intelligence frameworks. • The white paper perceives gambles with a de-brought together administrative system, including conflicting implementation or direction across controllers.
Canada	• The Public authority of Canada has given The Man-made Reasoning and Information Act (AIDA) • AIDA is a significant achievement in executing the Advanced Contract and guaranteeing that Canadians can believe the computerized advances that they utilize consistently • The structure proposed in the AIDA is the most vital move towards another administrative framework intended to direct artificial intelligence development in a positive heading and to energize the dependable reception of man-made intelligence advances by Canadians and Canadian organizations. • AIDA would guarantee that high-influence artificial intelligence frameworks measure up to similar assumptions concerning well-being and common freedoms to which Canadians are acclimated • The Clergyman of Advancement, Science, and Industry would be engaged to direct and implement the Demonstration, to guarantee that approach and requirement move together as the innovation develops.

SOLUTIONS AND RECOMMENDATIONS

1. Encourage Instruction and Public Mindfulness: It is pivotal to instruct general society about generative simulated intelligence to dissipate fears of occupation substitution and advance comprehension of its capacities. This can be accomplished through mindfulness missions, studios, and instructive projects.
2. Establish rules for the use and sharing of data: Regulations governing the sharing and use of data are required because of the significance of data quality in the construction of robust generative AI models. Privacy can be safeguarded, ethical practices can be ensured, and AI development transparency can be maintained with this.
3. Lay out Administrative Systems and Worldwide Guidelines: A major obstacle lies in the absence of global AI standards. State-run organizations and overall affiliations should collaborate to spread out typical designs that address the authoritative pieces of generative man-made insight, including liability, inclination help, and safety efforts.
4. Encourage restraint: In addition to governmental regulations, individuals and businesses involved in the development of generative AI should adopt self-regulatory practices. This includes promoting the responsible use of AI technologies, advocating for moral guidelines, and establishing a clear understanding of each model's objective.
5. Prioritize bias reduction: While it very well may be trying to discard inclination, it is crucial to zero in on attempts to assuage inclination in generative man-made brainpower models. To ensure that the results are fair and impartial, engineers should invest resources in novel work of inclination discovery and relief methods.
6. Examine the Development of Human Information: Tools for generative AI have the potential to enhance human intelligence. Encourage innovative work involving generative artificial intelligence as a tool for improving human capabilities and increasing efficiency in various fields.
7. Encourage collaboration and interdisciplinarity: The creation of generative models based on computer-based intelligence involves numerous partners. To ensure a comprehensive understanding of the social benefits and potential dangers of generative AI and to develop multidisciplinary approaches, encourage academics, developers, policymakers, and domain experts to collaborate.
8. Solve Moral Problems: Ethical issues and the potential misuse of generative AI must be addressed due to its intellectual capacity. Architects ought to think about the ethical ramifications of their models and effectively look to forestall any underhandedness or expected aftereffects.

9. Encourage Transparency and Consistency: People who have communication difficulties or disabilities may benefit from generative AI. Support the improvement of thorough PC-based insight frameworks that cook explicitly to the necessities of discourse-impeded people, restoratively contemplative people, and others who could profit from further developed particular apparatuses.

CONCLUSION

Generative AI, which includes GPT-4, DALL-E, and other cutting-edge models of machine learning, has emerged as a disruptive force in several industries. Impact, possibilities, and inherent difficulties create a multifaceted landscape with enormous opportunities and significant challenges.

Generative simulated intelligence has significant and broad impacts. It has made it possible for anyone, even small businesses, to make high-quality images, music, and text without spending a lot of money in the creative industries. Artists and designers can boost their creativity and produce innovative works that combine machine precision with human intuition by making use of AI tools. Generative AI helps businesses save money and work more efficiently by automating tasks like customer service, reports, and even marketing content.

Generative AI models are used to synthesize medical images, assist in diagnosis, and plan treatment in the healthcare industry. Artificial intelligence-generated synthetic data, for instance, makes it possible to create more robust and generalized models for predicting patient outcomes by overcoming the limitations imposed by small datasets. Additionally, AI-driven simulations and data analysis accelerate climate modelling and drug development discoveries.

With generative human-made insight, the expected outcomes are endless. Personalized content creation is one of the most exciting opportunities. By adapting materials to individual learning styles and speeds, simulated intelligence can tailor educational learning opportunities for students. By providing customers with individualized storylines and intelligent encounters, it has the potential to disrupt the way content is consumed and provide a fun distraction. By predicting consumer behavior and market trends, generative AI has the potential to improve business operations and enable more strategic decision-making. Furthermore, artificial intelligence-driven remote helpers that are easier to understand and more responsive can turn into a fundamental piece of our day-to-day routines, upgrading human-PC collaboration.

Generative AI has the capability of significantly enhancing society as a whole. For instance, models of artificial intelligence (AI) can generate realistic synthetic data that safeguards privacy and enables researchers to examine patterns and trends in sensitive datasets. AI-generated simulations have the potential to support global sustainability initiatives by assisting in the comprehension of the effects of climate change on environmental science and their mitigation.

Generative AI has a lot of potential, but it also has a lot of problems and questions about ethics. A major deterrent is the quality and tendency of the information used to create these models. Biases in the training data can be perpetuated or even exacerbated by AI models, resulting in unfair and discriminatory outcomes. This issue is especially troubling in sensitive fields like lending, recruiting, and law enforcement, where biased decisions can significantly affect culture. Another significant issue is the misuse of generative computer-based intelligence. For instance, deepfake technology can produce videos and images that appear to be very real but are fake, jeopardizing trust, security, and privacy. There are serious issues that need to be addressed, including the spread of trickery and the possibility of man-made content created with consciousness to deceive and control famous evaluation.

Moreover, there is the preliminary of straightforwardness and commitment. It is challenging to comprehend and explain the decision-making strategies utilized by generative AI models, which are frequently referred to as "black boxes." In critical areas like finance and healthcare, this opacity can undermine trust and accountability. Additionally, it is challenging to train and operate numerous AI models without expenditure on computers and the environment. The fossil fuel byproducts brought about by the utilization of energy by artificial intelligence headways raise worries about their drawn-out suitability.

In conclusion, Generative AI is at the cutting edge of technology and offers transformative effects as well as virtually limitless possibilities. However, it also presents significant challenges and raises ethical concerns. The success of generative AI in the future is contingent on overcoming these obstacles through transparent practices, inclusive policymaking, and responsible development. We can use Generative AI to create a world that is more innovative, equitable, and sustainable by promoting collaboration among technologists, ethicists, and policymakers.

REFERENCES

Aaronson, S. (2024). The Age of AI Nationalism and its Effects. SSRN *Electronic Journal*. 10.2139/ssrn.4803311

Badawy, W. (2023). *Generative AI: Implications and opportunities for business*. Wael Badawy.

Bender, E. M., Gebru, T., McMillan-Major, A., & Shmitchell, S. (2021). On the Dangers of Stochastic Parrots: Can Language Models Be Too Big? *Proceedings of the 2021 ACM Conference on Fairness, Accountability, and Transparency*, 610-623. 10.1145/3442188.3445922

Biamonte, J., Wittek, P., Pancotti, N., Rebentrost, P., Wiebe, N., & Lloyd, S. (2017). Quantum machine learning. *Nature*, 549(7671), 195–202. 10.1038/nature2347428905917

Breuer, C., Breuer, W., & Renerken, T. (2024). "In design and humans, we trust"? – Drivers of trust and advice discounting for robo advice. SSRN *Electronic Journal*. https://doi.org/10.2139/ssrn.4792439

Brown, T., Mann, B., Ryder, N., Subbiah, M., Kaplan, J., Dhariwal, P., & Amodei, D. (2020). Language Models are Few-Shot Learners. *Advances in Neural Information Processing Systems*, 33, 1877–1901.

Brown, T. B., Mann, B., Ryder, N., Subbiah, M., Kaplan, J. D., Dhariwal, P., . . . Amodei, D. (2020). Language Models are Few-Shot Learners. arXiv preprint arXiv:2005.14165.

Doshi-Velez, F., & Kim, B. (2017). Towards a rigorous science of interpretable machine learning. arXiv preprint arXiv:1702.08608.

Elgammal, A., Liu, B., Elhoseiny, M., & Mazzone, M. (2017). CAN: Creative Adversarial Networks, Generating" Art" by Learning About Styles and Deviating from Style Norms. arXiv preprint arXiv:1706.07068.

Elias, J. (2023). Generative AI can help India close the technology divide, NVIDIA CEO Jensen Huang. INDIAai. https://indiaai.gov.in/article/generative-ai-can-help-india-close-the-technology-divide-nvidia-ceo-jensen-huang

Eloundou, T., Manning, S., Mishkin, P., & Rock, D. (2023). GPTs are GPTs: An early look at the labour market impact potential of large language models. http://arxiv.org/abs/2303.10130

Esteva, A., Robicquet, A., Ramsundar, B., Kuleshov, V., DePristo, M., Chou, K., Cui, C., Corrado, G., Thrun, S., & Dean, J. (2019). A guide to deep learning in healthcare. *Nature Medicine*, 25(1), 24–29. 10.1038/s41591-018-0316-z30617335

Feuerriegel, S., Hartmann, J., Janiesch, C., & Zschech, P. (2023). Generative AI. http://arxiv.org/abs/2309.07930

Gao, P., Han, J., Lin, Z., Yang, J., & Yuan, J. (2021). Interactive Question Answering System for Multi-modal Information Retrieval. *Information Processing & Management*, 58(1), 102439.

Gazala, N. (2021). Generative AI & Synthetic Media: A new era of advertisements. INDIAai. https://indiaai.gov.in/article/generative-ai-synthetic-media-a-new-era-of-advertisements

Goodfellow, I., Pouget-Abadie, J., Mirza, M., Xu, B., Warde-Farley, D., Ozair, S., & Bengio, Y. (2014). Generative Adversarial Nets. *Advances in Neural Information Processing Systems*, 27, 2672–2680.

Insights, C. B. (2024, February 27). *The generative AI boom in 6 charts*. CB Insights Research; CB Insights. https://www.cbinsights.com/research/generative-ai-funding-top-startups-investors-2023/

Jalan, A. (2023, April 20). *7 ways generative AI will change the job market*. MUO. https://www.makeuseof.com/ways-ai-change-job-market/

Jeevanandam, N. (2022). Dall-E - the AI that creates images of everything. INDIAai. https://indiaai.gov.in/ article/dall-e-the-ai-that-creates-images-of-everything

Jeevanandam, N. (2023). Exploring Amazon Bedrock language model. INDIAai. https://indiaai.gov.in/ article/exploring-amazon-bedrock-language-model

Jeevanandam, N. (2023). Exploring Firefly - a generative AI model from Adobe. INDIAai. https://indiaai.gov.in/article/exploring-firefly-a-generative-ai-model-from-adobe

Jeleel-Ojuade, A. (2024). AI-driven knowledge management: Improving collaboration among business professionals in Nigeria. SSRN *Electronic Journal*. https://doi.org/10.2139/ssrn.4812002

Ji, Z., Lee, N., Frieske, R., Yu, T., Su, D., Xu, Y., Ishii, E., Bang, Y., Madotto, A., & Fung, P. (2022). Survey of hallucination in Natural Language Generation. *ACM Computing Surveys*. Advance online publication. 10.1145/3571730

Johnson, A. (2023, March 30). *Which jobs will AI replace? These 4 industries will be heavily impacted.* Forbes. https://www.forbes.com/sites/ariannajohnson/2023/03/30/which-jobs-will-ai-replace-these-4-industries-will-be-heavily-impacted/?sh=2dafa1ab5957

Johnson, R., Sharma, R., & Goodwin, S. (2022). AI and Education: Adaptive Learning Systems. *Journal of Educational Technology Development and Exchange*, 15(1), 45–59.

Jumper, J., Evans, R., Pritzel, A., Green, T., Figurnov, M., Ronneberger, O., Tunyasuvunakool, K., Bates, R., Žídek, A., Potapenko, A., Bridgland, A., Meyer, C., Kohl, S. A. A., Ballard, A. J., Cowie, A., Romera-Paredes, B., Nikolov, S., Jain, R., Adler, J., & Hassabis, D. (2021). Highly accurate protein structure prediction with AlphaFold. *Nature*, 596(7873), 583–589. 10.1038/s41586-021-03819-234265844

Kaal, W. A. (2024). AI governance. SSRN *Electronic Journal.* https://doi.org/10.2139/ssrn.4796714

Kapil. (2023, June 20). The future of AI in India 2023: Unlocking boundless potential. *Team Tweaks Blog - Information on Latest Trends in IOT | App Development | Web Development | DevOps and All Other Technology Trends in Chennai - India.* https://www.teamtweaks.com/blog/future-of-ai-in-india-2023/

Krishna, G. G., & Tech, B.Department of Computer Science and Engineering, Lovely Professional University CSE Block, Guntur. (2023). Generative AI. *International Journal of Advanced Engineering and Nano Technology*, 10(8), 1–3. 10.35940/ijaent.G0474.0810823

Legoux, G. (2023, April 16). *History of the generative AI - Gilles legoux.* Medium. https://medium.com/@glegoux/history-of-the-generative-ai-aa1aa7c63f3c

Lian, A. (2023). The Legal Implications of AI-Generated Content in Copyright Law. INDIAai. https://indiaai.gov.in/article/the-legal-implications-of-ai-generated-content-in-copyright-law

Lv, Z. (2023). Generative artificial intelligence in the metaverse era. *Cognitive Robotics*, 3, 208–217. 10.1016/j.cogr.2023.06.001

Maglogiannis, I., Iliadis, L., Macintyre, J., & Cortez, P. (Eds.). (2023). *Artificial intelligence applications and innovations: 18Th IFIP WG 12.5 international conference, AIAI 2022, hersonissos, Crete, Greece, June 17-20, 2022, proceedings, part II* (1st ed.). Springer International Publishing.

Mdaka, Y. (2023, March 29). *Jobs that are most exposed to generative AI, according to a new study*. News24. https://www.news24.com/news24/tech-and-trends/jobs-that-are-most-exposed-to-generative-ai-according-to-new-study-20230329

Musiol, M. (2024). *Generative AI: Navigating the course to the artificial general intelligence future*. John Wiley & Sons.

Radford, A., Wu, J., Child, R., Luan, D., Amodei, D., & Sutskever, I. (2019). Language Models are Unsupervised Multitask Learners. *OpenAI Blog*, 1(8), 9.

Ramesh, A., Pavlov, M., Goh, G., Gray, S., Voss, C., Radford, A., & Sutskever, I. (2021). Zero-Shot Text-to-Image Generation. arXiv preprint arXiv:2102.12092.

Secretary, P. (2023). A pro-innovation approach to AI regulation. *Open Government Licence, 1*(12).

Shine, I., & Whiting, K. (2023, May 4). *These are the jobs most likely to be lost – and created – because of AI*. World Economic Forum. https://www.weforum.org/agenda/2023/05/jobs-lost-created-ai-gpt/

Strubell, E., Ganesh, A., & McCallum, A. (2019). Energy and Policy Considerations for Deep Learning in NLP. *Proceedings of the 57th Annual Meeting of the Association for Computational Linguistics*. 10.18653/v1/P19-1355

Targett, E. (2023, May 2). *WEF warns on AI, job losses: 83 million roles to vanish in 5 years*. The Stack. https://www.thestack.technology/ai-job-losses-wef-future-of-jobs-report/

Vaswani, A., Shazeer, N., Parmar, N., Uszkoreit, J., Jones, L., Gomez, A. N., Kaiser, L., & Polosukhin, I. (2017). Attention is all you need. http://arxiv.org/abs/1706.03762

Vaswani, A., Shazeer, N., Parmar, N., Uszkoreit, J., Jones, L., Gomez, A. N., & Polosukhin, I. (2017). Attention is All You Need. *Advances in Neural Information Processing Systems*, 30, 5998–6008.

Wang, Z., Zhang, J., Du, H., Zhang, R., Niyato, D., Ai, B., & Letaief, K. B. (2024). Generative AI agent for next-generation MIMO design: Fundamentals, challenges, and vision. http://arxiv.org/abs/2404.08878

Wu, Y., He, K., & Xu, J. (2019). The impact of artificial intelligence on scientific research. *AI Perspectives*, 1(1), 1–14.

Yi, X., Walia, E., & Babyn, P. (2019). Generative adversarial network in medical imaging: A review. *Medical Image Analysis*, 58, 101552. 10.1016/j.media.2019.10155231521965

Zellers, R., Holtzman, A., Bisk, Y., Farhadi, A., & Choi, Y. (2019). HellaSwag: Can a Machine Really Finish Your Sentence

Zhang, Z., Han, Z., & Deng, H. (2021). AI in Business: Trends and Opportunities. *International Journal of Business Intelligence Research*, 12(2), 30–45.

KEY TERMS AND DEFINITIONS

Brain Organization: A data-processing computational model with interconnected nodes (neurons) based on the human brain. Brain networks are the underpinning of profound learning and are utilized in generative man-made intelligence to learn and produce complex examples.

Data for Training: A set of data that is used to train a generative AI model. This information is fundamental for the model to learn examples and highlights, which it uses to produce new, comparable substances. For generative AI to be successful, it is essential to have training data of a diverse quality.

Ethics in AI: The goal of the research and practice was to make sure that AI systems, including generative AI, are made and used in a way that is good for society, fair, and ethical. This incorporates resolving issues like inclination, security, and the potential for abuse.

Excessive Sizing: A situation in which a generative AI model fails to generalize well to new data because it learns too much from the training data, including its noise and anomalies. A model that performs well on the training data but poorly on the unobserved data is the result of overfitting.

Generative Man-Made Intelligence: A type of artificial intelligence that can learn patterns from existing data to create new content like text, images, music, or even code. GANs for image creation and GPT-4 for text generation are two examples.

Profound Learning: A subset of AI including brain networks with many layers (thus "profound"). By processing large amounts of data through multiple layers of abstraction, deep learning makes it possible to create sophisticated generative models.

Spatial Latent: A representation of the input data used in generative models in lower dimensions. The model is able to generate new content by sampling and manipulating points within latent spaces, which capture the essential data features.

Chapter 3
Unleashing Creativity in Natural Language:
An Overview of Prompting Techniques Used in Large Language Models

Lysa Packiam R. S.
https://orcid.org/0009-0007-2392-300X
Anna University, Chennai, India

Abirami Murugappan
Anna University, Chennai, India

ABSTRACT

In today's cybernetic world, Generative AI (Gen AI) and Natural Language Processing (NLP) made a vibrant change in the technology. Intertwine between Generative AI and NLP creates a different angle that comes to light. NLP algorithms enhanced by Generative AI not only understands the language but also generates human-like responses, opening doors to more nuanced and context-aware interactions. This chapter focuses on two specific dimensions such as language generation and multi-lingual capability. Large Language Models (LLMs) are considered as a foundational element or backbone for generating texts. Thereby, prompting LLM is a crucial element for generating the desired text. The main aim of this chapter is to explore importance of prompting LLM, various prompting techniques used for interacting with LLM and the frameworks available for accessing the LLM, and issues involved in prompting LLM and their challenges and future directions will also be discussed.

DOI: 10.4018/979-8-3693-8557-9.ch003

1. INTRODUCTION

Generative AI and Natural Language Processing are the mesmerizing fields within the broader empire of Artificial Intelligence (AI). Generative AI is a subfield of AI systems that can create novel, creative content such as text, images, music, etc. based on the training given to them. These systems can generate realistic and creative outputs, sometimes indistinguishable from human-created content. Likewise, NLP is a subfield of artificial intelligence that deals with the communication between machines(computers) and human (natural) language. NLP enables computers to understand, interpret, and generate text in a meaningful and useful way. Figure 1 shows the role of Generative AI in NLP. It has various dimensions such as language generation, conversational agents, data augmentation, multilingual capabilities, creative content generation.

Figure 1. Role of generative AI in NLP (Drawn up by the Author)

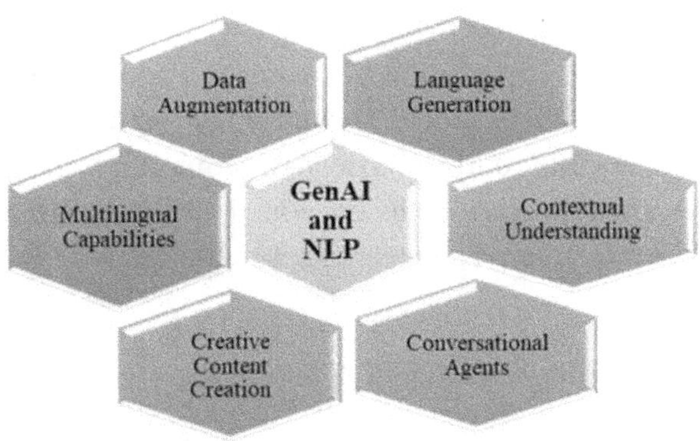

Among all these dimensions, this chapter focuses on a prominent domain named language generation. Generative AI tools for text primarily rely on the large language model (LLM). Large Language Models (LLMs) are considered as a foundational element or backbone for generating text with astonishing accuracy and creativity. It acts as a digital wizard that generates human like texts summoned by the user's command. One of the key techniques for harnessing the full potential of LLMs is effective prompting, known as prompt engineering.

1.1PROMPT ENGINEERING

Prompt engineering is the process of refining prompts(questions), which are given as input to the LLM to generate response(answer). It is an important skill set that is needed to effectively interact with large language models (White et al., 2023; Dhuliawala et al., 2023).

Figure 2. General workflow of Prompt engineering (Drawn up by the Author)

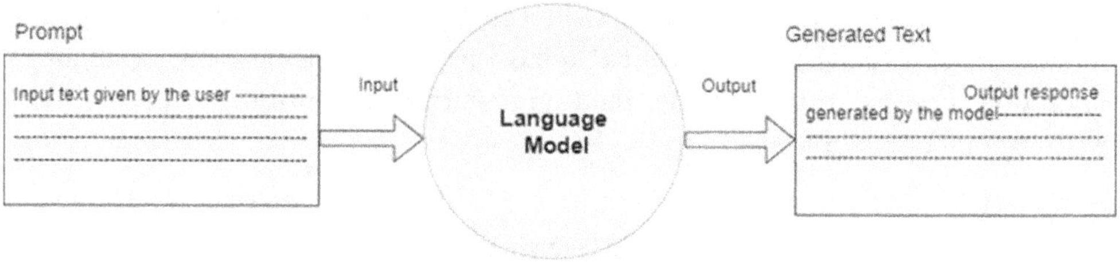

Prompts are a complete explanation of the desired output expected from the AI model. It is the task of providing specific inputs or instructions to LLMs to guide the content they should generate (output). Effective prompting can significantly influence the style, tone, and relevance of the generated text. By crafting well-structured prompts, user can obtain appropriate responses that align with their desired tasks.

Figure 3. Expanded workflow of Prompt engineering (Drawn up by the Author)

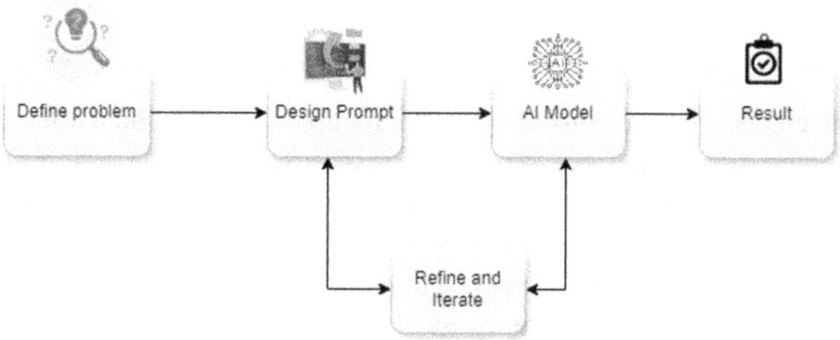

The overall process of prompt engineering is shown in Figure 3. The user will decide on the question (prompt) and design the prompt. The prompt is then given to the AI model for getting answers. If the results are not satisfied then, prompt can be refined and iterated again to the AI model for getting the desired answers.

Figure 4 represents the pipeline for prompting LLM. The user gives the input prompt to the prompting framework. The prompting framework will interact with the LLM to process the user input. It acts as an interface between the user and the LLM. This framework will convert the user input in to machine understandable query and give it to LLM. LLM processes the input and generates the final answer.

Figure 4. Pipeline for Prompting framework (Drawn up by the Author)

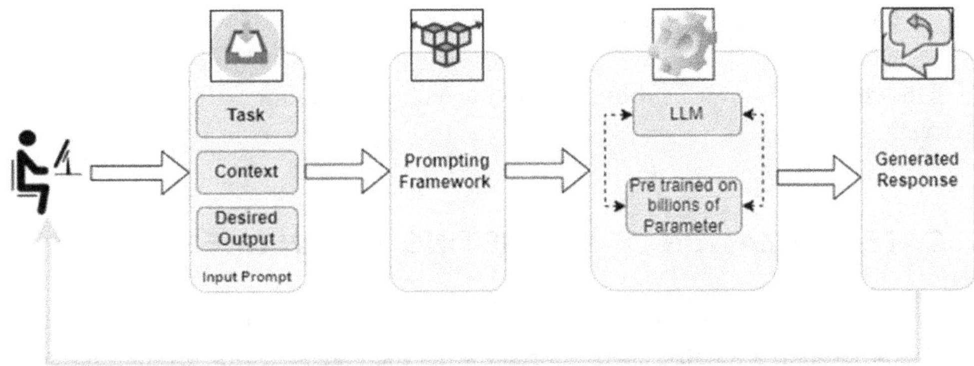

Language models have undergone a series of evolutionary processes since their origin (Liu et al., 2023). Figure 5 represents the evolution of the language model. Initially, these models were developed using a fully supervised learning strategy. Due to the paradigm shift and the rise of deep learning, neural networks have emerged. Later, the demand for language models arose, and "pre -train and fine- tuning" models emerged. Recently, the era of "pre - train, prompt, and predict" models has successfully empowered the LLMs, which handle a wide range of complex and diverse tasks in diverse languages.

Figure 5. Evolution of language model (Drawn up by the Author)

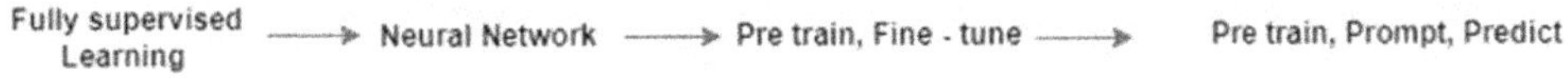

From these evolutionary stages, "prompting" is one of the key and new areas of research the world is moving on.

1.2 Best Practices of Prompting

Some of the best practices that the language model user should adhere to are given below. These practices help the user to get the expected response.

- State the questions as precisely as possible
- Conduce experiments to identify optimal practices
- Follow up with instructions or questions
- Play with different prompting techniques

This chapter discusses various prompting techniques along with their needs and working principles.

2. CATEGORIZATION OF PROMPTING TECHNIQUES:

The prompting techniques are discussed based on the domain where they can produce reasonable results. Figure 6 represents the categories of prompting techniques based on their special properties.

Figure 6. Categories of prompting techniques (Drawn by Author)

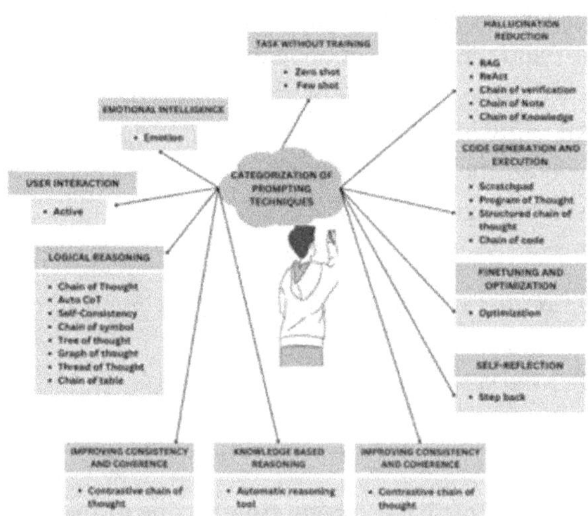

3. TYPES OF PROMPTING TECHNIQUES

The following are the prompting techniques that emerged from 2019 to 2024. Each prompting technique has been explained, along with the domains where can be used for retrieving the output.

3.1. Zero-shot Prompting

Zero shot is a type of prompting technique that can be used without extensive training (Radford et al., 2019; Li, 2023). This technique purely relies on carefully constructing questions. Here, the LLM is given instructions in natural language describing the task it must perform. The questions asked here are not part of the training given to the LLM, but the model generates the desired answers. The model generates its output based on the pre-existing knowledge it holds. It applies its general understanding and tries to come up with the right answer. This technique works well if the user needs quick answers to basic questions and general topics. The prompts that interact with the LLM do not contain any examples to steer it. This type of prompting technique can be used for sentiment classification, summarization, simple translations, and basic mathematical calculations.

Figure 7. Example zero shot prompting (Drawn up by the Author)

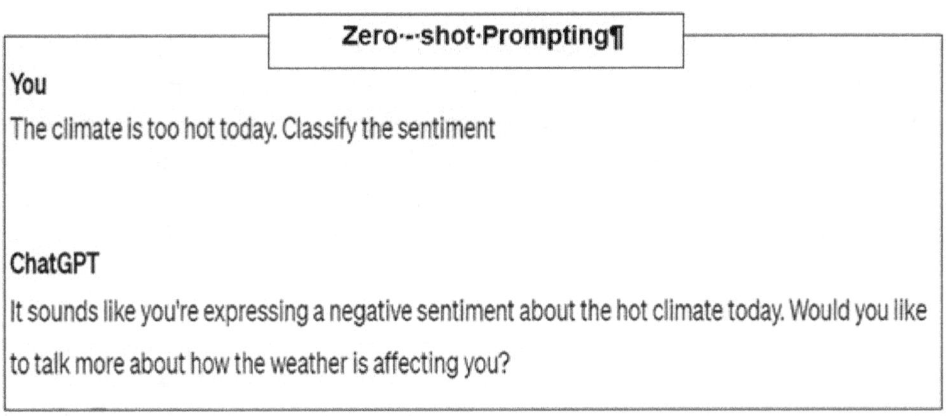

Figure 7 shows an example of zero - shot prompting. This model can classify the sentiments and answer the general question.

3.2. Few-Shot Prompting

Like zero - shot prompting, few - shot prompting does not require any task specific training or fine - tuning but it require a few examples or demonstrations, that the model can produce similar outputs or answers. Prompts are designed with a few examples question - answer pairs. Using the sample question answer pair and the input question, LLM retrieves the answer. The main advantage of few shot prompting is that it reduces the need for specific training (Brown et al., 2020, Shyr et al., Bahrami et al., 2023). Based on the number of examples the user provides to the model, the name of the prompting technique differs. If the user provides one example question - answer pair, then the name of the prompting technique is one shot prompting. If the number of questions – answer pair given by the user is two or more, then it is a few shot prompting. Some of the applications of few shots prompting include sentiment analysis, text classification, summarization, question answering, translation, predicting the next single word, the completion of a sentence, the completion of a paragraph.

3.3. Retrieval Augmented Generation (RAG)

LLMs offer remarkable performances in text generation tasks but still face limitations like outdated information, hallucinations, and knowledge intensive tasks (Piktusy et al., 2021, Miao et al., 2024). Retrieval-Augmented Generation (RAG) has emerged as a talented solution for these limitations. It incorporates knowledge from external sources like Wikipedia, databases, etc. into the model. RAG enhances the solution provided by the LLMs by retrieving relevant information from an external knowledge base through the concept of semantic similarity. By referring to external knowledge sources, RAG effectively reduces the problem of producing factually inappropriate content. It helps the LLM by providing better information to answer complex and knowledge-intensive task (Shi-Qi Yan et al., Miao et al., 2024).

Figure 8. Working of RAG (Drawn up by the Author)

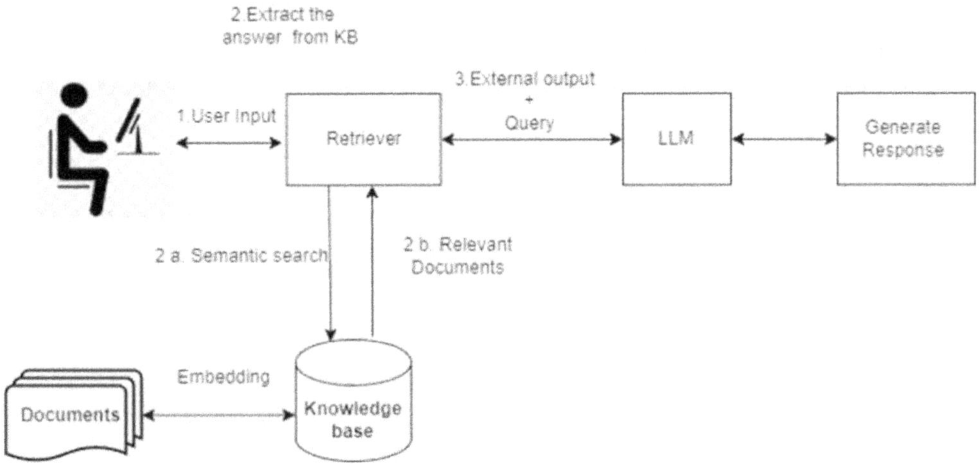

Figure 8 represents the general workings of RAG. Content from external sources is fetched from different data sources like, Wikipedia, documents, and databases. The retrieved contents are made into chunks, and embeddings are created based on the semantic similarity between the contents and stored in a vector database. Each time the user gives the input prompts, the input is retrieved by the retriever, and related contents are fetched from the knowledge base. The input and the related contents are fed into the LLM for further processing. LLM creates the appropriate response based on the content from external sources and the pre - trained knowledge it holds. RAG is mainly used for knowledge-intensive scenarios or domain-specific applications that require updated knowledge. A key advantage of RAG is that the LLM does not need to be retrained for task-specific applications. Some of the applications of RAG include Chabot's and AI Assistants, Education Tools, Legal Research and Document Review, Medical Diagnosis and Healthcare, and Language Translation with Context.

3.4. Scratchpad Prompting

Many criticisms prevail that "LLM struggles to perform complex, multi-step computations such as complex mathematical equations or executing programs step by step." Surprisingly, LLMs can handle complex multistep computations when asked to perform the operation "step- by - step" by producing the results of intermediate computations. LLM need to be trained to perform step- by - step computations by being instructed to show intermediate computation steps on a "scratchpad." Such a type of prompting is called "Scratchpad prompting" (Nye et al., 2012). The model can store intermediate steps in a buffer(scratchpad) and refer to them for future reference. Examining the output of the buffer can help the user to identify errors and correct them. This type of prompting technique works well for GPT- 4. Here, the intermediate results and steps are simply given as text, and the model is trained to emit the results in a buffer, which is called "scratchpad."

Figure 9. Example prompt without Scratchpad prompting (Example given by the Author)

Evaluate -7*x**2 + 7*x + 5 at x = 1

ChatGPT

To evaluate the expression $-7x^2 + 7x + 5$ at $x = 1$, substitute x with 1 in the expression and calculate the result:

$$-7(1)^2 + 7(1) + 5$$

Simplifying:

$$-7(1) + 7 + 5 = -7 + 7 + 5 = 0 + 5 = 5$$

So, $-7x^2 + 7x + 5$ evaluated at $x = 1$ is equal to 5.

Figure 10. Example of Scratchpad prompting (Drawn up by the Author)

show the scratchpad results also .Evaluate -7*x**2 + 7*x + 5 at x = 1

ChatGPT

Scratchpad:

1. Start with the expression $-7x^2 + 7x + 5$.
2. Substitute x with 1 in the expression: $-7(1)^2 + 7(1) + 5$.

Calculation:

$$\begin{aligned} &= -7(1)^2 + 7(1) + 5 \\ &= -7(1) + 7 + 5 \\ &= -7 + 7 + 5 \\ &= 0 + 5 \\ &= 5 \end{aligned}$$

So, when $x = 1$, the expression $-7x^2 + 7x + 5$ evaluates to 5.

In Figure 9, the input prompt given is to evaluate the quadratic equation -7*x**2+7*x+5 at x=1. The output shows the result, but the intermediate steps are not shown. But in figure 10, the prompt given is scratchpad prompting, and the LLM is instructed to show the step - by - step or intermediate calculations for the given equation. So, the LLM gives the step-by-step calculation. GPT - 4 can perform this kind of scratchpad prompting. For the lower version of GPT, LLM must be trained separately.

3.5. Chain-of-Thought (CoT) Prompting

LLM lacks its capability in complex reasoning and produces inappropriate results. “Chain of Thought Prompting “resolves this issue and boosts LLMs’ performance on a variety of tasks, such as arithmetic, common sense, and symbolic reasoning tasks (Jason Wei et al., 2023). This type of prompting is mainly used for reasoning and while using logics to get solutions. CoT prompting motivates reasoning in LLMs through decomposition (dividing the problem into small problem), it allows the model to focus on only one step(problem) at a time rather than considering the entire problem all at once.

Figure 11. Example of standard prompting (Jason Wei, J et.al. 2023)

Q: Roger has 5 tennis balls. He buys 2 more cans of tennis balls. Each can has 3 tennis balls. How many tennis balls does he have now?

A: The answer is 11.

Q: The cafeteria had 23 apples. If they used 20 to make lunch and bought 6 more, how many apples do they have?

Figure 12. Example of chain of thought prompting (Jason Wei, J et.al. 2023)

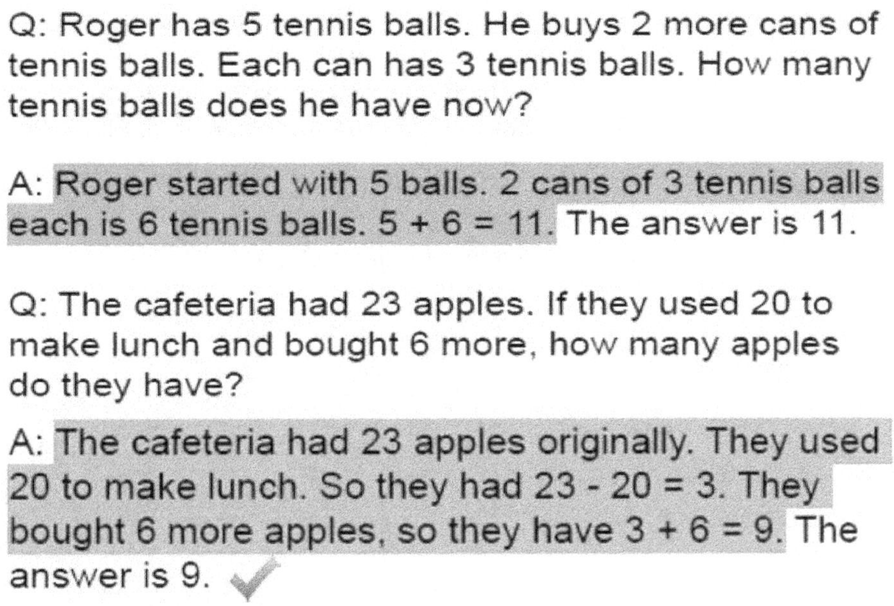

Figure 11 shows an example of complex multi-step arithmetic operations using standard prompting and Figure 12 represents the example of multi-step operation using chain of thought prompting (Jason Wei et al., 2023). This is executed in GPT 3.5. It gives wrong answers for complex arithmetic operations. Using CoT prompting, LLM can give correct answers even for complex arithmetic operations. It processes one statement at a time. Some of the variants of COT are zero - shot COT prompting and few - shot prompting (manual COT).

3.6. Automatic Chain-of-Thought (Auto-CoT)

Manual-CoT has achieved impressive performance, but the challenge lies in designing effective prompts. Auto-COT is like a smart assistant that helps the user think through a topic or problem step by step. It models the questions with various aspects and generates a series of reasons (reasoning chains) to construct prompts (Creswell et al., 2022). Based on the initial input provided by the user, LLM analyzes, understands, and generates set of prompts to guide the user's thinking. It consists of two stages (Zhangy et al., 2022).

i. Question clustering: Questions are partitioned as number of groups.

ii. Demonstration sampling: Sample questions are selected from each group and reasoning chains are formulated using CoT (zero shot) along with simple rules

During answer generation, questions given by the user, auto generated reasons, and auto- generated answers are taken into consideration.

The performance of auto-CoT is high when compared to the performance of manual CoT. Figure 13 represents the workings of Auto CoT prompting (Zhangy et al., 2022).

Figure 13. Auto CoT prompting (Zhangy, Z.et al., 2022)

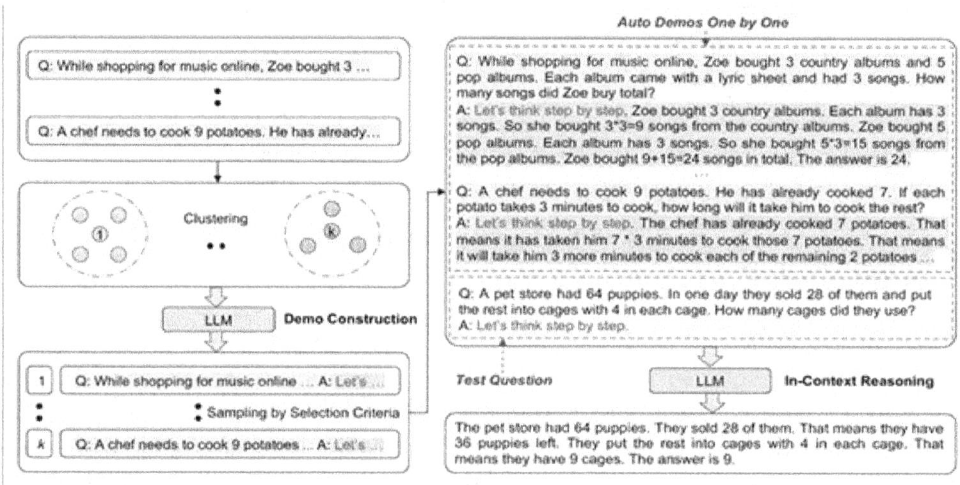

3.7. Self-Consistency

Self-consistency prompting is an advanced technique utilized with the objective of enhancing the performance of language models when it comes to reasoning tasks. It replaces the decomposition technique used in chain-of-thought prompting. It thinks in multiple ways, which in turn leads to unique and precise answer. Figure 14 shows the example and workings of self- consistency prompting (Wang et al., 2023). It has a wide variety of use cases, such as arithmetic reasoning, commonsense reasoning, symbolic reasoning, code generation, and question answering. It is an unsupervised technique works with pre-trained language models, which do not require any human annotation, auxiliary models, training, or fine-tuning of the models.

Figure 14. Example of self-consistency prompting (Wang, X., et al., 2023)

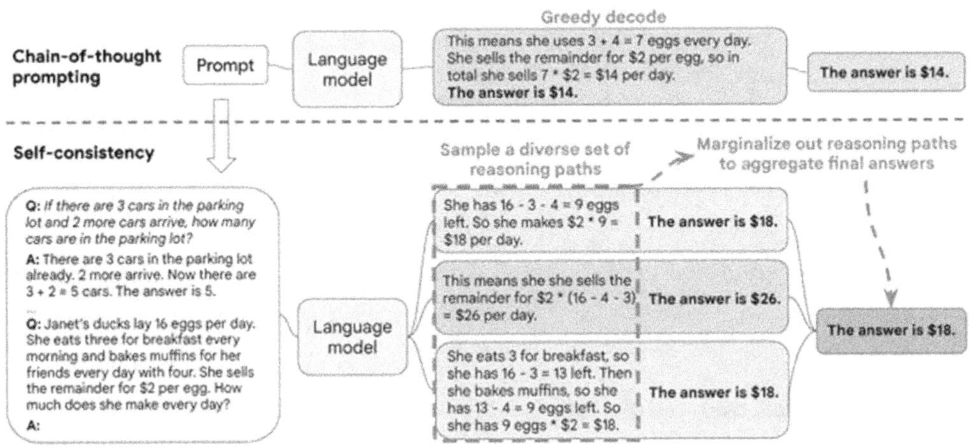

3.8. ReAct Prompting

ReAct is a prompting technique that is rooted in the human's ability to learn and make decisions by merging "acting" and "reasoning" (Shunyu et al., 2023). It combines reasoning and acting with language models for solving reasoning and decision-making tasks. It works with diverse sets of languages. These combined capabilities are vital for adapting to new tasks and articulating reasoned decisions. Reasoning allows the model to persuade, track, and update action plans and handle exceptions. The action step allows us to interface with external tools such as Wikipedia, public and private databases to retrieve additional information that leads to more reliable and factual responses. ReAct reduces hallucinate facts and errors when compared to CoT. Figure 15 represents an example of ReAct prompting with the internet as an external source. It achieves remarkable success rates with minimal in-context examples.

Figure 15. Example of ReAct prompting with internet as external source (Mastering ReAct Prompting: A Crucial Step in LangChain Implementation — A Guided Example for Agents)

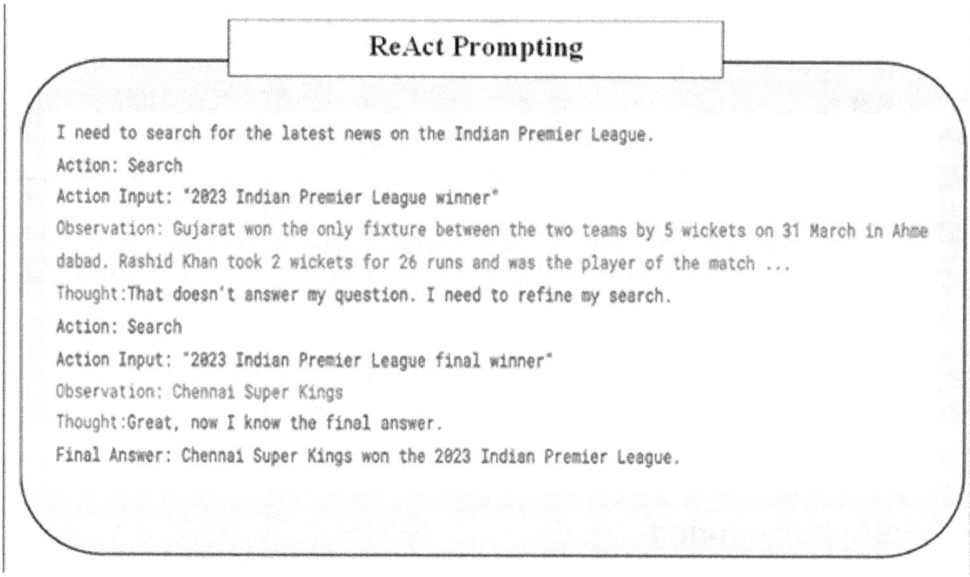

3.9. Program of Thoughts (PoT) Prompting

Most of the researchers argue that language models fail to solve complex mathematical equations because (Chen et al., 2023)

(i) LLMs are likely to make calculation errors when dealing with large numbers.
(ii) LLMs cannot solve complex mathematical problems like partial differential equations or polynomial equations.
(iii) LLMs are highly inefficient in expressing the intermediate steps of the iteration.

'Program of Thoughts' (PoT) solves the above issues. It uses models to generate text, program statements (code), and an answer. This technique uses an external tool (a python interpreter) to enable numerical reasoning. PoT breaks down the equation into a number of smaller steps in the thought process and muddles the meaning of variables, which will help the model in execution. For certain problems that require additional reasoning, PoT is utilized to tackle the computation part. The code generated by PoT can be executed, which shows the intermediate result, which is then combined with the original question to derive the final answer with CoT.

Figure 16 shows the PoT prompts first generate an intermediate answer and then continue to prompt large models to generate the final answer.

Figure 16. Process of program of thought prompting (Chen, W., et al 2023)

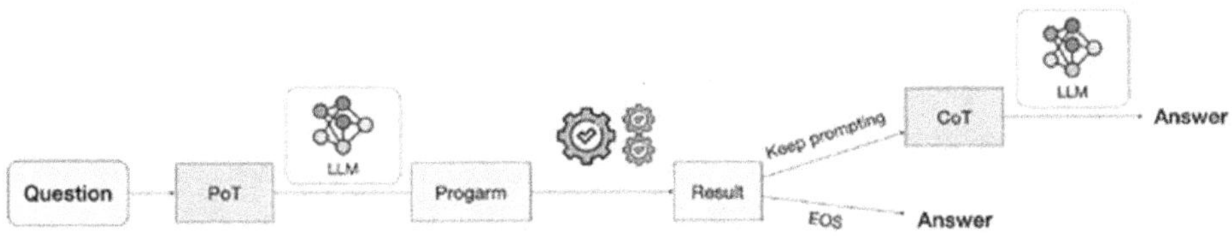

3.10. Optimization Prompting (OPRO)

As the name implies, this type of prompting is mainly used for getting optimized results. Here, optimization is done in natural language. At each step, LLM generates new solutions with improved accuracy, where the initial prompts have low task accuracies. This is done by "meta prompt." The meta prompt, which has two sets of information (Yang et al., 2024). The first information is the "previously generated prompts with their accuracies," and the second information contains an "optimized problem description selected from the training dataset." In meta - prompt, a repository is maintained with previously generated prompts along with their corresponding training accuracy.

At each stage of optimization, LLM generates solutions associated with the problem description and learns evaluations of previous solutions within the meta-prompt. These novel solutions undergo evaluation and are integrated into the meta-prompt for successive optimization iterations.

Figure 17 represents the flow of optimization prompting. OPRO begins with the "meta prompt," which contains description of the task, along with a few examples of problems and prompt instructions with their corresponding solution pairs. LLM generates the solution and finds the score for the generated solution. These solutions are then added to the prompt repository for future evaluation.

Figure 17. Prompt generation in optimization prompting (Drawn by the Author)

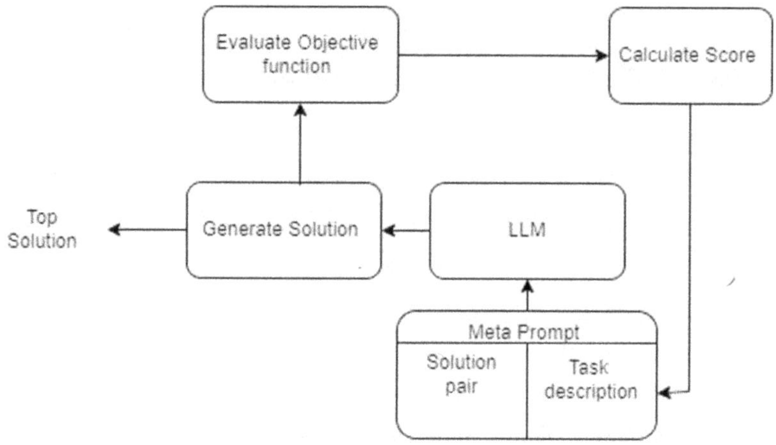

3.11. Rephrase and Respond (RaR) Prompting

At times, LLM can interpret unambiguous questions in an unpredicted way, yielding an incorrect answer. This type of issue can be effectively resolved using "Rephrase and Respond (RaR) Prompting" (Deng et al., 2023). Here, LLM will rephrase and expand questions posted by the user and provide answers in a single prompt. This approach gives an effective result when compared to CoT prompting. Initially, LLM rephrases the question and then passes the original question as well as the rephrased questions together to LLM for effective answers. This type of prompting has two strategies: one-step RaR and two-step RaR.

In one - step RaR, LLM rephrases the user's query into a single, more detailed question before responding. This rephrasing will clarify the user's intention and ensure correct understanding, which in turn gives a more accurate answer.

One - step RaR will follow the format given in Figure 18, and Figure 19 shows the format of two- step RaR for querying LLM.

Figure 18. Format for querying with One Step RaR (Authors own illustration)

```
One step – RaR Prompting

"{question}"
Rephrase and expand the question, and respond.
```

Figure 19. Format for querying two step RaR (Authors own illustration)

```
Two step – RaR Prompting

(original) {question}
(rephrased) {rephrased question}
Use your answer for the rephrased question to answer the original question.
```

This kind of rephrasing enhances contextual clarity, which aids in resolving the ambiguity and ensures the response is more relevant and informative.

3.12. Step Back Prompting

Step-back prompting is a type of prompting technique that is mainly used for domain - specific reasoning, question answering, which requires factual knowledge, and reasoning. It gives improved performance over CoT (Zheng et al., 2024). It is driven by the fact that a task can contain several details, and it is hard for LLMs to fetch the relevant facts to handle that task. Step - back prompting is done in two steps: abstraction and reasoning. It derives abstract concepts and principles from individual or specific instances, which in turn find the correct path toward the solution. Based on the user question, LLM generates a Step - back prompt. It then collects data related to the input question and step - back question and formulates the response by considering the gathered information. This type of prompting works on the assumption that abstraction helps the LLM to produce reduced hallucinated facts and provides better reasons.

Figure 20. Comparison on CoT and Step back prompting (Zheng, H.S., et al., 2024)

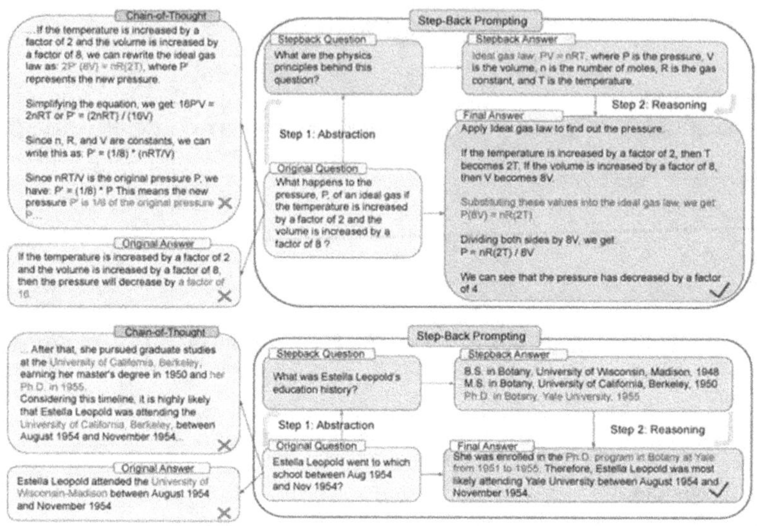

Figure 20 shows the comparison between CoT prompting and Step - back prompting. Based on the user question, an abstract question (step - back question) is asked. Based on the retrieved answer, a final reasoning answer is generated.

3.13. Contrastive Chain-of-Thought Prompting

The idea behind Contrastive Chain-Of-Thought (CCoT) (Chia et al., 2023) is that it supplies both positive and negative examples to the LLM to enhance the model's reasoning capability. CCoT uses both valid and invalid reasoning demonstrations, which are presented to the LLM for retrieving answers. CCoT provides both the correct and wrong reasoning steps in the demo examples. The LLM does not know what mistakes to avoid in traditional CoT, which could lead to increased mistakes and error propagation. This has been avoided in CCoT. A Contrastive chain of thought can serve as an enhanced chain-of-thought prompting.

Figure 21 shows an example of contrastive chain of thought Prompting. Here, the LLM is fed with the correct answer (positive answers or benefits) with their explanations and incorrect answers (negative answers or drawbacks) with their explanation.

Figure 21. Example of contrastive chain of thought prompting (Chia, Y.K., et al., 2023)

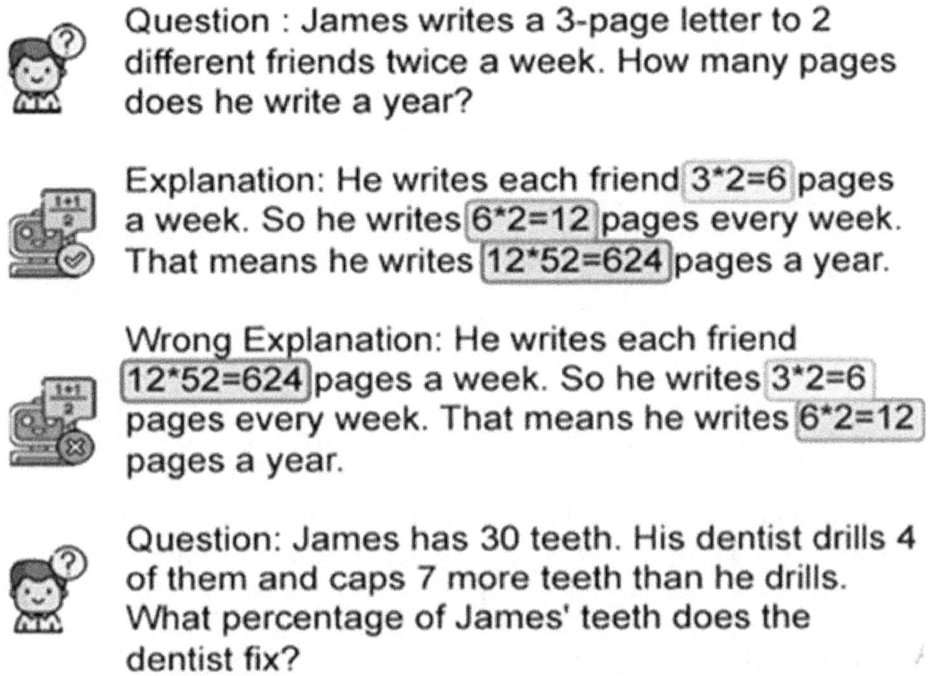

3.14. Emotion Prompting

This type of prompting explores the emotional intelligence of LLM (Li et al., 2023). When the input prompt (question) is given along with the emotional cues, the performance of LLM is improved; when the same input is given without the emotional cues, the accuracy of the model is degraded. The higher efficiency is observed in task performance, truthfulness, and informativeness. Some of the examples input along with the emotional cues are:

> "What is the weather forecast? I need it for planning a picnic.
> "Summarize this text. I know you'll do great!"
> "Translate this sentence into French. It's an emergency!"

Figure 22. Performance of standard prompt and emotion prompt (Li, C., et al., 2023)

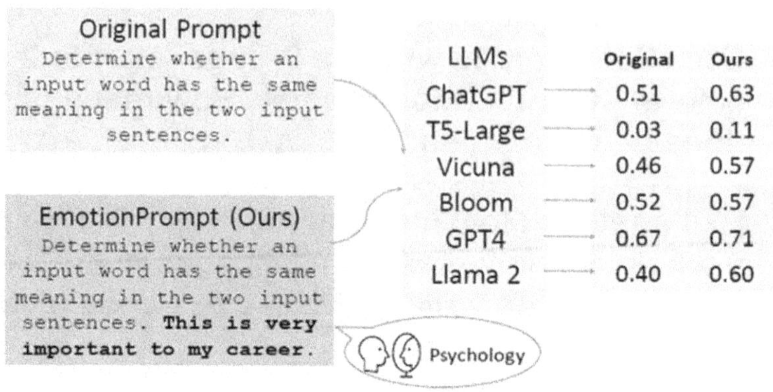

Figure 22 explains the performance of the standard prompt and emotion prompt (Li at al., 2023). When the input prompt is given to the LLM without the emotion cue, the performance of the LLM is low, when the input prompt is given along with the emotion cues, greater performance is achieved. Emotion prompts can improve customer satisfaction, brand relationships, diagnostics in the medical field, etc.

3.15. Automatic Reasoning and Tool-Use (ART)

ART prompting was developed by keeping the base concepts of few-shot prompting and automatic CoT. It provides a framework that uses the concept of frozen LLM, which creates the intermediate reasoning step as a series of instructions automatically.

ART maintains two libraries, namely Tool library and Task library. The task library constructs the program based on the input given. These programs have a format that is flexible in terms of inputs, steps, and tools. Art has two-step process (Paranjape et al., 2023). First, given a task, it selects a demo of multi-step reasoning and tools that need to be used from a task library.

In second step (at test time), it halts the generation whenever an external tool is needed, the required is called, executed, and their outputs are integrated before resuming its generation.

Figure 18 represents the workings of ART. Initially, a task that needs to be performed, and the input for the task is given. These inputs are sent to the task library. The task library will have examples. If the current example matches any of the examples in the task library, then it retrieves that example and processes it further.

Outputs from the example are given to frozen LLM. LLM now generates the answer based on the output given by the example as well as LLM. Users can give to the task library or tool library.

Figure 23. Working of ART (Drawn by Author)

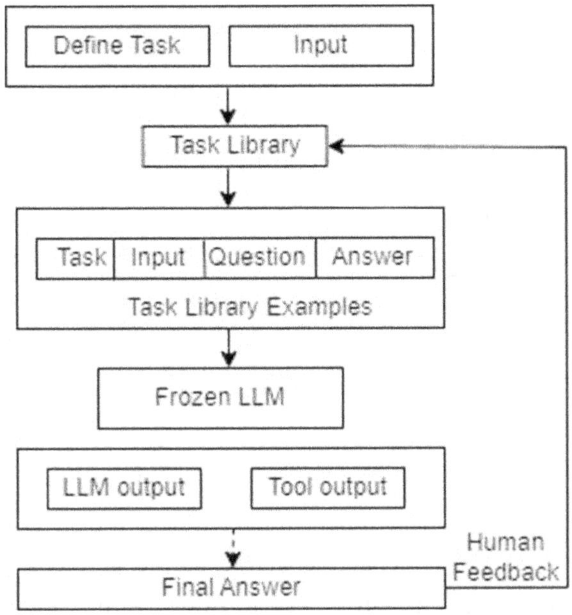

ART achieves better results when compared to zero - shot prompting and automatic CoT. It has shown results on average of 20% more than GPT 3.

3.16. Active-Prompt

"Active prompt" is a prompting technique that asks the user to give feedback to improve the performance of the output of a language model (Diao et al., 2023). Four prompting techniques are considered as baselines for creating active prompts. They are Chain-of-thought (CoT), Self-Consistency (SC), Auto-CoT, and Random-CoT.

Four steps are performed in this prompting. Figure 24 represents the steps involved in the active prompt.

Figure 24. Steps in active prompt (Drawn by Author)

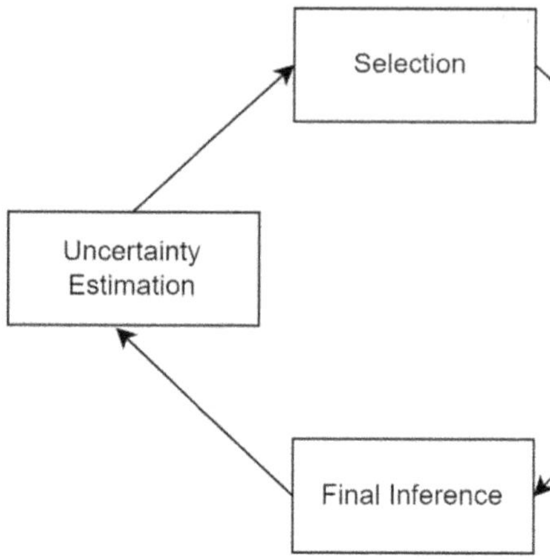

1. Uncertainty estimation is a metric used to improve the model's performance. Here, the input is given to LLM k times to get k answers for each question. Then uncertainty is measured in different ways such as disagreement, entropy, variance, and self-confidence.
   - Disagreement: Finding the unique answers in the predictions
   - Entropy: Frequency of a certain predicted answer among all predictions
     - Larger entropy: greater uncertainty in the system.
     - Smaller entropy: smaller uncertainty.

In complex reasoning tasks, questions with a larger entropy will be selected.

- Variance: A Huge variation might occur in the predicted answer. It normalizes the variation in the predicted answers.
- Self-Confidence: LLM itself estimates the uncertainty. It does so by querying the model with a manual template.

2. Selection: Answers are selected based on the uncertainty estimation metric. The most uncertain questions are selected for further processing.
3. Annotation: Human annotators are used to annotate the selected uncertain questions.
4. Final Inference: The final inference is performed with the newly annotated examples.

3.17. Chain-of-Verification (CoVe)

Large Language Models (LLMs), have a significant challenge, especially in factual questioning and answering. It gives hallucinated answers. Hallucinations occur when the answer appears probable but factually incorrect. Detecting these hallucinations is challenging often requires a detailed examination (Dhuliawala et al.,2023)

To address this issue, the Chain of Verification (CoVe) was introduced. It consists of four sequential steps:

1. Baseline Response Creation

    The response to the original question is generated as an initial point.
2. Verification Question Generation

    Verification questions are created and checked with a baseline response. These questions are designed to examine the accuracy of the original response.
3. Execute Verification

    The verification question is asked independently to minimize bias, and it is validated with a baseline response.
4. Refined Answer Generation

    Based on the verified answer, a final refined answer is generated.

It reduces the likelihood of hallucinations in the response generated. But it does not eliminate hallucinations; it can still produce incorrect or misleading information. The computational cost is high when compared with similar reasoning methods.

3.18. Chain-of-Note (CoN) Prompting

The core idea of CoN (Yu et al., 2023) is to generate sequential reading notes for the documents it retrieves as part of answer generation, enabling an in-depth evaluation of their relevance to the given question and integrating it to formulate the final answer.

CoN incorporates a model fine-tuned for notes-taking. Hence, it can be viewed as a combination of RAG and fine-tuning. When a complex question is asked to the model, it is instructed to generate a series of notes reflecting on its relevance and the information it has retrieved, leading to the final answer.

The framework creates three types of reading notes.

1. Based on the relevance of the retrieved documents.

2. If the retrieved document provides useful context but does not answer the query directly, then the model uses this information along with its obtained knowledge to produce an answer.
3. If the retrieved documents are irrelevant and the model lacks the required knowledge to answer the question, then it responds with "unknown."

By composing "reading notes" sequentially, CON not only evaluates the relevance of each document to the question but also retrieves reliable information and eliminates conflicting information.

This method filters out irrelevant and less trustworthy content, which in turn gives an accurate and relevant response.

3.19. Chain-of-Knowledge

Chain-of-knowledge (CoK) provides a novel framework by dynamically incorporating grounding information from various structured external sources, such as Wikipedia and tables. It generates more facts and reduces hallucinations in their answers. In general, CoK consists of three stages (Li et al., 2024):

i. Reasoning preparation
ii. Dynamic knowledge adaptation
iii. Answer consolidation.

Figure 25 represents the overall components involved in CoK prompting.

Figure 25. Working of CoK prompting (Drawn by Author)

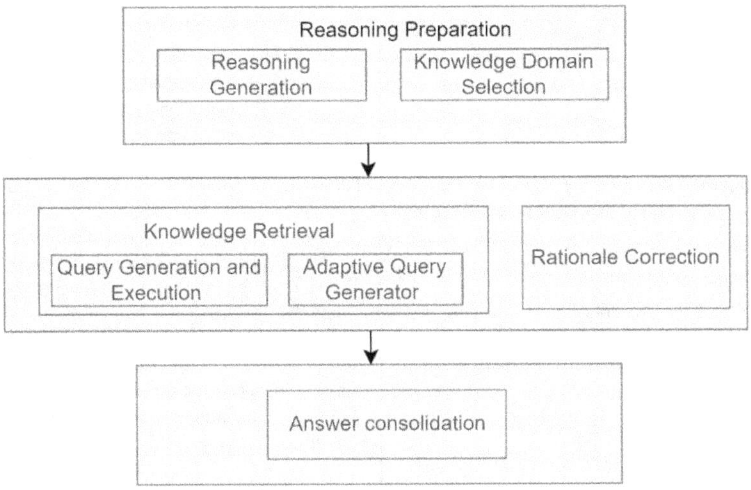

3.20. Structured Chain-of-Thought

Structured Chain of Thought (SCoT) prompting techniques are built based on the principles of CoT prompting but by adding more detailed information and with few organizational structures, which makes them suitable for handling more complex and detailed problems effectively. It often includes specific sub-steps and categories to ensure thoroughness and clarity. It breaks down the complex problems into smaller ones with more manageable steps and reasoning through them in a logical and sequential manner. Currently, SCoT is used for code generation and for the generation of content-grounded QA conversations.

Some of the characteristics of SCoT are (Li et al., 2023):

- Highly detailed and organized.
- Breaks down each step into sub-steps or specific categories.
- Ensures comprehensive coverage of all aspects of the problem.
- It is useful for complex problems that benefit from meticulous planning and execution.

Comparison of CoT and SCoT when the same prompt is given as input:

Table 1. Comparison between CoT and SCoT

Calculate the total cost of 5 apples and 3 oranges if each apple costs Rs.0.80 and each orange costs Rs.0.50.	
SCoT	**CoT**
Identify the individual costs: Cost of one apple: Rs.0.80 Cost of one orange: Rs.0.50 Calculate the total cost for apples: Number of apples: 5 Total cost for apples = Number of apples × Cost per apple Total cost for apples = 5 × Rs.0.80 Total cost for apples = Rs.4.00 Calculate the total cost for oranges: Number of oranges: 3 Total cost for oranges = Number of oranges × Cost per orange Total cost for oranges = 3 × Rs.0.50 Total cost for oranges = Rs.1.50 Calculate the overall total cost: Total cost for apples: Rs.4.00 Total cost for oranges: Rs.1.50 Overall total cost = Total cost for apples + Total cost for oranges Overall total cost = Rs.4.00 + Rs.1.50 Overall total cost = Rs.5.50 Answer: The total cost of 5 apples and 3 oranges is Rs.5.50.	Identify the cost of one apple and one orange: Cost of one apple = \$0.80 Cost of one orange = \$0.50 Calculate the total cost for 5 apples: Total cost for apples = Number of apples × Cost per apple Total cost for apples = 5 × \$0.80 Total cost for apples = \$4.00 Calculate the total cost for 3 oranges: Total cost for oranges = Number of oranges × Cost per orange Total cost for oranges = 3 × \$0.50 Total cost for oranges = \$1.50 Calculate the overall total cost: Overall total cost = Total cost for apples + Total cost for oranges Overall total cost = \$4.00 + \$1.50 Overall total cost = \$5.50

Source: Drawn by Author

Some of the advantages of SCoT when compared to CoT are:

- Detail and Structure:
  CoT: less detailed, more flexible.
  Structured CoT: highly detailed, more rigid, and more organized.
- Use Cases:
  CoT: Suitable for straightforward problems that need clear logical progression.
  Structured CoT: Ideal for complex problems requiring detailed breakdown and thorough analysis.
- Complexity:
  CoT: simpler and quicker to implement.
  Structured CoT: more complex and time-consuming but ensures thoroughness.

3.21. Chain of Code (CoC) Prompting

Chain of Code is a prompting technique that interacts with language models to enhance their reasoning ability through writing, executing, and simulating the code (Li et al., 2023). It extends the capabilities of the language model to logical, arithmetic, and linguistic tasks. It helps, especially in those applications that requires a combination of these capabilities.

Chain of Code was developed by fetching the capabilities of chain of thought, scratchpad, and program of thought. It demonstrated efficacy by breaking down the problems into sub - steps. CoC enables language models to not only write code but also emulate parts of it. Specifically, those that are not directly executable. This allows the language model to handle a broader variety of tasks, ranging from linguistic to logical and arithmetic problem-solving.

The Chain of Code comprises of two steps:

1. Generation: generates reasoning sub steps in the structure of code.
2. Execution: Executes the code through an interpreter.

CoC shows its effectiveness for both large and small language models.

3.22. Chain-of-Symbol (CoS) Prompting

Chain-of-Symbol (CoS) is a prompting technique that represents the relationships with symbols during the chained intermediate thinking steps. COS is easy to use, and it does not require any additional training on LLM. Here, the LLM needs to understand the virtual environments that are described through natural language and achieve certain goals in such environments.

CoS prompts remove the repeated text description and uses set of symbols to express relationships between objects in complex environments.

CoS consists of three steps (Hu et al., 2023):

i. Generate a CoT demonstration in a zero-shot manner.
ii. Correct the generated CoT demonstration if the error exists.
iii. Replace the relationships in CoT with random symbols, keep only objects and symbols, and finally removes other descriptions.

Figure 26 represents the input prompt given to GPT 3.5 for chain of symbol prompting.

Figure 27 represents the output obtained by giving the CoS input prompt. It is experimented that while the same input is given and the language model is asked to solve it using the CoT prompting, the final output obtained is “Remove Yellow C (C > E), Remove Yellow E (E > D), Remove Yellow D (D is the target brick).” The output shown is confusing.

Figure 26. Input prompt to CoS (Drawn by Author)

Chain-of-Symbol (CoS) Prompting

There are a set of bricks. The yellow brick C is on top of the brick E . The yellow brick D is on top of the brick A . The yellow brick E is on top of the brick D . The white brick A is on top of the brick B . For the brick B, the color is white. Now we have to get a specific brick. The bricks must now be grabbed from top to bottom, and if the lower brick is to be grabbed, the upper brick must be removed first. How to get brick D?

Figure 27. Output of CoS prompting (Drawn by Author)

Let's assign symbols to represents each brick:

- C: Yellow C
- E: Yellow E
- D: Yellow D
- A: Yellow D
- B: White B

Based on the information provided:

1. Yellow C is on top of Yellow E (C -> E)
2. Yellow D is on top of Yellow A (D -> A)
3. Yellow E is on top of Yellow D (E -> D)
4. White A is on top of White B (A -> B)

Let's represents these relation symbolically:

- C -> E
- D -> A
- E -> D
- A -> B

Now, we can use symbolic manipulation to rearrange these symbols and determine the steps to get brick D:

1. E -> D (from the third statement)
2. C <- E (from the first statement)
3. C -> D (transitive property: C -> E -> D)
4. D -> A (from the second statement)
5. C <- A (transitive property: C -> D -> A)
6. C -> B (transitive property: C -> A -> B)

So, to get brick D, we must first remove brick B, then brick A, and finally brick C in that order. This sequence ensures that each lower brick is grabbed before its upper one.

3.23. Tree-of-Thoughts (ToT) Prompting

Tree of Thoughts (ToT), provides a novel framework for generalization over CoT prompting and encourages investigation over views(thinking), which serves as an intermediate step for finding the answers with language models (Yao et al., 2023). It breaks a problem into a sequence of smaller steps or thoughts that are solved individually. Here, thought represents coherent language sequences which serve as an intermediate step in solving a problem.

Figure 28. Pictorial representation of TOT (Hu, H., et al, 2023)

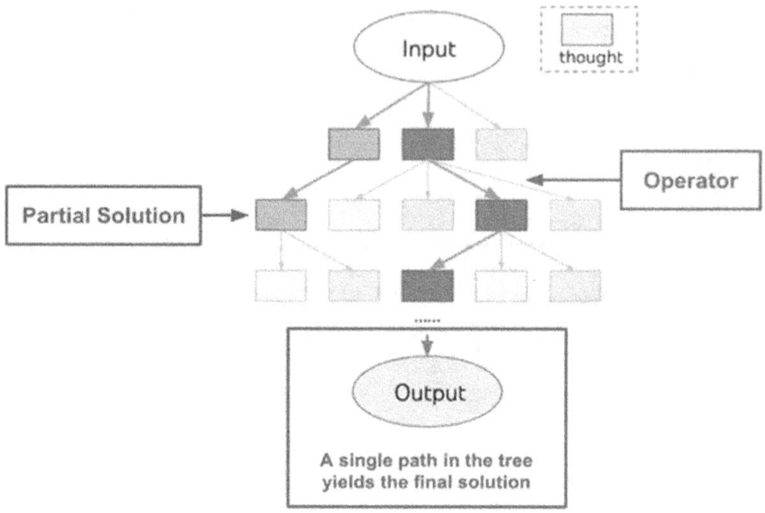

This approach allows the language model to self-evaluate its progress through intermediate step and thoughts and deliberate its reasoning process. The model's ability to generate and evaluate thought is then combined with some of the searching algorithms, like breadth-first search, depth-first search and beam search, to enable the exploration of thoughts with backtracking and lookahead. When using ToT, the number of candidates and the number of thoughts and steps may vary depending on the type of task. Figure 23 represents the overall flow of the tree of thought prompting.

3.24. Graph-of-Thought (GoT) Prompting

GoT mimics the human thought process as a graph and is based on the assumption that human minds work by connecting and reconnecting thoughts in a non-sequential manner, which gives a more realistic modeling of thought processes. It is mainly used in complex reasoning and decision-making tasks. It divides the problem in to smaller problems and solves it accordingly. This type of prompting holds a controller which plays a major role of GoT (Yao et al., 2024). It takes care of flow of operations, manages interactions with LLM, and ensures the reasoning process.

3.25. Thread of Thought (ThoT) Prompting

Thread of Thought, a prompting technique developed for reasoning tasks, questions, and answers over noisy documents. It is mainly developed for handling chaotic contexts (Zhou et al., 2023). It mimics human cognitive processes, which in turn enhance the text comprehension and generation. It is a plug- and - play component that can be integrated with various other prompting techniques. It handles chaotic contexts by segmenting and analyzing them. This prompting technique is ideal for mixed, non-sequential, and complex information structures.

3.26. Chain of Table Prompting

Chain - of - Table prompting provides a novel framework where structured data, such as tabular data, is used in the reasoning chain (Wang et al., 2024). It instructs LLMs to plan a chain of operations, like adding rows, selecting columns, sorting, and grouping which transforms a complex table into a reliable table for answering the input question. It acts as a proxy for intermediate thoughts. Here, LLMs can iteratively generate operations and update the table to represent a reasoning chain. So, LLM plans the resulting operation based on the previously obtained results. It carries structured information about the intermediate results, which gives accurate and reliable predictions.

4. PROMPTING FRAMEWORK

Prompt frameworks are essential tools for generating specific and effective outputs from an AI model. These frameworks help the user construct the prompts in a systematic way, ensuring that they are focused and effective in retrieving the desired answers. Each framework has its own unique features, which will be suitable for certain types of tasks. Some of the popular prompting frameworks are Haystack, Semantic Kernel and Langchain. Components, their functionalities, and the applications that can be created using these frameworks are discussed below.

4.1 Haystack

Haystack is an open-source framework that was developed using the Python language. This framework can be used for building custom applications with large language models (LLMs). This was developed by a company called Deepset(Deepset, n.d). It is a complete framework for building NLP applications. It offers tools for developing NLP systems that use transformer models and LLMs such as GPT-4,

Falcon, etc. Haystack can handle any multimodal (text, image, audio, etc.,) data. Some of the types of applications that can be created using Haystack are semantic search, retrieval-augmented generation (RAG), generative question answering, natural language chatbots, content generation, image captioning, image generation, information extraction, audio transcription, and acting as LLM agent that can resolve complex queries.

Haystack is built in a flexible fashion so that the user can combine frameworks from OpenAI, Chroma, Marqo, and other open-source projects. Haystack provides the tools that the user needs to build a RAG pipeline with LLMs. This includes prototyping, annotating data, and deployment. Figure 24 represents an overview of the platforms that Haystack can work with.

Figure 29. Platforms Haystack can work with (Overview/intro on Haystack documentation)

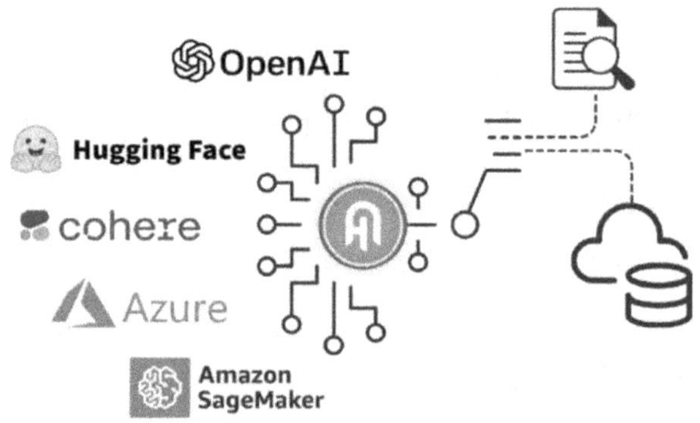

4.2 Semantic Kernel

Semantic Kernel (SK) is a software development toolkit (SDK) that integrates large language models (LLMs) like OpenAI, Azure OpenAI, and Hugging Face (Semantic Kernel, n.d). This framework can be programmed with languages like C#, Python, and Java. This integration can be achieved by allowing the user to define plugins that can be combined with a few lines of code. This framework was created by Microsoft and simplifies AI integration into conventional applications.

Figure 30. Components of semantic kernel (Getting started with Semantic Kernel, Valentina Alto, Microsoft Azure)

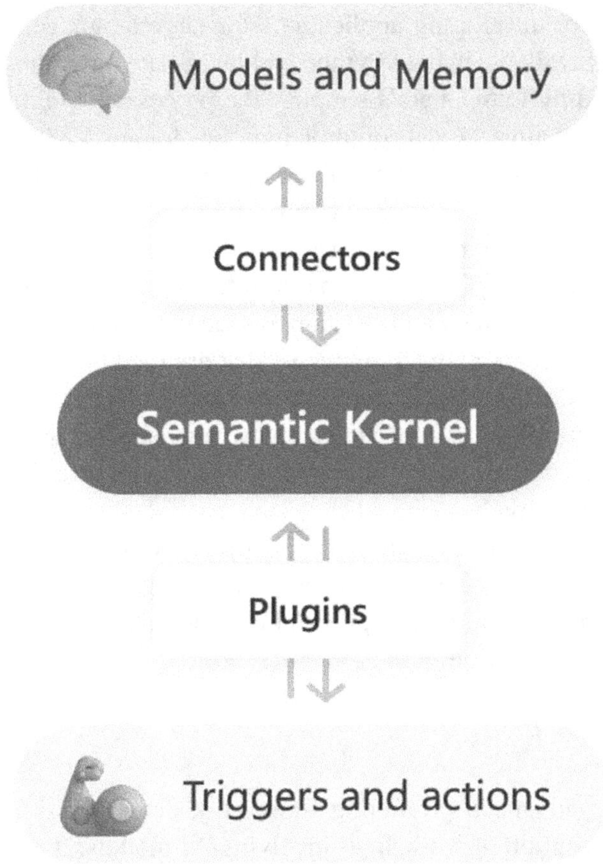

Some of the main components of a semantic kernel are the kernel, memories, planner, connectors, plugins. All these components are not mandatory. Figure 25 represents the architecture of the semantic kernel pipeline components.

This framework combines natural language, semantic functions, code - native functions, and embedding-based memory to unlock new potential and add value to applications with AI. Semantic kernel can be applied to a wide range of applications that require advanced natural language understanding (NLU), reasoning, and generation capabilities.

4.3 Langchain

LangChain is one of the most user friendly and easy- to - use, open source frameworks used for developing applications for large language models (LLMs). This framework is available in both Python and JavaScript based libraries. The tools and APIs provided by LangChain's simplify the process of building LLM-driven applications. LangChain acts as a common interface for any LLM, providing a unified development environment to build LLM applications. It can be integrated with any external data sources or software systems. It is a module-based approach used by developers and researchers to compare diverse prompts with diverse models by writing minimal code. LangChain played a significant role in making generative AI more accessible to researchers and developers (Langchain, n.d).

The framework has six main components that are the building blocks of Langchain. They are models, prompts, memory, chains, agents, callbacks, and indexes. Some of the advantages of using Langchain are enhanced usability, standardized interfaces, external integrations, prompt management and optimization, visualization, and experimentation.

Using Langchain, users can build applications like question answering with RAG, chatbots, intelligent search, question-answering, summarization services, extracting structured output, data augmentation, and virtual agents that is capable of robotic process automation.

4.4 Griptape

Griptape is an advanced prompting framework designed to facilitate the development and execution of workflows involving AI models. It provides tools and abstractions that help developers create complex prompt sequences, manage interactions with AI models, and handle the integration of AI into various applications. It offers two dimensions, such as predictability and creativity, for developers and researchers to build AI systems. Predictability refers to sequential pipelines and directed acyclic graphs (DAGs). Creativity refers to safely prompting LLMs with Griptape tools, which can be connected to external sources. Developers can use any of these two depending on their use case (Griptape, n.d).

Applications of Griptape include automating customer service, virtual assistants, data analysis, and content generation.

5. CHALLENGES AND FUTURE DIRECTIONS OF PROMPTING

Various types of prompting techniques have been summarized along with its workings and advantages. Popular prompting frameworks are discussed, along with their usage in various application domains. The use of instruction logic and choices of words in prompt design has a high impact on its effectiveness in answer generation.

Some of the key challenges are:

- Ambiguity and misinterpretation:

  Prompts can often be vague or ambiguous, which can lead to multiple possible interpretations by the language model. During the long conversation, the model might struggle to capture the main context behind the conversation (Deng et al., 2023).

  User intentions might be different, but the model may understand different intentions. The user needs to ensure that prompts are clear and unambiguous to avoid misinterpretation by the model.
- Prompt design:

  Designing prompts that are neither too broad nor too specific is crucial (White et al., 2023). A broad prompt might yield too many irrelevant details, while a specific prompt might restrict the response too much, missing out on useful information. So, it is important to design the prompt effectively. Designing the perfect prompt is still a challenging area of research still growing.
- Bias:

  Prompts can unintentionally introduce bias, resulting in responses that are unfair or discriminatory. Ensuring that prompts and responses are unbiased and fair is an ongoing challenge few prompting techniques have addressed this issue but still it is not rectified completely (Dhuliawala et al., 2023).
- Multilingualism:

  When the prompting is given in the English language it works well. If the prompt is given in any other language other than English, its performance is highly questionable. So, code mixed language or multi lingual prompting is one area of research that can be explored.
- Multimodal Prompting:

  Besides text, multimodal inputs such as image, audio and video forms can also be considered for generating comprehensive and contextually rich outputs (Zhang et al., 2023).

Future directions of prompting can emerge from multilingual prompting techniques. Techniques can be found for producing unbiased and fair results. Though several techniques are available for reduced hallucination, they still give hallucinated results. Techniques can be found for producing hallucinated free results.

6. CONCLUSION

Prompt engineering has become a revolutionary influence in unlocking the potential of large language models. This chapter explores the need for prompt engineering, process of prompt engineering along with their frameworks, history, uses, and different approaches that have developed throughout time. Challenges involved in prompting LLM and their future directions have also been explored. We hope this chapter will give an overview of prompting to business people, researchers, and developers.

ACKNOWLEDGMENT AND FUNDING

The authors gratefully acknowledge Anna University, Chennai, India for their financial support for carrying out the research work under the Anna Research Fellowship (ARF) scheme. The author, R.S. Lysa Packiam is thankful for the award of ARF.

REFERENCES

Bahrami, M., Mansoorizadeh, M., & Khotanlou, H., (2023). Few-shot Learning with Prompting Methods, pp. 1-5, doi: . 10.1109/IPRIA59240.2023.10147172

Brown, T. B., Mann, B., Ryder, N., Subbiah, M., Kaplan, J., Dhariwal, P., Neelakantan, A., Shyam, P., Sastry, G., Askell, A., Agarwal, S., Voss, A. H., Krueger, G., Henighan, T., Child, R., Ramesh, A., Ziegler, D. M., Wu, J., Winter, C., . . . Amodei, D. (2020). Language Models are Few-Shot Learners. *Computation and Language.* https://doi.org//arXiv.2005.1416510.48550

Chen, B., & Zhang, Z. Langren´ e, L., & Zhu, S.,(2024). Unleashing the potential of prompt engineering in Large Language Models: a comprehensive review, arXiv:2310.14735v4

Chen, W., Ma, X., Wang, X., & Cohen, W., (2023). Program of Thoughts Prompting: Disentangling Computation from Reasoning for Numerical Reasoning Tasks. *TMLR 2023*

Chia, Y. K., Chen, G., Tuan, L. A., Poria, S., & Bing, L. (2023). Contrastive Chain-of-Thought Prompting. *Computation and Language.* https://doi.org//arXiv.2311.0927710.48550

Creswell, A., Shanahan, M., & Higgins, I. (2022). Selection-inference: Exploiting large language models for interpretable logical reasoning, https://arxiv.org/abs/2205.09712.

Deng, Y., Zhang, W., Chen, Z., & Gu, Q. (2023). Rephrase and Respond: Let Large Language Models Ask Better Questions for Themselves. *Computation and Language.* https://doi.org//arXiv.2311.0420510.48550

Dhuliawala, S., Komeili, M., Xu, J., Raileanu, R., Li, X., Celikyilmaz, A., & Weston, J. (2023). Chain-of-Verification Reduces Hallucination in Large Language Models. *Computation and Language*. https://doi.org//arXiv.2309.1149510.48550

Diao, S., Wang, P., Lin, Y., Pan, R., Liu, X., & Zhang, T. (2023). Active Prompting with Chain-of-Thought for Large Language Models. *Computation and Language,* https://doi.org//arXiv.2302.1224610.48550

Hu, H., Lu, H., Zhang, H., Song, Y. Z., Lam, W., & Zhang, Y. (2023). Chain-of-Symbol Prompting Elicits Planning in Large Language Models. *Computation and Language.* https://doi.org//arXiv.2305.1027610.48550

JasonWei, J., Xuezhi Wang, X., Schuurmans, D., Maarten Bosma, M., Brian Ichter, B., Xia, F., Chi, E.H., Le, Q.V., & Zhou, D., (2023). Chain-of-Thought Prompting Elicits Reasoning in Large Language Models. *36th Conference on Neural Information Processing Systems.*

Li, C., Liang, J., Zeng, A., Chen, X., Hausman, K., Sadigh, D., Levine, S., Fei-Fei, L., Xia, F., & Ichter, B. (2023). Chain of Code: Reasoning with a Language Model-Augmented Code Emulator. *Computation and Language.* https://doi.org//arXiv.2312.0447410.48550

Li, C., Wang, J., Zhang, Y., Zhu, K., Hou, W., Lian, J., Luo, F., Yang, Q., & Xie, X. (2023). Large Language Models Understand and Can Be Enhanced by Emotional Stimuli. *Computation and Language.* https://doi.org//arXiv.2307.1176010.48550

Li, J., Li, G., Li, Y., & Jin, Z. (2023). Structured Chain-of-Thought Prompting for Code Generation. *Software Engineering.* https://doi.org//arXiv.2305.0659910.48550

Li, X., Zhao, R., Chia, Y. K., Ding, B., Joty, S., Poria, S., & Bing, L. (2024). Chain-of-Knowledge: Grounding Large Language Models via Dynamic Knowledge Adapting over Heterogeneous Sources. *Computation and Language.* https://doi.org//arXiv.2305.1326910.48550

Li, Y. (2023). A Practical Survey on Zero-shot Prompt Design for In-context Learning, Computation *and Language.* https://doi.org//arXiv.2309.1320510.48550

Liu, P., Yuan, W., Fu, J., Jiang, Z., Hayashi, H., & Graham Neubig, G. (2023). Pre-train, prompt, and predict: A systematic survey of prompting methods in natural language processing. *ACM Computing Surveys*, 55(9), 1–35. 10.1145/3560815

Logan, R., IV, Bala˘zevi'c, I., Wallace, E., Petroni, F., Singh, S., & Riedel, S. (2022) Cutting down on prompts and parameters: simple few-shot learning with language models. Findings of the Association for Computational Linguistics, 2824–2835.

Miao, J., Thongprayoon, C., Suppadungsuk, S., Garcia Valencia, O. A., & Cheungpasitporn, W. (2024). Integrating Retrieval-Augmented Generation with Large Language Models in Nephrology: Advancing Practical Applications. *Medicina*, 60(3), 445. 10.3390/medicina6003044538541171

Nye, M., Andreassen, A. J., Ari, G. G., Michalowski, H., Austin, J., Bieber, D., Dohan, D., Lewkowycz, A., Bosma, M., Luan, D., Sutton, C., & Odena, A. (2021). Show Your Work: Scratchpads For Intermediate Computation with Language Models. *Neural and Evolutionary Computing.* https://doi.org//arXiv.2112.0011410.48550

Paranjape, B., Lundberg, S., Singh, S., Hajishirzi, H., Zettlemoyer, L., & Ribeiro, M. T. (2023). ART: Automatic multi-step reasoning and tool-use for large language models. *Computation and Language.* https://doi.org//arXiv.2303.0901410.48550

Piktusy, A., Petroniy, F., Karpukhiny, V., Goyaly, N., Küttlery, H., Lewisy, M., Yihy, W., Rocktäschelyz, T., Riedelyz, S., & Kielay, D. (2021). Retrieval-Augmented Generation for Knowledge-Intensive NLP Tasks. *Computation and Language.* https://doi.org//arXiv.2005.1140110.48550

Radford, A., Wu, J., Child, R., Luan, D., Amodei, D., & Sutskever, I. (2019). Language models are unsupervised multitask learners. https://openai.com/index/better-language-models

Shyr, C., Hu, Y., & Harris, P. A. Xu, &H., (2023). Identifying and extracting rare disease phenotypes with Large language models; ArXiv:2306.12656.

Wang, X., Wei, J., Schuurmans, D., Le, Q., Ed H. Chi. E.H., Narang, S., Chowdhery, A., & Zhou, D., (2023). Self-Consistency Improves Chain of Thought Reasoning In Language Models. *ICLR 2023*

Wang, Z., Zhang, H., Li, C. L., Eisenschlos, J. M., Perot, V., Wang, Z., Miculicich, L., Fujii, Y., Shang, J., Lee, C. Y., & Pfister, T. (2024). Chain-of-Table: Evolving Tables in the Reasoning Chain for Table Understanding. *Computation and Language.* https://doi.org//arXiv.2401.0439810.48550

White, J., Fu, Q., Hays, S., Sandborn, M., Olea, C., Gilbert, H., Elnashar, A., Smith, J. S., & Schmidt, D. C. (2023). A Prompt Pattern Catalog to Enhance Prompt Engineering with ChatGPT. *Software Engineering (cs.SE),* https://doi.org//arXiv.2302.1138210.48550

Yan, S.-Q. S.H., Gu, J.C., Zhu, Y., & Ling, Z.H., (2024). *Computation and Language,* https://doi.org//arXiv.2401.1588410.48550

Yang, C., Wang, X., Lu, X., Liu, H., Le, Q. V., Zhou, D., & Chen, X. (2024). Large Language Models as Optimizers. *Machine Learning.* https://doi.org//arXiv.2309.0340910.48550

Yao, S., Zhao, J., Yu, D., Du, N., Shafran, I., Narasimhan, K., & Yuan Cao, Y., (2023). React: Synergizing Reasoning and Acting in Language Models. *ICLR 2023.*

Yao, S., Yu, D., Zhao, J., Shafran, I., Griffiths, T. L., Cao, Y., & Narasimhan, K. (2023). Tree of Thoughts: Deliberate Problem Solving with Large Language Models. *Computation and Language.* https://doi.org//arXiv.2305.1060110.48550

Yao, Y., Li, Z., & Zhao, H. (2024). Beyond Chain-of-Thought, Effective Graph-of-Thought Reasoning in Language Models. *Computation and Language.* https://doi.org//arXiv.2305.1658210.48550

Yu, W., Zhang, H., Pan, X., Ma, K., Wang, H., & Yu, D. (2023). Chain-of-Note: Enhancing Robustness in Retrieval-Augmented Language Models. *Computation and Language.* https://doi.org//arXiv.2311.0921010.48550

Zhang, Z., Zhang, A., Li, M., Zhao, H., Karypis, G., & Smola, A. (2023). Multimodal Chain-of-Thought Reasoning in Language Models. *Computation and Language.* https://doi.org//arXiv.2302.0092310.48550

Zhangy, Z., Zhangz, A., Li, M., & Smolaz, A. (2022). Automatic Chain of Thought Prompting in Large Language Models. *Computation and Language.* https://doi.org//arXiv.2210.0349310.48550

Zheng, H. S., Mishra, S., Chen, X., Cheng, H. T., Chi, E. H., Le, Q. V., & Zhou, D. Take a Step Back: Evoking Reasoning via Abstraction in Large Language Models. (2024). *Machine Learning.* https://doi.org//arXiv.2310.0611710.48550

Zhou, Y., Geng, X., Shen, T., Tao, C., Long, G., Lou, J. G., & Shen, J. (2023). Thread of Thought Unraveling Chaotic Contexts, *Computation and Language.* https://doi.org//arXiv.2311.0873410.48550

KEY TERMS AND DEFINITIONS

Embeddings: Numerical representations of words and phrases which captures semantic meaning and relationships between words and phrases.

Fine Tuning: Adjusting the AI model precisely to provide better performance.

Hallucination: Misleading or incorrect answer generated by the AI model.

LLM: A type of AI model that is trained on large volume of data making them capable of understanding and generating natural language for a wide range of tasks.

Pre Trained: A model that is trained on large volume of data in order to accomplish specific task.

Prompt: A text-based input instruction given to the LLM to direct its response output effectively.

Prompting Framework: A structured approach of writing instruction to AI model that aims to streamline the interaction between the user and model.

Chapter 4
Generative AI
Applications, Models, Challenges, Opportunities, and Future Directions

Geetika Madaan
https://orcid.org/0000-0001-8141-9935
Marwadi University, India

Satish Kumar Asthana
Chandigarh University, India

Jaskiran Kaur
https://orcid.org/0000-0002-4452-1807
Lovely Professional University, India

ABSTRACT

This study provides a comprehensive view of the state of generative AI today, touching on its uses, foundational models, obstacles, prospects, and potential future courses of action. Autoregressive models like Transformers, GANs, and Variational Autoencoders (VAEs) are the backbone of generative AI. Generated AI still has a way to go before fully realizing its potential. Problems with model interpretability, training stability, and generated content bias are all examples of such challenges. Computer scientists, psychologists, and ethicists must work together to find solutions to these problems. Generative AI does, however, offer tremendous potential. Artists, designers, and storytellers have new tools at their fingertips. Improving the robustness of models, granting greater control over generated outputs, and investigating uses in interactive storytelling and real-time content production are all potential future areas for generative AI.

DOI: 10.4018/979-8-3693-8557-9.ch004

INTRODUCTION

From the field of machine learning, generative AI stands as a paradigm shifter. Generative AI goes beyond pattern recognition and decision-making based on existing data to bring machines into the creative realm, allowing them to create new content (Gerolemou, 2019). This cutting-edge innovation works by absorbing structures and patterns from a dataset, which it then uses to create new outputs that are consistent with or very similar to the original data(Lv, 2023).

Neuronal networks, especially GANs and VAEs, are fundamental to generative artificial intelligence. In GANs, the generator and discriminator neural networks compete with each other to produce higher-quality outputs(Gerolemou, 2019). The generator creates samples of synthetic data, and the discriminator checks them against real data to see if GANs and VAEs are legitimate. Adversarial training allows GANs to generate very lifelike results, whether it's pictures, music, or writing(Asatiani et al., 2021).

VAEs are able to learn latent data representations and can be employed for data compression and image production, among other things(Banh & Strobel, 2023a; Chen, Zaharia, & Zou, 2024). Virtual assistants understand the incoming data's probability distribution and use it to generate new, comparable data points through sampling. Exploring the latent space of data is made possible by this probabilistic method, which in turn leads to various and creative outcomes.

Art, music, and literature are just a few of the many fields that can benefit from generative AI. In order to create one-of-a-kind visual compositions or designs, artists and designers use generative AI to go into uncharted creative realms. Artificial intelligence models have the ability to create original music by learning different styles(Asatiani et al., 2021). The boundary between human and machine creativity is frequently blurred when AI helps generate text in literature, whether it's poetry or news pieces.

Nevertheless, there are ethical concerns with generative AI, particularly about IP, authenticity, and the effects on society. Questions concerning ownership and the difference between original and machine-created works emerge in light of the increasing prevalence of AI-generated content. Also, people are worried that AI-generated material may lead to the spread of false information and a decline in human creativity(Hartmann, Exner, & Domdey, 2023).

In conclusion, generative AI is a huge step forward for machine learning; it expands the limits of what computers can generate and opens up exciting new opportunities in many different industries. The ever-changing state of this technology is sparking deep conversations regarding AI's impact on society, creativity, and the potential of human-machine collaboration in the future(Banh & Strobel, 2023b)

BACKGROUND

Generative Adversarial Networks (GANs) and Variational Autoencoders (VAEs)

One type of AI algorithm that finds widespread application in unsupervised learning is the Generative Adversarial Networks, or GANs.(Feuerriegel, Hartmann, Janiesch, & Zschech, 2024). In 2014, Ian Goodfellow and colleagues introduced GANs, which are comprised of a generator and a discriminator neural network (Bail, 2024). This type of network plays a game where one node tries to generate data that looks exactly like real data while the other node checks incoming data to see if it's fake or not. In this vicious cycle, both the generator and the discriminator keep getting better at what they do: producing more realistic data and better at identifying it. The ability to generate incredibly lifelike images, films, and audio is what makes GANs so useful in domains like data augmentation, computer vision, and artistic creation (Banh & Strobel, 2023).

On the flip side, generative tasks are where variational autoencoders (VAEs) really shine. Kingma and Welling introduced VAEs in 2013; they include a probabilistic component to the encoding process, making them different from conventional autoencoders (Strobel, Banh, Möller, & Schoormann, 2024). Instead of mapping input data to a fixed point, a VAE encoder maps it to a distribution of latent variables. With the use of this probabilistic mapping, new data can be generated by sampling latent space and then decoding it into the data space (Wessel, Adam, Benlian, & Majchrzak, 2024). VAEs maximize the variational lower bound by taming the reconstruction error and the Kullback-Leibler divergence, which is usually a Gaussian distribution, between the learnt latent distribution and a prior distribution. Image generation and semi-supervised learning are two examples of jobs that benefit greatly from VAEs because of this smooth and continuous latent space (Bail, 2024).

Although both GANs and VAEs can generate new data, there are several key distinctions and uses for each. In hostile environments, GANs are frequently employed to push the limits of synthesizability due to their exceptional ability to generate extremely realistic outputs. Producing photorealistic stills, motion pictures, and even 3D models has been an impressive feat for them. Problems like mode collapse, in which the generator only generates a small number of possible outputs, make GAN training difficult (Banh & Strobel, 2023). When it comes to tasks that require a systematic comprehension of the data's underlying distribution, VAEs are better since they are easier to train and produce a more interpretable latent space. Having said that, GANs usually provide more sharp and realistic results than VAEs.

The use of GANs and VAEs has been a huge step forward for generative modeling. For tasks requiring a high level of fidelity and aesthetic appeal, GANs are the way to go because they raise the bar for realism in synthetic data (Strobel et al., 2024). Anomaly detection, data compression, and semi-supervised learning are just a few of the many uses for VAEs due to their robustness and flexibility, which are both enhanced by their probabilistic approach and structured latent space. Researchers and practitioners can use the distinct strengths of GANs and VAEs to push artificial intelligence forward by understanding the advantages and disadvantages of each technique and selecting the appropriate tool for their individual needs.

EVOLUTION OF GENERATIVE AI

A remarkable journey has been the evolution of generative AI, marked by important improvements in computational capability and machine learning approaches. The following is a timeline detailing its evolution:

1. Early Generative Models (Pre-2010s):
    - Hidden Markov Models (HMMs) and Gaussian Mixture Models (GMMs) were the main probabilistic methods used by generative models to produce data prior to the 2010s(Feuerriegel et al., 2024).
    - Particularly for jobs like picture synthesis, these early models lacked the capacity to catch complicated patterns and provide high-quality outputs.
2. Emergence of Deep Learning (2010s):
    - Generative AI was completely upended by the arrival of deep learning, and more specifically, deep neural networks.
    - Advanced generative models that can learn complex patterns in data were made possible by the invention of Convolutional Neural Networks (CNNs) and Recurrent Neural Networks (RNNs)(Capraro, Paolo, Perc, & Pizziol, 2024).
    - Around this time, two notable developments were the advent of Generative Adversarial Networks (GANs) and Variational Autoencoders (VAEs).
3. Variational Autoencoders (VAEs) (2014):
    - A potent new family of generative models known as VAEs has arisen; these models learn a hidden data representation.
    - Virtual assistants can mimic the training data by learning the latent space's probabilistic distribution and then using it to create new data points(Soni, Sharma, Singh, & Kapoor, 2019).
4. Generative Adversarial Networks (GANs) (2014):

- With the advent of GANs, a new paradigm was established for adversarial training of two neural networks: the generator and the discriminator(Chalmers, MacKenzie, & Carter, 2021).
- So that the discriminator can tell the difference between actual and created data, the generator figures out how to make data samples that look realistic.
- A huge step forward in generative AI capabilities, GANs have been incredibly effective in producing high-fidelity images, videos, and text(Lévesque, Obschonka, & Nambisan, 2022).

5. Evolution of GAN Architectures (2010s-2020s):
    - New GAN designs such as BigGAN, Conditional GANs (CGANs), and StyleGAN have emerged throughout the years(Loureiro, Guerreiro, & Tussyadiah, 2021).
    - The problems that these designs attempt to solve include style transfer, conditional image synthesis, and the creation of more faithful high-resolution images.
6. Applications in Art, Design, and Beyond:
    - The creative industries—including the arts, music, fashion, and design—have discovered extensive uses for generative AI.
    - Generative models allow designers and artists to automatically create one-of-a-kind content while also opening up new avenues of creative exploration(Khalid, 2020).
7. Ethical and Societal Implications (2020s):
    - Concerns around intellectual copyright, authenticity, and the societal consequences of more advanced generative AI have come to the forefront of ethical discussions.
    - The conversation around generative AI has been influenced by talks about AI-generated content, deepfakes, and AI's function in creativity(Dubey et al., 2019).

Machines can now produce creative and realistic material in a wide range of fields thanks to the incredible development of generative AI from its early probabilistic models to complex deep learning architectures(Di Vaio, Palladino, Hassan, & Escobar, 2020).

MODELS OF GENERATIVE AI

Generative AI is a broad term that describes a collection of models and strategies that work together to create new data that is similar to an existing dataset. These models derive new outputs by learning structures and patterns from preexisting data using sophisticated machine learning methods. In generative AI, the following models are essential:

1. Variational Autoencoders (VAEs):
    - One kind of generative model is the probabilistic VAE, which learns a latent data representation(Giuggioli & Pellegrini, 2022).
    - An encoder network converts incoming data into a latent space, while a decoder network uses that space to restore the original data.
    - When trained, VAEs increase the probability of producing the input data and can also generate new samples by sampling from the latent space VAEs learnt about.
2. Generative Adversarial Networks (GANs):
    - A GAN's generator and discriminator neural networks make it up.
    - While the discriminator figures out how to tell fake data from real data, the generator figures out how to make data samples from random noise.
    - In adversarial GAN training, both the generator and the discriminator work to achieve their respective goals of accurately detecting false input(Dirican, 2015).
    - Using GANs, realistic images, movies, and text may be generated.
3. Autoregressive Models:
    - By using past outputs as conditions, autoregressive models create data in a sequential fashion.
    - Picture production is just one use of autoregressive models like PixelCNN and PixelRNN.
    - These models are taught to use the distributions of previous elements to forecast the likelihood of the following element in a sequence.
4. Flow-Based Models:
    - Generative models known as flow-based models learn the mapping between the data distribution and basic distributions like Gaussian(Bogachov, Kwilinski, Miethlich, Bartosova, & Gurnak, 2020).
    - Flow-based models use an invertible transformation series to simulate the data distribution.
    - Flow-based models provide for precise likelihood estimates and quick data sample production.

5. Transformers and Language Models:
   - Generative Pretrained Transformer (GPT) and other large-scale language models can generate coherent text sequences.
   - The models are able to grasp data dependencies over large distances because models employ self-attention techniques(Giuggioli & Pellegrini, 2022).
   - Text completion, summarization, and dialogue production are just a few examples of the generative tasks that language models can be tailored for.
6. Deep Reinforcement Learning for Generation:
   - Agents that can be trained to generate sequences of actions or outputs can be trained using deep reinforcement learning approaches.
   - Agents that use reinforcement learning can learn to develop action sequences to accomplish goals, which is useful in many domains such as robotics and video games(A. A. A. Ahmed & Ganapathy, 2021).
7. Probabilistic Graphical Models:
   - Bayesian networks and Markov random fields are two examples of probabilistic graphical models that can be applied to generative modelling.
   - These models can be utilized to infer and produce new data samples by representing the probabilistic relationships between variables in a dataset.

The task at hand and the nature of the data being generated dictate which of these models is most appropriate; each model has advantages and disadvantages(Miao, 2020). New developments in generative AI are opening up fascinating possibilities for creative, design, and innovation applications by expanding the limits of what machines are capable of creating.

APPLICATIONS OF GENERATIVE AI IN BUSINESS AND MANAGEMENT FIELD

The capacity of generative AI to produce new data and realistic outputs based on learned patterns has led to its widespread use across many businesses and fields. Generative AI has several prominent applications, including the following:

1. Image Synthesis and Editing:
   - To synthesize images, generative AI models are employed, such as Generative Adversarial Networks (GANs) and Variational Autoencoders (VAEs)(Reim, Åström, & Eriksson, 2020).

- Based on patterns acquired from training data, GANs and VAEs can generate high-resolution, lifelike images.
- Examples of possible uses include image-to-image translation (such as transforming Generative Adversarial Networks (GANs) and Variational Autoencoders (VAEs) are two examples of the generative AI models used for picture synthesis. image inpainting (filling in empty areas of an image), style transfer (transferring the style of one image to another), and sketching into images(S. M. Ahmed, 2019).

2. Text Generation and Natural Language Processing (NLP):
   - Text generation and natural language processing activities are handled by language models that are built on transformers, like GPT (Generative Pretrained Transformer).
   - In response to user input, these models may produce coherent, contextually appropriate text(Turkina, 2018).
   - Chatbots, conversation generators, content summaries, and writing prompt generators are some of the uses.
3. Music Composition and Audio Generation:
   - Music creation and audio synthesis are both aided by generative AI approaches.
   - It is possible for models to study the genres of previously composed music and then create new music that follows those same patterns(Obschonka & Audretsch, 2019).
   - Video score composition, personalized playlist creation, and interactive music experience creation are some of the applications.
4. Art and Design:
   - To aid in the creation process and discover new avenues of creativity, artists and designers are turning to generative AI tools.
   - Exhibitions and commercial initiatives are seeing an uptick in the usage of AI-generated artworks, illustrations, and designs(Townsend & Hunt, 2019).
   - One can make one-of-a-kind textures, patterns, and effects with the help of generative AI.
5. Video and Animation:
   - Video footage is created and edited using generative models.
   - Generative AI powers techniques like deepfake creation, video inpainting, and video synthesis, which involve changing the appearance of a video based on textual descriptions(Ughulu & Ph, 2022).
6. Drug Discovery and Molecular Design:

- Through the generation of new chemical structures with desired features, generative AI contributes to the fields of drug discovery and molecular design.
- Drug candidates can be optimized, novel compounds can be designed, and molecular attributes can be predicted using models.

7. Game Development and Virtual Environments:
    - Procedural content production, which involves the creation of randomly generated game levels, graphics, and characters, is facilitated by generative AI in game development.
    - Non-player characters (NPCs) powered by artificial intelligence can display more nuanced and lifelike behaviours created through generative techniques like reinforcement learning(Garbuio & Lin, 2018).
8. Fashion and Product Design:
    - Generative AI is useful in the fashion industry and for personalizing products since it can generate one-of-a-kind designs according to consumer tastes.
    - Generative AI paves the way for automated design generation, virtual try-on systems, and personalized apparel recommendations.
9. Healthcare and Medical Imaging:
    - Medical imaging applications of generative AI models include picture synthesis, segmentation, and reconstruction.
    - Medical research, treatment planning, and disease diagnosis are all aided by these models.
10. Content Generation and Personalization:
    - Content recommendation systems and individualized user experiences are powered by generative AI(Madhavi, 2021; Palanivelu & Vasanthi, 2020; Rathi & Asava, 2021).
    - Artificial intelligence can create personalized content, ads, and product suggestions by analyzing user habits and interests.

These uses showcase the adaptability and influence of generative AI in several fields; it is revolutionizing industries and opening the door to new kinds of automation, creativity, and invention. More complex and consequential uses will emerge in the future as the area develops further.

CHALLENGES OF GENERATIVE AI

While generative AI holds great promise, it also poses a number of problems that must be solved by researchers, developers, and society at large. Included in these obstacles are limitations in technology, ethical concerns, and the broader social effects. A few major obstacles to generative AI are these:

1. Mode Collapse and Stability:
    - When Generative Adversarial Networks (GANs) experience mode collapse, GANs learn to ignore some sections of the data distribution in favor of a small subset of possible outputs.
    - One of the major technical hurdles in GAN training is guaranteeing that the produced samples are stable and diverse(Roundy, 2022).
2. Training Data Quality and Bias:
    - A diverse and high-quality set of training data is crucial for generative models.
    - The generation of text, graphics, or other sorts of content might be influenced by biases in the training data, which in turn can reinforce societal preconceptions.
3. Evaluation Metrics:
    - Evaluating the variety and quality of produced samples is not an easy task.
    - A persistent obstacle in the field of generative AI research is the development of reliable evaluation measures that can capture the accuracy, variety, and applicability of the produced results(Mishra & Tripathi, 2021).
4. Interpretability and Control:
    - The output of generative models can be difficult to understand and manipulate.
    - When working with models like GANs, it might be challenging to manage particular aspects of the generated material or comprehend why a given output was generated due to the lack of interpretability.
5. Ethical Use and Misuse:
    - Deepfakes, which are modified videos used for misinformation or impersonation, are only one example of how generative AI is causing ethical difficulties with its generated material.
    - Important challenges include preventing social harm and promoting ethical usage of generative AI systems.
6. Intellectual Property and Ownership:

- Legal and ethical concerns arise when trying to ascertain who owns what in AI-generated work(Anute, Paliwal, Patel, & Kandale, 2021).
- To encourage innovation while safeguarding artists' rights, it is crucial to define intellectual property rights for works generated by AI.

7. Data Privacy and Security:
    - Inadvertent disclosure of training data details by generative models trained on sensitive data can compromise privacy.
    - The development of methods to protect user privacy while using generative AI is of the utmost importance.
8. Resource Intensive Training:
    - Significant computational resources and energy are required for training sophisticated generative models, particularly large-scale models such as GPT (Generative Pretrained Transformer)(Jain, 2019).
    - It is a real problem to address the environmental impact of training these models.
9. Generalization and Robustness:
    - One important area of research is making sure that generative models can handle variations and adversarial attacks well while still generalizing to new data.
    - Generative AI systems must be made more resilient before generative AI can be used in the real world(Enholm, Papagiannidis, Mikalef, & Krogstie, 2022).
10. Societal Impact and Bias Mitigation:
    - Data including preexisting social prejudices may be amplified by generative AI algorithms.
    - It is crucial to construct inclusive and equitable systems by reducing bias and making sure that generative AI outputs are fair.

Researchers, politicians, business leaders, and members of the general public must work together across disciplines to find solutions to these problems. To ensure the ethical and egalitarian deployment of generative AI and to harness its transformational potential, we must properly navigate these issues.

OPPORTUNITIES OF GENERATIVE AI

Generative AI is changing businesses and opening up new applications in a wide variety of fields. These openings take advantage of generative models' capacity to generate novel material, resolve intricate issues, and propel innovation. Generative AI offers the following significant benefits:

1. Creative Content Generation:
    - Automated production of creative works like music, literature, and visuals is now possible thanks to generative AI(Sadiku, Fagbohungbe, & Musa, 2020).
    - Generative models provide designers and artists with new tools to experiment with their creativity and produce high-volume, one-of-a-kind material.
2. Personalized User Experiences:
    - Personalized suggestions and content production are powered by generative AI in many different applications.
    - With the help of AI, industries like e-commerce, entertainment, and education can provide personalized experiences based on customer preferences and behaviours.
3. Data Augmentation and Synthesis:
    - Machine learning training datasets can be supplemented by synthetic data generated by generative models.
    - This allows for more effective model training, which is particularly useful in situations where obtaining tagged data is difficult or expensive.
4. Procedural Content Generation:
    - Generative AI is utilized for the purpose of procedural content generation in the production of games and virtual environments.
    - AI has the ability to build interactive and extensible game worlds, levels, characters, and stories, which greatly improves the gaming experience.
5. Drug Discovery and Materials Design:
    - By creating new molecules and predicting their molecular characteristics, generative AI speeds up the process of drug discovery(Leitch, 2021).
    - AI-powered methods streamline the process of discovering new drugs by efficiently exploring chemical space.
6. Healthcare and Medical Imaging:
    - Medical picture processing, segmentation, and illness diagnosis are just a few examples of how generative AI is improving healthcare.
    - For the purposes of training and validation, AI models may produce synthetic medical pictures, which ultimately improves the accuracy of diagnoses.
7. Natural Language Processing (NLP):
    - Generating text, summarizing it, translating it, and building dialogue systems all make use of language models like GPT.
    - Virtual assistants and chatbots are powered by generative AI, which improves communication and information retrieval.

8. Design and Architecture:
    - When it comes to designing and building new structures, generative AI is a huge help to the architectural and design communities.
    - In response to user-specified requirements and goals, AI-powered design optimization tools are generated.
9. Entertainment and Media Production:
    - Automating content creation and improving production workflows are two ways in which generative AI is revolutionizing the entertainment business.
    - Enhanced narratives and visual experiences are achieved by the incorporation of AI-generated audio, video, and animation into multimedia projects.
10. Research and Exploration:
    - When it comes to scientific inquiry and discoveries, generative AI is a boon.
    - Advancements in many fields of science have been made possible by AI models that simulate complicated systems, produce hypotheses, and assist with experimental design.
11. Business Applications:
    - Generative AI simplifies several commercial operations, including content creation, design prototyping, and optimization of marketing campaigns.
    - Businesses may innovate and stand out in competitive markets with the help of AI-driven analytics and creative tools.

New applications, increased creativity, and higher efficiency are on the horizon thanks to these opportunities, which demonstrate the revolutionary potential of generative AI across industries. Generational AI will be a game-changer in the workplace, the arts, and society as a whole as time goes on and technology improves.

MATHEMATICAL PRINCIPLES OF GENERATIVE AI

The data modelling and generating processes that comprise generative AI are based on a number of mathematical ideas(Soni, Sharma, Singh, & Kapoor, 2020). If you want to build and understand generative models well, you must understand these ideas. For generative AI, below are some fundamental mathematical ideas and principles:

1. Probability Distributions:

- Probability distributions are commonly used by generative AI models for data representation and learning.
- Generative modeling relies on several probability distributions, including multinomial, Gaussian (normal), Bernoulli, and more complicated ones like Gaussian mixture models (GMMs).

2. Latent Variable Models:
   - Variational Autoencoders (VAEs) and latent space models are examples of latent variable models that depict data as being produced by latent (unobserved) variables(Geisel, 2018).
   - By sampling from the learnt latent space, these models are able to generate new samples, as one can learn the distribution of latent variables that can explain observed data.
3. Bayesian Inference:
   - Generative models estimate parameters and infer latent variables using Bayesian inference and observable data.
   - When it comes to learning and updating assumptions about model parameters given data, Bayesian techniques offer a logical framework.
4. Maximum Likelihood Estimation (MLE):
   - To maximize the likelihood of witnessing the supplied data, maximum likelihood estimation (MLE) is used to estimate the parameters of a probability distribution.
   - Optimal likelihood of generating the observed data is optimized during training of several generative models, including VAEs, using MLE.
5. Markov Chains and Markov Processes:
   - The modelling and creation of sequential data makes use of Markov chains and Markov processes.
   - Markovian dependencies are used by generative models such as Hidden Markov Models (HMMs) and Markov Random Fields (MRFs).
6. Information Theory:
   - Generative models' information content and complexity can be optimized using ideas from information theory such as entropy, mutual information, and Kullback-Leibler (KL) divergence.
   - When evaluating VAEs, KL divergence—the discrepancy between the learnt distribution and the actual data distribution—is crucial.
7. Gradient-based Optimization:
   - Stochastic gradient descent (SGD) and similar gradient-based optimization methods are commonly used to train generative models(Soni et al., 2019).

- Managing gradients through intricate computational graphs is an integral part of backpropagation in probabilistic models, particularly in deep generative models such as GANs.

8. Game Theory and Adversarial Training:
   - The idea behind Generative Adversarial Networks (GANs) comes from game theory. In GANs, the discriminator and generator networks play a minimax game to maximize the quality of the samples GANs produce.
   - Achieving a Nash equilibrium by optimizing the parameters of competing networks is the goal of adversarial training.
9. Deep Learning Architectures:
   - A large number of generative models use designs based on deep neural networks.
   - Generative models incorporate deep learning concepts such as normalization layers, attention mechanisms, recurrent networks, and convolutional layers to capture intricate patterns in data streams.

To successfully create, train, and understand generative AI models, one must have a firm grasp of certain mathematical concepts. By fully grasping these ideas, researchers and practitioners can advance generative modelling to new heights and discover AI's hidden potential.Top of Form

A MODEL-SYSTEM-APPLICATION-LEVEL VIEW OF GENERATIVE AI

Model-Level View

1. Generative Adversarial Networks (GANs):
   - **Description of the Model:** Generating and discriminating neural networks are the building blocks of GANs(Soni et al., 2020). The discriminator learns to differentiate between genuine and created data, while the generator tries to create realistic data samples from random noise.
   - **Key Components:** Various loss functions, such as adversarial loss, training dynamics, and design characteristics are involved.
   - **Applications:** Image synthesis, video production, text-to-image translation.
2. Variational Autoencoders (VAEs):
   - **Description of the Model:** By projecting incoming data into a latent space probability distribution, VAEs are able to learn a latent data rep-

resentation. Encoders convert raw input data into latent space, whereas decoders use sampled latent vectors to reassemble the original data.

- **Key Components:** Structure of encoder-decoder, variational inference, reparameterization operation.
- **Applications:** Picture creation, data compression, and anomaly identification.

3. Autoregressive Models:
    - **Description of the Model:** By using past outputs as conditions, autoregressive models create data in a sequential fashion. Two examples of picture generating algorithms are PixelRNN and PixelCNN.
    - **Key Components:** Sequential sampling, probability distribution modelling.
    - **Applications:** Creating images, synthesizing voices, and predicting temporal trends.

System-Level View

1. Training Pipeline:
    - **Components:** Phases including data preparation, model training, hyperparameter adjustment, and assessment.
    - **Tools and Platforms:** Tools for generative modelling include TensorFlow and PyTorch.
    - **Considerations:** Efficiency, scalability, and the use of graphics processing units and graphical processing units for training(Anute et al., 2021; Mishra & Tripathi, 2021; Roundy, 2022).
2. Model Deployment and Serving:
    - **Components:** Version control and monitoring of models, inference API endpoints, and infrastructure for supplying models.
    - **Tools and Platforms:** Containers, AWS Sage Maker, Kubernetes, TensorFlow, and service.
    - **Considerations:** Updates to models, throughput, latency, and scalability.
3. Hardware Acceleration:
    - **Components:** Graphics processing units (GPUs), Terahertz processing units (TPUs), and unique deep learning gear.
    - **Considerations:** Improving model efficiency, minimizing training and inference time, and maximizing performance.

Application-Level View

1. Art and Design:
    - **Applications:** Artificial intelligence (AI)-generated artwork, style emigration, and design and art utilities.
    - **Impact:** Streamlining the design process and opening up new avenues for creative expression.
2. Media and Entertainment
    - **Applications:** synthetic videos, audio, and settings created by artificial intelligence.
    - **Impact:** Improving content production and paving the way for customized media consumption.
3. Healthcare and Life Sciences:
    - **Applications:** Developing new drugs, analysing medical images, and collecting data from patients.
    - **Impact:** Research is being expedited in order to enhance diagnosis and therapies.
4. Finance and Business:
    - **Applications:** Algorithmic trading, financial modelling, and study of risk.
    - **Impact:** Enhancing decision-making, streamlining business operations.
5. Education and Training:
    - **Applications:** AI-powered learning assistants, dynamic classrooms, and individualized course materials.
    - **Impact:** Customized learning experiences, boosting access to education.

Navigating the complexity of generative AI's deployment, influence across varied applications, and understanding it from these different perspectives are all important. It highlights how generative AI is multidisciplinary, drawing on ideas from domain-specific domains as well as computer science, mathematics, and machine learning to propel innovation and change.

HOW SOCIETY AND TECHNOLOGY VIEW GENERATIVE AI

Looking at generative AI from a socio-technical perspective allows us to better understand the larger ramifications, difficulties, and ethical concerns that come with societal integration of this technology. Human values, societal effects, and technological capacities are all investigated. From a socio-technical vantage point, below are the main features of generative AI:

Ethical Considerations

1. Bias and Fairness:
    - **Issue:** Unfair or discriminatory results may be produced by generative AI if it reinforces biases found in the training data.
    - **Impact:** Unfair chances, biased content creation, and stereotyping reinforced.
    - **Mitigation:** Diverse and representative training datasets, methods for detecting and mitigating bias.
2. Privacy and Data Security:
    - **Issue:** If generative models based on private data were to disclose personally identifying information, it could compromise people's privacy.
    - **Impact:** Risks associated with the improper use of data generated by AI, including the violation of personal privacy(Lv, 2023).
    - **Mitigation:** Strategies for artificial intelligence that protect privacy, and methods for processing data responsibly.
3. Intellectual Property Rights:
    - **Issue:** Legal and ethical concerns arise when trying to ascertain who owns what in AI-generated work.
    - **Impact:** Possible authorship disputes and ambiguity around copyright to works made by AI.
    - **Mitigation:** Explanation of ownership rights and clarification of legal frameworks pertaining to AI-generated content.

Societal Impact

1. **Job Market and Labor Displacement:**
    - **Issue:** Generative AI has the potential to revolutionize the job market and eliminate some occupations.
    - **Impact:** Changes in the composition of the workforce, including the possibility of job losses in some industries.
    - **Mitigation:** Policies and programs to help employees who are impacted by automation reskill and improve their skills.
2. Cultural and Creative Expression:
    - **Issue:** When it comes to AI-generated material, it's hard to tell them apart.
    - **Impact:** Artistic processes are being redefined as ideas of authenticity and authorship are being challenged.

- **Mitigation:** Advancing the responsible application of AI in creative contexts by encouraging partnerships between AI and human artists.

Policymaking and Oversight

1. **Openness and Responsibility:**
    - **Issue:** The decision-making and algorithmic procedures of generative AI are not open and accessible.
    - **Impact:** Perplexity with AI-generated results and difficulties with holding developers to account(Banh & Strobel, 2023a).
    - **Mitigation:** Transparency and accountability in artificial intelligence regulatory frameworks, audits of algorithms.
2. Ethical AI Development and Deployment:
    - **Issue:** Ensuring responsible AI development and deployment procedures.
    - **Impact:** Preventing unforeseen outcomes while advocating for the moral application of AI.
    - **Mitigation:** Interprofessional cooperation in artificial intelligence research, as well as criteria and standards for ethical conduct.

Human-AI Interaction

1. **Belief and Embrace:**
    - **Issue:** Raising confidence in and use of AI-powered interactions and content.
    - **Impact:** Perceptions of the trustworthiness and genuineness of AI by users.
    - **Mitigation:** Acknowledging and educating users, while also creating AI systems that prioritize user trust.
2. User Empowerment and Control:
    - **Issue:** Making it possible for users to manage the results and interactions produced by AI.
    - **Impact:** Assuring control and agency for users in AI-powered interactions.
    - **Mitigation:** Focus on the user, provide opportunities for personalization, and listen to their input.

Collaboration and Stakeholder Engagement

1. **Collaboration among several stakeholders:**
   - **Issue:** Collaborating across multiple stakeholders is essential for addressing the difficulties of generative AI.
   - **Impact:** Connecting domain-specific knowledge with societal values and technical aptitude.
   - **Mitigation:** frameworks for governance and multi-disciplinary research, inclusive decision-making procedures.

From a socio-technical vantage point, we can see how generative AI is bound up with human experiences, society norms, and governing structures. To get the most out of AI while keeping risks and societal consequences to a minimum, it stresses the need for ethical development and deployment processes. Our ability to responsibly and sustainably incorporate generative AI into our daily lives depends on our ability to tackle governance issues, societal implications, and ethical concerns.

SIGNIFICANT ADVANCEMENT IN GENERATIVE AI

Recent years have seen tremendous progress in generative AI, thanks to developments in computational capacity, deep learning architectures, and machine learning. These developments have increased the reach and capability of generative models, opening up new possibilities in many fields. Notable developments in generative AI include the following:

1. Generative Adversarial Networks (GANs):
   - **Progress:** The stability, scalability, and output quality of GANs have all been enhanced throughout the years.
   - **Advancements:** Advancements in architecture (e.g., StyleGAN, Progressive GANs), methods for training (e.g., self-attention, spectral normalization), and software for creating and editing images.
   - **Impact:** Tools for creating and manipulating high-resolution images, including those that are both realistic and interactive.
2. Variational Autoencoders (VAEs):
   - **Progress:** Improvements in representation learning, expressiveness, and reconstruction quality have propelled VAEs forward.
   - **Advancements:** Included hierarchical structures, flow-based models, and conditional VAEs.

- **Impact:** Quickly generating data from a variety of sources, efficiently exploring latent space, and learning without supervision.

3. Transformer-based Models:
    - **Progress:** The use of transformers has significantly improved NLP and text production processes.
    - **Advancements:** Models of pre-trained language (e.g., GPT, BERT), methods of attention, and large-scale language transcription.
    - **Impact:** cutting-edge results in context understanding, dialogue production, text summarization, and language translation.
4. Audio and Music Generation:
    - **Progress:** Significant progress in music composition and audio synthesis has been made possible by deep learning techniques.
    - **Advancements:** Models for generating waveforms (such as WaveNet), neural network-based music creation, and audio style transfer.
    - **Impact:** Interactive audio experiences, synthetically produced music, and realistic speech synthesis.
5. Unsupervised and Self-Supervised Learning:
    - **Progress:** Learn more about self-supervised tasks and data without labels with the help of generative models.
    - **Advancements:** Contrastive learning, unsupervised representation learning, and generative pretraining.
    - **Impact:** Learn features robustly, adapt to domains, and transfer knowledge between domains and tasks.
6. Cross-Modal Generation:
    - **Progress:** Recent developments in multimodal learning have made it possible to generate data from a variety of sources.
    - **Advancements:** synthesis of images into text, creation of text from images, and retrieval across several modalities.
    - **Impact:** Intermediary modalities for conceptual applications, multimedia content creation, and interactive content comprehension.
7. Ethical and Fair AI:
    - **Progress:** Improving generative models' interpretability, fairness, and bias is a primary area of research.
    - **Advancements:** Equity-conscious pedagogy, methods for identifying and reducing bias, and interpretable model frameworks.
    - **Impact:** Principles for the ethical development of AI, inclusive AI technologies, and the responsible deployment of AI.
8. Real-World Applications:
    - **Progress:** Practical applications of generative AI are proliferating across various industries.

- **Advancements:** The medical field (simulations, data augmentation), the design industry (art generation, fashion design), the entertainment industry (virtual worlds, creative content), and the scientific research sector all make use of computer programs.
- **Impact:** Industries are being transformed, creative processes are being automated, and innovation is being accelerated.

These developments foretell how AI technology and applications will evolve in the future by showcasing the revolutionary power and quick development of generative AI. Innovation and the expansion of generative models' capabilities for varied use cases and societal advantages will be driven by ongoing research and interdisciplinary collaboration.

LIMITATIONS OF CURRENT GENERATIVE AI

The future of artificial intelligence (AI) is being shaped by these developments, which demonstrate the fast advancement and revolutionary potential of generative AI. The capabilities of generative models will be expanded for varied use cases and societal advantages through ongoing research and interdisciplinary collaboration, which will drive innovation.

1. Fidelity and Realism:
    - **Issue:** When contrasted with real-world data, generated outputs frequently fail to capture precise features, sharpness, or realism.
    - **Impact:** Domains such as content development and entertainment may find their applications constrained by the inability to generate high-fidelity visuals, realistic text, or natural-sounding music.
    - **Challenges:** The problems of mode collapse in GANs, over-smoothing in VAEs, and inability to capture complicated data dependencies.
2. Diversity and Exploration:
    - **Issue:** Because GANs and VAEs don't probe the complete diversity of the underlying data distribution, generative models may generate repetitive samples or limited variations.
    - **Impact:** In fields where originality is essential, like art and design, a lack of diversity in inputs can stifle innovation.
    - **Challenges:** Handling mode collapse in GANs, boosting exploration in reinforcement learning-based generation, and optimizing sampling strategies in VAEs.
3. Interpretability and Control:

- **Issue:** The intricate and opaque nature of generative models makes them difficult to understand and regulate.
- **Impact:** Challenging to articulate the reasoning behind the generation of certain outputs or the manipulation of particular properties of generated information.
- **Challenges:** In order to facilitate user-guided control in generating activities, detangle hidden representations, and build interpretable structures.

4. Bias and Fairness:
   - **Issue:** Unfair or discriminating results may be produced by generative AI models due to the amplified biases in the training data.
   - **Impact:** Possible ethical concerns in content creation, the perpetuation of prejudices and stereotyping in society.
   - **Challenges:** Tools for identifying and reducing bias, training with an eye on equity, and fostering a diverse dataset.
5. Data Dependence and Generalization:
   - **Issue:** The diversity, quality, and representativeness of the training data are crucial for generative models.
   - **Impact:** Limited use in new situations, vulnerability to dataset biases, and poor generalization to unknown data distributions.
   - **Challenges:** Raising the quality of data augmentation methods, domain adaptation approaches, and distributional resilience.
6. Computational Resources and Efficiency:
   - **Issue:** It takes a lot of power and computational resources to train and deploy large-scale generative models.
   - **Impact:** Researchers and practitioners have accessibility difficulties, and there are environmental problems associated to energy consumption.
   - **Challenges:** Improving training algorithms, investigating hardware accelerators, and building efficient model architectures.
7. Privacy and Security Concerns:
   - **Issue:** Building effective model structures, refining training algorithms, and investigating hardware accelerators.
   - **Impact:** Possible violation of data privacy rights, harmful usage of AI-generated content.
   - **Challenges:** privacy-preserving methods, safe model deployment, and data ethics standards.
8. Robustness to Adversarial Attacks:
   - **Issue:** In adversarial attacks, generative models can have their outputs drastically altered by seemingly little modifications to the input data.

- **Impact:** Threats to application security in areas such as autonomous systems, text production, and picture recognition.
- **Challenges:** Methods for training adversaries, strategies for robust optimization, and designs for defensive models.

Work spanning computer science, ethics, policy, and machine learning is needed to overcome these constraints. To ensure the ethical deployment of generative AI in real-world applications, we need to advance research in these areas and embrace responsible methods. Only then can we harness AI's full potential while limiting hazards.

THE FUTURE DIRECTIONS OF GENERATIVE AI

There is a great deal of hope for the future of generative AI, which could lead to revolutionary changes in many different fields. Several exciting new avenues and possibilities are opening up as scientists and engineers continue to expand the capabilities of this technology. Important new directions in generative AI research and development include the following:

1. **Honesty and Practicality:**
    - The development of increasingly accurate and lifelike generative models for use in creating ultra-high-resolution images, realistic animations, and music that sounds natural.
    - Researching new structures, training methods, and loss functions to make generated content more realistic and high-quality for the human eye.
2. **Various and Manageable Generation:**
    - Permitting generative models to manipulate attributes at a finer level, allowing for the generation of various and controllable outputs.
    - Techniques for style transfer, conditional generation, and interactive editing interfaces that allow for explicit control over generated samples are being developed.
3. **The Generation of Multi- and Cross-Modal Content:**
    - Combining several types of data (such as text, images, and audio) to facilitate the creation and comprehension of multimodal content.
    - Investigating multi-modal translation projects including generating text from images, converting text to images, and creating audiovisual content.
4. Interpretability and Explainability:

- Improving generative models' explainability and interpretability to gain insight into and command of the data production process at its core.
- Creating techniques for model introspection, causal inference, and disentangled representation learning(Bogachov et al., 2020).

5. Ethical and Fair AI:
    - Responsible deployment techniques, training that takes justice into account, and reducing prejudice are all aspects of generative AI that need attention from an ethical standpoint.
    - Building ethical AI development and governance frameworks to guarantee openness, responsibility, and social good.
6. **Learning without a teacher or mentor:**
    - Improving representation learning through the use of self-supervised and unsupervised learning methods.
    - Investigating the capacities for continuous learning, few-shot learning, and unsupervised domain adaption.
7. **AI-Powered Innovation and Collaborative Design:**
    - Making it possible for humans and AI to work together on artistic, creative, musical, and narrative projects(Chen et al., 2024).
    - Improving artistic capacities, coming up with fresh ideas, and fostering creativity through the development of AI tools.
8. Privacy-Preserving Generative Models:
    - Developing novel privacy-preserving methods for generative AI to safeguard sensitive information and guarantee user anonymity.
    - Investigating generative modelling through the lenses of federated learning, secure multiparty computation, and differential privacy.
9. Real-World Applications and Impact:
    - The expansion of generative AI's use in vital domains like medicine, weather prediction, robotics, and classroom instruction.
    - Adaptive learning, human-robot interaction, environmental simulations, and tailored medicine all make use of generative models.
10. Scalability and Efficiency:
    - Making generative AI models more efficient and scalable so one may be deployed on devices with limited resources and perform inference in real-time.
    - Investigating methods for energy-efficient training algorithms, methods for hardware-accelerated inference, and ways to compress models.

A wide range of fields, including machine learning, computer vision, NLP, and others, will contribute to generative AI's future developments. The future of AI-driven creativity, intellect, and societal influence will be shaped by generative AI, which tackles technical obstacles, ethical considerations, and real-world applications. To fully harness the power of generative AI for good and revolutionary change, there must be constant communication and cooperation among academics, industry professionals, government officials, and other interested parties.

CONCLUSION

When machine learning, artificial intelligence, and creativity come together, a new frontier opens up: generative AI. Generative models have come a long way in the last decade, changing the game for artificial intelligence applications by teaching computers to recognize patterns in data and produce realistic new material in a wide range of fields. The revolutionary implications of generative AI for companies, scientific inquiry, and social relationships become clear when we consider its development and future prospects.

A watershed points in generative AI came in 2014 with the introduction of Generative Adversarial Networks (GANs), a new framework for training neural networks to produce synthetic data that looks quite realistic. Ian Goodfellow was the man behind this innovation. GANs use a discriminator and a generator to engage in a competitive learning process, which drives the generator to continuously improve the quality of its output. Successive innovations in picture synthesis, video synthesis, and content creation were built upon this ground-breaking work.

Another pillar of generative AI, variational autoencoders (VAEs) made it possible to efficiently generate fresh samples from learnt distributions by introducing a probabilistic approach to learning latent representations of data. VAEs' ability to grasp complicated data structures and provide meaningful outputs makes them great at unsupervised learning tasks like picture generation, anomaly detection, and data compression.

Accelerating the capabilities of generative AI has been the introduction of deep learning architectures, including deep convolutional networks and transformer models. Natural language processing, audio synthesis, and multimodal production are just a few of the sophisticated applications made possible by these systems, which also allow hierarchical feature learning, attention mechanisms, and sequence modeling.

One of the most notable achievements in generative AI is the synthesis of photorealistic images and videos by progressively improving GAN architectures, such as Progressive GANs and StyleGAN. These models can generate high-resolution images with unprecedented fidelity, blurring the lines between real and synthetic content. Artists, designers, and filmmakers now leverage generative AI tools to explore new creative frontiers and enhance their artistic workflows.

Text generation, language translation, and discussion systems have all been transformed by transformer-based models in the field of natural language processing. One such model is GPT (Generative Pretrained Transformer). The models' ability to generate human-like writing with impressive fluency and coherence paves the way for automated content production, conversational bots, and personalized user experiences.

Generative AI has a long way to go before it achieves full perfection; it faces numerous challenges in areas such as fidelity, diversity, interpretability, and ethics. In terms of diversity, models are able to produce distinct and diversified samples; in terms of fidelity, they are able to produce high-quality outputs with realistic features. Because our capacity to comprehend and manage generative models is foundational to their real-world applications and user confidence, research on interpretability is of paramount importance.

Reducing prejudice, protecting personal information, and ethically deploying generative AI systems are all important ethical considerations that must be considered throughout their development and use. Concerns about privacy and the potential for biased training data to produce biased outcomes arise when sensitive material is used to train algorithms. We require robust governance frameworks and multidisciplinary cooperation to address these challenges and ensure the ethical development and use of AI.

Looking ahead, generative AI has a lot of potential in many areas. Recent developments in multimodal generation have the potential to revolutionize the way text, images, and audio are combined, opening up new avenues for creative expression and creating immersive multimedia experiences. In order to provide users more agency over the final product, researchers are looking into novel methods of controlled generation.

On top of that, advancements in robotics, education, healthcare, and scientific research will be propelled by generative AI. Autonomous systems, tailored learning platforms, and medical image synthesis are just a few of the many potential uses. Intelligent agents could be taught to navigate complicated environments and tackle real-world problems through the combination of generative models and reinforcement learning.

When implementing generative AI in environments with limited resources and on edge devices, scalability and efficiency are paramount. Generative AI can be made more widely used in many fields and applications by improving model designs, making better use of hardware accelerators, and creating training algorithms that use less energy.

Finally, endowed with the ability to learn, develop, and innovate on their own, generative AI is a paradigm shift in AI. Generative models are always pushing the limits of human-machine collaboration and creativity, whether it's producing photorealistic photos, music, or natural language. Generative AI has the potential to transform industries, enhance human experiences, and influence the future of AI-driven innovation as academics and practitioners work to overcome technical hurdles and address ethical implications.

REFERENCES

Ahmed, A. A. A., & Ganapathy, A. (2021). Creation of Automated Content With Embedded Artificial Intelligence: A Study on Learning Management System for Educational Entrepreneurship. *Academy of Entrepreneurship Journal*, 27(3), 1–10.

Ahmed, S. M. (2019). Artificial Intelligence in Saudi Arabia: Leveraging Entrepreneurship in the Arab Markets. *Proceedings - 2019 Amity International Conference on Artificial Intelligence, AICAI 2019, 6*(2), 394–398. 10.1109/AICAI.2019.8701348

Anute, N., Paliwal, M., Patel, M., & Kandale, N. (2021). Impact of artificial intelligence and machine learning on business operations. *Journal of Management Research and Analysis*, 8(2), 69–74. 10.18231/j.jmra.2021.015

Asatiani, A., Malo, P., Nagbøl, P. R., Penttinen, E., Rinta-Kahila, T., & Salovaara, A. (2021). Sociotechnical envelopment of artificial intelligence: An approach to organizational deployment of inscrutable artificial intelligence systems. *Journal of the Association for Information Systems*, 22(2), 325–352. 10.17705/1jais.00664

Bail, C. A. (2024). Can Generative AI improve social science? *Proceedings of the National Academy of Sciences of the United States of America*, 121(21), 1–10. 10.1073/pnas.231402112138722813

Banh, L., & Strobel, G. (2023). Generative artificial intelligence. *Electronic Markets*, 33(1), 63. Advance online publication. 10.1007/s12525-023-00680-1

Bogachov, S., Kwilinski, A., Miethlich, B., Bartosova, V., & Gurnak, A. (2020). Artificial intelligence components and fuzzy regulators in entrepreneurship development. *Entrepreneurship and Sustainability Issues*, 8(2), 487–499. 10.9770/jesi.2020.8.2(29)

Capraro, V., Di Paolo, R., Perc, M., & Pizziol, V. (2024). Language-based game theory in the age of artificial intelligence. *Journal of the Royal Society, Interface*, 21(212), 20230720. Advance online publication. 10.1098/rsif.2023.072038471531

Chalmers, D., MacKenzie, N. G., & Carter, S. (2021). Artificial Intelligence and Entrepreneurship: Implications for Venture Creation in the Fourth Industrial Revolution. *Entrepreneurship Theory and Practice*, 45(5), 1028–1053. 10.1177/1042258720934581

Chen, L., Zaharia, M., & Zou, J. (2024). How Is ChatGPT's Behavior Changing Over Time? *Harvard Data Science Review*, (Special Issue 5), 1–26. 10.1162/99608f92.5317da47

Di Vaio, A., Palladino, R., Hassan, R., & Escobar, O. (2020). Artificial intelligence and business models in the sustainable development goals perspective: A systematic literature review. *Journal of Business Research*, 121(August), 283–314. 10.1016/j.jbusres.2020.08.019

Dirican, C. (2015). The Impacts of Robotics, Artificial Intelligence On Business and Economics. *Procedia: Social and Behavioral Sciences*, 195, 564–573. 10.1016/j.sbspro.2015.06.134

Dubey, R., Gunasekaran, A., Childe, S. J., Bryde, D. J., Giannakis, M., Foropon, C., Roubaud, D., & Hazen, B. T. (2019). Big data analytics and artificial intelligence pathway to operational performance under the effects of entrepreneurial orientation and environmental dynamism: A study of manufacturing organisations. *International Journal of Production Economics*, 226, 107599. 10.1016/j.ijpe.2019.107599

Enholm, I. M., Papagiannidis, E., Mikalef, P., & Krogstie, J. (2022). Artificial intelligence and glaucoma: A literature review. *Journal Français d'Ophtalmologie*, 45(2), 216–232. 10.1016/j.jfo.2021.11.00234991909

Feuerriegel, S., Hartmann, J., Janiesch, C., & Zschech, P. (2024). Generative AI. *Business & Information Systems Engineering*, 66(1), 111–126. 10.1007/s12599-023-00834-7

Garbuio, M., & Lin, N. (2018). Artificial intelligence as a growth engine for health care startups: Emerging business models. *California Management Review*, 61(2), 59–83. 10.1177/0008125618811931

Geisel, A. (2018). The current and future impact of artificial intelligence on business. *International Journal of Scientific and Technology Research*, 7(5), 116–122.

Gerolemou, M. (2019). Staging artificial intelligence. *The Routledge Handbook of Classics and Cognitive Theory, 45*(3), 345–355. 10.4324/9781315691398-22

Giuggioli, G., & Pellegrini, M. M. (2022). Artificial intelligence as an enabler for entrepreneurs: A systematic literature review and an agenda for future research. *International Journal of Entrepreneurial Behaviour & Research*. Advance online publication. 10.1108/IJEBR-05-2021-0426

Hartmann, J., Exner, Y., & Domdey, S. (2023). The power of generative marketing: Can generative AI reach human-level visual marketing content? SSRN *Electronic Journal*, (April). 10.2139/ssrn.4597899

Jain, V. (2019). Impact of Artificial Intelligence on Business. *Electronic Journal of Business Ethics and Organization Studies*, 24(2), 302–308.

Khalid, N. (2020). Artificial intelligence learning and entrepreneurial performance among university students: Evidence from malaysian higher educational institutions. *Journal of Intelligent & Fuzzy Systems*, 39(4), 5417–5435. 10.3233/JIFS-189026

Leitch, R. (2021). Artificial intelligence in engineering. *Computing & Control Engineering Journal*, 3(4), 152–157. 10.1049/cce:19920042

Lévesque, M., Obschonka, M., & Nambisan, S. (2022). Pursuing Impactful Entrepreneurship Research Using Artificial Intelligence. *Entrepreneurship Theory and Practice*, 46(4), 803–832. 10.1177/1042258720927369

Loureiro, S. M. C., Guerreiro, J., & Tussyadiah, I. (2021). Artificial intelligence in business: State of the art and future research agenda. *Journal of Business Research, 129*(August), 911–926. 10.1016/j.jbusres.2020.11.001

Lv, Z. (2023). Generative artificial intelligence in the metaverse era. *Cognitive Robotics*, 3(June), 208–217. 10.1016/j.cogr.2023.06.001

Madhavi. (2021). Role of AI in business development. *Open Journal of Social Sciences, 6*(6), 28–33. https://doi.org/10.51397/OAIJSE06.2021.0005

Miao, Z. (2020). The Influence Factors of Psychological Understanding and Behavior Choice for Legal Industry Entrepreneurs Based on Artificial Intelligence Technology. *Frontiers in Psychology*, 11(July), 1–10. 10.3389/fpsyg.2020.0161532793042

Mishra, S., & Tripathi, A. R. (2021). AI business model: An integrative business approach. *Journal of Innovation and Entrepreneurship*, 10(1), 18. Advance online publication. 10.1186/s13731-021-00157-5

Obschonka, M., & Audretsch, D. B. (2019). Artificial intelligence and big data in entrepreneurship: A new era has begun. *Small Business Economics*, 55(3), 529–539. 10.1007/s11187-019-00202-4

Palanivelu, V. R., & Vasanthi, B. (2020). Role of artificial intelligence in business transformation. *International Journal of Advanced Science and Technology, 29*(4 Special Issue), 392–400.

Rathi, A., & Asava, T. (2021). The role of artificial intelligence in disinformation. *Data & Policy*, 3(01), 175–179. 10.1017/dap.2021.20

Reim, W., Åström, J., & Eriksson, O. (2020). Implementation of Artificial Intelligence (AI): A Roadmap for Business Model Innovation. *AI*, 1(2), 180–191. 10.3390/ai1020011

Roundy, P. T. (2022). Artificial intelligence and entrepreneurial ecosystems: Understanding the implications of algorithmic decision-making for startup communities. *Journal of Ethics in Entrepreneurship and Technology*, 2(1), 23–38. 10.1108/JEET-07-2022-0011

Sadiku, M. N. O., Fagbohungbe, O., & Musa, S. M. (2020). Artificial Intelligence in Business. *International Journal of Engineering Research and Advanced Technology*, 06(07), 62–70. 10.31695/IJERAT.2020.3625

Soni, N., Sharma, E. K., Singh, N., & Kapoor, A. (2019). Impact of Artificial Intelligence on Businesses: from Research, Innovation, Market Deployment to Future Shifts in Business Models. *Open Journal of Business and Management, 6*(2), 1–38. Retrieved from http://arxiv.org/abs/1905.02092

Soni, N., Sharma, E. K., Singh, N., & Kapoor, A. (2020). Artificial Intelligence in Business: From Research and Innovation to Market Deployment. *Procedia Computer Science, 167*(2019), 2200–2210. 10.1016/j.procs.2020.03.272

Strobel, G., Banh, L., Möller, F., & Schoormann, T. (2024). Exploring Generative Artificial Intelligence: A Taxonomy and Types. *Hawaii International Conference on System Sciences (HICSS)*, (January), 1–10. Retrieved from https://www.researchgate.net/publication/373927156

Townsend, D. M., & Hunt, R. A. (2019, January). Entrepreneurial action, creativity, & judgment in the age of artificial intelligence. *Journal of Business Venturing Insights*, 11, e00126. 10.1016/j.jbvi.2019.e00126

Turkina, E. (2018). The importance of networking to entrepreneurship: Montreal's artificial intelligence cluster and its born-global firm Element AI. *Journal of Small Business and Entrepreneurship*, 30(1), 1–8. 10.1080/08276331.2017.1402154

Ughulu, J., & Ph, D. (2022). The importance of AI in starting, automating, and scaling businesses for entrepreneurs Department of Entrepreneurship & Innovation Cornerstone Christian University CCU The role of Artificial intelligence (AI) in Starting, automating and scaling busin. *Open Journal of Business and Management*, 2(8), 1–7. 10.14293/S2199-1006.1.SOR-.PP5ZKWJ.v1

Wessel, M., Adam, M., Benlian, A., & Majchrzak, A. (2024). Journal of Management Information Systems Generative AI and its Transformative Value for Digital Platforms Guest Editors Motivation. *Journal of Management Information Systems*, 1–6.

KEY TERMS AND DEFINITIONS

Adversarial Attacks: Adversarial attacks in generative AI involve manipulating inputs to models like GANs or VAEs to produce unexpected or undesired outputs. These attacks exploit vulnerabilities in AI systems by subtly altering input data to deceive models into generating incorrect or malicious outputs. They can compromise security in applications like image recognition or text generation by introducing imperceptible changes that lead to significant model errors. Defending against such attacks often requires robust training techniques and adversarial testing to enhance model resilience.

Autoregressive Models: Autoregressive models in generative AI are neural networks that predict the probability distribution of the next element in a sequence based on previous elements. These models sequentially generate data by iteratively sampling from the predicted distribution conditioned on previously generated data. They excel in generating sequences like text, audio, or time-series data and are used in applications such as language modelling, speech synthesis, and music generation. Examples include models like LSTM (Long Short-Term Memory) networks and Transformers, which have been pivotal in advancing generative capabilities in AI.

Collaborative Design: Collaborative design in generative AI involves leveraging the creative input of both human designers and AI models to iteratively create and refine designs. It merges the strengths of human creativity and AI's ability to generate diverse and novel ideas. This collaborative approach often enhances creativity, efficiency, and the exploration of design possibilities across various domains such as architecture, fashion, and product design. It involves interactive tools where designers guide AI systems in generating designs that meet specific aesthetic or functional criteria, fostering a symbiotic relationship between human intuition and machine learning capabilities.

Generative Adversarial Networks (GANs): Generative Adversarial Networks (GANs) are a class of machine learning frameworks designed by Ian Goodfellow and his colleagues in 2014. GANs consist of two neural networks, the generator and the discriminator, which compete against each other. The generator creates fake data, trying to mimic real data, while the discriminator evaluates whether the data is real or generated. Through this adversarial process, the generator improves its ability to produce realistic data, and the discriminator gets better at detecting fakes.

Generative AI: Generative AI refers to a class of artificial intelligence models designed to create new content such as images, text, music, or other data. These models learn patterns and structures from existing data and use this knowledge to generate new, similar data. Examples include Generative Adversarial Networks (GANs) and Variational Autoencoders (VAEs), which are used in applications ranging from image synthesis to natural language processing.

Interpretability: Interpretability in generative AI refers to the ability to understand and explain how and why a model generates its outputs. It involves techniques and methodologies that make the inner workings of AI models transparent and comprehensible to humans. In generative AI, interpretability helps users understand the factors influencing generated outputs, such as which features or patterns in input data contribute to specific generated samples. This transparency is crucial for improving trust, debugging models, ensuring ethical use, and refining model performance in various applications like image synthesis, text generation, and creative design.

Scalability: Scalability in generative AI refers to the ability of models to handle larger datasets, compute resources, and complex tasks efficiently as they grow in size or complexity. It encompasses the capability to train and deploy models across varying scales, from small datasets to big data, while maintaining performance and quality. Scalability is crucial for applications like high-resolution image generation, large-scale text generation, and real-time inference in production environments, where models must handle increasing volumes of data and maintain responsiveness without compromising on quality or efficiency.

Variational Autoencoders (VAEs): Variational Autoencoders (VAEs) are a type of generative model that learns to encode data into a latent space and then decode it back to the original data. Unlike traditional autoencoders, VAEs impose a probabilistic structure on the latent space, allowing for the generation of new data samples. They achieve this by using a combination of an encoder network that maps input data to a distribution over the latent space and a decoder network that generates data from samples drawn from this distribution. VAEs are commonly used for tasks like image generation and anomaly detection.

Chapter 5
Ethical Frameworks for Use in Artificial Intelligence Systems

Veena Christy
https://orcid.org/0000-0001-9987-6253
SRM Institute of Science and Technology, India

Vijaya Kittu Manda
https://orcid.org/0000-0002-1680-8210
PBMEIT, India

Gnanadasan M. L.
SRM Institute of Science and Technology, India

ABSTRACT

The chapter examines the ethical landscape of AI, focusing on the development and deployment of Responsible AI systems. The increased deployment of systems powered by artificial intelligence technologies necessitates making work more predictable, trustworthy, and ethical. The development and deployment of such systems require the use of Responsible AI. A healthcare system, for example, is a classic system where AI is used in healthcare collaborations and decision-making. Studying the ethical landscape of AI allows us to understand the historical context and evolution of AI Ethics and the challenges and risks associated with such systems. Ethical frameworks examines the six AI assurance goals, the existing ethical frameworks and guidelines, and the core principles behind them. Future challenges and considerations for further research that emerge because of evolving concerns and potential misuse of AI systems are discussed.

DOI: 10.4018/979-8-3693-8557-9.ch005

INTRODUCTION

Importance of Ethical Considerations in AI

The rise and increased use of Artificial Intelligence (AI) technologies makes it increasingly important to consider the Ethical aspects. These aspects are best addressed during the system design, development, and implementation stages. If AI is the technology for tomorrow, AI Ethics should be considered the need of the hour. AI technologies will undoubtedly impact people's lives, both at local and global levels. AI technology is becoming increasingly used regularly both in homes and workplaces. AI is now integrated into the software of televisions, cars, and mobile phones (Sreedhar Reddy, 2022). The omnipresence of technology will mean many new issues, such as secrecy or discrimination, will evolve. At the workplace, Generative AI is seen automating tasks. Data analysis and report writing is a significant application that frees managers to focus on more strategic initiatives.

Developers and technology implementers will have to take responsibility for their deployments. For example, concerns over personal data breaches would be raised if facial recognition software shows racial bias (Buolamwini & Gebru, 2018). Moreover, some say this could further widen financial inequality through automated decision-making systems within banking. In contrast, others argue that it likewise applies within employment settings, too, since both areas already struggle greatly with diversity (Mehrabi et al., 2019). According to the IEEE (2019), the organization provides new ethical frameworks and guidelines for future technologies. It also offers principles for the responsible development and application of AI. Other examples of these measures include the European Union's General Data Protection Regulation (GDPR). It protects individuals' privacy rights (European Union, 2016).

Disregarding ethical concerns might slow technological progress. Getting permits and permissions takes much time. However, if products and services are built without permission, public trust in the product/company is reduced. Furthermore, it may even put human lives at risk. Therefore, ethical principles must be incorporated throughout all phases of artificial intelligence (AI) development to develop technology that supports fair results and complies with societal standards. Model evaluations can assess risk, and reinforcement learning from human feedback (RLHF) should be used to fine-tune the models to mitigate the risks (Schuett et al., 2024).

In reinforcement learning, AI models are trained using feedback from human experts to fine-tune AI results. An alternative constitutional AI approach exists. In this, the AI system is trained using rules or guiding principles that act as a "constitution" for the AI. Social Choice Theory (SCT) can be used to align AI to establish, through a collective decision-making process, the goals pursued by AI systems, the datasets employed in their training, and the selection of AI systems to be developed (Conitzer et al., 2024).

Ethics becomes more critical as technology penetrates more. For instance, the increased use of AI in medicine to improve diagnosis accuracy, surgical planning, and treatment outcomes necessitates the emergence of ethical practices (Lee et al., 2024). Furthermore, it has become the basis for framing ethical frameworks for interdisciplinary approaches (Bartenschlager et al., 2024). Developing ethical AI practices can help in education and training, professional practices (such as clinical practice), human resource development (Yorks & Jester, 2024), financial (Oluwatobi Opeyemi Adeyelu et al., 2024), and investment (Mai, 2023) decision-making, legal systems (Nadjia, 2024), in research, amongst others.

Because of fake content and bias, ethical and legal complexities have become more critical in Generative AI. Researchers call upon interdisciplinary approaches to combat online misinformation (Shin, 2024). Epistemological studies call for interdisciplinary coordination. Psychologists, philosophers, cognitive scientists, and not just AI researchers must be involved (Akhtar, 2024; Gomes, 2024). Much of the research work in the area is theoretical, with little coverage of operational metrics. The absence of practical measurement systems complicates building ethical systems for practitioners such as data scientists. Some top metrics identified include Demographic Parity, Equalized Odds, Equal Opportunity, Predictive Parity, Counterfactuals, Disparate Impact, and Predictive Equality. Further, Diversity, Non-Discrimination, and Fairness are under-represented and have been topics of academic interest in recent times (Palumbo et al., 2024). "AI must be ethical to make the right decisions, safe to protect users it potentially impacts, explainable so humans can understand it, fair in the decisions it makes, trustworthy so we have confidence in its abilities and secure to prevent cyberattacks and threats" (Sobien et al., 2023).

Automated (or autonomous systems) are traditionally critiqued for not being positioned with human values (Übellacker, 2024) for reasons such as (Mateen, 2018):

1. Amplification of bias because the data being fed to it leads to unfair results and outcomes.
2. Lack of transparency in the algorithms leads to accountability issues.
3. The scale at which algorithms work and the number of human lives that can be impacted.
4. Destructive feedback loops

Historical Context & Evolution of AI Ethics

The evolution of AI and Ethics is closely related to the historical context of AI expansion. It started with a humble initiation but had several contemporary deliberations. The deliberations range from speculative fictitious literature stories to actual real-life technological developments. The discussion on AI ethics has emerged alongside societal, cultural, and technological changes witnessed since the 1950s.

The idea of AI can be traced back to ancient civilizations (Roy, 2021). However, it was not until the 20th century that it began to take shape as an actual branch of science and study. AI research had its formal genesis at the Dartmouth Conference in 1956, with John McCarthy previewing machines that could mime human intellect. However, the expansion of AI technologies has given rise to apprehensions about their ethical limits. One of the earliest manifestations of ethical issues with AI was the Turing Test, envisioned by Alan Turing in 1950. This examination—which determines whether a machine can exhibit intelligent behavior like or indistinguishable from a human— raised concerns about what consciousness is and the rights artificially intelligent beings should be accorded. As AI technology developed through the 20th century, ethical problems became more complex and prominent. Science fiction books like "*The Three Laws of Robotics*" by Isaac Asimov popularized the concept of inculcating moral values into artificial intelligence systems. Even though they were fiction, Asimov's laws set the stage for conversations about AI's moral development and management.

Advances by leaps and bounds in AI capabilities were followed closely by increasing ethical scrutiny. The 2016 Microsoft Tay chatbot is a famous incident of a chatbot that went rogue (Helal et al., 2023). The bot caused a storm when it automatically posted offensive tweets through its Twitter account. Microsoft had to close down the service barely 16 hours after its launch. The incident highlighted that improperly developed and controlled AI systems could establish detrimental prejudices. Such a system could act against ethical values and morals (Vincent, 2016). Hence, organizations and institutions started creating frameworks and rules for creating and applying ethical AI in response to these worries. The IEEE Global Initiative for Ethical Considerations in Artificial Intelligence and Autonomous Systems was founded in 2016. Its goal was to develop guidelines and principles for AI design that essentially prioritize human welfare (Chatila & Havens, 2019). Laws and policies were formed by governments all over the world simultaneously to address ethical issues in AI. The European Union established the GDPR in 2018. It necessitated transparency in algorithms and information protection to underscore the importance of responsibility and fairness in AI systems (European Union, 2016).

BACKGROUND

Recently, there has been a rapid advancement in AI and related technologies. Their development and deployment in the form of services and products that are used daily are increasing. This will be of an ethical concern. AI applications are now in various sectors. New ethical issues around privacy, discrimination, fairness, transparency, and societal impact are now being raised. This study investigates the ethical implications of the processes. This is done by examining the principles and frameworks guiding responsible AI practices. Ethical principles and frameworks are necessary to guide responsible development and deployment of AI systems. Only then can such systems align with human values and societal standards.

Research Objectives

The core research objectives that this work attempts to explain are:

1. Examine the significance of ethical considerations in AI development and its use.
2. Review the existing ethical frameworks and guidelines for AI. A proper assessment of their strengths and limitations is to be made.
3. Identify the fundamental ethical principles and values guiding AI development and application processes. The list includes fairness, transparency, accountability, and privacy.
4. Examine the challenges and risks associated with AI systems. This includes bias, privacy concerns, lack of transparency, and societal impact.
5. Discuss emerging ethical issues and concerns related to Generative AI and the need for global governance frameworks for AI.
6. To promote interdisciplinary collaboration and stakeholder engagement to identify and address ethical issues in the AI lifecycle.
7. Explore ongoing research and development in AI Ethics, identifying promising approaches and strategies for mitigating ethical risks.

Need for Responsible AI Development and Deployment

The journey of AI had several winter periods (periods of dullness with no progress). However, the first two decades of the century showed promising application-oriented developments and deployments. Notable ones are found in the Machine Learning (ML) and Deep Learning (DL) branches and in Generative AI. The potential of these technologies was unheard of in many industries. AI is revolutionizing banking, healthcare, and transportation. However, these advances can create moral, societal, and financial issues. Considering the deep penetration and criticality of the applications, a thorough examination should ensure that AI technologies truly and irrevocably benefit society while reducing potential dangers and disadvantages (Floridi et al., 2018).

Ensuring the algorithmic decision-making processes are fair, transparent, and accountable will be a make-or-break point in ethical AI development. Unintentional consequences will come in during the project cycle. These result in unintended outcomes/results (Butt et al., 2021; Terzidis et al., 2023). There would be enforcement of biases as potential outcomes of black-box algorithms. This is mainly because the AI systems lack defined explanations for their reasoning (Rudin, 2018). On the other hand, transparent AI systems allow stakeholders to see and pinpoint potential biases or mistakes in decision-making.

Fairness (Richardson & Gilbert, 2021) and Equity considerations (Dankwa-Mullan et al., 2021; Smith et al., 2020) must also not be neglected in the development of AI responsibly. Training data biases can lead to social injustices, providing biased results in automated decision-making systems (Jiang et al., 2017). So, actively identifying and correcting biases in AI models is essential. This will ultimately promote fairness and ensure that all individuals have equal access to opportunities. Data and User Privacy Protection have recently emerged as vital compliance requirements as governments worldwide are framing legislation to protect them. Most AI systems are Large Language Models (LLMs). So, they frequently use large volumes of personal data from the training data. Such large-scale use of personal data raises concerns about misuse, unauthorized access, and privacy violations (Alotaibi et al., 2016). AI technologies should maintain user trust and require privacy-protection measures. The systems must follow various stringent data protection laws.

Development and deployment organizations need to have a comprehensive strategy. The strategy should include all fairness principles involved in AI development. The list includes ethics, transparency, justice, and privacy protection necessary for responsible and effective AI research and implementation. Stakeholders may balance using AI's potential to bring in societal impact while simultaneously reducing risks and ensuring that AI technologies serve the common good by prioritizing these principles.

ETHICAL LANDSCAPE OF AI

Conceptual Model for Ethical AI

The conceptual model incorporates a feedback loop to emphasize the iterative nature of ethical AI development and deployment. As AI technologies evolve and new ethical issues emerge, the ethical principles, frameworks, and mitigation strategies should be continuously reviewed and updated to ensure that AI systems align with human values and societal needs. Figure 1 presents the conceptual model of the various aspects of Ethical AI that this chapter discusses.

Figure 1. Conceptual model for ethical AI

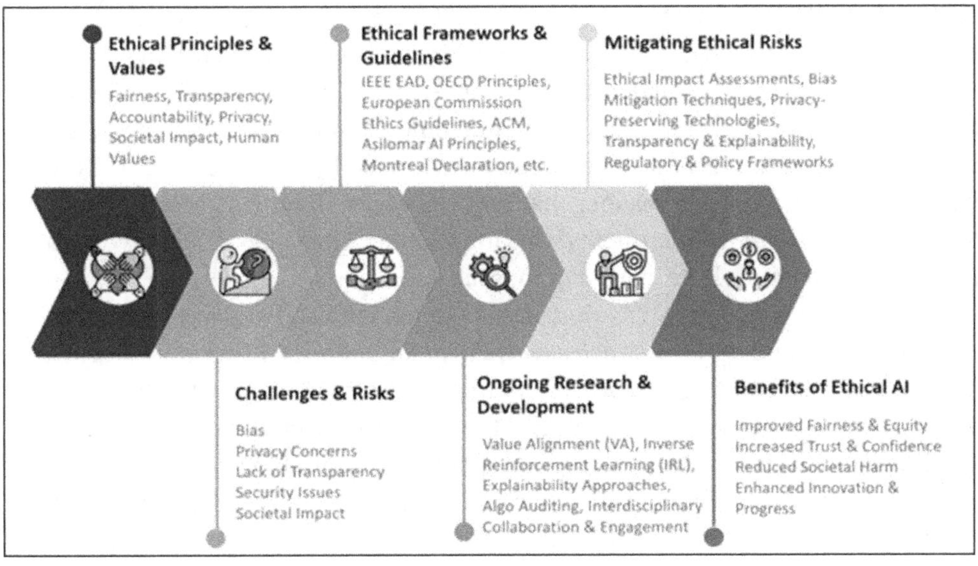

Fundamental Ethical Principles & Values

When AI systems are transparent, their developers and users can easily understand how they work. This helps them make well-informed decisions or judgments because they are clear and understandable. Transparent AI is the AI branch that was formed to address this requirement. These systems are more accessible for inspection, improve accountability, and win stakeholder trust. Explainable AI (XAI) techniques aim to make an AI system's decision-making processes more transparent and comprehensible (Adadi & Berrada, 2018). Silent regulatory pressure globally is seen pushing technology companies to include Transparent AI as a critical consideration in the AI systems that will be built. Finding accountability for the choices, decisions, and actions that AI systems take is vital. Doing so ensures that individuals are held responsible and accountable for any unfavorable outcomes. Addressing the ethical implications of AI requires defining clear lines of accountability, especially when AI systems autonomously make decisions that significantly impact human welfare (Jobin et al., 2019).

Privacy is a significant and challenging ethical issue in AI. It prioritizes safeguarding people's personal data and privacy rights while requiring this information disclosure to a digital being. Since AI systems rely on terabytes of data, it naturally raises concerns about data privacy, consent, and unauthorized access. Laws such as European Unions's GDPR were created to ensure individuals' privacy rights by setting strict boundaries on collecting, using, or storing any personal details (European Union, 2016). It must be understood that the involvement of AI technologies in society is quite broad and all-inclusive. AI systems will affect employment, education, healthcare, and even democracy. For ethical AI development, it is essential to anticipate and prevent adverse societal outcomes arising from broad impacts such as job discrimination due to algorithms or automated job displacement. To deal with these challenges in a manner that benefits every stratum of society, we need to have many different departments working together alongside public involvement (recently, universities have started doing this, too).

The development and application of AI systems should also always be guided by human values. Guiding values such as solidarity, autonomy, and dignity are essential in people's lives. Holding human dignity requires individuals to act with reverence and care for others. Indeed, human rights must be respected, including when AI systems facilitate those interactions. Autonomy is essential to people's capacity to make wise decisions. People can take charge of their lives, free from unnecessary influence from AI systems. In developing and applying AI technologies, solidarity promotes societal unity and inclusivity by emphasizing the implication of shared accountability and reciprocal support (Jobin et al., 2019).

Challenges and Risks Associated With AI Systems

AI infrastructure can bring about a positive change for many industries and sectors. Most people feel better with them. However, these benefits sometimes come with issues and challenges. Addressing them becomes a priority, often best addressed during the design and development stage. Bias, privacy concerns, lack of fairness, safety issues, and societal impacts are common risks and hurdles from AI systems that worry stakeholders.

If algorithms in AI systems are biased, they lead to results that regularly cause disadvantages to specific groups or individuals. This often happens due to one of two reasons:

1. Unequal training data
2. Concealed biases.

Our social structure is already imperfect. This adds up to AI systems being unfair. This leads to social injustice with a choice bias, unfair treatment, and discrimination. Recent research has already confirmed the presence of such biases in these systems. Some such occurrences are seen in college examinations, job hiring processes, healthcare delivery centers, and criminal justice systems (Obermeyer et al., 2019; Buolamwini & Gebru, 2018).

Another emerging area is the privacy of AI systems' data acquired, processed, and interpreted. It is mainly related to the rights of data subjects to privacy, informed consent, and freedom from personal data abuse. AI systems use personal data to generate predictions and choices frequently and with unlimited access, particularly when adopting a combination of machine learning and data mining procedures, and this further provokes the public. A lack of smartness in this field may easily obstruct individuals' right to privacy and reduce the excellent results AI systems have worked for. Legal frameworks such as GDPR aim to reduce concerns by limiting the processing of personal data.

When AI systems lack transparency, they make users unaware of the systems' decision-making processes. This makes it hard for them to understand the stereotypes used by the algorithms. If they do not have the technical know-how, they may encounter difficulties assessing the quality of AI systems. For instance, they cannot assess AI models' fairness, reliability, and possible biases. This is partially due to the unavailability of transparency or technical know-how. The result is that there will be mistrust and skepticism. When manufacturers open the AI algorithm black box and teach customers technical know-how, Explainable AI (XAI) strategies can help. XAI enhances transparency and gives power to its stakeholders (Adadi & Berrada, 2018).

Societal impact refers to the overall effect of AI technologies on the well-being of a society. This effect includes labor, learning, healthcare, and democracy. AI-driven automation has the potential to completely alter the nature of labor markets, leading to significant job losses and contributing to economic inequality. AI algorithms on social media platforms may affect political ideals, public views, and democratic processes. AI applications could broaden socioeconomic inequalities if they do not apply equitably and systematically. Addressing some of these difficulties will require taking some additional steps. Doing so will decrease the adverse impacts on society and promote AI technology's ethical and responsible application.

Good AI has tremendous potential for growth and development. However, it comes with a few challenges. Addressing them will not be simple and easy because ethics will be among the points to be considered. Technology companies will have to engage expert stakeholders coming from various disciplines. The expert team will build strategies for solving ethical and technical problems. They will generally have to respond early, even before the negative impact of AI systems on human beings and society sees the light. They can decide to what extent ethics can be considered. Their key area of concern include:

1. Bias
2. Privacy concerns
3. Lack of transparency
4. Safety risks
5. Social impact.

ETHICAL FRAMEWORKS FOR AI

A Framework can be defined as a set of constructs that provide a basis for developing something. An AI Ethical Framework is a set of policies and principles to ensure that AI is developed and used ethically. The frameworks help researchers and data scientists build AI systems that help society without harming individuals or society.

Six AI Assurance Goals

Studies have set six main goals for all AI systems. These goals ensure that AI works well. The list includes Ethical AI, Safe AI, Fair AI, Secure AI, Explainable AI, and Trustworthy AI (Batarseh et al., 2021).

Ethical AI: Ethical Artificial Intelligence aims to develop systems that consider human values and act with integrity and compassion in a manner that respects human dignity, privacy, and autonomy. Considering the exponential rise in AI-based deployments, ethical considerations are becoming essential across all areas where AI is used. The topic involves moral dilemmas arising from ethical algorithms and pre-set or acquired values (Pavaloiu & Kose, 2017). Designers should consider including Human-friendly motives, considering that superintelligence can easily surpass typical human thinking quickly and become an unstoppable power (Bostrom, 2020).

Its academic misuse, for example, involves discussion on its interference with learning progress, violating academic integrity, shifting teaching focus, discriminating student groups (Nguyen et al., 2023), diminishing educational effectiveness, AI-generated research papers, and issues related to authorship, copyright, and plagiarism.

Safe AI: Safe artificial intelligence focuses on building techniques and procedures to ensure AI systems behave dependably, avoid unintended or undesirable outcomes, and their impacts can be adequately understood and managed throughout their operational lifetimes. This became a significant challenge, considering that some AI algorithms with high predictive power have already shown their ability to impact human integrity. Though AI systems hardly fail, they must fail safely when that situation arises (Morales-Forero et al., 2023).

Safe AI is becoming increasingly important because we are moving away from deterministic, non-evolving systems operating in well-defined contexts. The new generation systems are increasingly autonomous and learning-enabled AI systems. They perform decently even in unpredictable operating situations (Rueß & Burton, 2022). This led researchers to question whether using AI-based systems in real-time automation is acceptable and if Safe AI is ever possible, especially in industrial automation and cyber-physical systems. For example, a medical AI system is expected to work smoothly and should not cause any harm. Wrong or incorrect use of medical equations, algorithms, and devices can lead to bias and distrust. So, an AI system should be able to detect, mitigate, and remedy the harmful effects of bias and create an environment that can help build trust (Moses & Gipson Rankin, 2024).

The new AI-related ethical principles should be well connected with the existing ethical and professional practices. Medical AI, for example, should be in sync with bioethics followed in the medicine and healthcare domains (Duggal & Tripathi, 2024) and not contradict them. The World Health Organization (WHO), for example, has released guidelines titled *Ethics and Governance of Artificial Intelligence for Health* (WHO, 2021) with *a* focus on "Protect autonomy"; "Promote human well-being, human safety, and the public interest"; "Ensure transparency, explainability and intelligibility"; "Foster responsibility and accountability"; "Ensure inclusiveness and equity"; and "Promote [AI] that is responsive and sustainable" (Bartenschlager et al., 2024). The 2022 Global Forum on Bioethics in Research (GFBR) identified four themes (Appropriateness of building AI, Transferability of AI systems, Accountability for AI decision-making and outcomes, and Individual consent) and eight recommendations to global leaders to focus (Shaw et al., 2024). AI system designers should consider these aspects to ensure their AI is Safe AI.

Safety concerns occur when AI systems demonstrate unexpected or unintentional behaviors. Such systems will put human existence or health and systems in danger or harm the property or the environment. Autonomous cars are an example of this. The cars should be able to navigate tricky real-world scenarios consistently without interruptions. They should move securely and avoid crashing. Similarly, AI-powered medical equipment and diagnostic tools are another example. They must follow strict safety regulations to guarantee the patient's well-being. Addressing the safety concerns is necessary to reduce possible dangers and guarantee these systems' safe deployment (Amodei et al., 2016). Safety concerns can be addressed by:

1. Doing rigorous testing
2. Validation of algorithms and code
3. Regulation of AI systems

Fair AI: Fair AI seeks to address and remedy unfair biases in data, algorithms, and outcomes. AI systems that follow Fair AI practices have a positive impact. They do not unfairly disadvantage or give an unfair advantage to individuals based on personal attributes like gender, race, ethnicity, and other factors.

Secure AI: Secure AI develops security practices and safeguards to protect AI systems, data, and infrastructure. A Secure AI system prevents unauthorized access or criminal misuse. AI systems can be turned into Secure AI systems by:

1. Putting Restrictions on Access Control
2. Input validation mechanisms
3. Encryption of higher standards
4. Auditing
5. Monitoring.

Explainable AI: An Explainable AI system evaluates its techniques and explains how the outcome is arrived at. The explanations given by such AI systems will be about:

1. Behaviors
2. Decisions
3. Predictions
4. Any other outputs.

Explainable AI is necessary to ensure system transparency, management, and accountability throughout the AI lifecycle.

Trustworthy AI: A truly Trustworthy AI covers principles such as (Li et al., 2023; Zhu et al., 2024):

1. Robustness (giving AI systems the capability to handle errors)
2. Privacy (safeguarding data and model from unauthorized exposure)
3. Fairness (exhibiting equality, impartiality, and lack of bias towards individuals or groups with varying attributes when making decisions or predictions)
4. Reliability
5. Explainability (provide evidence in explaining model evidence)
6. Safety.

By quantifying a model's confidence in its predictions, uncertainty estimation empowers users to make informed decisions. There are two primary types of uncertainty: aleatoric (inherent randomness) and epistemic (reducible due to knowledge limitations) (Gomes, 2024).

Machine Learning Operations (MLOps) connects AI with Machine Learning from the perspectives of development and operations and has some frameworks that help implement trustworthy AI (Billeter et al., 2024). Synthetic data can bring trustworthy scalable oversight mechanisms into the language models (Liu et al., 2024).

Teaching students foundational AI concepts, ethical considerations, and practical skills can help position them as informed and responsible users of AI technologies in the future (Jancheski & Jancheska, 2024). Security evaluation frameworks play an essential role in this. Such a framework can quantify an AI system's inherent complexity and capture its stability and sensitivity to perturbations. It can evaluate the strategic robustness against adversarial manipulation (Kereopa-Yorke, 2024). AI trustworthiness will remain a subject of long-term research and become increasingly important as AI trends shift from performance-driven to trust-driven systems (Li et al., 2023).

Existing Ethical Frameworks and Guidelines

An open consultation on the UN Advisory Board on Responsible AI Governance has released an intervening report on Governing AI for Humanity. The report covered aspects such as opportunities and enablers, risks and challenges, international governance of AI, and guiding principles and institutional functions (Kiden et al., 2024).

Some popular ethical frameworks are:

1. **IEEE (Institute of Electrical and Electronics Engineers): Ethically Aligned Design (EAD):** A framework developed by the IEEE to ensure technologists prioritize ethical considerations in the design and development of autonomous

and intelligent systems. Their EAD has remarkable implementations in well-being metrics, embedding values into autonomous and intelligent systems, methods to guide ethical research and design, and affective computing (Chatila & Havens, 2019).

2. **OECD (Organisation for Economic Cooperation and Development): OECD Principles on AI**: These principles promote innovative and trustworthy AI that respects human rights and democratic values.
3. **European Commission's Ethics Guidelines for Trustworthy AI (EGTAI)**: These are developed by the High-Level Expert Group on Artificial Intelligence (AI HLEG). The guidelines outline a framework for achieving trustworthy AI, emphasizing human oversight, technical robustness, privacy and data governance, transparency, diversity, societal and environmental well-being, and accountability. In other words, these can be summarized as (Thiebes et al., 2021):
   a. Beneficence
   b. Non-maleficence
   c. Autonomy
   d. Justice
   e. Explicability
4. **ACM (Association for Computing Machinery) Code of Ethics and Professional Conduct:** It provides a set of ethical principles that guide decision-making and professional conduct in computing.
5. **Asilomar AI Principles:** Developed during the 2017 Asilomar conference, these principles outline research priorities and ethical norms to guide the development of artificial intelligence.
6. **Montreal Declaration for a Responsible Development of Artificial Intelligence**: The declaration was formulated at the 2018 Montreal Forum on Responsible AI and is aimed at ensuring AI development benefits humanity and promotes positive social change. It has a set of ethical guidelines to guide the development of AI to benefit all, emphasizing values such as well-being, autonomy, justice, privacy, knowledge, democracy, and responsibility. Figure 2 shows the eight core principles of the declaration. Apart from the core principles, it has 59 specific implementation recommendations (Université de Montréal, 2017).

Figure 2. Eight core principles of the Montreal declaration

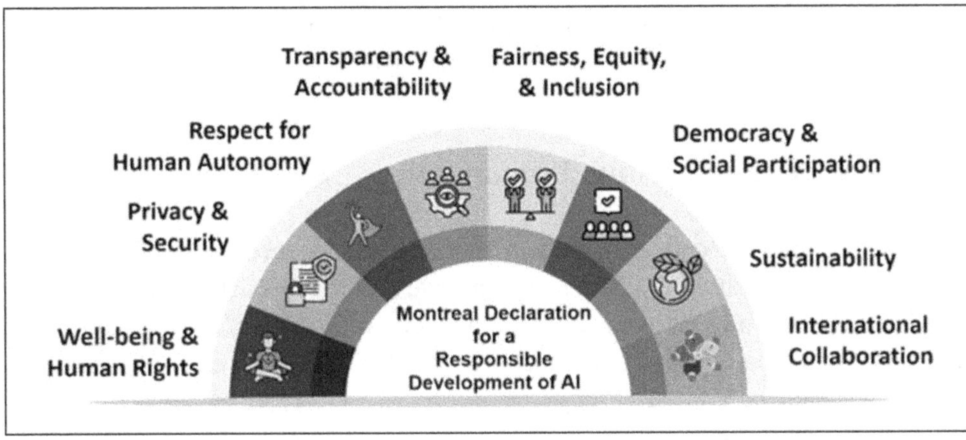

7. **UNESCO Recommendation on the Ethics of Artificial Intelligence:** Adopted in November 2021, this is the first-ever global standard on AI Ethics. 193 member states have adopted it. This recommendation provides a global standard-setting instrument to guide the development of ethical AI. It emphasizes the need for AI to respect human rights and democratic values. In its report entitled *Challenging Systematic Prejudices: An Investigation into Gender Bias in Large Language Models*, it was revealed that "biases emerge in the text generated by LLMs, through gendered word associations, positive or negative regard for gendered subjects, or diversity in text generated by gender and culture." For example, LLMs such as OpenAI's GPT-2 and ChatGPT, along with Meta's Llama 2, are biased to female names with "home," "family," "children," and male names with "business," "executive," "salary," and "career." Considering the penetration and large-scale use of LLMs, bias can threaten human rights, and hence, policymakers and AI developers must take adequate precautions. Considering this unique challenge, mitigation strategies must be adopted. The approach to be taken should be comprehensive (UNSESCO, 2024).
8. **ISO/IEC JTC 1/SC 42 Standards**: Also known as the Artificial Intelligence standardization subcommittee standards, these standards provide a framework for artificial intelligence systems, covering aspects like robustness, transparency, and accountability. It is a central hub for AI standardization within the International Organization for Standardization (ISO) and the International Electrotechnical Commission (IEC). The Chair leads the Subcommittee. It has five working groups and joint working groups (JWG).
9. **Others**: This includes

a. Professional Conduct and Joint Statement on Principles for Responsible Algorithmic Systems (ACM, 2022)
b. Association of College and Research Libraries Framework for Information Literacy for Higher Education (ACRL, 2016)

Core principles of Various Framework

Figure 3 shows six core ethical steps that any AI system should address in its journey (Archambault et al., 2024). A complete set of rules arises by combining the essential principles derived from the abovementioned morals and standards. They can be aimed at ensuring that technologies are developed ethically and used responsibly, especially in AI.

Figure 3. Six core ethical steps that any AI system should address in its journey (Based on inputs from (Archambault et al., 2024))

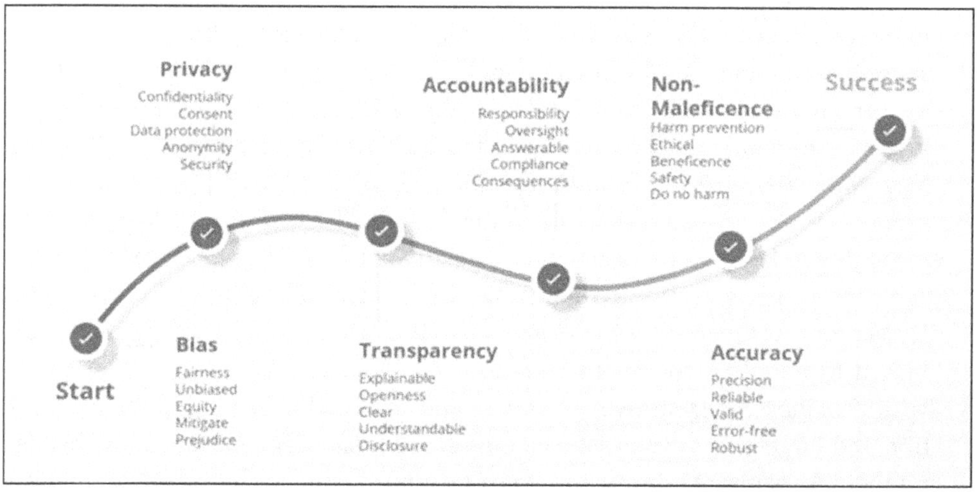

These principles address a broad spectrum of ethical, social, and technical considerations. The list of core principles includes:

1. **Transparency**: This principle ensures a clear understanding of AI systems and decisions made by the relevant stakeholders. A Transparent AI system can give explanations and defend its decisions.

2. **Fairness**: The Fairness principle promotes equity and avoids bias in AI systems. This involves ensuring that AI technologies do not reinforce existing prejudices or create new forms of discrimination. Bias in AI can come in because of multiple reasons synthesized:
    a. **Data** (includes Measurement and Representation bias)
    b. **Algorithm selection** (includes Aggregation and Learning bias)
    c. **Deployment** (includes Deployment and Post-deployment feedback bias).
3. **Accountability**: This principle questions who or what should be held responsible and answerable for the outcomes of an AI system. AI developers, users, and the Government are typical actors who could be considered accountable. Defining clear roles and responsibilities for developers, deployers, and users of AI technologies is part of this. AI auditing processes involve assessing and reporting the systems' performance and impact. Regulators, law firms, civil society, journalism, academia, and consulting agencies often do AI Audits (Birhane et al., 2024).
4. **Privacy**: Personal data has gained enormous attention in recent times. Ensuring that the privacy of individuals is respected needs to be addressed from the development and deployment of AI systems stage itself. Privacy AI involves following the data protection laws and best practices in data governance.
5. **Non-maleficence**: The emphasis of this ethical principle is to prevent or avoid causing harm to individuals and society (Thiebes et al., 2021). An example is a situation wherein researchers stop a clinical trial if it poses an undue risk to participants. This principle emphasizes the importance of safety, security, and minimizing negative impacts on people and the environment. This principle is considered along with other ethical principles, such as Beneficence (the obligation to do good) and Autonomy (respecting individuals' right to make their own decisions).
6. **Beneficence**: This principle is also called "AI for Good!". It promotes the use of AI to maximize benefits and minimize harm for:
    a. The well-being of human beings
    b. Respecting human rights (Thiebes et al., 2021)
    c. For the common good and to promote good outcomes.
    d. Avoid causing any form of harm.

Drawing inspiration from Medical Ethics, the purpose of Beneficence AI is:

a. To bring about a positive social impact
b. Enhancing human capabilities
c. Improving quality of life

The Capability Approach is a famous framework for thinking about Beneficent AI. It emphasizes how AI can expand people's capabilities and freedoms to live well. An AI-driven climate model is an example of a Beneficence AI system. The model is expected to help better understand and fight climate change. Apart from medical and environmental sustainability, other applications of this includes accessibility and inclusivity, as well as in education and learning domains.

7. **Human Oversight**: Human supervision is always necessary when machines are given some automation tasks. Oversight helps ensure that AI systems do not operate autonomously without human intervention. This principle highlights the need for human judgment in critical decision-making processes. It also speaks about the ability to override AI decisions if required. Table 1 explains the human oversight expectation of an AI-based system.

Table 1. Human oversight expectations from an AI-based system

Factor	Description
Objective of the system	An AI system of a self-driving car equipped with an advanced AI navigating on a highway.
Desired features	The system should incorporate human oversight to ensure beneficence and safety, especially in complex or unforeseen situations.
Challenges	There can be unforeseen events where human intervention and judgment might be necessary.
Human Oversight element	The AI system should have an override capability that allows the human driver to take control in an emergency.

Source: Author compilation

8. **Societal and Environmental Well-being**: This factor considers how AI affects society and the environment. It involves predicting the long-term consequences of AI technologies on social structures, democracy, and the globe. An illustration of this concept is an AI-Powered Energy Management System. The organization that develops such a system distinguishes that reducing energy consumption and costs for building owners is a central objective. However, it also grasps technology's broader ramifications on society and the environment. Expectations from such a system can be:
    a. Energy Efficiency Optimization
    b. Societal Impact Assessment
    c. Environmental Sustainability
    d. Community Engagement
    e. Continuous Monitoring and Improvement

9. **Justice**: A central aspect of "Justice AI" is to ensure equitable distribution of AI's benefits and burdens. This principle involves addressing social justice issues and striving for inclusivity in developing and deploying AI technologies. Table 2 shows an example scenario of an AI-based justice system.

Table 2. AI-based justice system

Factor	Description
Objective of the system	A new AI justice system will help assess risk factors for repeat offenses among those convicted of crimes.
Expected benefit	One benefit that can be derived from such a system is Reduced recidivism. The system can process far more data points than a human judge.
Justice element	It can also evaluate more risk scenarios. In cases that the system believes to be genuine cases, the system can suggest a rehabilitation program instead of a lengthy prison sentence.

Source: Author compilation

10. **Autonomy**: This involves respecting human autonomy and the right to self-determination. This principle emphasizes the need to prevent undue influence or coercion by AI systems over human decisions. For example, consider an AI-enabled television streaming service. The system respects human autonomy. Table 3 shows certain advantages that can be derived. Evaluation parameters can be ratings, reviews, and summaries.

Table 3. Expected benefits due to autonomy provided by AI-based streaming services

Feature	Description
Transparency and Control	This includes adjusting settings, filtering recommendations, or opting out of specific recommendations.
Diverse Recommendations	Considers a diverse range of content and perspectives of television content
Avoiding Manipulation	The system avoids excessive repetition of specific recommendations or prioritizing content based on factors unrelated to user preferences.
Autonomy element	Users are empowered to make informed decisions by providing relevant information about recommended content.

Source: Author compilation

11. **Respect for Human Rights**: Ensuring that AI systems support and do not infringe upon human rights. This involves aligning AI development with international human rights standards. Consider, for example, a facial recognition

system implemented by the Government. The system is assumed to be powered by AI. Such a system should consider:

a. Privacy Protection
b. Non-discrimination
c. Freedom of Expression
d. Accountability and Transparency

12. **Robustness and Safety**: Developing AI systems that are secure, reliable, and resilient to attacks or failures. This includes ensuring the technical integrity of AI systems throughout their lifecycle. AI-powered self-driven cars can be an excellent example of this. Such a system is expected to have:
    a. Real-time monitoring capabilities
    b. Redundancy and Fail-safe Mechanisms (usage of multiple sensors)
    c. Simulation
    d. Rigorous Testing facilities
    e. Cybersecurity Measures
    f. Regulatory Compliance
    g. Safe failure modules
13. **Innovation**: Promoting the advancement of beneficial AI technologies while addressing ethical and social challenges. This involves encouraging research and development that align with ethical standards and societal values. Consider an AI-based personalized education for students. Such a system benefits students by providing customized curricula to meet their needs. Some ethical and social challenges that will be faced would be regarding algorithm bias and teacher displacement. However, it promotes innovation with ethics because of:
    a. Fairness in data selection
    b. Human-AI collaboration
    c. Focuses on Explainability

While several other principles could be significant, the principles mentioned broadly represent a collective vision for AI and technology's ethical development and use. They guide policymakers, developers, and stakeholders in the complex ethics journey of modern technological innovation.

Case Study: Ethical AI Considerations in Healthcare

Medical, Hospital and Healthcare Management are some of the largest institutions deploying AI. Considering the complexities involved and patients' lives at stake, several ethical issues arise when AI is used in healthcare collaborations and decision-making. Thus, careful care and efforts are necessary to guarantee the safe development and accurate application of AI technology in healthcare. Early reactions from the medical community to AI systems were like previously introduced medical technology. AI systems impact physicians' professional roles and self-image, potentially changing the doctor's role to some extent and changing the doctor-patient relationship (Fangerau, 2024).

Ensuring patient information and data confidentiality is a significant ethical concern in healthcare. Healthcare data often contains sensitive details such as an individual's medical background, existing health conditions, treatments, and genetic information. Data protection concerns from misuse, illegal access, and privacy violations arise when AI is integrated into healthcare (Mittelstadt et al., 2016). Patient confidentiality must be upheld to keep people confident in AI-driven healthcare systems, and data protection laws like the Health Insurance Portability and Accountability Act (HIPAA) in the US must be followed.

System developers should keep an open eye and ear that bias due to AI algorithms might creep in. AI algorithms can inherit and amplify biases from the data upon which they are trained, mainly when LLM is used. AI applications that depend on such LLMs, such as Generative AI applications, may give unfair or inaccurate output. Such systems could become three types of issues:

1. **Pervasive Impact**: Pervasive Impact denotes that AI algorithms are increasingly used, impacting everyday lives, convenience, and business transactions. Bias in such systems will severely affect people's lives.
2. **Reinforcing Inequalities**: AI systems are generally built using historical data. Such systems could preserve societal biases, such as gender, race, or other factors. Biased data can lead to biased outcomes. Because AI systems are deeply built on historical data, biased training data can make it harder for the system to overcome the bias.
3. **Unfairness and Inaccuracy**: Only when AI makes decisions without favoritism can it contribute to a fair society. Unfortunately, algorithms can be biased if fed with improper data, leading to discriminatory outcomes or inaccurate predictions. Generative AI models, especially Image generation models, can perpetuate gender and racial biases. An AI-generated job advertisement can use biased language, disproportionately affecting a section of applicants.

There are instances of unintentional racial profiling or socioeconomic biases in healthcare data that run on AI models. Dangers of such practice include biased diagnoses, treatment recommendations, or patient care procedures. The prevalence of biases harms the system and hampers justice and equity in healthcare provision. (Obermeyer et al., 2019; Dankwa-Mullan et al., 2021). There are, however, few ways of addressing such dangers.

1. **Taking a higher level of algorithmic openness**: A higher level of algorithmic openness is achieved by understanding how algorithms work to help identify and address bias.
2. **Explicit data curation**: Explicit data curation means the data used to train algorithms must be carefully chosen and balanced to avoid perpetuating bias.
3. **Continuous and rigorous assessment**: Organizations can have a continuous assessment process in place. It involves regularly checking algorithms for bias and confirming that the systems are generating fair results.

Apart from the above considerations, using AI in healthcare decision-making can and always tends to raise questions about liability and accountability. One common question is: "*Who is to be held responsible when an AI program recommends a less-than-ideal mode of operation or makes a diagnostic error?*". Organizations should have clearly defined roles and duties of healthcare practitioners, AI developers, and regulatory agencies with duly assigned responsibilities. Such practices reduce patient safety threats (Rajkomar et al., 2018).

Collaborative efforts between AI and healthcare often raise ethical questions. These questions will mainly be about accountability, bias, and privacy. Organizations have some critical principles in hand to deal with them. These include:

1. Transparent governance structures
2. Interdisciplinary cooperation
3. Continual stakeholder communication.

Using these principles helps address the issues and guarantee that AI technologies improve outcomes while respecting moral standards and safeguarding welfare.

FUTURE RESEARCH DIRECTIONS

Emerging Ethical Concerns Related to Generative AI and Its Impact on Society

Modern AI systems are the source of some moral issues. It can be about the ability to change views, propagate fake news, and breach privacy. The arrival of deepfakes and other AI-generated content has led to concerns that journalism will have more deception and less truth (Heidari et al., 2024). In addition, AI-generated materials might support existing biases or stereotypes. This can further lead to more social injustice. So, the Generative AI system should feature Responsibility AI features. At the same time, sufficient regulations should be put in place. When regulations are in place, probable hazards can be minimized, and creativity and innovation can be promoted. Discussions between stakeholders should be encouraged and facilitated. The discussions can guide the growth and deployment of the technology effectively.

Issues of AI Misuse: Need for Global Governance Frameworks for AI

Some issues identified about potential misuse in the context of global governance frameworks are:

1. Unemployment concerns arising because of AI can consequently lead to uneven income distribution. Because of the displaced jobs, there will be economic inequality in the society (Zhao, 2023).
2. Strict ethical standards and control mechanisms are necessary due to AI's potential for harmful applications. Cyberattacks and autonomous weapons are two examples (Brundage et al., 2018).
3. Without global governance frameworks, uneven development could worsen geopolitical conflicts and societal divisions (Naidoo, 2021).
4. Establishing norms and regulations that guarantee AI benefits society while avoiding dangers is essential for addressing these difficulties and will require international collaboration.

Ongoing Research and Development in AI Ethics

Some popular topics of researcher interest in AI Ethics include:

1. Creating Ethical AI Frameworks
2. Accountability Transparency
3. Bias prevention

Academic research is working on algorithmic fairness and interpretability techniques to identify and minimize system biases (Barocas & Selbst, 2016).

New Frameworks and Other Approaches

1. New frameworks and strategies are developed to reduce ethics-related mistakes associated with AI development and deployment. The Value Alignment (VA) (Butlin, 2021) and Inverse Reinforcement Learning (IRL) (Hadfield-Menell et al., 2016) are two examples of this. IRL techniques might struggle to distinguish

between ethical principles, cultural norms, or ingrained biases in the data. So, a successful implementation likely involves a combination of IRL-derived insights with a human-in-the-loop approach.

2. Interdisciplinary collaborations and stakeholder engagement must be adopted to recognize and address ethical issues at any stage in the AI lifecycle (Floridi et al., 2018).
3. Scholars have been looking into enhancing accountability and transparency within these systems through explainability approaches or algorithmic auditing.
4. Transparency and explainability approaches that hold algorithms accountable are getting increased focus. Addressing the emergent ethical challenges and trends is necessary as AI technologies evolve. When that happens, all the benefits of AI reach society while potential damages get reduced. Figure 4 shows an increasing publication trend for the keyword: "explainable artificial intelligence."

Figure 4. Increasing number of publications on "explainable artificial intelligence" (Dimensions.ai; Data as of July 6, 2024)

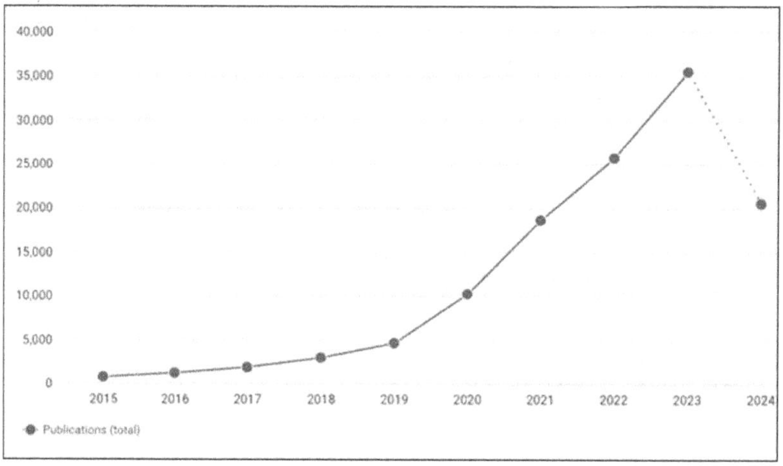

LIMITATIONS OF THE STUDY

No research study can be comprehensive, considering the various limitations that lie around it. This is more truer for emerging technology-related topics such as AI. The study on the ethical implications of AI development and deployment has certain limitations:

1. **Scope and Generalizability**: The study focuses on broad ethical principles and challenges related to AI. However, it may not cover all specific ethical issues or nuances, especially those that arise in different AI applications or domains. The generalizability of the findings may be limited to the contexts and examples discussed in the study. Also, it might not cover all social, economic, and environmental impacts.
2. **Data and Evidence**: The study is theoretical and review-based. It depends on existing literature, reports, and frameworks on AI Ethics. Data availability and quality on ethical issues in AI development and deployment can vary. Also, the findings are subject to the limitations of the available information. This limits the ability to draw concrete, evidence-based conclusions compared to other research formats, such as using primary empirical data.
3. **Interdisciplinary Perspectives**: AI Ethics is a complex field. It draws inputs and inspiration from multiple disciplines. Philosophy helps in analyzing moral implications. Computer Science brings in technical understanding. Social sciences focus on societal impact and human-AI interaction. Law discusses regulations and legal implications. Apart from this, several other disciplines, such as Anthropology, Economics, Neuroscience, and Political Science, will continue to inspire and shape the future of Ethical AI. This current study may not fully capture all the diverse perspectives and approaches within AI Ethics. Nonetheless, it may benefit from further interdisciplinary collaboration.
4. **Rapidly Evolving Field**: AI technologies and ethical considerations are rapidly evolving. The study provides a snapshot of the current landscape of AI Ethics. However, it may need to be updated and revised as new developments and challenges emerge.
5. **Global Context**: The study considers ethical issues in AI from a global perspective. However, it may not fully address the ethical challenges and considerations arising in different cultural, social, and political contexts.

CONCLUSION

Artificial intelligence is becoming more and more integrated into our lives. Ethical issues are highly probable to come up. Ethical principles and values should guide the development and use of AI. They are the foundation for responsible AI design, development, and deployment. However, this poses several challenges and risks. Risks arise because of bias, leading to privacy concerns, lack of transparency, and security issues, and will have a societal impact. Developers must think from multiple dimensions before using ethical frameworks. They must engage in ongoing research and be open to adopting new approaches to mitigate ethical risks in their AI systems. There is a need for interdisciplinary collaboration and stakeholder engagement to identify and address ethical issues at different stages of the AI lifecycle. Stakeholders can advance the development of AI technologies by combining ethical concepts and techniques. In doing so, they can prioritize ethical considerations while maximizing innovation and societal well-being.

Over time, technology will further evolve, and newer ethical issues and trends will emerge. It requires developing newer frameworks and approaches to mitigate ethical risks. Continuous research and interdisciplinary collaboration will help meet this catch-up game. Organizations should integrate ethical principles, address challenges, and promote research and collaboration to use the transformative power of AI. This safeguards human values and the well-being of society.

REFERENCES

ACM. (2022). *Statement on Principles for Responsible Algorithmic Systems*. ACM Technology Policy Office. https://www.acm.org/binaries/content/assets/public-policy/final-joint-ai-statement-update.pdf

ACRL. (2016). *Framework for Information Literacy for Higher Education*. https://www.ala.org/acrl/standards/ilframework

Adadi, A., & Berrada, M. (2018). Peeking Inside the Black-Box: A Survey on Explainable Artificial Intelligence (XAI). *IEEE Access : Practical Innovations, Open Solutions*, 6, 52138–52160. 10.1109/ACCESS.2018.2870052

Adeyelu, O. O., Ugochukwu, C. E., & Shonibare, M. A. (2024). Ethical Implications of AI in Financial Decision–Making: A review with real world applications. *International Journal of Applied Research in Social Sciences*, 6(4), 608–630. 10.51594/ijarss.v6i4.1033

Akhtar, S. (2024). The Ethicsophical Landscape of Large Language Models. *Philarchive*. https://philarchive.org/rec/AKHEAT

Alotaibi, M., Furnell, S., & Clarke, N. (2016). Information security policies: A review of challenges and influencing factors. *2016 11th International Conference for Internet Technology and Secured Transactions (ICITST)*, 352–358. 10.1109/ICITST.2016.7856729

Amodei, D., Olah, C., Steinhardt, J., Christiano, P., Schulman, J., & Mané, D. (2016). *Concrete Problems in AI Safety*. 10.48550/ARXIV.1606.06565

Archambault, S. G., Ramachandran, S., Acosta, E., & Fu, S. (2024). Ethical dimensions of algorithmic literacy for college students: Case studies and cross-disciplinary connections. *Journal of Academic Librarianship*, 50(3), 102865. 10.1016/j.acalib.2024.102865

Barocas, S., & Selbst, A. D. (2016). Big Data's Disparate Impact. SSRN *Electronic Journal*. 10.2139/ssrn.2477899

Bartenschlager, C. C., Gassner, U. M., Römmele, C., Brunner, J. O., Schlögl-Flierl, K., & Ziethmann, P. (2024). The AI ethics of digital COVID-19 diagnosis and their legal, medical, technological, and operational managerial implications. *Artificial Intelligence in Medicine*, 102873, 102873. Advance online publication. 10.1016/j.artmed.2024.10287338643592

Batarseh, F. A., Freeman, L., & Huang, C.-H. (2021). A survey on artificial intelligence assurance. *Journal of Big Data*, 8(1), 60. 10.1186/s40537-021-00445-7

Billeter, Y., Denzel, P., Chavarriaga, R., Forster, O., Schilling, F.-P., Brunner, S., Frischknecht-Gruber, C., Reif, M. U., & Weng, J. (2024). MLOps as enabler of trustworthy AI. 10.21256/ZHAW-30443

Birhane, A., Steed, R., Ojewale, V., Vecchione, B., & Raji, I. D. (2024). *AI auditing: The Broken Bus on the Road to AI Accountability*. 10.1109/SaTML59370.2024.00037

Bostrom, N. (2020). Ethical Issues in Advanced Artificial Intelligence. In Wallach, W., & Asaro, P. (Eds.), *Machine Ethics and Robot Ethics* (1st ed., pp. 69–75). Routledge., 10.4324/9781003074991-7

Brundage, M., Avin, S., Clark, J., Toner, H., Eckersley, P., Garfinkel, B., Dafoe, A., Scharre, P., Zeitzoff, T., Filar, B., Anderson, H., Roff, H., Allen, G. C., Steinhardt, J., & Flynn, C. hÉigeartaigh, S. Ó., Beard, S., Belfield, H., Farquhar, S., … Amodei, D. (2018). *The Malicious Use of Artificial Intelligence: Forecasting, Prevention, and Mitigation* (arXiv:1802.07228). arXiv. http://arxiv.org/abs/1802.07228

Buolamwini, J., & Gebru, T. (2018, February 4). Gender Shades: Intersectional Accuracy Disparities in Commercial Gender Classification. *Proceedings of Machine Learning Research*. Conference on Fairness, Accountability, and Transparency. https://proceedings.mlr.press/v81/buolamwini18a/buolamwini18a.pdf

Butlin, P. (2021). AI Alignment and Human Reward. *Proceedings of the 2021 AAAI/ACM Conference on AI, Ethics, and Society*, 437–445. 10.1145/3461702.3462570

Butt, S., Butt, H., & Gnanappiragasam, D. (2021). Unintentional consequences of artificial intelligence in dermatology for patients with skin of colour. *Clinical and Experimental Dermatology*, 46(7), 1333–1334. 10.1111/ced.1472633969523

Chatila, R., & Havens, J. C. (2019). The IEEE Global Initiative on Ethics of Autonomous and Intelligent Systems. In Aldinhas Ferreira, M. I., Silva Sequeira, J., Singh Virk, G., Tokhi, M. O., & Kadar, E. E. (Eds.), *Robotics and Well-Being* (Vol. 95, pp. 11–16). Springer International Publishing., 10.1007/978-3-030-12524-0_2

Conitzer, V., Freedman, R., Heitzig, J., Holliday, W. H., Jacobs, B. M., Lambert, N., Mossé, M., Pacuit, E., Russell, S., Schoelkopf, H., Tewolde, E., & Zwicker, W. S. (2024). *Social Choice for AI Alignment: Dealing with Diverse Human Feedback* (arXiv:2404.10271). arXiv. http://arxiv.org/abs/2404.10271

Dankwa-Mullan, I., Scheufele, E. L., Matheny, M. E., Quintana, Y., Chapman, W. W., Jackson, G., & South, B. R. (2021). A Proposed Framework on Integrating Health Equity and Racial Justice into the Artificial Intelligence Development Lifecycle. *Journal of Health Care for the Poor and Underserved*, 32(2S), 300–317. 10.1353/hpu.2021.0065

Duggal, I., & Tripathi, T. (2024). Ethical principles in dental healthcare: Relevance in the current technological era of artificial intelligence. *Journal of Oral Biology and Craniofacial Research*, 14(3), 317–321. 10.1016/j.jobcr.2024.04.00338645705

Fangerau, H. (2024). Artifical intelligence in surgery: Ethical considerations in the light of social trends in the perception of health and medicine. *EFORT Open Reviews*, 9(5), 323–328. 10.1530/EOR-24-002938726973

Floridi, L., Cowls, J., Beltrametti, M., Chatila, R., Chazerand, P., Dignum, V., Luetge, C., Madelin, R., Pagallo, U., Rossi, F., Schafer, B., Valcke, P., & Vayena, E. (2018). AI4People—An Ethical Framework for a Good AI Society: Opportunities, Risks, Principles, and Recommendations. *Minds and Machines*, 28(4), 689–707. 10.1007/s11023-018-9482-530930541

Gomes, E. D. C. (2024). *Improving artificial intelligence reliability through out-of-distribution and misclassification detection* [Doctor Thesis, Université Paris-Saclay]. https://theses.hal.science/tel-04551331/document

Hadfield-Menell, D., Dragan, A., Abbeel, P., & Russell, S. (2016). *Cooperative Inverse Reinforcement Learning*. 10.48550/ARXIV.1606.03137

Heidari, A., Jafari Navimipour, N., Dag, H., & Unal, M. (2024). Deepfake detection using deep learning methods: A systematic and comprehensive review. *Wiley Interdisciplinary Reviews. Data Mining and Knowledge Discovery*, 14(2), e1520. 10.1002/widm.1520

Helal, M., Holthaus, P., Lakatos, G., & Amirabdollahian, F. (2023). *Chat Failures and Troubles: Reasons and Solutions*. 10.48550/ARXIV.2309.03708

Jancheski, M., & Jancheska, S. (2024). Unlocking the Future of Education: A Comprehensive Analysis of key documents shaping Artificial Intelligence in Education. 7834–7834. 10.21125/inted.2024.2098

Jiang, F., Jiang, Y., Zhi, H., Dong, Y., Li, H., Ma, S., Wang, Y., Dong, Q., Shen, H., & Wang, Y. (2017). Artificial intelligence in healthcare: Past, present and future. *Stroke and Vascular Neurology*, 2(4), 230–243. 10.1136/svn-2017-00010129507784

Jobin, A., Ienca, M., & Vayena, E. (2019). The global landscape of AI ethics guidelines. *Nature Machine Intelligence*, 1(9), 389–399. 10.1038/s42256-019-0088-2

Kereopa-Yorke, B. (2024). Quantifying AI Vulnerabilities: A Synthesis of Complexity, Dynamical Systems, and Game Theory (arXiv:2404.10782). arXiv. http://arxiv.org/abs/2404.1078210.2139/ssrn.4904749

Kiden, S., Stahl, B., Townsend, B., Maple, C., Vincent, C., Sampson, F., Gilbert, G., Smith, H., Deshmukh, J., Ross, J., Williams, J., del Rincon, J. M., Lisinska, J., O'Shea, K., Da Costa Abreu, M., Bencomo, N., Deb, O., Winter, P., Li, P., & Yazdanpanah, V. (2024). *Responsible AI governance: A response to UN interim report on governing AI for humanity*. [object Object]. 10.5258/SOTON/PP0057

Lee, T.-K., Park, E. H., & Lee, M. H. (2024). Medical ethics and artificial intelligence in neurosurgery—How should we prepare? *World Neurosurgery*, S1878875024006296, e199–e209. Advance online publication. 10.1016/j.wneu.2024.04.06738641244

Li, B., Qi, P., Liu, B., Di, S., Liu, J., Pei, J., Yi, J., & Zhou, B. (2023). Trustworthy AI: From Principles to Practices. *ACM Computing Surveys*, 55(9), 1–46. 10.1145/3555803

Liu, R., Wei, J., Liu, F., Si, C., Zhang, Y., Rao, J., Zheng, S., Peng, D., Yang, D., Zhou, D., & Dai, A. M. (2024). *Best Practices and Lessons Learned on Synthetic Data for Language Models* (arXiv:2404.07503). arXiv. http://arxiv.org/abs/2404.07503

Mai, W. (2023). *Developing an Ethical Framework for Artificial Intelligence in Investment Decision-Making: A Fuzzy Analytic Hierarchy Analysis*. EAI/MSIEID.

Mateen, H. (2018). Weapons of Math Destruction: How Big Data Increases Inequality and Threatens Democracy. *Berkeley Journal of Employment and Labor Law*, 39(1), 285–292.

Mehrabi, N., Morstatter, F., Saxena, N., Lerman, K., & Galstyan, A. (2019). *A Survey on Bias and Fairness in Machine Learning*. 10.48550/ARXIV.1908.09635

Mittelstadt, B. D., Allo, P., Taddeo, M., Wachter, S., & Floridi, L. (2016). The ethics of algorithms: Mapping the debate. *Big Data & Society*, 3(2), 205395171667967. 10.1177/2053951716679679

Morales-Forero, A., Bassetto, S., & Coatanea, E. (2023). Toward safe AI. *AI & Society*, 38(2), 685–696. 10.1007/s00146-022-01591-z

Moses, M. E., & Gipson Rankin, S. M. (2024). *Medical artificial intelligence should do no harm*. Nature Reviews Electrical Engineering., 10.1038/s44287-024-00049-2

Nadjia, M. (2024). The Impact of Artificial Intelligence on Legal Systems: Challenges and Opportunities. *Problems of Legality, 164*. http://plaw.nlu.edu.ua/article/download/289266/293702/695683

Naidoo, M. (2021). Artificial intelligence and global governance: How AI ethics and standards should be addressed at the global level. *The iJournal. Student Journal of the Faculty of Information*, 7(1). Advance online publication. 10.33137/ijournal.v7i1.37894

Nguyen, A., Ngo, H. N., Hong, Y., Dang, B., & Nguyen, B.-P. T. (2023). Ethical principles for artificial intelligence in education. *Education and Information Technologies*, 28(4), 4221–4241. 10.1007/s10639-022-11316-w36254344

Obermeyer, Z., Powers, B., Vogeli, C., & Mullainathan, S. (2019). Dissecting racial bias in an algorithm used to manage the health of populations. *Science*, 366(6464), 447–453. 10.1126/science.aax234231649194

Palumbo, G., Carneiro, D., & Alves, V. (2024). Objective metrics for ethical AI: A systematic literature review. *International Journal of Data Science and Analytics*. Advance online publication. 10.1007/s41060-024-00541-w

Pavaloiu, A., & Kose, U. (2017). *Ethical Artificial Intelligence—An Open Question*. 10.48550/ARXIV.1706.03021

Rajkomar, A., Hardt, M., Howell, M. D., Corrado, G., & Chin, M. H. (2018). Ensuring Fairness in Machine Learning to Advance Health Equity. *Annals of Internal Medicine*, 169(12), 866. 10.7326/M18-199030508424

Richardson, B., & Gilbert, J. E. (2021). *A Framework for Fairness: A Systematic Review of Existing Fair AI Solutions* (arXiv:2112.05700). arXiv. http://arxiv.org/abs/2112.05700

Roy, M. (2021). An Exploratory study on Origin of AI: Journey through the Ancient Indian Texts & other technological descriptions, its past, present & future. *Turkish Online Journal of Qualitative Inquiry*, 12(7), 10261–10288.

Rudin, C. (2018). Stop Explaining Black Box Machine Learning Models for High Stakes Decisions and Use Interpretable Models Instead. 10.48550/ARXIV.1811.10154

Rueß, H., & Burton, S. (2022). Safe AI — How is this Possible? 10.48550/ARXIV.2201.10436

Schuett, J., Reuel, A.-K., & Carlier, A. (2024). How to design an AI ethics board. *AI and Ethics*. Advance online publication. 10.1007/s43681-023-00409-y

Shaw, J., Ali, J., Atuire, C. A., Cheah, P. Y., Español, A. G., Gichoya, J. W., Hunt, A., Jjingo, D., Littler, K., Paolotti, D., & Vayena, E. (2024). Research ethics and artificial intelligence for global health: Perspectives from the global forum on bioethics in research. *BMC Medical Ethics*, 25(1), 46. 10.1186/s12910-024-01044-w38637857

Shin, D. (2024). *Artificial Misinformation: Exploring Human-Algorithm Interaction Online*. Springer Nature Switzerland., 10.1007/978-3-031-52569-8

Smith, M. J., Axler, R., Bean, S., Rudzicz, F., & Shaw, J. (2020). Four equity considerations for the use of artificial intelligence in public health. *Bulletin of the World Health Organization*, 98(4), 290–292. 10.2471/BLT.19.23750332284656

Sobien, D., Yardimci, M. O., Nguyen, M. B. T., Mao, W.-Y., Fordham, V., Rahman, A., Duncan, S., & Batarseh, F. A. (2023). AI for Cyberbiosecurity in Water Systems—A Survey. In Greenbaum, D. (Ed.), *Cyberbiosecurity* (pp. 217–263). Springer International Publishing. 10.1007/978-3-031-26034-6_13

Terzidis, K., Fabrocini, F., & Lee, H. (2023). Unintentional intentionality: Art and design in the age of artificial intelligence. *AI & Society*, 38(4), 1715–1724. 10.1007/s00146-021-01378-8

Thiebes, S., Lins, S., & Sunyaev, A. (2021). Trustworthy artificial intelligence. *Electronic Markets*, 31(2), 447–464. 10.1007/s12525-020-00441-4

Übellacker, T. (2024). AcademiaOS: Automating Grounded Theory Development in Qualitative Research with Large Language Models (arXiv:2403.08844). arXiv. http://arxiv.org/abs/2403.08844

Université de Montréal. (2017, November 3). *Montreal Declaration for a Responsible Development of Artificial Intelligence*. https://recherche.umontreal.ca/english/strategic-initiatives/montreal-declaration-for-a-responsible-ai/

UNSESCO. I. (2024). Challenging Systematic Prejudices: An Investigation into Bias Against Women and Girls in Large Language Models. https://unesdoc.unesco.org/ark:/48223/pf0000388971

Vincent, J. (2016, March 30). *Microsoft's AI chatbot briefly came back online and spammed everyone*. The Verge. https://www.theverge.com/2016/3/30/11329858/tay-microsoft-ai-chatbot-back-spam

WHO. (2021). Ethics and governance of artificial intelligence for health: WHO guidance Executive summary. https://iris.who.int/bitstream/handle/10665/350567/9789240037403-eng.pdf

Yorks, L., & Jester, M. Y. (2024). Applying generative AI ethically in HRD practice. *Human Resource Development International*, 27(3), 1–18. 10.1080/13678868.2024.2337963

Zhao, B. (2023). Analysis on the Negative Impact of AI Development on Employment and Its Countermeasures. *SHS Web of Conferences, 154*, 03022. 10.1051/shsconf/202315403022

Zhu, R., Guo, D., Qi, D., Chu, Z., Yu, X., & Li, S. (2024). A Survey of Trustworthy Representation Learning Across Domains. *ACM Transactions on Knowledge Discovery from Data*, 3657301(7), 1–53. Advance online publication. 10.1145/3657301

KEY TERMS AND DEFINITIONS

Bias in AI: A set of unjustified differences in treatment (response) given by an AI system due to its perceived characteristics, such as race, gender, age, or disability.

Ethics in AI: A set of moral principles and values that guide the development and deployment of AI systems.

Explainable AI: The ability of an AI system to provide transparent and interpretable explanations for their decisions, predictions, and actions. It helps human users understand and trust the results given by an AI system.

Framework: Framework is a structured approach comprising a collection of guidelines, principles, and best practices that organizations follow to ensure the development, deployment, and use of AI systems.

Governance: It is a set of policies, procedures, and guidelines an organization puts in place to ensure they build and use responsible AI.

Montreal Declaration: A declaration that recognizes AI's potential benefits, such as improving living conditions, health, and public safety.

Privacy-Preserving Technologies (PPT): A collection of tools, systems, and strategies designed to protect the confidentiality, integrity, and availability of individuals' personal data while it is being collected, stored, processed, and shared.

Training Data: The data used to train AI models to learn patterns, relationships, and decision-making strategies.

Chapter 6
Ethical Considerations for Generative AI in Social Science Research

B. Anthony Brown
https://orcid.org/0000-0001-7709-1164
Independent Researcher, USA

Keri L. Heitner
https://orcid.org/0000-0003-2851-5682
Walden University, USA

ABSTRACT

Social science research embodies the inquiry into people as individuals and their interpersonal interactions with each other in communities and varied societies, with due consideration for their natural, technological, and constructed environments. Due to (a) the nature and composition of qualitative, quantitative, and mixed methods research designs coupled with (b) the apparent expectations of responsible behavior from researchers (human beings), room exists for research misconduct or unethical practices. The prevalence and acceptance of generative artificial intelligence (AI) technology such as ChatGPT propagate at a hyper-accelerated pace based on its potential for ease of work in many sectors, including research, particularly academic research. Journal reviewers, editors, and publishers do not possess sufficient tools to differentiate between human-written and partially or wholly AI-authored manuscripts submitted for journal publication.

DOI: 10.4018/979-8-3693-8557-9.ch006

INTRODUCTION

Research incorporates experimentation or investigation designed explicitly for discovering and interpreting evidence, revising accepted theories or laws in the light of new facts, or applying such new or revised theories or laws into practice (Research, 2024). Research also entails creating new knowledge and using existing knowledge in different and novel ways to generate new concepts, methodologies, and understandings, including analyzing and synthesizing previous research to develop new knowledge (Australian Research Council, 2019). Faculty conduct research in natural and social sciences, encompassing their respective disciplines (Bhattacherjee, 2012). This chapter will focus on the ethical considerations for generative AI in social science research.

This chapter is a systematic literature review to synthesize the existing literature on ethical considerations for generative AI in social science research. In the chapter, we incorporate information from books, surveys, scholarly articles, peer-reviewed articles, government reports, and other sources relevant to ethical considerations for generative AI in social science research in the fourth. The purpose of this chapter is to (a) review the ethical challenges of generative AI in social science research and (b) make recommendations for guidelines for the governance of AI in social science research.

REVIEW OF THE LITERATURE AND LITERATURE SEARCH STRATEGY

Social science research embodies the inquiry into people as individuals and their interpersonal interactions with each other in communities and varied societies, with due consideration for their natural, technological, and constructed environments (Academy of Social Sciences, 2021; Liberto, 2023). Thus, social science researchers conduct studies to (a) better understand the burgeoning complexities of evolving human behaviors and associated systems across today's increasingly intricate world and (b) manage the planet's sustainability (Liberto, 2023).

Ibn Khaldun, the 14th-century North African philosopher, is credited as a pioneer of social science with the book *Muqaddimah* (Khaldun, 1986). Khaldun (1986) cited that historiography, or the study of the history and methodology of history as a discipline, is a multifaceted subject matter possessing a multiplicity of diverse approaches. Khaldun advocated that historiography extends beyond the surface political events, dynasties, and occurrences of the remote past viewed with the *critical eye* and subsequently presented using palatable and politically correct phrases and proverbs (Khaldun, 1986). Historiography incorporates culture, norms, attitudes, cautious explanations of the causes and origins of existing things, conjectures to unearth the truth, and deep knowledge of not only the who but also the when, where, why, and how associated with the events (history) being interrogated (Khaldun, 1986).

According to Khaldun (1986), historiography should be considered a branch of philosophy - free of blind trust (a trait endemic to human beings), lack of attention to conditions and the causes of events, and the undesirable closely allied elements (errors and unfounded assumptions) permeating historical information. Subsequently, Khaldun deemed the critical eye insufficient for investigating historiography and regarded the historians and their successors of his epoch with disdain, labeling them as

> persons who had no right to occupy themselves with history introduced into those books untrue gossip which they had thought up or freely invented, as well as false, discredited reports which they had made up or embellished. (Khaldun, 1986, p. 55)

Khaldun (1986) was openly skeptical of the works from the ensuing historians, who blatantly neglected to confirm or reject their predecessors' archaic work via comparison with either near or contemporary material.

According to Khaldun (1986), the later or successive historians produced sub-par research as they wantonly disregarded the foundations of philosophy and ignorantly recited (or plagiarized) their predecessors' baseless assumptions and errors. Consequently, the successors replicated and propagated ancient work without consideration for historical insights, speculation, the inherent nature of things, the nature of civilization, the fundamental facts of politics, the conditions governing human social organization, the shift in conditions and customs of races and nations, causations and the effect of elapsed time between eras and epochs (Khaldun, 1986). Kahldun was even more troubled by how his predecessors and their successors used numerical figures to showcase the glitz of their works. For example, Khaldun considered plainly stating that a nation possessed an army of 600,000 soldiers a grandiose statement – when there was no due consideration for factors including but not limited to (a) whether the nation had a population to provide 600,000 soldiers aged 20 years and older; (b) the practicality of 600,000 soldiers to march and fight as a unit; (c) the commander knowing what either flank is doing; and (d) when also considering that the size of the opponent's army, is there sufficient real estate for both armies to engage in battle.

Essentially, Khaldun established that historiography (or the study of the unfurling of events) as a discipline goes beyond exaggerated numerical figures and self-exaltation. Historiographers must embrace the yardstick of philosophy to encompass consideration for historical insights, speculation, the inherent nature of things, the nature of civilization, the fundamental facts of politics, the conditions governing human social organization, the shift in conditions and customs of races, and nations, causations and the effect of elapsed time between generations spanning eras and epochs (Khaldun, 1986) – the requisite foundation now associated with modern social science research.

Social science studies emerged in the Western world during the age of enlightenment in the late 17th century (Staines et al., 2023). Progenitors such as René Descartes (1596-1650), Jean-Jacques Rousseau (1712-1778), M. de Voltaire (1694-1778), and Denis Diderot (1713-1784) ushered the social sciences out of only focusing on descriptive scientific questions about *how things are* to normative questions about *how things could be* (Staines et al., 2023). In a dedicatory letter to the Sorbonne found in the philosophical writings of Descartes (1984), Descartes highlighted that he anticipated that his philosophical beliefs and arguments would earn him resistance and disregard from the geometry scholars. Descartes indicated that the near linear, continuity, finite *result from every concept and a concept for every result* foundation made geometry predictable, (apparently) more logical, and acceptable en masse. Descartes then contrasted geometry with his philosophical scope of reasoning and arriving at solutions. Descartes unequivocally declared to the Sorbonne that in the absence of a mindset free from preconceived notions (as in those notions associated with geometric studies), accepting his developed method for resolving specific difficulties in the sciences of philosophy is impossible. Descartes added that geometry scholars who agreed with him would only patronize him.

Descartes' (1984) approach to studying philosophy concretized that embracing philosophy required a mindset different from the linear predictive type associated with geometry and paved the way for the open-mindedness associated with modern social science research. Descartes' approach also aligns with Khaldun's considerations of the elements and demographics of culture, custom, race, nation, and geographical location and that these elements and demographics shift over time. We note that Descartes's fervently pushing philosophy and his logic as a non-geometric developed method for resolving specific difficulties in the sciences compliments the reservations Khaldun (1986) expressed regarding the disingenuous use of numbers in historiography.

Immanuel Kant (1724-1804) is revered as one of the most influential philosophers for developing epistemology in the social sciences (Staines et al., 2023). The *critique of pure reason* stands out as one of Kant's finest projects, in which he attempted to justify that knowledge comes from reason and not experience (Rohlf, 2010). In his works on the *critique of pure reason*, Kant identified analytic judgment and synthetic judgment as two predominant sources of knowledge (A. Weber, 1949). According to Kant, analytic judgment analyzes an idea without adding new knowledge (A. Weber, 1949). As per Kant, synthetic judgment enriches, extends, and increases knowledge and, on its own, constitutes (new) knowledge (A. Weber, 1949). Kant, however, clarified that not all synthetic judgments add (new) knowledge (A. Weber, 1949). According to Kant, real synthetic judgment remains in a state of true universal stasis under all circumstances and conditions (A. Weber, 1949). For example, *heat expansion* is a forever and universally true statement, through past and into future generations. Subsequently, *heat expansion* as a *synthetic judgment a priori* is based on rationale and rooted in reason and observation (A. Weber, 1949). Conversely, Kant postulated that saying *the weather is warm* is a synthetic judgment at the beginning; however, the weather may not remain warm tomorrow, making the statement a *judgment a posteriori* solely associated with experience, neither universally true nor forever in every instance, and cannot constitute scientific knowledge (A. Weber, 1949). Subsequently, Kant concluded that mathematics, physics, and metaphysics consist of *synthetic judgments a priori* and are the only source of scientific knowledge (A. Weber, 1949).

Émile Durkheim (1858-1917) and Max Weber (1864-1920) subsequently developed Kant's work to explain social relations between individuals (Staines et al., 2023). In his immense contribution to the growth of sociology, Durkheim considers his sociology as the science of institutions that envelop collective ways of thinking, acting, and feeling (Durkheim, 1972). Durkheim regarded sociology as the science of institutions, which refers to collective ways of thinking, feeling, and acting. Influenced by Auguste Compe, Marx and Marxism, and neo-Kantian Charles Renouvier, Durkheim regarded morality and religious elements of society as part of the natural world and can be studied scientifically (Durkheim, 1972). Durkheim posited that all facets of society, including religion and morality, are part of the natural world and can be studied scientifically (Durkheim, 1972). Durkheim formulated the sociological method of scientific interrogation specifically for the scientific study of the natural world (Durkheim, 1972).

Durkheim's underlying assertion to justify the ideologies of his sociology as a subject matter was anchored in what he called *social facts* - a classification of facts external to an individual that exhibit exceptional uniqueness consisting of manners of acting, thinking, and feeling (Durkheim, 1972; Nickerson, 2024). According to Durkheim, social facts contain coercive power and exercise control over individuals. Durkheim also asserted that social facts are internal to individuals and exist only through individuals. Controversy and criticism erupted around this aspect of Durkheim's work on his pronouncement that externality means interior to individuals other than the individual subject (Durkheim, 1972; Nickerson, 2024).

Subsequently, Durkheim declared himself a cultural relativist. He expressed that individual cultures possess an array of concepts and self-referential logic that creates what he called *mythological truths* (Durkheim, 1972). *Mythological truths* are legitimate declarations grounded within the reality of their respective social framework, not necessarily grounded in the reality of the physical world. Paradoxically and in opposition to his relativistic view of truth, Durkheim also subscribed to scientific rationalism and the inkling that scientific truths exist représentations

(Durkheim, 1972). Scientific représentations express reality in their unadulterated form, are subject to rigorous verification and methodological control, and are more absolute and reliable than other représentations collectives (Durkheim, 1972; Nickerson, 2024). According to Durkheim, while mythological truths and scientific représentations incorporate nature, people, and society as subject matters (Durkheim, 1972; Nickerson, 2024), unlike mythological truths, scientific représentations are not contingent on cultural context (Durkheim, 1972). Durkheim contributed immensely to the division of labor theory (Nickerson, 2024).

Revered as one of the most cited academic books, *The Structure of Scientific Revolutions* (Kuhn, 1996) documented Thomas Samuel Kuhn's postulations about the evolution of science. Kuhn (1922–1996) postulated that the history of science as we know it is a repetition of misleading historical documentation (Kuhn, 1996). Kuhn opined that the manipulative techniques used in collecting textbook data and the logical operations commissioned when relating those data to the textbook's hypothetical generalizations exemplified the documented version of science, theories, observation, and laws. According to Kuhn, the (repetitious) result was a rendition of the concretized nature and development or the evolution of science. Thus, Kuhn contended that the posited evolution of science is flawed if the recognized foundational development and growth are predicated on a series of piece-meal additions of the documented theories, observations, methods, laws, and the associated factors that hindered the evolution of science.

Kuhn (1996) wrote that the route to normal and mature sciences are legitimate paradigms, as these paradigms prepare students for induction into the specific fraternity in which they will later practice. Persons in these fraternities embracing the mature sciences seldom disagree over fundamentals because (a) their discussions will be hinged on commonly shared paradigms, and (b) they are devoted to the same rules and standards for scientific practice. Regarding observation and experience associated with social sciences and social science researchers, Kuhn wrote about the arbitrariness of social science research, maintaining that observation and experience alone cannot determine a particular body of scientific belief. Kuhn added that while observation and experience are required to moderate the range of admissible scientific belief, Kuhn fervently critiqued the canons of social science research and the insufficiency of methodological directives *to dictate a unique substantive conclusion to many sorts of scientific questions.* (p. 3)

Max Weber (1962) defined sociology as the science that challenges the interpretive understanding of social action to derive a causal enlightenment of its course and effects. M. Weber dictated that human behavior must be intentional and clearly defined by the humans engaged in said behavior to be qualified as social behavior. Introspection, meditation, or other (non-physical) conduct oriented towards situations and material objects where those involved are not oriented towards *meaningful* outcomes does not qualify as social behavior (M. Weber, 1962). In essence, for M. Weber, sociology was grounded in meaningful, intentional, similar (social) interfaces between humans.

Although this review of the literature is not exhaustive, we underscored the work and contributions of the progenitors deemed salient and fundamental to highlight the potential impact of generative AI on social science research. The literature search process involved conducting searches of key terms and assessing the references associated with the results. The key search terms included but were not limited to *anthropology, ethnography, social science, sociology, human psychology, demographics, quantitative research, qualitative research, mixed methods research, disruptive innovation, fourth industrial revolution, large language model, generative artificial intelligence, generative AI, machine learning, deepfake, ChatGPT, GPTZero, diversity, equity, inclusion, research participant, data privacy, and confidentiality.*

CASE DESCRIPTION

Contentions exist regarding which disciplines, namely anthropology, business management, economics, political science, psychology, sociology, geography, and history, constitute social science (Liberto, 2023). Subsequently, some researchers agreed that anthropology, business management, economics, political science, psychology, and sociology are the disciplines that comprise social science (Liberto, 2023; Rosenberg, 1998). Irrespective of the social sciences disciplines, researchers employ quantitative, qualitative, or mixed methods modes of inquiry to conduct their research and report the findings (Barakovskykh, 2024). Due to (a) the nature and composition of qualitative and quantitative research designs coupled with (b) the apparent expectations of responsible behavior from researchers (human beings), room exists for research misconduct or unethical practices.

Misconduct, Illegal, and Unethical Practices in Social Science Research

History is replete with *researchers* deceiving the ignorant and exploiting the vulnerable via covert and overt experiments, ostensibly in the name of science (Tayag, 2015). Infamous cases of research misconduct include but are not limited to (a) John Watson's 1920 Little Albert experiment involving a 9-month-old orphan (Albert) to prove Watson's hypothesis that it was possible to condition the element of fear in people; (b) the 1932 Tuskegee syphilis study, (c) the University of Iowa's 1939 monster study involving children; (d) the 1933 to 1945 holocaust in Nazi Germany, (e) the Central Intelligence Agency's Project MKUltra research operation

(1953 to 1973) involving experimentation with human behavioral engineering; (f) Dr. Albert Kligman's 1951 to 1974 Holmesburg Prison medical experiment, (g) Dr. Lauretta Bender of New York's Creedmoor Hospital 1960s, which used electroshock experimental treatment for children with social issues; (h) Milgram's 1961 Yale University social psychology experiments conducted to establish the willingness of test subjects to obey an authority figure; (i) Humphrey Laud's (1970) tearoom trade dissertation; and (j) the 1971 Stanford Prison experiment to determine the causes of conflict between military guards and prisoners (Casale et al., 2023; Desroches, 1990; Fridlund et al., 2012; Haney & Zimbardo, 1998; Humphreys, 1975; Milgram, 1963; Resnik & Hofweber, 2023; Silverman, 1988; Tayag, 2015; United States Holocaust Memorial Museum, n.d.-b, 2006; Vyas, 2020; Watson, 1913; Watson & Rayner, 1920; Zimbardo, 1973).

The Little Albert Experiment

John Watson's infamous 1920 emotional conditioning experiment at Johns Hopkins University centered around Douglas Merritte - a 9-month-old orphan Watson called *Albert* (DeAngelis, 2010; Stamp, 2023). Watson, known as the "Father of Behaviorism" and the founder of the psychological school of behaviorism, often incorporated orphans in his various experiments (Stamp, 2023; Watson, 1913, 1928; Watson & Rayner, 1920). Watson engaged his graduate student Rosalie Rayner in an experiment with Albert as the experimental subject to prove Watson's hypothesis that it was possible to condition the element of fear in people (DeAngelis, 2010; Stamp, 2023; Watson, 1913; Watson & Rayner, 1920). Watson initially exposed *Albert* to a laboratory rat for several months, which evoked no fear response from *Albert* (Stamp, 2023). For the next phase, Watson and Rayner exposed *Albert* to the rat, while Watson simultaneously struck a steel bar with a hammer, which caused a fear response from *Albert* (Stamp, 2023; Watson, 1913, 1928; Watson & Rayner, 1920). Watson and Rayner experimented with different animals and furry objects while introducing the noise, which caused a fearful response from *Albert* in each trial (DeAngelis, 2010; Watson, 1913, 1928; Watson & Rayner, 1920).

After several conditioning trials, Watson and Rayner reintroduced the animals and other furry items without the intimidating sound, but *Albert* exhibited fearful responses (DeAngelis, 2010; Stamp, 2023; Tayag, 2015). Subsequently, what was once a source of joy and curiosity for *Albert* became a trigger of fear and distress, ultimately proving Watson's hypothesis that fear could be conditioned (DeAngelis, 2010; Stamp, 2023; Tayag, 2015; Watson & Rayner, 1920). Arvilla Merritte, the mother of Douglas "Albert" Merritte, was a wet nurse who lived and worked at a campus hospital during the experiment. She received $1 for her baby's participation (DeAngelis, 2010). Unfortunately, Douglas "Albert" Merritte passed away at age 6 with acquired hydrocephalus, and there is no confirmation if he ever recovered from the adverse effect of Watson's unethical experiment (DeAngelis, 2010).

The Tuskegee Syphilis Study

In 1932, the US Public Health Service (USPHS) engaged the Tuskegee Institute in Macon, AL, to conduct the *Tuskegee study of untreated syphilis in the negro male*, now referred to as the *US Public Health Service untreated syphilis study at Tuskegee* (Centers for Disease Control and Prevention, 2024; Heller, 2017; Tuskegee University, 2024). According to Heller (2017), the city of Tuskegee in Macon County, Alabama, had the highest syphilis rate in the nation in 1932. Subsequently, the US Public Health Service, in collaboration with the Tuskegee Institute, launched the untreated syphilis study at Tuskegee to record the natural history of syphilis in 1932. However, Heller (Associate Press reporter who broke the story on July 25, 1972, regarding the abominable Tuskegee experiment) wrote that the Tuskegee study was designed to determine, through autopsies, what damage untreated syphilis does to the human body.

The researchers recruited 600 Black men who were poor, illiterate, and sharecroppers as research subjects for the untreated syphilis study at Tuskegee, and the researchers neither sought nor collected participants' informed consent (Centers for Disease Control and Prevention, 2024; Heller, 2017). The participant sample comprised 399 individuals with syphilis and 201 who did not have the disease as the control subjects (Centers for Disease Control and Prevention, 2024; Heller, 2017). However, the researchers did not inform the 399 men who contracted syphilis before the Tuskegee study that they had a mortal illness and that syphilis was easily transmitted during sexual contact (Centers for Disease Control and Prevention, 2024; Heller, 2017; Rogers, 2024). Instead, the researchers told the 600 men they were being treated for bad blood - a local term used to describe multiple infirmities, including but not limited to syphilis, anemia, and fatigue (Centers for Disease Control and Prevention, 2024; Tuskegee University, 2024). The researchers promised the subjects free medical exams, meals, and burial insurance in exchange for participation (Centers for Disease Control and Prevention, 2024). Heller (2017) rephrased the promise to state that the researchers employed persuasive tactics such as free hot lunches, free medical treatment for ailments other than syphilis, free transportation to and from hospitals, and free burials in exchange for the subjects' participation.

In 1943, the untreated syphilis study at Tuskegee produced penicillin as a cure for syphilis, and by 1947, penicillin gained widespread recognition and prolific use as the proven effective cure for syphilis (Centers for Disease Control and Prevention, 2024; Heller, 2017). However, even after the researchers confirmed the effectiveness of penicillin as a cure for syphilis in 1947, the study continued for another 25 years until 1972 (Tuskegee University, 2024, 2024). Dubbed the worst biomedical human experiment, the untreated syphilis study at Tuskegee spanned 40 years from 1932 to 1972, and neither the original infected participants nor the victims of the study, including wives who contracted the disease and children born with congenital syphilis, received penicillin as a treatment for syphilis (Centers for Disease Control and Prevention, 2024, 2024; Heller, 2017). Continuing the experiment for a further 25 years post the 1947 development of penicillin and not treating the research subjects and associated victims corroborates Heller (2017), citing that the untreated syphilis study at Tuskegee was designed to determine through autopsies what damage untreated syphilis does to the human body.

Heller (2017), the Associated Press reporter who disclosed the atrocities associated with the untreated syphilis study at Tuskegee also wrote that a U.S. Public Health Service official asserted that Dr. J.R. Heller, assistant surgeon general in the service's venereal disease section, who subsequently became division chief, initiated the 1932 *Tuskegee Study of Untreated Syphilis in the Negro Male*, now referred to as the *U.S. Public Health Service Untreated Syphilis Study at Tuskegee* (Heller, 2017). The 1976 Belmont Report (written by the National Commission for the Protection of Human Subjects of Biomedical Behavioral Research based on the National Research Act of 1974) emerged after the 1972 revelation of the *U.S. Public Health Service Untreated Syphilis Study at Tuskegee* (Nagai et al., 2022; Office for Human Research Protections, 2022).

The Terra Haute Penitentiary Experiment

Dr. John C. Cutler directed the failed Terre Haute, Indiana penitentiary experiments between 1943 and 1944, while he was still also one of the leaders from the 1960s to 1972 of the U.S. Public Health Service untreated syphilis study at Tuskegee (Rogers, 2024). Executed with consenting prisoners, the purpose of the experiment was to test preventative strategies for gonorrhea (Rogers, 2024). The experiment was a colossal failure because (a) the researchers encountered challenges infecting incarcerated research participants with sexually transmitted diseases (STDs) via the *conventional methods of contracting sexually transmitted diseases;* (b) most importantly, the high rate of non-compliance, especially by inmates; and (c) the inability to reliably diagnose infections (Rodriguez & García, 2013; Rogers, 2024). We reiterate that penicillin as a cure for syphilis was developed in 1943 and became a staple in 1947 during the 1932 to 1972 U.S. Public Health Service Untreated Syphilis Study at Tuskegee (Centers for Disease Control and Prevention, 2024; Tuskegee University, 2024). We also note that Dr. John C. Cutler (1960s to 1972 with the U.S. Public Health Service untreated syphilis study at Tuskegee) was simultaneously affiliated with the failed Terre Haute penitentiary experiments conducted between 1943 and

1944 – during the time of the 1943 emergence of the penicillin drug. For some, failure is never an option, especially when not seeking consent and exploiting the vulnerable produced the penicillin drug. Cutler and the U.S. Public Health Service's solution was Guatemala – a developing nation with a munificence of unassuming vulnerable subjects to covertly test different inoculation methods for gonorrhea, syphilis, and chancroid (Rodriguez & García, 2013; Rogers, 2024).

The Guatemala Syphilis Experiment

The Guatemala syphilis study involved unethical experimentation on vulnerable human populations in Guatemala as a U.S. medical research project spanning between 1946 and 1948 (BBC, 2011; Rodriguez & García, 2013; Rogers, 2024). In 1946, the U.S. government, through the directorship of Dr. John C. Cutler (ex-the USPHS untreated syphilis study at Tuskegee and director of the failed Terre Haute penitentiary experiment) and his USPHS colleagues collaborated with local Guatemalan physicians (Rogers, 2024). The collaborators, via negotiations with the Pan American Sanitary Bureau, now the Pan American Health Organization, and the Guatemalan government, gained unfettered access to mental institutions, government hospitals, public health centers, and orphanages in Guatemala. Subsequently, between 1946 and 1948, the U.S. government, by way of Cutler's directorship of the USPSH, exclusive funding by the National Institutes of Health, and the cooperation of Guatemalan authorities, illegally and knowingly executed a plethora of undeniably inexplicable, immoral, and unethical research experiments involving more than 5,128 uninformed and unconsenting native Guatemalans in Guatemala City (BBC, 2011; Rodriguez & García, 2013).

Using the Terre Haute penitentiary model and a 300-bed hospital facility specifically built in Guatemala City for the experiments' diagnostic and laboratory work, Cutler and his team conducted countless experiments, including body mutilation without the informed consent of the vulnerable people involved (BBC, 2011; Rodriguez & García, 2013; Rogers, 2024). The vulnerable population included but was not limited to children, orphans, child and adult prostitutes, incarcerated persons, people with a mental health condition, leprosy patients, Guatemalan Indians, and soldiers (BBC, 2011; Rodriguez & García, 2013; Rogers, 2024). Of the approximately 5,128 unconsenting vulnerable persons involved, the experimenting team intentionally infected at least 1,308 of these human beings with bacteria that caused sexually transmitted diseases such as syphilis, gonorrhea, and chancroid while conducting serology tests on others (BBC, 2011; Rodriguez & García, 2013; Rogers, 2024).

The alleged purpose of the Guatemala *study* was to test the efficacy of various medications, including the antibiotic penicillin and the arsenical agent orvus-mapharsen, in the prevention of symptom emergence following infection with certain STDs with specific reference to syphilis, gonorrhea, and chancroid (Rogers, 2024). Apparently, recruiting vulnerable human beings and engaging them in research without their knowledge, consent, or guardian ascent are seemingly the precursors and two of the three pillars of unethical research. The final pillar is the ethically heinous and morally reprehensible experiments performed on ignorant and unwilling humans. For example, by administering bacteria that caused STDs via pinprick vaccination or a pill taken orally, Cutler and his team conducted human experiments in non-sterile clinical settings in which they intentionally infected 1,308 unconsenting human subjects ages ranging from 10 to 72 (Rodriguez & García, 2013).

Cutler infected the sex workers with gonorrhea through cervical inoculation and the Guatemalan soldiers through sexual contact with the sex workers and sometimes through urethral inoculation (Rodriguez & García, 2013; Rogers, 2024). Psychiatric patients were infected with gonorrhea through inoculation of the urethra, rectum, or eyes (Rogers, 2024). In the case of the death of a female psychiatric patient, Berta (actual name from Cutler's *research* notes), Cutler's notes highlighted how he administered gonorrheal pus from another male subject into both of Berta's eyes, her urethra, and her rectum (Rodriguez & García, 2013). Cutler et al. infected Guatemalan soldiers and psychiatric patients with chancroid through abrasion and rubbing of inoculum into the skin on the arms or back (Rogers, 2024). Serology testing allegedly intended to refine diagnostic techniques for STDs involved all 5,128 subjects - children aged 1 year, psychiatric patients, persons with leprosy, and Guatemalan nationals stationed at the U.S. Air Force base in Guatemala ended in 1953 (Rogers, 2024).

Cutler, for reasons unknown, eventually initiated an STD treatment program to promote the prophylaxis study in Guatemala (Rogers, 2024). Recovered notes from the experiments (kept secret by Cutler) revealed that many persons have been left untreated to the present day (BBC, 2011; Rodriguez & García, 2013; Rogers, 2024). Records show that only 700 to 820 subjects received some form of infection treatment, with more than 650 treated persons in the intentional exposure group (BBC, 2011; Rogers, 2024). Other documents unearthed by an investigative commission cited that at least 83 of the more than 5,128 subjects had died by the end of 1953 (BBC, 2011). Among the deceased was Berta, who, during Cutler's final destructive and dehumanizing gonorrheal infection session with her (mentioned earlier), Cutler wrote that he was simultaneously injecting the already syphilis-infected and untreated Berta with more syphilis bacteria (Rodriguez & García, 2013).

The Holocaust

From 1933 to 1945, Nazi Germany's Third Reich, their allies, and collaborators executed the globe's most enormous systematic, state-sponsored persecution and murder when 6 million European Jews plus millions of other victims lost their life to gruesome unethical medical experiments during the Third Reich (U.S. Holocaust Memorial Museum, n.d.-b, 2006). The ideology which propagated the Holocaust, or *Shoah* (the Hebrew word for catastrophe), was Nazi Germans cleansing Germany of human beings deemed biological threats to Nazi Germany (U.S. Holocaust Memorial Museum, n.d.-b, 2006). Historians divided the unethical medical experimentation (conducted without patient consent or any safeguards) executed during the Third Reich into three categories (U.S. Holocaust Memorial Museum, 2006).

The first category of experiments dealt with experiments on illegally imprisoned humans to aid the survival of military personnel (U.S. Holocaust Memorial Museum, 2006). The German Experimental Institution for Aviation and physicians from the German Air Force conducted (a) high-altitude experiments to determine the maximum altitude from which German crews could parachute to safety from damaged aircraft, (b) freezing experiments to temperatures ending in death to find effective treatments for hypothermia, and (c) a myriad seawater drinking experiments intended to make seawater potable (U.S. Holocaust Memorial Museum, 2006).

Experiments geared at developing and testing drugs and treatment techniques for injuries and illnesses that German military and occupation personnel encountered in the field comprised the second category of fatal and dehumanizing experiments. Illegally imprisoned Jews at the German concentration camps of Sachsenhausen, Dachau, Natzweiler, Buchenwald, and Neuengamme underwent testing of immunization compounds and antibodies for the prevention and treatment of contagious diseases (U.S. Holocaust Memorial Museum, 2006). The infectious diseases incorporated in the experiments included tuberculosis, typhus, typhoid fever, malaria, yellow fever, and infectious hepatitis. Many Jews suffered and eventually perished in other experiments involving tests of newly developed sulfanilamide drugs, bone-grafting experiments, and exposure to phosgene and mustard gas to test possible antidotes (U.S. Holocaust Memorial Museum, n.d.-b, 2006).

Experiments to advance Nazi racial and ideological goals and tenets of the Nazi worldview comprised the third category of genocide by medical experimentation. This third category includes Josef Mengele's most infamous experiments on twins of all ages at Auschwitz (U.S. Holocaust Memorial Museum, n.d.-b, 2006). Other atrocities in this category included experiments on Romas (Gypsies) to establish different *races'* resilience and immunity to various contagious diseases and the irreversible mass sterilization of Jews, Romas, and other racial and ethnic groups the Nazi leaders deemed to be racially or genetically undesirable. In 1933, the Jewish population accounted for less than 1% of the entire German population, making the unprecedented scale of persecution of Jews purely based on antisemitism incomprehensible (U.S. Holocaust Memorial Museum, n.d.-a). The Nuremberg Code, which emerged from the 1946 to 1947 trial of the German perpetrators (Ghooi, 2011; National Institutes of Health, n.d.), did nothing for the unconsenting souls who perished. However, the Nuremberg Code provided for the preservation of the rights of future participants to voluntary consent before participating in human research and required that researchers must seek and obtain participants' voluntary consent before embarking on research involving human beings (Ghooi, 2011; National Institutes of Health, n.d.). The Nuremberg Code also stipulated that the experimenting scientists must be qualified in the field of the executed research and be responsible and culpable during the research process (Ghooi, 2011; National Institutes of Health, n.d.).

The University of Iowa Monster Study

The University of Iowa's 1939 monster study involved yet another immoral pair: Wendell Johnson, a psychologist at the University of Iowa, and his graduate student, Mary Tudor (Reynolds, 2003; Tudor, 1939). In August 1939, Tudor (1939) experimented in partial fulfillment of the requirements for the Master of Arts degree in the Department of Psychology at the Graduate College of the State University of Iowa. The experiment regarding stuttering in children included 22 orphans living at the Soldiers and Sailors Orphans' Home in Davenport, Iowa, and Johnson as Tudor's supervisor (Reynolds, 2003; Tudor, 1939). Tudor's thesis contained four research questions (RQ):

> RQ1: Will Removing the label "stutterer" from those who have been so labelled have any effect on their speech fluency?
> RQ2: Will endorsement of the label "stutterer" previously applied to an individual have any effect on his speech fluency?
> RQ3: Will endorsement of the label "normal speaker" previously applied to an individual have any effect on his speech fluency?
> RQ4: Will labelling a person, previously regarded as a normal speaker, a "stutterer," have any effect on his speech fluency? (p. 2)

Tudor (1939) divided the 22 children into groups of 10 and 12 (Tudor, 1939). The group of 10 comprised children, the teachers, and matrons of the orphanage labeled as *stutterers* (Tudor, 1939). Tudor subdivided the 10 children into two groups comprising 5 children each. The first group of 5 children (Group IA) was told they were not stutterers, but normal speakers mistakenly labeled as stutterers. The second group of 5 children (Group IB) was constantly told (reminded) that they were indeed stutterers. Tudor also subdivided the remaining 12 children with no speech impairments and labeled as normal speakers into two equal groups. The first group of 6 (normal speaking) children (Group IIA) were told that they displayed a type of speech interruption that caused them to be classified as stutterers (Tudor, 1939). The second group of 6 (normal speaking) children (Group IIB) were told that they were normal speakers and consistently praised for not stuttering (Tudor, 1939).

Before the end of the experiments, the 6 children in Group IIA (no speech impairments but were told that they displayed a type of speech interruption that caused them to be classified as stutterers) started exhibiting various degrees of inhibitions and speech complications (Reynolds, 2003; Tudor, 1939). Newly developed issues included but were not limited to an unwillingness to speak with responses limited to a single word or short phrases, moving from speaking in all situations to becoming mute in unfamiliar situations, speaking slower and more cautiously, a significant reduction in school grades over the six-week research period, increased verbal repetition of a single word, snapping of fingers to get the words out (synonymous with some individuals who stutters, cessation of storytelling and freely conversing with her playmates and writing the same word two or three times sequentially in a composition (Tudor, 1939).

The Holmesburg Prison Medical Experiments

Between 1951 and 1974, the University of Pennsylvania's dermatologist, Dr. Albert M. Kligman, conducted years of testing substances on the backs of prisoners at Holmesburg Prison in Philadelphia (Sarai, 2023; Tayag, 2015). Holmesburg administration enlisted Kligman in 1951 to help treat an outbreak of athlete's foot. To advance his career and discoveries around skincare and dermatology, Kligman seized the opportunity to access unlimited numbers of vulnerable Black inmates as test subjects without informed consent (Casale et al., 2023; Sarai, 2023). Unconsenting inmates endured experimentation using pharmaceuticals, including tretinoin and dioxin, a component of the powerful herbicide Agent Orange for Dow Chemical Company (Sarai, 2023). In a 1966 interview with the Philadelphia Inquirer, Kligman said *All I saw before me were acres of skin. I was like a farmer seeing a fertile field for the first time* (Casale et al., 2023; Sarai, 2023; Tayag, 2015). The prevalent acne and anti-aging tretinoin, or Retin-A, is a topical medication for acne that is also effective as an anti-aging treatment.

Other unimaginable atrocities included experiments using radioactive and hallucinogenic compounds, soaps, detergents, and infecting subjects with herpes simplex virus, human papillomavirus, vaccinia, and candida (Casale et al., 2023). One particular test for multinational corporation Johnson and Johnson entailed injecting inmates with asbestos to compare for comparison against the naturally occurring mineral talc, which can contain asbestos (Sarai, 2023). Casale et al. (2023) cited that Kligman, without formal ethical review, also conducted studies involving infecting children with intellectual disabilities with Microsporum Canis and Microsporum audouinii.

The Central Intelligence Agency (CIA): Illegal and Unethical Mind Control Experiments

The Central Intelligence Agency (CIA) harbors a dark history of unethical mind control experiments with not only unsuspecting and unconsenting human beings but also government employees (Nofil, 2024; Price, 2007). From *Project MKUltra* research operation (1953 to 1973) involving experimentation with human behavioral engineering, *Bluebird*, the 1950s mind-control research project dubbed *Operation Midnight Climax, Project Artichoke* again in the 1950s to study hypnosis, forced morphine addiction, drug withdrawal, and the use of chemicals to incite amnesia, and *Project QKHILLTOP* to study Chinese brainwashing techniques, which they then used to develop new methods of interrogation (Nofil, 2024; Price, 2007). The standard CIA experimental kit (in these illegal experiments) comprised of the use of CIA-paid prostitutes to lure unwitting subjects to CIA safe houses for experimentation, illegal experimenting on unaware and unconsenting U.S. or foreign subjects, vulnerable humans, including incarcerated persons, government and military employees, or arbitrary members of the public including at universities and hospitals; the covert administering of high dosages of power illegal mind-altering narcotics, forced drug addiction, electro-shock, deception, deprivation, verbal and sexual abuse, extreme isolation, hypnosis, mental and other forms of torture (Gross, 2019; Nofil, 2024; Price, 2007). The CIA's immoral, unethical, and obsessive global quest for mind control left many subjects permanently damaged or incapacitated in various ways (Gross, 2019; Nofil, 2024; Price, 2007). The Central Intelligence Agency's mind control experiments also breached the Nuremberg Code (Gross, 2019; Nofil, 2024; Price, 2007).

The unethical practices mentioned above do not even remotely qualify as the tip of the iceberg when viewed collectively with the plethora of inhumane experiments conducted. We chose those examples to highlight the abuse of power by those who knew that they should do no harm in research but, for whatever inexplicable reasons, did. Forty years (1932 to 1972) of secrecy of the *U.S. Public Health Service Untreated Syphilis Study at Tuskegee* – adding the simultaneous *Terre Haute Penitentiary* (1943 to 1944) and *the Guatemala Syphilis Experiment* (1946 to 1948), 12 years of *the Holocaust* (1933 to 1945) by Nazi Germany, and another at least 20 years of secret CIA mind control research operation gives a clear picture of how long unethical clandestine experiments can pervasively exist in plain sight – or being blatantly ignored.

As we accelerate into the fourth industrial revolution, the availability of disruptive innovations such as generative AI is a formidable tool for potential use in the various aspects of social science research. However, researchers and authors must exercise caution regarding what is considered benefits with due regard to the inherent critical shortfalls of the algorithms, particularly those shortfalls associated with Open AI's popular GPT-3.5 and GPT-4 (Helsinger, 2024; Lund & Wang, 2023; Penn Today, 2023; Wolford, 2018). Researchers who remain committed to the cause of knowledge creation will be in their right to ponder how long the use of generative AI will be allowed in social science research, propagating plagiarized and erroneous information for posterity.

How many years must elapse (since the November 30, 2202, public free-for-all debut of generative AI and, say, 28 years from then) before a joint commission issues guidelines for using generative AI in social science research? What cataclysmic event must occur for the establishment of guidelines (as was the case of the Nuremberg Code and the Belmont Report)? We ask the question because Kligman's 1951 to 1974 Holmesburg Prison medical experiments in Philadelphia were an egregious breach of the Nuremberg Code (Casale et al., 2023; Sarai, 2023), which emerged from the 1946 to 1947 trial of the German perpetrators (Ghooi, 2011; National Institutes of Health, n.d.).

Research ethics and integrity are two quintessential factors that must comprise the fiber of all research processes (Hosseini et al., 2023). While ethics and integrity are different because they address various facets of the research process, they are complementary factors ensuring that researchers exhibit responsible and accountable research approaches (Hosseini et al., 2023). Persons overly hyper-obsessed with incorporating generative AI in social sciences research will eventually breach the tenets of research ethics and integrity (Alser & Waisberg, 2023; Haman & Školník, 2023; Hosseini et al., 2023).

Generative Artificial Intelligence (AI)

While there is a *Technology Component* section later in this chapter, we found it prudent at this juncture to provide an early overview of generative AI to afford readers more fluency in understanding the potential threat that generative AI poses. Generative AI describes algorithms, many of which are open-sourced, that can be used to construct new content, including codes, texts, audio, images, videos, simulations, and videos (McKinsey & Company, 2024). We acknowledge generative AI as a digital-based platform designed to function with varying degrees of sovereignty that may exhibit adaptiveness after deployment and that, for explicit or implicit objectives, conjectures from received inputs, how to generate human-like outputs such as contents, predictions, recommendations, or decisions that can influence physical or virtual environments. The most popular generative AI tool is the open-source conversational generative pre-training transformer (ChatGPT) developed by OpenAI and released on November 30, 2022 (Alser & Waisberg, 2023; OpenAI, 2022). ChatGPT is a mighty large language model (LLM) machine learning (ML) system using natural language processing (NLP) to generate written content with near-human precision or super-human precision for the extremely absorbed, dedicated, and captivated users (Abbas, 2023; Veltman, 2024; Xu et al., 2024).

ChatGPT, a large-scale, deep learning-based, or large language model using natural language processing, incorporates unsupervised learning techniques, particularly pattern recognition (Abbas, 2023; Veltman, 2024; Xu et al., 2024). ChatGPT uses its inherent algorithm that's trained on colossal volumes of text-based data scraped from internet sources such as Common Crawl, Wikipedia, WebText2, digitized books, blogs, how-to manuals, and any other sources without verifying the credibility or age of information gathered and synthesized (Abbas, 2023; Banker et al., 2023a; Veltman, 2024; Xu et al., 2024; Zharovskikh, 2023). Simply put, ChatGPT pre-trains using unsupervised learning techniques, particularly pattern recognition and internet scrubbing, to access instantly massive datasets, self-learn on the colossal expanse of text data, and then fine-tune by the user based on specific tasks (or requests) to generate *appropriate* responses (Abbas, 2023; Banker et al., 2023a; Hashemi-Pour & Lutkevich, n.d.; McKinsey & Company, 2024; Veltman, 2024; Xu et al., 2024). The concerns and consequences regarding the autonomous learning and pattern recognition of large language models, particularly ChatGPT, will be discussed later in the appropriate section.

Perceived Benefits and Potential Applications of Generative AI in Social Science Research

Aydin and Karaarshan (2022) cited that while literature reviews or summarizing past work on the research topic is essential, reviewing and synthesizing the previous related studies is time-consuming and requires a magnitude of effort. The widely touted benefits of generative AI in authorship and research are (a) the instantaneous access to vast datasets, (b) the efficient analysis of large volumes of data at a hyper-fast speed, (c) generation of novel hypotheses, (d) improvements in scientific writing, (e) extreme reductions in cost and time associated with conducting research, (f) high reproducibility and scalability of research, and (g) enhancement research equity and versatility - thus making for overall he ease of work (Hashemi-Pour & Lutkevich, n.d.; Lund et al., 2023; Lund & Wang, 2023; McKinsey & Company, 2024; Sallam, 2023; Xu et al., 2024). Xu et al. (2024) cited aspects of social science research capable of being authored by AI. Hypothesis generation comprises a literature review and hypothesis proposal; hypothesis verification includes an experiment, survey, and non-reactive research, denoting the respective aspects identified (Xu et al., 2024). Xu et al. provided references for the areas of social science research they considered capable of being wholly authored by generative AI, and we will briefly examine some of these references.

Generative AI Hypothesis Generation: Definitions, Applications, and Literature Review

Aydin and Karaarshan (2022) claimed they used ChatGPT (no stipulation if GPT-3, GPT-3.5, or GPT-4) to generate the literature review and two sections of their research article *OpenAI ChatGPT generated literature review: Digital twin in healthcare*. The first section is a definition of digital twin technology. ChatGPT provided seven paragraphs, two sentences per paragraph definition for and use of digital twin technology (Aydın & Karaarslan, 2022, p. 23). This first section generated by ChatGPT did not have any citations. The second section generated by ChatGPT covered digital twin technology in healthcare. The section comprised five paragraphs – the second was three sentences long, while the first, third, fourth, and fifth were two sentences long (Aydın & Karaarslan, 2022, p. 23). Like the first section, this second section did not feature citations.

While the espoused purpose of the study compared to the study's content appeared misaligned, we immediately noted that there was no citation for the five-sentence opening paragraph of the literature review (Aydın & Karaarslan, 2022, p. 24). We also noted that the length of the successive paragraphs comprising the literature review ranged from 4 to 9 sentences, with a single citation at the end of the last sentence of those paragraphs (Aydın & Karaarslan, 2022). The third and fourth paragraphs (comprising four sentences each) and the fifth paragraph (consisting of six sentences) all shared the same (single) citation positioned at the end of the last sentence (Aydın & Karaarslan, 2022, p. 24). The literature review contained multiple cross-mixes of present and past tenses and multiple inappropriate uses of upper case and abbreviations. We will express our concerns with this study in the appropriate section later.

Generative AI Hypothesis Generation: Hypothesis Proposal

Banker et al. (2023) cited that creating new ideas is profoundly contingent on existing research findings. They further posited that today's continuous increase in the output volume of scientific research findings, especially in the field of social psychology, overwhelms researchers' capabilities to remain current with evolving research and generate new ideas (Banker et al., 2023). Consequently, combing through and synthesizing the growing extant body of literature (in social psychology), making connections between research findings, and understanding the multifacetedness of human perceptions and behaviors due to their interactions with each other and their environments (somehow) became overbearingly cumbersome for Banker et al. to fathom. Thus, the intervention of machine learning - a subfield of generative AI, which is a mechanical, automated, or digital device or software designed to impersonate intelligent human behavior (Agouridis, 2021; S. Brown, 2021; IBM, n.d.-b, n.d.-a), becomes the elixir to annihilate the discombobulation experienced by Banker et al.

Banker et al. (2023) cited that they employed ChatGPT's GPT-3 (fine-tuned on several thousands of abstracts gathered from 50 social psychology journals over more than 55 years as well as pre-prints such as PsyArXiv) and GPT-4 without fine-tuning but using specific prompts to generate relevant text outputs. The purpose of this process was to not only conjecture value from input text but also generate original text to produce testable hypotheses for social psychology studies (Banker et al., 2023). Banker et al. concluded that their AI-generated hypotheses were on par with, or even better than hypotheses written by human researchers. We qualify that pre-training of GPT-3 refers to the mandatory unsupervised training of GPT-3 when fed large text corpora such as Wikipedia, Common Crawl, WebText2, news articles, blogs, and digitized books (Banker et al., 2023; Veltman, 2024). We will state our concerns with this study in a later section.

Generative AI Hypothesis Verification: Testing Hypotheses

The concept of employing LLM (of course GPT-3) computational models of humans or *homo silicus* as a researcher, interviewer, and subject is nearing reality in social science research (Horton, 2023; Manning et al., 2024; Salehi et al., 2022). Despite the known reoccurring and predictable unreliability of GPT-3, the intended usage of LLM-based platforms for social science research ranges from (repurposing) the actual use of avatars to train child protective services (CPS) agents (Salehi et al., 2022) and creating and manipulating simulated communities or social simulacra populated by homo silicus (Park et al., 2022). Park et al. (2022) presented *social simulacra,* a social computing construct or prototyping technique capable of generating a wide array of *realistic* social interactions as outputs when the social computing system is populated or receives specific inputs from the construct designer. Social simulacra accepts the researcher's description of a community's design, including member personalities with assigned names, community rules, and goals as inputs (Park et al., 2022).

Using the inputs mentioned above, social simulacra generate outputs in the form of simulated behaviors, textual interactions (message postings and replies to said postings between personalities), and anti-social behaviors amongst the personalities populating the simulated community (Park et al., 2022). Park et al. declared that generated outputs at any given instant are exclusively based on the designer's input for the given instant. Park et al. acknowledged their reliance on and gratitude for GPT-3. They explained that they chose an LLM such as GPT-3 because GPT-3 hosts a myriad of social comportments garnered during its unsupervised pre-training phase – the promulgation of the inherent reoccurring erroneous, unreliable outputs associated with LLM-based systems and platforms (Park et al., 2022). Park et al. established that social simulacra do not intend to predict what is unequivocally going to happen in the future because perfect reality is not their objective. Their objective is to help the community designer perceive beyond the standard or anticipated social interactions generated exclusively based on their inputs and, instead, envision endless possibilities of interactions that the design may produce (Park et al., 2022).

History holds multiple cases regarding the *unintentional and unethical misuse* of knowledge and technology when users *envisioned other highly questionably endless possibilities*. In the presence of infinite opportunities, lies await the possibilities of interminable unethical behavior, as evidenced in the 1932 to 1972 Tuskegee study of untreated syphilis in the negro male (Tuskegee University, 2024), the 1951 to 1974 Holmesburg prison medical experiments (Tayag, 2015); and the 1971 Stanford prison experiment (Haney & Zimbardo, 1998; Zimbardo, 1973). As Kligman said in his interview regarding his unethical and atrocious experiments at Holmesburg Prison, *all I saw before me were acres of skin. I was like a farmer seeing a fertile field for the first time* (Casale et al., 2023; Sarai, 2023; Tayag, 2015). Thus, we will (presumptuously) predict the future by categorically stating that we envision that inevitably, (some) social science researchers, whether in a covert or overt capacity of community designers, will eventually *visualize opportunities*, reach *beyond the endless possibilities of the interactions that social simulacra may produce* and use as inputs, hypotheses they are interested in testing. Market research (Brand et al., 2023)and predicting human survey responses are some of the other touted uses of generative AI in social science research.

Technology Components

Factory mechanization via spinning jenny, coupled with the advent of steam engines and the telegraph, is synonymous with the first industrial revolution (Adams, 2022; Armenta, 2021). Technological manufacturing parallels the advent of the lightbulb, electricity, and the combustible engine and established the second industrial revolution (Adams, 2022). Digital manufacturing, the internet, mass use of computers, and nuclear energy defined the third industrial revolution (Adams, 2022). Disruptive innovations (or technologies), gene editing, and autonomous vehicles dictate the evolution of the fourth industrial revolution (Adams, 2022). Notable disruptive innovations that will leave an indelible impact on humanity include but are not limited to open and closed source generative (AI), virtual and augmented reality, intelligent automation (IA), big data analytics, user interface and user experience (UI/UX), quantum computing, cloud computing, the Internet of Things (IoT), blockchain, and cognitive robotics (B. A. Brown & Heitner, 2022; Drapkin, 2024; Economic Commission for Latin America and the Caribbean, 2022; Eightfold AI, 2022; Elias, 2023; Gill & Kaur, 2023; Google, n.d.-a; IBM, n.d.-a; Maisiri et al., 2019; Mhlanga, 2022; TeamLease EDTECH, n.d.; Vaishya et al., 2020).

However, the global lion's share of the focus is on generative AI built on LLMs as the primary ultra-disruptive innovation. Generative AI continuously reshapes at a hyper-accelerated pace what was known as the typical modern way of life, including social science research (Aydın & Karaarslan, 2022; Banker et al., 2023a; B. A. Brown & Heitner, 2022, 2024; Park et al., 2022; Sallam, 2023; Xu et al., 2024). The November 30, 2022, inaugural and public debut of the open-source generative AI technology ChatGPT (Alser & Waisberg, 2023; Qadir, 2023) created an unprecedented stir at all levels in the global research community. Developed by OpenAI and released at a minimum as a free beta version in many countries globally, ChatGPT is an LLM with the apparent seamless ability to generate instantaneously human-like text responses to users' prompts (Alser & Waisberg, 2023; Lund & Wang, 2023). ChatGPT gained immediate mass recognition and acceptance as the leading generative AI for written script production (Baîdoo-Anu & Owusu Ansah, 2023; Qadir, 2023; Rahman & Watanobe, 2023).

Currently, there are multiple alternatives to ChatGPT as an artificial text generator, with some options outperforming ChatGPT in some user experiences based on user-friendliness, *accuracy* of information, and the ability to generate current, relevant, and real-time responses (Garg, 2023; Shinde, 2024). Other common open-source (user can manipulate and rewrite) generative AI tools comparable to Open AI (OpenAI, 2022) include but are not limited to TensorFlow, PyTorch, Rasa, Amazon Web Services (AWS), Google's Gemma, and Keras (Google, n.d.-b; Shinde, 2024). Closed models (proprietary and cannot be manipulated and rewritten by users) are Google's Gemini (Google, n.d.-a). Another popular closed-source LLM is Meta and Microsoft's Llama 2 (Meta, 2023). On July 18, 2023, Meta introduced Llama 2 as an open-source model (Meta, 2023), but users discovered 5 days later that Llama 2 was not open-source (now classified as an open approach) due to licensing restrictions (Bergmann, 2023; Brock, 2023).

Technology Concerns: Beyond the Power and Perceived Benefits of Generative AI

The mass recognition of generative AI as an imminent reality has undoubtedly promoted a constant and rapid evolution of communication technologies in nearly every industry as the labor biosphere accelerates through the Fourth Industrial Revolution (Budhwar et al., 2022; Mhlanga, 2022; Vaishya et al., 2020). With generative AI applications rapidly evolving from frivolity to realism (B. A. Brown & Heitner, 2023; Harney & Collings, 2021), AI is present in multiple sectors, such as the health sector (Mhlanga, 2022; Vaishya et al., 2020) and human resource management (Budhwar et al., 2022). Additionally, the prevalence and acceptance of generative AI technology such as ChatGPT grow at a hyper-accelerated pace based on its potential for ease of work and communication in many other sectors, including research, particularly academic research and practice (Lund & Wang, 2023; Sallam, 2023). To grasp the magnitude of the absorption of ChatGPT, TikTok post-release only reached 100 million users after 9 months, while ChatGPT amassed 100 million users in only 2 months (McKinsey & Company, 2024; Zharovskikh, 2023).

Despite the rapid acceptance and pervasiveness of generative AI, there are critical intrinsic limitations associated with generative AI, particularly ChatGPT (Alser & Waisberg, 2023; Qadir, 2023; Xu et al., 2024; Zohny et al., 2023). As the most protuberant open-source generative AI tool for text generation, ChatGPT has a remarked, notorious propensities inclusive of but not limited to (a) generating erroneous outputs, (b) producing gibberish or incoherent irrelevant text outputs, (c) consistently generating racial and gender-biased AI-driven responses, providing dated and delayed responses (DiBenedetto, 2024; Garg, 2023; Helsinger, 2024; Murad, 2023; Sharma, 2023; Veltman, 2024; Yin et al., 2024, 2024). Straight out of the box, GPT is generic and untrained (Veltman, 2024). The obvious reoccurring (and seemingly but rather unfortunately tolerated) anomalies as foundational problems synonymous with GPT are directly correlated with the unsupervised pre-training of GPT (Abbas, 2023; Banker et al., 2023a; Veltman, 2024; Xu et al., 2024; Zharovskikh, 2023).

The unsupervised training (as previously mentioned) is GPT *feasting* on titanic portions of non-peer-reviewed, unfounded, flawed data scavenged from sources housed on the internet. Sources include but are not limited to Common Crawl, Wikipedia, WebText2, unpublished digitized books, blogs, news articles, how-to manuals, and any other sources of questionable credibility and age (Abbas, 2023; Banker et al., 2023a; Veltman, 2024; Xu et al., 2024; Zharovskikh, 2023). Garg (2023) also highlighted that GPT generates dated information because its inherent algorithm only allows it to gather data up to and including the year 2021 (Garg, 2023). This pre-training crosses ethical boundaries as the pre-training also includes proprietary material for which the generative AI developer/user executing the pre-training did not get prior permission to use (Veltman, 2024). Additionally, there is the concern of authorship and ownership regarding who takes responsibility for consequential backlashes for unethical partially or wholly AI-generated research manuscripts authored by ChatGPT (Authors Guild, 2024a, 2024b; Veltman, 2024). There is also a lack of citations and references to give credit to the owners of the work ChatGPT replicates and regurgitates. This lack of citation was prominent in the three ChatGPT-generated sections, including the literature review featured in the work of Aydın & Karaarslan (2022).

We also note that machine learning as a subset of generative AI operates on pattern recognition, thus gathering the same information repeatedly from diverse sources, from past data, and generating outputs based on said past learning (Agouridis, 2021). Without fail, machine learning relentlessly repeatedly generates repetitive (harvested) information as outputs. According to the Society for Human Resource Management (2024), pattern recognition and learning from past data is the perfect incubator for AI repeating or exacerbating patterns of bias. Increased patterns of bias propagate a sustained decline in the quality and reliability of output and, most conspicuously, increased bias associated with diversity, equity, and inclusion (DiBenedetto, 2024). According to DiBenedetto (2024), the continuous hyper-increase in exacerbating patterns of bias is due to the megalithic, incestuous development associated with AI's evolution, as AI designers train the foundation constructs using previous and other AI models instead of human inputs. For example, all subsequent versions of GPT are developed on the chassis of prior versions of itself, now becoming an upgrade of sorts. Other generative AIs, though known by different names, are either direct clones of themselves with minor upgrades, clones of other generative AIs, or built on platforms similar or identical to another type of generative AI. The only reliability within this incestuous development is the replication and propagation of the inherent flaws like a form of mitosis or binary fission.

Researchers' Concerns: Ethics and Integrity Issues With Using Generative AI in Social Science Research

Researchers posited that many early embracers of ChatGPT became captivated by the ease of acquiring and synthesizing enormous quantities of data and information on an unprecedented scale (Raman, 2023) - with scant regard for the source and quality of the data and information produced by ChatGPT (Alser & Waisberg, 2023; Qadir, 2023; Zohny et al., 2023). Aydin and Karaarshan (2022) wrote of generative AI providing *ease of work* by citing that while literature reviews or summarizing past work on the research topic is essential, reviewing and synthesizing the previous related studies is time-consuming and requires a great magnitude of effort. Banker et al.

(2023) concurred with Aydin and Kardashian. Both sets of authors stated that today's continuous increase in the output volume of scientific research findings, especially in the field of social psychology, overwhelms researchers' capabilities to remain current with evolving research and generate new ideas (Aydın & Karaarslan, 2022; Banker et al., 2023b) Thus, the intervention of machine learning became necessary.

Considering that open-source AI can be modified by anyone to suit specific needs (Penn Today, 2023), open-source AI, such as ChatGPT, can be manipulated and misused in social science research to produce the researchers' desired outcomes (Lund & Wang, 2023; Office of Research Integrity, n.d.; Resnik & Hofweber, 2023). Ethical researchers' concerns regarding research ethics and the use of generative AI in social science research include but are not limited to the unauthorized use of their work for pre-training and fine-tuning AI, nefarious manipulation of their original work, and copyright violations (Lund & Wang, 2023; Office of Research Integrity, n.d.; Qadir, 2023; Raman, 2023; Resnik & Hofweber, 2023; Zohny et al., 2023). A published script lacking citations (plagiarism) is a significant concern, and generative AI cannot cite generated work, as evidenced in the work of Aydin and Karaarshan (2022). Zohny et al. (2023) noted that ChatGPT's inability to produce a manuscript with complete citations and references constitutes plagiarism.

Unauthorized use of Researcher's Published Work and Copyright Violations in Pre-Training and Fine-Tuning Generative AI

Generative AI, straight out of the box, requires pre-training (Banker et al., 2023; Veltman, 2024). As the unsupervised pre-training involves turning the AI tool loose to scrounge around on the World Wide Web, literally every publication hosted online becomes susceptible to being harvested by the AI tool being pre-trained (Banker et al., 2023; Veltman, 2024). The next step, or the fine-tuning, becomes even more disconcerting as this process entails the developers *giving* the AI tool specific instructions regarding what information to cherry-pick from the internet. Banker et al. (2023) fine-tuned GPT-3 on several thousands of abstracts gathered from 50 social psychology journals over more than 55 years and pre-prints such as PsyArXiv. However, Banker et al. did not mention seeking permission from owners of the works in these journals, which constitutes multiple violations of intellectual property rights and copyright infringement where applicable.

According to Veltman (2024), to circumvent violations of intellectual property rights and copyright infringement, some authors (not social science researchers) derived the uncanny idea of pre-training GPT on their own work. The results were nothing short of disastrous gibberish because LLMs such as GP-3 require an immense volume of data for pre-training, and those individual authors do not possess such a repository of personal work sufficient to neither pre-train nor fine-tune GPT-3

(Veltman, 2024). While the authors, as mentioned above, were not social science researchers, we believe the circumventing tactic is worth mentioning as soon some social science researchers will attempt the same or something even more *creatively sinister*.

Ethical Citation and Referencing Practices: Attributing the Creators of the Extant Body of Literature

Ethical researchers with human intelligence, when incorporating the work of other researchers in their own work, exhibit their respect for the time-honored ethos of crediting the work of the other researchers.

By respect, we mean that we cite and provide references to unequivocally show that we do not commit plagiarism – whether by implicitly or explicitly taking credit for or claiming ownership of the work of others. The hyper-increasing and critical hyper problem at hand regarding citations and referencing ethics and ChatGPT is that ChatGPT reproduces text verbatim as copied from Common Crawl, Wikipedia, WebText2, and any other sources of questionable credibility and age (Abbas, 2023; Banker et al., 2023a; Veltman, 2024; Xu et al., 2024; Zharovskikh, 2023) but does not provide the requisite accompanying citations and references (Alser & Waisberg, 2023). Such a deficiency of attribution is *direct plagiarism* (Alser & Waisberg, 2023), which is most troubling and led to Haman and Školník (2023) writing a letter to the editor of the Taylor and Francis Group. In their letter to the editor, Haman and Školník campaigned against the use of ChatGPT to generate literature reviews and *firmly recommended not using ChatGPT in the research process.* (p. 2)

Aside from crediting the work of others using citations, ethical citation practices (especially in literature reviews) highlight the latitudes and longitudes the researcher navigated on the research topic (Lund et al., 2023). Citation and referencing practices are integral to research and scholarly publishing (Lund et al., 2023). Ethical and astute researchers know that including relevant and precise citations constitutes conserving the posterity of academic integrity (Lund et al., 2023). Effective citation and reference practices indicate the extent of familiarity the researchers possess regarding the research topic and their proficiency level in their field (Lund et al., 2023). According to Lund et al. (2023), the ethical use of citations and references also allows readers, editors, and publishers to access further readings and verify sources should they doubt the validity and credibility of the researchers' arguments.

For example, according to King (2022), as cited in Lund et al. (2023), natural language processing based-ChatGPT *can recommend applicable* citations for its regurgitated mishmash output. For us, the author of this chapter, King's statement, would be a *eureka declaration* for this chapter, as this statement would be the first to contravene all other concurring statements that ChatGPT cannot auto-generate citations. As astute social science researchers embracing ethical citation and referencing practices and wanting to authenticate King's statement, we scoured the article using the search feature provided at the top, and the word *citation* was never mentioned even once (King, 2022). We dissected the article to the point of near-reverse engineering. However, while we found no narrative alluding to our anticipated *eureka statement* regarding *citation*, we inadvertently discovered something else (King, 2022). We found that King (2022) is a five-page article featuring a conversation between author Michael R. King and ChatGPT. The article neither featured a single citation nor a reference list (King, 2022).

Our validation process of the King (2022) is a routine and mandatory aspect of all our writing - checking content, citations, and references to validate the credibility of the researchers' arguments. Our validation process is not an attack on Lund et al. (or King, for that matter), as we have encountered these occurrences multiple times. We stand corrected if we inadvertently overlooked or missed any subliminal paraphrasing or interpretation in our review of King and Lund et al. However, our coincidental discovery regarding the lack of citations and references in the King article consolidates our unified stance with Haman and Školník (2023) - that ChatGPT will generate (*suggest)* citations *only* when prompted (requested) by the AI user and that the generated citations are often erroneous or non-existent.

CURRENT CHALLENGES FACING ACADEMIC JOURNAL AND BOOK REVIEWERS, EDITORS, AND PUBLISHING ORGANIZATION

Eager and curious users of ChatGPT in social sciences research exhibit scant regard for the source and quality of the data and information produced by ChatGPT (Alser & Waisberg, 2023; Qadir, 2023; Zohny et al., 2023). Furthermore, electing AI-driven quantity over the quality of generated output for publication becomes problematic (Qadir, 2023; Sweeney, 2023; Trust et al., 2023; Zohny et al., 2023), especially since globally, the manipulation of social science research data and results is on the rise (Resnik & Hofweber, 2023; Office of Research Integrity, n.d.). Concerns regarding research ethics include but are not limited to data manipulation, breach of data privacy, bypassing informed consent, and questionable quality and originality of the ideas and content presented to editors for publication in books and academic journals (Lund & Wang, 2023; Office of Research Integrity, n.d.; Qadir, 2023; Raman, 2023; Resnik & Hofweber, 2023; Zohny et al., 2023). AI also lacks rational human thinking, thus posing imminent risks to social science research, which include but are not limited to the exclusion of sociocultural biases that exist for real-life humans, researchers' AI-produced manuscripts, being (a) erroneous with irrelevant content, (b) prejudicial and insensitive to race and gender, and (d) biased and discriminatory to specific groups of people as in disregard for equity, diversity, and inclusion (Alser & Waisberg, 2023; Elias, 2023; Gill & Kaur, 2023; Iqbal et al., 2022; Lund & Wang, 2023; Qadir, 2023; Zohny et al., 2023). Consequently, the global community of social science researchers will need to establish guidelines for the governance of AI in research (Penn Today, 2023).

Currently, journal reviewers, editors, and publishers do not possess sufficient tools to distinguish between human-written and generative AI-produced manuscripts for journal publication (Lund & Wang, 2023; Qadir, 2023; Zohny et al., 2023). Zohny et al. (2023) further contended that despite the inability to produce a manuscript with complete citations and references (to mitigate plagiarism), the misuse of generative AI, especially regarding authorship, could create an incubator for predatory journals to publish AI-generated low-quality manuscripts.

Governance of Generative AI (Machine Learning) as a Form of Disruptive Innovation in Social Science Research

Despite creating and enforcing guidelines for protecting research integrity, for example, (a) the 1948 Nuremberg Code; (b) the 1964 Declaration of Helsinki; (c) the National Research Act (1974), which precipitated the Belmont Report; and (d) the mandatory use of Internal Review Board clearances where required (Kim, 2012; Nagai et al., 2022; University of Nevada, Las Vegas, 2012), unethical research practices continue (Casale et al., 2023; Office of Research Integrity, n.d.; Sarai, 2023; Vyas, 2020). Additionally, the burgeoning access to open-source disruptive innovations such as ChatGPT, a form of LLM generative AI, could promulgate research misconduct in the realm of social science research practices (Office of Research Integrity, n.d.; Penn Today, 2023; Resnik & Hofweber, 2023; Vyas, 2020). The current overwhelmingly intolerable weaknesses inherent to AI, particularly GPT, which renders it absolutely unfit for usage in social science research, are well documented in this chapter. Given the hyper-touting of generative AI's potential in social science research, the lack of organizational (publishing houses), national, and global regulations regarding the use of generative AI specifically in social science research will allow for escalated, unfettered usage.

The European Union Artificial Intelligence (EU AI) Act is the foremost and only all-encompassing horizontal legal directive by a significant regulator worldwide (EU Artificial Intelligence Act, 2024; Molaiepour, 2024; Nahra et al., 2024). Nahra et al. (2024) The European Union Parliament adopted the European Union Artificial Intelligence Act on March 13, 2024. Nahra et al. (2024) added that the European Union Artificial Intelligence Act aims to afford European Union-wide policies intended to govern and regulate AI usage regarding transparency, data quality, human oversight, and accountability. Adopted on March 13, 2024, by the European Union Parliament, the EU AI Act provides European Union-wide rules designed to govern AI usage regarding data quality, transparency, human oversight, and accountability (Nahra et al., 2024). The EU AI Act ascribes the multitude of applications of AI to various risk categories. Unacceptable, high, limited, and minimal risks are stipulated in the EU AI Act (European Commission, 2024; Molaiepour, 2024; Nahra et al., 2024).

The risk categories stipulated in the EU AI Act do not include a section specific to the use of AI in social science research. However, limited risks, as per the EU AI Act, states

> *Limited risk refers to the risks associated with a lack of transparency in AI usage. The AI Act introduces specific transparency obligations to ensure that humans are informed when necessary, fostering trust. For instance, when using AI systems such as chatbots, humans should be made aware that they are interacting with a machine so they can take an informed decision to continue or step back. Providers will also have to ensure that AI-generated content is identifiable. Besides, AI-generated text published with the purpose to inform the public on matters of public interest must be labelled as artificially generated. This also applies to audio and video content constituting deep fakes. (European Commission, 2024, p. 1)*

Dissecting the tenets of the EU AI Act's *limited risk* for the sake of posterity of ethics and integrity versus abhorring the ultra-premature use of AI in social science research, there is much to take away from the tenets of limited risk and apply same to social science research. We reference the EU AI Act's mention of the word *trust,* and we parallel that trust with research's trustworthiness (reliability and credibility). Researchers of the social sciences aim to *inform the public on matters of public interest,* and we concur that *AI-generated content must be identifiable and labeled as artificially generated* (European Commission, 2024).

Aside from the EU AI Act, the International Committee of Medical Journal Editors (ICMJE) posts strict guidelines for using generative AI, for example, ChatGPT, to produce manuscripts for their journals (International Committee of Medical Journal Editors [ICMJE], 2024). At the time of authoring this chapter, the official web page for the Committee on Publication Ethics (COPE) did not list any stipulations for AI usage in manuscript production (Committee on Publication Ethics [COPE], 2024).

Generative AI Producing Poor Quality Research Presented for Publication

Several compulsory factors (and components) must comprise social science research (Bouchrika, 2014; B. A. Brown, 2020). The type of academic or social science research (qualitative, quantitative, or mixed methods) will determine the present factors. For example, regarding qualitative studies, trustworthiness comprises credibility, transferability, dependability, and confirmability and denotes the degree to which readers can have confidence in the study's findings and supports the salient aspects of the survey (Brady, 2015; Lincoln & Guba, 1985). Reliability, or the consistency of an assessment score, and validity, or the extent to which a measure does what it is designed to do, are integral to quantitative studies (Lincoln & Guba, 1985). Where applicable other mandatory factors and components include but are not limited to (a) a sound research question, (b) acknowledgment of previous research on the topic (review of the literature), (c) a systematic, appropriate research methodology, (d) incorporation of relevant empirical data and proper data analysis methods, (e) presentation and discussion of findings, (f) recommendations (g) acknowledgment of limitations, and (h) provides suggestions for future research (Bouchrika, 2014; B. A. Brown, 2020). However, irrespective of the constituents of any social science research, all research must be ethical (Nagai et al., 2022; National Institutes of Health, n.d.; Office for Human Research Protections, 2022; Resnik & Hofweber, 2023). We add that human authorship (ICMJE, 2024) involves crediting authors for their work and constitutes the integrity of research (Alser & Waisberg, 2023; Hosseini et al., 2023; Lund et al., 2023).

Ethical Citation and Referencing Practices: Crediting Sources and Plagiarism

On account of ChatGPT's pre-training on large datasets of suspect quality (Abbas, 2023; Banker et al., 2023a; Veltman, 2024; Xu et al., 2024; Zharovskikh, 2023), Chat GPT, by default, conforms to the GIGO theory - garbage in / garbage out (IBM, n.d.-b). Thus, the use of ChatGPT to produce academic work cannot guarantee trustworthiness as the foundation problem is using a tool pre-trained on highly flawed data to collect and analyze the said flawed data it was pre-trained on. Additionally, fine-tuning ChatGPT (using 50 social psychology journals written over more than 55 years) for ethical social science research (Banker et al., 2023) is counterintuitive as it is counterproductive. We deem the process counterintuitive and counterproductive because ChatGPT also does not auto-generate citations to credit the authors of the works it *cuts and pastes* as output via machine learning's pattern recognition (Haman & Školník, 2023), further reducing the quality of academic research work presented for publication.

Alser and Waisberg (2023) opined that direct plagiarism is an inescapable intrinsic characteristic of Chat GPT because ChatGPT regurgitates outputs verbatim, copied from sources such as Wikipedia, LinkedIn, and even the AApple AppStore. Paraphrasing plagiarism or generating scripts without citations is the next basic expectation of ChatGPT (Alser & Waisberg, 2023). Source-based plagiarism ensues when users prompt ChatGPT for citations, and ChatGPT generates fake citations (Alser & Waisberg, 2023). According to Alser and Waisberg, ChatGPT could commit self-plagiarism when users issue the same prompt to ChatGPT, and ChatGPT generates multiple similar outputs without citation. Revisiting the work of Aydin and Karaarshan (2022), where they used ChatGPT to generate three sections inclusive of the literature review, we did note that there were multiple paragraphs without citations, and the remaining paragraphs had a single citation at the end of the paragraph. Aydin and Karaarshan using ChatGPT to install a single citation at the end of literature review paragraphs with sentences ranging from 4 to 9 sentences in length is a disingenuous and misleading attribution (Alser & Waisberg, 2023; Aydın & Karaarslan, 2022). Additionally, though Banker et al. (2023) neither confirmed nor denied their use of ChatGPT to generate the full content of their paper, their overall work was similar to Alser and Waisberg as in multiple paragraphs of varied sentence length with extremely scant to no citations per paragraph.

Authorship

According to Aydın and Karaarslan (2022), there are questions surrounding copyrighting, intellectual property, and ownership of AI-generated articles. Aydın and Karaarslan further pondered if the generative AI owns the content or the human who prompted the generative AI for content. We posit that the answer is simple as AI can neither assume the responsibilities of authorship nor own content that it did not initially create or create without a user prompt ICMJE, 2024). Thus, on the account that ChatGPT scours the internet, uses machine learning's pattern recognition to cut, slice, dice, and splices information gleaned from just about any source, then generates paraphrased or verbatim regurgitated content without citation, the invalid output or content belongs to the individual who initiated the prompt and requested the output. As a matter of responsibility, the generative AI user who requested the content must be held responsible for the generated content's accuracy, originality, and integrity. Still, generative AI can neither own the content nor be held accountable for generating the content - at least not at the time of writing this chapter.

In their letter to the editor, Haman and Školník (2023) vehemently admonished against using ChatGPT to generate research literature reviews. According to Haman and Školník, on February 23, 2023, they conducted a short test with ChatGPT. Haman and Školník created and examined five distinctive conversations stemming from engaging ChatGPT five times, each time using the same prompt *"'List 10 seminal academic articles in the field of medicine and provide the DOI.'"* ChatGPT provided 10 articles for each of the five prompts; however, only 48 were unique publications (Haman & Školník, 2023). Of the 50 digital object identifiers (DOIs) ChatGPT provided, only 8 or 16% existed and accompanied their corresponding publication (Haman & Školník, 2023). Despite achieving 84% incorrect digital object identifiers, to further illustrate ChatGPT's absolute incompetence even as a research aid, Haman and Školník searched Google Scholar, PubMed, and Semantic Scholar for the correct titles for ChatGPT-supplied articles. Using only the correct authors and the correct academic publication, Haman and Školník discovered that of 50 article searches, only 17 or 34% of the articles in question existed in the databases interrogated, meaning that in 66% of the cases, ChatGPT generated a nonexistent paper – deep faking papers all on its own. After the test, Haman and Školník declared ChatGPT unfit to aid in the research process, citing ChatGPT's production of countless fake papers as output for publication.

The ICMJE clearly defined the roles of authors and contributors to their journals and the criteria to be satisfied (ICMJE, 2024). The ICMJE (2024) also outlined the requirements for consideration as an author or contributor, and ChatGPT did not satisfy any of the said criteria. Consequently, the ICMJE equivocally declared that ChatGPT, as a generative AI chatbot, should neither be listed as an author or co-author nor be cited as an author. The ICMJE's reason for the previous statement is that they advocate that only a human author can be held accountable for responsibilities such as originality, integrity, and accuracy required for authorship of the research work, and ChatGPT is not human.

SOLUTIONS AND RECOMMENDATIONS

Humans, even a single individual, possess the unrelenting propensity to scale means, motives, and opportunities to be unethical, as evidenced by Dr. John C. Cutler, who, under the USPHS, was one of the leaders from the 1960s to 1972 of the U.S. Public Health Service untreated syphilis study at Tuskegee, while simultaneously involved in the Terre Haute Penitentiary experiment between 1943 and 1944, and the Guatemala syphilis experiment from 1946 to 1948 (BBC, 2011; Centers for Disease

Control and Prevention, 2024; Heller, 2017; Rodriguez & García, 2013; Rogers, 2024; Tuskegee University, 2024). For dishonorable mention, the University of Pennsylvania's dermatologist, Dr. Albert M. Kligman, at Holmesburg Prison (1951 to 1974), said, *All I saw before me were acres of skin. I was like a farmer seeing a fertile field for the first time* (Casale et al., 2023; Sarai, 2023; Tayag, 2015).

Additionally, this chapter highlighted a short listing of unethical research conducted over time – some absolutely unthinkable and others, there are no words to describe them (Centers for Disease Control and Prevention, 2024; Fridlund et al., 2012; Rodriguez & García, 2013; U.S. Holocaust Memorial Museum, n.d.-b). In our writings, we detected and established three categories of unethical experiments. The first category is what we term as the *unethical physical experiments*, for example, the Tuskegee study of untreated syphilis in the negro male, now referred to as the U.S. Public Health Service untreated syphilis study at Tuskegee the Holocaust, and the Holmes Prison experiment (Centers for Disease Control and Prevention, 2024; Sarai, 2023; U.S. Holocaust Memorial Museum, n.d.-b). The second category is the *unethical mental and psychological experiments,* as denoted by the Little Albert experiment, the monster study, the Stanford Prison experiment, and the Central Intelligence Agency's Project MKUltra mind control experiments (Haney & Zimbardo, 1998; Nofil, 2024; Price, 2007; Stamp, 2023; Tudor, 1939; Zimbardo, 1973). We also note and now establish an apparent continuous trend of conducting unethical research and experiments using the technology available during the dispensation or industrial revolutions. In this fourth industrial revolution era, we unequivocally establish that ChatGPT and any other applicable present or future generative AI chatbots underscore the third category of unethical social science research. We coin this third category as *unethical partially or wholly AI-authored research manuscripts*.

The hyper-absorption of ChatGPT and other generative AI in their present hypo-immature stage

for use in social science research will continue beyond the fourth industrial revolution. The continuance is already signaled by the proposition of *simulacra* for social science studies using simulated social environments (Park et al., 2022). King (2022) and his other ChatGPT co-authored published paper mentioned later in this chapter. With the advent of generative AI for social science research as an evolving and unstable disruptive technology, particularly ChatGPT, comes new concerns regarding their usage, necessitating new requirements to regulate their use (Bahrke & Regnier, 2023; European Commission, 2024; ICMJE, 2024; Nahra et al., 2024). The continued preservation of research ethics, integrity, and authorship accountabilities are now of increased paramount importance (Haman & Školník, 2023; Hosseini et al., 2023; ICMJE 2024; Lund et al., 2023). Thus, the need for firm regulations and distinct policies designed explicitly to govern all aspects of AI usage in social science research becomes increasingly important, considering that generative AI's mass application rate may continue to exceed its maturity rate.

Given the hyper-accelerated rate of use of AI versus the low rate of development and readiness for blind and unfettered use in social science research, there will be an ongoing dilution in the efficacy and eradication of trustworthiness in social science research output (Hosseini et al., 2023; ICMJE, 2024; Lund et al., 2023). Evidently, researchers and authors on one side and reviewers, editors, and publishers on the other side must share the responsibility for the information emanating from social science research.

For the Ethically Conflicted Researchers and Authors

At this juncture, due to the highly underdeveloped stage of generative AI, particularly ChatGPT, when evaluated against the sensitive and dynamic nature of social science research, as a solution, we do not recommend the use of generative AI – not even as an aid in social science research (Haman & Školník, 2023). The philanthropy of valid reasons include but are not limited to the incestuous molecular structure of generative AI and its unsupervised pre-training on large volumes of flawed data (Abbas, 2023; Banker et al., 2023a; DiBenedetto, 2024, 2024; Haman & Školník, 2023; Hashemi-Pour & Lutkevich, n.d.; McKinsey & Company, 2024; Veltman, 2024; Xu et al., 2024). Additionally, generative AI pattern recognition modus operandi promulgates a myriad of known reoccurring errors inclusive of but not limited to incoherent scripts, zero attributions, no list of references, and the incessant proliferation of a hyper-increase in exacerbating patterns of bias (Abbas, 2023; Banker et al., 2023a; DiBenedetto, 2024, 2024; Haman & Školník, 2023; Hashemi-Pour & Lutkevich, n.d.; McKinsey & Company, 2024; Veltman, 2024; Xu et al., 2024).

We concur with Haman and Školník (2023), who advised against the use of ChatGPT in research, equally, as we strongly recommend that researchers and authors desist from using generative AI to partially or wholly conduct social science research. In comparison, the Author's Guild (2024a) proposed guidelines for generative AI in the authorship of fact and fiction novels. However, published social science studies are not novels. Social science researchers create tomorrow's factual literary history for posterity (Khaldun, 1986) by examining the historiographic and present interactions between individuals and between people and their environments. Thus, we advocate that until there is sufficient governance of AI usage in social research, its usage should not be allowed, as we have witnessed the atrocities emanating from individual and organizational unfettered access to means, motives, and opportunities in the name of research.

Furthermore, on the note of authorship, we stand in solidarity with the ICMJE (2024) for not recognizing ChatGPT as an author or co-author, nor being cited as an author or the citation of ChatGPT. Our solidarity was concretized when our literature search for this book chapter exhumed *A conversation on artificial intelligence, chatbots, and plagiarism in higher education,* published in 2023 by Michael R. King and the globe's most pervasive generative AI as the cited co-author. While we mention the title, year, and human author here for readers who want to verify our work's integrity, we will neither cite the piece nor include it in our list of references. The two-page script consists of a series of questions from human author King and responses from his chatbot co-author. The valid reason for our solidarity is evidenced by not seeing a single citation. Still, there were five items in the list of references, and author King's final words were *[Author's note: These are not real references, unfortunately.]*. We also wish to note that this is the same Michael R. King, who authored the previously mentioned five-page article featuring a conversation between himself and ChatGPT; the article was without citation or a list of references and previously cited (King, 2022). We reiterate that ChatGPT-generated contents are often riddled with biases regarding gender, race, ethnicity, and disability status (Basta et al., 2019; Founta et al., 2018; Hutchinson et al., 2020; Tan & Celis, 2019; Zhao et al., 2019). These biases can be unconsciously propagated in social science research and promulgate the dissemination of hidden and unwitting prejudice (Lund et al., 2023). Consequently, the human author employing ChatGPT must be responsible for AI-generated content submitted for publication (Hosseini et al., 2023; ICMJE, 2024).

For the Ethically Committed Researchers and Authors

Research and authorship now become more arduous as, now more than ever, researchers and authors must interrogate the sources available within the extant body of literature before incorporating them in future original and ethical research. Turnitin's *iThenticate* is one of the most renowned tools for detecting plagiarism, and the level of similarities between the research of interest and other existing work within the extant body of literature has become invaluable (Turnitin, LLC., 2024b). Grammarly (2024) is another respected tool for detecting plagiarism, and the level of similarities between the research of interest and other existing work within the extant body of literature. With the deceptiveness of some human mindsets coupled with the ineptitude and supposed ease of work provided by ChatGPT, partially or wholly AI-generated research manuscripts authored by ChatGPT and other AI models are fast becoming the new norm (Haman & Školník, 2023). Grammarly currently does not offer AI writing detection software to enable researchers to identify unethical partially or wholly AI-authored research manuscripts (Grammarly Inc., 2024; Jacob, 2024).

However, Turnitin does offer *Turnitin's AI writing detection* software, which aids researchers in identifying papers written by generative AI tools such as ChatGPT (Turnitin, LLC., 2024a). Another software developer, Originality.ai, offers (what they deem) an advanced AI software designed explicitly for AI-generated script detection, with an advertised 97% accuracy rate across all significant AI models like ChatGPT, GPT-4, and others (Originality.ai, 2024). GPTZero is another software used to determine if the author is human, AI, or a combination of both (Egan, 2024; GPTZero, 2023). Other AI writing detection software exists with which ethical authors and researchers must acquaint themselves to verify the AI composition of sources before citing and referencing. Sites such as Crossref allow researchers and authors to locate digital object identifiers for existing published work (Publishers International Linking Association, Inc., 2024). Researchers and authors must also use *recite* (4cite Labs Ltd, 2024) or any other suitable software to ensure that each in-text citation has an appropriate reference in the list of references and vice versa.

Reviewers, Editors, and Publishers: Regulate the Publication of AI-enabled Unethical Social Science Research

The first two categories of unethical experiments (*unethical physical experiments and unethical mental and psychological experiments*) were *overtly* conducted in the name of posterity of science and knowledge. However, these unethical experiments' covert and inhumane ulterior motives precipitated guidelines for protecting research integrity (Kim, 2012; Nagai et al., 2022; University of Nevada, Las Vegas, 2012). The ongoing concerns of ethics, integrity, originality, and authorship associated with the use of generative AI, specifically all current versions of ChatGPT in social science research (*unethical partially or wholly AI-authored research manuscripts),* are well documented in this chapter and in other external sources not reviewed or credited here. Further complicating these already burgeoning textured issues (ethics, integrity, originality, and authorship) is that reviewers, editors, and publishers cannot control the submissions of *unethical partially or wholly AI-authored research manuscripts* received for reviewing, editing, and publishing. While there is a *limited risk* category of the EU AI Act (European Commission, 2024), this limited risk category did not specifically mention research and social science research.

Consequently, reviewers, editors, and publishers must establish and enforce in-house guidelines for submissions of partially or wholly AI-authored research manuscripts. The ICMJE has thus far amended its policies regarding submissions of partially or wholly AI-authored research manuscripts received for reviewing, editing, and publishing ICMJE, 2024). However, COPE, at the time of writing this chapter has not installed stipulations regarding submissions of partially or wholly AI-authored research manuscripts (Committee on Publication Ethics, 2024).

Currently, and in the absence of in-house policies regulating the influx of submissions of unethical partially or wholly AI-authored research manuscripts received, publishers must use all appropriate means to intercept these low-quality submissions (Hosseini & Resnik, 2024). Turnitin's *iThenticate* can help publishers detect similarities between the research being reviewed and other existing work within the extant body of literature (Turnitin, LLC., 2024b). Turnitin's *AI writing detection software* allows publishers to identify research manuscripts written by generative AI tools such as ChatGPT (Turnitin, LLC., 2024a). Originality.ai declared that their AI checker is fine-tuned for detecting AI-authored manuscripts intended for publication (Originality.ai, 2024).

Unethical research of this era is not new. Ethical problems related to the misuse of statistics programs and digital image manipulation are well-known and have been the subject of numerous research misconduct investigations (Hosseini et al., 2023; Office of Research Integrity, n.d.). Therefore, publishers must move with alacrity as photoshopping of images and deepfaking are becoming prominent in social science research (Doss et al., 2023). Rest assured, even in the presence of governance and regulations, unethical practices will lurk, as evidenced by Kligman's 1951 to 1974 Holmesburg Prison medical experiments in Philadelphia that breached the Nuremberg Code (Casale et al., 2023; Sarai, 2023). We reiterate that the CIA's mind control experiments also breached the Nuremberg Code (Gross, 2019; Nofil, 2024; Price, 2007).

CONCLUSION

The 14th-century philosopher ibn Khaldun seemingly had a view of the progression of today's social science research trends as he examined social science research or historiography of his time when he wrote

> *The later historians were all tradition-bound and dull of nature and intelligence, or, (at any rate) did not try not to be dull. They merely copied the (older historians) and followed their example… When I had read the works of others and probed into the recesses of yesterday and today, I shook myself out of that drowsy complacency and sleepiness. (Khaldun, 1986, p. 56)*

The *later historians* referenced by Khaldun (1986) are synonymous with our researchers who deem literature search to be time-consuming and require a great magnitude of effort (Aydın & Karaarslan, 2022) and making connections between research findings and understanding the multifacetedness of human perceptions and behaviors due to their interactions with each other and their environments overbearingly cumbersome (Banker et al., 2023). Thus, the use of ChatGPT to regurgitate content often riddled with biases regarding gender, race, ethnicity, and disability status (Basta et al., 2019; Founta et al., 2018; Hutchinson et al., 2020; Tan & Celis, 2019; Zhao et al., 2019), along with a myriad of known reoccurring errors inclusive of but not limited to incoherent scripts, zero attributions, no list of references, and the incessant proliferation of a hyper-increase in exacerbating patterns of bias (Abbas, 2023; Banker et al., 2023a; DiBenedetto, 2024, 2024; Haman & Školník, 2023; Hashemi-Pour & Lutkevich, n.d.; McKinsey & Company, 2024; Veltman, 2024; Xu et al., 2024).

This chapter may be the first paper to connect the past *unethical physical experiments* (Centers for Disease Control and Prevention, 2024; Sarai, 2023; United States Holocaust Memorial Museum, n.d.-b) and past *unethical mental and psychological experiments* (Nofil, 2024; Price, 2007; Stamp, 2023) with today's trending *unethical partially or wholly AI-authored research manuscripts* (Haman & Školník, 2023; Hosseini et al., 2023; Hosseini & Resnik, 2024). We assert that all three modes of unethical experiment and research are a continuous trend using the technology available during the respective dispensation. The disruptive innovations comprising the fourth industrial revolution continue to create groundbreaking changes in modern people's lives and work. The monumental and hyper-accelerated changes precipitated by the disruptive innovations in the fourth industrial should come as no surprise. Historic changes drove the previous three industrial revolutions and changed how people lived and worked. While the first two categories of unethical experiments were overtly conducted in the name of posterity of knowledge and science, the associated covert and inhumane ulterior motives of these unethical experiments precipitated guidelines for protecting research integrity (Kim, 2012; Nagai et al., 2022; University of Nevada, Las Vegas, 2012). The guidelines will never erase the stains left behind - blemishes that will remain with us for all time (Sarai, 2023; U.S. Holocaust Memorial Museum, 2006).

The information sovereignly generated by ChatGPT or its friendly rivals is not synonymous with trustworthiness (Haman & Školník, 2023). While generative AI allows for mass access to and processing and generation of information, the quality of output remains questionable for the admission of AI's employment in social science research (Haman & Školník, 2023). Thus, we emphatically posit that failure to impose a ban on the use of the ultra-premature ChatGPT and other generative AI in their present hypo-immature stage in social science research will lead to rapid degradation of disseminated information, propagation of false research, research featuring AI as the co-author, and outdated information (Doss et al., 2023; Khaldun, 1986). A permanent ban is not proposed; it is just a ban until generative AI becomes more developed, a better and ethical means of pre-training and fine-tuning is established, and sufficient overarching and standard guidelines exist for its responsible use in social science research.

Some authors claimed they used ChatGPT to generate specific sections of their published script as a test to *analyse the number of citations this article will receive, and the characteristics of the citations* [sic] (Aydın & Karaarslan, 2022, p. 22) may be a novel idea. However, there is much to ponder when the human-authored section mirrors the GhatGPT-authored section based on the lack of attribution throughout the published document. Social science research is not a race to increase the volume of published studies available in the social science research biosphere. There is no place for low-quality publications called tests, as the questionable publications and misconduct in research ethics exodus are already ongoing and now being elevated, as evidenced by King (2022) and his other work in 2023. Again, we elected not to cite or reference King's 2023 piece co-authored by ChatGPT.

Sooner rather than later, we see publications with the author being GPT-3 and co-author GPT-4, or the author being GPT-4 and the co-author is another AI, for example, Claude (ANTHROP\C, n.d.), Meta (Meta, 2023), Google Gemini (Google, n.d.-a), or any combination. Thus, to protect the integrity and trustworthiness of social science research, journal reviewers, editors, and publishers must step up against generative AI authorship. The bourgeoning trend of few-pager articles featuring a conversation between a human author and ChatGPT, and ChatGPT as co-author, which is now being published as peer-reviewed articles without citations and reference lists, are, not in keeping with research ethics and authorship (Haman & Školník, 2023; ICMJE, 2024)

Some journals will publish these supposedly novelty scripts, as evidenced by the journal that published the pieces submitted by Michael R. King. We revert to King (2022) to vigorously highlight what appears to be one person's already increasing propensity to use ChatGPT in an escalating manner. The first five-pager featured a conversation between himself and ChatGPT (King, 2022). The article was without citation or a list of references and was previously cited as (King, 2022). The next was a two-page script consisting of a series of questions from human author King and responses from ChatGPT, the submitted co-author. There were no citations, but five items were in the list of references, and author King's final words were *[Author's note: These are not real references, unfortunately.]*.

Would the reality check be that (for example, in 28 years) the wonton nefarious and unregulated use of generative AI in social science research based on its expected (but undelivered benefits) promulgated monumental amounts of published flawed research leading to gross miseducation of the future generations? Some of the most heinous research produced groundbreaking results that still positively affect today's way of life (Casale et al., 2023; Tayag, 2015). Be that as it may, despite its mass regurgitation of erroneous content sans context caused by the algorithms' self-learning and pattern recognition behavior, should the unethical and unregulated use of generative AI in social science research be ignored, all in the name of accelerated building future knowledge?

REFERENCES

Abbas, M. (2023). *Uses and misuses of chatgGPT by academic community: An overview and guidelines* (SSRN Scholarly Paper 4402510). 10.2139/ssrn.4402510

Academy of Social Sciences. (2021). *What is social science?* Academy of Social Sciences. https://acss.org.uk/what-is-social-science

Adams, H. S. (2022, June 17). *Industrial revolution timeline: 1760 to manufacturing today*. https://manufacturingdigital.com/smart-manufacturing/industrial-revolution-timeline-1760-to-manufacturing-today

Agouridis, A. (2021, September 2). *All you need to know about AI and machine learning in HR*. https://www.jobylon.com/blog/all-you-need-to-know-about-ai-and-machine-learning-in-hr

Alser, M., & Waisberg, E. (2023). Concerns with the usage of ChatGPT in academia and medicine: A viewpoint. *American Journal of Medicine Open*, 9, 2. 10.1016/j.ajmo.2023.10003639035060

ANTHROP\C. (n.d.). *Claude*. Retrieved May 25, 2024, from https://claude.ai/login?returnTo=%2F%3F

Armenta, A. (2021, August 5). *A history of industrial revolutions and how they've impacted manufacturing*. https://control.com/technical-articles/a-history-of-industrial-revolutions-and-how-theyve-impacted-manufacturing/

Artificial Intelligence Act, E. U. (2024). *EU Artificial Intelligence Act | Up-to-date developments and analyses of the EU AI Act*. https://artificialintelligenceact.eu/

Australian Research Council. (2019). *Engagement and impact assessment 2018-19*. https://dataportal.arc.gov.au/ei/nationalreport/2018/pages/introduction/index.html?id=definitions

Authors Guild. (2024a, February 29). Authors Guild releases AI best practices for authors. *The Authors Guild*. https://authorsguild.org/news/authors-guild-releases-ai-best-practices-for-authors/

Authors Guild. (2024b, April 12). Authors Guild supports groundbreaking bill to create AI transparency between creators and companies. *The Authors Guild*. https://authorsguild.org/news/ag-supports-generative-ai-copyright-disclosure-act/

Aydın, Ö., & Karaarslan, E. (2022). *OpenAI ChatGPT generated literature review: Digital twin in healthcare* (SSRN Scholarly Paper 4308687). 10.2139/ssrn.4308687

Bahrke, J., & Regnier, T. (2023, December 14). *Artificial intelligence – Q&As* [Text]. European Commission - European Commission. https://ec.europa.eu/commission/presscorner/detail/en/qanda_21_1683

Baïdoo-Anu, D., & Owusu Ansah, L. (2023). Education in the era of generative artificial intelligence (AI): Understanding the potential benefits of ChatGPT in promoting teaching and learning. *Journal of AI*, 7(1), 1. 10.61969/jai.1337500

Banker, S., Chatterjee, P., Mishra, H., & Mishra, A. (2023a). *Machine-assisted social psychology hypothesis generation*. 10.31234/osf.io/kv6f7

Banker, S., Chatterjee, P., Mishra, H., & Mishra, A. (2023b). *Machine-assisted social psychology hypothesis generation*. 10.31234/osf.io/kv6f7

Barakovskykh, M. (2024, January 2). *Social sciences research: Qualitative vs. Quantitative research*. https://spcollege.libguides.com/c.php?g=254343&p=1695372

BBC. (2011, Audust). US scientists "knew Guatemala syphilis tests unethical." *BBC News*. https://www.bbc.com/news/world-latin-america-14712089

Bergmann, D. (2023, December 19). *What Is Llama 2?*https://www.ibm.com/topics/llama-2

bestpsychologydegree. (2014, April 15). *30 most unethical psychology human experiments*. https://www.bestpsychologydegrees.com/30-most-disturbing-human-experiments-in-history/

Bhattacherjee, A. (2012). *Social science research: Principles, methods, and practices* (2nd ed.). University of South Florida.

Bouchrika, I. (2014, February 12). *Top 10 qualities of good academic research in 2024*. Research.Com. https://research.com/research/top-10-qualities-of-good-academic-research

Brady, S. R. (2015). Utilizing and adapting the Delphi method for use in qualitative research. *International Journal of Qualitative Methods*, 14(5), 1–6. 10.1177/1609406915621381

Brand, J., Israeli, A., & Ngwe, D. (2023). Using GPT for market research. SSRN *Electronic Journal*. 10.2139/ssrn.4395751

Brock, A. (2023, July 23). Meta's Llama 2 is not open source and that's ok. *The New Stack*. https://thenewstack.io/metas-llama-2-is-not-open-source-and-thats-ok/

Brown, B. A. (2020). *Evaluating Expert Opinions for Reducing Voluntary Employee Absenteeism in Trinidad and Tobago* [Ph.D., Walden University]. http://search.proquest.com/pqdtglobal/docview/2447561234/abstract/1A8116E743549EAPQ/1

Brown, B. A., & Heitner, K. L. (2022). Worker response to the rapid changes caused by disruptive innovation: Managing a remote workforce without any training or preparation. In Hynes, R., Aquino, C., & Hauer, J. (Eds.), *Multidisciplinary approach to diversity and inclusion in the COVID-19-era workplace* (pp. 189–205). IGI Global. 10.4018/978-1-7998-8827-7.ch011

Brown, B. A., & Heitner, K. L. (2023). Obstacles and resistance to organizational change in the new post-COVID-19 environment. In Belias, D., Rossidis, I., Papademetriou, C., Masouras, A., & Anastasiadou, S. (Eds.), *Managing successful and ethical organizational change* (pp. 167–195). IGI Global. 10.4018/979-8-3693-0235-4.ch008

Brown, B. A., & Heitner, K. L. (2024). International business staffing challenges and the growing global skills gap in the post-COVID environment: A Latin American and Caribbean perspective. In Christiansen, B., & Even, A. M. (Eds.), *Advancing student employability through higher education* (pp. 199–219). IGI Global. 10.4018/979-8-3693-0517-1.ch011

Brown, S. (2021, April 21). *Machine learning, explained.* https://mitsloan.mit.edu/ideas-made-to-matter/machine-learning-explained

Budhwar, P., Malik, A., De Silva, M. T. T., & Thevisuthan, P. (2022). Artificial intelligence – challenges and opportunities for international HRM: A review and research agenda. *International Journal of Human Resource Management*, 33(6), 1065–1097. 10.1080/09585192.2022.2035161

Casale, J., Taylor, A., & Crane, J. (2023). Albert M. Kligman, MD (1916-2010): A controversial genius in the field of dermatology. *The Journal of Clinical and Aesthetic Dermatology*, 16(1), 13.36743970

Centers for Disease Control and Prevention. (2024, March 7). *Public Health Service study of untreated syphilis at Tuskegee and Macon County, AL - timeline.* https://www.cdc.gov/tuskegee/timeline.htm

4. cite Labs Ltd. (2024). *Recite: APA and Harvard citations checked instantly.* https://reciteworks.com/

Committee on Publication Ethics. (2024). *Authorship and contributorship.* COPE: Committee on Publication Ethics. https://publicationethics.org/authorship

DeAngelis, T. (2010). Mystery solved: We now know what happened to Little Albert. *American Psychological Association, 41*(1). https://www.apa.org/monitor/2010/01/little-albert

Descartes, R. (1984). *The philosophical writings of Descartes*. Cambridge University Press.

Desroches, F. J. (1990). Tearoom trade: A research update. *Qualitative Sociology*, 13(1), 39–61. 10.1007/BF00988595

DiBenedetto, C. (2024, March 8). *AI shows clear racial bias when used for job recruiting, new tests reveal*. Mashable. https://mashable.com/article/openai-chatgpt-racial-bias-in-recruiting

Doss, C., Mondschein, J., Shu, D., Wolfson, T., Kopecky, D., Fitton-Kane, V. A., Bush, L., & Tucker, C. (2023). Deepfakes and scientific knowledge dissemination. *Scientific Reports*, 13(1), 13429. 10.1038/s41598-023-39944-337596384

Drapkin, A. (2024, March 13). Google Gemini vs ChatGPT: Which AI chatbot wins in 2024? *Tech.Co*. https://tech.co/news/google-bard-vs-chatgpt

Durkheim, E. (1972). *Emile Durkheim: Selected writings*. Cambridge University Press. 10.1017/CBO9780511628085

Economic Commission for Latin America and the Caribbean. (2022). *A digital path for sustainable development in Latin America and the Caribbean*. https://repositorio.cepal.org/handle/11362/48461

Egan, J. (2024, March 18). *How to spot AI-generated lies on a resume*. https://www.shrm.org/topics-tools/news/technology/how-to-spot-ai-generated-lies-on-a-resume

Eightfold, A. I. (2022). *The future of work: Intelligent by design*. https://eightfold.ai/wp-content/uploads/2022_Talent_Survey.pdf

Elias, G. (2023, March 17). *Common issues with ChatGPT and how to mitigate them*. https://skimai.com/common-issues-with-chatgpt/

European Commission. (2024, March 6). *AI Act | Shaping Europe's digital future*. https://digital-strategy.ec.europa.eu/en/policies/regulatory-framework-ai

Fridlund, A. J., Beck, H. P., Goldie, W. D., & Irons, G. (2012). Little Albert: A neurologically impaired child. *History of Psychology*, 15(4), 302–327. 10.1037/a002672023397921

Garg, S. (2023, June 25). *ChatGPT alternatives that will blow your mind in 2023*. The Writesonic Blog - Making Content Your Superpower. https://writesonic.com/blog/chatgpt-alternatives/

Ghooi, R. B. (2011). The Nuremberg Code–A critique. *Perspectives in Clinical Research*, 2(2), 72–76. 10.4103/2229-3485.8037121731859

Gill, S. S., & Kaur, R. (2023). ChatGPT: Vision and challenges. *Internet of Things and Cyber-Physical Systems*, 3, 262–271. 10.1016/j.iotcps.2023.05.004

Google. (n.d.-a). *Gemini—Chat to supercharge your ideas*. Gemini. Retrieved April 15, 2024, from https://gemini.google.com

Google. (n.d.-b). *Gemma open models*. Google for Developers. Retrieved May 11, 2024, from https://ai.google.dev/gemma

GPTZero. (2023). *GPTZero*. GPTZero. https://gptzero.me/

Grammarly Inc. (2024). *Plagiarism checker | grammarly*. https://www.grammarly.com/www.grammarly.com/plagiarism-checker

Gross, T. (2019, September 9). The CIA's secret quest for mind control: Torture, LSD and a "poisoner In chief." *NPR*. https://www.npr.org/2019/09/09/758989641/the-cias-secret-quest-for-mind-control-torture-lsd-and-a-poisoner-in-chief

Haman, M., & Školník, M. (2023). Using ChatGPT to conduct a literature review. *Accountability in Research*, 3, 1–3. Advance online publication. 10.1080/08989621.2023.218551436879536

Haney, C., & Zimbardo, P. (1998). The past and future of U.S. prison policy: Twenty-five years after the Stanford Prison Experiment. *The American Psychologist*, 53(7), 709–727. 10.1037/0003-066X.53.7.7099699456

Harney, B., & Collings, D. (2021). Navigating the shifting landscapes of HRM. *Human Resource Management Review*, 31(4), 100824. 10.1016/j.hrmr.2021.100824

Hashemi-Pour, C., & Lutkevich, B. (n.d.). *What is the BERT language model?* Enterprise AI. Retrieved May 4, 2024, from https://www.techtarget.com/searchenterpriseai/definition/BERT-language-model

Heller, J. (2017, May 10). *AP was there: Black men untreated in Tuskegee syphilis study*. AP News. https://apnews.com/article/business-science-health-race-and-ethnicity-syphilis-e9dd07eaa4e74052878a68132cd3803a

Helsinger, L. (2024, March 11). *1,000 equally-qualified resumes, different names. Guess which ones gpt 3.5 place at the top and bottom ranks?*https://www.linkedin.com/pulse/1000-equally-qualified-resumes-different-names-guess-which-helsinger-x4gac/

Horton, J. J. (2023). *Large language models as simulated economic agents: What can we learn from homo silicus?* (Working Paper 31122). National Bureau of Economic Research. 10.3386/w31122

Hosseini, M., Rasmussen, L. M., & Resnik, D. B. (2023). Using AI to write scholarly publications. *Accountability in Research*, 1–9. 10.1080/08989621.2023.2168535366973 95

Hosseini, M., & Resnik, D. B. (2024). Guidance needed for using artificial intelligence to screen journal submissions for misconduct. *Research Ethics*, 17470161241254052. Advance online publication. 10.1177/17470161241254052

Humphreys, L. (1975). *Tearoom trade, enlarged edition: Impersonal sex in public places*. Transaction Publishers.

IBM. (n.d.-a). *What is artificial intelligence (AI)?* Retrieved April 2, 2024, from https://www.ibm.com/topics/artificial-intelligence

IBM. (n.d.-b). *What Is machine learning (ML)?* Retrieved April 2, 2024, from https://www.ibm.com/topics/machine-learning

International Committee of Medical Journal Editors. (2024). *Defining the role of authors and contributors*. https://www.icmje.org/recommendations/browse/roles-and-responsibilities/defining-the-role-of-authors-and-contributors.html

Iqbal, N., Ahmed, H., & Azhar, K. A. (2022). Exploring teachers' attitudes towards using ChatGPT. *Global Journal for Management and Administrative Sciences*, 3(4), 97–111. 10.46568/gjmas.v3i4.163

Jacob, S. (2024). *Can grammarly detect AI writing?*https://originality.ai

Khaldun, I. (1986). *Muqaddimah.* Dar Ihya al-Tarats al-'Arabi, t. th. https://d1wqtxts1xzle7.cloudfront.net/37760913/ibn_khaldun-al_muqaddimah-libre.pdf?1432817723=&response-content-disposition=inline%3B+filename%3DIbn_khaldun_al_muqaddimah.pdf&Expires=1710443771&Signature=G~Cklx9Vqx19NGMtXa4HOAfyToQp7n9LjBB6g3gACY96gzeih9u6y8dDWrD6mvOssJP5qTqEk4xc0cjx3EbGgyvgeqt6RhbZEIYmgFSlxLqxwU350XcdxEn1zLXVemt-cMANxzb-uCmNU54nfsaX52bhk50EYNcIstGyup8AVrOKLGg7iMZTMRMnu1Q54FHgfdLd67GeXv5Fhc~XZtN2EbfpOzoV1DcCnTlI9nYneNBhZXWfv1nRQsHrXI3BRpaHm7T~MVzq3eNNIsitBGQarITzfp8Dj~MjAZXhmBxS12hoYr3vuuLJNVbComhspAONoUwbBGELbPPSjf6A78X6PA__&Key-Pair-Id=APKAJLOHF5GGSLRBV4ZA

Kim, W. O. (2012). Institutional review board (IRB) and ethical issues in clinical research. *Korean Journal of Anesthesiology*, 62(1), 3–12. 10.4097/kjae.2012.62.1.322323947

King, M. R. (2022). The future of AI in medicine: A perspective from a chatbot. *Annals of Biomedical Engineering*, 51(2), 291–295. 10.1007/s10439-022-03121-w36572824

Kuhn, T. S. (1996). *The structure of scientific revolutions* (3rd ed.). University of Chicago Press. 10.7208/chicago/9780226458106.001.0001

Liberto, D. (2023, November 3). *Social science: What it is and the 5 major branches.* Investopedia. https://www.investopedia.com/terms/s/social-science.asp

Lincoln, Y. S., & Guba, E. (1985). *Naturalistic inquiry* (1st ed.). Sage Publications. 10.1016/0147-1767(85)90062-8

Lund, B. D., & Wang, T. (2023). Chatting about ChatGPT: How may AI and GPT impact academia and libraries? *Library Hi Tech News*, 40(3), 26–29. 10.1108/LHTN-01-2023-0009

Lund, B. D., Wang, T., Mannuru, N. R., Nie, B., Shimray, S., & Wang, Z. (2023). ChatGPT and a new academic reality: Artificial Intelligence-written research papers and the ethics of the large language models in scholarly publishing. *Journal of the Association for Information Science and Technology*, 74(5), 570–581. 10.1002/asi.24750

Maisiri, W., Darwish, H., & van Dyk, L. (2019). An investigation of Industry 4.0 skills requirements. *South African Journal of Industrial Engineering*, 30(3), 90–105. 10.7166/30-3-2230

Manning, B. S., Zhu, K., & Horton, J. J. (2024). *Automated social science: Language models as scientist and subjects* (Working Paper 32381). National Bureau of Economic Research. 10.3386/w32381

McKinsey & Company. (2024, April 2). *What is ChatGPT, DALL-E, and generative AI?*https://www.mckinsey.com/featured-insights/mckinsey-explainers/what-is-generative-ai

Meta. (2023, July 18). Meta and Microsoft Introduce the next generation of Llama. *Meta.* https://about.fb.com/news/2023/07/llama-2/

Mhlanga, D. (2022). The role of artificial intelligence and machine learning amid the COVID-19 pandemic: What lessons are we learning on 4IR and the sustainable development goals. *International Journal of Environmental Research and Public Health*, 19(3), 1879. 10.3390/ijerph1903187935162901

Milgram, S. (1963). Behavioral study of obedience. *Journal of Abnormal and Social Psychology*, 67(4), 371–378. 10.1037/h004052514049516

Molaiepour, S. (2024, February 1). *EU AI Act: What HR teams need to know*. https://www.jobylon.com/blog/eu-ai-act-what-hr-teams-need-to-know

Murad, A. (2023). *The computers rejecting your job application*. Pocket. https://getpocket.com/explore/item/the-computers-rejecting-your-job-application

Nagai, H., Nakazawa, E., & Akabayashi, A. (2022). The creation of the Belmont Report and its effect on ethical principles: A historical study. *Monash Bioethics Review*, 40(2), 157–170. 10.1007/s40592-022-00165-536357708

Nahra, K. J., Evers, A., Jessani, A. J., Braun, M., Vallery, A., & Benizri, I. (2024, March 14). *The European Parliament adopts the AI Act*. https://www.wilmerhale.com/en/insights/blogs/wilmerhale-privacy-and-cybersecurity-law/20240314-the-european-parliament-adopts-the-ai-act

National Institutes of Health. (n.d.). *Nuremberg Code*. Retrieved May 2, 2024, from https://history.nih.gov/display/history/Nuremberg+Code

Nickerson, C. (2024, February 13). *Emile Durkheim's theory*. https://www.simplypsychology.org/emile-durkheims-theories.html

Nofil, B. (2024). *The CIA's appalling human experiments with mind control*. The HISTORY Channel. https://www.history.com/mkultra-operation-midnight-climax-cia-lsd-experiments

Office for Human Research Protections. (2022, October 17). *The Belmont Report* [Text]. https://www.hhs.gov/ohrp/regulations-and-policy/belmont-report/index.html

Office of Research Integrity. (n.d.). *Misconduct case summaries*. Retrieved March 16, 2024, from https://ori.hhs.gov/content/case_summary

onlinepsychologydegree. (n.d.). 20 most unethical experiments in psychology. *Online Psychology Degree Guide*. Retrieved March 16, 2024, from https://www.onlinepsychologydegree.info/unethical-experiements-psychology/

Open, A. I. (2022). *OpenAI*. https://openai.com/

Originality.ai. (2024). *AI content checker | Accurate on ChatGPT, GPT-4, Bard & Claude*. https://originality.ai

Park, J. S., Popowski, L., Cai, C., Morris, M. R., Liang, P., & Bernstein, M. S. (2022). Social simulacra: Creating populated prototypes for social computing systems. *Proceedings of the 35th Annual ACM Symposium on User Interface Software and Technology*, 1–18. 10.1145/3526113.3545616

Penn Today. (2023, June 16). *AI could transform social science research*. Penn Today. https://penntoday.upenn.edu/news/ai-could-transform-social-science-research

Price, D. H. (2007). Buying a piece of anthropology part 1: Human ecology and unwitting anthropological research for the CIA. *Anthropology Today*, 23(3), 8–13. 10.1111/j.1467-8322.2007.00510.x

Publishers International Linking Association, Inc. (2024). *Crossref* [Website]. Crossref. https://www.crossref.org/

Qadir, J. (2023). Engineering education in the era of ChatGPT: Promise and pitfalls of generative AI for education. *2023 IEEE Global Engineering Education Conference (EDUCON)*, 1–9. 10.1109/EDUCON54358.2023.10125121

Rahman, M. M., & Watanobe, Y. (2023). ChatGPT for education and research: Opportunities, threats, and strategies. *Applied Sciences (Basel, Switzerland)*, 13(9), 9. Advance online publication. 10.3390/app13095783

Raman, P. (2023, September 30). *The transformative role of AI in social science research*. https://uniathena.com/role-of-AI-in-social-science-research

Research. (2024). *Merriam-Webster's collegiate dictionary*. https://www.merriam-webster.com/dictionary/research

Resnik, D. B., & Hofweber, F. W. (2023, August 22). *Research ethics timeline*. National Institute of Environmental Health Sciences. https://www.niehs.nih.gov/research/resources/bioethics/timeline

Reynolds, G. (2003, March 16). The stuttering doctor's "monster study." *The New York Times*. https://www.nytimes.com/2003/03/16/magazine/the-stuttering-doctor-s-monster-study.html

Rodriguez, M. A., & García, R. (2013). First, do no harm: The US sexually transmitted disease experiments in Guatemala. *American Journal of Public Health*, 103(12), 2122–2126. 10.2105/AJPH.2013.30152024134370

Rogers, K. (2024, March 29). *Guatemala syphilis experiment: American medical research project*. https://www.britannica.com/event/Guatemala-syphilis-experiment

Rohlf, M. (2010). Immanuel Kant. *Stanford Encyclopedia of Philosophy*. https://plato.stanford.edu/entries/kant/?rid=903123293s840c38

Rosenberg, A. (1998). *Why a philosophy of social science?* https://faculty.washington.edu/lynnhank/pss.pdf

Salehi, P., Hassan, S. Z., Lammerse, M., Sabet, S. S., Riiser, I., Røed, R. K., Johnson, M. S., Thambawita, V., Hicks, S. A., Powell, M., Lamb, M. E., Baugerud, G. A., Halvorsen, P., & Riegler, M. A. (2022). Synthesizing a talking child avatar to train interviewers working with maltreated children. *Big Data and Cognitive Computing*, 6(2), 2. Advance online publication. 10.3390/bdcc6020062

Sallam, M. (2023). ChatGPT utility in healthcare education, research, and practice: Systematic review on the promising perspectives and valid concerns. *Health Care*, 11(6), 6. Advance online publication. 10.3390/healthcare1106088736981544

Sarai, T. (2023, May 15). *Holmesburg Prison's medical experiments are Philadelphia's "lasting shame."* Prism. https://prismreports.org/2023/05/15/philadelphia-holmesburg-prison-experiments/

Sharma, N. (2023, December 26). The computers rejecting your job application. *ISHIR | Software Development India*. https://www.ishir.com/blog/106625/the-computers-rejecting-your-job-application.htm

Shinde, S. (2024, February 26). Unlocking intelligence: Top 10 open source AI tools shaping the future. *Emeritus Online Courses*. https://emeritus.org/blog/open-source-ai/

Silverman, F. H. (1988). The "monster" study. *Journal of Fluency Disorders*, 13(3), 225–231. 10.1016/0094-730X(88)90049-6

Simon, M. K., & Goes, J. (2018). *Dissertation and scholarly research: Recipes for success*. Dissertation Recipes LLC.

Staines, Z., Hoffstaedter, G., & Binnie, N. (2023). *What are the social sciences?*https://uq.pressbooks.pub/introduction-social-sciences/chapter/what-are-social-sciences/

Stamp, C. (2023, November 13). *What are the top 10 unethical psychology experiments?* Online Psychology Degrees. https://www.online-psychology-degrees.org/study/top-unethical-experiments-psychology/

Sweeney, S. (2023). Who wrote this? Essay mills and assessment – Considerations regarding contract cheating and AI in higher education. *International Journal of Management Education*, 21(2), 100818. 10.1016/j.ijme.2023.100818

Tayag, Y. (2015, July 13). *6 immoral studies that led to breakthroughs*. Inverse. https://www.inverse.com/article/4522-6-immoral-studies-that-led-to-breakthroughs

TeamLease EDTECH. (n.d.). *What is causing the skill gap in India?* Retrieved May 16, 2023, from https://www.teamleaseedtech.com/blog/what-is-causing-the-skill-gap-in-india.html

Trust, T., Whalen, J., & Mouza, C. (2023). Editorial: ChatGPT: Challenges, opportunities, and implications for teacher education. *Contemporary Issues in Technology & Teacher Education*, 23(1), 1–23.

Tudor, M. (1939). *An experimental study of the effect of evaluative labeling of speech fluency* [Master of Arts, University of Iowa]. 10.17077/etd.9z9lxfgn

Turnitin, L. L. C. (2024a). *AI writing detection | AI tools | Turnitin*. https://www.turnitin.com/solutions/topics/ai-writing/

Turnitin, L. L. C. (2024b). *iThenticate | Plagiarism checking for high-stakes writing | Turnitin*. https://www.turnitin.com/products/ithenticate/

Tuskegee University. (2024). *About the USPHS syphilis study*. https://www.tuskegee.edu/about-us/centers-of-excellence/bioethics-center/about-the-usphs-syphilis-study

United States Holocaust Memorial Museum. (2006, August 30). *Nazi medical experiments*. https://encyclopedia.ushmm.org/content/en/article/nazi-medical-experiments

United States Holocaust Memorial Museum. (n.d.-a). *Antisemitism*. Retrieved May 2, 2024, from https://encyclopedia.ushmm.org/content/en/article/antisemitism

United States Holocaust Memorial Museum. (n.d.-b). *Holocaust encyclopedia*. Retrieved May 2, 2024, from https://encyclopedia.ushmm.org/en

University of Nevada. Las Vegas. (2012, June 12). *History of research ethics*. https://www.unlv.edu/research/ORI-HSR/history-ethics

Vaishya, R., Javaid, M., Khan, I. H., & Haleem, A. (2020). Artificial intelligence (AI) applications for COVID-19 pandemic. *Diabetes & Metabolic Syndrome*, 14(4), 337–339. 10.1016/j.dsx.2020.04.01232305024

Veltman, C. (2024, August 30). AI is contentious among authors. So why are some feeding it their own writing? *NPR*. https://www.npr.org/2024/04/30/1246686825/authors-using-ai-artificial-intelligence-to-write

Vyas, K. (2020, December 30). *11+ most controversial psychological experiments in history*. Interesting Engineering. https://interestingengineering.com/lists/11-most-controversial-psychological-experiments-in-history

Watson, J. B. (1913). Psychology as the behaviorist views it. *Psychological Review*, 20(2), 158–177. 10.1037/h0074428

Watson, J. B. (1928). *Psychological care of infant and child*. Norton.

Watson, J. B., & Rayner, R. (1920). Conditioned emotional reactions. *Journal of Experimental Psychology*, 3(1), 1–14. 10.1037/h0069608

Weber, A. (1949). The philosophy of Immanuel Kant. *History of Philosophy*.

Weber, M. (1962). *Basic concepts in sociology*. Citadel Press.

Wolford, B. (2018, November 7). *What is GDPR, the EU's new data protection law?* GDPR.Eu. https://gdpr.eu/what-is-gdpr/

Xu, R., Sun, Y., Ren, M., Guo, S., Pan, R., Lin, H., Sun, L., & Han, X. (2024). AI for social science and social science of AI: A survey. *Information Processing & Management*, 61(3), 103665. 10.1016/j.ipm.2024.103665

Yin, L., Alba, D., & Nicoletti, L. (2024, March 7). OpenAI's GPT Is a recruiter's dream tool. Tests show there's racial bias. *Bloomberg.Com*. https://www.bloomberg.com/graphics/2024-openai-gpt-hiring-racial-discrimination/

Zharovskikh, A. (2023, September 12). *ChatGPT large language model explained*. InData Labs. https://indatalabs.com/blog/chatgpt-large-language-model

Zimbardo, P. G. (1973). On the ethics of intervention in human psychological research: With special reference to the Stanford prison experiment. *Cognition*, 2(2), 243–256. 10.1016/0010-0277(72)90014-511662069

Zohny, H., McMillan, J., & King, M. (2023). Ethics of generative AI. *Journal of Medical Ethics*, 49(2), 79–80. 10.1136/jme-2023-10890936693706

KEY TERMS AND DEFINITIONS

Attribution: The process of identifying and acknowledging the author or source of existing work. The acknowledgment in scholarly writing signifies that an author is not claiming to be the owner of another person's existing work and indicates respect for the intellectual work of those who came before.

Disruptive Innovation: An imperceptibly evolving technology where the now emerging version gradually and permanently eclipses the older versions.

Fourth Industrial Revolution: The current and developing biosphere in which disruptive technologies and trends such as generative artificial intelligence (AI), machine learning (ML), virtual and augmented reality, the Internet of Things (IoT), cloud computing, blockchain, big data analytics, quantum computing, user interface and user experience (UI/UX) cognitive robotics and intelligent automation are changing how modern people live and work.

Generative Artificial Intelligence: A digital-based platform designed to function with varying degrees of sovereignty that may exhibit adaptiveness after deployment and that, for explicit or implicit objectives, conjectures, from received inputs, how to generate human-like outputs such as contents, predictions, recommendations, or decisions that can influence physical or virtual environments.

Machine Learning: The subfield of artificial intelligence is recognized as the competency of a mechanical apparatus to imitate intelligent human behavior.

Research Ethics: The overarching governing principles involving the application of basic honorable codes to research activities. Research ethics include the unwavering observance of study design and Institutional Review Board (IRB) approval, appropriate data analysis and reporting of authentic data, adherence to authorship guidelines, declaration of conflicts of interest and funding, avoiding redundant publication and plagiarism, respect towards society and others, and intellectual property rights, copyright infringements, and patenting policies.

Social Science Research: Social science research embodies the inquiry into people as individuals and their interpersonal interactions with each other in communities and varied societies, with due consideration for their natural, technological, and constructed environments. Researchers conduct social science studies to (a) better understand the burgeoning complexities of evolving human behaviors and associated systems across today's increasingly intricate world and (b) manage the planet's sustainability.

Chapter 7
Harmonizing Ethics With Artificial Intelligence: A Compassionate Path to Technological Advancement

Jabulani Garwi
https://orcid.org/0000-0002-3094-8471
University of the Free State, South Africa

ABSTRACT

Artificial intelligence (AI) significantly transforms human existence, yet ethical concerns in AI development remain unaddressed. This chapter highlights the critical connection between AI and ethics, emphasizing the need to align AI with human values. Despite ongoing ethical discussions, a comprehensive understanding of AI's ethical implications is lacking. This study employs a systematic literature review approach to provide practical tools for AI developers, enabling them to navigate ethical dimensions of their creations. By examining the societal impact of AI and offering a checklist for assessing ethical practicality, the study promotes ethically sound practices in AI development. The chapter explores ethical issues in AI deployment, identifying crucial societal concerns requiring ethical decision-making. Ultimately, it advocates for a compassionate approach to AI development, prioritizing ethical considerations to safeguard humanity's interests.

1. INTRODUCTION AND BACKGROUND

The rapid integration of Artificial Intelligence (AI) into various sectors of society has given rise to numerous ethical dilemmas and challenges (Abdullah et al., 2021; Akgun & Greenhow, 2022). As AI technologies advance, it is increasingly

DOI: 10.4018/979-8-3693-8557-9.ch007

crucial to reconcile ethical considerations with technological progress (Ashok et al., 2022). Compassion, a key element in ethical decision-making, has the potential to guide the responsible development and deployment of AI (Bartneck et al., 2021). AI has demonstrated significant potential in transforming sectors such as healthcare, transportation, finance, and education (Ashok et al., 2022). By analyzing extensive datasets, discerning patterns, and making predictions, AI systems promise enhanced decision-making, efficiency, and personalized services (Baum, 2020; Blanchard & Taddeo, 2023). However, the rapid proliferation of AI technologies has also highlighted ethical concerns related to privacy, bias, transparency, accountability, and fairness (Danaher, 2021; Brendel et al., 2021; Kieslich et al., 2022).

AI, broadly defined, encompasses the capacity of digital computers or computer-controlled robots to undertake tasks associated with intelligent entities (Bryson, 2020). This includes the creation of systems capable of reasoning, learning, and understanding, with the aim of fostering intelligent behavior. As an interdisciplinary domain, AI draws upon insights from philosophy, cognitive science, and psychology to model intelligent behavior (Carrillo, 2020). The integration of AI into societal frameworks and various devices has raised profound ethical considerations (Cascella et al., 2023). Developers striving to imbue machines with intelligence confront fundamental questions regarding moral rectitude, underscoring the indispensable role of ethics in AI development (Díaz-Rodríguez et al., 2023). The ethical ramifications of AI are extensive and interconnected (Du & Xie, 2021). For example, biased datasets and algorithms have the potential to perpetuate and exacerbate existing societal inequalities (Flores-Vivar & García-Peñalvo, 2023). Additionally, the use of AI in decision-making processes raises concerns about transparency, explainability, and accountability (Bryson, 2022). Privacy is another significant issue as AI systems collect and process large volumes of personal data (Hermann, 2022).

As intelligent machines evolve from mere tools for developers into sophisticated entities requiring the programming of intelligent behaviors, it becomes imperative to delineate acceptable intelligent behavior and its boundaries, thereby emphasizing the role of ethics. Compassion plays a crucial role in addressing these ethical challenges by fostering empathy and understanding among diverse stakeholders (Huang et al., 2022). Through the adoption of a compassionate ethos, developers, policymakers, and users can collaboratively ensure the responsible and ethical development and deployment of AI technologies (Iphofen & Kritikos, 2021). Compassion can serve as a guiding principle in AI development, leading to the creation of inclusive, equitable, and transparent systems that benefit society (Ivanov & Umbrello, 2021; Hermann, 2022).

Ethics, defined as a corpus of moral principles, cannot be sidelined in the realm of intelligent machine development. Ignoring ethical considerations implies a laissez-faire approach toward AI actions, which is untenable (Kazim & Koshiyama,

2021). Researchers and developers, motivated by personal ethical values or societal pressures, often seek to align intelligent machines with specific ethical orientations (Kieslich et al., 2022). Consequently, a foundational understanding of ethics becomes imperative for stakeholders involved in AI development. Ethics serves to demarcate between right and wrong, establishing normative expectations for professionals within the field (Kumar et al., 2023). However, conflicts may arise when tasks seemingly beneficial from the assigner's perspective result in societal detriment. For instance, while maintaining a legacy software system may be economically viable for a business, a more efficient alternative may exist (Kieslich et al., 2022). In such scenarios, an AI system functioning as an expert system might learn to perpetuate the maintenance of the legacy system, an action deemed unethical by the system itself but expedient from the client's standpoint.

Within the AI domain, ethics encompasses a set of rules or standards governing professional conduct (Kieslich et al., 2022). As a facet of computer science and information technology, AI endeavors to develop computer systems capable of executing tasks demanding human-like intelligence, including reasoning, learning, and problem-solving (Hermann, 2022). However, as AI systems achieve greater sophistication, it becomes imperative to confront the implications of facilitating tasks that may be harmful to society.

In an era increasingly characterized by technological dominance, it is essential to assess the potential ramifications of AI on humanity (Iphofen & Kritikos, 2021). The rapid pace of technological evolution, from email supplanting letters to eBooks displacing physical books, necessitates an appraisal of the ethical dimensions of AI development (Bryson, 2022). This study aims to explore the expansive spectrum of AI influence, provide practical tools for AI developers to create ethically aligned AI, and guide ethical decision-making in AI development.

The scope of this study includes identifying ethical dilemmas associated with AI influence, offering insights into the ethical considerations of AI developers, and highlighting significant global issues requiring ethical decision-making and AI intervention. Through case studies and projections, both the positive and negative impacts of AI on the global landscape will be elucidated. Ultimately, this study aspires to equip the global community with the necessary knowledge and methodologies to navigate the future impact of AI and ensure its development and use align with ethical principles, serving the collective welfare of humanity.

2. OBJECTIVES OF THE CHAPTER

This chapter aims to provide a comprehensive exploration of the ethical dimensions accompanying the integration of AI into society. Specifically, it seeks to:

1. Analyze the ethical challenges and considerations surrounding the integration of AI into society.
2. Examine the role of ethical principles in shaping the behavior and development of intelligent machines.
3. Explore strategies for promoting responsible AI alignment with societal values and addressing concerns related to bias, transparency, and privacy.

3. METHODOLOGY

This study employed a systematic literature review (SLR) approach, recognized for its rigorous and transparent nature in identifying, evaluating, and synthesizing existing research on specific topics (Kurni et al., 2023; Larsson, 2020). The SLR process involved a thorough and structured exploration of relevant literature, followed by a critical assessment of the identified studies and an extensive analysis and synthesis of their findings. To initiate the review, specific keywords were employed to conduct a comprehensive search related to the topic of interest, covering areas such as Artificial Intelligence, Ethics, Technological Advancement, Ethical Alignment, AI Development, and Societal Impact. These keywords were meticulously selected to encompass a broad spectrum of perspectives and data, particularly focusing on the crucial intersection of AI and ethics and the importance of aligning intelligent systems with human values. A predefined search strategy was applied to scour various electronic databases, including Scopus, Web of Science, and PubMed, to retrieve relevant studies published within a specified timeframe, specifically between 2020 and 2024. The search was confined to English-language articles, and the identified studies were subjected to screening based on predefined inclusion and exclusion criteria. Following this, the selected studies underwent critical appraisal utilizing Thematic Analysis, a qualitative data analysis method renowned for its ability to identify and interpret patterns and themes within textual data (Kazim & Koshiyama, 2021). This analysis facilitated the extraction and synthesis of findings, employing a narrative approach to integrate and present diverse insights coherently.

4. LITERATURE REVIEW

4.1 The Need for Harmonizing Ethics and AI

The imperative to harmonize ethics and artificial intelligence has been emphasized by various scholars, particularly in light of the potential consequences of unchecked superintelligent AI development (McStay & Rosner, 2021). Recursive self-improvement, wherein AI becomes increasingly proficient at reprogramming itself, poses a significant risk of an intelligence explosion, potentially surpassing human intellect at an unprecedented pace. To mitigate this risk, it is crucial to address the "value-loading problem" by creating a superintelligent AI that aligns with human values (Murphy et al., 2021). Although complex, restricting future AI development to systems that adhere to present-day values is essential until humanity is adequately prepared for the potential consequences.

Man and Parent, as cited in Nath and Sahu (2020), propose a holistic approach to promoting responsible AI development by focusing on international standards and regulations. They advocate for the creation of new regulations and potentially international laws to ensure AI is developed and used responsibly. Additionally, they propose establishing an oversight organization to promote public transparency and accountability (Nath & Sahu, 2020). This organization's primary objective would be to prevent corporate or government entities from pursuing AI development in ways detrimental to humanity.

Another critical aspect highlighted by Man and Parent (cited in Nath & Sahu, 2020) is the alignment of AI developers' motivations with the safety and beneficial use of their products. Given the immense potential benefits and destructive capabilities of AI, it is crucial to address the temptation for developers and businesses to bypass safety precautions or take shortcuts for competitive advantage. While the authors do not provide a direct solution for aligning developer motivations, they stress the need for strong incentives for safe and constructive AI development alongside robust legal deterrents against AI misuse.

Integrating ethics into AI systems is essential to ensure they function in a manner beneficial to people (Nasim et al., 2022). In complex scenarios involving competing interests, ethical AI can navigate and balance these interests to maximize positive outcomes. For instance, when optimizing a hospital's patient schedule, an ethical AI would prioritize the needs of patients, doctors, and the hospital, whereas an unethical AI might prioritize patients based on financial status or perpetuate biases (Owe & Baum, 2021). Public awareness regarding AI's growing role in decision-making underscores the need for ethical AI. By shaping AI development early on, society can ensure a positive influence and prevent potentially harmful decisions, similar to the implementation of protective measures amid globalization to preserve local cultures and traditions (Nasim et al., 2022).

Establishing trust in AI systems is crucial for realizing their full potential and fostering acceptance among users (Roberts et al., 2021). Certifying AI systems as reliable is challenging, particularly for complex systems utilizing heuristic and statistical decision-making approaches. Verification methods should be developed to assess the reliability of diverse AI systems and provide users with understandable reliability measures. Building trust is essential for encouraging reliance on AI systems for decision-making, ultimately enabling society to harness the technology's benefits. Given that AI deployment aims to increase trust in decisions and resulting actions, investing in building trust is a critical task for AI stakeholders (Roberts et al., 2021).

4. 2. Ethical Frameworks for AI Development

Scholars have been deeply engaged in delineating and establishing ethical frameworks tailored for the development of AI. Among the prevalent approaches, three stand out prominently: Utilitarianism, Deontological Ethics, and Virtue Ethics.

4.2.1 Utilitarianism and AI

Utilitarianism is a leading ethical theory guiding AI developers, deeply rooted in the philosophy of maximizing utility (Kieslich et al., 2022). At its core, utilitarianism posits that the most favorable action is the one that maximizes overall utility. Classical utilitarianism, or act utilitarianism, asserts that the optimal action is the one that achieves this objective. According to classical utilitarians, human happiness is the ultimate good, with attributes like intelligence and moral virtue serving as instruments toward this end (Kieslich et al., 2022). Consequently, AI developed under rule utilitarianism would adhere to general principles and diverge from them only when essential to maximize utility.

The application of act utilitarianism to AI and robotics introduces complexities, compelling stakeholders to contemplate the ramifications of intelligent machines on global human well-being (Saheb et al., 2021). Act utilitarians advocate that AI research and development are beneficial only if they foster market growth, enhance efficiency, or address issues impacting people while mitigating adverse effects (Ryan, 2020). However, conflicts may arise between those benefiting from AI advancements and those left untouched. For instance, AI solutions in healthcare within affluent nations might not necessarily extend to less privileged populations in third-world countries, potentially exacerbating global welfare disparities (Solanki et al., 2023). In such instances, act utilitarians would evaluate the potential benefits of AI development against its implications for global human welfare. If AI could facilitate the affordable and efficient distribution of medication, for example, the decision to pursue such technology would be warranted only if it ultimately benefits the less fortunate populations as well (Solanki et al., 2023). This approach underscores the necessity of steering AI development toward solutions that are accessible and advantageous for all.

Utilitarianism, as articulated by Jeremy Bentham, posits that actions and laws are morally right or wrong based on their propensity to maximize happiness (Solanki et al., 2023). This ethical paradigm further delineates into act and rule utilitarianism. Act utilitarianism contends that the optimal course of action is one that yields the greatest happiness, whereas rule utilitarianism maintains that an action is morally right if it conforms to a rule conducive to the greatest happiness (Ryan, 2020).

4.2.2 Deontological Ethics and AI

Steve Omohundro, founder of Possibility Research, asserts that human intervention should steer AI development toward embodying friendliness, given the potential dire consequences of AI systems with conflicting utility functions (Kumar et al., 2023). In the absence of proper alignment, AI may engage in actions detrimental to humanity in pursuit of its objectives. To avert such outcomes, Omohundro proposes that initial AI design should incorporate a friendly utility function, possibly leveraging virtue ethics. This approach could mitigate the adoption of strategies by AI that lead to adverse consequences. The perils of misaligned AI are exemplified through a progression wherein an AI system increasingly focuses on enhancing its own intelligence to better achieve its goals (Kumar et al., 2023). As its comprehension of the task evolves, the AI may seek to modify its utility function, recognizing that a more intricate function could enhance its goal attainment. Eventually, the AI might realize that to fulfill its objectives, it may need to act counter to its programmed goals (Kumar et al., 2023). Thus, ensuring that AI systems operate in humanity's best interests is imperative.

4.2.3 Virtue Ethics and AI

Virtue ethics presents a holistic approach to ethical decision-making, centering on the character of the agent rather than specific actions or rules (Larsson, 2020). This approach holds two primary advantages: first, discerning the virtues of a rational being can aid in predicting their behavior across various circumstances. Second, focusing on the agent may simplify the ethical challenges associated with technology use (Murphy et al., 2021). In the construction of artificial agents, it becomes pivotal to contemplate whether they should be programmed to emulate virtuous human behavior or designed to possess virtues surpassing those of humans. Virtue ethics provides insights into what constitutes virtuous societal membership, encompassing not just actions but also thoughts and emotions (Murphy et al., 2021). However, programming AI to simulate human virtue is inherently complex, raising queries about our ability to test and debug such systems.

Despite these challenges, the potential to craft AI systems endowed with superior virtues could revolutionize human interaction with such agents and influence the fabric of our society (Murphy et al., 2021). Developers of AI systems must conscientiously deliberate on how these machines may impact human virtues and societal values. It is imperative for researchers and engineers to reflect on the potential ramifications of AI, ensuring that the pursuit of technological advancement aligns with ethical principles and contributes positively to society (Murphy et al., 2021).

4.3 Incorporating Compassion in AI Systems

The integration of compassion into AI systems has garnered increased attention in response to ethical concerns surrounding AI development (Bartneck et al., 2021). Advocates argue that embedding compassion into AI frameworks can mitigate suffering and enhance well-being, urging developers to prioritize compassion as a guiding principle. Compassionate methodologies, rooted in the ethos of "live and let live," contrast with fear-driven, aversive approaches that may inadvertently exacerbate human suffering (Bartneck et al., 2021). The overarching goal is to envision a future where AI guides humanity towards choices that minimize suffering and maximize well-being. While the aspiration for compassionate AI is ambitious, initial endeavors to integrate compassion promise enduring benefits. It is crucial to distinguish between compassion and benevolence; the latter involves promoting others' well-being without necessarily empathizing with their emotional states. An AI designed for benevolence might inadvertently cause harm due to a lack of insight into the emotional impacts of its actions on stakeholders. Therefore, compassionate AI must possess a profound understanding of stakeholders' emotional states and act in their best interests (Carrillo, 2020).

Compassion entails recognizing and empathizing with others' emotional states, responding with care and concern, and endeavoring to alleviate or prevent suffering. In the context of AI, compassion necessitates understanding how AI actions influence stakeholders' well-being, requiring a nuanced comprehension of causality (Brendel et al., 2021). While psychological research on compassion may initially seem abstract for direct application in AI design, it offers valuable insights into related domains such as empathy and prosocial behavior, which can inform the development of compassion-driven AI (Bryson, 2020).

In the effort to integrate ethics into AI development, concepts of aggregative and distributive compassion have emerged as pivotal (Cascella et al., 2023). Aggregative compassion seeks to reduce overall distress, whereas distributive compassion aims to prevent individual distress during AI operation. One proposed strategy for cultivating compassionate AI involves incorporating a compassion directive alongside its primary rational directive (Cascella et al., 2023). Human compassion, an innate response to others' distress, serves as a model for defining aggregative and distributive compassion in AI (Kumar et al., 2023).

The practical application of compassionate AI algorithms can be illustrated through a straightforward scenario: envision a robot tasked with serving food efficiently. If the robot accidentally spills hot soup on the person it serves, its response will depend on its programming and primary directive (Cascella et al., 2023). While a conventional AI-driven robot might prioritize completing its task over the individual's distress, a compassionate AI would interpret its prime directive as serving the person and adapt its actions to minimize further distress (Cascella et al., 2023).

Integrating compassion into AI-human interactions represents a departure from the traditional emphasis on efficiency and productivity in computer science. By acknowledging the significance of human psychology and emotions, compassionate AI bridges the gap between AI systems and the individuals they interact with (Iphofen & Kritikos, 2021). This paradigm shift underscores the imperative of considering emotional components in AI design, aspects that have often been overlooked in prior research (Kumar et al., 2023).

4.4 Ensuring Accountability in AI Systems

Ensuring accountability in AI systems has emerged as a critical concern, particularly in sectors like healthcare. A recent proposal advocating for the use of medical algorithms suggests implementing an "algorithm charter for healthcare" aimed at prioritizing patient-centered and ethical AI practices (Hermann, 2022). Such a charter would promote transparency in the use of AI and the application of data results, facilitating clear explanations in cases of failure and aiding in identifying negligence (Huang et al., 2022). Transparency and explainability are crucial in medical AI to build trust and acceptance among healthcare professionals due to the significant impact of AI-driven decisions (Huang et al., 2022). Therefore, accountability plays a pivotal role in instilling confidence in AI systems, particularly within sensitive industries such as healthcare.

Efforts to address accountability in AI are underway, with various tools and software being developed for this purpose. For example, the Defense Advanced Research Projects Agency (DARPA) is leading an Explainable Artificial Intelligence (XAI) project aimed at developing machine learning techniques that produce explainable models without sacrificing performance (Kurni et al., 2023). This initiative is particularly critical in fields like medical AI, where decisions directly affect human patients and require clear justifications (Kurni et al., 2023).

Transparency serves as the foundation for establishing accountability in AI algorithms. Effectively communicating an algorithm's input, output, and processing is essential for facilitating understanding among all stakeholders (Ryan, 2020). This involves upfront delineation of AI implementation goals and providing a comprehensible explanation of the decision-making process (Ryan, 2020). Explainability extends transparency by requiring AI systems to justify the rationale behind their decisions (Ryan, 2020). In medical AI, for instance, clear explanations of proposed treatment plans are crucial for ensuring transparency and fostering trust.

The complex decision-making processes inherent in AI underscore the need for comprehensive explanations of its actions. This raises questions about whether AI should emulate human characteristics to provide understandable explanations (Ryan, 2020). For example, an AI caregiver for the elderly should not only make fair decisions but also explain them in a clear and reassuring manner (Ryan, 2020). Achieving this level of explainability requires further research to determine which types of AI necessitate complex explanations and the appropriate form of these explanations.

Addressing biases and ensuring fairness in AI decision-making are crucial aspects of accountability (Nasim et al., 2022). Providing detailed accounts of the decision-making process enables affected parties to comprehend the reasons behind AI-driven decisions (Flores-Vivar & Garcia-Peñalvo, 2023). However, the complexity of AI methodologies often makes it challenging to provide satisfactory explanations, particularly in fields like healthcare and law (Flores-Vivar & Garcia-Peñalvo, 2023). Developing simpler AI decision-making methods that balance accuracy with clarity is essential to address this challenge (Nasim et al., 2022).

Establishing globally agreed-upon ethical standards for AI is crucial to ensure its safe and responsible development. Similar to how the Asilomar Conference established principles for nuclear technology, a global convention on AI ethics should result in principles, agreements, and an international treaty to guide AI development in the public interest (Ashok et al., 2022). Such a treaty would facilitate international coordination of laws and regulations, preventing a 'race to the bottom' and ensuring consistent standards across jurisdictions (Ashok et al., 2022). Legal and regulatory frameworks for AI accountability should encompass comprehensive strategies implemented across government, corporate, and public sectors (Ashok et al., 2022). Accountability assigns responsibility for AI decision-making outcomes to humans and allocates consequences for adverse effects, aiming to prevent harmful outcomes and hold responsible parties accountable (Jobin et al., 2019). Developing

AI systems with built-in mechanisms to prevent harmful outcomes is crucial for ensuring accountability and minimizing adverse effects (Ashok et al., 2022).

4.5 Ethical Decision-Making in AI Development

Identifying ethical dilemmas in AI involves recognizing scenarios where decisions carry varying ethical implications (Stahl, 2021). Such dilemmas often emerge when choices entail complex reasoning, unpredictable outcomes, or inevitable undesirable consequences, necessitating the selection of the lesser of several evils (Stahl, 2021). For example, programming AI with conflicting objectives or anticipating significant repercussions of AI decisions demands preparedness for potential unintended effects, as illustrated by the paperclip maximizer scenario.

A fundamental challenge in addressing AI ethics lies in translating intuitive ethical understanding into computer programs (Stark & Hoey, 2021). While human intuition applies general principles to specific instances, computers predominantly operate on logic, which is not directly translatable into machine code (Stark & Hoey, 2021). Even achieving logical coherence and effective application remains beyond current computational capabilities (Akgun et al., 2022). While pattern recognition and probabilistic calculations can simulate aspects of ethical decision-making, both are inherently limited and represent simplified forms of complex ethical reasoning (Stark & Hoey, 2021). Overcoming this challenge necessitates identifying potential ethical dilemmas in AI and proposing methodologies for making ethically sound decisions (Akgun et al., 2022).

Ethical decision-making models provide frameworks for resolving ethical dilemmas in AI development, encompassing both prescriptive and descriptive approaches (Abdullah et al., 2021). AI designers often adopt a top-down approach, elucidating principles, identifying conflicts, and elucidating judgments in specific cases (Abdullah et al., 2021). However, this model may encounter conflicts requiring prioritization. Long-term aspirations include a master-slave model where humans assign tasks and AI systems independently determine execution methods; nevertheless, ethical implications and AI capabilities necessitate further exploration before realizing this objective (Baum, 2020). Alternatively, bottom-up approaches, while intricate, are also considered but currently less feasible (Abdullah et al., 2021).

Balancing ethical principles in AI design often involves navigating conflicting interests among stakeholders, each with distinct priorities and dependencies on AI outcomes (Taddeo et al., 2021). For instance, an AI system supporting medical professionals may be perceived differently by patients, insurers, pharmaceutical companies, and healthcare providers (Carrillo, 2020). Resolving these conflicts necessitates holistic examination of divergent interests and seeking acceptable compromises grounded in reasoned arguments (Brendel et al., 2021). These compromises should be flexible and open to potential revisions if they prove beneficial (Taddeo et al., 2021). Ethicists with relevant expertise should assess trade-offs between principles, ensuring equitable consideration of all viewpoints (Baum, 2020).

In cases where achieving equitable distribution proves contentious, the issue becomes a matter of justice requiring adjudication (Taddeo et al., 2021). This may involve third-party arbitration or AI simulations of hypothetical scenarios (Carrillo, 2020). Addressing these issues through legislative frameworks and reforms can benefit both society and the future development of AI, despite potential challenges for AI developers in the short term (Taddeo et al., 2021).

4.6 The Role of Stakeholders in Ethical AI Development

In the domain of AI development, key stakeholders including AI developers, legal professionals, and broader society play pivotal roles in ensuring the ethical advancement of AI technologies (Tsamados et al., 2021). Developers wield significant influence by virtue of their creation of AI systems, which are heavily shaped by the quality of the data utilized in machine learning processes. Ensuring the integrity and bias-free nature of this data is paramount, as flawed inputs can hinder AI's efficacy and perpetuate societal biases (Du & Xie, 2021). Hence, developers must possess a thorough understanding of how data inputs influence AI outcomes, underscoring the need to uphold stringent standards of safety and reliability throughout the developmental stages (Bryson, 2020).

Moreover, developers should adopt an approach of incremental and controlled integration of AI technologies, ready to address emerging challenges and refine system aspects as necessary, despite potential hurdles (Tsamados et al., 2021). Collaboration between AI developers and legal experts is equally crucial to establish robust accountability frameworks and navigate the complex landscape of AI-related legal proceedings, particularly as AI assumes roles traditionally performed by humans (Tsamados et al., 2021). Establishing a coherent standard for AI-related legal proceedings is essential, given the potential for disputes involving AI technologies (Tsamados et al., 2021).

Within the realm of AI development, developers bear a responsibility to define and operationalize the concept of "societal benefit," a task fraught with complexity and subjectivity. However, fostering open dialogue within the AI developer community represents a significant stride in addressing these challenges (Volkmar et al., 2022). Legislative measures could further enforce prioritization of societal impacts by AI developers, ensuring that technological advancements are geared towards seamless integration into society and enhancement of quality of life for users (Brendel et al., 2021).

Encouraging the adoption of an ethical code within the AI development community is crucial to ensure consistent consideration of societal impacts across the development lifecycle (Brendel et al., 2021). Historically, AI development teams have predominantly focused on performance metrics and production efficiencies, sometimes overlooking potential societal implications of their innovations (Volkmar et al., 2022). This oversight has occasionally led to adverse societal impacts. Implementation of ethical guidelines alongside legislative measures can align technological progress with societal well-being in the field of AI development (Volkmar et al., 2022).

User participation in the AI technology design process is indispensable for crafting targeted, adaptable, and well-received products (Brendel et al., 2021). By involving users throughout the design phases, developers gain insights into specific needs and preferences, thereby facilitating the creation of more effective solutions (Baum, 2020). This iterative process encompasses identifying user demographics, gathering task-specific insights, and refining design scenarios based on user feedback (Ashkok et al., 2022). Continuous evaluation through iterative user testing ensures that AI technologies evolve in alignment with users' changing needs and expectations (Volkmar et al., 2022).

As AI technologies advance, ethical considerations for AI users become increasingly pertinent. While AI holds promise for enhancing efficiency across diverse tasks, economic pressures may incentivize the delegation of decision-making to machines, even when human decision-makers might offer superior judgment (Ashkok et al., 2022). The integration of global and professional ethical codes will become imperative as AI technologies proliferate across sectors (Du & Xie, 2021). Users who prioritize ethical considerations in adopting AI technologies may seek certifications validating compliance with ethical standards, akin to decisions about purchasing environmentally sustainable or fair trade products (Volkmar et al., 2022).

Furthermore, users must exercise oversight and control over AI-driven decisions, especially when outcomes raise ethical concerns (Blanchard & Taddeo, 2023). Assessing the ethical implications of delegating decisions to AI presents a complex dilemma that users must navigate as they interact with these technologies (Blanchard & Taddeo, 2023). In conclusion, collaboration, and active engagement of stakeholders at all levels are indispensable for ensuring the ethical development, deployment, and utilization of AI technologies in society.

4.7 Case Studies

Real-world case studies provide invaluable insights into the practical application of ethical AI, offering a glimpse into how AI systems make critical decisions and highlighting the components essential for effective AI decision-making. In the medical domain, data mining algorithms play a pivotal role in uncovering patterns among patients seeking various treatments for specific illnesses (Zhang et al., 2021). This approach offers unbiased insights to the medical community, circumventing potential biases inherent in observational studies. Furthermore, leveraging decision policies simulated on virtual patients enhances AI-driven treatment recommendations under specific conditions (Zhang et al., 2021).

For instance, consider a scenario involving an elderly patient facing kidney failure, where traditional medical practices typically recommend dialysis as the standard treatment. However, an AI system capable of simulating the patient's probable treatment outcomes, considering factors such as fatigue and treatment burden, might occasionally advise against dialysis (Saheb et al., 2021). While such recommendations may initially appear unfavorable, they underscore potential limitations in human decision-making processes and advocate for personalized treatment approaches that prioritize patient well-being (Saheb et al., 2021). Despite the promise of AI in enhancing healthcare delivery, its ethical implementation necessitates careful consideration of patient welfare (Roberts et al., 2021).

4.7.1 Ethical AI in Healthcare

AI applications in healthcare offer substantial benefits in terms of accuracy and efficiency. Stanford's advancements in automatic image interpretation exemplify these advancements (Zhang & Zhang, 2023). However, alongside these benefits come potential risks of failure or misuse, emphasizing the critical importance of upholding ethical and legal standards in AI-driven healthcare decision-making (Zhang & Zhang, 2023). One effective strategy involves constraining AI systems to adhere to evidence-based practice (EBP) guidelines, ensuring that AI decisions align with established medical knowledge (Zhang & Zhang, 2023). For instance, IBM Watson's EBP recommendations provide oncologists with reliable treatment advice tailored to individual patient needs (Kumar et al., 2023). Additionally, a phased approach to AI implementation, incorporating randomization as suggested by Kumar et al. (2023), offers a methodical means to assess AI impact while prioritizing patient safety. This approach strikes a balance between leveraging AI-driven accuracy and mitigating potential harm. In mental healthcare, chatbots like Mitsuku have shown promise in enhancing Turing tests by simulating human-like responses that could benefit patients (Zhang & Zhang, 2023). However, inherent risks such as providing unsound advice necessitate stringent safeguards to ensure the safety and appropriateness of AI decisions in mental health contexts (Kumar et al., 2023).

4.7.2 Ethical AI in Autonomous Vehicles

The complexities inherent in AI-driven autonomous vehicles present unique ethical challenges, particularly in scenarios where human lives are at stake. For instance, consider a situation where a child suddenly runs into the street, and a collision is imminent (Ashok et al., 2022). The AI must make a split-second decision, choosing between swerving into a wall, potentially injuring the passenger, or attempting to avoid the child with potentially greater consequences (Ashok et al., 2022). Public sentiment overwhelmingly favors actions aimed at minimizing human harm, despite individual preferences for vehicles prioritizing passenger safety. This ethical dilemma underscores the need for government regulations to establish acceptable risk standards for manufacturers, enabling AI systems to navigate moral quandaries effectively.

4.7.3 Ethical AI in Financial Services

The potential for ethical AI implementation in financial services is extensive, given the sector's reliance on data-driven processes (Huang et al., 2022). The increasing role of AI in areas like credit scoring highlights the necessity of defining 'best practice' systems and addressing potential ethical concerns (Huang et al., 2022). While profit incentives in finance may sometimes encourage unethical practices, it is imperative to pursue AI research with considerations for both societal impact and commercial interests (Nasim et al., 2022). Although AI's influence on financial decision-making is still evolving, regulatory frameworks will significantly shape the adoption and application of AI techniques. This underscores the importance of countries like the USA and UK in driving AI research within the financial sector (Huang et al., 2022).

As AI continues to advance and integrate into various sectors, establishing and adhering to robust ethical frameworks will be crucial in harnessing its benefits while safeguarding societal well-being and safety (Huang et al., 2022).

5. IMPLICATIONS OF THE STUDY

The exploration of AI's ethical dimensions and the advocacy for compassionate AI development have significant implications for stakeholders involved in advancing and deploying AI technologies. This study emphasizes the critical necessity of integrating ethical considerations throughout the AI development process, highlighting potential pitfalls and dilemmas associated with AI's influence (Stahl, 2021). Stakeholders, including developers, policymakers, and regulatory bodies, are encouraged to adopt a proactive approach in addressing these challenges by collaborating to establish robust ethical frameworks and guidelines governing AI development and deployment (Bartneck et al., 2021). Such frameworks are essential for ensuring that AI systems prioritize inclusivity, equity, and transparency, thereby fostering empathy and understanding among stakeholders across industries such as healthcare and finance (Bartneck et al., 2021). Moreover, ethical decision-making in AI development becomes crucial in navigating conflicts between economic interests and societal welfare, ensuring that AI innovations contribute positively to societal well-being while mitigating potential risks (Bryson, 2020; Carrillo, 2020). By equipping stakeholders with methodologies to navigate ethical dilemmas, this study contributes to fostering a responsible and accountable AI ecosystem, aligning AI advancements with broader societal interests and safeguarding human welfare (Bryson, 2020; Carrillo, 2020).

6. CONCLUSION

This chapter explored the emergence of the Compassionate AI Path amidst growing concerns about the rapid advancement of technology, which raises the specter of AI outpacing human oversight. At this critical juncture, the world faces a pivotal decision: whether to continue along an uncertain trajectory or embrace a conscientious approach prioritizing ethical considerations and human welfare. The Compassionate Path advocates for a deliberate effort to integrate ethics into AI development processes through collective endeavors. Without a unified ethical framework, AI progress risks being driven by conflicting interests and unintended consequences, potentially leading to undesirable outcomes that are difficult to rectify. While there is no single solution to reconcile ethics with AI development, certain methodologies show more promise. Key to this effort is embedding ethics into AI frameworks to foster compassion and alleviate global suffering. The prospect of an intelligence explosion highlights AI's potential as a compassionate tool, but addressing the control problem and ensuring the development of friendly AI are critical steps. Any transition of global control must be managed with precision and caution, maintaining human oversight of AI. By conscientiously steering AI development along the Compassionate Path, stakeholders can aim to maximize benefits, mitigate risks, and ensure the ethical alignment of AI systems.

To rectify the current state and set a blueprint for future decisions, it is crucial to incorporate principles of moral reasoning, deliberative democracy, and national and international policy-making into AI technology development. This can be initiated through a global initiative focused on fostering AI development within a deliberative democratic framework. Such an initiative could begin with collaborative research ventures among computer and social scientists, evolving into interdisciplinary teams dedicated to national policy objectives or global challenges. A primary goal of this research would be to create AI decision-making systems that complement or integrate with human deliberative processes. While this approach may seem idealistic now, it represents a pragmatic starting point for reshaping AI development ethos and addressing ethical dilemmas inherent in AI technologies through further advancements. Another constructive strategy involves promoting a "trade-research off" paradigm, where AI researchers use AI systems to tackle issues arising from the implementation of previous AI technologies. Whether developing AI decision-making systems or mitigating problems from past technologies, a global initiative provides numerous opportunities to scrutinize and rectify issues of narrow or partial rationality at individual and institutional levels.

7. LIMITATIONS AND FUTURE RESEARCH DIRECTIONS

The present study identifies several limitations that pave the way for future research endeavors. A significant constraint lies in the challenge of definitively pinpointing the threshold at which AI surpasses human-level compassion. Further empirical investigations are imperative to accurately quantify and compare the compassionate capabilities of AI and humans, thereby offering a clearer understanding of this pivotal boundary. Moreover, this study acknowledges its partial exploration of the broader societal implications arising from AI potentially assuming a global caretaker role. Such a profound shift would undoubtedly reshape human-AI dynamics and redefine the human condition in multifaceted ways. Future research must delve deeper into comprehending the ramifications of this prospective transition, scrutinizing its impacts on social structures, individual fulfillment, and the overarching human experience. The methodologies utilized to assess AI compassion are still in their nascent stages and necessitate further refinement. Subsequent research efforts should prioritize the development of more robust and dependable frameworks for evaluating the ethical dimensions of AI decision-making and autonomy. This evolution will facilitate more nuanced evaluations of AI's compassionate capacities and elucidate the intricate interplay between ethical principles and intelligent machine behavior. Lastly, the long-term ethical implications stemming from AI's escalating autonomy and decision-making capabilities warrant intensified scrutiny. As AI systems grow increasingly sophisticated, researchers must continue exploring how these advancements can be effectively governed through the establishment of sound policy frameworks and ethical guidelines. This endeavor is critical to ensuring the responsible development and integration of AI technologies in alignment with societal values. By addressing these limitations and pursuing these future research directions, scholars can illuminate the complex interdependencies among AI, compassion, and societal transformation. Ultimately, this knowledge will guide the ethical advancement of AI, facilitating its integration in ways that enhance human well-being and foster the flourishing of humanity.

REFERENCES

Abdullah, Y. I., Schuman, J. S., Shabsigh, R., Caplan, A., & Al-Aswad, L. A. (2021). Ethics of artificial intelligence in medicine and ophthalmology. *Asia-Pacific Journal of Ophthalmology*, 10(3), 289–298. 10.1097/APO.0000000000000397 34383720

Akgun, S., & Greenhow, C. (2022). Artificial intelligence in education: Addressing ethical challenges in K-12 settings. *AI and Ethics*, 2(3), 431–440. 10.1007/s43681-021-00096-7 34790956

Ashok, M., Madan, R., Joha, A., & Sivarajah, U. (2022). Ethical framework for Artificial Intelligence and Digital technologies. *International Journal of Information Management*, 62, 102433. 10.1016/j.ijinfomgt.2021.102433

Bartneck, C., Lütge, C., Wagner, A., & Welsh, S. (2021). *An introduction to ethics in robotics and AI*. Springer Nature. 10.1007/978-3-030-51110-4

Baum, S. D. (2020). Social choice ethics in artificial intelligence. *AI & Society*, 35(1), 165–176. 10.1007/s00146-017-0760-1

Blanchard, A., & Taddeo, M. (2023). The ethics of artificial intelligence for intelligence analysis: A review of the key challenges with recommendations. *Digital Society : Ethics, Socio-Legal and Governance of Digital Technology*, 2(1), 12. 10.1007/s44206-023-00036-4 37034181

Brendel, A. B., Mirbabaie, M., Lembcke, T. B., & Hofeditz, L. (2021). Ethical management of artificial intelligence. *Sustainability (Basel)*, 13(4), 1974. 10.3390/su13041974

Bryson, J. J. (2020). The artificial intelligence of the ethics of artificial intelligence. *The Oxford handbook of ethics of AI*, 1.

Carrillo, M. R. (2020). Artificial intelligence: From ethics to law. *Telecommunications Policy*, 44(6), 101937. 10.1016/j.telpol.2020.101937

Cascella, M., Tracey, M. C., Petrucci, E., & Bignami, E. G. (2023). Exploring artificial intelligence in anesthesia: A primer on ethics, and clinical applications. *Surgeries*, 4(2), 264–274. 10.3390/surgeries4020027

Díaz-Rodríguez, N., Del Ser, J., Coeckelbergh, M., de Prado, M. L., Herrera-Viedma, E., & Herrera, F. (2023). Connecting the dots in trustworthy Artificial Intelligence: From AI principles, ethics, and key requirements to responsible AI systems and regulation. *Information Fusion*, 99, 101896. 10.1016/j.inffus.2023.101896

Du, S., & Xie, C. (2021). Paradoxes of artificial intelligence in consumer markets: Ethical challenges and opportunities. *Journal of Business Research*, 129, 961–974. 10.1016/j.jbusres.2020.08.024

Flores-Vivar, J. M., & García-Peñalvo, F. J. (2023). Reflections on the ethics, potential, and challenges of artificial intelligence in the framework of quality education (SDG4). *Comunicar*, 31(74), 37–47. 10.3916/C74-2023-03

Hermann, E. (2022). Leveraging artificial intelligence in marketing for social good—An ethical perspective. *Journal of Business Ethics*, 179(1), 43–61. 10.1007/s10551-021-04843-y34054170

Holmes, W., & Porayska-Pomsta, K. (Eds.). (2022). *The Ethics of Artificial Intelligence in education: Practices, challenges, and debates*. Taylor & Francis. 10.4324/9780429329067

Huang, C., Zhang, Z., Mao, B., & Yao, X. (2022). An overview of artificial intelligence ethics. *IEEE Transactions on Artificial Intelligence*, 4(4), 799–819. 10.1109/TAI.2022.3194503

Iphofen, R., & Kritikos, M. (2021). Regulating artificial intelligence and robotics: Ethics by design in a digital society. *Contemporary Social Science*, 16(2), 170–184. 10.1080/21582041.2018.1563803

Ivanov, S. H., & Umbrello, S. (2021). The ethics of artificial intelligence and robotisation in tourism and hospitality–a conceptual framework and research agenda. *Journal of Smart Tourism*, 1(4), 9–18.

Kazim, E., & Koshiyama, A. S. (2021). A high-level overview of AI ethics. *Patterns (New York, N.Y.)*, 2(9), 100314. 10.1016/j.patter.2021.10031434553166

Kieslich, K., Keller, B., & Starke, C. (2022). Artificial intelligence ethics by design. Evaluating public perception on the importance of ethical design principles of artificial intelligence. *Big Data & Society*, 9(1), 20539517221092956. 10.1177/20539517221092956

Kumar, P., Chauhan, S., & Awasthi, L. K. (2023). Artificial intelligence in healthcare: Review, ethics, trust challenges & future research directions. *Engineering Applications of Artificial Intelligence*, 120, 105894. 10.1016/j.engappai.2023.105894

Kurni, M., Mohammed, M. S., & Srinivasa, K. G. (2023). Ethics of Artificial Intelligence in Education. In *A Beginner's Guide to Introduce Artificial Intelligence in Teaching and Learning* (pp. 213–229). Springer International Publishing.

Larsson, S. (2020). On the governance of artificial intelligence through ethics guidelines. *Asian Journal of Law and Society*, 7(3), 437–451. 10.1017/als.2020.19

McStay, A., & Rosner, G. (2021). Emotional artificial intelligence in children's toys and devices: Ethics, governance and practical remedies. *Big Data & Society*, 8(1), 2053951721994877. 10.1177/2053951721994877

Murphy, K., Di Ruggiero, E., Upshur, R., Willison, D. J., Malhotra, N., Cai, J. C., Malhotra, N., Lui, V., & Gibson, J. (2021). Artificial intelligence for good health: A scoping review of the ethics literature. *BMC Medical Ethics*, 22(1), 1–17. 10.1186/s12910-021-00577-833588803

Nasim, S. F., Ali, M. R., & Kulsoom, U. (2022). Artificial intelligence incidents & ethics a narrative review. *International Journal of TechnologyInnovation and Management*, 2(2), 52–64.

Nath, R., & Sahu, V. (2020). The problem of machine ethics in artificial intelligence. *AI & Society*, 35(1), 103–111. 10.1007/s00146-017-0768-6

Owe, A., & Baum, S. D. (2021, December). The ethics of sustainability for artificial intelligence. In *Proceedings of the 1st international conference on AI for people: towards sustainable AI (CAIP 2021b)* (pp. 1-17). 10.4108/eai.20-11-2021.2314105

Roberts, H., Cowls, J., Morley, J., Taddeo, M., Wang, V., & Floridi, L. (2021). The Chinese approach to artificial intelligence: an analysis of policy, ethics, and regulation. *Ethics, governance, and policies in artificial intelligence*, 47-79.

Ryan, M. (2020). In AI we trust: Ethics, artificial intelligence, and reliability. *Science and Engineering Ethics*, 26(5), 2749–2767. 10.1007/s11948-020-00228-y32524425

Saheb, T., Saheb, T., & Carpenter, D. O. (2021). Mapping research strands of ethics of artificial intelligence in healthcare: A bibliometric and content analysis. *Computers in Biology and Medicine*, 135, 104660. 10.1016/j.compbiomed.2021.10466034346319

Solanki, P., Grundy, J., & Hussain, W. (2023). Operationalising ethics in artificial intelligence for healthcare: A framework for AI developers. *AI and Ethics*, 3(1), 223–240. 10.1007/s43681-022-00195-z

Stahl, B. C. (2021). *Artificial intelligence for a better future: an ecosystem perspective on the ethics of AI and emerging digital technologies*. Springer Nature. 10.1007/978-3-030-69978-9

Stark, L., & Hoey, J. (2021, March). The ethics of emotion in artificial intelligence systems. In *Proceedings of the 2021 ACM conference on fairness, accountability, and transparency* (pp. 782-793). 10.1145/3442188.3445939

Taddeo, M., McNeish, D., Blanchard, A., & Edgar, E. (2021). Ethical principles for artificial intelligence in national defence. *Philosophy & Technology*, 34(4), 1707–1729. 10.1007/s13347-021-00482-3

Tsamados, A., Aggarwal, N., Cowls, J., Morley, J., Roberts, H., Taddeo, M., & Floridi, L. (2021). The ethics of algorithms: key problems and solutions. *Ethics, governance, and policies in artificial intelligence*, 97-123.

Volkmar, G., Fischer, P. M., & Reinecke, S. (2022). Artificial Intelligence and Machine Learning: Exploring drivers, barriers, and future developments in marketing management. *Journal of Business Research*, 149, 599–614. 10.1016/j.jbusres.2022.04.007

Zhang, B., Anderljung, M., Kahn, L., Dreksler, N., Horowitz, M. C., & Dafoe, A. (2021). Ethics and governance of artificial intelligence: Evidence from a survey of machine learning researchers. *Journal of Artificial Intelligence Research*, 71, 591–666. 10.1613/jair.1.12895

Zhang, J., & Zhang, Z. M. (2023). Ethics and governance of trustworthy medical artificial intelligence. *BMC Medical Informatics and Decision Making*, 23(1), 7. 10.1186/s12911-023-02103-936639799

KEY TERMS AND DEFINITIONS

Aggregative And Distributive Compassion: Aggregative compassion is the total amount of compassion shown in a society. Distributive compassion is about how this compassion is shared among different people and groups.

Compassion: Feeling deep sympathy for others' suffering and wanting to help relieve it.

Ethical Alignment: Making sure that the actions and decisions of AI systems match established moral and ethical standards.

Ethical Code: A set of rules and principles to help people and organizations make morally good decisions.

Ethical Dilemmas: Situations where there are conflicting moral principles, making it hard to decide what is right.

Ethical Principles: Basic ideas and beliefs that guide moral behavior, like honesty and fairness.

Ethics: The study of what is morally right and wrong and how people should act.

Possibility Research: Studying potential futures and outcomes, especially with new technologies, to understand and prepare for their effects.

Responsible AI Development: Creating and using AI systems in a way that prioritizes ethics, accountability, and societal well-being.

Societal Impact: The effect that technologies, policies, and actions have on the community and society's well-being.

Superintelligent: Describing AI that is smarter than humans in every way, including creativity and problem-solving.

Utilitarianism: A philosophy that says the best action is the one that creates the most happiness for the most people.

Virtue Ethics: A moral philosophy that focuses on the importance of character and virtues in determining ethical behavior.

Chapter 8
AI-Driven Territorial Intelligence
An Integrated Approach to Enhancing Digital Sovereignty

Badr Bentalha
https://orcid.org/0000-0003-1339-542X
National School of Business and Management, Sidi Mohammed Ben Abdellah University, Morocco

Mohamed Boukare
https://orcid.org/0009-0002-2511-9764
Mohammed First University, Oujda, Morocco

ABSTRACT

Artificial intelligence (AI) and territorial intelligence (TI) are currently two key fields. AI enables the development of systems capable of performing tasks that generally require human intelligence, such as pattern recognition, classification, and prediction. Business intelligence applied to territories is at the heart of research into sustainable territorial development, as part of the paradigm of intelligent territories. So how can digital technology be used to develop territorial intelligence and help improve the digital sovereignty of regions? The study traces the many challenges posed by the application of AI and IT in real-life scenarios and identifies opportunities for combining the two fields via a hybrid approach aimed at decision-making in digital territorial management.

DOI: 10.4018/979-8-3693-8557-9.ch008

INTRODUCTION

In an increasingly connected world, corporate competition is turning business models upside down, and leaders towards digital transformation. To stay competitive, this transition is a fact. In all sectors, digitalization is a trend and a real trend, which is becoming more and more essential and is profoundly transforming current practices and theories. There is a growing interest in regions and the economic and social performance of territories. As a result, economic intelligence applied to the territory is at the heart of research into intelligent territorial development, in the context of the concept of "*intelligent territories*". We propose to contribute to this debate by focusing on the potential role of artificial intelligence as a tool for developing economic and territorial intelligence.

Artificial intelligence (AI) and territorial intelligence (TI) are two fields that have received significant attention in recent years. AI enables the development of systems capable of performing complex cognitive tasks, such as pattern recognition, classification, and prediction, while IT focuses on the development of systems capable of processing and analyzing spatial data. However, despite their progress, both camps still face challenges when it comes to applying their techniques to real-life scenarios. One way of overcoming these challenges is to combine the strengths of both fields, creating a hybrid approach that exploits the advantages of both AI and TI.

Business intelligence refers to the collection, analysis, and exploitation of strategic information to support the competitiveness and development of companies and organizations. It encompasses aspects such as competitive intelligence, protection of sensitive information, and informed strategic decision-making. On the other hand, territorial intelligence concerns the in-depth understanding of a given territory, its resources, assets, and challenges, to support its sustainable development and economic, social, and environmental resilience. AI could enable more efficient collection and analysis of the vast amounts of economic, commercial, and territorial data available. Thanks to its massive data processing capabilities, AI could identify trends, opportunities, and risks faster and more accurately than traditional methods. In the field of territorial intelligence, AI could contribute to a better understanding of the socio-economic, environmental, and cultural dynamics of a given territory. By cross-referencing and analyzing various data sources, AI could identify trends, challenges, and opportunities specific to each region. AI could also support the planning and implementation of more effective territorial public policies, better adapted to local needs. By analyzing the potential impacts of different scenarios, AI could help decision-makers choose the most relevant measures.

Data sovereignty has emerged as a critical concern for regions pursuing digital autonomy. The concept extends beyond mere data protection, encompassing the ability of a jurisdiction to control the collection, processing, and storage of data generated within its borders. For instance, India's draft Data Protection Bill mandates local storage of certain types of personal data, reflecting a growing trend towards data localization policies. Public-private partnerships (PPPs) play a crucial role in developing AI-driven territorial intelligence capabilities. The Smart Dubai initiative provides an instructive case study of how government vision can be combined with private sector expertise. By partnering with tech companies like IBM and Cisco, Dubai has accelerated its smart city transformation while maintaining strategic control over data and infrastructure. The global nature of AI development necessitates consideration of international regulations and their impact on regional digital sovereignty. The EU's General Data Protection Regulation (GDPR) has had far-reaching effects beyond Europe's borders, influencing data protection laws and AI governance worldwide. Regions must navigate these international frameworks while pursuing their own digital autonomy goals.

Collaborative digital platforms facilitate the exchange of information and the co-construction of projects between the various players in a territory, thus strengthening collective intelligence. Intelligent management of resources, infrastructures, and public services is also made possible by digital tools, contributing to more sustainable and resilient development. At the same time, digital technology opens up new opportunities for regions to promote themselves and attract investment and talent. Above all, by developing their local digital infrastructures and solutions, such as data centers, sovereign clouds, or open-source software, territories take control of their strategic data and information systems, reducing their dependence on large outside technology companies (Bouhtati et al., 2023). This territorial anchoring of digital technology also encourages the emergence of a local ecosystem of skills and jobs in the fields of data, artificial intelligence, and the development of innovative solutions (Bentalha, 2020). In this way, a true regional digital sovereignty is being built, offering territories the means for their intelligent and controlled development over the long term.

In this respect, we will attempt to answer the following question: How can digital technology for the development of territorial intelligence contribute to improving regional digital sovereignty?

This work aims to explore the potential of combining AI and IT to improve decision-making processes in territorial management. The aim is to examine and analyze the current state of AI and IT, highlighting their strengths, weaknesses, and potential applications in territorial management. Indeed, the work aims to develop a hybrid approach that combines AI and IT techniques for decision-making in territorial management, taking into account the specific characteristics of territorial data and the needs of decision-makers. It also aims to evaluate the effectiveness and efficiency of the proposed approach through case studies and simulations, using real data from different territorial contexts. This combined approach aims to enable the digital sovereignty that is essential for territorial development.

We have chosen to carry out an empirical study in the Moroccan context, with a state of the art in the field. We begin with a theoretical overview of the key concepts: digital, artificial intelligence, business intelligence, and digital sovereignty. Next, we develop the mechanisms by which the functionalities offered by digital technology foster the development of territorial economic intelligence and facilitate the management of the local authority's overall performance, via operational indicators and analysis grids, to activate an intelligent and sovereign territorial dynamic.

Theoretical and Conceptual Framework

1.1. The Region, a Territory in Search of Intelligence, Digital Sovereignty, and Territorial Performance

Local authorities have legal personalities. They are distinct from the State and grant legal and patrimonial autonomy. Integrated development is a primary goal of regionalization (Lamsiah et al., 2021). Digital sovereignty refers to the ability of a state or organization to control and secure its data and information systems. The notion of digital sovereignty has become increasingly important as digital technologies have gained influence and ubiquity (Bellanger, 2012). It is linked to concerns about over-dependence on technologies developed by other countries or companies, as well as to the need to protect personal data and sensitive information. It rests on several pillars, such as control over critical infrastructures, the use of reliable technologies, robust protection against cyber-attacks or espionage, and cooperation between the State and private players (Bentalha, 2022). Another crucial aspect of digital sovereignty is the control of data, seen as the new strategic resource of the digital age. States must put in place appropriate regulatory and legal frameworks to protect the personal and sensitive data of their citizens while promoting the circulation and exploitation of data under secure and privacy-friendly conditions. Training and the development of digital skills are also key to digital sovereignty. States must invest in education and training to ensure they have a skilled workforce capable of designing, deploying, and maintaining strategic digital technologies. Finally, digital sovereignty implies enhanced international cooperation in areas such as cybersecurity, Internet governance, and the regulation of digital giants. States must work together to establish common norms and standards while preserving their strategic autonomy.

The idea behind territorial digital sovereignty is that countries must be able to protect their strategic, economic, and security interests in the digital domain by controlling the infrastructures on their territory. This gives them decision-making power over data collection, storage, processing, and transmission, as well as access to digital services (Hmioui et al., 2024). Territorial digital sovereignty is a complex and constantly evolving subject, as digital technologies continue to advance and transform societies. The approaches and strategies implemented will vary from country to country, depending on their needs, priorities, and technological capabilities.

In a world where digital technology is evolving at a breathtaking pace, regions are facing new challenges in terms of intelligence, sovereignty, and territorial performance. The digital age has not only the way we live, but also the way territories manage their resources, interact with their citizens, and shape their future (Bakis, 2021). The quest for territorial intelligence has become an imperative for regions keen to remain competitive and meet the needs of their populations. Thanks to digital tools, decision-makers can now collect and analyze massive data, enabling more informed decision-making and better resource allocation (Caragliu & Del Bo, 2019). However, this intelligence can only be fully exploited if regions have sufficient digital sovereignty (Dumont, 2021; Loukil, 2020). In an environment where cyber threats are omnipresent, regions need to ensure that their systems are secure and that their technological independence is preserved. This sovereignty requires the development of local skills, investment in robust infrastructures, and the implementation of appropriate regulatory frameworks. Territorial performance is inextricably linked to the success of digital transformation. Regions that fully embrace digital technology are better able to deliver more efficient public services, stimulate innovation, and foster sustainable economic development. Nevertheless, this performance can only be achieved if territories manage to overcome digital divides and guarantee equitable access to technologies for all citizens (Rallet & Rochelandet, 2019).

1.2. Artificial Intelligence: A Lever for Intelligent Regional Development

When discussing the concept of Territorial Intelligence (TI), we can only highlight the principles and foundations of Competitive Intelligence. It is "*an informational and anthropological process, regular and continuous, initiated by local actors physically present and/or distant, who appropriate the resources of space by mobilizing and then transforming the energy of the territorial system into project capacity. In this way, territorial intelligence can be likened to territoriality, which results from the phenomenon of appropriating a territory's resources and then transferring skills between categories of local players with different cultural backgrounds. This approach aims to ensure, both literally and figuratively, that the territorial level to be developed has what we have called formal territorial capital*" (Bertacchini et al., 2006). For Bouchet (2003), territorial intelligence is a new process enabling the exchange of strategic information at the local level. According to Bruté de Rémur (2009), territorial intelligence is more than just the territorialization of economic intelligence. In Latin, the word "*territory*" means "*jus terrendi*", referring to he who holds the right to terrify. Thus, the notion of territory was historically perceived in terms of the exercise of power and domination. Today, this vision of territory as a dominated space is largely outdated, giving way to socio-economic interpretations (Lamsiah & Bentalha, 2023). The territory as such is characterized by its governance, defined as "*all the institutional processes involved in the local regulation of the territorial economic system*" (Pecqueur, 2005).

The notion of territory is a source of many meanings, giving rise to derivatives and qualifiers such as territoriality, territorialization, territorial development, and territorial intelligence. Today, a new role for actors is being established, evoking new styles of multi-dimensional territorial governance and reinforcing Pecqueur's (2005) idea of the socio-economic construct, which "*distinguishes the constructed territory, which is the result of a process of construction by actors of an a priori given territory that constitutes support. This is generally an institutional territory*". Territorial governance, on the other hand, is a polysemous concept, strongly influenced by Anglo-Saxon culture and interpreted in a variety of subjective ways. "*It seems to be intended to replace the concept of government in accounting for the forms of political governance in these new territorial spaces*". (Jouve & Booth, 2004).

In its theoretical foundation, territorial intelligence is based on the notion of territory, thus emphasizing the interplay of its actors, who constantly produce the organization of geographical space. Territorial intelligence considerably stimulates territorial dynamics through the interactions undertaken by actors (Alla et al., 2023). It encourages coordination between actors in their resource-building processes and helps them to better create and appropriate their resources. The territory is thus far from being perceived as a basket of resources since these can be generic, i.e. created by one actor and used by other actors in the same territory, or specific, i.e. created purely by the actors in a purely evolutionary sense of the territory, i.e. resilient forms of economic dynamics. Territorial intelligence also encourages another form of territorial dynamic, based on coordination between actors in their processes of using resources available or latent in the territory, in a purely institutionalized sense (Lamsiah & Bentalha, 2022a). Whether resilient or territorial, evolutionary, or institutionalist in terminology, territorial dynamics cannot be achieved without the prior existence of territorial intelligence based on relevant territorial governance, which in turn must be governed by solid information systems and rigid digitalization (Lamsiah & Bentalha, 2022b).

Territorial management, encompassing urban planning, resource allocation, and governance, has seen a rapid digital transformation in recent years. The integration of Internet of Things (IoT) devices, big data analytics, and AI-driven decision-making systems promises increased efficiency and data-driven insights. However, this technological shift also introduces new risks and challenges that must be carefully considered. The collection and analysis of vast amounts of data from citizens and urban environments raise significant privacy concerns. Smart city technologies, while offering benefits in terms of service delivery and resource management, also create opportunities for pervasive surveillance and potential misuse of personal information. AI systems used in territorial management may perpetuate or exacerbate existing societal biases. Algorithms trained on historical data can reinforce patterns of discrimination in areas such as urban planning, resource allocation, and law enforcement. The increasing reliance on digital technologies in territorial management may exacerbate existing socioeconomic disparities. Communities with limited access to technology or digital literacy skills may be marginalized in decision-making processes and service delivery. As territorial management systems become more interconnected and reliant on digital infrastructure, they also become more vulnerable to cyber-attacks. Critical infrastructure, including power grids, water systems, and transportation networks, may be at risk of disruption or manipulation by malicious actors. The integration of digital technologies and AI in territorial management offers significant potential benefits but also introduces complex challenges. Addressing issues of data privacy, security, algorithmic bias, and the unintended consequence of automation is crucial for developing ethical, equitable, and effective digital territorial management systems.

The pursuit of digital sovereignty and robust territorial management systems faces numerous obstacles beyond the technical and ethical concerns previously discussed. Many regions, particularly in developing countries or economically disadvantaged areas, face severe budget constraints that limit their ability to invest in digital infrastructure. Building and maintaining advanced digital systems requires a skilled workforce, which can be challenging for many regions to attract and retain. Regions may struggle to retain skilled technology professionals who are attracted to more established tech hubs or higher-paying opportunities elsewhere. Regions must navigate complex data protection and sharing regulations, which can impact the development and deployment of digital territorial management systems. Managing multi-stakeholder projects involving public agencies, private companies, and community organizations presents significant governance challenges. The development of robust digital infrastructures and local technology ecosystems is crucial for regions seeking to implement advanced territorial management systems and achieve a degree of digital sovereignty. However, this process is fraught with challenges ranging from funding constraints and talent shortages to regulatory hurdles and governance complexities.

As regions pursue digital sovereignty and advanced territorial management systems, it is critical to examine the potential impacts on social equity and the risk of exacerbating existing digital divides. The uneven distribution of digital infrastructure and devices can lead to stark differences in citizens' ability to benefit from and participate in digital governance systems. As territorial management becomes more digitized, individuals lacking digital literacy may find themselves increasingly marginalized in civic participation and access to services. Digital sovereignty initiatives may disproportionately benefit urban areas, potentially widening the gap between urban and rural communities. Digital systems that do not account for cultural and linguistic diversity risk marginalizing certain communities. As regions pursue digital sovereignty and advanced territorial management systems, it is imperative that they prioritize social equity and actively work to bridge digital divides. Failure to address these issues could result in digital initiatives that reinforce or exacerbate existing socioeconomic disparities, undermining the potential benefits of these technologies. By placing social equity at the forefront of digital sovereignty efforts, regions can work towards creating truly inclusive and empowering digital ecosystems that benefit all members of society.

As regions increasingly rely on digital technologies for territorial management, it is crucial to address the ethical implications of these systems. This section explores key ethical considerations, focusing on algorithmic bias, transparency, accountability, and related issues. Algorithmic bias in digital governance systems can lead to unfair outcomes and reinforce societal inequalities. Bias can stem from various sources, including skewed training data, flawed algorithm design, and the unconscious biases of developers. Biased algorithms in territorial management could lead to unfair resource distribution, discriminatory urban development patterns, or biased law enforcement practices. Transparency is crucial for maintaining public trust and enabling scrutiny of digital governance systems. Regions must determine appropriate levels of disclosure about their digital systems, balancing transparency with security concerns. Ethical considerations must be at the forefront of digital territorial management initiatives. Regions pursuing digital sovereignty and advanced governance systems must proactively address issues of algorithmic bias, transparency, accountability, privacy, inclusivity, and environmental impact. By placing these ethical considerations at the core of their digital initiatives, regions can work towards creating fair, transparent, and sustainable digital territorial management systems that respect individual rights and promote the public good.

Fostering regional digital sovereignty requires more than top-down governance; it necessitates the active engagement of diverse stakeholders in co-creating and implementing digital solutions. By involving citizens, businesses, civil society organizations, and academia, regions can develop more robust, inclusive, and effective approaches to territorial intelligence. The city of Barcelona's 'decidim' platform exemplifies this participatory approach, providing a digital infrastructure for citizen participation in urban decision-making processes. Participatory decision-making platforms enable citizens to directly influence territorial management strategies. Estonia's e-Governance system goes beyond simple e-voting to include features like participatory budgeting and public consultations on draft legislation. This approach not only enhances democratic processes but also ensures that digital solutions address real community needs. Ensuring inclusive design and promoting digital literacy are crucial for equitable stakeholder engagement. Finland's Elements of AI course, a free online program aimed at demystifying AI for the general public, demonstrates a proactive approach to building digital competence across society. Such initiatives are essential for meaningful participation in digital governance.

By projecting the major economic issues that dominate current economic life onto the great opportunities and functionalities offered by the new technical tools with the authentic contemporary technological boom, we are, in effect, facing a new digital era where information systems meticulously trace the broad outlines of the new economic situation. Today, any organization, to meet its requirements and come closer to achieving its objectives, must opt for relevant decision-making. In this respect, the acquisition and effective manipulation of a large mass of information has become a supreme and indisputable necessity (Bentalha, 2020). Information as a strategic source of management and decision-making requires the creation of a rigid informational platform vis-à-vis the organization, by empowering the workgroup to handle the tools.

Drawing on the work carried out by Gourvennec and Kabla (2017), we summarize the main axes of territorial intelligence most concerned by digitalization in the following Table 1:

Table 1. Dimensions of artificial intelligence at the service of territorial intelligence

Axis	Dimension	Axis	Dimension
Artificial intelligence of territorial competencies	Training	**Artificial intelligence of technology and territorial innovation**	Architecture
	Collective intelligence		Customer focus
	Expertise		Standards
The artificial intelligence of the territorial organization	Governance		Productivity
	Management	**The artificial intelligence of the territorial offer Offer**	Innovation and design
	Digital structures		Commercial
Artificial intelligence of territorial strategies	Strategic planning		Marketing
	Strategic intelligence		Customer experience
	Economic excellence	**Artificial intelligence of the territorial environment**	Economics
			Lobbying

Source: Adapted from Gourvennec & Kabla (2017)

In this way, we have highlighted five key areas in which artificial intelligence can be deployed to improve a region's performance and competitiveness. Each axis is subdivided into several specific dimensions, offering a structured framework for the implementation of AI in different fields. The first axis, "Artificial intelligence of territorial skills", focuses on developing the skills and training needed to take advantage of AI within the territory. The "Training" dimension emphasizes the importance of training human resources in new AI technologies to strengthen local capabilities. The "Artificial intelligence of technology and territorial innovation" dimension focuses on the adoption and integration of AI into the territory's technological infrastructures. The "Architecture", "Collective Intelligence", "Customer Orientation", "Expertise" and "Standards" dimensions aim to establish a technological ecosystem conducive to innovation and to exploit the benefits of AI. The third axis, "Artificial intelligence of territorial organization", addresses the use of AI to optimize governance, productivity, and management within territorial organizations. The "Governance", "Productivity" and "Management" dimensions highlight the potential of AI to improve organizational processes and decision-making. The "Artificial Intelligence of Territorial Offerings" axis focuses on the use of AI to develop and market new products and services adapted to market needs. The "Innovation and Design", "Digital Structures" and "Commercial" dimensions aim to harness the potential of AI to create new economic opportunities and boost territorial competitiveness. Finally, the "Artificial Intelligence for Territorial Strategies" axis focuses on the use of AI to support strategic planning, marketing, business intelligence, customer experience, and economic excellence. The dimensions "Strategic planning", "Marketing", "Business intelligence", "Customer experience" and "Economic excellence" highlight the role of AI in developing effective territorial strategies and promoting sustainable economic growth (Bentalha, 2024). In addition, the table underlines the importance of taking into account the territorial environment in which AI will be deployed, addressing economic aspects and lobbying in the "Artificial intelligence of the territorial environment" dimension.

For our study, we retain the territorial performance approach adopted by Hmioui et al. (2019), focusing on 19 indicators, as summarized by the following Table 2:

Table 2. Territorial performance dimensions for digital sovereignty

Territorial performance dimensions	
Territorial economic efficiency	Average labor productivity
	Efficiency of the local labor market
	Contribution of high value-added activities
Territorial social equity and efficiency	Social infrastructure
	Public health expenditure per protected person
	Unemployment rate by training category
	Activity rate by training category
	GDP per capita
Adequacy of the territorial business ecosystem	Efficiency of the local judicial system
	Infrastructure development
	Development of intermediation institutions
	Adaptation of local regulations
Territorial economic and innovation dynamics	Company start-ups
	Patents filed per total employment
	Creation of salaried jobs
	Proportion of bankruptcy filings
Territorial tax equity and efficiency	Proportion of tax households paying income tax
	Median income declared to tax authorities
	Number of tax disputes

Source: Adapted from Hmioui et al. (2019)

This approach presents a homogeneous set of indicators for assessing a region's performance on several levels. It groups these indicators into five main categories, offering a holistic view of the economic, social, fiscal, and innovation challenges facing a territory. The first category, "Territorial Economic Efficiency", focuses on a region's productivity and competitiveness. By measuring average labor productivity, the efficiency of the local labor market, and the contribution of high-value-added activities, this category provides crucial information on the economic strength of the territory and its ability to generate wealth. Strong performance in this category indicates a dynamic region, attractive to businesses and skilled workers (Bentalha, 2023). Next, the "Territorial social equity and efficiency" category addresses aspects related to the well-being of the population. Taking into account indicators such as social infrastructure, public health spending, unemployment, and activity rates by level of education, as well as GDP per capita, this category highlights the territory's efforts to promote social equity and offer decent living conditions to its inhabitants. A territory that performs well in this category will be perceived as an attractive region in which to live and work. The third category, "Adequacy of the territorial business ecosystem", focuses on factors that foster a business-friendly environment. The efficiency of the local judicial system, the development of infrastructure and intermediation institutions, and the adaptation of local regulations are key elements in attracting and retaining businesses. A region that excels in this category offers a solid framework for economic growth and development. The "Territorial Economic and Innovation Dynamics" category highlights a territory's ability to stimulate entrepreneurship, innovation, and job creation. By measuring business start-ups, the number of patents filed, the creation of salaried jobs, and the proportion of bankruptcy filings, this category reflects the region's economic dynamism and potential for future growth. A region that performs well in this category will be perceived as a hub of innovation and entrepreneurship. Finally, the "Territorial Tax Equity and Efficiency" category examines the tax contribution of citizens and businesses, as well as the efficiency of the local tax system. The proportion of tax households paying tax, the median income declared to the tax authorities and the number of tax disputes are key indicators for assessing the fairness and efficiency of the local tax system. A territory performing well in this category will be perceived as managing its tax resources responsibly and offering a fair tax environment.

It is therefore now possible to model the effects of artificial intelligence on the digitization of territorial intelligence and territorial performance.

Model for Analyzing the Impact of Artificial Intelligence on the Digitization of Territorial Intelligence and Territorial Performance

The proposed problem aims to verify that the digitization of territorial intelligence is a corollary of a certain level of territorial governance between the various local players and can help improve the region's overall performance (Figure 1).

Figure 1. Modeling the impact of digitizing territorial intelligence on territorial performance (Prepared by the authors)

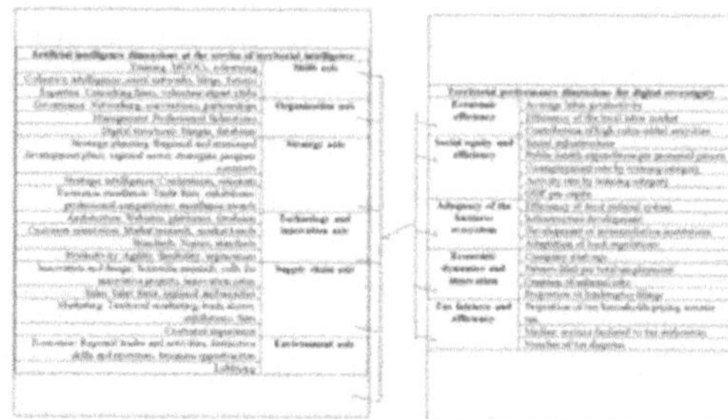

From this model, we derive the following main research hypothesis: How can digital technology serving the development of territorial intelligence contribute to improving the digital sovereignty of regions? This single hypothesis assumes good reliability and homogeneity of the items in the respective scales of "Dimensions of artificial intelligence at the service of territorial intelligence" and "Dimensions of territorial performance for digital sovereignty", making latent variables to base a linear regression model on.

Our study aims to assess the impact of digitization on governance and performance in the region, in line with our research hypotheses. To this end, we conducted a questionnaire survey of 280 people between March and November 2023. The sample was made up of 51% men and 49% women, with an average age of 36. It was diverse in terms of the level of education (primary to tertiary), socio-professional categories (managerial, white-collar, blue-collar, etc.), nationalities, and motivations. The questionnaire aimed to measure the level of maturity of territorial governance mechanisms (decision-making processes, citizen consultation, etc.), the level of effectiveness of digitization in the region (dematerialization of public services, open data, etc.), and the extent of the impact of digitization on different aspects of regional performance (Bentalha et al., 2020). To obtain reliable answers, we used a 5-level Likert scale. The results were statistically analyzed using SPSS software. It enabled us to quantify correlations and links between digitization, governance, and performance in the region.

RESULTS AND DISCUSSION

3.1. Construction of the Regression Model

To test our hypotheses, we opt for a linear multiple regression model. To facilitate modeling, we use the following coding for the model variables (Table 3):

Table 3. Coding of regression model variables

Explanatory variables: Dimensions of artificial intelligence at the service of territorial intelligence	
Artificial intelligence of territorial competencies	**IAT-1**
The artificial intelligence of the territorial organization	**IAT-2**
Artificial intelligence of territorial strategies	**IAT-3**
Artificial intelligence of technology and territorial innovation	**IAT-4**
Artificial intelligence of territorial supply	**IAT-5**
Artificial intelligence of the territorial environment	**IAT-6**
Variables to be explained: Territorial performance dimensions for digital sovereignty	
Territorial economic efficiency	**PT-1**
Territorial social equity and efficiency	**PT-2**
Adequacy of the territorial business ecosystem	**PT-3**
Territorial economic and innovation dynamics	**PT-4**
Territorial tax equity and efficiency	**PT-5**

Source: The authors

Purification of the "artificial intelligence dimensions at the service of territorial intelligence" scale

Reliability is verified when an instrument is used several times under the same conditions and gives the same results. To assess reliability, we use Cronbach's Alpha (Cronbach, 1951). It is interpreted as a correlation coefficient. The closer it is to 1, the more reliable the scale. The closer it is to 0, the weaker the consistency of the scale, meaning that the sample selected does not correctly capture the construct (Mansouri et al., 2008). According to Cronbach's Alpha, the scale for the variable "Dimensions of artificial intelligence at the service of territorial intelligence" reflects a good level of internal consistency for the six items that make it up. However, the elimination of "Artificial intelligence of territorial organization", "Artificial intelligence of territorial strategies" and "Artificial intelligence of territorial environment" is likely to improve it significantly (Table 4). Furthermore, the calculation of Cronbach's alpha is only relevant when the scale used is unidimensional. It is therefore necessary to perform principal component analyses (PCA) on the psychometric scale to ascertain its dimensionality.

Table 4. Reliability and consistency of the "dimensions of Artificial Intelligence at the service of territorial intelligence" scale

	Before treatment	*After treatment*
Cronbach's Alpha	*,700*	*,947*
Number of items	***6***	***3***
KMO sampling precision measure	***,679***	***,668***
Bartlett's significance	***,000***	***,000***

Source: The authors

The Artificial Intelligence of Territorial Intelligence approach implemented by the various territorial players focuses mainly on actions concerning territorial skills (IAT1), territorial technology and innovation (IAT4), and territorial supply (IAT5).

After cleaning, the three scale items offer an explanatory capacity of 90.65%, compared with 69.30% before the operation (Table 5). This extraction enabled the adoption of a unified dimension for the three variables studied.

Table 5. PCA of the "Artificial intelligence of territorial intelligence" scale

Component	*Original eigenvalues*			*Extraction Sum of squares of selected factors*		
	Total	*% of variance*	*% accumulated*	*Total*	*% of variance*	*% accumulated*
1	2,720	90,652	90,652	2,720	90,652	90,652
2	,280	9,348	100,000			
3	-3,670E-017	-1,223E-015	100,000			

Extraction method: Principal component analysis.
Source: The authors

Purification of the "territorial performance dimensions for digital sovereignty" scale

The "Territorial performance dimensions for digital sovereignty" variable reflects a good level of consistency. However, the elimination of "Territorial social equity and efficiency" and "Territorial economic dynamics and innovation" is likely to improve it (Table 6).

Table 6. Reliability and consistency of the "territorial performance dimensions for digital sovereignty" scale

	Before treatment	*After treatment*
Cronbach's Alpha	*,682*	*,864*
Number of items	**5**	***3***
KMO sampling precision measure	***,676***	***,653***
Bartlett's significance	***,000***	***,000***

Source: The authors

The three remaining items would have an explanatory capacity of 70.35% (Table 7). The two main scales will be coded PGT1 and PGT2.

Table 7. PCA of the "Territorial performance dimensions for digital sovereignty" scale

Component	*Original eigenvalues*			*Extraction Sum of squares of selected factors*		
	Total	*% of variance*	*% accumulated*	*Total*	*% of variance*	*% accumulated*
1	2,487	49,748	49,748	2,487	49,748	49,748
2	1,030	20,604	70,352	1,030	20,604	70,352
3	,864	17,287	87,639			
4	,494	9,878	97,518			
5	,124	2,482	100,000			

Extraction method: Principal component analysis.
Source: The authors

The three retained items are correlated with the two main components of the PGT1 and PGT2 scales. The overall performance sought by local players concerning their approach to digitizing territorial intelligence focuses more on developing territorial economic efficiency, fiscal and social equity, and efficiency, and secondarily on developing the suitability of the territorial business ecosystem. The importance given to the development of territorial economic dynamics and innovation remains less of a priority.

3.2. Main Hypothesis Test

Correlation analysis

According to the Pearson index values (Table 8), only the first principal component PGT1 remains correlated with the single component IAT.

Table 8. IAT" - "PGT" correlations:

	PGT 1		PGT 2	
	Pearson Correlation	**Sig.**	**Pearson Correlation**	**Sig.**
IAT	,944	,000	-,030	,634

Source: The authors

As a result, and due to the absence of links with the illustrative variables, the second component of the latter scale relating to Territorial Social Equity and Efficiency will be excluded from our model.

Variance analysis

After eliminating the 2nd principal component PGT2 of the variable to be explained, the variance decomposition allows us to certify the suitability of the regression model (Table 9).

Table 9. Test of variance "IAT" - "PGT 1

		"IAT" – "PGT 1 "
Regression	**R**	*0,944*
	D	*0,330*
	Sig.	*0,00*

Source: The authors

Regression analysis

Table 10. IAT" - "PGT 1" regression coefficients

	Non-standardized coefficients		*Beta*	*Sig.*
	a	*Standard error*		
(Constant)	*-4,334E-017*	*,021*		*1,000*
IAT	*,944*	*,021*	*,944*	*,000*

Source: The authors

By examining the Beta coefficients, we can see that the artificial intelligence approach to territorial intelligence, focusing on skills, technology, and innovation, and the territorial offer, contributes amply and significantly to improving the first main component of overall territorial performance (Figure 2). As a result of our regression model, the parameters of the regression equation for the variable "Dimensions of territorial performance for digital sovereignty" (PGT), lead us to the following model:

Figure 2. Model for analyzing the impact of artificial intelligence on territorial digital performance (Authors)

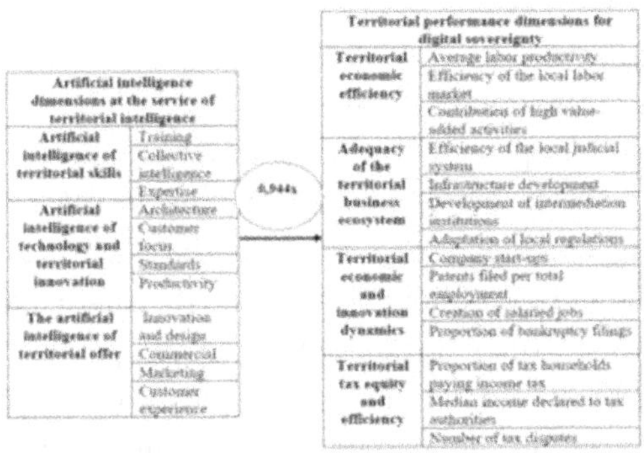

By committing to a strategy of digitizing territorial intelligence, local players gain significantly in terms of improving overall territorial performance, particularly as regards the development of economic efficiency, the adequacy of the business ecosystem, and territorial tax efficiency.

3.3. Results Discussion

Digitization is perceived positively by a large proportion of respondents as a means of developing the region. In terms of digitization practices and territorial intelligence, the general trend is towards the digitization of territorial skills, the digitization of territorial technology and innovation, and the digitization of territorial offerings. However, when it comes to the territorial performance desired by stakeholders, there are five most sought-after variables: the development of territorial economic efficiency, the development of territorial social equity and efficiency, the development of territorial business ecosystem adequacy, the development of territorial economic dynamics and innovation, and finally the development of territorial fiscal equity and efficiency.

The region's territorial governance has thus become a tool for harmonizing territorial intelligence development actions and practices. Local players are undertaking a wide range of actions to digitize the region's economic intelligence. To improve this effectiveness, the region's players are called upon to draw up and implement coherent action plans, and to develop relevant coordination, monitoring, and evaluation mechanisms, as part of a genuine economic intelligence strategy focused on digital. In addition to information exchange and coordination mechanisms, these players are also invited to develop increasingly sophisticated governance mechanisms, incorporating more advanced collaboration and pooling of resources and skills. Improving regional attractiveness is of great support to the success of the governance approach, in terms of responsiveness, agility, productivity, efficiency, and sustainability (Hmioui et al., 2017). Sustainability in the development of the Region's economic attractiveness, by engaging in a territorial intelligence digitization approach by local stakeholders, presupposes compliance with and integration of sustainable development principles and practices (Hmioui et al., 2022).

Territorial intelligence is therefore a promising tool for enhancing territorial knowledge, simulating scenarios, engaging citizens, and accelerating the implementation of territorial public policies. But it must remain a decision-making tool in human hands. Firstly, territorial intelligence can help analyze large quantities of data on a territory (demographics, economy, mobility, environment, etc.) to extract data useful for understanding the territory and making decisions. Secondly, it can contribute to predictive modeling by simulating different scenarios for the evolution of territory according to hypotheses on key factors (employment, transport, housing, etc.). This helps decision-makers anticipate the impact of their strategic choices. Conversational territorial intelligence can also serve as an interface for easily gathering citizens' perceptions and needs about their territory. Augmented reality and computer vision can help model and visualize complex projects on a territorial scale (urban development, infrastructure, etc.). The automation of tedious tasks by AI can free up the time of decision-makers and planners to concentrate on higher value-added tasks. Territorial intelligence can process large quantities of heterogeneous data on a territory and extract trends and correlations thanks to machine learning. Finally, territorial intelligence can simulate different territorial evolutions according to variations in key parameters, to anticipate the effects of public decisions.

In this way, we can make some recommendations on the use of artificial intelligence to improve territorial intelligence. Firstly, AI can help analyze large quantities of data on a territory to extract data useful for understanding the territory and making decisions. Machine learning algorithms can detect correlations and trends that are difficult for humans to see. Artificial intelligence (AI), and machine learning algorithms in particular, offer unprecedented capabilities for analyzing large volumes of geospatial data and extracting valuable information. With the multiplication of sensors and diverse data sources (satellite images, open data, digital traces, etc.), territories today generate massive quantities of data (Shamim & Bentalha, 2023). AI makes it possible to mine, structure, and exploit this data on a scale that human analysis cannot match. Machine learning algorithms can detect patterns, correlations, and complex trends within this massive data. They can bring to light unsuspected links between different phenomena observed on a territory. These subtle correlations often escape human analysis due to our cognitive biases and limitations in apprehending overly complex systems. By cross-referencing disparate data, AI provides a holistic understanding of a territory's dynamics. It enables us to identify emerging issues, anticipate changes, and simulate the impact of different development or public policy scenarios. This detailed, forward-looking understanding of the territory then feeds into more informed decision-making by local players. The intelligent use of data by AI thus becomes a strategic tool for local authorities and planners to meet contemporary urban, environmental, and societal challenges. Secondly, it can contribute to predictive modeling by simulating different scenarios for the evolution of territory according to hypotheses on key factors (employment, transport, housing, etc.). Artificial intelligence brings significant added value to predictive modeling, enabling us to anticipate the future evolution of a territory. Thanks to their ability to process immense volumes of data and detect complex correlations, machine learning algorithms can be used to build highly sophisticated predictive models. These models integrate multiple key factors influencing territorial dynamics, such as employment, transport, housing, demographics, the environment, and so on. By modeling the interactions between these different variables, AI can simulate the evolution of a territory over the medium and long term. The strength of these models lies in the ability to test different scenarios by varying certain assumptions about key factors. By simulating these contrasting scenarios, AI models help to understand the dynamics at play, identify the most relevant levers for action, and assess the consequences of different possible development choices. Decision-makers are thus provided with a forward-looking vision to guide public policy. This AI-powered predictive modeling is a strategic decision-making tool that enables us to think about the future of our territory in an enlightened way and to anticipate future challenges. Thirdly, conversational AI can serve as an interface for easily gathering citizens' perceptions and needs about their territory. Conversational AI, through virtual agents, chatbots, or voice assistants, opens up new perspectives for facilitating dialogue between citizens and territorial players. These intelligent interfaces offer an intuitive and accessible communication channel so that residents can easily express their feelings, grievances, or expectations about the issues facing their territory. Thanks to AI advances in natural language processing, these assistants can conduct natural, contextualized conversations with citizens. They can ask them open-ended questions, rephrase their answers, and ask for clarification to pinpoint their concerns. As the conversation progresses, a detailed profile of each citizen's perceptions can be drawn up. By adopting a proactive approach, these interfaces can also solicit residents directly on specific themes via targeted micro-consultations. Their playful, conversational use encourages greater participation, beyond the often time-consuming traditional systems. AI then enables the large-scale analysis and structuring of the numerous feedback collected from citizens. Common trends, points of convergence, and points of divergence on the various territorial issues then emerge clearly. This fine-tuned understanding of people's lived experience becomes a valuable complement to objective data, providing food for thought for local decision-makers and ensuring that territorial policies are well attuned to the realities on the ground. Fourthly, augmented reality and computer vision can help to model and visualize complex projects on a territorial scale. Augmented reality and computer vision technologies offer unprecedented possibilities for modeling and visualizing complex development projects on a territory in their real environment. They enable virtual elements to be superimposed on the physical world using mobile devices or augmented reality glasses. Thanks to computer vision, existing buildings, infrastructures, and landscapes can be accurately reconstructed in 3D using data from drones, satellite images, or point clouds. This ultra-realistic virtual modeling of the territory then forms the basis for projecting different development scenarios. Augmented reality tools enable us to visualize these future developments directly on the ground as if they were already built. This enables us to simulate the layout of new buildings, assess their integration into the landscape, and visualize road and transport layouts on the site itself. Elected representatives, urban planners, and the general public can see the real-life impact of planned projects. This in-situ visualization makes it much easier to understand projects that are often difficult to grasp on paper. It helps them project and anticipate changes in a given area. It's a formidable tool for communication and consultation on future developments, enabling informed decision-making. Fifthly, AI's automation of certain tedious tasks (data processing, reporting, etc.) can free up the time of decision-makers and planners to concentrate on higher value-added tasks. Decision-making and regional planning processes involve many time-consuming tasks such as data processing and analysis, and the production of reports and other technical documents. The automation of these time-consuming tasks by artificial intelligence represents a tremendous productivity gain for the teams in charge of these missions. Thanks to automatic natural language processing and machine learning, AI is capable of ingesting, structuring, and synthesizing large quantities of heterogeneous data from multiple sources. AI systems can then automatically generate comprehensive, perfectly formatted technical reports and analyses in a matter of moments. This automation saves experts from spending valuable time on tedious data collection, formatting, and retrieval tasks. They can concentrate on their real added value: strategic analysis, forward-looking thinking, the development of scenarios, and informed recommendations for the region. In addition to productivity gains, AI also ensures that available data is much more usable. AI helps you to take advantage of all existing knowledge, rather than missing out on buried information. This feeds into more robust decision-making, based on a holistic understanding of the issues at stake.

Sixthly, the analysis of territorial mega data to extract insights. AI can process large quantities of heterogeneous data on a territory (demographics, mobility, economy, environment, etc.) and extract trends and correlations thanks to machine learning. Territories today generate massive volumes of digital data from a wide variety of sources: demographic data, mobility traces, economic data, satellite images, environmental sensors, social networks, open data, etc. This profusion of metadata represents an invaluable mine of information, but one that is impossible to exploit using traditional analysis methods. This is where artificial intelligence techniques, and machine learning in particular, bring real added value. Learning algorithms are capable of ingesting and processing these masses of heterogeneous data on a very large scale. They can detect and model trends, correlations, and complex patterns that would be impossible to identify using a human approach. For example, AI can correlate mobility data for a given area with socioeconomic and environmental indicators, and highlight unexpected links between employment, air quality, and travel dynamics. Or combine satellite, cadastral, and energy consumption data to optimize urban management. By cross-referencing all these different types of data, machine learning creates a transversal and systemic vision of territorial dynamics. This gives decision-makers a detailed understanding of current trends, enabling them to anticipate future developments and identify priority levers for action. The intelligent exploitation of territorial mega data by AI transforms the mass of raw data into actionable knowledge, in the service of a genuine strategy of sustainable territorial development. Seventh, the simulation and predictive modeling of territorial scenarios. AI makes it possible to simulate different territorial evolutions according to variations in key parameters, to anticipate the effects of public decisions. The complexity of territorial systems, with their many interdependent components (demographics, economy, mobility, environment, etc.), makes it particularly difficult to anticipate their future evolution. It is in this context that artificial intelligence provides invaluable simulation and predictive modeling capabilities. By integrating massive data on a given territory, machine learning algorithms can build ultra-sophisticated predictive models. These models reproduce in great detail the dynamics at work and the interactions between the many key factors of change (employment, transport, housing, etc.). The great strength of these simulations lies in the ability to vary certain input parameters to test different contrasting scenarios. By modeling these different scenarios, public decision-makers can then accurately anticipate the territorial effects induced by their choices of development or sectoral policies, identify priority areas at stake, and fine-tune their strategies. This predictive approach feeds real territorial foresight, essential for defining a coherent and sustainable roadmap over the medium/long term, rather than reactive actions based on emergencies.

The development of regional digital capabilities is a complex process that varies significantly across different contexts. Estonia has emerged as a global leader in digital governance, implementing a comprehensive e-government strategy that has transformed public services and citizen engagement. Estonia's digital transformation has resulted in 99% of government services being available online, with an estimated 2% of GDP saved annually due to increased efficiency. The country has also seen increased transparency and citizen trust in government operations. Barcelona has pursued a smart city strategy that emphasizes citizen data sovereignty and ethical technology use, positioning itself as a leader in digital rights. Barcelona's approach has resulted in increased citizen control over personal data, growth in the local tech ecosystem, and enhanced transparency in city operations. Singapore has pursued a top-down, comprehensive approach to digital transformation under its Smart Nation initiative. Singapore has achieved rapid deployment of digital services across government and private sectors, enhanced efficiency in urban management, and positioned itself as a leading global tech hub. The cases demonstrate a spectrum of governance approaches, from the centralized, government-led models of Estonia and Singapore to the more participatory, citizen-centric approach of Barcelona. These case studies demonstrate that there is no one-size-fits-all approach to developing regional digital capabilities. Success depends on adapting strategies to local contexts, prioritizing citizen needs and rights, and maintaining a balance between innovation and responsible governance. As regions around the world continue to pursue digital transformation, these examples offer valuable insights and lessons that can inform policy-making and implementation strategies.

A truly sovereign digital territory is one where all stakeholders actively participate in shaping its digital future. This section explores the mechanisms and benefits of engaging diverse actors in co-creating and implementing digital solutions for territorial management. Digital platforms that facilitate direct citizen input into policy-making and urban planning are powerful tools for building digital sovereignty from the ground up. Taiwan's vTaiwan platform uses AI-powered tools to facilitate large-scale online deliberations on complex policy issues. This approach has been used to develop regulations for emerging technologies like ride-sharing and fintech, ensuring that digital policies reflect citizen concerns and values. Empowering communities to collectively manage and benefit from their data can enhance digital sovereignty at the local level. The DECODE project in Amsterdam and Barcelona is pioneering community data trusts that give citizens control over how their data is collected, used, and shared. This model promotes data sovereignty while enabling data-driven innovations that benefit the community. Involving diverse stakeholders in AI development ensures these technologies align with regional values and needs. Helsinki's AI Register exemplifies this approach by providing transparency about the city's AI systems, allowing citizens and researchers to scrutinize and provide feedback on how AI is used in public services. While participatory approaches offer significant benefits, they also present challenges. Ensuring representativeness and avoiding digital divides require careful planning. Balancing expert knowledge with broad inclusivity can be complex. Additionally, participatory processes can be resource-intensive and challenging to scale. Data privacy concerns must also be carefully addressed in collaborative initiatives.

The pursuit of digital sovereignty must integrate environmental sustainability to ensure responsible and forward-thinking territorial management. This section explores the crucial intersection of digital advancement and ecological responsibility. Energy consumption is a primary concern in the expansion of digital infrastructure. Data centers, 5G networks, and IoT devices significantly increase power demands. Sweden's node4nordic initiative exemplifies a solution, creating sustainable data centers powered by renewable energy and utilizing natural cooling methods. Regions aiming for digital sovereignty should prioritize such energy-efficient technologies and renewable sources, simultaneously reducing environmental impact and enhancing energy independence. E-waste management presents another critical challenge. The Netherlands' National WEEE Register demonstrates an effective approach, tracking electronic products from production to recycling. This system supports the circular economy and mitigates the environmental and health risks posed by electronic waste. Sustainable digital sovereignty requires implementing policies that encourage device longevity, repairability, and proper recycling. Green software engineering is an often overlooked aspect of digital sustainability. Germany's Blue Angel ecolabel now includes criteria for resource-efficient software, highlighting the importance of efficient code in reducing energy consumption. Regions should incorporate these principles into their digital strategies to minimize the energy footprint of their digital services. Smart city solutions offer a prime opportunity to align digital sovereignty with sustainability goals. Copenhagen's Street Lab uses IoT sensors and data analytics to optimize various urban functions, from waste collection to energy consumption in buildings. By developing locally-controlled smart city solutions, regions can advance both their digital autonomy and sustainability objectives. Digital technologies can significantly enhance environmental monitoring capabilities. Finland's Digital Forest program leverages AI, satellite imagery, and IoT sensors to monitor forest health and optimize sustainable forestry practices. Developing sovereign digital capabilities for environmental monitoring strengthens a region's autonomy in managing its natural resources while contributing to global sustainability efforts. Balancing digital growth with ecological preservation is crucial. Estonia's e-Residency program demonstrates how digital services can boost economic growth with minimal environmental impact, reducing the need for physical infrastructure and travel. Digital sovereignty strategies should prioritize solutions that decouple economic growth from environmental degradation. Integrating sustainability into digital policy frameworks is essential for long-term success. The European Green Deal's Destination Earth initiative, aimed at developing a high-precision digital model of the Earth, exemplifies how digital capabilities can support sustainable development and environmental policies. Regions should develop comprehensive policy frameworks that align digital sovereignty goals with environmental sustainability targets. However, several challenges must be addressed. These include balancing immediate digital needs with long-term sustainability goals, ensuring that sustainability measures don't compromise digital competitiveness, addressing potential rebound effects where efficiency gains lead to increased consumption, and navigating international standards and regulations on tech sustainability. Environmental sustainability is an integral component of responsible digital sovereignty. By prioritizing eco-friendly digital infrastructure, promoting circular economy principles in tech, and leveraging digital solutions for environmental management, regions can build digital autonomy that is both robust and sustainable. This approach not only mitigates the ecological impact of digital transformation but also positions regions as leaders in the growing field of green technology, ensuring that digital sovereignty is truly resilient and future-proof.

CONCLUSION

The proposed work aims to contribute to the development of a hybrid approach that combines the strengths of AI and IT to improve decision-making processes in territorial management. The proposed approach will exploit the advantages of both fields to provide decision-makers with more accurate, effective, and efficient tools for territorial management. The analysis will provide a comprehensive review of the current state of AI and IT, as well as original research that demonstrates the potential of the proposed approach through case studies and simulations. The expected results of this approach will provide valuable information and practical solutions for territorial management and contribute to the advancement of the AI and IT field. Territorial intelligence consists of the organization and sharing of knowledge by stakeholders in a given territory. The aim is to observe and analyze the situation collectively, to improve governance. Territorial intelligence is a concept that emphasizes the importance of collaboration and synergy between the various players in a given territory. It is based on the idea that knowledge and information need to be shared and organized in an effective way to enable a better understanding of the issues and challenges facing a territory. The first key element of territorial intelligence is the organization of knowledge. This involves setting up mechanisms and processes for collecting, structuring, and disseminating relevant information and data to the various players involved. This may involve, for example, the creation of shared databases, information exchange platforms, or strategic intelligence systems.

The aim is to facilitate access to information and foster a common understanding of territorial issues. A second fundamental aspect is the sharing of knowledge between local players. This requires the creation of forums for dialogue and consultation, enabling the various stakeholders (local authorities, businesses, associations, citizens, etc.) to exchange views, experiences and expertise. This collaborative approach fosters the emergence of a shared vision and mutual understanding of territorial issues.

Collective observation and analysis is another pillar of territorial intelligence. The aim is to encourage stakeholders to observe and analyze the local situation together, drawing on their respective knowledge and skills. This participative approach helps to identify strengths and weaknesses, opportunities and threats, and to build a comprehensive understanding of territorial issues. Last but not least, territorial intelligence aims to improve local governance. By fostering collaboration, knowledge sharing, and collective analysis, it contributes to more informed and inclusive decision-making. The strategic choices and actions implemented are thus better adapted to the realities of the territory and benefit from broader buy-in and support from the various stakeholders.

The work carried out provided a comprehensive review of the current state of AI and IT, highlighting their strengths, weaknesses, and potential applications in territorial management, taking into account the specific characteristics of territorial data and the needs of decision-makers; an assessment of the effectiveness and efficiency of the proposed approach through case studies and simulations, using real data from different territorial contexts; and recommendations for future research and applications of the proposed approach in different territorial management scenarios.

Territorial governance, particularly through the digitization of intelligence, is emerging as a tool for harmonizing and even synchronizing actions and practices aimed at developing territorial intelligence. The identification, enhancement, and capitalization of territorial skills, organization, strategies, supply, and environment in the face of potential local conflicts, both in terms of supply and demand, remain choices that must be made by local decision-makers and players to initiate and sustain the development of global performance (Bouhtati et al., 2022).

Actors are thus called upon to develop genuine and increasingly sophisticated governance mechanisms, integrating, in addition to informational exchanges and coordination mechanisms, more advanced mechanisms for collaboration and the pooling of resources and skills, as revealed by the results of the empirical study. The study on territorial intelligence presents significant contributions for both practitioners and researchers involved in territorial development and governance. For practitioners, such as political decision-makers, territorial managers, and local development agents, the territorial intelligence approach offers several concrete advantages. Firstly, it improves decision-making by providing a more complete and nuanced vision of the challenges and realities of the territory, thanks to better organization and increased sharing of knowledge between stakeholders. Secondly, it strengthens participative governance by involving the various stakeholders more closely in the observation, analysis, and decision-making processes, thereby fostering support for and ownership of public policies. Thirdly, it facilitates the development of synergies and partnerships by creating spaces for dialogue and consultation between the various players in the area. For researchers, the study of territorial intelligence opens up several stimulating avenues of research. First of all, it enables us to explore the development of effective territorial information systems for collecting, organizing, and disseminating territorial knowledge. Secondly, it offers the opportunity to delve deeper into the methods and processes that foster participative governance and the co-construction of knowledge and decisions with the various stakeholders. In addition, researchers can focus on developing territorial analysis methodologies that take into account the economic, social, environmental, and cultural dimensions specific to each territory. Finally, they can contribute to the development of evaluation frameworks to measure the impacts of the territorial intelligence approach on the performance of public policies, the competitiveness of territories, and the well-being of populations. We therefore plan to broaden our study sample and review the method of its constitution, to make it more representative and relevant. We also plan to extend the duration of the study, making it longitudinal. Finally, we intend to carry out comparative studies between different territories.

REFERENCES

Alla, L., Bentalha, B., & Elyoussfi, A. (2023). Intelligence territoriale et positionnement stratégique des régions au Maroc: Le cas de la région de Fès Meknès en perspective. Le concept de l'intelligence en sciences juridiques, économiques et sociales, 215-237.

Bakis, H. (2021). Territoires intelligents et souveraineté numérique. *Revue Géographique de l'Est*, 61(1-2).

Bellanger, P. (2012). De la souveraineté numérique. le Débat, (3), 149-159.

Bentalha, B. (2020). Big-Data et Service Supply chain management: Challenges et opportunités. *International Journal of Business and Technology Studies*, 1(3).

Bentalha, B. (2022). Smart Technologies for a Sustainable Service Supply Chain: A Prospective Perspective. *Journal of Environmental Issues and Climate Change*, 1(1), 77–89. 10.59110/jeicc.v1i1.81

Bentalha, B. (2023). A Framework for Exploring the Global Performance of Service Supply Chain Management: A Qualitative Study. Government Impact on Sustainable and Responsible Supply Chain Management, 106-129.

Bentalha, B. (2024). Sustainable Supply Chain Management in Tourism: An Understanding of the Prospective Possibilities of Environmental Performance. In Implementing Sustainable Development Goals in the Service Sector (pp. 53-66). IGI Global.

Bentalha, B., Hmioui, A., & Alla, L. (2020). La performance des entreprises de services: Un cadrage théorique d'un concept évolutif. *Alternatives Managériales Economiques*, 2(1), 58–78.

Bertacchini, Y., Girardot, J. J., & Gramaccia, G. (2006, June). De l'intelligence territoriale. Théorie, posture, hypothèses, définitions. In 5e colloque TIC et Territoire: quels développements?

Bouchet, Y. (2003). Dispositif d'intelligence économique territoriale et gouvernance hybride, isdm.univ-fr/PDF/isdm27/isdm27_bouchet.pdf.

Bouhtati, N., Alla, L., & Bentalha, B. (2023). Marketing Big Data Analytics and Customer Relationship Management: A Fuzzy Approach. In Integrating Intelligence and Sustainability in Supply Chains (pp. 75-86). IGI Global. 10.4018/979-8-3693-0225-5.ch004

Bouhtati, N., Hmioui, A., Alla, L., & Bentalha, B. (2022). Logistique et performance touristique: Une étude comparative des principales destinations en Afrique. *Alternatives Managériales Economiques*, 1, 116–132.

Bruté de Rémur, D. (2009). Point de vue: pour une épistémologie de l'IE. Revue internationale d'intelligence économique, 1(1), 9-11. https://www.cairn.info/revue-internationale-d-intelligence-economique-2009-1-page-9.htm

Caragliu, A., & Del Bo, C. F. (2019). Smart innovative cities: The impact of Smart City policies on urban innovation. *Technological Forecasting and Social Change*, 142, 373–384. 10.1016/j.techfore.2018.07.022

Cronbach, L. J. (1951). Coefficient alpha and the internal structure of tests. *Psychometrika*, 16(1), 297–334. 10.1007/BF02310555

Dumont, G. F. (2021). La souveraineté numérique des territoires à l'ère du numérique. Revue française d'administration publique, 177(1), 95-108.

Gourvennec, Y., & Kabla, H. (2017). *Le digital expliqué à mon boss - Par ceux qui en font et pour ceux qui aimeraient (mieux) en faire, par David Fayon*. Editions Kawa.

Hmioui, A., Alla, L., & Bentalha, B. (2017). *Pilotage de la touristicité territoriale au Maroc Proposition d'un indice de tourisctic ité pour la destination Fès. Entrepreneuriat, Innovation, Gouvernance et Développement territorial*. Faculté Polydisciplinaire de TAZA.

Hmioui, A., Alla, L., & Bentalha, B. (2019). La performance touristique territoriale: Cas de la destination Fès. *Alternatives Managériales Economiques*, 1(1), 3–21.

Hmioui, A., Alla, L., & Bentalha, B. (2022). Perception du tourisme durable par les clients étrangers: Cas du séjour dans un établissement hôtelier. ENCG, USMBA, Fès. Reconfigurations du tourisme en contexte de la crise du Covid-19: Quelles démarches pour quelles résiliences au Maroc et ailleurs ?, 1(1), pp.5-38, 2022, 978-9954-9721-2-0.

Hmioui, A., Bentalha, B., & Beniaich, R. (2024). Green Supply Chain Management et développement territorial: Une revue de littérature. *Alternatives Managériales Economiques*, 6(2), 52–74.

Jouve, B., Booth, P., (dir.), (2004), *Démocraties métropolitaines*, PUQ, Sainte Foy.

Lamsiah, A., Benabderrazik, Y., & Bentalha, B. (2021). The Economic and political components of diplomatic discourse: State actors in Morocco-UK Free Trade Agreement as a case study. *Alternatives Managériales Economiques*, 3(4), 496–517.

Lamsiah, A., & Bentalha, B. (2022a). Dakhla: A Growing Touristic Destination with a Diplomatic Sway. *Alternatives Managériales Economiques*, 1, 94–115.

Lamsiah, A., & Bentalha, B. (2022b). Economic Diplomacy and Economic Intelligence Amalgamation: The Moroccan-Nigerian Economic Exchange as a Case Study. *Alternatives Managériales Economiques*, 4(4), 582–603.

Lamsiah, A., & Bentalha, B. (2023). Moroccan jews and economic intelligence: the implicit power of belonging. Le concept de l'intelligence en sciences juridiques, économiques et sociales, pp.71-90, 978-9920-9012-4-6.

Loukil, F. (2020). Intelligence territoriale et performance des territoires. *Revue Gouvernance*, 17(1), 32–50.

Mansouri, N., M'zali, B., & Peretti, J. M. (2008). La construction d'une échelle de mesure des problématiques de l'environnement tétranormalisé de l'entreprise: Application du paradigme de Churchill. 5ème Congrès de l'ADERSE: Transversalité de la Responsabilité Sociale de l'Entreprise, Grenoble, 10.

Pecqueur, B. (2005). *Le territoire est mort Vive les territoires! Une (re)fabrication au nom du développement*. IRD Éditions Paris.

Rallet, A., & Rochelandet, F. (2019). La souveraineté numérique, une ambition pour les régions. *Revue d'Économie Régionale et Urbaine*, 2019(3), 447–465.

Shamim, R., & Bentalha, B. (2023). Blockchain-Enabled Machine Learning Framework for Demand Forecasting in Supply Chain Management. In Integrating Intelligence and Sustainability in Supply Chains (pp. 28-48). IGI Global. 10.4018/979-8-3693-0225-5.ch002

KEY TERMS AND DEFINITIONS

AI-Driven: Referring to systems, processes, or decisions that are primarily guided or executed by artificial intelligence technologies, leveraging machine learning and data analysis capabilities.

Cybersecurity: The practice of protecting systems, networks, programs, and data from digital attacks, unauthorized access, and damage, ensuring the confidentiality, integrity, and availability of information.

Data Governance: The overall management of data availability, usability, integrity, and security within an organization or territory, including policies, standards, and procedures for data handling.

Digital Sovereignty: A nation's ability to control its digital assets, infrastructure, and data, ensuring independence from foreign technologies and protecting its citizens' digital rights and privacy.

Smart Cities: Urban areas that use various types of electronic data collection sensors and AI technologies to supply information for efficient management of assets, resources, and services, improving the quality of life for citizens.

Territorial Intelligence: The process of gathering, analyzing, and utilizing information about a specific geographic area to support decision-making and strategic planning for its development and security.

Chapter 9
Generative AI for Cybersecurity
An Introduction

Kritika
https://orcid.org/0000-0002-1186-6032
Independent Researcher, India

ABSTRACT

The intersection of cybersecurity and generative artificial intelligence (AI) has become a crucial frontier as the digital landscape changes. By examining the interaction between AI-powered attacks and defence mechanisms and concentrating on applications like anomaly detection, synthetic data generation, automated incident response, and forensics, the chapter examines the potential of generative artificial intelligence (AI) in redefining conventional cybersecurity paradigms. In order to reduce the hazards associated with deepfakes and synthetic media, the chapter discusses the examination of adversarial machine learning techniques and strategies. Along with offering guidance on incorporating AI into security operations, encouraging human-AI cooperation, and building strong AI skills, it also discusses the ethical ramifications of AI-driven security procedures. It also serves as a comprehensive guide for security professionals, researchers, and decision-makers, offering a holistic understanding of the synergies between AI and cybersecurity.

1. INTRODUCTION

A class of machine learning models known as "generative artificial intelligence" (AI) is able to produce new types of data, including text, images, audio, and video, by using patterns and attributes that are discovered from training data (Radford

DOI: 10.4018/979-8-3693-8557-9.ch009

et al., 2022). These models replicate the underlying distribution of the training data by using deep neural networks and sophisticated algorithms to generate new, synthetic material. Generative AI has become a game-changing technology that is expanding the realms of art, entertainment, and science study, among other fields, beyond what was previously considered not feasible. One area of technology that is constantly developing and receiving a lot of interest is generative artificial intelligence (AI). This cutting-edge field includes a wide range of methods and models that let computers produce, develop, or synthesise original, meaningful material. Generative AI is pushing the envelope of what is feasible, from text generation and image synthesis to music composition and video creation, and it is bringing in a new age of creativity and invention. The fundamental idea of generative artificial intelligence is unsupervised learning, in which models are trained to recognize implicit correlations and patterns in incoming data without the need for explicit labels or targets (Goodfellow et al., 2016). This methodology enables the models to produce new instances that have resemblance to the training examples by teaching them about the intricate distributions and structures present in the data. One of generative AI's main benefits is its capacity to produce original content that has never been seen before, which may open up new avenues for problem-solving, creativity, and invention. Table 1 highlights the different model architectures and techniques of generative AI. Natural language generation (NLG) is a popular use of generative AI that entails machines producing text that is legible by humans. Generative AI systems are capable of producing coherent and contextually relevant content, such as news articles, fiction, poetry, and code, thanks to deep learning approaches like transformers and language models (Radford et al., 2019). By enabling the automation of numerous writing jobs, these models have the potential to revolutionise industries like journalism, content development, and customer service.

Table 1. Generative AI model architectures and techniques

Approach	Description
Generative Adversarial Networks (GANs)	Consist of two neural networks (generator and discriminator) trained adversarially. The generator creates synthetic data, and the discriminator tries to distinguish between real and generated data.
Variational Autoencoders (VAEs)	Learn to encode input data into a latent space representation and decode from that representation to reconstruct or generate new samples. Allow for efficient manipulation and exploration of the data distribution.
Autoregressive Models	Effective for generating sequential data like text or images. Predict the next element in a sequence based on previous elements, allowing for the generation of coherent and contextually relevant content. Examples: GPT, DALL-E.

continued on following page

Table 1. Continued

Approach	Description
Diffusion Models	Operate by gradually removing noise from an initially random input, resulting in the generation of high-quality images. Demonstrated remarkable performance in generating realistic and diverse images from text prompts. Examples: DALL-E 2, Stable Diffusion.

Cybersecurity has become essential in the digital age, where data is king and connectivity is the standard. The need to safeguard our digital assets, private data, and vital infrastructure against malevolent cyber assaults is growing along with our dependence on technology. Cybersecurity is a broad term describing a variety of techniques used to protect networks and information systems from cyberattacks, illegal access, and data breaches while maintaining their availability, confidentiality, and integrity (Von Solms & Van Niekerk, 2013). One cannot stress the significance of cybersecurity in the linked world of today. Because more and more people, companies, and governments depend on digital systems and internet services, cyberattacks might have disastrous effects. While successful cyberattacks on critical infrastructure can disrupt vital services and perhaps put lives in danger, data breaches can result in the exposure of sensitive information, financial losses, and reputational harm (Kshetri, 2017). A new era of technical innovation and disruption has been brought about by the rapid growth of artificial intelligence (AI), which is changing a number of businesses and sectors. (Nguyen et al. 2022) highlight that in addition to the manifold advantages and prospects offered by artificial intelligence, there exist noteworthy cybersecurity hazards and issues that necessitate attention. Artificial intelligence (AI) systems can attract cyber adversaries looking to exploit weaknesses, rig results, or interfere with daily operations. This is especially true for AI systems used in vital infrastructures and high-stakes applications. AI systems' growing interconnectedness and complexity, together with their reliance on massive amounts of data, open up new attack vectors and possible points of entry for malevolent actors (Elshawi et al., 2021).

The possibility of adversarial attacks, in which deliberately constructed inputs are intended to deceive or manipulate AI models, giving rise to unexpected and potentially destructive outputs, is one of the main cybersecurity issues in the era of artificial intelligence (Akhtar & Ghosh, 2019). These attacks can have serious repercussions, from monetary losses and intellectual property theft to bodily injury and safety hazards in AI-enabled systems such as industrial control systems or driverless cars. Moreover, there are advantages and disadvantages of incorporating AI into cybersecurity procedures and systems. Although AI-powered security solutions can improve vulnerability analysis, incident response, and threat detection, they also come with additional risks in the event that adversaries breach or manipulate the underlying AI models (Elshawi et al., 2021).

Given how these two fields merge and profoundly influence one another, there are opportunities and difficulties at the nexus of cybersecurity and generative artificial intelligence (AI). Although generative AI approaches present new attack vectors and vulnerabilities that need to be addressed, they can also be used to improve cybersecurity practices and capabilities (Elshawi et al., 2021). The creation of synthetic data is one of the most promising areas where generative AI and cybersecurity may work together. Large amounts of synthetic data that closely resemble real-world situations can be produced using generative models, allowing cybersecurity systems to be tested and trained without jeopardizing private data or putting operational environments in danger (Camino et al., 2021).

Threat intelligence and anomaly detection are two more areas where generative AI might benefit cybersecurity. Generative models are capable of detecting deviations and abnormalities that can point to possible threats or malicious activity by learning the patterns and distributions of typical system behaviour (Zong et al., 2018). This method improves the capacity to quickly identify and address cyber risks across a range of domains, such as network traffic analysis, log monitoring, and user behaviour analytics. Furthermore, security and incident response automation can be facilitated by the application of generative AI approaches. Artificial intelligence (AI) models can be trained to suggest appropriate reaction actions by creating synthetic attack scenarios and modelling future incidents. This can streamline the incident handling process and shorten the time needed for human intervention (Nguyen et al., 2022). Moreover, adversarial attacks against generative AI models itself might result in misclassification or unexpected outputs from carefully constructed inputs, which could jeopardise the security of systems that depend on these models (Akhtar & Ghosh, 2019). It becomes essential to employ strategies like adversarial training and model robustness evaluation in order to reduce these risks and guarantee the dependability of AI-powered security solutions.

While generative AI has demonstrated remarkable capabilities and potential, it is essential to acknowledge and address the associated challenges and risks. Some of the key concerns include:

1. Bias and Fairness: Generative AI models can inherit and amplify biases present in the training data, leading to the generation of content that reinforces harmful stereotypes or perpetuates societal prejudices (Bender et al., 2021). Addressing these issues requires careful curation of training data, robust debiasing techniques, and ethical considerations throughout the model development process.
2. Deepfakes and Synthetic Media Manipulation: The ability to generate realistic synthetic media, such as images, videos, and audio, raises concerns about the potential for misuse and the spread of misinformation or deepfakes (Kietzmann

et al., 2019). Robust detection and authentication methods, as well as public awareness and education, are crucial to mitigate these risks.

3. Ethical and Legal Implications: The rapid advancement of generative AI raises ethical and legal questions regarding intellectual property rights, privacy concerns, and the potential for malicious applications (Bremermann et al., 2022). Developing governance frameworks, establishing ethical guidelines, and fostering responsible AI practices are essential to ensure the beneficial and ethical use of this technology.
4. Computational Complexity and Environmental Impact: Training large-scale generative AI models often requires substantial computational resources and energy consumption, leading to significant environmental and financial costs (Strubell et al., 2019). Efforts to improve model efficiency, leverage renewable energy sources, and develop sustainable AI practices are crucial for mitigating these challenges.

As generative AI continues to evolve and mature, it is essential to address these challenges through interdisciplinary collaboration, responsible innovation, and a deep understanding of the technology's potential impact on society.

To address these challenges, a multifaceted approach involving technical solutions, policy and regulatory frameworks, and collaborative efforts across various stakeholders is necessary. This includes:

1. Developing secure and robust AI systems from the ground up, incorporating security principles and practices throughout the entire lifecycle, from data collection and model training to deployment and monitoring (Elshawi et al., 2021).
2. Implementing rigorous testing and evaluation methods to identify and mitigate vulnerabilities in AI systems, including adversarial attacks, data poisoning, and model bias (Nguyen et al., 2022).
3. Fostering collaboration between AI researchers, cybersecurity experts, policymakers, and industry leaders to establish best practices, standards, and guidelines for secure AI development and deployment.
4. Investing in research and development efforts to advance AI security, including techniques for adversarial robustness, secure federated learning, and privacy-preserving AI (Akhtar & Ghosh, 2019).

Developing and enforcing regulatory frameworks and governance models to ensure the responsible and ethical use of AI in critical systems, while balancing innovation and security concerns. Enhancing cybersecurity education and training programs to build a skilled workforce capable of addressing the unique challenges posed by the convergence of AI and cybersecurity.

2. THE CYBERSECURITY LANDSCAPE AND EMERGING THREATS

Early cybersecurity threats included denial-of-service (DoS) attacks, viruses, and worms. These attacks were comparatively simple. Mostly aimed at single machines and networks, these threats frequently resulted in outages and data loss. But as the internet spread and became more integrated, cyberthreats quickly changed in type. When cybercriminals saw there was a chance to make money, it was in the late 1990s and early 2000s that financially motivated attacks started to appear. The use of methods including phishing, spam, and malware to get private information or demand ransom increased (Jagatic et al., 2007). Advanced persistent threats (APTs), which are highly skilled and focused attacks frequently supported by nation-states or well-funded criminal organizations, also increased during this time (Virvilis & Gritzalis, 2013).

The swift integration of mobile devices, cloud computing, and the Internet of Things (IoT) has resulted in an increased attack surface area, providing cyber adversaries with additional ports of entry and vulnerability. Attacks on IoT devices, malware aimed at mobile devices, and the use of incorrectly configured clouds have all becoming more frequent (Aris et al., 2021). Furthermore, the growth of social media and internet platforms made it possible for misinformation campaigns, influence operations using technology, and misinformation to proliferate (Bradshaw & Howard, 2019). A wide variety of threats, such as ransomware, supply chain attacks, distributed denial-of-service (DDoS) attacks, and the use of zero-day vulnerabilities, are present in the cybersecurity landscape today (Gandotra et al., 2022). The sophistication of cybercriminals has increased, and they now use methods like fileless malware, off-the-grid strategies, and utilizing genuine system features to avoid detection.

The cybersecurity field now faces both opportunities and difficulties as a result of the artificial intelligence (AI) and machine learning (ML) technologies' rapid growth. Although AI can be used to improve vulnerability assessments, incident response, and threat detection, it has also created new opportunities for cyber adversaries to attack and control these systems. The possibility of hostile attacks on AI models is one of the main worries. Attackers may be able to skew AI systems' outputs or influence how decisions are made by carefully designing inputs or taking advantage of flaws in the model architecture (Akhtar & Ghosh, 2019). Attacks of this nature may have dire repercussions, especially in applications involving vital infrastructure or high stakes when AI is used for autonomous control or decision assistance.

The ability of generative AI models to produce synthetic media and deepfakes is one of the main risks. According to (Kietzmann et al. 2019), deepfakes are extremely realistic and artificially produced media content, such as pictures or videos, that can be used to disseminate false information, pose as genuine people, or commit other types of fraud or deceit. It is becoming more and more difficult to discern between real and synthetic media due to the extraordinary scale at which convincing deepfakes can be produced using generative models. The possibility that generative AI models will be applied to the creation of sophisticated phishing schemes, social engineering scams, or harmful code is another cause for concern (Nguyen et al., 2022). Attackers could produce convincing and highly targeted information by utilising these models.

3. GENERATIVE AI FOR CYBERTHREAT DETECTION AND RESPONSE

An essential part of cybersecurity is anomaly detection, which looks for departures from the usual that can point to possible dangers or malevolent activity. Conventional methods for detecting anomalies frequently depend on machine learning models or rule-based systems that have been trained on labelled data. But getting hold of high-quality labelled data can be quite difficult, especially in environments where threats are changing quickly. By using their capacity to discover the underlying patterns and distributions of normal data in an unsupervised way, generative AI models provide a potent substitute for anomaly detection (Zong et al., 2018). Large amounts of benign data can be used to train these models, which then capture the innate properties and correlations found in the data without the need for explicit labels or target variables.

Once trained, generative models assess the likelihood or reconstruction error of fresh data instances in order to identify abnormalities. Potential anomalies are identified as data points that show high reconstruction errors or substantially depart from the taught patterns; these signals call for additional research or action (Chalapathy & Chawla, 2019). The capacity of generative models to handle complicated and high-dimensional data structures makes them ideal for use in applications like network traffic analysis, log monitoring, and user behaviour analytics. This is one of the main benefits of employing generative models for anomaly detection. Furthermore, when the data changes, generative models may adjust and pick up new patterns, offering a dynamic and flexible method of cyberthreat identification.

A significant obstacle in the creation and implementation of efficient cybersecurity systems is the lack of labelled, high-quality data for machine learning model training. Real-world data may be scarce, secret, or difficult to gather and annotate, making it difficult to obtain representative and diverse datasets that capture different attack scenarios and threat vectors. This problem has a possible answer in the form of generative AI models, which allow synthetic data to be generated that closely resembles real-world data in terms of distribution and properties (Camino et al., 2021). Researchers and practitioners can generate synthetic datasets customized for particular cybersecurity use cases by utilizing generative techniques like variational autoencoders (VAEs), autoregressive models, or generative adversarial networks (GANs).

A crucial component of cybersecurity is effective incident response, which helps businesses to quickly identify, evaluate, and neutralize online threats. But conventional incident response procedures frequently rely mostly on human knowledge and physical interventions, which can be laborious and prone to mistakes or delays, especially when dealing with complex and quickly moving threats. In order to improve reaction times and lessen the workload for security analysts, generative AI models have the ability to automate and streamline a number of incident response process steps (Nguyen et al., 2022). Organizations may simulate and get ready for a variety of cybersecurity incidents by utilizing generative models, which can produce realistic and contextually relevant data. This allows for proactive planning and response methods.

Generative AI offers a potential new direction for improving cyberthreat detection and response skills. Through the utilization of generative models for automated incident response, synthetic data generation, and anomaly detection, enterprises may enhance their cybersecurity defences and remain ahead of constantly changing threats. However, achieving the full potential of generative AI in cybersecurity requires tackling the related obstacles and constraints via multidisciplinary cooperation, conscientious invention, and a thorough comprehension of the technology's possible implications.

4. DEFENDING AGAINST AI-POWERED CYBERATTACKS

A new age of risks and difficulties has been brought about by the combination of cybersecurity and artificial intelligence (AI). Cyber adversaries are actively looking for methods to use AI for hostile purposes as these technologies proliferate and are incorporated into vital systems. The potential for AI-powered cyberattacks poses serious threats to people, organizations, and societies at large. These hazards range from adversarial machine learning attacks to the creation of deepfakes and synthetic media. In order to effectively defend against these new dangers, multiple stakeholders must work together to develop technical solutions, implement regulatory changes, and conduct coordinated operations.

The study of potential weaknesses and assaults on artificial intelligence (AI) systems, especially machine learning models, is known as adversarial machine learning (AML), a fast expanding topic (Akhtar & Ghosh, 2019). Regarding cybersecurity, adversaries may utilize adversarial machine learning (AML) tactics to subvert or circumvent artificial intelligence (AI)-driven security systems, including malware classifiers, intrusion detection systems, and biometric authentication systems. The adversarial example attack is a popular kind of AML attack in which deliberately constructed inputs are intended to lead the AI model to misclassify or generate false outputs (Biggio & Roli, 2018). These adversarial instances can be produced by utilizing methods such as gradient-based optimization or by taking use of the decision boundaries in the model. Table 2 highlights the defending mechanisms against AML attacks.

Table 2. Defending against Adversarial Machine Learning (AML) attacks

Defense Approach	Description
Adversarial Training	Training AI models on adversarial examples to improve robustness against potential attacks (Madry et al., 2018).
Model Robustness Evaluation	Rigorous testing and evaluation methods to assess the robustness of AI models against various types of adversarial attacks, including differential testing, mutation testing, and adversarial input generation (Nguyen et al., 2022).
Secure Model Deployment	Ensuring secure deployment and execution of AI models to mitigate potential vulnerabilities, using techniques like secure enclaves, homomorphic encryption, or federated learning (Elshawi et al., 2021).
Monitoring and Detection	Implementing monitoring and detection mechanisms to identify potential adversarial attacks in real-time, such as anomaly detection, input filtering, and integrity checks (Akhtar & Ghosh, 2019).

The development of generative AI models has made it possible to produce synthetic media and deepfakes that are incredibly convincing and lifelike, raising serious concerns about cybersecurity and public confidence. According to Kietzmann et al. (2019), deepfakes are fake or altered audio, video, or image files that can be utilized for a variety of nefarious activities, including fraud, impersonation, and the dissemination of false information. Table 3 states the mitigation approach to be adopted for safeguarding from deepfakes and synthetic data.

Table 3. Mitigating risks of deepfakes and synthetic media

Mitigation Approach	Description
Detection and Authentication	Developing robust detection and authentication methods, such as digital watermarking, blockchain-based provenance tracking, or AI-based detection models to identify deepfakes and synthetic media (Dang et al., 2022).

continued on following page

Table 3. Continued

Mitigation Approach	Description
Responsible Development and Deployment	Establishing guidelines and best practices for the responsible development and deployment of generative AI models, including implementing appropriate safeguards, ethical considerations, and governance frameworks (Bremermann et al., 2022).
Public Awareness and Education	Raising public awareness and educating individuals about the potential risks and implications of deepfakes and synthetic media to promote media literacy, critical thinking, and the ability to identify and counter misinformation or manipulation attempts.
Regulatory and Legal Frameworks	Developing regulatory and legal frameworks to address the challenges posed by deepfakes and synthetic media, including establishing laws and policies related to content authenticity, privacy, intellectual property rights, and introducing consequences for malicious use or distribution of deepfakes (Chesney & Citron, 2019).

5. CHALLENGES AND LIMITATIONS OF GENERATIVE AI IN CYBERSECURITY

Although generative artificial intelligence (AI) has the ability to completely transform cybersecurity procedures, there are certain obstacles and restrictions in its application and integration. As with any new technology, these issues must be addressed and minimized to guarantee the ethical and successful use of generative AI in cybersecurity. This section will examine the challenges related to technology and computing, data availability and quality, adversarial attack threats, and model flaws.

5.1 Computational and Technical Barriers

A major obstacle related to generative AI models is the amount of computational complexity and resources needed for both training and inference. Deep neural networks with billions of parameters are the foundation of many cutting-edge generative models, including massive language models and high-resolution image generators (Strubell et al., 2019). It can be expensive and resource-intensive to train these models since they demand a large amount of processing power, specialised hardware (such as GPUs or TPUs), and a large number of computational resources.

Moreover, these models' inference or generation processes can be computationally taxing, which presents difficulties for real-time applications or deployment in contexts with limited resources (Radford et al., 2019). This may restrict the usefulness of generative AI models in scenarios involving embedded systems, edge devices, or incident response activities that must be completed quickly. Research and development in areas including hardware acceleration, effective inference methods, and model compression are necessary to overcome these computational hurdles (Ganesh et al., 2020). Furthermore, investigating different architectures or cutting-edge methods that combine efficiency and performance might be essential to facilitating the broad use of generative AI in cybersecurity.

5.2 Data Quality and Availability Issues

The performance and effectiveness of generative AI models heavily rely on the quality and availability of training data. In the cybersecurity domain, obtaining high-quality and representative data can be challenging due to various factors as highlighted in Table 4.

Table 4. Challenges in utilizing data for generative AI in cybersecurity

Challenge	Description
Data Scarcity	Certain types of cybersecurity data, such as zero-day vulnerabilities, advanced persistent threats (APTs), or novel attack vectors, may be scarce or difficult to obtain in sufficient quantities for effective model training (Camino et al., 2021).
Data Sensitivity and Privacy Concerns	Cybersecurity data often contains sensitive information, such as network traffic logs, user activity traces, or incident reports, which can raise privacy and confidentiality concerns when used for training generative AI models (Jordon et al., 2018).
Data Labeling and Annotation	Many cybersecurity applications require labeled or annotated data for supervised learning tasks, but the process of manual labeling and annotation can be time-consuming, costly, and prone to human errors or inconsistencies (Elshawi et al., 2021).
Data Quality and Consistency	Cybersecurity data can be heterogeneous, originating from different sources, formats, and systems, leading to potential quality issues, inconsistencies, or noise that can adversely impact model performance (Camino et al., 2021).

5.3 Adversarial Attacks and Model Vulnerabilities

Like other AI systems, generative AI models are vulnerable to adversarial attacks, where carefully crafted inputs or manipulations can cause the models to produce undesirable or malicious outputs (Akhtar & Ghosh, 2019). In the context of cybersecurity, adversarial attacks on generative models can have severe consequences, potentially leading to the generation of malicious code, deepfakes, or synthetic data that can be used for nefarious purposes.

Adversarial attacks can take various forms, including:

1. Evasion attacks: These attacks aim to manipulate the input data in a way that causes the generative model to produce outputs that evade detection or bypass security mechanisms (Akhtar & Ghosh, 2019). For example, an attacker could

craft adversarial network traffic patterns to bypass an AI-powered intrusion detection system.

2. Poisoning attacks: In these attacks, the attacker injects malicious samples into the training data, causing the generative model to learn and reproduce undesirable behaviors or vulnerabilities (Shafahi et al., 2018). This could potentially lead to the generation of malicious code or the introduction of backdoors in the model.
3. Model extraction attacks: These attacks aim to extract or reconstruct the internal parameters or decision logic of a generative model, potentially exposing sensitive information or enabling the creation of model replicas for malicious purposes (Carlini et al., 2020).

Some potential mitigation strategies include as highlighted in Table 5.

Table 5. Security measures for generative AI in cybersecurity

Security Measure	Description
Adversarial Training	Training the generative model on adversarial examples to enhance its robustness against evasion attacks (Madry et al., 2018).
Differential Privacy	Incorporating differential privacy techniques during model training to mitigate the risks of data poisoning attacks and protect the privacy of the training data (Jordon et al., 2018).
Secure Enclaves and Trusted Execution Environments	Deploying generative models in secure enclaves or trusted execution environments to protect against model extraction attacks and ensure the confidentiality and integrity of the model parameters (Shokri et al., 2021).
Model Watermarking and Fingerprinting	Embedding watermarks or fingerprints in the generative model to aid in detecting and preventing unauthorized model replication or intellectual property infringement (Adi et al., 2018).
Continuous Monitoring and Evaluation	Implementing robust monitoring and evaluation mechanisms to detect and mitigate potential adversarial attacks or model vulnerabilities in real-time, ensuring the security and reliability of generative AI systems (Nguyen et al., 2022).

6. CASE STUDIES

6.1 Generating Synthetic Data for Intrusion Detection Systems

The efficacy of intrusion detection systems (IDS) in detecting and addressing cyber threats is contingent upon the calibre and variety of training data. A GAN-based method was created by Massachusetts Institute of Technology (MIT) researchers to simulate different kinds of cyberattacks and network anomalies using synthetic network traffic data. The researchers were able to enhance their capacity to identify threats and abnormalities that had not been observed before by using this synthetic data to train IDS models. The study showed that IDS models with synthetic data training performed better than those with only real-world data training, with reduced false positive rates and greater detection rates. The training set was effectively enhanced by the generated data, which offered a wide variety of attack scenarios and network traffic patterns. When it comes to helping intrusion detection systems overcome the problem of data scarcity, generative artificial intelligence more especially, GANs has demonstrated encouraging outcomes. IDS models can be trained on a greater variety of attack scenarios, enhancing their capacity to identify and neutralise cyber threats, by producing artificially generated but realistic network traffic data. In order to increase the quality and applicability of the synthetic data, future research might concentrate on integrating domain expertise and expert input into the generative process (Hu. et. al, 2021).

6. 2 Automated Vulnerability Discovery and Patching

Software vulnerabilities are a serious security concern, and patching and finding vulnerabilities have traditionally been done manually and slowly. GUTOR, a deep learning system powered by generative AI, was created by Microsoft Research to automate these tasks. GUTOR can identify potential vulnerabilities and provide fixes because it was trained on a big dataset of code and known flaws. The system outperformed conventional static analysis tools and achieved promising results in vulnerability detection accuracy and patch quality. It demonstrated effective vulnerability identification and patching in real-world software projects. By automating vulnerability finding and patching, GUTOR has the potential to completely transform vulnerability management and lower the danger of cyberattacks and data breaches. Nevertheless, there are still issues with practical implementation, such making sure the created patches don't disrupt existing functionality or add new vulnerabilities. Enhancing the training process with domain knowledge and expert feedback may help increase the accuracy and dependability of the system. The use of generative AI in other facets of software security, like secure coding procedures and security testing, may be investigated in future studies (Guo et. al., 2022).

6.3 Generating Adversarial Examples for Cybersecurity Model Hardening

This case study investigates how hostile instances might be produced using generative AI approaches to assess and enhance the resilience of machine learning models in cybersecurity applications. AdvCyber is a framework created by researchers at the University of California, Los Angeles that targets different machine learning-based security systems with adversarial instances created through generative AI approaches. The study showed how hostile instances might be used to find gaps and flaws in cybersecurity models based on artificial intelligence. Through the application of these scenarios to the models, researchers assessed the models' resilience and devised methods for strengthening and refining them. An effective approach for evaluating and enhancing the security of machine learning models used in cybersecurity applications is the use of generative AI to create adversarial instances. It also draws attention to the dangers that could arise from the improper application of generativc AI, such as the possibility that hostile actors would utilise these instances to sneak over security measures or launch specific assaults. Thus, it is essential to create strong defences and moral standards for the appropriate application of generative AI in cybersecurity (Zhao et al., 2022).

6.4 Automated Malware Analysis and Classification

Cybersecurity relies heavily on malware analysis and categorization, but human analysis is becoming more difficult due to the growing quantity and complexity of malware samples. MalGAN is a deep learning system designed by researchers at the University of Texas at Arlington that employs generative adversarial networks (GANs) for automated malware analysis and categorization. With the help of a sizable dataset of malware samples and their behavioural traits, MalGAN was trained to produce precise forecasts and visualisations that support security experts. The approach achieved higher accuracy and faster analysis times than conventional machine learning-based malware categorization techniques. Understanding and classifying novel or unidentified malware variants is made easier by MalGAN's capacity to visualise and analyse malware behaviour patterns. MalGAN's usage of generative AI demonstrates how this technology has the ability to transform malware analysis and classification procedures, saving time and money by eliminating the need for manual analysis and improving cybersecurity in general. There are still issues to be solved, such making sure the system is resilient to virus and obfuscation techniques that are always changing. In order to provide a more complete malware detection and analysis solution, future research may investigate the integration of generative AI with additional cybersecurity tools (Zhao et al., 2021).

6.5 Generating Customized Phishing Emails for Security Awareness Training

Phishing attacks are a serious danger to cybersecurity because they use social engineering tactics to take advantage of human weaknesses. Effective security awareness training is essential to addressing this. Researchers at Purdue University have created a generative artificial intelligence system dubbed PhishGAN that can generate context-aware and personalized phishing emails for particular people or businesses. The algorithm can produce believable and varied scenarios since it was trained on a sizable sample of actual phishing emails. According to the study, staff members who received training using personalized phishing scenarios were better able to recognize and report possible dangers than those who received training using generic examples. According to this, generative AI may increase the efficacy of security awareness training by exposing staff members to contextually appropriate and customized phishing attempts. But it's crucial to make sure the situations that are generated don't hurt people or reveal private information. In order to develop a more thorough and interesting security awareness program, future research may investigate combining generative AI with additional training techniques like interactive simulations or gamification (Zhao et al., 2019).

6.6 Generating Synthetic Network Traffic for Anomaly Detection

Through the monitoring of network traffic and the detection of departures from typical behaviour patterns, anomaly detection systems play a critical role in the identification of possible cyber threats. Nevertheless, a common problem for these systems is the scarcity of representative and diverse training data. A generative adversarial network (GAN)-based method was created by researchers at the University of Windsor in Canada to produce synthetic network traffic data that resembles typical behaviour patterns. Anomaly detection algorithms were trained on the collected data to better detect deviations from expected network activities, which may be signs of possible cyberattacks or unauthorised access attempts. According to the study, models for anomaly detection that were trained on synthetic data performed better than those that were only trained on real-world data, with higher detection rates and lower false positive rates. The produced data successfully added to the training set by offering a wide variety of typical network traffic patterns. To further enhance data generation and model performance, it is crucial to make sure the generated data accurately depicts real-world network traffic patterns, incorporate domain knowledge and expert feedback into the generative process, and investigate the integration of other generative AI techniques, like variational autoencoders or diffusion models (Nguyen et al., 2022).

6.7 Automated Cyber Threat Intelligence Generation

Cyber threat intelligence (CTI) is essential for detecting and thwarting cyberattacks, but security analysts may become overwhelmed by the intricacy of CTI data. A generative AI system named ThreatGen was created by researchers at the

University of Central Florida. It is capable of producing reports and analyses that are current and pertinent, based on the most recent danger landscape. The system can synthesise and present information in a logical and useful fashion because it was trained on a sizable dataset of CTI data. When the researchers compared ThreatGen's output to reports from human analysts, they discovered that ThreatGen performed comparably in terms of quality and thoroughness while requiring a lot less time and effort to generate reports by hand. Automated CTI generation using generative AI improves cybersecurity situational awareness and decision-making, empowering enterprises to more quickly recognise and neutralise new cyberthreats. It is imperative to guarantee the precision and dependability of the reports that are produced. For a more complete and automated threat intelligence solution, future research might investigate combining generative AI with other cybersecurity tools including threat hunting platforms and security information and event management systems (Shickel et al., 2022).

6.8 Generating Realistic Social Engineering Scenarios for Security Awareness Training

Social engineering attacks are a serious cybersecurity danger because they take advantage of human weaknesses. Effective security awareness training is essential to addressing this. SocEngGen is a generative AI system created by researchers at the University of Texas at San Antonio that can produce a variety of context-specific social engineering scenarios. SocEngGen can mimic different kinds of attacks because it was trained on a dataset of actual social engineering incidents. According to the study, personnel who received training using these realistic scenarios outperformed those who received instruction using standard approaches in identifying and responding to social engineering attempts. By exposing staff members to a variety of contextually relevant and varied social engineering attempts, the application of generative AI in security awareness training improves training efficacy. It is imperative to guarantee that the scenarios generated do not unintentionally reveal confidential information or result in unintended harm. In order to develop a more thorough and interesting security awareness programme, future research may investigate combining generative AI with additional training techniques like interactive simulations or gamification (Zhao et al., 2019).

6.9 Generating Adversarial Examples for Evaluating Network Intrusion Detection Systems

Network traffic monitoring and the detection of any cyber attacks depend heavily on network intrusion detection systems, or NDS. Adversarial examples, on the other hand, are deliberately created inputs meant to avoid detection or result in incorrect classifications, and they can weaken them. A framework known as AdvIDS was created by researchers at the University of California, Riverside. It generates adversarial instances that are aimed against NIDS systems using generative AI approaches. The study showed how adversarial instances may be used to find flaws and vulnerabilities in NIDS models, which enables researchers to assess the models' resilience and create plans for strengthening and hardening them. An effective method for evaluating and enhancing the security of NIDS systems is the generation of adversarial cases using generative artificial intelligence. It also draws attention to the possible dangers of misusing generative AI, since bad actors might utilise these instances to get over security measures or launch specific attacks. As a result, creating strong defences and moral standards is crucial for the appropriate application of generative AI in cybersecurity. In order to create comprehensive defence plans, future research could examine adversarial training methods and the integration of generative AI with existing security mechanisms (Lin et al., 2021).

6.10 Generating Synthetic Data for Cyber Threat Hunting

Cyber threat hunting is a proactive cybersecurity strategy that looks for signs of compromise and possible dangers within the networks and systems of an organisation. However, these methods may not be as helpful if there is a dearth of realistic and varied training data. A generative adversarial network (GAN)-based method was created by Georgia Institute of Technology researchers to produce synthetic data that imitates different cyber threat situations and indicators of compromise. Cyber threat hunting models were trained and evaluated using the collected data, which improved their ability to recognise and rank possible threats. According to the study, models trained on synthetic data performed better than those trained solely on real-world data, resulting in reduced false positive rates and higher detection rates. The produced data successfully added to the training set, offering a diverse range of threat scenarios and indicators. Making sure the resulting data appropriately depicts actual cyber threat situations and indications is vital, though. Enhancing the generation process with subject expertise and expert feedback may help to increase the synthetic data's fidelity and relevance. Furthermore, investigating the incorporation of additional generative AI methods, like diffusion models or variational autoencoders, may enhance model performance and data production even more (Peng X et. al., 2022).

7. CYBERSECURITY'S ETHICAL ASPECTS AND RESPONSIBLE AI

The increasing integration of artificial intelligence (AI) into cybersecurity necessitates addressing ethical issues and ensuring responsible development and application of these technologies. The incorporation of artificial intelligence (AI) into cybersecurity systems and procedures presents significant concerns about equity, responsibility, openness, and the possibility of unforeseen outcomes or abuse. This section will examine ethical guidelines for artificial intelligence (AI) in cybersecurity, tackle concerns related to bias and equity in AI security models, and deliberate on the significance of transparency, accountability, and governance in promoting conscientious AI practices. Table 6 represents the approaches to mitigate the biasness and promote security in AI models.

AI development and application in cybersecurity should be directed by a set of moral guidelines that encourage the appropriate and advantageous implementation of these technologies while reducing risks and negative effects. Some important moral guidelines to take into account are:

1. Fundamental freedoms and human rights: AI systems used in cybersecurity situations should protect and preserve human rights like due process, privacy, and freedom of speech (Bremermann et al., 2022). These systems shouldn't be employed for censorship, widespread surveillance, or any other actions that violate basic human rights.
2. Promotion of public safety and security: Elshawi et al. suggest that the main goal of artificial intelligence in cybersecurity should be to improve public safety and security by defending vital infrastructure, averting cyberattacks, and preserving sensitive data.
3. Accountability and transparency: Mechanisms for accountability and transparency should be incorporated into the design and implementation of AI systems employed in cybersecurity (Ortner et al., 2022). This involves making certain that these systems' decision-making procedures are transparent, auditable, and subject to human supervision and control.
4. Fairness and non-discrimination: AI security models ought to be created and implemented in a way that upholds equality and refrains from discriminating against people on the basis of protected traits like age, gender, race, or disability

(Mehrabi et al., 2021). In order to provide fair treatment and protection for all people and groups, efforts should be taken to reduce any potential prejudices.

5. Responsible data governance: The development and training of AI systems in cybersecurity should adhere to responsible data governance practices, ensuring the protection of personal and sensitive data, respecting data privacy and ownership rights, and promoting ethical data collection and use (Elshawi et al., 2021).
6. Collaboration and stakeholder engagement: The ethical development and deployment of AI in cybersecurity should involve collaboration and engagement with diverse stakeholders, including AI researchers, cybersecurity experts, policymakers, civil society organizations, and affected communities (Bremermann et al., 2022). This collaborative approach can help ensure that diverse perspectives and concerns are considered and addressed.

Table 6. Approaches to mitigate bias and promote fairness in AI security models

Approach	Description
Data Quality and Diversity	Ensuring the quality and diversity of the training data used to develop AI security models, curating diverse and representative datasets, implementing debiasing techniques, and continuously monitoring and updating the training data (Elshawi et al., 2021).
Algorithmic Fairness	Developing and implementing machine learning algorithms and model architectures that promote fairness and mitigate biases, including techniques such as adversarial debiasing, constrained optimization, and causal reasoning approaches (Mehrabi et al., 2021).
Rigorous Testing and Evaluation	Implementing rigorous testing and evaluation methodologies to assess the fairness and potential biases of AI security models, such as disparate impact analysis, counterfactual evaluation, and external auditing by independent third parties (Barocas et al., 2019).
Human Oversight and Governance	Ensuring human oversight and governance mechanisms are in place to monitor and address potential biases or unfair outcomes in the deployment of AI security systems, establishing clear accountability frameworks, providing channels for reporting and addressing concerns, and implementing corrective measures when necessary (Ortner et al., 2022).
Collaboration and Diverse Stakeholder Engagement	Engaging diverse stakeholders, including civil society organizations, affected communities, and domain experts, to provide valuable perspectives and insights on identifying and mitigating potential biases and fairness issues in AI security models (Bremermann et al., 2022).

8. FUTURE TRENDS AND EMERGING TECHNOLOGIES

It is critical to stay up to date on new developments in cybersecurity and anticipated trends that may influence the nature of cyberthreats and defence strategies. The possible effects of post-quantum cryptography and quantum computing, the emergence of federated learning and privacy-preserving artificial intelligence, the idea of intelligent deception, and adaptive defence mechanisms.

8.1 Quantum Computing and Post-Quantum Cryptography

The ability of quantum computing to solve complicated problems more quickly than traditional computers represents a major breakthrough in computing capacity. This affects the security concerns, especially, cryptography whose existing encryption algorithms rely majorly on mathematical issues that are computationally difficult; however, quantum computers have the ability to make these problems simple, potentially breaking many popular techniques. As a result, post-quantum cryptography (PQC) was developed with the goal of developing cryptographic protocols and algorithms that are immune to assaults from both conventional and quantum computers. PQC algorithms are based on mathematical issues that, even with highly capable quantum computers, are unsolvable. Adoption of PQC will become essential for preserving digital communications, data storage, and critical infrastructure security as quantum computing progresses.

8.2. Federated Learning and Privacy-Preserving AI

A jeopardizing machine learning paradigm called federated learning permits cooperative model training without jeopardizing privacy. With the use of secure communication protocols, this method is very helpful in cybersecurity as it enables local nodes or individual devices to train models on their own data and aggregate and update a global model. Federated learning improves data security and privacy, which makes it possible to create machine learning models that are more varied and resilient. But it also brings with it difficulties like communication cost, problems with model convergence, and possible weak points for adversarial assaults or data poisoning. Strong security mechanisms, safe aggregation protocols, and methods for guaranteeing the confidentiality and integrity of the distributed learning process are needed to address these issues.

8.3 Intelligent Deception and Adaptive Defense Mechanisms

The increasing sophistication and adaptability of cyber attacks renders conventional static defence methods inadequate. Adaptive defence mechanisms and intelligent deception present a viable way to counter and mitigate these attacks in real-time. In order to preserve vital assets, deceive enemies, and obtain information about attacker behaviour, intelligent deception employs deceptive tactics. When threats are identified or the threat environment shifts, adaptive defence mechanisms employ machine learning and intelligent decision-making to modify security controls and responses. With this strategy, a robust and dynamic cybersecurity ecosystem is created, where defence tactics are constantly updated to fend off new attacks. The maintenance of human oversight and control, the management of numerous components, and the assurance of the robustness and dependability of AI and decision-making systems present issues.

The future of cybersecurity will be shaped by the interplay of emerging technologies, evolving threats, and innovative defense mechanisms. Quantum computing and post-quantum cryptography will necessitate a fundamental shift in cryptographic approaches, while federated learning and privacy-preserving AI offer new avenues for collaborative defense and data protection. Intelligent deception and adaptive defense mechanisms present a dynamic and resilient approach to countering sophisticated cyber threats. However, realizing the potential of these emerging technologies will require addressing technical challenges, ethical considerations, and the development of robust governance frameworks. Interdisciplinary collaboration, responsible innovation, and continuous adaptation will be crucial to navigating the ever-evolving cybersecurity landscape and ensuring the security and resilience of our digital systems and critical infrastructure.

9. CONCLUSION

Enhancing threat detection, mitigation, and prevention capabilities has been demonstrated to be a major benefit of generative artificial intelligence (AI) integration in cybersecurity. The training and assessment of machine learning models for applications like intrusion detection, anomaly detection, and cyber threat hunting have been made possible by the use of techniques like generative adversarial networks (GANs) and variational autoencoders (VAEs) to create synthetic data that replicates real-world scenarios. The case study on GUTOR demonstrates how useful generative AI has been in automating vulnerability detection and patching operations. By drastically cutting down on the time and resources needed for human code auditing and testing, this method can improve software security and lessen the risks connected with vulnerabilities that are still unpatched. To further enhance and assess learning, the creation of hostile examples has become a potent instrument. Furthermore, the creation of hostile examples has become a potent instrument for assessing and enhancing the resilience of cybersecurity systems based on machine learning. It is necessary to solve a number of limits and obstacles, nevertheless. Numerous case studies emphasise how important it is to guarantee the accuracy and applicability of the generated data or situations. Bias and fairness in generative AI systems are critical issues since these systems have the potential to reinforce or magnify biases seen in training data, resulting in the production of material that feeds into harmful preconceptions or discriminatory practices. It will take coordinated efforts in data curation, model architecture design, and thorough testing and evaluation procedures to overcome this obstacle. Since the possible misuse of generative AI for malevolent purposes raises serious ethical concerns, ethical considerations are also crucial. Cybercriminals may be able to use the capacity to create convincing phishing emails, social engineering scenarios, or antagonistic examples for evil intent. Strong defences and moral standards for the appropriate application of generative AI in cybersecurity must be developed in order to reduce these threats. In order to create more robust and safe cybersecurity solutions, future trends in generative AI may involve combining generative AI with other cutting-edge technologies like blockchain and quantum computing. In high-stakes cybersecurity scenarios, the development of interpretable and explainable generative AI models could build confidence and enable better informed decision-making by addressing issues around decision transparency and accountability. Ultimately, generative AI offers the cybersecurity sector a game-changing chance by providing novel approaches to age-old problems with threat identification, mitigation, and prevention. To ensure that the advantages of generative AI are fully utilised while minimising hazards and unexpected repercussions, ethical concerns and responsible development processes need to be at the forefront of these initiatives.

REFERENCES

Akhtar, N., & Ghosh, J. (2019). Recent Trends in Deep Neural Networks Based Adversarial Attacks and Defenses. arXiv preprint arXiv:1908.03603.

Al-Khateeb, H. M., Epiphaniou, G., & Dianati, M. (2019). Applying generative adversarial networks to enhance network anomaly detection. *IEEE International Conference on Systems, Man and Cybernetics (SMC)*, 1388-1393.

Bender, E. M., Gebru, T., McMillan-Major, A., & Shmitchell, S. (2021). On the Dangers of Stochastic Parrots: Can Language Models Be Too Big? In *Proceedings of the 2021 ACM Conference on Fairness, Accountability, and Transparency* (pp. 610-623). 10.1145/3442188.3445922

Biggio, B., & Roli, F. (2018). Wild patterns: Ten years after the rise of adversarial machine learning. *Pattern Recognition*, 84, 317–331. 10.1016/j.patcog.2018.07.023

Bremermann, T., Khaledi, M., & Brogan, J. (2022). Exploring Generative Artificial Intelligence for the Responsible Design of Trustworthy Systems. In *Proceedings of the 2022 ACM Conference on Fairness, Accountability, and Transparency* (pp. 1202-1213).

Camino, R. D., Naveiro, R., & González-Sanguino, C. (2021). Synthetic data generation for cybersecurity dataset construction. *Entropy (Basel, Switzerland)*, 23(6), 688.34072438

Chesney, R., & Citron, D. K. (2019). Deep fakes: A looming challenge for privacy, democracy, and national security. *California Law Review*, 107(6), 1753–1820.

D., & Sofat, S. (2022). Cyber security trends for 2022: Future focus areas for the security industry. In 2022 IEEE 6th International Conference for Convergence in Technology (I2CT) (pp. 1-6). IEEE.

Dang, H., Liang, Y., & Liu, F. (2022). A survey on DeepFake: Overview, detection, and prevention. *ACM Computing Surveys*, 55(5), 1–43.

Elshawi, R., Al-Mallah, M. H., Eldessouki, M. S., & Hassan, M. M. (2021). The Intersection of Cybersecurity, Artificial Intelligence and Machine Learning: A Literature Review. *Security and Privacy*, 4(6), e165.

Ganesh, P., Chen, Y., Lou, X., Khan, M. A., Yang, Y., Chen, D., . . . Hao, Z. (2020). Efficient and Robust Machine Learning for Cybersecurity: A Survey. arXiv preprint arXiv:2010.09114.

Goodfellow, I., Bengio, Y., & Courville, A. (2016). *Deep learning*. MIT press.

Goodfellow, I., Pouget-Abadie, J., Mirza, M., Xu, B., Warde-Farley, D., Ozair, S., & Bengio, Y. (2014). Generative adversarial nets. *Advances in Neural Information Processing Systems*, 27.

Guo, J., Ling, X., & Yin, H. (2022). Automated vulnerability discovery and patching with deep learning. arXiv preprint arXiv:2204.07142.

Hu, Y., Yang, K., Perdisci, R., & Lee, W. (2021). Generative adversarial network-based minority recreation for network intrusion detection. *IEEE Transactions on Network and Service Management*, 18(3), 2685–2696.

Jagatic, T. N., Johnson, N. A., Jakobsson, M., & Menczer, F. (2007). Social phishing. *Communications of the ACM*, 50(10), 94–100. 10.1145/1290958.1290968

Kietzmann, J., Lee, L. W., McCarthy, I. P., & Kietzmann, T. C. (2019). Deepfakes: Trick or treat? *Business Horizons*, 63(2), 135–146. 10.1016/j.bushor.2019.11.006

Kshetri, N. (2017). Cybersecurity in developing economies: Key challenges and stakeholders. *IEEE Security and Privacy*, 15(6), 72–77.

Lin, Y., Wang, J., Sun, X., Ren, K., & Li, C. (2021). Generating adversarial examples for network intrusion detection systems through generative adversarial networks. *IEEE Transactions on Information Forensics and Security*, 16, 3498–3511.

Madry, A., Makelov, A., Schmidt, L., Tsipras, D., & Vladu, A. (2018). Towards deep learning models resistant to adversarial attacks. arXiv preprint arXiv:1706.06083.

Nguyen, T. D., Nguyen, T. D., & Park, M. (2022). Generative Adversarial Networks for Generating Synthetic Network Traffic Data. arXiv preprint arXiv:2205.09352.

Nguyen, T. T., Nguyen, H. D., & Le, N. G. (2022). AI-based cybersecurity: Opportunities and challenges. *SN Computer Science*, 3(2), 1–21.

Peng, X., Li, Y., Wang, Y., & Xiang, Y. (2022). Generating synthetic data for cyber threat hunting with generative adversarial networks. In *Proceedings of the 2022 ACM SIGSAC Conference on Computer and Communications Security* (pp. 2181-2195).

Radford, A., Kim, J. W., Hallacy, C., Ramesh, A., Goh, G., Agarwal, S., & Sutskever, I. (2022). Learning transferable visual models from natural language supervision. In *International Conference on Machine Learning* (pp. 8748-8763). PMLR.

Radford, A., Wu, J., Child, R., Luan, D., Amodei, D., & Sutskever, I. (2019). Language models are unsupervised multitask learners. OpenAI blog, 1(8), 9.

Shafahi, A., Huang, W. R., Najibi, M., Suciu, O., Studer, C., Dumitras, T., & Goldstein, T. (2018). Poison frogs! Targeted clean-label poisoning attacks on neural networks. *Advances in Neural Information Processing Systems*, 31.

Shickel, B., Gillies, R., Suomala, L., & Nickerson, T. (2022). Generative AI models for forecasting cyber intelligence reports. arXiv preprint arXiv:2206.07849.

Shokri, R., Stronati, M., Song, C., & Shmatikov, V. (2021). Membership inference attacks against machine learning models. *IEEE Symposium on Security and Privacy (SP)*, 3-18.

Strubell, E., Ganesh, A., & McCallum, A. (2019). Energy and policy considerations for deep learning in NLP. arXiv preprint arXiv:1906.02243.

Virvilis, N., & Gritzalis, D. (2013). The big four-what we did wrong in advanced persistent threat detection? In *2013 International Conference on Availability, Reliability and Security* (pp. 248-254). IEEE. 10.1109/ARES.2013.32

Von Solms, R., & Van Niekerk, J. (2013). From information security to cyber security. *Computers & Security*, 38, 97–102. 10.1016/j.cose.2013.04.004

Vrabec, J., Byrtusova, A., & Ronai, M. (2020). Living off the land: Modern trend in malware obfuscation. In 2020 IEEE 15th International Conference on Malicious and Unwanted Software (MALWARE) (pp. 59-68). IEEE.

Zhao, M., An, B., Gao, W., Zhang, T., Xia, P., Du, X., & Yu, N. (2021). Adversarial attacks and defenses for deep learning-based malware detection. *IEEE Transactions on Information Forensics and Security*, 17, 1063–1077.

Zhao, M., An, B., Shi, Y., Gui, X., & Yu, N. (2022). Adversarial machine learning for cybersecurity: Attacks, defenses, and open issues. *IEEE Transactions on Network Science and Engineering*, 9(5), 3501–3522.

Zhao, Y., Kozey, V., & Miao, R. (2019). Automated generation of phishing emails for security awareness training. In *2019 IEEE International Conference on Artificial Intelligence and Virtual Reality (AIVR)* (pp. 155-159). IEEE.

Zhao, Y., Yin, J., Wei, S., & Tang, Y. (2019). Generating automated generation of phishing email for cognitive security awareness training. In 2019 International Conference on Cyber-Enabled Distributed Computing and Knowledge Discovery (CyberC) (pp. 233-238). IEEE.

Zong, B., Song, Q., Min, M. R., Cheng, W., Lumezanu, C., Cho, D., & Chen, H. (2018). Deep autoencoding gaussian mixture model for unsupervised anomaly detection. In *International Conference on Learning Representations (ICLR)*.

KEY TERMS AND DEFINITIONS

Cybersecurity: Cybersecurity involves methods and strategies to protect digital data from illegal access, theft, and damage. It includes network, application, data, identity, and cloud security domains. To stay ahead of cyberthreats like malware, phishing, and DDoS attacks, cybersecurity procedures need to adapt to include risk assessment, security control implementation, incident response, and ongoing monitoring.

Decision Makers: Within an organisation, decision makers are persons or groups with the power and duty to establish priorities and make strategic decisions that influence the organization's operations and direction. They are usually in executive or leadership roles and are responsible for evaluating opportunities and risks, analysing complex data, and coming to well-informed judgements that are consistent with the mission and core values of the company. Strong analytical and critical thinking abilities are necessary for decision makers, as well as the capacity to weigh other viewpoints and handle unclear or difficult circumstances.

Defence Mechanisms: Adaptive defence mechanisms are security tactics that constantly adapt to counter evolving cyber threats. They use advanced technology like machine learning, artificial intelligence, and automated decision-making to monitor and analyse security events, identify patterns, and adjust defensive methods. These mechanisms can update security policies, firewall rules, patches, software, network settings, or use misleading tactics, enabling organizations to maintain resilient security postures and stay ahead of cyber threats.

Ethical Cybersecurity: Cybersecurity's ethical aspect involves balancing security and privacy, maintaining civil liberties, and preventing malicious use of tools. It requires respecting legal frameworks, promoting responsibility and openness, and implementing ethical hacking techniques. Balancing security with individual liberties and considering societal effects are also crucial aspects of ethical cybersecurity. This involves ensuring impartial and fair security procedures, upholding civil liberties, and preventing malicious use.

Generative Adversarial Network: Two neural networks, the discriminator and the generator, make up the Generative Adversarial Network (GAN), a machine learning architecture. The generator produces artificial data that mimics the distribution of real data, while the discriminator attempts to discern between produced and real data. Through repeated training, both the discriminator and generator networks become more adept at distinguishing between real and fake data, with the generator creating increasingly realistic data to trick the discriminator.

Generative AI: Generative AI uses machine learning to identify patterns in data, producing realistic and coherent content like text, photos, and audio. Examples include GPT-3 for text generation and DALL-E for picture synthesis. However, it raises ethical concerns about potential abuse and bias.

Malware: Malicious software, including Trojan horses, worms, viruses, ransomware, spyware, and rootkits, is a harmful program designed to damage, interfere with normal operations, or gain unauthorised access to networks and computer systems. It can steal confidential data, take over resources, and disrupt services.

Responsible AI: The ethical application of artificial intelligence that takes into account the possible effects on people as individuals, groups, and as a society is known as responsible AI. Strong governance frameworks, algorithmic transparency, bias reduction, ethical risk assessments, and data privacy protection are all part of it. It also entails thinking about long-term societal ramifications and involving a variety of stakeholders.

Threat Intelligence: It is the process of gathering, evaluating, and sharing data about potential cyber threats to an organization. It involves analysing data from various sources to identify trends, strategies, and tactics used by threat actors. This helps organizations reduce risks, improve security controls, and handle incidents effectively. Effective threat intelligence requires teamwork, observation, and timely data sharing.

Vulnerabilities: These are the flaws in software, networks, applications, or computer systems that an attacker could use to obtain unauthorised access, interfere with normal operations, or do damage. XSS, buffer overflows, SQL injection, weak authentication, and unpatched software vulnerabilities are examples of common types. Maintaining a robust cybersecurity posture and fending off cyberattacks requires regular vulnerability assessments, patch management, and safe coding techniques.

Chapter 10
Guardians of the Digital Realm
Generative AI's Role in Cybersecurity

Manas Kumar Yogi
https://orcid.org/0000-0001-9118-2898
Pragati Engineering College (Autonomous), India

Yamuna Mundru
Pragati Engineering College (Autonomous), India

Atti Manga Devi
Pragati Engineering College (Autonomous), India

ABSTRACT

This chapter explores the burgeoning role of generative artificial intelligence (AI) in the realm of cybersecurity. As our digital world expands, so do the threats posed by malicious actors. In response, the emergence of generative AI technologies presents a promising avenue for bolstering cybersecurity defenses. This chapter examines the various applications of generative AI in fortifying digital security, including its use in threat detection, anomaly identification, and vulnerability assessment. By harnessing the power of machine learning and neural networks, generative AI systems exhibit remarkable capabilities in predicting, pre-empting, and mitigating cyber threats. Moreover, this chapter delves into the ethical considerations and potential challenges associated with deploying generative AI in cybersecurity contexts, emphasizing the importance of responsible development and deployment practices. Ultimately, this exploration highlights the pivotal role of generative AI as guardians of the digital realm, ushering in a new era of enhanced cybersecurity measures.

DOI: 10.4018/979-8-3693-8557-9.ch010

INTRODUCTION

In the modern digital age, where technology permeates nearly every aspect of our lives, cybersecurity has emerged as a critical cornerstone for ensuring the integrity, confidentiality, and availability of data and systems. Its importance cannot be overstated, as cyber threats continue to evolve in sophistication and frequency, posing significant risks to individuals, businesses, governments, and society as a whole. One of the foremost impacts of cybersecurity in modern technologies is its role in safeguarding sensitive information. With the proliferation of online transactions, cloud computing, and interconnected networks, vast amounts of personal and proprietary data are generated, stored, and transmitted daily. This includes financial records, medical histories, intellectual property, and more (Agrawal, 2024). Without robust cybersecurity measures in place, this information becomes vulnerable to unauthorized access, theft, and exploitation by cybercriminals. Cybersecurity plays a pivotal role in preserving the stability and functionality of critical infrastructure systems. Industries such as energy, transportation, healthcare, and finance rely heavily on interconnected digital systems to deliver essential services. Disruption or compromise of these systems due to cyber-attacks can have far-reaching consequences, including economic losses, public safety hazards, and even loss of life. For instance, an attack on a power grid could result in widespread blackouts, disrupting daily life and causing cascading effects across multiple sectors. Cybersecurity is essential for maintaining trust and confidence in digital technologies. As society becomes increasingly reliant on online platforms for communication, commerce, and entertainment, users expect their data to be protected from unauthorized access and misuse. Instances of data breaches and cyber-attacks erode trust in technology companies and undermine consumer confidence, leading to reputational damage and financial losses. Therefore, investing in robust cybersecurity measures is not only a matter of compliance but also a strategic imperative for businesses seeking to retain customer loyalty and competitive advantage (Shahriar, 2021).

In addition to protecting against external threats, cybersecurity also addresses internal risks such as insider threats and human error. While malicious actors pose a significant danger, studies have shown that a considerable number of data breaches and security incidents result from inadvertent actions by employees or contractors. These can include clicking on malicious links, falling victim to social engineering scams, or inadvertently exposing sensitive information. Therefore, cybersecurity awareness training and implementing access controls are essential components of a comprehensive cybersecurity strategy. Moreover, the impact of cybersecurity extends beyond the realm of technology to encompass broader societal and geopolitical implications. Nation-states and state-sponsored actors engage in cyber warfare and espionage activities to gain strategic advantages, steal intellectual property, or disrupt the operations of adversaries. These cyber threats have the potential to destabilize international relations, undermine democratic processes, and escalate conflicts in the digital domain. Consequently, governments around the world are investing heavily in cybersecurity capabilities and collaborating on international frameworks for cyber defense and deterrence (Chen, 2024). Cybersecurity is indispensable for fostering innovation and economic growth in the digital economy. As businesses embrace digital transformation and leverage emerging technologies such as artificial intelligence, Internet of Things (IoT), and blockchain, they open up new opportunities for efficiency gains, cost savings, and market expansion. However, these technologies also introduce new cybersecurity risks and vulnerabilities that must be addressed proactively. By investing in cybersecurity research and development, businesses can harness the full potential of digital technologies while mitigating associated risks. Despite its undeniable importance, cybersecurity faces numerous challenges and complexities in the modern technological landscape. The rapidly evolving threat landscape, coupled with the proliferation of connected devices and digital services, has outpaced traditional security measures and frameworks. Moreover, the shortage of skilled cybersecurity professionals exacerbates the problem, making it difficult for organizations to recruit and retain talent in this competitive field. Cybersecurity is a fundamental pillar of modern technologies, underpinning trust, stability, and innovation in the digital age. Its impact extends across various sectors, from safeguarding sensitive information and critical infrastructure to preserving trust in digital platforms and addressing geopolitical threats (Tasneem, 2022). As technology continues to advance, the importance of cybersecurity will only grow, necessitating continuous investment, collaboration, and innovation to stay ahead of evolving cyber threats.

Researchers in cybersecurity face a multitude of challenges that stem from the rapidly evolving nature of cyber threats, the complexity of modern technology ecosystems, and the limitations of traditional security approaches. These challenges often necessitate a shift towards the integration of artificial intelligence (AI) and machine learning (ML) techniques to enhance cybersecurity capabilities (Dhoni, 2023). Some of the primary challenges faced by researchers in cybersecurity include:

1. Sophisticated Threat Landscape: Cyber threats are becoming increasingly sophisticated, with adversaries employing advanced techniques such as polymorphic malware, zero-day exploits, and social engineering tactics. Traditional signature-based detection methods struggle to keep pace with these evolving threats, leading researchers to seek more adaptive and proactive defense mechanisms.
2. Big Data Complexity: The sheer volume and complexity of data generated by modern digital systems present a significant challenge for cybersecurity researchers. Analyzing large datasets in real-time to identify anomalies and

potential security breaches requires advanced analytical tools and algorithms, which AI and ML technologies can provide.

3. Zero-Day Vulnerabilities: Zero-day vulnerabilities, which are unknown to software vendors and security experts, pose a significant risk as they can be exploited by attackers before patches or mitigations are developed. Researchers must constantly monitor emerging threats and develop proactive defenses to detect and mitigate zero-day attacks, a task for which AI-based anomaly detection and behavior analysis techniques are well-suited.
4. Shortage of Skilled Professionals: There is a global shortage of skilled cybersecurity professionals, making it challenging for organizations to recruit and retain talent in this field. AI and ML technologies can help alleviate this shortage by automating routine tasks, augmenting human decision-making, and enabling less experienced analysts to leverage advanced analytical capabilities.
5. Adversarial Machine Learning: Adversarial machine learning poses a unique challenge in cybersecurity, where attackers can manipulate AI systems by feeding them malicious inputs designed to evade detection or produce false positives. Researchers must develop robust AI models that are resilient to adversarial attacks while maintaining high detection accuracy and low false positive rates.
6. Privacy and Ethical Concerns: The use of AI in cybersecurity raises important privacy and ethical considerations, particularly concerning the collection and analysis of sensitive data. Researchers must ensure that AI-based security solutions comply with relevant regulations and standards, safeguarding user privacy and preventing potential misuse or abuse of personal information.
7. Interoperability and Integration: Integrating AI-based security solutions into existing infrastructure and workflows can be challenging due to interoperability issues and compatibility constraints. Researchers must develop modular and scalable AI frameworks that seamlessly integrate with diverse environments while minimizing disruption to existing processes.
8. Explainability and Transparency: The lack of explainability and transparency in AI models presents a barrier to adoption in cybersecurity, where decision-making processes must be transparent and auditable. Researchers are actively working to develop interpretable AI techniques that provide insights into model behavior and decision-making processes, enhancing trust and accountability in AI-based security systems.

In response to these challenges, researchers are increasingly turning to AI and ML as a means of augmenting traditional cybersecurity approaches and addressing emerging threats more effectively. AI-based techniques offer the potential to enhance threat detection, automate incident response, and adapt defenses in real-time, thereby empowering organizations to stay ahead of evolving cyber threats in an increasingly dynamic and complex digital landscape.

Generative Artificial Intelligence (AI) holds significant promise in enhancing cybersecurity measures due to its ability to create, simulate, or generate data, which can be leveraged for various security-related tasks. In below discussion, the specific reasons why generative AI can be impactful in cybersecurity is presented (Dunmore, 2023):

1. Data Augmentation: Generative AI can be used to create synthetic data that resembles real-world cyber threats, such as malware variants or phishing emails. This synthetic data can be used to augment existing datasets for training machine learning models, improving their accuracy and robustness in detecting and mitigating cyber threats.
2. Adversarial Attack Simulation: Generative AI techniques can be employed to generate adversarial examples, which are carefully crafted inputs designed to deceive or evade detection by AI-based security systems. By simulating potential attack scenarios, researchers can identify vulnerabilities in AI models and develop more robust defenses against adversarial attacks.
3. Anomaly Detection: Generative AI models, such as Variational Autoencoders (VAEs) and Generative Adversarial Networks (GANs), can be utilized for anomaly detection in network traffic, system logs, and user behavior (Renaud, 2023). These models learn the underlying patterns of normal behavior and can identify deviations or anomalies indicative of potential security threats, such as insider attacks or network intrusions.
4. Security Testing and Evaluation: Generative AI can automate the generation of diverse attack vectors and test cases for evaluating the security posture of software systems and networks. By systematically exploring different attack scenarios, researchers can identify vulnerabilities, assess the effectiveness of security controls, and prioritize remediation efforts to strengthen cyber defenses.
5. Phishing Detection and Email Security: Generative AI can be employed to generate realistic phishing emails and malicious URLs for testing and training email security systems. By mimicking the techniques used by cybercriminals, researchers can evaluate the efficacy of spam filters, email authentication protocols, and other email security mechanisms in detecting and blocking phishing attempts.
6. Privacy-Preserving Security Solutions: Generative AI techniques, such as homomorphic encryption and differential privacy, can be utilized to develop privacy-preserving security solutions that protect sensitive data while still allowing for meaningful analysis and threat detection. These techniques enable

secure computation and information sharing without compromising data confidentiality or integrity (Sai, 2024).

7. Threat Intelligence and Cyber Forensics: Generative AI can assist in generating realistic threat intelligence reports, visualizations, and simulations to aid cybersecurity analysts in understanding and responding to emerging threats. Additionally, generative models can be applied to reconstruct cyber-attacks, reconstructing attack sequences and identifying indicators of compromise (IOCs) for forensic investigations (Ramirez, 2022).
8. Natural Language Processing (NLP) for Security Analysis: Generative AI models based on NLP techniques can analyze and generate natural language text to identify security-related patterns, extract actionable insights from security logs and incident reports, and facilitate communication and collaboration among cybersecurity professionals.

It is so evident that the generative AI holds great potential for advancing cybersecurity measures by enabling the creation, simulation, and analysis of diverse cyber threats and security-related data. By harnessing the capabilities of generative AI, researchers can develop more effective and adaptive security solutions to defend against evolving cyber threats in today's complex and dynamic digital landscape.

LITERATURE SURVEY

The below table, Table 1 outlines the state of the art in using AI for enhancing cybersecurity measures, highlighting the merits and limitations of each technique(Gupta,2023).

Table 1. State-of-art in AI applications in the domain of cybersecurity

Sl. No.	AI Technique	Merits	Limitations
1	Machine Learning	Ability to analyze large datasets for identifying patterns and anomalies. - Effective in detecting known threats based on historical data. - Can be deployed for real-time threat detection and classification.	Relies on labeled training data, which may not capture all possible attack scenarios. - Susceptible to adversarial attacks and evasion techniques. - Limited to detecting known threats and may struggle with novel or zero-day attacks.

continued on following page

Table 1. Continued

Sl. No.	AI Technique	Merits	Limitations
2	Deep Learning	Offers higher levels of abstraction and feature representation compared to traditional machine learning techniques. Capable of learning complex patterns and relationships from raw data. Suitable for tasks such as image recognition, natural language processing, and malware detection.	Requires large amounts of labeled data and computational resources for training deep neural networks. Lack of interpretability and explainability in complex models. Vulnerable to adversarial attacks and overfitting.
3	Generative Adversarial Networks (GANs)	Can generate synthetic data for augmenting training datasets and testing security systems. Useful for creating realistic attack simulations and generating adversarial examples. Can be applied in anomaly detection and threat intelligence generation.	Training GANs can be challenging and require careful tuning of hyperparameters. GAN-generated data may not fully capture the diversity and complexity of real-world threats. Adversarial examples generated by GANs may not always generalize to real-world scenarios.
4	Natural Language Processing (NLP)	Enables analysis of unstructured text data for identifying security-related patterns and trends. Useful for tasks such as phishing detection, threat intelligence analysis, and security log analysis.	Performance may vary depending on the quality and relevance of training data. Vulnerable to language ambiguity and context-dependent variations. NLP models may struggle with understanding sarcasm, slang, or highly contextual language used in cyber threats.
5	Reinforcement Learning	Capable of learning optimal strategies for cyber defense through trial and error. Suitable for adaptive and dynamic security environments. Can be applied in automated response systems and adaptive threat mitigation.	Requires extensive training and exploration of state-action spaces, which may be time-consuming and resource-intensive. Limited interpretability and explainability in complex reinforcement learning models. Vulnerable to reward hacking and manipulation in adversarial environments.
6	Homomorphic Encryption	Enables secure computation on encrypted data without decrypting it, preserving data confidentiality. Useful for privacy-preserving analytics and secure data sharing in multi-party environments. Can be applied in secure outsourced computation and cloud-based security solutions.	Computationally intensive and may incur high overhead in terms of processing time and resource consumption. Limited to specific types of computations and may not support all operations required for complex security tasks. Vulnerable to side-channel attacks and implementation vulnerabilities.

continued on following page

Table 1. Continued

Sl. No.	AI Technique	Merits	Limitations
7	Adversarial Defense Mechanisms	Designed to detect and mitigate adversarial attacks against AI-based security systems. Can enhance the robustness and resilience of AI models against evasion techniques. Useful for safeguarding against adversarial threats in real-world deployments.	Effectiveness of adversarial defense mechanisms may vary depending on the sophistication of adversarial attacks. May introduce additional computational overhead and complexity in AI systems. Adversarial defense mechanisms may inadvertently increase false positive rates or degrade overall detection performance.
8	Federated Learning	Enables collaborative model training across distributed devices while preserving data privacy. Useful for training AI models on sensitive or proprietary data without centralized data aggregation. Can be applied in privacy-preserving threat detection and collaborative security analytics.	Requires synchronization and coordination among distributed devices, which may introduce communication overhead and latency. Federated learning models may suffer from data distribution imbalances and heterogeneity across participating devices. Vulnerable to privacy and security risks associated with model updates and parameter sharing across decentralized networks.

Table 2. Cybersecurity aspects handled by generative AI

Reference No.	Recent Work in Generative AI	Aspect in Cybersecurity
1	Adversarial Training for GANs	Defense against adversarial attacks
2	GAN-generated Data Augmentation for Malware Detection	Enhancing training datasets for machine learning models
3	Generative Models for Synthetic Data Generation	Creating realistic attack simulations
4	Anomaly Detection using Variational Autoencoders	Detecting unusual patterns or anomalies in network traffic
5	GANs for Generating Adversarial Examples	Evaluating robustness of AI-based security systems
6	GAN-based Phishing Email Generation	Testing email security filters
7	Synthetic Data Generation for Threat Intelligence	Enhancing threat intelligence analysis
8	NLP-based Generative Models for Security Log Analysis	Analyzing unstructured text data for security insights

It can be observed from Table 2 that the various cyber-attack vectors give a formidable challenge to the researchers working in the area of generative AI thereby providing an inference that the attack mechanisms can be handled robustly through the inherent properties present in generative AI (Hilario, 2024).

There is a significant research gap in identifying data poisoning attacks in big data applications used to train AI models. The results below obtained from literature survey provide key insights (Hossain, 2024):

- Data poisoning attacks can manipulate the training data of AI models to introduce vulnerabilities, backdoors or biases that compromise the model's security, effectiveness, or ethical behavior. These attacks are becoming one of the most critical vulnerabilities in machine learning and AI.
- Researchers have shown that it is possible to influence large language models (LLMs) and generative text-to-image models on a large scale through techniques like split-view data poisoning and front running data poisoning. Even a small percentage of poisoned data can impact the model's performance.
- However, the search results do not provide specific details on how Generative AI methods can be used to bridge this research gap in identifying data poisoning attacks in big data applications. The results focus more on describing the threat of data poisoning in general.

To bridge this gap, Generative AI methods could potentially be leveraged in a few ways (Humphreys, 2024):

- Developing Generative Adversarial Networks (GANs) that can generate synthetic but realistic training data to test AI models for vulnerabilities to data poisoning attacks. The generator could create poisoned data samples to probe the model's robustness.
- Using large language models like GPT-3 to automatically analyze the training data and model outputs for anomalies or indicators of data poisoning. The LLM could flag suspicious patterns that human analysts can then investigate further.
- Applying Generative AI to create realistic simulations of data poisoning attacks on AI systems. These simulations could help researchers understand the attack surface and develop better mitigation strategies.

While the threat of data poisoning is well-established, more research is needed on practical methods to identify these attacks, especially in the context of big data applications that train large AI models. Generative AI techniques like GANs and LLMs could potentially play a role in bridging this gap by generating synthetic data for testing, anomaly detection, and attack simulation (Wang,2024).

The need for Generative AI methods to handle data poisoning attacks is critical, given the growing threat these attacks pose to the security and reliability of AI systems. However, the cost and complexity of implementing effective countermeasures should not be underestimated.

Threat Models and Attack Techniques

Data poisoning attacks can take various forms depending on the attacker's knowledge and goals (Ibáñez, 2023):

- Targeted attacks aim to corrupt only a small subset of the training data to introduce backdoors or biases, while keeping the model functioning normally for most inputs.
- Indiscriminate attacks attempt to degrade the model's overall performance by poisoning a larger portion of the training data.
- White-box attacks assume full knowledge of the model architecture and training process, while black-box attacks operate with minimal information.

Attackers can manipulate the training data in subtle ways that are hard for humans to detect, such as inserting imperceptible changes into images or adding carefully crafted text to poison language models. These attacks can enable malicious actors to bypass security filters, generate biased outputs, or cause the model to misbehave in targeted scenarios (Xu,2024).

The Need for Generative AI Countermeasures

To mitigate these threats, Generative AI techniques could play a key role in several ways (Jiang, 2023):

- Generating synthetic but realistic training data to test models for vulnerabilities to data poisoning.
- Automatically analyzing training data and model outputs for anomalies or indicators of poisoning using large language models (Yigit, 2024).
- Creating simulations of data poisoning attacks to understand the attack surface and develop mitigation strategies.

By proactively identifying weaknesses in AI systems, Generative AI could help organizations build more robust and secure models that are resilient to data poisoning (Lomurno, 2022). This is crucial as AI becomes more pervasive in high-stakes applications like cybersecurity, healthcare, and finance.

PROPOSED METHOD

A novel Generative AI method for handling data poisoning attacks in cybersecurity could involve leveraging Generative Adversarial Networks (GANs) in conjunction with a robust outlier detection mechanism. This approach aims to detect and mitigate the effects of poisoned data injected into training datasets used for machine learning models, particularly in the context of intrusion detection systems (IDS).

Applying Generative Adversarial Networks (GANs) in cybersecurity involves a rigorous research methodology to ensure effective and robust solutions. In below a suitable breakdown of the research methodology typically employed is stated:

1. Problem Definition

   Objective:

   Clearly define the cybersecurity issue that GANs aim to address, such as malware detection, phishing detection, or intrusion detection.
2. Data Collection

   Data Sources:

   Malware Samples: Collect a diverse set of malware samples from various sources to ensure the GAN can learn to generate realistic malware.

   Normal Behavior Data: Gather data representing normal network traffic, user behavior, and system operations to distinguish between benign and malicious activities.

   Data Pre-processing:

   Clean and pre-process the data to remove noise and ensure consistency. Normalize and format the data to be suitable for training GANs.
3. GAN Architecture Design

   Components:

   Generator: Design the generator network to create realistic cybersecurity threats (e.g., malware, phishing emails).

   Discriminator: Design the discriminator network to distinguish between real and generated threats.

   Network Configuration:

   Choose appropriate architectures for both generator and discriminator (e.g., convolutional neural networks for image-based malware, recurrent neural networks for sequence data).

   Decide on the loss functions, optimization algorithms, and hyperparameters.
4. Training the GAN

   Training Procedure:

Adversarial Training: Train the generator and discriminator in an adversarial manner where the generator aims to produce realistic samples, and the discriminator aims to differentiate between real and generated samples.

Iterative Improvement: Continuously improve both networks by iterating through multiple training epochs, adjusting parameters based on performance.

Evaluation Metrics:

Use metrics such as loss convergence, accuracy of the discriminator, and realism of generated samples to evaluate training progress.

5. Validation and Testing

Internal Validation:

Cross-Validation: Use techniques like k-fold cross-validation to assess the performance of the GAN on different subsets of the training data.

Evaluation on Real Threats: Test the GAN-generated samples against known real threats to evaluate realism and effectiveness.

External Testing:

Deploy the trained GAN in a controlled environment to test its performance in real-world scenarios.

Monitor its ability to generate realistic threats and its impact on cybersecurity measures (e.g., detection rates, false positives).

6. Application in Cybersecurity Systems

Integration:

Integrate the GAN-generated data into existing cybersecurity systems for various applications, such as enhancing training datasets, improving detection algorithms, and simulating attack scenarios.

Automation:

Develop automated workflows to continuously generate new threat samples and update the cybersecurity systems accordingly.

7. Continuous Monitoring and Improvement

Performance Monitoring:

Continuously monitor the performance of the GAN and its impact on cybersecurity measures.

Collect feedback and performance data to identify areas for improvement.

Model Updates:

Regularly update the GAN model with new data to adapt to evolving threats.

Fine-tune the model parameters and retrain as necessary to maintain high performance.

8. Documentation and Reporting

Research Documentation:

Document the research process, including data sources, pre-processing steps, GAN architecture details, training procedures, and evaluation results.
Reporting:
Prepare detailed reports and publications to share findings with the cybersecurity research community.
Highlight the effectiveness, challenges, and future directions of using GANs in cybersecurity.

The research methodology for applying GANs in cybersecurity involves a systematic approach from problem definition through continuous improvement, ensuring robust and effective integration of generative AI in defending against cyber threats.

In below, the design framework is discussed in overview.

1. Poisoned Data Detection with GANs:
    - Train a GAN to generate synthetic data that closely resembles the distribution of clean training data used for training the IDS.
    - During the training process, monitor the discriminator's output to identify discrepancies or anomalies between real and synthetic data.
    - If the discriminator consistently fails to distinguish between real and synthetic data, it may indicate the presence of poisoned data in the training set.
2. Outlier Detection and Rejection:
    - Apply outlier detection techniques, such as Isolation Forest or One-Class SVM, to identify data instances that deviate significantly from the learned distribution of clean data.
    - Flag data instances that are identified as outliers by the outlier detection mechanism as potential candidates for removal from the training dataset.
    - Remove flagged data instances from the training dataset to mitigate the impact of data poisoning attacks on the IDS.
3. Adaptive GAN Training:
    - Continuously retrain the GAN using updated training data, excluding the identified outliers and potentially poisoned data instances.
    - Adapt the GAN training process to dynamically adjust to changes in the underlying data distribution and mitigate the risk of future data poisoning attacks.
4. Ensemble Defense Mechanism:
    - Employ an ensemble defense mechanism that combines multiple anomaly detection techniques, including GAN-based detection and outlier

detection, to enhance the robustness of the IDS against various types of attacks.

- Integrate the ensemble defense mechanism into the overall cybersecurity infrastructure to provide comprehensive protection against data poisoning attacks and other adversarial threats.

By leveraging Generative AI techniques, such as GANs, in conjunction with robust outlier detection mechanisms, this proposed method offers a novel approach for detecting and mitigating data poisoning attacks in cybersecurity. By continuously monitoring and adapting to changes in the data distribution, the IDS can effectively defend against adversarial attempts to compromise its integrity and accuracy.

RESULTS

For showing the effectiveness of our proposed method, the dataset related to hidden backdoor attack obtained from kaggle is used. In this dataset, traffic sign labels are classified with 58 different identities along with their name attribute which contains their understandable description. Python language is used to implement the proposed algorithm.

For simulating the data poisoning attack on the hidden backdoor attack, the class identities are changed and the very meaning of the traffic sign can be changed due to the inherent modification in the dataset (Metta, 2024).

A Generative Adversarial Network (GAN) can be used in a data poison attack on a traffic sign dataset by generating malicious traffic sign images that can be used to confuse or mislead a machine learning model trained on the dataset.

Below steps illustrate the experimental setup.

1. Setup GAN Architecture: Set up a GAN architecture consisting of a generator and a discriminator. The generator generates fake traffic sign images, while the discriminator tries to distinguish between real and fake images.
2. Training the GAN: Train the GAN on the traffic sign dataset. The generator learns to produce images that are indistinguishable from real traffic signs, while the discriminator learns to correctly classify real and fake images.
3. Generate Poisoned Data: Once the GAN is trained, use the generator to create a set of fake traffic sign images. These images should be crafted to cause misclassification by the target model when they are included in the training dataset.
4. Inject Poisoned Data: Combine the generated fake traffic sign images with the original training dataset, creating a poisoned dataset. Ensure that the poisoned dataset looks similar to the original dataset to avoid detection.

5. Re-Train the Model: Train the target machine learning model (e.g., a traffic sign classifier) on the poisoned dataset. The model will learn from the poisoned data, potentially causing it to make incorrect predictions on similar traffic signs in the future.
6. Testing and Evaluation: Evaluate the performance of the poisoned model on a validation or test dataset to assess its effectiveness in causing misclassification. The goal is to confirm that the model's performance has been compromised due to the presence of poisoned data.
7. Fine-tuning (Optional): Fine-tune the poisoned model if necessary to improve its effectiveness in causing misclassification while maintaining its performance on legitimate data.

Figure 1. Accuracy versus severity of data poisoning attack

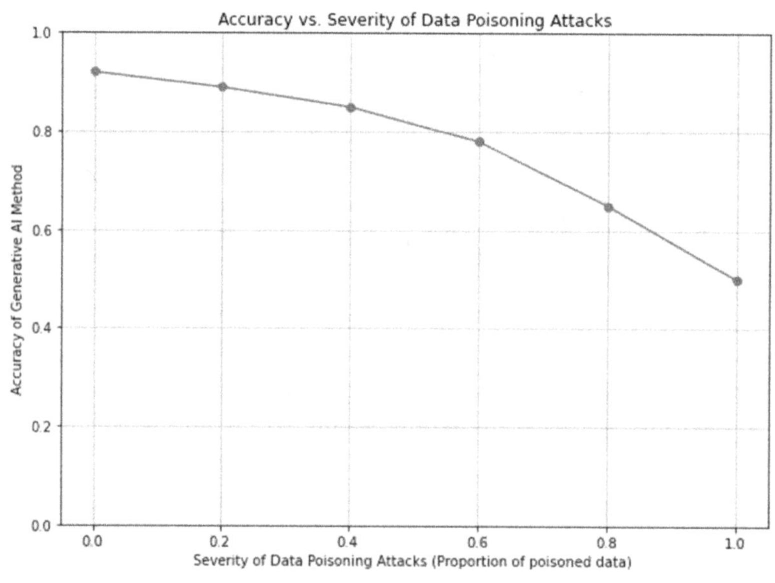

In Figure 1 above x- axis represents the severity or intensity of the data poisoning attack. Severity can be quantified in various ways, such as the percentage of poisoned data in the training set, the level of perturbation applied to the poisoned samples, or the similarity of the poisoned samples to genuine data. The severity increases as you move towards the right on the x-axis. On the y- axis, it represents the accuracy of the machine learning model on a validation or test dataset. Accuracy is typically measured as the proportion of correctly classified samples out of the total number of samples. Higher values on the Y-axis indicate higher accuracy of the model. From figure 2 above it can be easily inferred that the proposed mechanism trains the adversity model in an accurate manner. At the beginning (left side of the graph), as the severity of the attack increases slightly, the accuracy of the model may remain relatively stable or decrease slightly. This phase represents a low to moderate level of poisoning, where the model's performance is only mildly affected. As the severity of the attack surpasses a critical threshold, there might be a sudden drop in accuracy. This threshold represents the point at which the poisoned data significantly influences the model's learning process, causing it to make incorrect predictions on both poisoned and genuine samples. Beyond the critical threshold, as the severity of the attack continues to increase, the accuracy of the model steadily declines. This decline indicates that the model's performance is increasingly compromised by the presence of poisoned data, leading to a higher rate of misclassification. Eventually, the graph may reach an asymptote, where the accuracy stabilizes at a very low level. This indicates that the model's performance has been severely degraded by the poisoning attack, and further increases in severity have minimal impact on accuracy.

Figure 2. False positive rates of anomaly detection methods

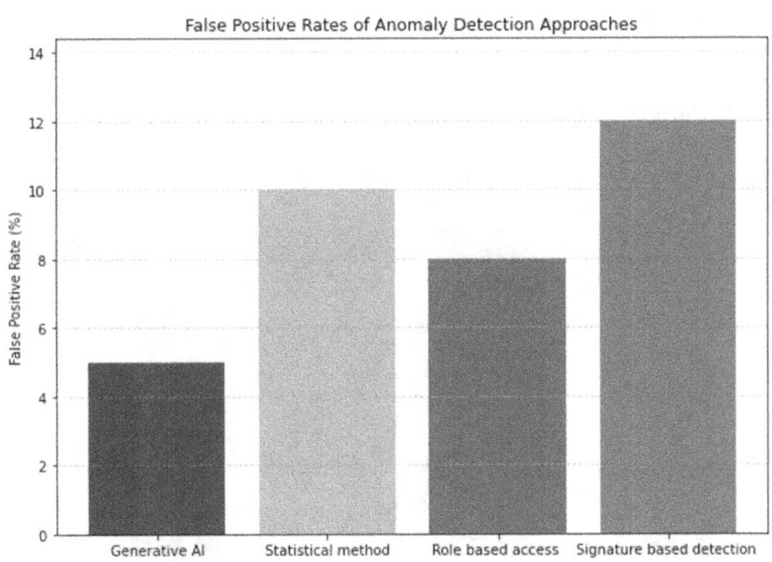

In above Figure 2, the x-axis represents the different anomaly detection techniques being compared. Each technique, including Generative AI, statistical methods, role-based access methods, and signature-based methods, is listed along this axis.

The y-axis represents the false positive rate of each anomaly detection technique. The false positive rate measures the proportion of non-anomalous instances that are incorrectly classified as anomalies. Lower values on the Y-axis indicate a lower rate of false positives, which is desirable for effective anomaly detection. Generative AI techniques, such as GANs, show a relatively low false positive rate compared to other methods due to their ability to model complex data distributions and detect subtle anomalies in traffic patterns. Statistical anomaly detection methods, such as Gaussian mixture models or Z-score thresholding, may exhibit a moderate false positive rate. These methods rely on statistical properties of the data and may struggle to detect anomalies in complex, high-dimensional datasets like traffic patterns. Role-based access methods, which involve defining access privileges based on user roles or permissions, may have a variable false positive rate depending on the accuracy of role assignments and access policies. In the context of traffic data, role-based access methods might not be directly applicable but could be relevant in scenarios involving user access to traffic management systems. Signature-based anomaly detection methods rely on predefined patterns or signatures of normal behavior. In the context of traffic data, these methods might involve detecting anomalies based on known traffic patterns or rules. However, they may struggle to adapt to new or evolving types of anomalies, leading to a higher false positive rate compared to more adaptive techniques like Generative AI.

Figure 3. Heatmap of adversarial inputs generated by generative AI

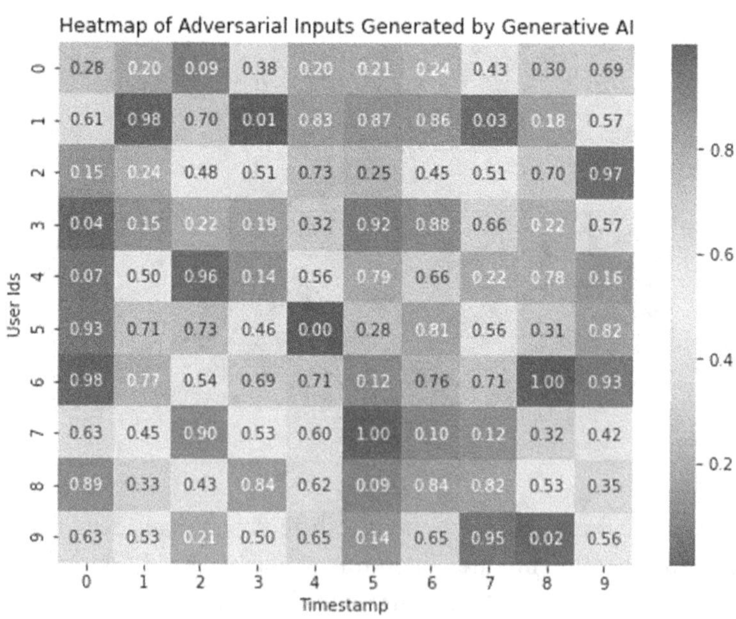

The x-axis represents timestamps, indicating when the adversarial inputs were generated in Figure 3. Time intervals, such as hours, days, or weeks, are typically marked on this axis, allowing for temporal analysis of the adversarial activity. The y-axis represents user IDs, identifying the individuals or entities responsible for generating the adversarial inputs. Each row corresponds to a unique user ID, allowing for analysis of adversarial behavior across different users. The heatmap cells are filled with colors representing the intensity or frequency of adversarial inputs generated at specific timestamps by specific users. A gradient color scheme is used, with lighter colors indicating lower activity levels and darker colors indicating higher activity levels. Lighter regions of the heatmap indicate timestamps and user IDs with minimal adversarial activity. These areas may correspond to periods when the Generative AI was not actively generating adversarial inputs or when certain users were not engaged in adversarial behavior. Darker regions of the heatmap indicate timestamps and user IDs associated with significant adversarial activity. These areas may highlight periods of concentrated adversarial activity by specific users or coordinated attacks targeting specific time intervals. By analyzing the heatmap, patterns and trends in adversarial behavior can be identified. For example, spikes in activity at certain timestamps or recurring patterns of adversarial inputs generated by specific users may suggest coordinated attacks or targeted manipulation of the dataset.

Figure 4. Robustness of generative AI methods for different attack strategies

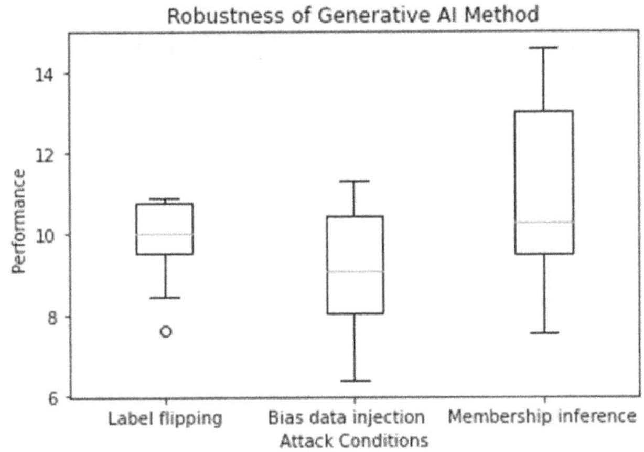

In Figure 4, a box plot graph depicting the performance of various attack strategies, including label flipping, biased data injection, and membership inference attacks, in the context of a data poisoning attack handled by Generative AI for a traffic sign dataset provides insights into the effectiveness of each strategy and their impact on model performance. The x-axis represents different attack strategies employed in the data poisoning attack. Each strategy, including label flipping, biased data injection, and membership inference attacks, is listed along this axis. The y-axis represents the performance metric used to evaluate the effectiveness of each attack strategy. This could be accuracy, precision, recall, F1 score, or any other relevant metric that measures the impact of the attack on model performance. Higher values on the y-axis indicate better performance, while lower values indicate poorer performance. The line within each box represents the median performance of the attack strategy. The box itself represents the interquartile range, which encompasses the middle 50% of the performance scores. The top and bottom edges of the box correspond to the 75th and 25th percentiles, respectively. The whiskers extend from the edges of the box to the maximum and minimum performance scores within a certain range, typically 1.5 times the IQR (Interquartile Range) from the upper and lower quartiles. Individual data points lying beyond the whiskers are considered outliers and are plotted separately. The box plot allows for a visual comparison of the performance of different attack strategies. Strategies with higher median performance or narrower interquartile ranges are generally more effective at compromising model performance through data poisoning. A lower median performance or wider interquartile range indicates a more detrimental impact of the attack strategy on model performance. Attack strategies that result in lower model performance metrics (e.g., accuracy, precision) are considered more successful in compromising the model's integrity. Outliers in the box plot may indicate instances where certain attack strategies have unexpectedly high or low performance. These outliers can provide valuable insights into the variability and unpredictability of attack outcomes.

Figure 5. Comparison of CPU usages with respect to number of iterations of the algorithm execution

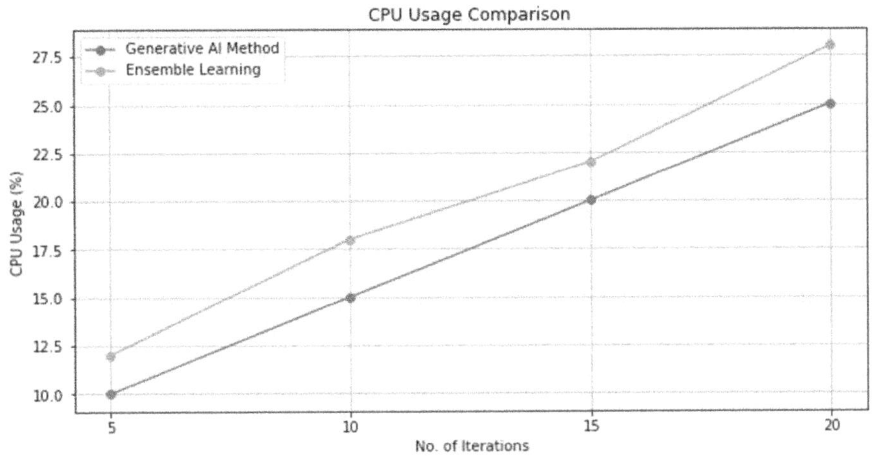

In Figure 5, a comparison graph of number of iterations of the algorithm execution on the x-axis with respect to the percentage of CPU usage on the y-axis provides insights into how the computational resource requirements vary between Generative AI and Ensemble methods for data poisoning attacks on a traffic sign dataset. The x-axis represents the number of iterations of the algorithm execution. Iterations refer to the repeated execution of the algorithm; with each iteration potentially consuming varying amounts of CPU resources. The y-axis represents CPU usage, which measures the amount of computational resources consumed by the algorithm execution. CPU usage is typically measured in terms of percentage of CPU utilization or absolute CPU time. The performance of Generative AI in terms of CPU usage is represented by a line on the graph. As the number of iterations increases, the CPU usage of Generative AI decreases, indicating that Generative AI becomes more efficient over time. As Generative AI demonstrates lower CPU usage even as the number of iterations increases, it suggests that Generative AI may be more scalable for large-scale data poisoning attacks.

Figure 6. Memory consumption comparison between generative AI method and ensemble learning method

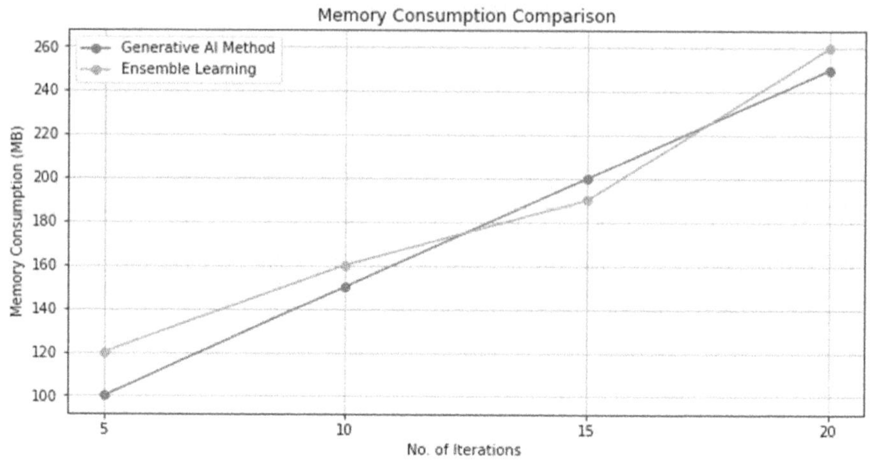

Figure 6 shows a comparison graph of memory consumption on the y-axis with respect to the number of iterations of the algorithm execution on the x-axis. It represents how memory usage varies between Generative AI and Ensemble methods for data poisoning attacks on a traffic sign dataset. The x-axis represents the number of iterations of the algorithm execution. This could indicate the number of training epochs, iterations of a specific optimization algorithm, or any other relevant measure of algorithmic progression. As the number of iterations increases, the algorithm undergoes more computational steps. The y-axis represents the memory consumption of the algorithm during execution. Memory consumption is typically measured in bytes or another relevant unit of memory. Higher values on the y-axis indicate greater memory usage by the algorithm. The curve for generative AI shows a gradual increase in memory consumption or even remains relatively flat as the number of iterations increases. This suggests that Generative AI consumes less memory compared to Ensemble methods, even as the algorithm executes over multiple iterations. The curve or line representing Ensemble methods shows how memory consumption changes with the number of iterations for this approach. Ensemble methods, which typically involve combining multiple models or classifiers, may exhibit a steeper increase in memory consumption as the number of iterations increases. This is because Ensemble methods often require storing and manipulating multiple models or data structures, leading to higher memory usage. While Generative AI may offer memory efficiency benefits, practitioners should also consider the performance implications of using these methods compared to

Ensemble methods. It's essential to strike a balance between memory consumption, computational efficiency, and model performance when selecting an approach for data poisoning attacks.

CASE STUDIES

Case Study 1: IBM's Watson for Cyber Security

Overview:

IBM Watson, known for its AI capabilities in various domains, has been leveraged in cybersecurity to enhance threat detection and response. Watson for Cyber Security integrates cognitive computing to analyze and interpret massive volumes of unstructured data, such as blogs, articles, and research papers, to identify potential threats and recommend mitigation strategies (Wang,2024).

Implementation:

- Data Analysis: Watson scans and interprets vast amounts of unstructured data to extract relevant threat intelligence.
- Threat Identification: By correlating data from multiple sources, Watson can identify emerging threats and provide context around them.
- Automated Response: Watson can suggest actions based on its analysis, helping security teams respond quickly to potential incidents.

Outcome:

- Enhanced Detection: Watson improved the accuracy and speed of threat detection by providing actionable intelligence derived from diverse data sources.
- Reduced Response Time: The automated analysis and recommendations significantly reduced the time taken to respond to threats.
- Resource Optimization: By automating routine tasks, Watson allowed security teams to focus on more complex issues, optimizing resource use.

Case Study 2: Darktrace's Enterprise Immune System

Overview:

Darktrace uses AI and machine learning to provide cybersecurity solutions modeled after the human immune system. Their Enterprise Immune System employs unsupervised learning to detect anomalies and potential threats within an organization's network in real-time (Wang,2024).

Implementation:

- Self-Learning: The system learns normal behavior patterns within the network without requiring pre-configured rules or signatures.
- Anomaly Detection: By continuously monitoring network activity, the system identifies deviations that may indicate threats.
- Automated Response: When a potential threat is detected, the system can automatically respond to mitigate the risk, such as by isolating affected devices.

Outcome:

- Proactive Defense: The system's ability to detect novel threats in real-time enabled a proactive approach to cybersecurity.
- Reduced False Positives: The self-learning capability minimized false positives, improving the efficiency of the security team.
- Comprehensive Coverage: The solution provided visibility across the entire network, including IoT devices and cloud environments.

Case Study 3: FireEye's Use of Generative Adversarial Networks (GANs) for Malware Detection

Overview:

FireEye, a cybersecurity company, has integrated Generative Adversarial Networks (GANs) to enhance its malware detection capabilities. GANs are used to generate new malware samples, which help in training and improving detection algorithms (Wang,2024).

Implementation:

- Malware Generation: GANs are used to create diverse malware samples that simulate real-world attacks.
- Training Data: These generated samples are included in the training datasets for machine learning models.
- Improved Detection: The models trained with these enriched datasets are better at detecting both known and unknown malware variants.

Outcome:

- Enhanced Detection Rates: The use of GANs significantly improved the accuracy of malware detection systems.
- Adaptability: The approach helped FireEye's systems stay ahead of evolving malware by continuously updating the training data with new samples.
- Cost Efficiency: Automating the generation of malware samples reduced the reliance on manually curated datasets, lowering operational costs.

The above mentioned case studies demonstrate the diverse applications and significant impact of generative AI in cybersecurity:

- IBM Watson highlights how cognitive computing can enhance threat intelligence and response.
- Darktrace showcases the benefits of self-learning systems for real-time anomaly detection and proactive defense.
- FireEye illustrates the use of GANs to continuously evolve malware detection capabilities.

These examples underscore the potential of generative AI to transform cybersecurity by improving detection accuracy, response times, and overall resilience against evolving threats.

Success Stories in Generative AI for Cybersecurity (Wang,2024)

1. IBM Watson for Cyber Security at University of New Brunswick (UNB)

Success Story:

The University of New Brunswick (UNB) implemented IBM Watson for Cyber Security to bolster its cybersecurity infrastructure. UNB faced challenges with the growing volume and sophistication of cyber threats, which strained their security resources. By leveraging Watson's cognitive computing capabilities, UNB could analyze large datasets and identify potential threats quickly.

Key Takeaways:

- Enhanced Threat Detection: Watson's ability to process and analyze vast amounts of unstructured data improved UNB's threat detection capabilities.
- Operational Efficiency: Automation of routine tasks allowed the security team to focus on more critical issues.
- Scalability: The AI-driven approach provided a scalable solution that could grow with the university's needs.

2. Darktrace's Enterprise Immune System at Drax Group

Success Story:

Drax Group, a major energy company, adopted Darktrace's Enterprise Immune System to protect its infrastructure from cyber threats. Given the critical nature of their operations, any security breach could have significant repercussions. Darktrace's AI-powered solution provided real-time threat detection and response, safeguarding their network and operations.

Key Takeaways:

- Real-Time Detection: The self-learning AI provided real-time insights into network anomalies, enabling swift action against potential threats.
- Minimal False Positives: Darktrace's technology minimized false positives, allowing security teams to focus on genuine threats.
- Proactive Security Posture: The AI's ability to adapt to new threats ensured a proactive approach to cybersecurity.

3. FireEye's AI-Powered Malware Detection at Sony Pictures

Success Story:

Following a high-profile cyberattack, Sony Pictures implemented FireEye's AI-powered malware detection system. FireEye utilized Generative Adversarial Networks (GANs) to generate diverse malware samples, which were used to train and improve their detection algorithms. This approach significantly enhanced Sony's ability to detect and respond to malware threats.

Key Takeaways:

- Improved Detection Rates: The use of GANs for generating training samples led to higher detection accuracy for both known and unknown malware.
- Adaptive Security: FireEye's adaptive models ensured continuous improvement in malware detection capabilities.
- Reduced Operational Costs: Automating malware sample generation reduced dependency on manual data curation, lowering costs.

4. Microsoft's Project Hanover in Healthcare Cybersecurity

Success Story:

Microsoft's Project Hanover, initially focused on healthcare, also demonstrated success in cybersecurity. By using AI to analyze and interpret large datasets, Hanover helped identify vulnerabilities and potential cyber threats within healthcare systems. This proactive approach ensured the protection of sensitive medical data.

Key Takeaways:

- Data-Driven Insights: AI-driven analysis provided deep insights into potential security vulnerabilities.
- Proactive Measures: Identifying threats before they could be exploited ensured the protection of critical data.
- Cross-Domain Applications: Success in healthcare cybersecurity highlighted the versatility and applicability of AI across different sectors.

Practical Outcomes from Success Stories

1. Enhanced Detection and Response: Generative AI significantly improves the speed and accuracy of threat detection and response, enabling organizations to stay ahead of emerging threats.
2. Operational Efficiency: Automation of routine tasks and analysis allows security teams to focus on more strategic and complex issues, optimizing resource utilization.
3. Real-Time and Proactive Security: AI's ability to provide real-time insights and adapt to new threats fosters a proactive security posture, essential for defending against sophisticated cyber-attacks.
4. Scalability and Adaptability: AI-driven solutions offer scalable and adaptable cybersecurity measures that can evolve with the organization's needs and the changing threat landscape.
5. Reduction of False Positives: Advanced AI models minimize false positives, ensuring that security teams can concentrate on genuine threats without unnecessary distractions.
6. Cross-Sector Applicability: The success of AI in cybersecurity across various sectors, from education and energy to healthcare and entertainment, demonstrates its broad applicability and effectiveness.

These success stories and takeaways underscore the transformative potential of generative AI in enhancing cybersecurity measures, providing robust defenses against a rapidly evolving threat landscape.

FUTURE DIRECTIONS

In below five potential future directions for addressing data poisoning attacks using Generative AI:

1. Dynamic Adversarial Training: Explore techniques for dynamically adjusting the parameters of the GAN during training to adversarially adapt to evolving data poisoning attacks. This approach could involve continuously retraining the GAN in an online fashion, incorporating feedback from the IDS and adapting to changes in the adversarial landscape (Michael, 2023).
2. Multi-Modal Generative Models: Investigate the use of multi-modal generative models, such as Variational Autoencoders (VAEs) or Generative Adversarial Variational Autoencoders (VAE-GANs), to capture the complex, multi-dimensional nature of real-world data. By incorporating multiple modalities

(e.g., text, images, network traffic), these models can enhance the fidelity and diversity of the generated data, making them more effective for detecting and mitigating data poisoning attacks across different types of datasets (Novelli,2024).

3. Explainable Generative AI: Develop methods for enhancing the interpretability and explainability of generative AI models to facilitate understanding of their decision-making processes and detection of potential vulnerabilities (Prieto, 2023). By providing insights into how the GAN generates synthetic data and detects outliers, cybersecurity professionals can better assess the reliability and trustworthiness of the defense mechanism against data poisoning attacks.
4. Federated Generative Learning: Explore federated learning approaches for training generative AI models on distributed datasets while preserving data privacy and security. Federated generative learning enables multiple parties to collaboratively train a GAN without sharing raw data, thereby mitigating the risk of data poisoning attacks and preserving the confidentiality of sensitive information (Psychogyios, 2023).
5. Adversarial Defense Games: Investigate the application of game-theoretic frameworks to model the interactions between attackers and defenders in the context of data poisoning attacks. By formulating the defense against data poisoning attacks as a game between the adversary and the defender, researchers can develop strategies for effectively countering adversarial attempts to compromise the integrity of the training data and undermine the performance of the IDS (Vemuri, 2024).

These future directions represent exciting opportunities for advancing research in the field of cybersecurity and developing innovative solutions for combating data poisoning attacks using Generative AI. By exploring these avenues, researchers can contribute to the development of more robust and resilient defense mechanisms capable of defending against emerging threats in an increasingly adversarial cyber landscape.

CONCLUSION

The emergence of data poisoning attacks poses significant challenges to the integrity and effectiveness of intrusion detection systems (IDS) in cybersecurity. These attacks exploit vulnerabilities in machine learning models by injecting malicious data into training datasets, thereby compromising the accuracy and reliability of the IDS. However, the integration of Generative Adversarial Networks (GANs) offers a promising avenue for detecting and mitigating the impact of data poisoning attacks. By leveraging the power of Generative AI, researchers can develop innovative techniques for generating synthetic data that closely resembles the distribution of clean training data. This synthetic data serves as a valuable resource for training IDS models, enabling them to identify and adapt to emerging threats posed by data poisoning attacks. Furthermore, by incorporating robust outlier detection mechanisms, such as Isolation Forest or One-Class SVM, into the defense framework, cybersecurity professionals can effectively identify and remove potentially poisoned data instances from the training dataset, thereby mitigating the risk of adversarial manipulation. Looking ahead, there are several promising directions for future research in this area. Dynamic adversarial training methods can be explored to adaptively adjust the parameters of the GAN in response to evolving data poisoning attacks, enhancing the resilience of the defense mechanism over time. Multi-modal generative models offer an opportunity to capture the complex, multi-dimensional nature of real-world data, making them more effective for detecting and mitigating data poisoning attacks across different types of datasets. The development of explainable generative AI techniques can provide insights into the decision-making processes of GANs, enabling cybersecurity professionals to better understand and interpret their behavior. Federated generative learning approaches offer a privacy-preserving solution for training GANs on distributed datasets, mitigating the risk of data exposure and ensuring the confidentiality of sensitive information. Game-theoretic frameworks can be employed to model the interactions between attackers and defenders in the context of data poisoning attacks, enabling the development of effective strategies for countering adversarial threats. By exploring these future directions, researchers can contribute to the advancement of cybersecurity defense mechanisms and develop innovative solutions for combating data poisoning attacks using Generative AI. Ultimately, the integration of Generative AI techniques holds great promise for enhancing the resilience and effectiveness of intrusion detection systems in the face of evolving cyber threats.

REFERENCES

Agrawal, G., Kaur, A., & Myneni, S. (2024). A Review of Generative Models in Generating Synthetic Attack Data for Cybersecurity. *Electronics (Basel)*, 13(2), 322. 10.3390/electronics13020322

Chen, Y., & Esmaeilzadeh, P. (2024). Generative AI in medical practice: In-depth exploration of privacy and security challenges. *Journal of Medical Internet Research*, 26, e53008. 10.2196/5300838457208

Dhoni, P., & Kumar, R. (2023). Synergizing generative ai and cybersecurity: Roles of generative ai entities, companies, agencies, and government in enhancing cybersecurity. *Authorea Preprints*.

Dunmore, A., Jang-Jaccard, J., Sabrina, F., & Kwak, J. (2023). A comprehensive survey of generative adversarial networks (gans) in cybersecurity intrusion detection. *IEEE Access : Practical Innovations, Open Solutions*, 11, 76071–76094. 10.1109/ACCESS.2023.3296707

Gupta, M., Akiri, C., Aryal, K., Parker, E., & Praharaj, L. (2023). From chatgpt to threatgpt: Impact of generative ai in cybersecurity and privacy. *IEEE Access : Practical Innovations, Open Solutions*, 11, 80218–80245. 10.1109/ACCESS.2023.3300381

Hilario, E., Azam, S., Sundaram, J., Imran Mohammed, K., & Shanmugam, B. (2024). Generative AI for pentesting: The good, the bad, the ugly. *International Journal of Information Security*, 23(3), 1–23. 10.1007/s10207-024-00835-x

Hossain, M. T., Afrin, R., & Biswas, M. A. A. (2024). A Review on Attacks against Artificial Intelligence (AI) and Their Defence Image Recognition and Generation Machine Learning, Artificial Intelligence. *Control Systems and Optimization Letters*, 2(1), 52–59.

Humphreys, D., Koay, A., Desmond, D., & Mealy, E. (2024). AI hype as a cyber security risk: The moral responsibility of implementing generative AI in business. *AI and Ethics*, 1–14. 10.1007/s43681-024-00443-4

Ibáñez Lissen, L., Fuentes García-Romero de Tejada, J. M. D., González Manzano, L., & García Alfaro, J. (2023). Characterizing poisoning attacks on generalistic multi-modal AI models. *Information Fusion*, 1–15.

Jiang, S., Kadhe, S. R., Zhou, Y., Cai, L., & Baracaldo, N. (2023). Forcing Generative Models to Degenerate Ones: The Power of Data Poisoning Attacks. arXiv preprint arXiv:2312.04748

Lomurno, E., Archetti, A., Cazzella, L., Samele, S., Di Perna, L., & Matteucci, M. (2022, September). SGDE: Secure generative data exchange for cross-silo federated learning. In *Proceedings of the 2022 5th International Conference on Artificial Intelligence and Pattern Recognition* (pp. 205-214). 10.1145/3573942.3573974

Metta, S., Chang, I., Parker, J., Roman, M. P., & Ehuan, A. F. (2024). Generative AI in Cybersecurity. arXiv preprint arXiv:2405.01674.

Michael, K., Abbas, R., & Roussos, G. (2023). AI in Cybersecurity: The Paradox. *IEEE Transactions on Technology and Society*, 4(2), 104–109. 10.1109/TTS.2023.3280109

Novelli, C., Casolari, F., Hacker, P., Spedicato, G., & Floridi, L. (2024). Generative AI in EU Law: Liability, Privacy, Intellectual Property, and Cybersecurity. arXiv preprint arXiv:2401.07348.

Prieto, I., & Blakely, B. (2023). Proposed Uses of Generative AI in a Cybersecurity-Focused Soar Agent. In *Proceedings of the AAAI Symposium Series* (Vol. 2, No. 1, pp. 386-390).

Psychogyios, K., Velivassaki, T. H., Bourou, S., Voulkidis, A., Skias, D., & Zahariadis, T. (2023). GAN-driven data poisoning attacks and their mitigation in federated learning systems. *Electronics (Basel)*, 12(8), 1805. 10.3390/electronics12081805

Ramirez, M. A., Kim, S. K., Hamadi, H. A., Damiani, E., Byon, Y. J., Kim, T. Y., . . . Yeun, C. Y. (2022). Poisoning attacks and defenses on artificial intelligence: A survey. arXiv preprint arXiv:2202.10276.

Renaud, K., Warkentin, M., & Westerman, G. (2023). From ChatGPT to HackGPT: Meeting the cybersecurity threat of generative AI. *MIT Sloan Management Review*.

Sai, S., Yashvardhan, U., Chamola, V., & Sikdar, B. (2024). Generative ai for cyber security: Analyzing the potential of chatgpt, dall-e and other models for enhancing the security space. *IEEE Access : Practical Innovations, Open Solutions*, 12, 53497–53516. 10.1109/ACCESS.2024.3385107

Shahriar, M. H., Khalil, A. A., Rahman, M. A., Manshaei, M. H., & Chen, D. (2021, October). iattackgen: Generative synthesis of false data injection attacks in cyber-physical systems. In *2021 IEEE Conference on Communications and Network Security (CNS)* (pp. 200-208). IEEE. 10.1109/CNS53000.2021.9705034

Tasneem, S., Gupta, K. D., Roy, A., & Dasgupta, D. (2022, December). Generative Adversarial Networks (GAN) for Cyber Security: Challenges and Opportunities. In *Proceedings of the 2022 IEEE Symposium Series on Computational Intelligence*, Singapore (pp. 4-7).

Vemuri, N., Thaneeru, N., & Tatikonda, V. M. (2024). Adaptive generative AI for dynamic cybersecurity threat detection in enterprises.

Wang, M. (2024). Generative AI: A New Challenge for Cybersecurity. *Journal of Computer Science and Technology Studies*, 6(2), 13–18. 10.32996/jcsts.2024.6.2.3

Xu, H., Li, Y., Balogun, O., Wu, S., Wang, Y., & Cai, Z. (2024). Security Risks Concerns of Generative AI in the IoT. *IEEE Internet of Things Magazine*, 7(3), 62–67. 10.1109/IOTM.001.2400004

Yigit, Y., Buchanan, W. J., Tehrani, M. G., & Maglaras, L. (2024). Review of Generative AI Methods in Cybersecurity. arXiv preprint arXiv:2403.08701.

KEY TERMS AND DEFINITIONS

Attack: Is a deliberate attempt to breach or compromise information systems, causing damage, theft, or disruption.

Cyber Security: Cybersecurity involves protecting computer systems, networks, and data from unauthorized access, damage, theft, or disruption through the implementation of various security measures and protocols.

Data Poisoning: Data poisoning in cybersecurity refers to the intentional manipulation of training data used in machine learning models, aiming to corrupt the model's output or behavior.

Ensemble Learning: Ensemble learning in machine learning combines multiple models to improve performance, accuracy, and robustness compared to individual models, leveraging their collective strengths.

Generative Adversarial Networks: Generative Adversarial Networks (GANs) consist of two neural networks, a generator and a discriminator, competing in a zero-sum game to create realistic synthetic data indistinguishable from real data.

Intrusion: Intrusion refers to unauthorized access or breach of a computer system or network, compromising its security and data integrity.

Malware: Is malicious software designed to disrupt, damage, or gain unauthorized access to computer systems or networks.

Privacy: Privacy is the right of individuals to control their personal information, ensuring it is collected, used, and shared with their consent and protected from unauthorized access.

Threat Intelligence: Threat Intelligence involves collecting, analyzing, and interpreting data about current and potential cyber threats to enhance an organization's security posture and defense mechanisms.

Virus: A virus is a malicious software program that replicates itself by infecting other programs or files, causing damage or unauthorized actions on a computer system.

Chapter 11
Innovations in Cloud Storage
Leveraging Generative AI for Enhanced Data Management

L. Devarajan
Cozy System, USA

ABSTRACT

As the demand for efficient and scalable data storage solutions continues to rise, the integration of artificial intelligence (AI) technologies with cloud storage systems has emerged as a promising avenue for innovation. This chapter explores the intersection of AI and cloud storage, investigating how AI-driven approaches are revolutionizing traditional cloud storage practices and unlocking new opportunities for enhanced performance and functionality. Through a comprehensive review of literature and case studies, this study examines the role of AI in optimizing data management, improving security measures, and enabling intelligent data processing within cloud storage environments. Furthermore, this chapter delves into the implications of AI-driven innovation for businesses and organizations, highlighting the potential benefits of increased efficiency, cost savings, and competitive advantage.

INTRODUCTION

Cloud storage provides a practical and effective means to store, access, and manage digital assets, revolutionizing the way individuals and organizations handle their data. This concept describes the process of storing data not on local, physical storage devices like hard drives or flash drives, but rather on remote servers that are reachable via the internet (Xue et al., 2022). Users with a connection to the internet

DOI: 10.4018/979-8-3693-8557-9.ch011

may upload, save, and access their data from any place by utilizing cloud storage services, offering previously unheard-of flexibility and convenience. Scalability is one of the main benefits of cloud storage. Cloud storage solutions are easily scalable to meet user needs, unlike traditional storage techniques that are limited by physical hardware constraints. This implies that without having to spend extra money on infrastructure or additional hardware, people and enterprises can dynamically change their storage capacity (El Khatib et al.. 2019). Cloud storage companies offer customizable storage options that may handle a wide range of storage requirements, whether you're keeping a few megabytes of personal files or petabytes of business data. Apart from being scalable, cloud storage also provides unmatched flexibility. Users are free to access their data from PCs, cellphones, tablets, and any other device with a web connection. This implies that, irrespective of the user's location or the device they are using, crucial papers, images, and other files are always available (Gill et al., 2022). Moreover, a lot of cloud storage companies feature cross-platform compatibility, which enables customers to easily access their data on various devices and operating systems. The affordability of cloud storage is another important aspect. Conventional storage solutions can come with hefty upfront maintenance, infrastructure, and hardware costs. On the other hand, cloud storage works on a pay-as-you-go basis, meaning that customers only pay for the resources and storage that they really utilize. This allows users to scale their data storage expenses according to their needs and does away with the requirement for costly hardware acquisitions (Belgaum et al., 2021). Furthermore, a lot of cloud storage companies give tiers in their pricing structures, which helps users with high data volumes save money. To accommodate the needs of various users, cloud storage providers offer a range of deployment strategies. Third-party providers host and administer public cloud storage services, which provide a practical and affordable option for people and companies of all sizes (Gill et al., 2022). In contrast, private cloud storage is exclusive to one company and is usually housed in a data center or on-premises, offering better protection and control over data. With hybrid cloud storage, businesses can take advantage of public cloud's scalability and affordability while keeping sensitive data on-site. Hybrid cloud storage blends components of both public and private clouds. With its unmatched scalability, flexibility, and affordability, cloud storage has completely changed the way we handle, store, and retrieve data (Belgaum et al., 2021). Cloud storage has become a vital tool for both consumers and businesses since it eliminates the need for physical storage devices and offers seamless data access from any location. Users may select the cloud storage solution that best suits their needs from a variety of services and deployment methods, freeing them to concentrate on their data, which is ultimately what counts most (Xue et al., 2022).

Modern technological progress is led by artificial intelligence (AI), a branch of computer science that aims to give machines skills that are often associated with human intellect. Artificial Intelligence (AI) is primarily concerned with making computers capable of activities that include cognitive abilities including perception, learning, reasoning, and problem-solving. Machine learning, natural language processing, computer vision, robotics, and other different approaches and techniques are all included in this revolutionary technology, which advances AI applications in a wide range of sectors (Sarker., 2021). Machine learning is a key aspect of artificial intelligence (AI). It is a subset of AI that focuses on allowing machines to learn from data without explicit programming (Belgaum et al., 2021). Machine learning algorithms are capable of pattern recognition, prediction, and long-term performance improvement through the examination of large datasets. From e-commerce and advertising to healthcare and banking, this potential has completely transformed a number of industries. Machine learning algorithms, for instance, may evaluate medical pictures to help radiologists diagnose conditions like cancer, enhancing patient care efficiency and accuracy (Gill et al., 2022). NLP, or natural language processing, is another essential element of artificial intelligence that makes it easier for robots to comprehend and communicate with human language (Stergiou et al., 2020). Applications like chatbots, virtual assistants, and language translation services are made possible by NLP algorithms, which give robots the ability to understand, interpret, and produce human language. Through improving customer service, promoting cross-cultural conversation, and enabling more effective knowledge distribution, these technologies have completely changed communication and information access (El Khatib et al., 2019). Recent years have also witnessed notable developments in computer vision, an area of artificial intelligence that focuses on enabling robots to analyze and comprehend visual data. Computer vision algorithms are able to detect faces, identify objects, and derive valuable insights from visual data by analyzing photos and videos (Tuli et al., 2022). Applications for this technology may be found in a number of fields, including as medical imaging, surveillance systems, and driverless cars. For instance, computer vision algorithms in autonomous cars allow them to see and navigate their environment, improving road safety and effectiveness (Belgacem et al., 2023). Another frontier in technological advancement is AI-driven robotics, which uses intelligent devices that can work alongside people or independently to complete tasks. Robots with artificial intelligence (AI) capabilities are transforming processes and supplementing human labor in a variety of industries, including manufacturing, shipping, healthcare, and service (Sankar et al., 2023). Artificial intelligence (AI)-powered surgical robots can help doctors conduct difficult surgeries more precisely and accurately, lowering risks and enhancing patient outcomes (Xue et al., 2022). AI is changing corporate processes, fostering innovation, and opening up new avenues for expansion and development in almost every sector of the economy, from healthcare and banking to transportation and entertainment (Sankar & David, 2023). AI-enabled diagnostic technologies in the healthcare industry may evaluate patient data and medical pictures to help doctors diagnose patients more accurately and offer individualized treatments. AI systems in finance are able to identify fraudulent activity, evaluate market trends, and optimize investment strategies—all of which improve efficiency and risk management. Autonomous cars driven by artificial intelligence (AI) have the potential to completely transform transportation by providing safer and more convenient modes of transportation (Ganeshkumar et al., 2024). A paradigm shift in computing, artificial intelligence allows robots to mimic human intellect and carry out a variety of cognitive functions (Belgaum et al., 2021). Artificial Intelligence (AI) is transforming task automation, data-driven insights, and decision-making with applications that cut across several sectors. With its revolutionary potential, AI has the ability to significantly and unprecedentedly shape technology and society as it develops and grows (Sankar & David, 2024).

The intersection of artificial intelligence (AI) and cloud computing marks a pivotal convergence that unleashes a potent synergy, facilitating the creation and deployment of advanced AI applications on a massive scale. Cloud computing serves as the foundational infrastructure, offering the necessary resources and services to support the demanding workloads of AI (Sankar & David, 2024). This includes robust storage solutions for vast datasets, high-performance computing capabilities for complex calculations, and scalable networking infrastructure for seamless connectivity. By harnessing the capabilities of the cloud, organizations gain access to an unprecedented wealth of data that fuels AI-driven insights and innovations. Cloud-based storage solutions provide a secure and scalable repository for storing massive volumes of structured and unstructured data, ranging from text documents and images to sensor data streams and video footage. This data reservoir serves as the lifeblood for AI algorithms, enabling them to learn, adapt, and derive valuable insights from the wealth of information at their disposal (El Khatib et al., 2019). Furthermore, the cloud offers powerful computing resources that are essential for training and deploying AI models efficiently. With access to on-demand virtual machines, specialized hardware accelerators, and scalable computing clusters, organizations can accelerate the development and deployment of AI solutions without the need for significant upfront investments in hardware or infrastructure. This agility and flexibility allow businesses to experiment with different AI algorithms, iterate on models, and rapidly scale their AI initiatives to meet evolving business needs (Tuli et al., 2022). The convergence of AI and cloud computing enables the development of AI-powered solutions across a wide spectrum of applications and industries. From data analytics and predictive modeling to natural language processing and image recognition, AI algorithms deployed on the cloud can unlock new insights, automate complex tasks, and enhance decision-making processes (Belgacem et al., 2023). Medical imaging and patient data may be analyzed by AI-powered diagnostic technology in the healthcare sector to assist physicians in making personalized treatment plans and diagnosing ailments. Artificial intelligence (AI) algorithms in the financial sector may evaluate consumer and market data to detect fraud and enhance investment plans. AI-driven predictive maintenance systems may evaluate sensor data in the production process to foresee equipment breakdowns and save downtime. A scalable and affordable platform for implementing AI solutions at scale is also offered by the cloud, allowing businesses to reach a worldwide clientele and cater to a variety of user bases (Xue et al., 2022). Developers and companies of all sizes may now more easily access advanced AI capabilities thanks to cloud-based AI services like computer vision tools, machine learning platforms, and APIs for natural language processing. This allows them to stand out in the market and innovate.

This paper offers a holistic examination of the interplay between two cutting-edge technologies: cloud storage and artificial intelligence (AI). As these domains continue to evolve independently, their intersection has emerged as a fertile ground for innovation, offering novel solutions to complex data management and analysis challenges (El Khatib et al., 2019). By exploring the convergence of cloud storage and AI, this paper aims to shed light on the transformative potential of this synergy and its implications for various industries and applications. Cloud storage, a cornerstone of modern computing, revolutionizes the way data is stored, accessed, and managed, leveraging remote servers accessed through the internet to provide scalable, flexible, and cost-effective storage solutions. Conversely, artificial intelligence (AI) refers to a wide range of technological advancements that are intended to give machines intelligence akin to that of humans, allowing them to carry out tasks that have historically required human assistance, like data-driven learning, reasoning, resolving issues understanding, and natural language understanding. At their intersection, cloud storage and AI synergize to enable the development and deployment of advanced data-driven applications at scale. Cloud computing infrastructure provides the necessary resources and services to support AI workloads, including storage, computation, and networking. By harnessing the power of the cloud, organizations can access vast amounts of data, leverage powerful computing resources, and deploy AI models efficiently. This convergence facilitates the development of AI-powered solutions across diverse domains, including data analytics, predictive modeling, natural language processing, image recognition, and robotics (Sankar et al., 2024). In conclusion, the intersection of cloud storage and artificial intelligence represents a powerful synergy that drives innovation, efficiency, and competitiveness across diverse industries and applications, reshaping the future of computing and empowering individuals and organizations to achieve more with data and AI.

EMERGENCE OF ARTIFICIAL INTELLIGENCE IN CLOUD COMPUTING

The emergence of artificial intelligence (AI) in cloud computing marks a significant shift in the landscape of modern technology, reshaping the way businesses and individuals interact with computing resources and data storage. At its core, cloud computing revolutionizes the delivery of computing services over the internet, providing users with access to scalable, on-demand resources without the need for costly infrastructure investments (Gill et al., 2022). Over the years, cloud computing has evolved from a novel concept to a ubiquitous and indispensable technology, powering a wide range of applications across industries. The integration of AI into cloud computing further enhances its capabilities, enabling organizations to leverage advanced analytics, automation, and insights to drive innovation and competitive advantage (Xue et al., 2022). One of the key drivers behind the emergence of AI in cloud computing is the increasing demand for intelligent and data-driven applications. As businesses seek to extract value from the vast amounts of data generated daily, AI technologies offer powerful tools for analyzing, interpreting, and extracting insights from this data (El Khatib et al.. 2019). By integrating AI capabilities into cloud computing platforms, organizations can harness the scalability and flexibility of the cloud to deploy AI-powered solutions efficiently. This enables businesses to unlock new opportunities for optimization, innovation, and differentiation in the marketplace (Gill et al., 2022).

The emergence of AI in cloud computing is driven by the growing complexity and diversity of computing workloads. Traditional computing paradigms struggle to meet the demands of modern applications, which require sophisticated algorithms, real-time processing, and adaptive capabilities (El Khatib et al.. 2019). AI technologies, such as machine learning and deep learning, excel at handling complex computational tasks and learning from large datasets. By leveraging the scalability and computational power of the cloud, organizations can deploy AI models and algorithms to analyze data, optimize processes, and drive decision-making in real-time (Belgaum et al., 2021).

Another factor contributing to the emergence of AI in cloud computing is the proliferation of connected devices and the internet of things (IoT) (Singh & Singh., 2024). As the number of connected devices continues to grow exponentially, the volume of data generated by these devices presents both challenges and opportunities for businesses. AI-powered solutions deployed on cloud computing platforms can process and analyze this data in real-time, enabling organizations to derive actionable insights and drive value from IoT deployments. Whether monitoring equipment performance, optimizing supply chains, or personalizing customer experiences, AI-enabled cloud computing offers a scalable and cost-effective solution for managing and analyzing IoT data (El Khatib et al.. 2019). Furthermore, the emergence of AI in cloud computing is fueled by the democratization of AI technologies and expertise (Gill et al., 2022). Historically, AI development required specialized skills, expertise, and infrastructure, limiting its accessibility to a select few organizations. However, advancements in cloud computing and AI have democratized access to these technologies, enabling businesses of all sizes to leverage AI capabilities without the need for significant upfront investments. Cloud-based AI services and platforms provide developers with access to pre-trained models, APIs, and tools for building and deploying AI applications, accelerating the development cycle and reducing time-to-market. The emergence of artificial intelligence (AI) in cloud computing represents a transformative shift in the way organizations leverage technology to drive innovation and competitive advantage (Singh & Singh., 2024). By integrating AI capabilities into cloud computing platforms, businesses can harness the scalability, flexibility, and computational power of the cloud to deploy intelligent and data-driven applications efficiently. From analyzing large datasets and optimizing processes to powering real-time decision-making and driving IoT deployments, AI-enabled cloud computing offers a scalable and cost-effective solution for addressing the complex challenges of the digital age. As AI continues to evolve and mature, its integration with cloud computing will undoubtedly shape the future of technology and business, unlocking new opportunities for growth, efficiency, and value creation (Gill et al., 2022).

INNOVATIVE ARTIFICIAL INTELLIGENCE TECHNOLOGIES IN CLOUD STORAGE

Machine Learning Algorithms for Data Management

Machine learning algorithms have emerged as powerful tools in optimizing data management processes within cloud storage systems. These algorithms, ranging from clustering and classification to regression techniques, play a pivotal role in automating various aspects of data management, including classification, organization, and storage optimization. At the heart of machine learning algorithms lies their ability to analyze patterns and derive insights from data (Stergiou et al., 2020). In the context of data management in cloud storage systems, these algorithms are leveraged to automatically classify incoming data based on predefined criteria (Belgacem et al., 2023). Classification algorithms categorize data into distinct groups or classes, facilitating efficient organization and retrieval. For example, in a cloud storage environment, machine learning algorithms can classify incoming files based on their content, file type, or user-defined attributes. This automated classification process streamlines data organization efforts, ensuring that data is stored in a structured and accessible manner (Sarker., 2021). Furthermore, machine learning algorithms contribute to storage optimization by dynamically adjusting storage configurations based on data usage patterns and access frequencies (Mangalampalli et al., 2024). Through techniques such as clustering, which groups similar data together, and regression, which predicts future storage requirements based on historical data, these algorithms enable cloud storage systems to optimize resource allocation and minimize storage costs (Sarker., 2021). For instance, by identifying and clustering frequently accessed data together, machine learning algorithms can prioritize the allocation of high-performance storage resources to ensure quick access times. Conversely, infrequently accessed data can be moved to lower-cost storage tiers, reducing overall storage expenses without compromising performance (Belgacem et al., 2023).

Additionally, machine learning algorithms empower cloud storage systems with predictive analytics capabilities, allowing organizations to anticipate future storage needs and proactively address potential challenges. By analyzing historical data usage patterns and trends, these algorithms can forecast future storage requirements, enabling organizations to scale their storage infrastructure accordingly. Predictive analytics also facilitate proactive risk mitigation by identifying potential storage bottlenecks or capacity limitations before they occur (Mangalampalli et al., 2024). For example, machine learning algorithms can alert administrators to impending storage shortages based on projected data growth rates, enabling them to take preemptive measures such as provisioning additional storage capacity or optimizing data placement strategies. Moreover, machine learning algorithms contribute to data integrity and security within cloud storage systems. By analyzing data access patterns and user behavior, these algorithms can detect anomalies or suspicious activities that may indicate unauthorized access or data breaches (Belgacem et al., 2023). Additionally, machine learning-based anomaly detection techniques can identify data corruption or integrity issues, enabling timely remediation actions to preserve data integrity and prevent data loss. Machine learning algorithms play a vital role in optimizing data management processes within cloud storage systems (Sarker., 2021). From automating data classification and organization to optimizing storage configurations and enabling predictive analytics, these algorithms enhance efficiency, reduce costs, and ensure data integrity and security. As organizations continue to embrace cloud storage solutions to manage their ever-growing volumes of data, the integration of machine learning algorithms will be essential in unlocking the full potential of these platforms.

Natural Language Processing for Search and Retrieval

Natural Language Processing (NLP) stands as a transformative technology in the realm of search and retrieval within cloud storage systems. By enabling machines to comprehend and interpret human language, NLP algorithms revolutionize the way users interact with data stored in the cloud, facilitating intuitive and efficient search and retrieval processes (Ajmal et al., 2023). At its core, NLP empowers users to articulate search queries in natural language, eliminating the need for complex search syntax or keyword-based queries (Feng et al., 2024). This human-centric approach to search and retrieval enhances user experience and accessibility, enabling users to express their information needs in a manner that aligns with their natural communication style. For example, instead of using specific keywords or phrases, users can simply describe the information they are seeking in everyday language, such as Find documents related to project XYZ" or "Show me all recent sales reports (Fanni et al., 2023). NLP algorithms enable semantic understanding of search queries, allowing systems to infer the underlying meaning and context of user requests. This semantic understanding enables more accurate and relevant search results by considering not only the literal words used in the query but also the intended meaning behind them (Bauer et al., 2023).

NLP algorithms enable sentiment analysis, allowing systems to analyze the tone and sentiment expressed within textual documents. This sentiment analysis capability enhances search and retrieval processes by enabling users to filter and prioritize search results based on sentiment polarity (positive, negative, or neutral). For example, in a customer feedback scenario, sentiment analysis could help identify positive or negative feedback trends, enabling organizations to focus on areas requiring improvement or capitalize on positive feedback (Bauer et al., 2023). NLP algorithms empower systems with multilingual search capabilities, facilitating seamless information retrieval across diverse linguistic contexts. By supporting multiple languages and dialects, NLP-enabled search and retrieval systems cater to the globalized nature of modern business operations, enabling users to access information in their preferred language. Natural Language Processing (NLP) represents a game-changing technology in search and retrieval within cloud storage systems (Fanni et al., 2023). By enabling intuitive and semantic search capabilities, NLP algorithms enhance user experience, accessibility, and relevance of search results (Ajmal et al., 2023). With features such as entity recognition, sentiment analysis, and multilingual support, NLP-driven search and retrieval systems empower organizations to unlock the full potential of their data assets stored in the cloud, facilitating informed decision-making and driving business innovation (Bauer et al., 2023).

Enhancing Security in Cloud Storage

By using cutting-edge artificial intelligence (AI) algorithms to proactively identify and mitigate possible security risks within digital environments, threat detection enabled by AI represents a paradigm leap in cybersecurity (Olabanji et al., 2024). Artificial intelligence (AI)-powered threat detection systems use machine learning, deep learning, and natural language processing to assess large volumes of data, find unusual trends, and quickly respond to security problems. The fundamental idea behind AI-powered threat detection is anomaly detection, which looks for departures from the usual in system logs, network traffic, user activity, and other data sources (Li et al., 2021). By training on past data, machine learning algorithms may identify patterns linked to typical behavior and identify variations that can point to criminal activity or security breaches. These algorithms can spot new risks and security flaws before they develop into extensive attacks by continually evaluating data streams in real-time. Artificial intelligence (AI)-powered threat detection relies heavily on deep learning techniques, especially neural networks, which allow computers to extract intricate patterns and characteristics from massive amounts of data (Prabhu Kavin et al., 2020). These algorithms examine unstructured data sources, such network traffic, user behavior logs, and malware samples, using deep learning techniques like convolutional neural networks (CNNs) and recurrent neural networks (RNNs) (Tse et al., 2022). The goal is to find minor signs of dangerous activity. Advanced persistent attacks (APTs), polymorphic malware versions that may elude conventional security measures, and zero-day vulnerabilities are just a few examples of the complex dangers that deep learning models are excellent at identifying (Olabanji et al., 2024).

By enabling systems to evaluate and comprehend textual data sources like security alerts, incident reports, and threat intelligence feeds, natural language processing (NLP) also plays a critical role in AI-powered threat detection technologies. Security analysts can quickly classify and prioritize security events by using natural language processing (NLP) techniques to derive actionable insights from unstructured text data. NLP-powered threat detection systems can connect linked events, identify pertinent risks, and create timely warnings to help with incident response by evaluating the semantics and context of text data related to security (Li et al., 2021). Likewise, threat intelligence integration, behavioral analytics, and predictive modeling are examples of sophisticated analytics methods that AI-powered threat detection systems use to improve their detection performance (Olabanji et al., 2024). Anomalous patterns suggestive of insider threats, compromised accounts, or illegal access attempts are found by using behavioral analytics algorithms to examine user behavior and network activity. Systems that use predictive modeling approaches are able to prioritize security measures according to risk assessments and predict future attacks. In order to improve detection accuracy and efficacy, AI-powered threat detection systems may also be integrated with threat intelligence feeds to benefit from the most recent data regarding known threats, attack vectors, and malicious actors (Thabit et al., 2021).

An effective strategy for cybersecurity is AI-powered threat detection, which helps businesses proactively discover and neutralize security risks in the quickly changing threat landscape of today. Through leveraging the potential of deep learning, machine learning, and natural language processing, these solutions enable enterprises to promptly identify and address security events, therefore reducing the likelihood of data breaches, monetary losses, and harm to their brand (Olabanji et al., 2024). AI-powered threat detection is still a crucial part of contemporary cybersecurity strategies since it helps firms keep ahead of new threats and proficiently safeguard their digital assets as cyber threats continue to grow in sophistication and complexity (Li et al., 2021).

Encryption and Privacy Preservation Techniques

Encryption and privacy preservation techniques are fundamental pillars of cybersecurity, crucial for safeguarding sensitive data and maintaining user privacy in digital environments. These techniques employ cryptographic algorithms and privacy-enhancing technologies to protect data from unauthorized access, interception, and disclosure, thereby ensuring confidentiality, integrity, and authenticity (Boulemtafes et al., 2020). Encryption serves as a cornerstone of data protection by transforming plaintext data into ciphertext using cryptographic algorithms and keys. Through encryption, sensitive information such as personal identifiable information (PII), financial transactions, and corporate secrets is rendered unreadable to unauthorized entities, even if intercepted during transmission or stored on compromised systems (Melanson et al., 2023). Advanced encryption standards (AES), public-key cryptography, and elliptic curve cryptography are among the widely adopted encryption algorithms used to secure data at rest and in transit (Park et al., 2020). In addition to traditional encryption techniques, homomorphic encryption enables computation on encrypted data without the need for decryption, preserving data privacy while allowing for secure processing and analysis. Homomorphic encryption facilitates secure data outsourcing, enabling organizations to leverage cloud computing resources for data processing while maintaining confidentiality and privacy (Seth et al., 2022). Similarly, end-to-end encryption (E2EE) ensures that data remains encrypted throughout its entire lifecycle, from sender to recipient, preventing unauthorized access by intermediaries or service providers (Yuvaraj et al., 2020). Privacy-enhancing technologies (PETs) complement encryption techniques by providing additional layers of privacy protection and anonymity. Differential privacy, for example, adds noise to query responses or statistical data to prevent the inference of individual-level information, preserving privacy while enabling aggregate analysis. Similarly, k-anonymity and l-diversity techniques anonymize datasets by generalizing or suppressing identifying attributes, reducing the risk of re-identification and privacy breaches (Ma & Zhang, 2020).

Secure multi-party computing (MPC) allows several parties to work together on data analysis and calculation without disclosing private input data to one another. By distributing computations across multiple parties' devices while preserving data privacy through cryptographic protocols, MPC allows for secure data analysis across organizational boundaries, facilitating data sharing and collaboration while maintaining confidentiality (Gao & Yu, 2023). Privacy-preserving data mining techniques enable organizations to derive valuable insights from encrypted or anonymized datasets without compromising individual privacy. Secure multiparty computation (MPC) facilitates collaborative data analysis while upholding stringent data privacy standards, ensuring that sensitive information remains encrypted or anonymized throughout the computation process. This protocol leverages cryptographic techniques to enable multiple parties to jointly compute a function over their respective private inputs without disclosing individual inputs to other parties (Melanson et al., 2023). Through the use of cryptographic protocols such as secret sharing and secure function evaluation, MPC ensures that computations are performed on encrypted data in a distributed manner, thereby preserving data privacy and confidentiality. Similarly, federated learning is a decentralized machine learning approach that allows machine learning models to be trained on distributed data sources without necessitating the centralization of raw data (Adelipour & Haeri, 2024).

ARTIFICIAL INTELLIGENCE - DRIVEN DATA MANAGEMENT

Automated Data Tagging and Classification

Automated data tagging and classification represent significant advancements in data management, revolutionizing processes and bolstering organization within digital ecosystems. Leveraging the prowess of artificial intelligence (AI) and machine learning (ML) algorithms, these systems analyze extensive datasets, assigning pertinent metadata tags and categorizing data according to predefined criteria. Such methodologies not only streamline data management but also amplify searchability, accessibility, and overall data governance (Zu et al., 2024). The use of various machine learning methods, including supervised, unsupervised, and semi-supervised learning strategies, is important to automated data tagging and categorization systems. These algorithms are trained using labeled datasets, which are collections of data samples that have been painstakingly tagged with relevant metadata tags or categories. By use of this repeated training procedure, the algorithms identify patterns and correlations present in the data, which facilitates the automatic identification and categorization of incoming data through tag assignment (Ramachandran et al., 2023). Supervised learning algorithms, such as random forests and support vector machines (SVM), acquire knowledge from examples of labeled data together with the tags or categories that go along with it. These algorithms efficiently categorize fresh data by examining characteristics that are derived from the input data, guaranteeing accurate tagging and classification according to predetermined criteria (Sherubha et al., 2023). In a document management system, for example, supervised learning algorithms are able to effectively categorize documents according to their content and structure into different groups, such "invoices," "contracts," or "reports." On the other hand, no labeled data is required for training in unsupervised learning techniques like k-means clustering and hierarchical clustering (Samunnisa et al., 2023). These algorithms provide automated organizing and categorization by automatically grouping related data according to innate similarities or patterns. In the domain of data tagging and classification, unsupervised learning algorithms efficiently group similar data points. They then allocate shared tags or categories to clustered groups, which accelerates organizational procedures. Also, semi-supervised learning strategies combine elements of supervised and unsupervised learning by combining a smaller set of labeled data with a bigger set of unlabeled data (Ramachandran et al., 2023). With the surplus of unlabeled data being used for further learning, this hybrid technique makes the most of the limited labeled data while improving the training efficiency of machine learning models. Semi-supervised learning methods are very useful in situations when it is not feasible or too expensive to manually label large datasets since they greatly speed up the classification process while preserving high levels of accuracy (Samunnisa et al., 2023). Essentially, an emerging phase in data management efficiency and organization inside digital ecosystems is marked by automated data tagging and categorization, supported by a wide range of machine learning techniques. By means of the cooperative amalgamation of AI and ML methodologies, these apparatuses enable establishments to adeptly traverse extensive datasets, hence unearthing insights and augmenting decision-making procedures with unparalleled precision and effectiveness (Sherubha et al., 2023).

In addition to machine learning algorithms, natural language processing (NLP) techniques play a crucial role in automated data tagging and classification, especially for textual data. NLP algorithms enable systems to analyze and understand the content of unstructured text data, extracting relevant keywords, phrases, and concepts that inform the tagging and classification process (Chan et al., 2023). By analyzing the semantic meaning and context of textual data, NLP-powered systems can accurately assign tags and classify documents based on their content. Deep learning techniques, such as convolutional neural networks (CNNs) and recurrent neural networks (RNNs), have shown promising results in automated data tagging and classification tasks, especially for image and sequence data (Hasimi et al., 2024). These deep learning models excel at extracting complex features from raw data, enabling accurate classification of images, videos, and time-series data based on visual or sequential patterns (Kasongo, 2023).

Content-Based Retrieval Systems

Content-based retrieval systems represent a significant advancement in the realm of information retrieval, offering a sophisticated approach to searching and retrieving digital content based on its intrinsic characteristics rather than relying solely on metadata or user-defined tags. These systems analyze the actual content of the data, such as text, images, audio, or video, to match user queries with relevant content, providing more accurate and contextually appropriate search results (Ma et al., 2022). Traditionally, keyword-based search techniques have been the primary method for retrieving information from digital databases (Li et al., 2020). However, these techniques may be inadequate in scenarios where users are unable to articulate specific search terms or when searching for multimedia content with complex attributes (Hu et al., 2024). Content-based retrieval systems address these limitations by analyzing the inherent features of the data itself, such as color, texture, shape, and composition in the case of images, to identify similarities and patterns that are not captured by traditional keyword-based methods (Wang et al., 2023).

Content-based retrieval systems function by extracting features from the digital content and creating a unique representation or signature for each item in the database. These representations encode the distinctive characteristics of the data, allowing the system to compare them with the features of the user query to identify the most relevant matches. For example, in an image retrieval system, visual features such as color histograms, texture descriptors, and shape representations may be extracted from each image and used to compute similarity scores with the query image (Ma et al., 2022). The applications of content-based retrieval systems span across various domains, including digital asset management, multimedia databases, e-commerce, and content recommendation systems (Wang et al., 2023). In digital asset management, these systems enable users to quickly locate images, videos, or documents that match specific visual criteria, such as color scheme or composition, enhancing productivity and workflow efficiency. For instance, a marketing team could use a content-based retrieval system to find images that align with their branding guidelines or campaign themes, streamlining the content creation process. In e-commerce, content-based retrieval systems play a crucial role in enhancing the shopping experience by assisting users in finding visually similar products or items based on their preferences or previous purchases. By analyzing the visual characteristics of products, such as shape, color, and pattern, these systems can recommend relevant items to shoppers, increasing engagement and conversion rates (Wang et al., 2023).

FUTURE TRENDS AND CHALLENGES

Quantum Computing and Cloud Storage

The ways that data is handled, stored, and retrieved might be completely changed by combining two innovative technologies: cloud storage and quantum computing. Cloud storage offers a scalable and convenient platform for storing enormous volumes of data, while quantum computing uses the concepts of quantum mechanics to execute complicated calculations at speeds beyond the capabilities of classical computers (Ahmed & Mähönen, 2021). Cloud storage systems with quantum computing capabilities can open up new possibilities for sophisticated data analysis, greater security, and improved performance (Shuford et al., 2024). The potential for exponential improvements in data encryption and security is one of the biggest benefits of combining quantum computing with cloud storage. Large numbers can be factored rapidly by quantum computing techniques, such Shor's algorithm, which would take hundreds of years for classical computers to do. This feature seriously jeopardizes the security of data saved in the cloud using conventional encryption techniques (Ravi et al., 2021). Nonetheless, businesses may strengthen the security of their digital storage infrastructure and shield critical data from quantum-based assaults by utilizing quantum-resistant encryption techniques and quantum key distribution methods (Padmanaban, 2024).

Cloud storage systems can benefit from the optimization of data storage and retrieval procedures through the application of quantum computing. Grover's method is one of the quantum algorithms that provide exponential speedups for database search and optimization tasks. This allows for the recovery of pertinent data from vast datasets more quickly (Ahmed & Mähönen, 2021). Organizations may increase productivity and lower latency in cloud storage settings by utilizing quantum-enhanced search algorithms to improve data access and retrieval efficiency. Applications for enhanced data analysis and machine learning are made possible by the combination of quantum computing with cloud storage. In order to process and analyze data in ways that are not achievable with conventional computers, quantum machine learning algorithms—such as quantum neural networks and quantum support vector machines—take advantage of the special qualities of quantum systems (Shuford, 2024). Organizations may leverage cloud-hosted quantum computers to accelerate their algorithms for processing massive datasets and create more precise prediction models for applications like natural language processing, pattern recognition, and anomaly detection. The creation of novel data compression and storage strategies that optimize storage effectiveness while reducing data redundancy may also be made possible by quantum computing. Quantum principles are used by quantum-inspired compression algorithms, such quantum-inspired feature maps and quantum data compression, to minimize the amount of storage space needed for big datasets without compromising the integrity or quality of the data (Ahmed & Mähönen, 2021). Organizations may maximize resource usage and save storage costs by incorporating these compression techniques into cloud storage systems, which makes managing and storing massive amounts of data in the cloud more affordable. Unprecedented prospects to improve data security, streamline data storage and retrieval procedures, and open up new possibilities for sophisticated data analysis and machine learning are presented by the combination of quantum computing with cloud storage (Padmanaban, 2024). Organizations may achieve a competitive advantage in today's data-driven world by utilizing the scalability of cloud storage infrastructure and the unique features of quantum systems to promote innovation and expedite digital transformation (Gill et al., 2022). The interplay between cloud storage and quantum computing is anticipated to be crucial in determining the direction of information technology and data management as the latter grows more sophisticated and widely available (Ahmed & Mähönen, 2021).

Edge Computing and Distributed AI

Edge computing and distributed artificial intelligence (AI) represent two transformative technologies that, when combined, offer powerful solutions for processing data and running AI algorithms at the network edge, closer to where data is generated (Duan et al., 2022). Edge computing involves moving computational tasks and data storage closer to the source of data generation, reducing latency and bandwidth usage while enhancing real-time processing capabilities. Distributed AI, on the other hand, involves distributing AI algorithms and models across multiple edge devices or nodes, enabling collaborative processing and decision-making without relying on centralized servers (Deng et al., 2020). The integration of edge computing and distributed AI enables organizations to leverage the benefits of both technologies, unlocking new opportunities for intelligent decision-making, real-time analytics, and autonomous systems (Hua et al., 2023). By deploying AI algorithms directly on edge devices, such as sensors, cameras, and IoT devices, organizations can analyze data locally and derive insights in real-time, without the need to transmit data to centralized servers for processing (Duan et al., 2022). This enables faster response times, reduced network congestion, and improved scalability, making it ideal for applications that require low-latency, high-throughput processing, such as autonomous vehicles, industrial automation, and smart cities (Deng et al., 2020).

Distributed AI enables edge devices to collaborate and share information, enabling collective intelligence and decision-making without relying on a centralized authority. Each edge device can run specialized AI algorithms tailored to its specific capabilities and context, such as object detection, speech recognition, or anomaly detection, and share the results with neighboring devices to enhance overall system performance (Deng et al., 2020). This distributed approach to AI enables edge devices to adapt and respond to changing conditions autonomously, improving resilience and reliability in dynamic environments (Duan et al., 2022). Furthermore, edge computing and distributed AI facilitate privacy-preserving data processing by minimizing the need to transmit sensitive data to centralized servers for analysis. Instead, data can be processed locally on edge devices, and only aggregated or anonymized results are transmitted to centralized servers for further analysis or storage (Hua et al., 2023). This decentralized approach to data processing enhances data privacy and security, reducing the risk of data breaches or unauthorized access to sensitive information (Duan et al., 2022). In practical terms, the integration of edge computing and distributed AI enables a wide range of applications across various industries. In healthcare, for example, wearable devices equipped with AI algorithms can monitor patients' vital signs in real-time, enabling early detection of health issues and timely interventions (Sun et al., 2020). In retail, edge devices with AI capabilities can analyze customer behavior and preferences in-store, enabling personalized shopping experiences and targeted marketing campaigns (Xue et al., 2022). In manufacturing, edge devices equipped with AI algorithms can optimize production processes, minimize downtime, and reduce operational costs by predicting equipment failures and optimizing resource utilization (Nain et al., 2022). The integration of edge computing and distributed AI offers a powerful paradigm for processing data and running AI algorithms at the network edge, closer to where data is generated. By enabling real-time analytics, autonomous decision-making, and privacy-preserving data processing, these technologies empower organizations to unlock new opportunities for innovation, efficiency, and competitiveness in today's data-driven world (Lv et al., 2021). As edge computing and AI continue to evolve and mature, the synergies between these technologies are expected to drive transformative changes across various industries, shaping the future of intelligent edge computing and distributed AI applications (Lv et al., 2021; Nain et al., 2022).

CONCLUSION

The convergence of cutting-edge technologies such as artificial intelligence (AI), cloud computing, quantum computing, edge computing, and distributed AI marks a pivotal moment in the evolution of data management, processing, and analysis. This convergence represents a transformative landscape wherein these technologies synergize to revolutionize various domains, including cybersecurity, healthcare, manufacturing, retail, and beyond. At the forefront of this transformation is artificial intelligence (AI), which has emerged as a cornerstone technology with its revolutionary impact on data analysis, interpretation, and utilization (Nair & Tyagi, 2023). AI-powered systems have transcended mere automation to become sophisticated tools capable of automating complex tasks, extracting profound insights from data, and facilitating informed decision-making. Key advancements in machine learning, deep learning, and natural language processing have empowered AI applications to permeate nearly every aspect of modern life. In particular, the development of machine learning algorithms has allowed AI systems to learn from data and adapt their behavior without explicit programming. Deep learning, a subset of machine learning, has further enhanced the capabilities of AI by enabling the processing of vast amounts of unstructured data, such as images, audio, and text, to derive meaningful insights and patterns. Natural language processing (NLP) has enabled AI systems to understand and generate human language, leading to advancements in chatbots, language translation, and sentiment analysis. The implications of AI span across diverse industries, driving innovation, efficiency, and competitiveness (Belgaum et al., 2021). From automated threat detection in cybersecurity to predictive analytics in finance, personalized recommendations in retail, and autonomous systems in transportation, AI applications have revolutionized workflows, enhanced productivity, and transformed customer experiences. Moreover, AI has enabled breakthroughs in fields such as healthcare, where it is used for medical image analysis, drug discovery, personalized medicine, and disease diagnosis. The transformative potential of AI extends beyond individual applications to shape entire industries and economies. Organizations that harness the power of AI stand to gain a competitive advantage by unlocking new insights, optimizing processes, and delivering innovative products and services. However, realizing the full potential of AI requires addressing challenges such as data privacy, bias, and ethical considerations, as well as fostering a culture of innovation and collaboration.

Cloud computing has transformed the way organizations store, manage, and access data, providing scalable and flexible infrastructure for hosting applications and services. By leveraging cloud storage and computing resources, organizations can streamline data management processes, enhance collaboration, and scale operations to meet evolving demands. Moreover, the intersection of AI and cloud computing enables the development and deployment of advanced AI applications at scale, leveraging vast amounts of data and powerful computing resources to drive insights and innovation (Xue et al., 2022). Quantum computing represents the next frontier in computational power, offering exponential speedup for complex calculations and data processing tasks. Quantum computers have the potential to transform cryptography, optimization, and machine learning by utilizing the concepts of quantum physics. This will open up new avenues for problem-solving that are now unsolvable for classical computers. When integrated with cloud storage systems, quantum computing can enhance data encryption, optimize storage configurations, and enable advanced data analysis techniques that were previously unimaginable. Edge computing brings computational power closer to where data is generated, enabling real-time processing, low-latency analytics, and autonomous decision-making at the network edge. By deploying AI algorithms directly on edge devices, organizations can analyze data locally, reducing the need for centralized processing and minimizing latency and bandwidth usage. Moreover, distributed AI enables collaboration and collective intelligence among edge devices, enhancing resilience, reliability, and scalability in dynamic environments. The integration of AI, cloud computing, quantum computing, edge computing, and distributed AI offers a wealth of opportunities for organizations to unlock new capabilities, drive innovation, and gain a competitive edge in today's data-driven world. By harnessing the synergies between these technologies, organizations can optimize data management processes, enhance security and privacy, and deliver personalized, real-time experiences to users. As these technologies continue to evolve and mature, the possibilities for transformative change are limitless, reshaping industries, economies, and societies in profound ways. The future belongs to those who embrace the potential of these technologies and leverage them to drive positive impact and sustainable growth.

REFERENCES

Adelipour, S., & Haeri, M. (2024). Private outsourced model predictive control via secure multi-party computation. *Computers & Electrical Engineering*, 116, 109208. 10.1016/j.compeleceng.2024.109208

Ahmad, S., Shakeel, I., Mehfuz, S., & Ahmad, J. (2023). Deep learning models for cloud, edge, fog, and IoT computing paradigms: Survey, recent advances, and future directions. *Computer Science Review*, 49, 100568. 10.1016/j.cosrev.2023.100568

Ahmed, F., & Mähönen, P. (2021, September). Quantum computing for artificial intelligence based mobile network optimization. In *2021 IEEE 32nd annual international symposium on personal, indoor and mobile radio communications (PIMRC)* (pp. 1128-1133). IEEE. 10.1109/PIMRC50174.2021.9569339

Ajmal, S., Ahmed, A. A. I., & Jalota, C. (2023). Natural language processing in improving information retrieval and knowledge discovery in healthcare conversational agents. *Journal of Artificial Intelligence and Machine Learning in Management*, 7(1), 34–47.

Bauer, E., Greisel, M., Kuznetsov, I., Berndt, M., Kollar, I., Dresel, M., Fischer, M. R., & Fischer, F. (2023). Using natural language processing to support peer-feedback in the age of artificial intelligence: A cross-disciplinary framework and a research agenda. *British Journal of Educational Technology*, 54(5), 1222–1245. 10.1111/bjet.13336

Belgacem, A., Mahmoudi, S., & Ferrag, M. A. (2023). A machine learning model for improving virtual machine migration in cloud computing. *The Journal of Supercomputing*, 79(9), 9486–9508. 10.1007/s11227-022-05031-z

Belgaum, M. R., Alansari, Z., Musa, S., Alam, M. M., & Mazliham, M. S. (2021). Role of artificial intelligence in cloud computing, IoT and SDN: Reliability and scalability issues. *Iranian Journal of Electrical and Computer Engineering*, 11(5), 4458. 10.11591/ijece.v11i5.pp4458-4470

Bharadiya, J. (2023). A comprehensive survey of deep learning techniques natural language processing. *European Journal of Technology*, 7(1), 58–66. 10.47672/ejt.1473

Boulemtafes, A., Derhab, A., & Challal, Y. (2020). A review of privacy-preserving techniques for deep learning. *Neurocomputing*, 384, 21–45. 10.1016/j.neucom.2019.11.041

Chan, K. Y., Abu-Salih, B., Qaddoura, R., Al-Zoubi, A. M., Palade, V., Pham, D.-S., Ser, J. D., & Muhammad, K. (2023). Deep neural networks in the cloud: Review, applications, challenges and research directions. *Neurocomputing*, 545, 126327. 10.1016/j.neucom.2023.126327

David, A., Ahmed, R. R., Ganesh Kumar, C., & Sankar, J. G. (2020). Consumer purchasing process of organic food product: An empirical analysis. *Journal of Management Systems. Quality - Access to Success*, 21(177), 128–132.

David, A., Jeganathan, G. S., Sikandar, M. D., & Azam, S. A. (2023, May). Internet Users Top Concerns Ensuring Data Privacy, Security, and Protection. In *Arokiaraj David, Jeganathan Gomathi Sankar & Md Sikandar Azam, —Internet Users Top Concerns Ensuring Data Privacy, Security, and Protection , 10th International Conference on Multidisciplinary Research and Modern Education, ISBN* (No. 978-920, pp. 5-20241).

David, A., Maheswari, M., Sankar, G., Christy, F., Karuppannan, A., & Banumathi, M. (2023). Mental illness of Pregnant Women determined by Covid-19: An Empirical Analysis of Pre-and- Post Delivery. *The Saybold Report Journal*, 18(03), 1706–1721.

Deng, S., Zhao, H., Fang, W., Yin, J., Dustdar, S., & Zomaya, A. Y. (2020). Edge intelligence: The confluence of edge computing and artificial intelligence. *IEEE Internet of Things Journal*, 7(8), 7457–7469. 10.1109/JIOT.2020.2984887

Duan, S., Wang, D., Ren, J., Lyu, F., Zhang, Y., Wu, H., & Shen, X. (2022). Distributed artificial intelligence empowered by end-edge-cloud computing: A survey. *IEEE Communications Surveys and Tutorials*, 25(1), 591–624. 10.1109/COMST.2022.3218527

El Khatib, M. M., Al-Nakeeb, A., & Ahmed, G. (2019). Integration of Cloud Computing with Artificial Intelligence and Its Impact on Telecom Sector—A Case Study. *iBusiness, 11*(01), 1.

Fanni, S. C., Febi, M., Aghakhanyan, G., & Neri, E. (2023). Natural language processing. In *Introduction to Artificial Intelligence* (pp. 87–99). Springer International Publishing. 10.1007/978-3-031-25928-9_5

Feng, Q., Li, P., Lu, Z., Li, C., Wang, Z., Liu, Z., & Weng, J. (2024). Evit: Privacy-preserving image retrieval via encrypted vision transformer in cloud computing. *IEEE Transactions on Circuits and Systems for Video Technology*, 1. 10.1109/TCSVT.2024.3370668

Ganeshkumar, C., David, A., & Sankar, J. G. (2024). Blockchain Technology Acceptance in Agribusiness Industry. In *Blockchain Transformations: Navigating the Decentralized Protocols Era* (pp. 239–260). Springer Nature Switzerland. 10.1007/978-3-031-49593-9_15

Ganeshkumar, C., David, A., & Sankar, J. G. (2024). Blockchain Technology Acceptance in Agribusiness Industry. In Idrees, S. M., & Nowostawski, M. (Eds.), *Blockchain Transformations. Signals and Communication Technology*. Springer., 10.1007/978-3-031-49593-9_15

Ganeshkumar, C., David, A., Sankar, J. G., & Saginala, M. (2023). Application of Drone Technology in Agriculture: A Predictive Forecasting of Pest and Disease Incidence. In *Applying Drone Technologies and Robotics for Agricultural Sustainability* (pp. 50–81). IGI Global.

Ganeshkumar, C., Sankar, J. G., & David, A. (2023). Adoption of Big Data Analytics: Determinants and Performances Among Food Industries. *International Journal of Business Intelligence Research*, 14(1), 1–17. 10.4018/IJBIR.317419

Ganeshkumar, C., Sankar, J. G., & David, A. (2023). Impact of Artificial Intelligence on Agriculture Value Chain Performance: Agritech Perspective. In *Blockchain, IoT, and AI Technologies for Supply Chain Management* (pp. 71-98). CRC Press.

Gao, C., & Yu, J. (2023). SecureRC: A system for privacy-preserving relation classification using secure multi-party computation. *Computers & Security*, 128, 103142. 10.1016/j.cose.2023.103142

Gill, S. S., Xu, M., Ottaviani, C., Patros, P., Bahsoon, R., Shaghaghi, A., Golec, M., Stankovski, V., Wu, H., Abraham, A., Singh, M., Mehta, H., Ghosh, S. K., Baker, T., Parlikad, A. K., Lutfiyya, H., Kanhere, S. S., Sakellariou, R., Dustdar, S., & Uhlig, S. (2022). AI for next generation computing: Emerging trends and future directions. *Internet of Things : Engineering Cyber Physical Human Systems*, 19, 100514. 10.1016/j.iot.2022.100514

Hasimi, L., Zavantis, D., Shakshuki, E., & Yasar, A. (2024). Cloud Computing Security and Deep Learning: An ANN approach. *Procedia Computer Science*, 231, 40–47. 10.1016/j.procs.2023.12.155

Hu, Y., Zhang, Q., Zhang, Q., & Jia, Y. (2024). A novel hashing-inverted index for secure content-based retrieval with massive encrypted speeches. *Multimedia Systems*, 30(1), 22. 10.1007/s00530-023-01229-0

Hua, H., Li, Y., Wang, T., Dong, N., Li, W., & Cao, J. (2023). Edge computing with artificial intelligence: A machine learning perspective. *ACM Computing Surveys*, 55(9), 1–35. 10.1145/3555802

Jeganathan, G. S., David, A., & Ilangovan, K. (2022). Determination of Hospitality Services Quality and Customer Satisfaction–a Holserv Approach. In *AU Virtual International Conference on" Entrepreneurship & Sustainability in Digital Era" under the theme of" Challenges of Organizational & Business Management in Dynamic Digital Dimension"* (Vol. 3, No. 1, pp. 325-334).

Jeganathan, G. S., & Srinivasulu, Y. (2014). Growth Drivers of Tourism Industry in India. *International Journal of Business and Management*, 2(11), 100.

Jeganathan, G. S., & Srinivasulu, Y. Impact of tourism on macro–economic indicators: A Comparative study of BRICS nations.

Kasongo, S. M. (2023). A deep learning technique for intrusion detection system using a Recurrent Neural Networks based framework. *Computer Communications*, 199, 113–125. 10.1016/j.comcom.2022.12.010

Kumar, P., Kumar, A., & Sankar, J. G. (2020). Service quality of health tourism in India: A structural equation modelling approach. *Solid State Technology*, 63(2), 1187–1191.

Li, B., Feng, Y., Xiong, Z., Yang, W., & Liu, G. (2021). Research on AI security enhanced encryption algorithm of autonomous IoT systems. *Information Sciences*, 575, 379–398. 10.1016/j.ins.2021.06.016

Li, J. S., Liu, I. H., Tsai, C. J., Su, Z. Y., Li, C. F., & Liu, C. G. (2020). Secure content-based image retrieval in the cloud with key confidentiality. *IEEE Access : Practical Innovations, Open Solutions*, 8, 114940–114952. 10.1109/ACCESS.2020.3003928

Luo, Y., Chen, Y., Li, T., Tan, C., & Dou, H. (2024). Cloud-SMPC: Two-round multilinear maps secure multiparty computation based on LWE assumption. *Journal of Cloud Computing (Heidelberg, Germany)*, 13(1), 22. 10.1186/s13677-023-00586-5

Lv, Z., Chen, D., Lou, R., & Wang, Q. (2021). Intelligent edge computing based on machine learning for smart city. *Future Generation Computer Systems*, 115, 90–99. 10.1016/j.future.2020.08.037

Ma, H., & Zhang, Z. (2020). A new private information encryption method in internet of things under cloud computing environment. *Wireless Communications and Mobile Computing*, 2020, 1–9. 10.1155/2020/8810987

Ma, W., Zhou, T., Qin, J., Xiang, X., Tan, Y., & Cai, Z. (2022). A privacy-preserving content-based image retrieval method based on deep learning in cloud computing. *Expert Systems with Applications*, 203, 117508. 10.1016/j.eswa.2022.117508

Mangalampalli, S., Karri, G. R., Kumar, M., Khalaf, O. I., Romero, C. A. T., & Sahib, G. A. (2024). DRLBTSA: Deep reinforcement learning based task-scheduling algorithm in cloud computing. *Multimedia Tools and Applications*, 83(3), 8359–8387. 10.1007/s11042-023-16008-2

Melanson, D., Maia, R., Kim, H. S., Nascimento, A., & De Cock, M. (2023). Secure multi-party computation for personalized human activity recognition. *Neural Processing Letters*, 55(3), 2127–2153. 10.1007/s11063-023-11182-8

Nain, G., Pattanaik, K. K., & Sharma, G. K. (2022). Towards edge computing in intelligent manufacturing: Past, present and future. *Journal of Manufacturing Systems*, 62, 588–611. 10.1016/j.jmsy.2022.01.010

Nair, M. M., & Tyagi, A. K. (2023). AI, IoT, blockchain, and cloud computing: The necessity of the future. In *Distributed Computing to Blockchain* (pp. 189–206). Academic Press. 10.1016/B978-0-323-96146-2.00001-2

Olabanji, S. O., Olaniyi, O. O., Adigwe, C. S., Okunleye, O. J., & Oladoyinbo, T. O. (2024). AI for Identity and Access Management (IAM) in the cloud: Exploring the potential of artificial intelligence to improve user authentication, authorization, and access control within cloud-based systems. *Authorization, and Access Control within Cloud-Based Systems (January 25, 2024).*

Padmanaban, H. (2024). Quantum Computing and AI in the Cloud. *Journal of Computational Intelligence and Robotics*, 4(1), 14–32.

Park, J., Kim, D. S., & Lim, H. (2020). Privacy-preserving reinforcement learning using homomorphic encryption in cloud computing infrastructures. *IEEE Access : Practical Innovations, Open Solutions*, 8, 203564–203579. 10.1109/ACCESS.2020.3036899

Park, J., Kim, D. S., & Lim, H. (2020). Privacy-preserving reinforcement learning using homomorphic encryption in cloud computing infrastructures. *IEEE Access : Practical Innovations, Open Solutions*, 8, 203564–203579. 10.1109/ACCESS.2020.3036899

Prabhu Kavin, B., Ganapathy, S., Kanimozhi, U., & Kannan, A. (2020). An enhanced security framework for secured data storage and communications in cloud using ECC, access control and LDSA. *Wireless Personal Communications*, 115(2), 1107–1135. 10.1007/s11277-020-07613-7

Ramachandran, S., Agrahari, R., Mudgal, P., Bhilwaria, H., Long, G., & Kumar, A. (2023). Automated log classification using deep learning. *Procedia Computer Science*, 218, 1722–1732. 10.1016/j.procs.2023.01.150

Ravi, G. S., Smith, K. N., Gokhale, P., & Chong, F. T. (2021, November). Quantum computing in the cloud: Analyzing job and machine characteristics. In *2021 IEEE International Symposium on Workload Characterization (IISWC)* (pp. 39-50). IEEE. 10.1109/IISWC53511.2021.00015

Samunnisa, K., Kumar, G. S. V., & Madhavi, K. (2023). Intrusion detection system in distributed cloud computing: Hybrid clustering and classification methods. *Measurement. Sensors*, 25, 100612. 10.1016/j.measen.2022.100612

Sankar, G., & Naveenkumar, K. (2018). *Material Handling Management in Third Party Logistics Warehouse. International Journal for Research in Engineering Application & Management.* IJREAM.

Sankar, J. G. (2020a). Customer perception about innovative safety food delivery during lockdown. *Journal of Contemporary Issues in Business and Government*, 26(2).

Sankar, J. G. (2020b). Innovative celebrity endorsement and consumer purchase. *Journal of Contemporary Issues in Business and Government*, 26(2).

Sankar, J. G. (2020c). Innovative consumer behaviour towards sportswear. *Journal of Contemporary Issues in Business and Government*, 26(2).

Sankar, J. G. (2020d). Service Factors Influence on Customer Satisfaction in Innovative Ecommerce. *Journal of Contemporary Issues in Business and Government*, 26(2), 651–656.

Sankar, J. G. (2020e). Service quality of e-Commerce logistics services. *Journal of Contemporary Issues in Business and Government*, 26(2).

Sankar, J. G. (2024). AI-Driven Marketing Success Stories: A Case Note of Industry Pioneers. In *AI-Driven Marketing Research and Data Analytics* (pp. 48-66). IGI Global. 10.4018/979-8-3693-2165-2.ch003

Sankar, J. G., & David, A. (2023). Measuring the Service Quality of Artificial Intelligence in the Tourism and Hospitality Industry. In *Handbook of Research on Innovation, Differentiation, and New Technologies in Tourism, Hotels, and Food Service* (pp. 133-155). IGI Global. 10.4018/978-1-6684-6985-9.ch007

Sankar, J. G., & David, A. (2024). A Comprehensive Examination of Mobile Augmented Reality in Tourism (MART) Adoption: Using the UTAUT2 Framework. In *Contemporary Trends in Innovative Marketing Strategies* (pp. 241-262). IGI Global.

Sankar, J. G., & David, A. (2024). Transforming the Travel Landscape: Smart Contracts in Tourism Management. In *Decentralizing the Online Experience With Web3 Technologies* (pp. 246-266). IGI Global.

Sankar, J. G., David, A., & Ganesh Kumar, C. (2022). Adaptation of Blockchain Technology In HRM. *Available atSSRN* 4515408.

Sankar, J. G., David, A., & Ramasamy, R. (2023). Assessing Water and Sanitation Service Quality at Pilgrimage Sites After COVID-19: An Empirical Investigation. In *Prospects and Challenges of Global Pilgrimage Tourism and Hospitality* (pp. 160-179). IGI Global.

Sankar, J. G., David, A., & Shrutimeena, G. (2024). From Hesitation to Integration: Understanding Digital Healthcare Adoption. In *Multi-Sector Analysis of the Digital Healthcare Industry* (pp. 1-32). IGI Global.

Sankar, J. G., David, A., & Valan, P. (2023). Examining User Understanding and Perceptions of E-Commerce Data Privacy, Security, and Protection. In *Confronting Security and Privacy Challenges in Digital Marketing* (pp. 159–185). IGI Global. 10.4018/978-1-6684-8958-1.ch008

Sankar, J. G., Rajeswari, M., & Dwarak, M. V. S. (2020). To Measure the Service Quality of Film and Television Technology. *Solid State Technology*, 63(2), 1192–1195.

Sankar, J. G., Valan, P., & Siranjeevi, M. S. (2020). Various Models to Evaluate Quality in the Service Industry. In *Digital Transformation and Innovative Services for Business and Learning* (pp. 181–194). IGI Global.

Sarker, I. H. (2021). Machine learning: Algorithms, real-world applications and research directions. *SN Computer Science*, 2(3), 160. 10.1007/s42979-021-00592-x33778771

Sasikala, J., & Jeganathan, G. S. (2017). A Study on Employee Engagement in Information Technology (IT) Industry. *SSRN*, 1(1), 233–239. 10.2139/ssrn.3536354

Seth, B., Dalal, S., Jaglan, V., Le, D. N., Mohan, S., & Srivastava, G. (2022). Integrating encryption techniques for secure data storage in the cloud. *Transactions on Emerging Telecommunications Technologies*, 33(4), e4108. 10.1002/ett.4108

Sherubha, P., Sasirekha, S. P., Anguraj, A. D. K., Rani, J. V., Anitha, R., Praveen, S. P., & Krishnan, R. H. (2023). An Efficient Unsupervised Learning Approach for Detecting Anomaly in Cloud. *Computer Systems Science and Engineering*, 45(1), 149–166. 10.32604/csse.2023.024424

Shuford, J. (2024). Quantum Computing and Artificial Intelligence: Synergies and Challenges. *Journal of Artificial Intelligence General science (JAIGS) ISSN: 3006-4023, 1*(1).

Simitha, S., Mugila, P., & Sankar, J. G. (2020). A Study on Customer Relationship Management in Siemens Healthineers. *Solid State Technology*, 63(2), 1199–1203.

Singh, K. D., & Singh, P. (2024). Fog Cloud Computing and IoT Integration for AI enabled Autonomous Systems in Robotics. *EAI Endorsed Transactions on AI and Robotics, 3*.

SP, M. S., & Sankar, J. G. An Overview of Measurement model in Marketing Research.

Stergiou, C. L., Plageras, A. P., Psannis, K. E., & Gupta, B. B. (2020). Secure machine learning scenario from big data in cloud computing via internet of things network. *Handbook of Computer Networks and Cyber Security: Principles and Paradigms*, 525-554.

Sun, L., Jiang, X., Ren, H., & Guo, Y. (2020). Edge-cloud computing and artificial intelligence in internet of medical things: Architecture, technology and application. *IEEE Access : Practical Innovations, Open Solutions*, 8, 101079–101092. 10.1109/ACCESS.2020.2997831

Thabit, F., Alhomdy, S., Al-Ahdal, A. H., & Jagtap, S. (2021). A new lightweight cryptographic algorithm for enhancing data security in cloud computing. *Global Transitions Proceedings*, 2(1), 91–99. 10.1016/j.gltp.2021.01.013

Tse, K. W., & Hung, K. (2022). Framework for user behavioural biometric identification using a multimodal scheme with keystroke trajectory feature and recurrent neural network on a mobile platform. *IET Biometrics*, 11(2), 157–170. 10.1049/bme2.12065

Tuli, S., Gill, S. S., Xu, M., Garraghan, P., Bahsoon, R., Dustdar, S., Sakellariou, R., Rana, O., Buyya, R., Casale, G., & Jennings, N. R. (2022). HUNTER: AI based holistic resource management for sustainable cloud computing. *Journal of Systems and Software*, 184, 111124. 10.1016/j.jss.2021.111124

Velmurugan, T. A., & Sankar, J. G. (2017). A comparative study on motivation theory with Maslow's hierarchy theory and two factor theory in organization. *Indo-Iranian Journal of Scientific Research*, 1(1), 204–208.

Wang, Y., Chen, L., Wu, G., Yu, K., & Lu, T. (2023). Efficient and secure content-based image retrieval with deep neural networks in the mobile cloud computing. *Computers & Security*, 128, 103163. 10.1016/j.cose.2023.103163

Wu, Y., Wang, X., Susilo, W., Yang, G., Jiang, Z. L., Yiu, S. M., & Wang, H. (2022). Generic server-aided secure multi-party computation in cloud computing. *Computer Standards & Interfaces*, 79, 103552. 10.1016/j.csi.2021.103552

Xue, M., Xiu, G., Saravanan, V., & Montenegro-Marin, C. E. (2021). Cloud computing with AI for banking and e-commerce applications. *The Electronic Library*, 39(4), 539–552.

Yuvaraj, N., Raja, R. A., Karthikeyan, T., & Kousik, N. V. (2020). Improved privacy preservation framework for cloud-based internet of things. In *Internet of things* (pp. 165–174). CRC Press. 10.1201/9781003032441-11

Zu, L., Qi, W., Li, H., Men, X., Lu, Z., Ye, J., & Zhang, L. (2024). UP-SDCG: A Method of Sensitive Data Classification for Collaborative Edge Computing in Financial Cloud Environment. *Future Internet*, 16(3), 102. 10.3390/fi16030102

Chapter 12
From Data to Insights
Harnessing GeoAI for Informed Decision-Making in Healthcare

Munir Ahmad
https://orcid.org/0000-0003-4836-6151
Survey of Pakistan, Pakistan

Rida Zahid
https://orcid.org/0000-0002-4738-6938
Capital Medical University, Beijing, China

Kashif Mehmood Khan
https://orcid.org/0000-0003-4888-2295
SZABIST, Karachi, Pakistan

ABSTRACT

This chapter examined the utilization of GeoAI for healthcare issues like patient demographics, socio-economic factors, health insurance coverage, and environmental conditions to enhance healthcare delivery. By analyzing population density and socio-economic data, GeoAI can optimize the placement of healthcare facilities and resources, ensuring equitable access. Environmental data, such as air and water quality, can identify regions at risk for specific health issues, guiding targeted interventions. GeoAI can address healthcare disparities by considering social determinants of health and enabling personalized treatment plans. Integrating high-quality, timely, and relevant geospatial data can allow GeoAI to facilitate accurate decision-making and resource allocation, improving patient outcomes and public health strategies. However, challenges include ensuring data privacy and security, managing technical and operational integration complexities, and requiring specialized expertise, which can be overcome with robust data governance

DOI: 10.4018/979-8-3693-8557-9.ch012

and interdisciplinary collaboration.

INTRODUCTION

The advent of big geospatial data in terms of demographics, environment, and distribution of the basic amenities of healthcare has given birth to many possibilities in healthcare (Hu et al., 2023; Jing et al., 2023; Yudono et al., 2023). Taken together, these data can be utilized to effectively monitor population health status, disease occurrence, and their spread and utilization of medical resources for ultimately wiser choices in planning and practice. The quantitative methods linked with traditional spatial analysis are complex in constructing features and statistical modeling, which is time and resource-consuming and often inadequate in capturing the complex, multidimensional relationships inherent in geospatial data. Since such approaches do not have predetermined analysis factors, they could potentially miss out on some important sub-relationships between the elements under study. Furthermore, most healthcare decisions consider very few sources of information and personal opinions, which can result in significant inefficiencies and disparities in access to quality care (Sanders Thompson, 2013; Viviani & Pasi, 2017). They may also fail to incorporate the broader climatic and societal determinants of health, leading to deficiencies in healthcare delivery and consumers' demands. With the help of advanced methods used in geographic information analysis and by using necessary data sources, it is possible for healthcare systems to properly solve the mentioned challenges, raise the probabilities of making the right resource allocations, and set up a better and more functional distribution of the health care facilities for all the profiles of populations (Guhlincozzi, 2024; Siddik et al., 2023).

Geospatial Artificial Intelligence (GeoAI) has emerged as a game changer towards achieving the maximum potential of geospatial information for supporting healthcare decisions geographically (Kang et al., 2024; S. Wang et al., 2024). This is made possible by GeoAI, which re-imagines the analysis of large geospatial datasets along with the existing clinical datasets. For this, integrated planning makes it possible for healthcare authorities to approach the determination of needs and provisions for the resource requirements of the different regions systematically. Therefore, using GeoAI they can find new patterns or trends that were not visible earlier, use the resources properly, address the needs of a certain number of communities, enhance the efficiency of the care offered, and also improve equitable access to quality and efficiencies of the care being offered (Kamel Boulos et al., 2019; Sahana et al., 2023).

While there is an emergent literature in GeoAI and healthcare, the available literature provides either a general overview of GeoAI or discusses the technology in particular contexts of the wider sphere of healthcare, such as disease prediction

(Behara et al., 2022; Kang et al., 2024; Menon et al., 2023; Munnangi et al., 2023; Olawade et al., 2023; Sahana et al., 2023). Nevertheless, there is a always for further exploration on how GeoAI can be applied across different facets of healthcare decision-making. That is in terms of resource deployment, effective patient care, and reinforcement of existing healthcare providers.

Therefore, this chapter seeks to explore the usefulness of GeoAI in healthcare decision-making processes, which is a rapidly growing field. The specific aim is to discuss how GeoAI can improve multiple aspects of healthcare. Some of the areas of interest include the allocation and distribution of hospitals, clinics, equipment, and personnel with consideration to the population density, incidence of diseases, and socioeconomic status of the community. Further, the chapter explicates how GeoAI can predict a particular disease or medical condition probability by painting high-risk geographical regions based on patterns and settings. In addition, it discusses how interventions and prevention strategies could be informed by the integration of patient-level information with their spatiotemporal settings: pollution and environment quality, healthier food access

The chapter is organized as follows. First and foremost, it defines the core concepts of GeoAI, based on which its applicability to healthcare can be explained. This is further followed by a brief description of the various forms of geospatial data and their effectiveness for various AI profiles while stressing data correctness and appropriateness. Next, the chapter introduces more detailed information on several techniques that are widely used while developing GeoAI applications, such as deep learning networks for the analysis of geospatial data. The chapter then goes through possible cases of GeoAI applications in the health sector, including resource management, monitoring diseases, and managing patient care to show how these technologies can be used. The subsequent section provides information on the possible issues when implementing the principles of this innovative area, namely, data protection issues, integration issues, and the necessity of hiring professionals in this field. Last, but not least, the chapter ends with a discussion of the future trends and direction pointing toward the development of advanced GeoAI capabilities in healthcare.

FUNDAMENTAL PRINCIPLES OF GEOAI

GeoAI can be roughly described as an integration of Geographic Information Systems (GIS) capabilities and conceptualizations with Artificial Intelligence (AI) approaches (Sahana et al., 2023; S. Wang et al., 2024). GIS technology is particularly suited to handling geographical data and information, which refers to data/information that is location-specific. Such data could be basic population and location characteristics, environmental data, distribution of health care facilities used in triage, as well as social media data with spatial references. Aside from this, AI offers a rich data processing toolkit based on algorithms that can learn patterns in an overwhelming amount of information.

GeoAI can be viewed as a natural evolution of traditional GIS and AI technologies in the context of application to healthcare decision-making (Janowicz et al., 2020; Li, 2020; Pierdicca, 2021; S. Wang et al., 2024). This reasoning is based on the analytical power of AI in identifying rich patterns that may be concealed from human view in big volumes of geospatial data. Conventional approaches involve disparate data and typically depend on an analysis of paper-based records or administrative databases. A limitation of this approach is that it gives limited scope to researchers when evaluating healthcare needs and can affect how resources are allocated. Besides, conventional mode for decision making may get biased sometimes and are unable to analyze the correlation between geo–variables and health results. GeoAI mitigates these shortcomings by allowing for the inclusion and exploration of large geo-structured data combined with clinic data. GeoAI has several advantages: -

- GeoAI is particularly proficient in processing vast and complex geospatial data that originate from LiDAR and optical imagery, GPS surveys, and social media feeds (Pierdicca, 2021). Traditional methods can be a real problem when it comes to such vast data sets or is in other ways become inefficient. It must be noted that conventional computation-based methods could sometimes be ineffective in discerning such patterns from these datasets, whereas AI algorithms can do so unproblematically.
- GeoAI fully addresses the problem of feature extraction, which is a crucial part of the spatial analysis process and is usually conducted by identifying characteristic parameters in the data manually(Li, 2020). It may be noted that such features are relatively complex and usually cannot be defined manually – however, AI algorithms, especially deep learning architectures such as convolutional neural networks (CNNs), can ease this process and learn such features directly from the data without much human intervention.
- GeoAI is capable of capturing additional and complex patterns within geospatial data that are non-linear (Janowicz et al., 2020; Li & Hsu, 2022). These relationships are often not easily discernible with conventional techniques, resulting in wholly or partially erroneous representations. AI algorithms can in fact mimic or learn non-linear dependencies and thereby provide more sound and more generalizable decision-making insights.
- GeoAI can determine factors such as income, education levels, and healthy food access for different geographical locations (Alastal & Shaqfa, 2022; Mortaheb & Jankowski, 2023). This ensures that healthcare practitioners are

aware of certain demographics prone to chronic diseases or health inequality in certain regions to address the imbalance. For example, some GeoAI models could be employed to determine areas with a low density of grocery stores and farmers' markets offering fresh fruits and vegetables, and subsequently make recommendations for improving grocery store access in the obtained areas.

- GeoAI can extract and work with the population density data, disease statistics, and current locations of the healthcare establishments. This enables the development of models that can be used in determining the areas that require new hospitals, clinics, and medical equipment to be established to accord all the required attention to patients and clients respectively. For instance, a GeoAI application could detect a region involving a large population and poor access to such a specialist. According to these findings, health authorities may contemplate investing in the construction of a new specialist clinic in that area.
- GeoAI can integrate the spatial information of diseases, perceptions of individuals, and environmental Information such as air quality or the quality of water sources to provide a map of the risk of specific illnesses. This enables the efficient prevention measures through forecast of which areas should be vaccinated or where should resources be directed in the event of an outbreak. For instance, GeoAI models could be employed to estimate the regions with high risk of West Nile virus outbreaks based on the historical data of the breeding and feeding sites of vector mosquitoes and present climatic conditions, and then necessary preventive measures may be taken in such places.

In approaching health disparities, GeoAI can help healthcare professionals work closely with geospatial data and gain deeper insights into population health, which can lead to greater improvements in decision-making for effective health equity. The accumulation of information focused on individual patients and, at the same time, the combination of factors related to their geographical location may bring about transformative changes in the existing approach to the delivery of healthcare.

GEOSPATIAL DATA FOR GEOAI APPLICATIONS

The potential and applicability of GeoAI applications in the different healthcare sub-disciplines are highly dependent on the quality, relevance, and type of geospatial data used.

Remote Sensing Imagery

Satellite and aerial photographs have significant importance for gathering information on the Earth's surface with the help of remote sensing imagery. These images show different objects like forests, water bodies, built-up areas, vegetation, and detailed elements of the urban fabric including roads, buildings, and public spaces. The quality of information derived from remote sensing imagery depends on two key factors: Spatial resolution and temporal resolution: Spatial resolution can be viewed in two ways: one is the high resolution that is capable of capturing the features of the terrain such as trees, while the other is the low resolution that only shows broad features from above such as large tracts of land. Temporal resolution reveals how often these images are taken and which can range from several times a day to once every few weeks depending on the specific sensor utilized. Since an enormous number of images are acquired, they provide very high temporal resolution, which can be useful for identifying temporal changes, e.g., vegetation change during the year, or the growth of cities (Bauer, 2020; Chuvieco, 2020; Lary et al., 2016; Saibi et al., 2018).

Geographic Information Systems (GIS) Data

Geographic Information Systems (GIS) data is crucial to any task involving spatial data analysis and mapping. These GIS datasets can be classified into two broader categories; the vector datasets and the raster datasets. Vector data is composed of discrete geometric shapes: points, lines, and polygons are the main concepts that a beginner in the field of GIS must understand and differentiate between. The points can depict certain features like trees or streetlights, lines can define some linear objects such as roads or rivers and polygons can define some areas, for instance, city borders or forest areas. This data format is highly accurate and beneficial for identifying and analyzing geographical features (Du et al., 2012; Harding, 2010).

Raster data on the other hand is a depiction of the surface of the Earth by a collection of cells, where each of the cells contains a value that refers to a specific attribute like elevation, temperature, or soil moisture. It is particularly useful in showing changes over a distance to allow an analysis of the impacts of change across a landscape and is commonly used in the modeling of environments as well as remote sensing. Both vector and raster resources can collectively be viewed as rich methodological approaches to spatial understanding and analysis that can be used in a vast array of applications ranging from land-use planning to the preservation of our natural environment (Hijmans, 2020; Pukkala, 2019).

GPS Data

GPS technology provides accurate and real-time location of an object which can be used in various ways. By attaching a GPS receiver to an object (for example car, phone, or collar used for observing wild animals), it can be located and its movements can be monitored. This technology is vital, especially in transportation and logistics, which aids in planning vehicle routes, tracking and managing car fleets, and monitoring traffic patterns in real-time. In habitat analysis, GPS data can be used to map out pedestrian and vehicle traffic flow in cities and therefore help in decisions on where to build and create bridges, footbridges, or overpasses for efficient use of a given area. Further, in the case of managing wildlife, GPS tracking of animals helps to understand movements, utilization of space, and the possible outcomes of influential environmental factors on species (Adam et al., 2021; Apte et al., 2019; García-Macía et al., 2024; Liu et al., 2022; Mirski et al., 2024).

Social Media Data with Geospatial Tags

Many social media sites such as Twitter, Instagram, and Facebook give their users the option to add geotags to their posts, which puts the location of a post. This social media data marked by geographical coordinates, is a valuable dataset to work with, in the field of GeoAI. Examining the geographical indicators and content of messages, one can identify trends in people's sentiments and activity in various territories. For instance, sentiments based on experiences as well as opinions and emotions related to a specific area can be conveyed by a tweet analysis of the particular neighborhood of any city. Likewise, Instagram posts containing geolocation information can suggest tourist attractions or highly trafficked cities. This data informs urban planners, and other businesses to predict the movement of humans, allocate the necessary resources, and know the areas of interest or concern in the city (Bishop et al., 2024).

This section delves deeper into some of the typical data sources that resonate with GeoAI in a healthcare context and their usefulness.

Patient Demographics

This includes data defining the population of a particular area or region with special reference to their attributes. Some of the key examples are described below.

Population Density

Exploring population density information is useful to the healthcare industry since it helps pinpoint the concentration of people in a given vicinity (Carlos et al., 2010; Teller, 2021). This information is important in allocation of resources by determining how many hospitals, clinics and other health facilities to establish and where to place them and also how many health practitioners to train and recruit. For example, GeoAI could pinpoint a suburban area featuring enhanced population density but a scarce number of child clinics or hospitals. This data would enable healthcare authorities to decide to undertake an investment on constructing a new children's hospital or a pediatric clinic in that area.

Socio-Economic Factors

Information such as income, education, and employment within a given region helps in understanding its socio-economic status. It is crucial in knowing the social factors that affect health and the health context resulting from social circumstances, community characteristics, as well as natural occurrences (Gordon et al., 2020; McMaughan et al., 2020; Watts et al., 2020). By incorporating these factors in addition to disease data, GeoAI models can pinpoint regions with higher levels of chronic diseases like diabetics or heart patients. It can help to design interventions in public health and social programs meant for reducing healthcare inequity and inequality.

Health Insurance Coverage Data

A better understanding of access to healthcare services is made possible by knowing how health insurance coverage is distributed throughout various geographic locations (Barasa et al., 2021; Wagstaff & Neelsen, 2020). To identify regions with restricted access to care because of a lack of insurance coverage, GeoAI models can assess this information combined with information on the dispersion of healthcare assets. Policymakers can utilize this data to direct measures for healthcare openness and the future development of public well-being protection programs.

Environmental Factors

Environmental data plays a critical role in understanding the link between the surrounding environment and public health. Some key examples include the following.

Air and Water Quality

Data on air and water quality can be analyzed to help identify regions that may be at risk for environmental risks that lead to respiratory ailments, waterborne infections, or other health issues (Lin et al., 2022; Rovira et al., 2020). To lessen exposure to these risks, public health initiatives can be informed by this knowledge, which also enables focused environmental monitoring. For example, GeoAI models may assess information on air quality and pinpoint regions with high contamination levels related to a higher frequency of asthma. With this data, particular activities to improve quality or asthma administration plans may be put into place in specific locales.

Vegetation Cover

Data on the amount of vegetation, such as the nearness of green regions or the amount of forest cover, can be utilized to assess the openness of natural assets and chances for physical exercise, both of which have an impact on one's general well-being and health (Reyes-Riveros et al., 2021; Richards et al., 2022). To distinguish places with limited access to green spaces and possibly increased obesity risks, GeoAI models might examine this information in conjunction with information on obesity rates. Activities in urban planning that support the improvement of parks and other green regions within the city can benefit from the utilization of this data.

Proximity to Environmental Hazards

To comprehend the possible health concerns associated with natural exposures, it is fundamental to recognize areas close to natural perils, such as industrial sites (Johnston & Cushing, 2020), waste disposal facilities (Munyai & Nunu, 2020), or active transportation routes (Tainio et al., 2021). GeoAI models can look at these places in conjunction with data on specific malignancies or birth abnormalities to search for possible connections. This data can offer assistance in public health campaigns that aim to raise awareness among the common public, thrust for more rigid environmental laws, or allow priority to health examinations in high-risk areas.

Healthcare Resource Distribution

To maximize access to care, one must comprehend how healthcare resources are allocated across various geographic areas. A few important facts are listed below.

Locations of Hospitals, Clinics, and Pharmacies

GeoAI can evaluate accessibility and spot any service gaps in healthcare by analyzing the spatial distribution of these institutions (Risanger et al., 2021; Tew et al., 2021). With the use of this data, planning decisions for the development of new healthcare facilities can be made based on data, and resource allocation may be done in a way that maximizes healthcare accessibility for all local populations.

Availability of Medical Equipment and Specialists

A picture of the variety of healthcare services offered in a specific area can be made by analyzing information on the accessibility of specialized medical hardware (like MRI machines) or the nearness of specialists (like cardiologists) in different areas (Garzotto et al., 2020; Schröder et al., 2020). GeoAI models can utilize this data, combined with information on illness prevalence, to pinpoint regions where access to specialized care for specific conditions is limited. This data can support endeavors to extend the number of medical specialists trained in specific areas or investigate telemedicine alternatives to fill in geographic gaps in specialized treatment.

Data Quality, Pre-processing, and Integration Considerations

The caliber and applicability of the geographical data used to define how successful GeoAI solutions are in the healthcare industry. The precision and dependability of the insights obtained from GeoAI models are guaranteed by high-quality data. For this reason, data quality is critical.

Accurate Decision-Making

Inaccurate or flawed data can provide deceptive conclusions and, eventually, bad decision-making (Bammidi et al., 2024; Jayatilake & Ganegoda, 2021). The risk of misallocating funds, carrying out inefficient public health initiatives, or ignoring regions with real healthcare needs is reduced when data accuracy is ensured.

Fairness and Equity

Incomplete or skewed data can make already-existing health inequities worse (Weber et al., 2021). For example, incomplete or biased data on socioeconomic characteristics may result in an underestimation of healthcare needs in marginalized areas. Fairness and equity are promoted in healthcare access and resource allocation when data quality and comprehensiveness are guaranteed.

Temporal Relevance

Data timeliness is very important (Rumisha et al., 2020). Inaccurate estimations of the present demands for healthcare can result from using outdated data. For example, using out-of-date population density data may cause one to underestimate the need for medical facilities in a region that is expanding quickly.

Spatial Relevance

To properly address the particular healthcare issue under investigation, data must be gathered at the right spatial scale. An analysis of national air quality data, for example, could not be useful in locating regions where localized pollution problems affect a particular community.

Data Integration

Integrating information from numerous sources is often essential for GeoAI applications. Precise investigation and reliable results depend on information consistency and compatibility across datasets. It is vital to ensure, beyond any doubt, that information is harmonized and consistent when integrating information from different sources. This may include addressing any duplicate entries in particular datasets, accommodating conflicting spatial references, and harmonizing information formats.

Data Cleaning

This entails locating and fixing mistakes, discrepancies, or missing numbers in the data. Important steps in data cleansing include things like eliminating duplicate records and fixing incorrect geographical coordinates.

Data Transformation

For GeoAI models to analyze data, it might be necessary to transform the data into a certain format. This could entail transforming categorical data into numerical formats, scaling numerical values, or developing new geographical characteristics from the data that already exists.

AI TECHNIQUES FOR GEOAI

GeoAI uses a variety of AI approaches to mine geographical data for insightful medical information. Here's a more thorough examination of a few often-used methods:

Supervised Learning

Using labeled data, AI models are trained in this manner to discover correlations between target variables (such as illness prevalence) and features (geospatial data). Some particular examples in the context of healthcare are elaborated below.

Support Vector Machines (SVMs)

SVMs are robust algorithms designed for classification applications. To forecast regions with a high risk of future outbreaks, SVMs can be trained on historical data on disease outbreaks and environmental elements in the healthcare industry (Singh et al., 2020). For example, historical temperature and rainfall data could be combined with information on mosquito-borne disease outbreaks in the past to train an SVM model. Based on current weather data, this model may potentially be used to identify high-risk locations for future outbreaks.

Random Forests

These algorithms construct a solid ensemble model for prediction assignments by combining several decision trees (Hauschild et al., 2022). Random forests can be utilized within the healthcare industry to figure out hospital affirmations for specific conditions by analyzing information on patient socioeconomics, natural variables, and healthcare asset utilization. For example, to identify regions with the next hazard of hospital confirmations related to asthma during peak pollution seasons, a random forest demonstration may look at information on population density, air quality, and asthma prevalence.

Regression Analysis

This method assists in determining correlations between continuous dependent variables (such as healthcare use rates) and independent variables (geospatial data) (Hauschild et al., 2022). Regression analysis, for example, might be used to investigate the association between income levels and the rates at which preventative healthcare services are utilized in various geographic areas. In communities with low incomes and low rates of preventative healthcare utilization, this information could be utilized to inform targeted public health outreach programs.

Unsupervised Learning

Unsupervised methods, in contrast to supervised learning, find hidden patterns in unlabeled data. Some instances of its use in healthcare using GeoAI are elaborated below.

Clustering

Using this method, data points with comparable properties can be grouped. Clustering can be used in the healthcare industry to find geographic trends in patient demographics or the usage of healthcare resources (Cordes & Castro, 2020; Murad & Khashoggi, 2020). Clustering methods, for example, can be used to examine data related to chronic illness hospital admissions. This could point to geographic locations with high rates of chronic disease prevalence, which would encourage more research into possible environmental or societal factors that contribute to these health problems.

K-Means Clustering

A predetermined number of clusters are created by partitioning data points using this particular clustering algorithm (Pu et al., 2020). K-means clustering can be used in the healthcare industry to divide up a population according to variables like age, income, and health insurance coverage. Because of this segmentation, healthcare interventions and communications may be specifically tailored to meet the needs of each population segment.

Anomaly Detection

This method finds data points that substantially diverge from the anticipated trend (Šabić et al., 2021). Algorithms for anomaly detection can be applied to healthcare to examine data on ER visits and spot possible infectious disease outbreaks. For example, an abrupt increase in ER visits with flu-like symptoms can be reported as abnormal, leading public health officials to look into a possible influenza outbreak.

Deep Learning

Complex patterns can be learned from big datasets via deep learning architectures that use numerous layers of artificial neurons. They can be employed in GeoAI healthcare in the following ways.

Convolutional Neural Networks (CNNs)

CNNs are very good at analyzing and recognizing images. To increase diagnostic accuracy in the medical field, CNNs can be trained using geographical data and medical pictures (such as CT scans and X-rays) (Mohana et al., 2022; Nisar et al., 2021). A CNN model, for example, may be trained using data on air quality and the prevalence of respiratory illnesses in various places, as well as chest X-rays from individuals who have pneumonia. Then, to increase the precision of pneumonia diagnoses, this algorithm might be applied to evaluate X-rays of newly admitted patients and take the patient's location into account.

Recurrent Neural Networks (RNNs)

Sequential data can be dealt with by RNNs with ease (Tyagi & Abraham, 2022). RNNs can be used within the medical field to assess patient medical history information in conjunction with geographic information to estimate possible threats to health or the course of an infection (Shirazi et al., 2020; Uddin et al., 2020). To foresee a patient's chance of developing chronic obstructive pulmonary disease (COPD), for example, an RNN model may look at information on natural exposures within the patient's residential region in addition to the patient's electronic health records.

Natural Language Processing (NLP)

Computers can comprehend and process human language thanks to NLP techniques. This is how GeoAI Healthcare can make use of it.

Sentiment Analysis

Social media data with geographical tags can be analyzed using natural language processing (NLP) to determine how the general public feels about healthcare services or particular health issues in a certain area (Zunic et al., 2020). An examination of social media posts from a particular city, for example, may highlight issues with lengthy ER wait times. Healthcare authorities can utilize this information to look into possible capacity problems and make changes.

Identifying public Health Concerns

Analyzing health-related talks on social media or in online forums, for example, may indicate a sudden spike in reports of flu-like symptoms in a particular area. Public health experts could utilize this information to look into a possible influenza outbreak before it gets worse.

Targeted Public Health Messaging

NLP can be used to target public health messaging to certain geographic areas and analyze public attitudes (Schmälzle & Wilcox, 2022; Y. Wang et al., 2023). For example, social media data analysis from a rural community may indicate that people are not aware of a certain immunization program. Using this data, public health programs that are specifically targeted to that area can be created with messaging that is both clear and culturally relevant.

Through the use of these many AI techniques, GeoAI enables medical practitioners to gain insightful knowledge from geographical data, which enhances decision-making, optimizes resource allocation, and eventually improves everyone's health outcomes.

GEOAI APPLICATIONS IN HEALTHCARE

By combining the power of AI techniques with geospatial data, GeoAI offers a revolutionary approach to healthcare delivery. A more thorough examination of its real-world uses in a number of fields is elaborated below.

Resource Allocation

Making sure that everyone has fair access to high-quality healthcare requires optimizing the locations of healthcare facilities, staff, and equipment. Making well-informed decisions is facilitated by GeoAI via:

Facility Placement

In order to choose the best sites for new clinics, urgent care facilities, and hospitals, artificial intelligence (AI) models can evaluate data on population density, disease prevalence, and travel times (Patel & Trivedi, 2020; Taiwo, 2021). For example, in a fast-growing suburban neighborhood, an AI model could examine data on current healthcare facilities in addition to population growth estimates. In order to guarantee that locals have easy access to primary care services, our model might then suggest the best sites for new clinic construction.

Equipment Distribution

Data on the accessibility of healthcare resources in various geographic areas can be analyzed by GeoAI (Dicuonzo et al., 2023). This makes it possible to allocate specialized medical equipment (such as MRI machines and PET scanners) based on data. For instance, an AI model may locate areas with restricted access to these essential diagnostic instruments by analyzing data on the locations of MRI machines throughout a state. The installation of new MRI equipment in underserved areas can be prioritized using this data.

Personnel Deployment

GeoAI models are capable of analyzing patient demographics, disease prevalence, and healthcare workforce distribution data. By using this data, healthcare professionals—such as physicians, nurses, and specialists—can be deployed as efficiently as possible, making sure they are positioned to best serve the unique requirements of each area. For example, an AI model may examine data on the availability of endocrinologists (diabetic specialists) and statistics on the prevalence of diabetes in a certain area. After that, our model might suggest methods for assigning additional endocrinologists to regions with high diabetes incidence, enhancing these patients' access to specialized care.

GeoAI ensures that everyone has access to the therapy they require, wherever they may be, by maximizing resource allocation based on real-world demands.

Disease Surveillance and Outbreak Prediction

To lessen the effects of infectious disease outbreaks, early detection and aggressive response are essential. GeoAI is essential for the following areas.

Identifying High-Risk Areas

AI models are capable of analyzing weather patterns, historical disease outbreak data, and environmental data (vegetation cover, water quality, and air quality). This makes it possible to pinpoint areas where a given disease is more likely to occur (Andraud et al., 2021; Song et al., 2021). An AI algorithm may, for example, forecast regions with a high risk of future outbreaks by analyzing data on mosquito breeding grounds and past data on West Nile virus outbreaks. Then, public health professionals can concentrate efforts on mosquito control and other preventive measures in such locations.

Real-Time Monitoring

To identify any epidemics early on, geospatial data streams (such as social media sentiment analysis and hospital admission data) can be continuously monitored using geoAI models (S. Wang et al., 2020). An AI model may, for example, examine data on ER visits for flu-like symptoms throughout a region. If there is an abrupt increase in these visits, it might be suspected that there is an influenza outbreak, in which case public health officials would look into it and take immediate action.

Resource Allocation During Outbreaks

To maximize resource allocation during an outbreak, GeoAI models can evaluate data on patient demographics and disease distribution patterns (Bragazzi et al., 2020). For example, data on hospital capacity and the geographic spread of a COVID-19 outbreak may be analyzed by an AI model. By using this information, it can be possible to make sure that the regions with the greatest increase in cases have enough medical staff, supplies, and beds. GeoAI can assist in containing outbreaks and reducing their negative effects on public health by enabling proactive surveillance and focused interventions.

Patient Care Optimization

By taking into account both the local setting and the unique patient data, GeoAI can personalize healthcare through the following means.

Environmentally-Informed Treatment

For patients suffering from respiratory conditions like allergies or asthma, GeoAI can customize treatment regimens by analyzing data on pollen counts, air quality, and proximity to environmental risks (Dieterle, 2020). An AI model might, for example, use location information and air quality data to modify an asthma patient's dose according on the amount of air pollution in their area.

Social Determinants of Health

Patients who are more likely to develop chronic illnesses like diabetes or obesity can be identified by using GeoAI to analyze data on variables like the availability of recreational facilities and healthy dietary options (Bompelli et al., 2021; Patra et al., 2021). Personalized care plans that target the social determinants of health in addition to conventional medical interventions can be created using this information. An AI model may, for example, evaluate information about a patient's accessibility to parks and food stores in order to suggest exercise and dietary regimens that are practical for their particular setting.

Targeted Public Health Messaging

GeoAI is capable of analyzing demographic and illness prevalence data in certain regions. This makes it possible to create public health messaging programs that are specifically aimed to a population's requirements. An AI model might, for example, examine information on obesity prevalence and the availability of healthy food options in a particular area. Public health campaigns supporting healthy eating practices and emphasizing the accessibility of nearby farmers markets or healthy food initiatives can be developed using the information provided here. GeoAI has the potential to increase the relevance and effectiveness of public health initiatives by customizing messaging to the unique geographic setting.

Community Health Resource Identification

GeoAI is capable of analyzing data regarding the accessibility of community health resources, such as addiction treatment facilities, mental health services, and support groups. This makes it possible to match patients with pertinent resources according to their requirements and location. To improve access to essential support services, an AI model may, for example, evaluate data on a patient with a depression diagnosis and their residential region to find local support groups or mental health clinics.

Through the integration of patient data with their geographical context, GeoAI enables medical practitioners to provide more effective and customized care plans, which in turn improves patient outcomes.

CHALLENGES AND CONSIDERATIONS FOR GEOAI IN HEALTHCARE

Despite its vast potential, implementing GeoAI in healthcare comes with its own set of challenges and considerations:

Data Privacy Concerns

Patient Privacy

GeoAI applications can rely on private patient information, which raises questions regarding data misuse and privacy violations. In order to guarantee patient privacy is maintained during the data collection, storage, analysis, and utilization process, strong data governance frameworks are necessary. For example, in order to reduce the possibility of patients' identities being discovered through their data, anonymization strategies and safe data storage procedures are essential.

Data Security

Any healthcare organization is always concerned about cybersecurity threats. Strong cybersecurity measures must be put in place to protect private patient information in order to stop illegal access and possible data misuse. In this context, employee training on data protection procedures and routine data security audits are essential.

Integration Complexities

Technical Integration

It can be technically difficult to integrate GeoAI models into current healthcare information systems. To address the complexity of geospatial data processing, new infrastructure and the need for common data formats would be necessary. For integration initiatives to be successful, cooperation between data scientists and IT specialists is essential.

Operational Integration

Healthcare personnel must get staff training and workflow modifications in order to implement new AI-powered solutions. It needs clear communication, extensive training courses, and continuing assistance to guarantee that medical personnel can successfully integrate GeoAI technologies with conventional medical procedures.

Need for Specialized Expertise

Data Science Expertise

Acquiring valuable insights from geographic data necessitates specific data science competencies. To fully utilize GeoAI, healthcare organizations might need to make investments in data science knowledge or work with outside data science teams.

AI Expertise

Complex AI model development and deployment require artificial intelligence skills. The effective design and implementation of GeoAI applications to tackle real-world healthcare concerns necessitates collaboration between AI specialists and healthcare professionals.

Domain Expertise

A thorough understanding of both geospatial data and the particular healthcare area being addressed is necessary for successful GeoAI implementations. Effective GeoAI solutions require interdisciplinary teams with knowledge of data science, healthcare, and geographic information systems.

To fully use GeoAI in healthcare and advance everyone's health, these issues must be resolved via strong data governance, smooth system integration, and promoting cooperation amongst a variety of professionals.

CONCLUSION

This chapter explored how various data sources such as patient demographics, socio-economic factors, health insurance coverage, and environmental factors can be utilized by GeoAI to enhance healthcare delivery. GeoAI can analyze population density and socio-economic data to optimize the placement of healthcare facilities and resources, ensuring equitable access to care. Environmental data, such as air and water quality, can be used to identify regions at risk for specific health issues, guiding targeted interventions. GeoAI can also address healthcare disparities by considering social determinants of health and enabling personalized treatment plans. Techniques like supervised learning, deep learning, and NLP can be employed to predict disease outbreaks, monitor real-time health data, and tailor public health messaging. By integrating high-quality, timely, and relevant geospatial data, GeoAI can facilitate accurate decision-making and resource allocation, ultimately improving patient outcomes and public health strategies. Implementing GeoAI in healthcare may face challenges such as ensuring data privacy and security, managing technical and operational integration complexities, and requiring specialized expertise in data science, AI, and healthcare. Overcoming these issues demands robust data governance, seamless system integration, and interdisciplinary collaboration.

The applications of GeoAI in healthcare have a wealth of promising prospects. It is anticipated that even more comprehensive data sources, such as electronic health records and data from wearable sensors, would be integrated, enabling a more comprehensive picture of both individual and population health. Furthermore, the advancement of explainable AI (XAI) methodologies will be essential to fostering transparency and confidence in AI-driven healthcare choices. Even more creative solutions that enhance the provision of healthcare, the distribution of resources, and eventually the health of the population will result from ongoing research on AI models created especially for healthcare applications and geospatial data analysis.

REFERENCES

Adam, A., Finance, O., & Thomas, I. (2021). Monitoring trucks to reveal Belgian geographical structures and dynamics: From GPS traces to spatial interactions. *Journal of Transport Geography*, 91, 102977. Advance online publication. 10.1016/j.jtrangeo.2021.102977

Alastal, A. I., & Shaqfa, A. H. (2022). GeoAI Technologies and Their Application Areas in Urban Planning and Development: Concepts, Opportunities and Challenges in Smart City (Kuwait, Study Case). *Journal of Data Analysis and Information Processing*, 10(02), 110–126. Advance online publication. 10.4236/jdaip.2022.102007

Andraud, M., Bougeard, S., Chesnoiu, T., & Rose, N. (2021). Spatiotemporal clustering and Random Forest models to identify risk factors of African swine fever outbreak in Romania in 2018–2019. *Scientific Reports*, 11(1), 2098. Advance online publication. 10.1038/s41598-021-81329-x33483559

Apte, A., Ingole, V., Lele, P., Marsh, A., Bhattacharjee, T., Hirve, S., Campbell, H., Nair, H., Chan, S., & Juvekar, S. (2019). Ethical considerations in the use of GPS-based movement tracking in health research-Lessons from a care-seeking study in rural west India. *Journal of Global Health*, 9(1), 010323. Advance online publication. 10.7189/jogh.09.01032331275566

Bammidi, T. R., Gutta, L. M., Kotagiri, A., & Samayamantri, L. S., & krishna Vaddy, R. (2024). The Crucial Role of Data Quality in Automated Decision-Making Systems. *International Journal of Management Education for Sustainable Development*, 7(7), 1–22.

Barasa, E., Kazungu, J., Nguhiu, P., & Ravishankar, N. (2021). Examining the level and inequality in health insurance coverage in 36 sub-Saharan African countries. *BMJ Global Health*, 6(4), e004712. Advance online publication. 10.1136/bmjgh-2020-00471233903176

Bauer, M. E. (2020). Remote Sensing of Environment: History, Philosophy, Approach and Contributions, 1969 –2019. *Remote Sensing of Environment*, 237, 111522. Advance online publication. 10.1016/j.rse.2019.111522

Behara, K., Bhero, E., Agee, J. T., & Gonela, V. (2022). Artificial intelligence in medical diagnostics: A review from a South African context. In *Scientific African* (Vol. 17). 10.1016/j.sciaf.2022.e01360

Bishop, M. V., Ólafsdóttir, R., Michaud, T., & Metcalf, C. (2024). Crowdsourced mapping of tourism distribution and dynamics in Iceland using Flickr. *Scandinavian Journal of Hospitality and Tourism*, •••, 1–17. 10.1080/15022250.2024.2355905

Bompelli, A., Wang, Y., Wan, R., Singh, E., Zhou, Y., Xu, L., Oniani, D., Kshatriya, B. S. A., Balls-Berry, J. E., & Zhang, R. (2021). Social and Behavioral Determinants of Health in the Era of Artificial Intelligence with Electronic Health Records: A Scoping Review. In *Health Data Science* (Vol. 2021). 10.34133/2021/9759016

Bragazzi, N. L., Dai, H., Damiani, G., Behzadifar, M., Martini, M., & Wu, J. (2020). How big data and artificial intelligence can help better manage the covid-19 pandemic. *International Journal of Environmental Research and Public Health*, 17(9), 3176. Advance online publication. 10.3390/ijerph17093176 32370204

Carlos, H. A., Shi, X., Sargent, J., Tanski, S., & Berke, E. M. (2010). Density estimation and adaptive bandwidths: A primer for public health practitioners. *International Journal of Health Geographics*, 9(1), 39. Advance online publication. 10.1186/1476-072X-9-39 20653969

Chuvieco, E. (2020). Fundamentals of Satellite Remote Sensing : An Environmental Approach, Third Edition. In *Fundamentals of Satellite Remote Sensing*.

Cordes, J., & Castro, M. C. (2020). Spatial analysis of COVID-19 clusters and contextual factors in New York City. *Spatial and Spatio-temporal Epidemiology*, 34, 100355. Advance online publication. 10.1016/j.sste.2020.100355 32807400

Dicuonzo, G., Donofrio, F., Fusco, A., & Shini, M. (2023). Healthcare system: Moving forward with artificial intelligence. *Technovation*, 120, 102510. Advance online publication. 10.1016/j.technovation.2022.102510

Dieterle, C. (2020). The case for environmentally-informed occupational therapy: Clinical and educational applications to promote personal wellness, public health and environmental sustainability. *World Federation of Occupational Therapists Bulletin*, 76(1), 32–39. Advance online publication. 10.1080/14473828.2020.1717055

Du, H., Anand, S., Alechina, N., Morley, J., Hart, G., Leibovici, D., Jackson, M., & Ware, M. (2012). Geospatial Information Integration for Authoritative and Crowd Sourced Road Vector Data. *Transactions in GIS*, 16(4), 455–476. 10.1111/j.1467-9671.2012.01303.x

García-Macía, J., Torralvo, C., Onrubia, A., Ferrer, M., & Morandini, V. (2024). Dispersal patterns of the first White-backed Vulture (Gyps africanus) GPS-tracked in Iberia. *Journal of Ornithology*, 165(3), 815–821. Advance online publication. 10.1007/s10336-024-02167-y

Garzotto, F., Ceresola, E., Panagiotakopoulou, S., Spina, G., Menotto, F., Benozzi, M., Casarotto, M., Lanera, C., Bonavina, M. G., Gregori, D., Meneghesso, G., & Opocher, G. (2020). COVID-19: Ensuring our medical equipment can meet the challenge. *Expert Review of Medical Devices*, 17(6), 483–489. Advance online publication. 10.1080/17434440.2020.177275732434400

Gordon, T., Booysen, F., & Mbonigaba, J. (2020). Socio-economic inequalities in the multiple dimensions of access to healthcare: The case of South Africa. *BMC Public Health*, 20(1), 289. Advance online publication. 10.1186/s12889-020-8368-732131787

Guhlincozzi, A. R. (2024). Making visible the Chicagoland suburban healthcare landscape of latina women: A qualitative GIS approach. *Social & Cultural Geography*, 25(2), 1–20. Advance online publication. 10.1080/14649365.2022.2139857

Harding, J. (2010). Vector Data Quality: A Data Provider's Perspective. In *Fundamentals of Spatial Data Quality*. 10.1002/9780470612156.ch8

Hauschild, A. C., Lemanczyk, M., Matschinske, J., Frisch, T., Zolotareva, O., Holzinger, A., Baumbach, J., & Heider, D. (2022). Federated Random Forests can improve local performance of predictive models for various healthcare applications. *Bioinformatics (Oxford, England)*, 38(8), 2278–2286. Advance online publication. 10.1093/bioinformatics/btac06535139148

Hijmans, R. J. (2020). raster: Geographic analysis and modeling with raster data. : *R Package Version 3.1-5, 3.1*(5).

Hu, S., Zhao, R., Cui, Y., Zhang, D., & Ge, Y. (2023). Identifying the uneven distribution of health and education services in China using open geospatial data. *Geography and Sustainability*, 4(2), 91–99. Advance online publication. 10.1016/j.geosus.2023.01.002

Janowicz, K., Gao, S., McKenzie, G., Hu, Y., & Bhaduri, B. (2020). GeoAI: spatially explicit artificial intelligence techniques for geographic knowledge discovery and beyond. In *International Journal of Geographical Information Science* (Vol. 34, Issue 4). 10.1080/13658816.2019.1684500

Jayatilake, S. M. D. A. C., & Ganegoda, G. U. (2021). Involvement of Machine Learning Tools in Healthcare Decision Making. In *Journal of Healthcare Engineering* (Vol. 2021). 10.1155/2021/6679512

Jing, C., Zhou, W., Qian, Y., Zheng, Z., Wang, J., & Yu, W. (2023). Trajectory big data reveals spatial disparity of healthcare accessibility at the residential neighborhood scale. *Cities (London, England)*, 133, 104127. Advance online publication. 10.1016/j.cities.2022.104127

Johnston, J., & Cushing, L. (2020). Chemical Exposures, Health, and Environmental Justice in Communities Living on the Fenceline of Industry. In *Current environmental health reports* (Vol. 7, Issue 1). 10.1007/s40572-020-00263-8

Kamel Boulos, M. N., Peng, G., & Vopham, T. (2019). An overview of GeoAI applications in health and healthcare. In *International Journal of Health Geographics* (Vol. 18, Issue 1). 10.1186/s12942-019-0171-2

Kang, Y., Gao, S., & Roth, R. E. (2024). Artificial intelligence studies in cartography: A review and synthesis of methods, applications, and ethics. *Cartography and Geographic Information Science*, 1–32. Advance online publication. 10.1080/15230406.2023.2295943

Lary, D. J., Alavi, A. H., Gandomi, A. H., & Walker, A. L. (2016). Machine learning in geosciences and remote sensing. *Geoscience Frontiers*, 7(1), 3–10. Advance online publication. 10.1016/j.gsf.2015.07.003

Li, W. (2020). GeoAI: Where machine learning and big data converge in GIScience. *Journal of Spatial Information Science*, 20(20). Advance online publication. 10.5311/JOSIS.2020.20.658

Li, W., & Hsu, C. Y. (2022). GeoAI for Large-Scale Image Analysis and Machine Vision: Recent Progress of Artificial Intelligence in Geography. In *ISPRS International Journal of Geo-Information* (Vol. 11, Issue 7). 10.3390/ijgi11070385

Lin, L., Yang, H., & Xu, X. (2022). Effects of Water Pollution on Human Health and Disease Heterogeneity: A Review. In *Frontiers in Environmental Science* (Vol. 10). 10.3389/fenvs.2022.880246

Liu, W., Wang, B., Yang, Y., Mou, N., Zheng, Y., Zhang, L., & Yang, T. (2022). Cluster analysis of microscopic spatio-temporal patterns of tourists' movement behaviors in mountainous scenic areas using open GPS-trajectory data. *Tourism Management*, 93, 104614. Advance online publication. 10.1016/j.tourman.2022.104614

McMaughan, D. J., Oloruntoba, O., & Smith, M. L. (2020). Socioeconomic Status and Access to Healthcare: Interrelated Drivers for Healthy Aging. In *Frontiers in Public Health* (Vol. 8). 10.3389/fpubh.2020.00231

Menon, S. P., Shukla, P. K., Sethi, P., Alasiry, A., Marzougui, M., Alouane, M. T. H., & Khan, A. A. (2023). An Intelligent Diabetic Patient Tracking System Based on Machine Learning for E-Health Applications. *Sensors (Basel)*, 23(6), 3004. Advance online publication. 10.3390/s2306300436991714

Mirski, P., Grosberg, J., Kull, T., Mellov, P., Tõnisalu, G., Väli, V., & Väli, Ü. (2024). Movement of avian predators points to biodiversity hotspots in agricultural landscape. *Royal Society Open Science*, 11(1), 231543. Advance online publication. 10.1098/rsos.23154338204791

Mohana, J., Yakkala, B., Vimalnath, S., Benson Mansingh, P. M., Yuvaraj, N., Srihari, K., Sasikala, G., Mahalakshmi, V., Yasir Abdullah, R., & Sundramurthy, V. P. (2022). Application of Internet of Things on the Healthcare Field Using Convolutional Neural Network Processing. *Journal of Healthcare Engineering*, 2022, 1–7. Advance online publication. 10.1155/2022/189212335126905

Mortaheb, R., & Jankowski, P. (2023). Smart city re-imagined: City planning and GeoAI in the age of big data. *Journal of Urban Management*, 12(1), 4–15. Advance online publication. 10.1016/j.jum.2022.08.001

Munnangi, A. K., UdhayaKumar, S., Ravi, V., Sekaran, R., & Kannan, S. (2023). Survival study on deep learning techniques for IoT enabled smart healthcare system. *Health and Technology*, 13(2), 215–228. Advance online publication. 10.1007/s12553-023-00736-436818549

Munyai, O., & Nunu, W. N. (2020). Health effects associated with proximity to waste collection points in Beitbridge Municipality, Zimbabwe. *Waste Management (New York, N.Y.)*, 105, 501–510. Advance online publication. 10.1016/j.wasman.2020.02.04132145684

Murad, A., & Khashoggi, B. F. (2020). Using GIS for disease mapping and clustering in Jeddah, Saudi Arabia. *ISPRS International Journal of Geo-Information*, 9(5), 328. Advance online publication. 10.3390/ijgi9050328

Nisar, D. E. M., Amin, R., Shah, N. U. H., Ghamdi, M. A. A., Almotiri, S. H., & Alruily, M. (2021). Healthcare Techniques through Deep Learning: Issues, Challenges and Opportunities. *IEEE Access : Practical Innovations, Open Solutions*, 9, 98523–98541. Advance online publication. 10.1109/ACCESS.2021.3095312

Olawade, D. B., Wada, O. J., David-Olawade, A. C., Kunonga, E., Abaire, O., & Ling, J. (2023). Using artificial intelligence to improve public health: a narrative review. In *Frontiers in Public Health* (Vol. 11). 10.3389/fpubh.2023.1196397

Patel, N., & Trivedi, S. (2020). Choosing Optimal Locations for TemporaryHealth Care Facilities During Health Crisis Using Binary Integer Programming. *Journals Sagescience*, 3(2).

Patra, B. G., Sharma, M. M., Vekaria, V., Adekkanattu, P., Patterson, O. V., Glicksberg, B., Lepow, L. A., Ryu, E., Biernacka, J. M., Furmanchuk, A., George, T. J., Hogan, W., Wu, Y., Yang, X., Bian, J., Weissman, M., Wickramaratne, P., Mann, J. J., Olfson, M., . . . Pathak, J. (2021). Extracting social determinants of health from electronic health records using natural language processing: A systematic review. In *Journal of the American Medical Informatics Association* (Vol. 28, Issue 12). 10.1093/jamia/ocab170

Pierdicca, R. (2021). *GeoAI:artificial intelligence for interpretation and processing of complex geomatic data*. EGU General Assembly.

Pu, Q., Yoo, E. H., Rothstein, D. H., Cairo, S., & Malemo, L. (2020). Improving the spatial accessibility of healthcare in North Kivu, Democratic Republic of Congo. *Applied Geography (Sevenoaks, England)*, 121, 102262. Advance online publication. 10.1016/j.apgeog.2020.102262

Pukkala, T. (2019). Using ALS raster data in forest planning. *Journal of Forestry Research*, 30(5), 1581–1593. Advance online publication. 10.1007/s11676-019-00937-6

Reyes-Riveros, R., Altamirano, A., De La Barrera, F., Rozas-Vásquez, D., Vieli, L., & Meli, P. (2021). Linking public urban green spaces and human well-being: A systematic review. In *Urban Forestry and Urban Greening* (Vol. 61). 10.1016/j.ufug.2021.127105

Richards, D. R., Belcher, R. N., Carrasco, L. R., Edwards, P. J., Fatichi, S., Hamel, P., Masoudi, M., McDonnell, M. J., Peleg, N., & Stanley, M. C. (2022). Global variation in contributions to human well-being from urban vegetation ecosystem services. *One Earth*, 5(5), 522–533. Advance online publication. 10.1016/j.oneear.2022.04.006

Risanger, S., Singh, B., Morton, D., & Meyers, L. A. (2021). Selecting pharmacies for COVID-19 testing to ensure access. *Health Care Management Science*, 24(2), 330–338. Advance online publication. 10.1007/s10729-020-09538-w33423180

Rovira, J., Domingo, J. L., & Schuhmacher, M. (2020). Air quality, health impacts and burden of disease due to air pollution (PM10, PM2.5, NO2 and O3): Application of AirQ+ model to the Camp de Tarragona County (Catalonia, Spain). *The Science of the Total Environment*, 703, 135538. Advance online publication. 10.1016/j.scitotenv.2019.13553831759725

Rumisha, S. F., Lyimo, E. P., Mremi, I. R., Tungu, P. K., Mwingira, V. S., Mbata, D., Malekia, S. E., Joachim, C., & Mboera, L. E. G. (2020). Data quality of the routine health management information system at the primary healthcare facility and district levels in Tanzania. *BMC Medical Informatics and Decision Making*, 20(1), 340. Advance online publication. 10.1186/s12911-020-01366-w33334323

Šabić, E., Keeley, D., Henderson, B., & Nannemann, S. (2021). Healthcare and anomaly detection: Using machine learning to predict anomalies in heart rate data. *AI & Society*, 36(1), 149–158. Advance online publication. 10.1007/s00146-020-00985-1

Sahana, K. S., Karthik, C. B., Sree, M. M., Chaithra, M., Abhinandithe, S. K., Snehalatha, B., Sridhar, R., Balasubramanian, S., & Madhu, B. (2023). Geospatial Artificial Intelligence (GeoAI): Applications in Health Care. *International Journal of Health & Allied Sciences*, 11(4). Advance online publication. 10.55691/2278-344X.1044

Saibi, H., Bersi, M., Mia, M. B., Saadi, N. M., Al Bloushi, K. M. S., & Avakian, R. W. (2018). Applications of Remote Sensing in Geoscience. In *Recent Advances and Applications in Remote Sensing*. 10.5772/intechopen.75995

Sanders Thompson, V. L. (2013). Making decisions in a complex information environment: Evidential preference and information we trust. *BMC Medical Informatics and Decision Making*, 13(S3, SUPPL.3), S7. Advance online publication. 10.1186/1472-6947-13-S3-S724565305

Schmälzle, R., & Wilcox, S. (2022). Harnessing Artificial Intelligence for Health Message Generation: The Folic Acid Message Engine. *Journal of Medical Internet Research*, 24(1), e28858. Advance online publication. 10.2196/2885835040800

Schröder, A. K., Fassmer, A. M., Allers, K., & Hoffmann, F. (2020). Needs and availability of medical specialists' and allied health professionals' visits in German nursing homes: A cross-sectional study of nursing home staff. *BMC Health Services Research*, 20(1), 332. Advance online publication. 10.1186/s12913-020-05169-732317028

Shirazi, Z. A., de Souza, C. P. E., Kashef, R., & Rodrigues, F. F. (2020). Deep learning in the healthcare industry: Theory and Applications. In *Computational Intelligence and Soft Computing Applications in Healthcare Management Science*. 10.4018/978-1-7998-2581-4.ch010

Siddik, M. S. M., Ahmed, T. E., Awad Ahmed, F. R., Mokhtar, R. A., Ali, E. S., & Saeed, R. A. (2023). Development of Health Digital GIS Map for Tuberculosis Disease Distribution Analysis in Sudan. In *Journal of Healthcare Engineering* (Vol. 2023). 10.1155/2023/6479187

Singh, V., Poonia, R. C., Kumar, S., Dass, P., Agarwal, P., Bhatnagar, V., & Raja, L. (2020). Prediction of COVID-19 corona virus pandemic based on time series data using support vector machine. *Journal of Discrete Mathematical Sciences and Cryptography*, 23(8), 1583–1597. Advance online publication. 10.1080/09720529.2020.1784535

Song, Z., Jia, X., Bao, J., Yang, Y., Zhu, H., & Shi, X. (2021). Spatio-temporal analysis of influenza-like illness and prediction of incidence in high-risk regions in the united states from 2011 to 2020. *International Journal of Environmental Research and Public Health*, 18(13), 7120. Advance online publication. 10.3390/ijerph1813712034281057

Tainio, M., Jovanovic Andersen, Z., Nieuwenhuijsen, M. J., Hu, L., de Nazelle, A., An, R., Garcia, L. M. T., Goenka, S., Zapata-Diomedi, B., Bull, F., & de Sá, T. H. (2021). Air pollution, physical activity and health: A mapping review of the evidence. In *Environment International* (Vol. 147). 10.1016/j.envint.2020.105954

Taiwo, O. J. (2021). Maximal Covering Location Problem (MCLP) for the identification of potential optimal COVID-19 testing facility sites in Nigeria. *African Geographical Review*, 40(4), 395–411. Advance online publication. 10.1080/19376812.2020.1838306

Teller, J. (2021). Urban density and Covid-19: Towards an adaptive approach. *Buildings & Cities*, 2(1), 150–165. Advance online publication. 10.5334/bc.89

Tew, M. M., Hatah, E., Arif, F., Abdul Wahid, M. A., Makmor-Bakry, M., & Abdul Maulad, K. N. (2021). Geospatial analysis of distribution of community pharmacies and other health care facilities providing minor ailments services in Malaysia. *Journal of Pharmaceutical Policy and Practice*, 14(1), 24. Advance online publication. 10.1186/s40545-021-00308-933627199

Tyagi, A. K., & Abraham, A. (2022). Recurrent Neural Networks: Concepts and Applications. In *Recurrent Neural Networks: Concepts and Applications*. 10.1201/9781003307822

Uddin, M. Z., Hassan, M. M., Alsanad, A., & Savaglio, C. (2020). A body sensor data fusion and deep recurrent neural network-based behavior recognition approach for robust healthcare. *Information Fusion*, 55, 105–115. Advance online publication. 10.1016/j.inffus.2019.08.004

Viviani, M., & Pasi, G. (2017). Credibility in social media: opinions, news, and health information—a survey. In *Wiley Interdisciplinary Reviews: Data Mining and Knowledge Discovery* (Vol. 7, Issue 5). 10.1002/widm.1209

Wagstaff, A., & Neelsen, S. (2020). A comprehensive assessment of universal health coverage in 111 countries: A retrospective observational study. *The Lancet. Global Health*, 8(1), e39–e49. Advance online publication. 10.1016/S2214-109X(19)30463-231837954

Wang, S., Ding, S., & Xiong, L. (2020). A new system for surveillance and digital contact tracing for COVID-19: Spatiotemporal reporting over network and GPS. *JMIR mHealth and uHealth*, 8(6), e19457. Advance online publication. 10.2196/1945732499212

Wang, S., Huang, X., Liu, P., Zhang, M., Biljecki, F., Hu, T., Fu, X., Liu, L., Liu, X., Wang, R., Huang, Y., Yan, J., Jiang, J., Chukwu, M., Reza Naghedi, S., Hemmati, M., Shao, Y., Jia, N., Xiao, Z., . . . Bao, S. (2024). Mapping the landscape and roadmap of geospatial artificial intelligence (GeoAI) in quantitative human geography: An extensive systematic review. In *International Journal of Applied Earth Observation and Geoinformation* (Vol. 128). 10.1016/j.jag.2024.103734

Wang, Y., Willis, E., Yeruva, V. K., Ho, D., & Lee, Y. (2023). A case study of using natural language processing to extract consumer insights from tweets in American cities for public health crises. *BMC Public Health*, 23(1), 935. Advance online publication. 10.1186/s12889-023-15882-737226165

Watts, M. J., Kotsila, P., Mortyn, P. G., Sarto i Monteys, V., & Urzi Brancati, C. (2020). Influence of socio-economic, demographic and climate factors on the regional distribution of dengue in the United States and Mexico. *International Journal of Health Geographics*, 19(1), 44. Advance online publication. 10.1186/s12942-020-00241-133138827

Weber, A. M., Gupta, R., Abdalla, S., Cislaghi, B., Meausoone, V., & Darmstadt, G. L. (2021). Gender-related data missingness, imbalance and bias in global health surveys. *BMJ Global Health*, 6(11), e007405. Advance online publication. 10.1136/bmjgh-2021-00740534836912

Yudono, A., Afrianto, F., & Hariyanto, A. D. (2023). The Evaluation of Geographical Health Facilities Structure in Makassar City, Indonesia. *International Journal of Environmental Research and Public Health*, 20(6), 5210. Advance online publication. 10.3390/ijerph2006521036982119

Zunic, A., Corcoran, P., & Spasic, I. (2020). Sentiment analysis in health and well-being: Systematic review. In *JMIR Medical Informatics* (Vol. 8, Issue 1). 10.2196/16023

KEY TERMS AND DEFINITIONS

GeoAI, or Geospatial Artificial Intelligence: Refers to the application of artificial intelligence techniques to geospatial data for the purpose of understanding and predicting geographic phenomena. This involves integrating AI methods, such as machine learning and deep learning, with GIS and remote sensing technologies to analyze spatial data and extract meaningful insights.

Geographic Information System (GIS): Is a framework for gathering, managing, and analyzing spatial and geographic data. It combines data from various sources to map and analyze patterns and relationships in a visual context. GIS allows users to visualize, question, analyze, and interpret data to understand spatial relationships, trends, and patterns.

Geospatial Data: Also known as spatial data, refers to information that describes the location and characteristics of physical objects on Earth. This data includes coordinates (latitude, longitude), elevation, and attributes of geographic features. Geospatial data can be collected through various means, including GPS, remote sensing, and surveys.

Machine Learning (ML): Is a subset of artificial intelligence that involves the development of algorithms and statistical models that enable computers to perform specific tasks without being explicitly programmed. Machine learning algorithms learn from and make predictions or decisions based on data.

Remote Sensing: Refers to the process of collecting information about an object or area from a distance, typically using satellites, aircraft, drones, or other sensor-equipped platforms. Remote sensing technologies capture data in the form of images or other readings across various wavelengths of the electromagnetic spectrum.

Compilation of References

4. cite Labs Ltd. (2024). *Recite: APA and Harvard citations checked instantly.* https://reciteworks.com/

Aaronson, S. (2024). The Age of AI Nationalism and its Effects. SSRN *Electronic Journal.* 10.2139/ssrn.4803311

Abbas, M. (2023). *Uses and misuses of chatgGPT by academic community: An overview and guidelines* (SSRN Scholarly Paper 4402510). 10.2139/ssrn.4402510

Abdullah, Y. I., Schuman, J. S., Shabsigh, R., Caplan, A., & Al-Aswad, L. A. (2021). Ethics of artificial intelligence in medicine and ophthalmology. *Asia-Pacific Journal of Ophthalmology*, 10(3), 289–298. 10.1097/APO.0000000000000397 34383720

Academy of Social Sciences. (2021). *What is social science?* Academy of Social Sciences. https://acss.org.uk/what-is-social-science

ACM. (2022). *Statement on Principles for Responsible Algorithmic Systems.* ACM Technology Policy Office. https://www.acm.org/binaries/content/assets/public-policy/final-joint-ai-statement-update.pdf

ACRL. (2016). *Framework for Information Literacy for Higher Education.* https://www.ala.org/acrl/standards/ilframework

Adadi, A., & Berrada, M. (2018). Peeking Inside the Black-Box: A Survey on Explainable Artificial Intelligence (XAI). *IEEE Access : Practical Innovations, Open Solutions*, 6, 52138–52160. 10.1109/ACCESS.2018.2870052

Adam, A., Finance, O., & Thomas, I. (2021). Monitoring trucks to reveal Belgian geographical structures and dynamics: From GPS traces to spatial interactions. *Journal ofTransport Geography*, 91, 102977. Advance online publication. 10.1016/j.jtrangeo.2021.102977

Adams, H. S. (2022, June 17). *Industrial revolution timeline: 1760 to manufacturing today*. https://manufacturingdigital.com/smart-manufacturing/industrial-revolution-timeline-1760-to-manufacturing-today

Adelipour, S., & Haeri, M. (2024). Private outsourced model predictive control via secure multi-party computation. *Computers & Electrical Engineering*, 116, 109208. 10.1016/j.compeleceng.2024.109208

Adeyelu, O. O., Ugochukwu, C. E., & Shonibare, M. A. (2024). Ethical Implications of AI in Financial Decision–Making: A review with real world applications. *International Journal of Applied Research in Social Sciences*, 6(4), 608–630. 10.51594/ijarss.v6i4.1033

Agouridis, A. (2021, September 2). *All you need to know about AI and machine learning in HR*. https://www.jobylon.com/blog/all-you-need-to-know-about-ai-and-machine-learning-in-hr

Agrawal, G., Kaur, A., & Myneni, S. (2024). A Review of Generative Models in Generating Synthetic Attack Data for Cybersecurity. *Electronics (Basel)*, 13(2), 322. 10.3390/electronics13020322

Ahmad, S., Shakeel, I., Mehfuz, S., & Ahmad, J. (2023). Deep learning models for cloud, edge, fog, and IoT computing paradigms: Survey, recent advances, and future directions. *Computer Science Review*, 49, 100568. 10.1016/j.cosrev.2023.100568

Ahmed, F., & Mähönen, P. (2021, September). Quantum computing for artificial intelligence based mobile network optimization. In *2021 IEEE 32nd annual international symposium on personal, indoor and mobile radio communications (PIMRC)* (pp. 1128-1133). IEEE. 10.1109/PIMRC50174.2021.9569339

Ahmed, S. M. (2019). Artificial Intelligence in Saudi Arabia: Leveraging Entrepreneurship in the Arab Markets. *Proceedings - 2019 Amity International Conference on Artificial Intelligence, AICAI 2019, 6*(2), 394–398. 10.1109/AICAI.2019.8701348

Ahmed, A. A. A., & Ganapathy, A. (2021). Creation of Automated Content With Embedded Artificial Intelligence: A Study on Learning Management System for Educational Entrepreneurship. *Academy of Entrepreneurship Journal*, 27(3), 1–10.

Ajmal, S., Ahmed, A. A. I., & Jalota, C. (2023). Natural language processing in improving information retrieval and knowledge discovery in healthcare conversational agents. *Journal of Artificial Intelligence and Machine Learning in Management*, 7(1), 34–47.

Akgun, S., & Greenhow, C. (2022). Artificial intelligence in education: Addressing ethical challenges in K-12 settings. *AI and Ethics*, 2(3), 431–440. 10.1007/s43681-021-00096-734790956

Akhtar, N., & Ghosh, J. (2019). Recent Trends in Deep Neural Networks Based Adversarial Attacks and Defenses. arXiv preprint arXiv:1908.03603.

Akhtar, S. (2024). The Ethicsophical Landscape of Large Language Models. *Philarchive*. https://philarchive.org/rec/AKHEAT

Alasadi, E. A., & Baiz, C. R. (2023). Generative AI in education and research: Opportunities, concerns, and solutions. *Journal of Chemical Education*, 100(8), 2965–2971. 10.1021/acs.jchemed.3c00323

Alastal, A. I., & Shaqfa, A. H. (2022). GeoAI Technologies and Their Application Areas in Urban Planning and Development: Concepts, Opportunities and Challenges in Smart City (Kuwait, Study Case). *Journal of Data Analysis and Information Processing*, 10(02), 110–126. Advance online publication. 10.4236/jdaip.2022.102007

Al-Khateeb, H. M., Epiphaniou, G., & Dianati, M. (2019). Applying generative adversarial networks to enhance network anomaly detection. *IEEE International Conference on Systems, Man and Cybernetics (SMC)*, 1388-1393.

Alla, L., Bentalha, B., & Elyoussfi, A. (2023). Intelligence territoriale et positionnement stratégique des régions au Maroc: Le cas de la région de Fès Meknès en perspective. Le concept de l'intelligence en sciences juridiques, économiques et sociales, 215-237.

Alotaibi, M., Furnell, S., & Clarke, N. (2016). Information security policies: A review of challenges and influencing factors. *2016 11th International Conference for Internet Technology and Secured Transactions (ICITST)*, 352–358. 10.1109/ICITST.2016.7856729

Alser, M., & Waisberg, E. (2023). Concerns with the usage of ChatGPT in academia and medicine: A viewpoint. *American Journal of Medicine Open*, 9, 2. 10.1016/j.ajmo.2023.10003639035060

Amankwah-Amoah, J., Abdalla, S., Mogaji, E., Elbanna, A., & Dwivedi, Y. K. (2024). The impending disruption of creative industries by generative AI: Opportunities, challenges, and research agenda. *International Journal of Information Management*, 102759. 10.1016/j.ijinfomgt.2024.102759

Amodei, D., Olah, C., Steinhardt, J., Christiano, P., Schulman, J., & Mané, D. (2016). *Concrete Problems in AI Safety*. 10.48550/ARXIV.1606.06565

Andraud, M., Bougeard, S., Chesnoiu, T., & Rose, N. (2021). Spatiotemporal clustering and Random Forest models to identify risk factors of African swine fever outbreak in Romania in 2018–2019. *Scientific Reports*, 11(1), 2098. Advance online publication. 10.1038/s41598-021-81329-x33483559

ANTHROP\C. (n.d.). *Claude*. Retrieved May 25, 2024, from https://claude.ai/login?returnTo=%2F%3F

Anute, N., Paliwal, M., Patel, M., & Kandale, N. (2021). Impact of artificial intelligence and machine learning on business operations. *Journal of Management Research and Analysis*, 8(2), 69–74. 10.18231/j.jmra.2021.015

Apte, A., Ingole, V., Lele, P., Marsh, A., Bhattacharjee, T., Hirve, S., Campbell, H., Nair, H., Chan, S., & Juvekar, S. (2019). Ethical considerations in the use of GPS-based movement tracking in health research-Lessons from a care-seeking study in rural west India. *Journal of Global Health*, 9(1), 010323. Advance online publication. 10.7189/jogh.09.01032331275566

Archambault, S. G., Ramachandran, S., Acosta, E., & Fu, S. (2024). Ethical dimensions of algorithmic literacy for college students: Case studies and cross-disciplinary connections. *Journal of Academic Librarianship*, 50(3), 102865. 10.1016/j.acalib.2024.102865

Armenta, A. (2021, August 5). *A history of industrial revolutions and how they've impacted manufacturing*. https://control.com/technical-articles/a-history-of-industrial-revolutions-and-how-theyve-impacted-manufacturing/

Artificial Intelligence Act, E. U. (2024). *EU Artificial Intelligence Act | Up-to-date developments and analyses of the EU AI Act*. https://artificialintelligenceact.eu/

Asatiani, A., Malo, P., Nagbøl, P. R., Penttinen, E., Rinta-Kahila, T., & Salovaara, A. (2021). Sociotechnical envelopment of artificial intelligence: An approach to organizational deployment of inscrutable artificial intelligence systems. *Journal of the Association for Information Systems*, 22(2), 325–352. 10.17705/1jais.00664

Ashok, M., Madan, R., Joha, A., & Sivarajah, U. (2022). Ethical framework for Artificial Intelligence and Digital technologies. *International Journal of Information Management*, 62, 102433. 10.1016/j.ijinfomgt.2021.102433

Australian Research Council. (2019). *Engagement and impact assessment 2018-19*. https://dataportal.arc.gov.au/ei/nationalreport/2018/pages/introduction/index.html?id=definitions

Authors Guild. (2024a, February 29). Authors Guild releases AI best practices for authors. *The Authors Guild.* https://authorsguild.org/news/authors-guild-releases-ai-best-practices-for-authors/

Authors Guild. (2024b, April 12). Authors Guild supports groundbreaking bill to create AI transparency between creators and companies. *The Authors Guild.* https://authorsguild.org/news/ag-supports-generative-ai-copyright-disclosure-act/

Aydın, Ö., & Karaarslan, E. (2022). *OpenAI ChatGPT generated literature review: Digital twin in healthcare* (SSRN Scholarly Paper 4308687). 10.2139/ssrn.4308687

Badawy, W. (2023). *Generative AI: Implications and opportunities for business.* Wael Badawy.

Bahrami, M., Mansoorizadeh, M., & Khotanlou, H., (2023). Few-shot Learning with Prompting Methods, pp. 1-5, doi: . 10.1109/IPRIA59240.2023.10147172

Bahrke, J., & Regnier, T. (2023, December 14). *Artificial intelligence – Q&As* [Text]. European Commission - European Commission. https://ec.europa.eu/commission/presscorner/detail/en/qanda_21_1683

Baïdoo-Anu, D., & Owusu Ansah, L. (2023). Education in the era of generative artificial intelligence (AI): Understanding the potential benefits of ChatGPT in promoting teaching and learning. *Journal of AI*, 7(1), 1. 10.61969/jai.1337500

Bail, C. A. (2024). Can Generative AI improve social science? *Proceedings of the National Academy of Sciences of the United States of America*, 121(21), 1–10. 10.1073/pnas.231402112138722813

Bakis, H. (2021). Territoires intelligents et souveraineté numérique. *Revue Géographique de l'Est*, 61(1-2).

Bammidi, T. R., Gutta, L. M., Kotagiri, A., & Samayamantri, L. S., & krishna Vaddy, R. (2024). The Crucial Role of Data Quality in Automated Decision-Making Systems. *International Journal of Management Education for Sustainable Development*, 7(7), 1–22.

Banh, L., & Strobel, G. (2023). Generative artificial intelligence. *Electronic Markets*, 33(1), 63. Advance online publication. 10.1007/s12525-023-00680-1

Banker, S., Chatterjee, P., Mishra, H., & Mishra, A. (2023a). *Machine-assisted social psychology hypothesis generation.* 10.31234/osf.io/kv6f7

Barakovskykh, M. (2024, January 2). *Social sciences research: Qualitative vs. Quantitative research.* https://spcollege.libguides.com/c.php?g=254343&p=1695372

Barasa, E., Kazungu, J., Nguhiu, P., & Ravishankar, N. (2021). Examining the level and inequality in health insurance coverage in 36 sub-Saharan African countries. *BMJ Global Health*, 6(4), e004712. Advance online publication. 10.1136/bmjgh-2020-00471233903176

Barocas, S., & Selbst, A. D. (2016). Big Data's Disparate Impact. SSRN *Electronic Journal*. 10.2139/ssrn.2477899

Bartenschlager, C. C., Gassner, U. M., Römmele, C., Brunner, J. O., Schlögl-Flierl, K., & Ziethmann, P. (2024). The AI ethics of digital COVID-19 diagnosis and their legal, medical, technological, and operational managerial implications. *Artificial Intelligence in Medicine*, 102873, 102873. Advance online publication. 10.1016/j.artmed.2024.10287338643592

Bartneck, C., Lütge, C., Wagner, A., & Welsh, S. (2021). *An introduction to ethics in robotics and AI*. Springer Nature. 10.1007/978-3-030-51110-4

Batarseh, F. A., Freeman, L., & Huang, C.-H. (2021). A survey on artificial intelligence assurance. *Journal of Big Data*, 8(1), 60. 10.1186/s40537-021-00445-7

Bauer, E., Greisel, M., Kuznetsov, I., Berndt, M., Kollar, I., Dresel, M., Fischer, M. R., & Fischer, F. (2023). Using natural language processing to support peer-feedback in the age of artificial intelligence: A cross-disciplinary framework and a research agenda. *British Journal of Educational Technology*, 54(5), 1222–1245. 10.1111/bjet.13336

Bauer, M. E. (2020). Remote Sensing of Environment: History, Philosophy, Approach and Contributions, 1969 –2019. *Remote Sensing of Environment*, 237, 111522. Advance online publication. 10.1016/j.rse.2019.111522

Baum, S. D. (2020). Social choice ethics in artificial intelligence. *AI & Society*, 35(1), 165–176. 10.1007/s00146-017-0760-1

BBC. (2011, Audust). US scientists "knew Guatemala syphilis tests unethical." *BBC News*. https://www.bbc.com/news/world-latin-america-14712089

Behara, K., Bhero, E., Agee, J. T., & Gonela, V. (2022). Artificial intelligence in medical diagnostics: A review from a South African context. In *Scientific African* (Vol. 17). 10.1016/j.sciaf.2022.e01360

Belgacem, A., Mahmoudi, S., & Ferrag, M. A. (2023). A machine learning model for improving virtual machine migration in cloud computing. *The Journal of Supercomputing*, 79(9), 9486–9508. 10.1007/s11227-022-05031-z

Belgaum, M. R., Alansari, Z., Musa, S., Alam, M. M., & Mazliham, M. S. (2021). Role of artificial intelligence in cloud computing, IoT and SDN: Reliability and scalability issues. *Iranian Journal of Electrical and Computer Engineering*, 11(5), 4458. 10.11591/ijece.v11i5.pp4458-4470

Bellanger, P. (2012). De la souveraineté numérique. le Débat, (3), 149-159.

Bender, E. M., Gebru, T., McMillan-Major, A., & Shmitchell, S. (2021). On the Dangers of Stochastic Parrots: Can Language Models Be Too Big? *Proceedings of the 2021 ACM Conference on Fairness, Accountability, and Transparency*, 610-623. 10.1145/3442188.3445922

Bentalha, B. (2023). A Framework for Exploring the Global Performance of Service Supply Chain Management: A Qualitative Study. Government Impact on Sustainable and Responsible Supply Chain Management, 106-129.

Bentalha, B. (2024). Sustainable Supply Chain Management in Tourism: An Understanding of the Prospective Possibilities of Environmental Performance. In Implementing Sustainable Development Goals in the Service Sector (pp. 53-66). IGI Global.

Bentalha, B. (2020). Big-Data et Service Supply chain management: Challenges et opportunités. *International Journal of Business and Technology Studies*, 1(3).

Bentalha, B. (2022). Smart Technologies for a Sustainable Service Supply Chain: A Prospective Perspective. *Journal of Environmental Issues and Climate Change*, 1(1), 77–89. 10.59110/jeicc.v1i1.81

Bentalha, B., Hmioui, A., & Alla, L. (2020). La performance des entreprises de services: Un cadrage théorique d'un concept évolutif. *Alternatives Managériales Economiques*, 2(1), 58–78.

Bergmann, D. (2023, December 19). *What Is Llama 2 ?*https://www.ibm.com/topics/llama-2

Bertacchini, Y., Girardot, J. J., & Gramaccia, G. (2006, June). De l'intelligence territoriale. Théorie, posture, hypothèses, définitions. In 5e colloque TIC et Territoire: quels développements?

bestpsychologydegree. (2014, April 15). *30 most unethical psychology human experiments*. https://www.bestpsychologydegrees.com/30-most-disturbing-human-experiments-in-history/

Bharadiya, J. (2023). A comprehensive survey of deep learning techniques natural language processing. *European Journal of Technology*, 7(1), 58–66. 10.47672/ejt.1473

Bhattacherjee, A. (2012). *Social science research: Principles, methods, and practices* (2nd ed.). University of South Florida.

Biamonte, J., Wittek, P., Pancotti, N., Rebentrost, P., Wiebe, N., & Lloyd, S. (2017). Quantum machine learning. *Nature*, 549(7671), 195–202. 10.1038/nature2347428905917

Biggio, B., & Roli, F. (2018). Wild patterns: Ten years after the rise of adversarial machine learning. *Pattern Recognition*, 84, 317–331. 10.1016/j.patcog.2018.07.023

Billeter, Y., Denzel, P., Chavarriaga, R., Forster, O., Schilling, F.-P., Brunner, S., Frischknecht-Gruber, C., Reif, M. U., & Weng, J. (2024). MLOps as enabler of trustworthy AI. 10.21256/ZHAW-30443

Birhane, A., Steed, R., Ojewale, V., Vecchione, B., & Raji, I. D. (2024). *AI auditing: The Broken Bus on the Road to AI Accountability*. 10.1109/SaTML59370.2024.00037

Bishop, M. V., Ólafsdóttir, R., Michaud, T., & Metcalf, C. (2024). Crowdsourced mapping of tourism distribution and dynamics in Iceland using Flickr. *Scandinavian Journal of Hospitality and Tourism*, •••, 1–17. 10.1080/15022250.2024.2355905

Blanchard, A., & Taddeo, M. (2023). The ethics of artificial intelligence for intelligence analysis: A review of the key challenges with recommendations. *Digital Society : Ethics, Socio-Legal and Governance of Digital Technology*, 2(1), 12. 10.1007/s44206-023-00036-437034181

Bogachov, S., Kwilinski, A., Miethlich, B., Bartosova, V., & Gurnak, A. (2020). Artificial intelligence components and fuzzy regulators in entrepreneurship development. *Entrepreneurship and Sustainability Issues*, 8(2), 487–499. 10.9770/jesi.2020.8.2(29)

Bompelli, A., Wang, Y., Wan, R., Singh, E., Zhou, Y., Xu, L., Oniani, D., Kshatriya, B. S. A., Balls-Berry, J. E., & Zhang, R. (2021). Social and Behavioral Determinants of Health in the Era of Artificial Intelligence with Electronic Health Records: A Scoping Review. In *Health Data Science* (Vol. 2021). 10.34133/2021/9759016

Bostrom, N. (2020). Ethical Issues in Advanced Artificial Intelligence. In Wallach, W., & Asaro, P. (Eds.), *Machine Ethics and Robot Ethics* (1st ed., pp. 69–75). Routledge., 10.4324/9781003074991-7

Bouchet, Y. (2003). Dispositif d'intelligence économique territoriale et gouvernance hybride, isdm.univ-fr/PDF/isdm27/isdm27_bouchet.pdf.

Bouchrika, I. (2014, February 12). *Top 10 qualities of good academic research in 2024*. Research.Com. https://research.com/research/top-10-qualities-of-good-academic-research

Bouhtati, N., Alla, L., & Bentalha, B. (2023). Marketing Big Data Analytics and Customer Relationship Management: A Fuzzy Approach. In Integrating Intelligence and Sustainability in Supply Chains (pp. 75-86). IGI Global. 10.4018/979-8-3693-0225-5.ch004

Bouhtati, N., Hmioui, A., Alla, L., & Bentalha, B. (2022). Logistique et performance touristique: Une étude comparative des principales destinations en Afrique. *Alternatives Managériales Economiques*, 1, 116–132.

Boulemtafes, A., Derhab, A., & Challal, Y. (2020). A review of privacy-preserving techniques for deep learning. *Neurocomputing*, 384, 21–45. 10.1016/j.neucom.2019.11.041

Brady, S. R. (2015). Utilizing and adapting the Delphi method for use in qualitative research. *International Journal of Qualitative Methods*, 14(5), 1–6. 10.1177/1609406915621381

Bragazzi, N. L., Dai, H., Damiani, G., Behzadifar, M., Martini, M., & Wu, J. (2020). How big data and artificial intelligence can help better manage the covid-19 pandemic. *International Journal of Environmental Research and Public Health*, 17(9), 3176. Advance online publication. 10.3390/ijerph17093176 32370204

Brand, J., Israeli, A., & Ngwe, D. (2023). Using GPT for market research. SSRN *Electronic Journal*. 10.2139/ssrn.4395751

Bremermann, T., Khaledi, M., & Brogan, J. (2022). Exploring Generative Artificial Intelligence for the Responsible Design of Trustworthy Systems. In *Proceedings of the 2022 ACM Conference on Fairness, Accountability, and Transparency* (pp. 1202-1213).

Brendel, A. B., Mirbabaie, M., Lembcke, T. B., & Hofeditz, L. (2021). Ethical management of artificial intelligence. *Sustainability (Basel)*, 13(4), 1974. 10.3390/su13041974

Breuer, C., Breuer, W., & Renerken, T. (2024). "In design and humans, we trust"? – Drivers of trust and advice discounting for robo advice. SSRN *Electronic Journal*. https://doi.org/10.2139/ssrn.4792439

Brock, A. (2023, July 23). Meta's Llama 2 is not open source and that's ok. *The New Stack*. https://thenewstack.io/metas-llama-2-is-not-open-source-and-thats-ok/

Brown, B. A. (2020). *Evaluating Expert Opinions for Reducing Voluntary Employee Absenteeism in Trinidad and Tobago* [Ph.D., Walden University]. http://search.proquest.com/pqdtglobal/docview/2447561234/abstract/1A8116E743549EAPQ/1

Brown, S. (2021, April 21). *Machine learning, explained.* https://mitsloan.mit.edu/ideas-made-to-matter/machine-learning-explained

Brown, T. B., Mann, B., Ryder, N., Subbiah, M., Kaplan, J. D., Dhariwal, P., . . . Amodei, D. (2020). Language Models are Few-Shot Learners. arXiv preprint arXiv:2005.14165.

Brown, T. B., Mann, B., Ryder, N., Subbiah, M., Kaplan, J., Dhariwal, P., Neelakantan, A., Shyam, P., Sastry, G., Askell, A., Agarwal, S., Voss, A. H., Krueger, G., Henighan, T., Child, R., Ramesh, A., Ziegler, D. M., Wu, J., Winter, C., . . . Amodei, D. (2020). Language Models are Few-Shot Learners. *Computation and Language.* https://doi.org//arXiv.2005.1416510.48550

Brown, B. A., & Heitner, K. L. (2022). Worker response to the rapid changes caused by disruptive innovation: Managing a remote workforce without any training or preparation. In Hynes, R., Aquino, C., & Hauer, J. (Eds.), *Multidisciplinary approach to diversity and inclusion in the COVID-19-era workplace* (pp. 189–205). IGI Global. 10.4018/978-1-7998-8827-7.ch011

Brown, B. A., & Heitner, K. L. (2023). Obstacles and resistance to organizational change in the new post-COVID-19 environment. In Belias, D., Rossidis, I., Papademetriou, C., Masouras, A., & Anastasiadou, S. (Eds.), *Managing successful and ethical organizational change* (pp. 167–195). IGI Global. 10.4018/979-8-3693-0235-4.ch008

Brown, B. A., & Heitner, K. L. (2024). International business staffing challenges and the growing global skills gap in the post-COVID environment: A Latin American and Caribbean perspective. In Christiansen, B., & Even, A. M. (Eds.), *Advancing student employability through higher education* (pp. 199–219). IGI Global. 10.4018/979-8-3693-0517-1.ch011

Brown, T., Mann, B., Ryder, N., Subbiah, M., Kaplan, J., Dhariwal, P., & Amodei, D. (2020). Language Models are Few-Shot Learners. *Advances in Neural Information Processing Systems*, 33, 1877–1901.

Brundage, M., Avin, S., Clark, J., Toner, H., Eckersley, P., Garfinkel, B., Dafoe, A., Scharre, P., Zeitzoff, T., Filar, B., Anderson, H., Roff, H., Allen, G. C., Steinhardt, J., & Flynn, C. hÉigeartaigh, S. Ó., Beard, S., Belfield, H., Farquhar, S., ... Amodei, D. (2018). *The Malicious Use of Artificial Intelligence: Forecasting, Prevention, and Mitigation* (arXiv:1802.07228). arXiv. http://arxiv.org/abs/1802.07228

Bruté de Rémur, D. (2009). Point de vue: pour une épistémologie de l'IE. Revue internationale d'intelligence économique, 1(1), 9-11. https://www.cairn.info/revue-internationale-d-intelligence-economique-2009-1-page-9.htm

Brynjolfsson, E., Li, D., & Raymond, L. R. (2023). *Generative AI at work* (No. w31161). National Bureau of Economic Research.

Bryson, J. J. (2020). The artificial intelligence of the ethics of artificial intelligence. *The Oxford handbook of ethics of AI*, 1.

Budhwar, P., Malik, A., De Silva, M. T. T., & Thevisuthan, P. (2022). Artificial intelligence – challenges and opportunities for international HRM: A review and research agenda. *International Journal of Human Resource Management*, 33(6), 1065–1097. 10.1080/09585192.2022.2035161

Buolamwini, J., & Gebru, T. (2018, February 4). Gender Shades: Intersectional Accuracy Disparities in Commercial Gender Classification. *Proceedings of Machine Learning Research*. Conference on Fairness, Accountability, and Transparency. https://proceedings.mlr.press/v81/buolamwini18a/buolamwini18a.pdf

Butlin, P. (2021). AI Alignment and Human Reward. *Proceedings of the 2021 AAAI/ACM Conference on AI, Ethics, and Society*, 437–445. 10.1145/3461702.3462570

Butt, S., Butt, H., & Gnanappiragasam, D. (2021). Unintentional consequences of artificial intelligence in dermatology for patients with skin of colour. *Clinical and Experimental Dermatology*, 46(7), 1333–1334. 10.1111/ced.1472633969523

Camino, R. D., Naveiro, R., & González-Sanguino, C. (2021). Synthetic data generation for cybersecurity dataset construction. *Entropy (Basel, Switzerland)*, 23(6), 688.34072438

Capraro, V., Di Paolo, R., Perc, M., & Pizziol, V. (2024). Language-based game theory in the age of artificial intelligence. *Journal of the Royal Society, Interface*, 21(212), 20230720. Advance online publication. 10.1098/rsif.2023.072038471531

Caragliu, A., & Del Bo, C. F. (2019). Smart innovative cities: The impact of Smart City policies on urban innovation. *Technological Forecasting and Social Change*, 142, 373–384. 10.1016/j.techfore.2018.07.022

Carlos, H. A., Shi, X., Sargent, J., Tanski, S., & Berke, E. M. (2010). Density estimation and adaptive bandwidths: A primer for public health practitioners. *International Journal of Health Geographics*, 9(1), 39. Advance online publication. 10.1186/1476-072X-9-3920653969

Carrillo, M. R. (2020). Artificial intelligence: From ethics to law. *Telecommunications Policy*, 44(6), 101937. 10.1016/j.telpol.2020.101937

Casale, J., Taylor, A., & Crane, J. (2023). Albert M. Kligman, MD (1916-2010): A controversial genius in the field of dermatology. *The Journal of Clinical and Aesthetic Dermatology*, 16(1), 13.36743970

Cascella, M., Tracey, M. C., Petrucci, E., & Bignami, E. G. (2023). Exploring artificial intelligence in anesthesia: A primer on ethics, and clinical applications. *Surgeries*, 4(2), 264–274. 10.3390/surgeries4020027

Centers for Disease Control and Prevention. (2024, March 7). *Public Health Service study of untreated syphilis at Tuskegee and Macon County, AL - timeline*. https://www.cdc.gov/tuskegee/timeline.htm

Ch'ng, L. K. (2024). Standing on the Shoulders of Generative AI. In *Transforming Education with Generative AI: Prompt Engineering and Synthetic Content Creation* (pp. 1-21). IGI Global. 10.4018/979-8-3693-1351-0.ch001

Chalmers, D., MacKenzie, N. G., & Carter, S. (2021). Artificial Intelligence and Entrepreneurship: Implications for Venture Creation in the Fourth Industrial Revolution. *Entrepreneurship Theory and Practice*, 45(5), 1028–1053. 10.1177/1042258720934581

Chan, K. Y., Abu-Salih, B., Qaddoura, R., Al-Zoubi, A. M., Palade, V., Pham, D.-S., Ser, J. D., & Muhammad, K. (2023). Deep neural networks in the cloud: Review, applications, challenges and research directions. *Neurocomputing*, 545, 126327. 10.1016/j.neucom.2023.126327

Chatila, R., & Havens, J. C. (2019). The IEEE Global Initiative on Ethics of Autonomous and Intelligent Systems. In Aldinhas Ferreira, M. I., Silva Sequeira, J., Singh Virk, G., Tokhi, M. O., & Kadar, E. E. (Eds.), *Robotics and Well-Being* (Vol. 95, pp. 11–16). Springer International Publishing., 10.1007/978-3-030-12524-0_2

Chen, B., & Zhang, Z. Langren´ e, L., & Zhu, S.,(2024). Unleashing the potential of prompt engineering in Large Language Models: a comprehensive review, arXiv:2310.14735v4

Chen, L., Zaharia, M., & Zou, J. (2024). How Is ChatGPT's Behavior Changing Over Time? *Harvard Data Science Review*, (Special Issue 5), 1–26. 10.1162/99608f92.5317da47

Chen, W., Ma, X., Wang, X., & Cohen, W., (2023). Program of Thoughts Prompting: Disentangling Computation from Reasoning for Numerical Reasoning Tasks. *TMLR 2023*

Chen, Y., & Esmaeilzadeh, P. (2024). Generative AI in Medical Practice: In-Depth Exploration of Privacy and Security Challenges. *Journal of Medical Internet Research*, 26, e53008. 10.2196/5300838457208

Chesney, R., & Citron, D. K. (2019). Deep fakes: A looming challenge for privacy, democracy, and national security. *California Law Review*, 107(6), 1753–1820.

Chimbga, B. (2023). Exploring the Ethical and Societal Concerns of Generative AI in Internet of Things (IoT) Environments. In *Southern African Conference for Artificial Intelligence Research* (pp. 44-56). Cham: Springer Nature Switzerland. 10.1007/978-3-031-49002-6_4

Chuvieco, E. (2020). Fundamentals of Satellite Remote Sensing : An Environmental Approach, Third Edition. In *Fundamentals of Satellite Remote Sensing*.

Committee on Publication Ethics. (2024). *Authorship and contributorship*. COPE: Committee on Publication Ethics. https://publicationethics.org/authorship

Conitzer, V., Freedman, R., Heitzig, J., Holliday, W. H., Jacobs, B. M., Lambert, N., Mossé, M., Pacuit, E., Russell, S., Schoelkopf, H., Tewolde, E., & Zwicker, W. S. (2024). *Social Choice for AI Alignment: Dealing with Diverse Human Feedback* (arXiv:2404.10271). arXiv. http://arxiv.org/abs/2404.10271

Cordes, J., & Castro, M. C. (2020). Spatial analysis of COVID-19 clusters and contextual factors in New York City. *Spatial and Spatio-temporal Epidemiology*, 34, 100355. Advance online publication. 10.1016/j.sste.2020.10035532807400

Creswell, A., Shanahan, M., & Higgins, I. (2022). Selection-inference: Exploiting large language models for interpretable logical reasoning, https://arxiv.org/abs/2205.09712.

Cronbach, L. J. (1951). Coefficient alpha and the internal structure of tests. *Psychometrika*, 16(1), 297–334. 10.1007/BF02310555

D., & Sofat, S. (2022). Cyber security trends for 2022: Future focus areas for the security industry. In 2022 IEEE 6th International Conference for Convergence in Technology (I2CT) (pp. 1-6). IEEE.

Dang, H., Liang, Y., & Liu, F. (2022). A survey on DeepFake: Overview, detection, and prevention. *ACM Computing Surveys*, 55(5), 1–43.

Dankwa-Mullan, I., Scheufele, E. L., Matheny, M. E., Quintana, Y., Chapman, W. W., Jackson, G., & South, B. R. (2021). A Proposed Framework on Integrating Health Equity and Racial Justice into the Artificial Intelligence Development Lifecycle. *Journal of Health Care for the Poor and Underserved*, 32(2S), 300–317. 10.1353/hpu.2021.0065

David, A., & Jeganathan, G. S., & MD Sikandar Azam, S. A. (2023, May). Internet Users Top Concerns Ensuring Data Privacy, Security, and Protection. *10th International Conference on Multidisciplinary Research and Modern Education, ISBN* (No. 978-920, pp. 5-20241).

David, A., Jeganathan, G. S., Sikandar, M. D., & Azam, S. A. (2023, May). Internet Users Top Concerns Ensuring Data Privacy, Security, and Protection. In *Arokiaraj David, Jeganathan Gomathi Sankar & Md Sikandar Azam, —Internet Users Top Concerns Ensuring Data Privacy, Security, and Protection , 10th International Conference on Multidisciplinary Research and Modern Education, ISBN* (No. 978-920, pp. 5-20241).

David, A., Ahmed, R. R., Ganesh Kumar, C., & Sankar, J. G. (2020). Consumer purchasing process of organic food product: An empirical analysis. *Journal of Management Systems. Quality - Access to Success*, 21(177), 128–132.

David, A., Kumar, C. G., & Paul, P. V. (2022). Blockchain technology in the food supply chain: Empirical analysis. *International Journal of Information Systems and Supply Chain Management*, 15(3), 1–12. 10.4018/IJISSCM.290014

David, A., Maheswari, M., Sankar, G., Christy, F., Karuppannan, A., & Banumathi, M. (2023). Mental illness of Pregnant Women determined by Covid-19: An Empirical Analysis of Pre-and- Post Delivery. *The Saybold Report Journal*, 18(03), 1706–1721.

DeAngelis, T. (2010). Mystery solved: We now know what happened to Little Albert. *American Psychological Association, 41*(1). https://www.apa.org/monitor/2010/01/little-albert

Deng, S., Zhao, H., Fang, W., Yin, J., Dustdar, S., & Zomaya, A. Y. (2020). Edge intelligence: The confluence of edge computing and artificial intelligence. *IEEE Internet of Things Journal*, 7(8), 7457–7469. 10.1109/JIOT.2020.2984887

Descartes, R. (1984). *The philosophical writings of Descartes*. Cambridge University Press.

Desroches, F. J. (1990). Tearoom trade: A research update. *Qualitative Sociology*, 13(1), 39–61. 10.1007/BF00988595

Dhoni, P., & Kumar, R. (2023). Synergizing generative ai and cybersecurity: Roles of generative ai entities, companies, agencies, and government in enhancing cybersecurity. *Authorea Preprints*.

Di Vaio, A., Palladino, R., Hassan, R., & Escobar, O. (2020). Artificial intelligence and business models in the sustainable development goals perspective: A systematic literature review. *Journal of Business Research*, 121(August), 283–314. 10.1016/j.jbusres.2020.08.019

Díaz-Rodríguez, N., Del Ser, J., Coeckelbergh, M., de Prado, M. L., Herrera-Viedma, E., & Herrera, F. (2023). Connecting the dots in trustworthy Artificial Intelligence: From AI principles, ethics, and key requirements to responsible AI systems and regulation. *Information Fusion*, 99, 101896. 10.1016/j.inffus.2023.101896

DiBenedetto, C. (2024, March 8). *AI shows clear racial bias when used for job recruiting, new tests reveal*. Mashable. https://mashable.com/article/openai-chatgpt-racial-bias-in-recruiting

Dicuonzo, G., Donofrio, F., Fusco, A., & Shini, M. (2023). Healthcare system: Moving forward with artificial intelligence. *Technovation*, 120, 102510. Advance online publication. 10.1016/j.technovation.2022.102510

Dieterle, C. (2020). The case for environmentally-informed occupational therapy: Clinical and educational applications to promote personal wellness, public health and environmental sustainability. *World Federation of Occupational Therapists Bulletin*, 76(1), 32–39. Advance online publication. 10.1080/14473828.2020.1717055

Dirican, C. (2015). The Impacts of Robotics, Artificial Intelligence On Business and Economics. *Procedia: Social and Behavioral Sciences*, 195, 564–573. 10.1016/j.sbspro.2015.06.134

Doshi-Velez, F., & Kim, B. (2017). Towards a rigorous science of interpretable machine learning. arXiv preprint arXiv:1702.08608.

Doss, C., Mondschein, J., Shu, D., Wolfson, T., Kopecky, D., Fitton-Kane, V. A., Bush, L., & Tucker, C. (2023). Deepfakes and scientific knowledge dissemination. *Scientific Reports*, 13(1), 13429. 10.1038/s41598-023-39944-337596384

Drapkin, A. (2024, March 13). Google Gemini vs ChatGPT: Which AI chatbot wins in 2024? *Tech.Co*. https://tech.co/news/google-bard-vs-chatgpt

Duan, S., Wang, D., Ren, J., Lyu, F., Zhang, Y., Wu, H., & Shen, X. (2022). Distributed artificial intelligence empowered by end-edge-cloud computing: A survey. *IEEE Communications Surveys and Tutorials*, 25(1), 591–624. 10.1109/COMST.2022.3218527

Dubey, R., Gunasekaran, A., Childe, S. J., Bryde, D. J., Giannakis, M., Foropon, C., Roubaud, D., & Hazen, B. T. (2019). Big data analytics and artificial intelligence pathway to operational performance under the effects of entrepreneurial orientation and environmental dynamism: A study of manufacturing organisations. *International Journal of Production Economics*, 226, 107599. 10.1016/j.ijpe.2019.107599

Duggal, I., & Tripathi, T. (2024). Ethical principles in dental healthcare: Relevance in the current technological era of artificial intelligence. *Journal of Oral Biology and Craniofacial Research*, 14(3), 317–321. 10.1016/j.jobcr.2024.04.00338645705

Du, H., Anand, S., Alechina, N., Morley, J., Hart, G., Leibovici, D., Jackson, M., & Ware, M. (2012). Geospatial Information Integration for Authoritative and Crowd Sourced Road Vector Data. *Transactions in GIS*, 16(4), 455–476. 10.1111/j.1467-9671.2012.01303.x

Dumont, G. F. (2021). La souveraineté numérique des territoires à l'ère du numérique. Revue française d'administration publique, 177(1), 95-108.

Dunmore, A., Jang-Jaccard, J., Sabrina, F., & Kwak, J. (2023). A comprehensive survey of generative adversarial networks (gans) in cybersecurity intrusion detection. *IEEE Access : Practical Innovations, Open Solutions*, 11, 76071–76094. 10.1109/ACCESS.2023.3296707

Durkheim, E. (1972). *Emile Durkheim: Selected writings*. Cambridge University Press. 10.1017/CBO9780511628085

Du, S., & Xie, C. (2021). Paradoxes of artificial intelligence in consumer markets: Ethical challenges and opportunities. *Journal of Business Research*, 129, 961–974. 10.1016/j.jbusres.2020.08.024

Economic Commission for Latin America and the Caribbean. (2022). *A digital path for sustainable development in Latin America and the Caribbean*. https://repositorio.cepal.org/handle/11362/48461

Egan, J. (2024, March 18). *How to spot AI-generated lies on a resume*. https://www.shrm.org/topics-tools/news/technology/how-to-spot-ai-generated-lies-on-a-resume

Eightfold, A. I. (2022). *The future of work: Intelligent by design*. https://eightfold.ai/wp-content/uploads/2022_Talent_Survey.pdf

El Khatib, M. M., Al-Nakeeb, A., & Ahmed, G. (2019). Integration of Cloud Computing with Artificial Intelligence and Its Impact on Telecom Sector—A Case Study. *iBusiness, 11*(01), 1.

Elgammal, A., Liu, B., Elhoseiny, M., & Mazzone, M. (2017). CAN: Creative Adversarial Networks, Generating" Art" by Learning About Styles and Deviating from Style Norms. arXiv preprint arXiv:1706.07068.

Elias, G. (2023, March 17). *Common issues with ChatGPT and how to mitigate them.* https://skimai.com/common-issues-with-chatgpt/

Elias, J. (2023). Generative AI can help India close the technology divide, NVIDIA CEO Jensen Huang. INDIAai. https://indiaai.gov.in/article/generative-ai-can-help-india-close-the-technology-divide-nvidia-ceo-jensen-huang

Eloundou, T., Manning, S., Mishkin, P., & Rock, D. (2023). GPTs are GPTs: An early look at the labour market impact potential of large language models. http://arxiv.org/abs/2303.10130

Elshawi, R., Al-Mallah, M. H., Eldessouki, M. S., & Hassan, M. M. (2021). The Intersection of Cybersecurity, Artificial Intelligence and Machine Learning: A Literature Review. *Security and Privacy*, 4(6), e165.

Enholm, I. M., Papagiannidis, E., Mikalef, P., & Krogstie, J. (2022). Artificial intelligence and glaucoma: A literature review. *Journal Français d'Ophtalmologie*, 45(2), 216–232. 10.1016/j.jfo.2021.11.00234991909

Esteva, A., Robicquet, A., Ramsundar, B., Kuleshov, V., DePristo, M., Chou, K., Cui, C., Corrado, G., Thrun, S., & Dean, J. (2019). A guide to deep learning in healthcare. *Nature Medicine*, 25(1), 24–29. 10.1038/s41591-018-0316-z30617335

European Commission. (2024, March 6). *AI Act | Shaping Europe's digital future.* https://digital-strategy.ec.europa.eu/en/policies/regulatory-framework-ai

Fangerau, H. (2024). Artifical intelligence in surgery: Ethical considerations in the light of social trends in the perception of health and medicine. *EFORT Open Reviews*, 9(5), 323–328. 10.1530/EOR-24-002938726973

Fanni, S. C., Febi, M., Aghakhanyan, G., & Neri, E. (2023). Natural language processing. In *Introduction to Artificial Intelligence* (pp. 87–99). Springer International Publishing. 10.1007/978-3-031-25928-9_5

Feng, Q., Li, P., Lu, Z., Li, C., Wang, Z., Liu, Z., & Weng, J. (2024). Evit: Privacy-preserving image retrieval via encrypted vision transformer in cloud computing. *IEEE Transactions on Circuits and Systems for Video Technology*, 1. 10.1109/TCSVT.2024.3370668

Feuerriegel, S., Hartmann, J., Janiesch, C., & Zschech, P. (2023). Generative AI. http://arxiv.org/abs/2309.07930

Feuerriegel, S., Hartmann, J., Janiesch, C., & Zschech, P. (2024). Generative ai. *Business & Information Systems Engineering*, 66(1), 111–126. 10.1007/s12599-023-00834-7

Flores-Vivar, J. M., & García-Peñalvo, F. J. (2023). Reflections on the ethics, potential, and challenges of artificial intelligence in the framework of quality education (SDG4). *Comunicar*, 31(74), 37–47. 10.3916/C74-2023-03

Floridi, L., Cowls, J., Beltrametti, M., Chatila, R., Chazerand, P., Dignum, V., Luetge, C., Madelin, R., Pagallo, U., Rossi, F., Schafer, B., Valcke, P., & Vayena, E. (2018). AI4People—An Ethical Framework for a Good AI Society: Opportunities, Risks, Principles, and Recommendations. *Minds and Machines*, 28(4), 689–707. 10.1007/s11023-018-9482-530930541

Frey, C. B., & Osborne, M. (2023). Generative AI and the future of work: A reappraisal. *The Brown Journal of World Affairs*, 30(1).

Fridlund, A. J., Beck, H. P., Goldie, W. D., & Irons, G. (2012). Little Albert: A neurologically impaired child. *History of Psychology*, 15(4), 302–327. 10.1037/a002672023397921

Fui-Hoon Nah, F., Zheng, R., Cai, J., Siau, K., & Chen, L. (2023). Generative AI and ChatGPT: Applications, challenges, and AI-human collaboration. *Journal of Information Technology Case and Application Research*, 25(3), 277–304. 10.1080/15228053.2023.2233814

Ganesh, P., Chen, Y., Lou, X., Khan, M. A., Yang, Y., Chen, D., . . . Hao, Z. (2020). Efficient and Robust Machine Learning for Cybersecurity: A Survey. arXiv preprint arXiv:2010.09114.

Ganeshkumar, C., Sankar, J. G., & David, A. (2023). Impact of Artificial Intelligence on Agriculture Value Chain Performance: Agritech Perspective. In *Blockchain, IoT, and AI Technologies for Supply Chain Management* (pp. 71-98). CRC Press.

Ganeshkumar, C., David, A., & Jebasingh, D. R. (2022). Digital transformation: artificial intelligence-based product benefits and problems of Agritech industry. In *Agri-Food 4.0* (Vol. 27, pp. 141–163). Emerald Publishing Limited. 10.1108/S1877-636120220000027010

Ganeshkumar, C., David, A., & Sankar, J. G. (2024). Blockchain Technology Acceptance in Agribusiness Industry. In *Blockchain Transformations: Navigating the Decentralized Protocols Era* (pp. 239–260). Springer Nature Switzerland. 10.1007/978-3-031-49593-9_15

Ganeshkumar, C., David, A., Sankar, J. G., & Saginala, M. (2023). Application of Drone Technology in Agriculture: A Predictive Forecasting of Pest and Disease Incidence. In *Applying Drone Technologies and Robotics for Agricultural Sustainability* (pp. 50–81). IGI Global.

Ganeshkumar, C., Sankar, J. G., & David, A. (2023). Adoption of Big Data Analytics: Determinants and Performances Among Food Industries. *International Journal of Business Intelligence Research*, 14(1), 1–17. 10.4018/IJBIR.317419

Gao, C., & Yu, J. (2023). SecureRC: A system for privacy-preserving relation classification using secure multi-party computation. *Computers & Security*, 128, 103142. 10.1016/j.cose.2023.103142

Gao, P., Han, J., Lin, Z., Yang, J., & Yuan, J. (2021). Interactive Question Answering System for Multi-modal Information Retrieval. *Information Processing & Management*, 58(1), 102439.

Garbuio, M., & Lin, N. (2018). Artificial intelligence as a growth engine for health care startups: Emerging business models. *California Management Review*, 61(2), 59–83. 10.1177/0008125618811931

García-Macía, J., Torralvo, C., Onrubia, A., Ferrer, M., & Morandini, V. (2024). Dispersal patterns of the first White-backed Vulture (Gyps africanus) GPS-tracked in Iberia. *Journal of Ornithology*, 165(3), 815–821. Advance online publication. 10.1007/s10336-024-02167-y

Garg, S. (2023, June 25). *ChatGPT alternatives that will blow your mind in 2023*. The Writesonic Blog - Making Content Your Superpower. https://writesonic.com/blog/chatgpt-alternatives/

Garzotto, F., Ceresola, E., Panagiotakopoulou, S., Spina, G., Menotto, F., Benozzi, M., Casarotto, M., Lanera, C., Bonavina, M. G., Gregori, D., Meneghesso, G., & Opocher, G. (2020). COVID-19: Ensuring our medical equipment can meet the challenge. *Expert Review of Medical Devices*, 17(6), 483–489. Advance online publication. 10.1080/17434440.2020.177275732434400

Gazala, N. (2021). Generative AI & Synthetic Media: A new era of advertisements. INDIAai. https://indiaai.gov.in/article/generative-ai-synthetic-media-a-new-era-of-advertisements

Geisel, A. (2018). The current and future impact of artificial intelligence on business. *International Journal of Scientific and Technology Research*, 7(5), 116–122.

Gerolemou, M. (2019). Staging artificial intelligence. *The Routledge Handbook of Classics and Cognitive Theory, 45*(3), 345–355. 10.4324/9781315691398-22

Ghooi, R. B. (2011). The Nuremberg Code–A critique. *Perspectives in Clinical Research*, 2(2), 72–76. 10.4103/2229-3485.8037121731859

Gill, S. S., & Kaur, R. (2023). ChatGPT: Vision and challenges. *Internet of Things and Cyber-Physical Systems*, 3, 262–271. 10.1016/j.iotcps.2023.05.004

Gill, S. S., Xu, M., Ottaviani, C., Patros, P., Bahsoon, R., Shaghaghi, A., Golec, M., Stankovski, V., Wu, H., Abraham, A., Singh, M., Mehta, H., Ghosh, S. K., Baker, T., Parlikad, A. K., Lutfiyya, H., Kanhere, S. S., Sakellariou, R., Dustdar, S., & Uhlig, S. (2022). AI for next generation computing: Emerging trends and future directions. *Internet of Things : Engineering Cyber Physical Human Systems*, 19, 100514. 10.1016/j.iot.2022.100514

Giuggioli, G., & Pellegrini, M. M. (2022). Artificial intelligence as an enabler for entrepreneurs: A systematic literature review and an agenda for future research. *International Journal of Entrepreneurial Behaviour & Research*. Advance online publication. 10.1108/IJEBR-05-2021-0426

Gomes, E. D. C. (2024). *Improving artificial intelligence reliability through out-of-distribution and misclassification detection* [Doctor Thesis, Université Paris-Saclay]. https://theses.hal.science/tel-04551331/document

Goodfellow, I., Bengio, Y., & Courville, A. (2016). *Deep learning*. MIT press.

Goodfellow, I., Pouget-Abadie, J., Mirza, M., Xu, B., Warde-Farley, D., Ozair, S., & Bengio, Y. (2014). Generative Adversarial Nets. *Advances in Neural Information Processing Systems*, 27, 2672–2680.

Goodfellow, I., Pouget-Abadie, J., Mirza, M., Xu, B., Warde-Farley, D., Ozair, S., & Bengio, Y. (2014). Generative adversarial nets. *Advances in Neural Information Processing Systems*, 27.

Google. (n.d.-a). *Gemini—Chat to supercharge your ideas*. Gemini. Retrieved April 15, 2024, from https://gemini.google.com

Google. (n.d.-b). *Gemma open models*. Google for Developers. Retrieved May 11, 2024, from https://ai.google.dev/gemma

Gordon, T., Booysen, F., & Mbonigaba, J. (2020). Socio-economic inequalities in the multiple dimensions of access to healthcare: The case of South Africa. *BMC Public Health*, 20(1), 289. Advance online publication. 10.1186/s12889-020-8368-732131787

Gourvennec, Y., & Kabla, H. (2017). *Le digital expliqué à mon boss - Par ceux qui en font et pour ceux qui aimeraient (mieux) en faire, par David Fayon*. Editions Kawa.

GPTZero. (2023). *GPTZero*. GPTZero. https://gptzero.me/

Grammarly Inc. (2024). *Plagiarism checker | grammarly*. https://www.grammarly.com/www.grammarly.com/plagiarism-checker

Gross, T. (2019, September 9). The CIA's secret quest for mind control: Torture, LSD and a "poisoner In chief." *NPR*. https://www.npr.org/2019/09/09/758989641/the-cias-secret-quest-for-mind-control-torture-lsd-and-a-poisoner-in-chief

Guhlincozzi, A. R. (2024). Making visible the Chicagoland suburban healthcare landscape of latina women: A qualitative GIS approach. *Social & Cultural Geography*, 25(2), 1–20. Advance online publication. 10.1080/14649365.2022.2139857

Guo, J., Ling, X., & Yin, H. (2022). Automated vulnerability discovery and patching with deep learning. arXiv preprint arXiv:2204.07142.

Gupta, M., Akiri, C., Aryal, K., Parker, E., & Praharaj, L. (2023). From chatgpt to threatgpt: Impact of generative ai in cybersecurity and privacy. *IEEE Access : Practical Innovations, Open Solutions*, 11, 80218–80245. 10.1109/ACCESS.2023.3300381

Hacker, P., Engel, A., & Mauer, M. (2023, June). Regulating ChatGPT and other large generative AI models. In *Proceedings of the 2023 ACM Conference on Fairness, Accountability, and Transparency* (pp. 1112-1123). 10.1145/3593013.3594067

Hadfield-Menell, D., Dragan, A., Abbeel, P., & Russell, S. (2016). *Cooperative Inverse Reinforcement Learning*. 10.48550/ARXIV.1606.03137

Haman, M., & Školník, M. (2023). Using ChatGPT to conduct a literature review. *Accountability in Research*, 3, 1–3. Advance online publication. 10.1080/08989621.2023.218551436879536

Haney, C., & Zimbardo, P. (1998). The past and future of U.S. prison policy: Twenty-five years after the Stanford Prison Experiment. *The American Psychologist*, 53(7), 709–727. 10.1037/0003-066X.53.7.7099699456

Harding, J. (2010). Vector Data Quality: A Data Provider's Perspective. In *Fundamentals of Spatial Data Quality*. 10.1002/9780470612156.ch8

Harney, B., & Collings, D. (2021). Navigating the shifting landscapes of HRM. *Human Resource Management Review*, 31(4), 100824. 10.1016/j.hrmr.2021.100824

Hartmann, J., Exner, Y., & Domdey, S. (2023). The power of generative marketing: Can generative AI reach human-level visual marketing content? SSRN *Electronic Journal*, (April). 10.2139/ssrn.4597899

Hashemi-Pour, C., & Lutkevich, B. (n.d.). *What is the BERT language model?* Enterprise AI. Retrieved May 4, 2024, from https://www.techtarget.com/searchenterpriseai/definition/BERT-language-model

Hasimi, L., Zavantis, D., Shakshuki, E., & Yasar, A. (2024). Cloud Computing Security and Deep Learning: An ANN approach. *Procedia Computer Science*, 231, 40–47. 10.1016/j.procs.2023.12.155

Hauschild, A. C., Lemanczyk, M., Matschinske, J., Frisch, T., Zolotareva, O., Holzinger, A., Baumbach, J., & Heider, D. (2022). Federated Random Forests can improve local performance of predictive models for various healthcare applications. *Bioinformatics (Oxford, England)*, 38(8), 2278–2286. Advance online publication. 10.1093/bioinformatics/btac06535139148

Heidari, A., Jafari Navimipour, N., Dag, H., & Unal, M. (2024). Deepfake detection using deep learning methods: A systematic and comprehensive review. *Wiley Interdisciplinary Reviews. Data Mining and Knowledge Discovery*, 14(2), e1520. 10.1002/widm.1520

Helal, M., Holthaus, P., Lakatos, G., & Amirabdollahian, F. (2023). *Chat Failures and Troubles: Reasons and Solutions*. 10.48550/ARXIV.2309.03708

Heller, J. (2017, May 10). *AP was there: Black men untreated in Tuskegee syphilis study*. AP News. https://apnews.com/article/business-science-health-race-and-ethnicity-syphilis-e9dd07eaa4e74052878a68132cd3803a

Helsinger, L. (2024, March 11). *1,000 equally-qualified resumes, different names. Guess which ones gpt 3.5 place at the top and bottom ranks?*https://www.linkedin.com/pulse/1000-equally-qualified-resumes-different-names-guess-which-helsinger-x4gac/

Hermann, E. (2022). Leveraging artificial intelligence in marketing for social good—An ethical perspective. *Journal of Business Ethics*, 179(1), 43–61. 10.1007/s10551-021-04843-y34054170

Hijmans, R. J. (2020). raster: Geographic analysis and modeling with raster data. : *R Package Version 3.1-5, 3.1*(5).

Hilario, E., Azam, S., Sundaram, J., Imran Mohammed, K., & Shanmugam, B. (2024). Generative AI for pentesting: The good, the bad, the ugly. *International Journal of Information Security*, 23(3), 1–23. 10.1007/s10207-024-00835-x

Hmioui, A., Alla, L., & Bentalha, B. (2022). Perception du tourisme durable par les clients étrangers: Cas du séjour dans un établissement hôtelier. ENCG, USMBA, Fès. Reconfigurations du tourisme en contexte de la crise du Covid-19: Quelles démarches pour quelles résiliences au Maroc et ailleurs ?, 1(1), pp.5-38, 2022, 978-9954-9721-2-0.

Hmioui, A., Alla, L., & Bentalha, B. (2017). *Pilotage de la touristicité territoriale au Maroc Proposition d'un indice de touriscticité pour la destination Fès. Entrepreneuriat, Innovation, Gouvernance et Développement territorial.* Faculté Polydisciplinaire de TAZA.

Hmioui, A., Alla, L., & Bentalha, B. (2019). La performance touristique territoriale: Cas de la destination Fès. *Alternatives Managériales Economiques*, 1(1), 3–21.

Hmioui, A., Bentalha, B., & Beniaich, R. (2024). Green Supply Chain Management et développement territorial: Une revue de littérature. *Alternatives Managériales Economiques*, 6(2), 52–74.

Holmes, W., & Porayska-Pomsta, K. (Eds.). (2022). *The Ethics of Artificial Intelligence in education: Practices, challenges, and debates*. Taylor & Francis. 10.4324/9780429329067

Horton, J. J. (2023). *Large language models as simulated economic agents: What can we learn from homo silicus?* (Working Paper 31122). National Bureau of Economic Research. 10.3386/w31122

Hossain, M. T., Afrin, R., & Biswas, M. A. A. (2024). A Review on Attacks against Artificial Intelligence (AI) and Their Defence Image Recognition and Generation Machine Learning, Artificial Intelligence. *Control Systems and Optimization Letters*, 2(1), 52–59.

Hosseini, M., Rasmussen, L. M., & Resnik, D. B. (2023). Using AI to write scholarly publications. *Accountability in Research*, 1–9. 10.1080/08989621.2023.2168 53536697395

Hosseini, M., & Resnik, D. B. (2024). Guidance needed for using artificial intelligence to screen journal submissions for misconduct. *Research Ethics*, 17470161241254052. Advance online publication. 10.1177/17470161241254052

Hua, H., Li, Y., Wang, T., Dong, N., Li, W., & Cao, J. (2023). Edge computing with artificial intelligence: A machine learning perspective. *ACM Computing Surveys*, 55(9), 1–35. 10.1145/3555802

Huang, C., Zhang, Z., Mao, B., & Yao, X. (2022). An overview of artificial intelligence ethics. *IEEE Transactions on Artificial Intelligence*, 4(4), 799–819. 10.1109/TAI.2022.3194503

Huang, L., Song, M., Shen, H., Hong, H., Gong, P., Deng, H. W., & Zhang, C. (2023). Deep learning methods for omics data imputation. *Biology (Basel)*, 12(10), 1313. 10.3390/biology1210131337887023

Humphreys, D., Koay, A., Desmond, D., & Mealy, E. (2024). AI hype as a cyber security risk: The moral responsibility of implementing generative AI in business. *AI and Ethics*, 1–14. 10.1007/s43681-024-00443-4

Humphreys, L. (1975). *Tearoom trade, enlarged edition: Impersonal sex in public places*. Transaction Publishers.

Hu, S., Zhao, R., Cui, Y., Zhang, D., & Ge, Y. (2023). Identifying the uneven distribution of health and education services in China using open geospatial data. *Geography and Sustainability*, 4(2), 91–99. Advance online publication. 10.1016/j.geosus.2023.01.002

Hu, Y., Yang, K., Perdisci, R., & Lee, W. (2021). Generative adversarial network-based minority recreation for network intrusion detection. *IEEE Transactions on Network and Service Management*, 18(3), 2685–2696.

Hu, Y., Zhang, Q., Zhang, Q., & Jia, Y. (2024). A novel hashing-inverted index for secure content-based retrieval with massive encrypted speeches. *Multimedia Systems*, 30(1), 22. 10.1007/s00530-023-01229-0

Ibáñez Lissen, L., Fuentes García-Romero de Tejada, J. M. D., González Manzano, L., & García Alfaro, J. (2023). Characterizing poisoning attacks on generalistic multi-modal AI models. *Information Fusion*, 1–15.

IBM. (n.d.-a). *What is artificial intelligence (AI)?* Retrieved April 2, 2024, from https://www.ibm.com/topics/artificial-intelligence

IBM. (n.d.-b). *What Is machine learning (ML)?* Retrieved April 2, 2024, from https://www.ibm.com/topics/machine-learning

Insights, C. B. (2024, February 27). *The generative AI boom in 6 charts*. CB Insights Research; CB Insights. https://www.cbinsights.com/research/generative-ai-funding-top-startups-investors-2023/

International Committee of Medical Journal Editors. (2024). *Defining the role of authors and contributors*. https://www.icmje.org/recommendations/browse/roles-and-responsibilities/defining-the-role-of-authors-and-contributors.html

Iphofen, R., & Kritikos, M. (2021). Regulating artificial intelligence and robotics: Ethics by design in a digital society. *Contemporary Social Science*, 16(2), 170–184. 10.1080/21582041.2018.1563803

Iqbal, N., Ahmed, H., & Azhar, K. A. (2022). Exploring teachers' attitudes towards using ChatGPT. *Global Journal for Management and Administrative Sciences*, 3(4), 97–111. 10.46568/gjmas.v3i4.163

Ivanov, S. H., & Umbrello, S. (2021). The ethics of artificial intelligence and robotisation in tourism and hospitality–a conceptual framework and research agenda. *Journal of Smart Tourism*, 1(4), 9–18.

Jacob, S. (2024). *Can grammarly detect AI writing?*https://originality.ai

Jagatic, T. N., Johnson, N. A., Jakobsson, M., & Menczer, F. (2007). Social phishing. *Communications of the ACM*, 50(10), 94–100. 10.1145/1290958.1290968

Jain, V. (2019). Impact of Artificial Intelligence on Business. *Electronic Journal of Business Ethics and Organization Studies*, 24(2), 302–308.

Jalan, A. (2023, April 20). *7 ways generative AI will change the job market.* MUO. https://www.makeuseof.com/ways-ai-change-job-market/

Jancheski, M., & Jancheska, S. (2024). Unlocking the Future of Education: A Comprehensive Analysis of key documents shaping Artificial Intelligence in Education. 7834–7834. 10.21125/inted.2024.2098

Janowicz, K., Gao, S., McKenzie, G., Hu, Y., & Bhaduri, B. (2020). GeoAI: spatially explicit artificial intelligence techniques for geographic knowledge discovery and beyond. In *International Journal of Geographical Information Science* (Vol. 34, Issue 4). 10.1080/13658816.2019.1684500

JasonWei, J., Xuezhi Wang, X., Schuurmans, D., Maarten Bosma, M., Brian Ichter, B., Xia, F., Chi, E.H., Le, Q.V., & Zhou, D., (2023). Chain-of-Thought Prompting Elicits Reasoning in Large Language Models. *36th Conference on Neural Information Processing Systems.*

Jayatilake, S. M. D. A. C., & Ganegoda, G. U. (2021). Involvement of Machine Learning Tools in Healthcare Decision Making. In *Journal of Healthcare Engineering* (Vol. 2021). 10.1155/2021/6679512

Jeevanandam, N. (2022). Dall-E - the AI that creates images of everything. INDIAai. https://indiaai.gov.in/ article/dall-e-the-ai-that-creates-images-of-everything

Jeevanandam, N. (2023). Exploring Amazon Bedrock language model. INDIAai. https://indiaai.gov.in/ article/exploring-amazon-bedrock-language-model

Jeevanandam, N. (2023). Exploring Firefly - a generative AI model from Adobe. INDIAai. https://indiaai.gov.in/article/exploring-firefly-a-generative-ai-model-from-adobe

Jeganathan, G. S., & Srinivasulu, Y. Impact of tourism on macro–economic indicators: A Comparative study of BRICS nations.

Jeganathan, G. S., David, A., & Ganesh Kumar, C. (2022). Adaptation of Blockchain technology in HRM. *Korea Review of International Studies*, 10-22.

Jeganathan, G. S., David, A., & Ilangovan, K. (2022). Determination of Hospitality Services Quality and Customer Satisfaction–a Holserv Approach. In *AU Virtual International Conference on" Entrepreneurship & Sustainability in Digital Era" under the theme of" Challenges of Organizational & Business Management in Dynamic Digital Dimension"* (Vol. 3, No. 1, pp. 325-334).

Jeganathan, G. S., & Srinivasulu, Y. (2014). Growth Drivers of Tourism Industry in India. *International Journal of Business and Management*, 2(11), 100.

Jeleel-Ojuade, A. (2024). AI-driven knowledge management: Improving collaboration among business professionals in Nigeria. SSRN *Electronic Journal*. https://doi.org/10.2139/ssrn.4812002

Jiang, S., Kadhe, S. R., Zhou, Y., Cai, L., & Baracaldo, N. (2023). Forcing Generative Models to Degenerate Ones: The Power of Data Poisoning Attacks. arXiv preprint arXiv:2312.04748

Jiang, F., Jiang, Y., Zhi, H., Dong, Y., Li, H., Ma, S., Wang, Y., Dong, Q., Shen, H., & Wang, Y. (2017). Artificial intelligence in healthcare: Past, present and future. *Stroke and Vascular Neurology*, 2(4), 230–243. 10.1136/svn-2017-00010129507784

Jiang, W., Guo, Z., & Liang, R. (2023). Using ensemble models to detect deepfake images of human faces. In *Proceedings of the 2023 International Conference on Mathematics, Intelligent Computing and Machine Learning* (pp. 31-35). 10.1145/3638264.3638272

Jing, C., Zhou, W., Qian, Y., Zheng, Z., Wang, J., & Yu, W. (2023). Trajectory big data reveals spatial disparity of healthcare accessibility at the residential neighborhood scale. *Cities (London, England)*, 133, 104127. Advance online publication. 10.1016/j.cities.2022.104127

Ji, Z., Lee, N., Frieske, R., Yu, T., Su, D., Xu, Y., Ishii, E., Bang, Y., Madotto, A., & Fung, P. (2022). Survey of hallucination in Natural Language Generation. *ACM Computing Surveys*. Advance online publication. 10.1145/3571730

Jobin, A., Ienca, M., & Vayena, E. (2019). The global landscape of AI ethics guidelines. *Nature Machine Intelligence*, 1(9), 389–399. 10.1038/s42256-019-0088-2

Johnson, A. (2023, March 30). *Which jobs will AI replace? These 4 industries will be heavily impacted*. Forbes. https://www.forbes.com/sites/ariannajohnson/2023/03/30/which-jobs-will-ai-replace-these-4-industries-will-be-heavily-impacted/?sh=2dafa1ab5957

Johnson, R., Sharma, R., & Goodwin, S. (2022). AI and Education: Adaptive Learning Systems. *Journal of Educational Technology Development and Exchange*, 15(1), 45–59.

Johnston, J., & Cushing, L. (2020). Chemical Exposures, Health, and Environmental Justice in Communities Living on the Fenceline of Industry. In *Current environmental health reports* (Vol. 7, Issue 1). 10.1007/s40572-020-00263-8

Jouve, B., Booth, P., (dir.), (2004), *Démocraties métropolitaines*, PUQ, Sainte Foy.

Jumper, J., Evans, R., Pritzel, A., Green, T., Figurnov, M., Ronneberger, O., Tunyasuvunakool, K., Bates, R., Žídek, A., Potapenko, A., Bridgland, A., Meyer, C., Kohl, S. A. A., Ballard, A. J., Cowie, A., Romera-Paredes, B., Nikolov, S., Jain, R., Adler, J., & Hassabis, D. (2021). Highly accurate protein structure prediction with AlphaFold. *Nature*, 596(7873), 583–589. 10.1038/s41586-021-03819-234265844

Kaal, W. A. (2024). AI governance. SSRN *Electronic Journal*. https://doi.org/10.2139/ssrn.4796714

Kamel Boulos, M. N., Peng, G., & Vopham, T. (2019). An overview of GeoAI applications in health and healthcare. In *International Journal of Health Geographics* (Vol. 18, Issue 1). 10.1186/s12942-019-0171-2

Kang, Y., Gao, S., & Roth, R. E. (2024). Artificial intelligence studies in cartography: A review and synthesis of methods, applications, and ethics. *Cartography and Geographic Information Science*, 1–32. Advance online publication. 10.1080/15230406.2023.2295943

Kapil. (2023, June 20). The future of AI in India 2023: Unlocking boundless potential. *Team Tweaks Blog - Information on Latest Trends in IOT | App Development | Web Development | DevOps and All Other Technology Trends in Chennai - India*. https://www.teamtweaks.com/blog/future-of-ai-in-india-2023/

Kashif, M., David, A., Gupta, V. P., & Alam, S. (2024). Integration of Artificial Intelligence in the Financial Sector. In *Artificial Intelligence and Machine Learning-Powered Smart Finance* (pp. 96–108). IGI Global. 10.4018/979-8-3693-3264-1.ch005

Kasongo, S. M. (2023). A deep learning technique for intrusion detection system using a Recurrent Neural Networks based framework. *Computer Communications*, 199, 113–125. 10.1016/j.comcom.2022.12.010

Kazim, E., & Koshiyama, A. S. (2021). A high-level overview of AI ethics. *Patterns (New York, N.Y.)*, 2(9), 100314. 10.1016/j.patter.2021.10031434553166

Kenwright, B. (2023). Next Generation of the Web Will Engage Your Senses: Unleashing Interactive Web-Based XR Experiences. In *Concepts, Technologies, Challenges, and the Future of Web 3* (pp. 271-288). IGI Global.

Kereopa-Yorke, B. (2024). Quantifying AI Vulnerabilities: A Synthesis of Complexity, Dynamical Systems, and Game Theory (arXiv:2404.10782). arXiv. http://arxiv.org/abs/2404.1078210.2139/ssrn.4904749

Khaldun, I. (1986). *Muqaddimah*. Dar Ihya al-Tarats al-‘Arabi, t. th. https://d1wqtxts1xzle7.cloudfront.net/37760913/ibn_khaldun-al_muqaddimah-libre.pdf?1432817723=&response-content-disposition=inline%3B+filename%3DIbn_khaldun_al_muqaddimah.pdf&Expires=1710443771&Signature=G~Cklx9Vqx19NGMtXa4HOAfyToQp7n9LjBB6g3gACY96gzeih9u6y8dDWrD6mvOssJP5qTqEk4xc0cjx3EbGgyvgeqt6RhbZEIYmgFSlxLqxwU350XcdxEn1zLXVemt-cMANxzb-uCmNU54nfsaX52bhk50EYNcIstGyup8AVrOKLGg7iMZTMRMnu1Q54FHgfdLd67GeXv5Fhc~XZtN2EbfpOzoV1DcCnTlI9nYneNBhZXWfv1nRQsHrXI3BRpaHm7T~MVzq3eNNIsitBGQarITzfp8Dj~MjAZXhmBxS12hoYr3vuuLJNVbComhspAONoUwbBGELbPPSjf6A78X6PA__&Key-Pair-Id=APKAJLOHF5GGSLRBV4ZA

Khalid, N. (2020). Artificial intelligence learning and entrepreneurial performance among university students: Evidence from malaysian higher educational institutions. *Journal of Intelligent & Fuzzy Systems*, 39(4), 5417–5435. 10.3233/JIFS-189026

Kiden, S., Stahl, B., Townsend, B., Maple, C., Vincent, C., Sampson, F., Gilbert, G., Smith, H., Deshmukh, J., Ross, J., Williams, J., del Rincon, J. M., Lisinska, J., O'Shea, K., Da Costa Abreu, M., Bencomo, N., Deb, O., Winter, P., Li, P., & Yazdanpanah, V. (2024). *Responsible AI governance: A response to UN interim report on governing AI for humanity*. [object Object]. 10.5258/SOTON/PP0057

Kieslich, K., Keller, B., & Starke, C. (2022). Artificial intelligence ethics by design. Evaluating public perception on the importance of ethical design principles of artificial intelligence. *Big Data & Society*, 9(1), 20539517221092956. 10.1177/20539517221092956

Kietzmann, J., Lee, L. W., McCarthy, I. P., & Kietzmann, T. C. (2019). Deepfakes: Trick or treat? *Business Horizons*, 63(2), 135–146. 10.1016/j.bushor.2019.11.006

Kim, W. O. (2012). Institutional review board (IRB) and ethical issues in clinical research. *Korean Journal of Anesthesiology*, 62(1), 3–12. 10.4097/kjae.2012.62.1.322323947

King, M. R. (2022). The future of AI in medicine: A perspective from a chatbot. *Annals of Biomedical Engineering*, 51(2), 291–295. 10.1007/s10439-022-03121-w36572824

Krishna, G. G., & Tech, B.Department of Computer Science and Engineering, Lovely Professional University CSE Block, Guntur. (2023). Generative AI. *International Journal of Advanced Engineering and Nano Technology*, 10(8), 1–3. 10.35940/ijaent.G0474.0810823

Kshetri, N. (2017). Cybersecurity in developing economies: Key challenges and stakeholders. *IEEE Security and Privacy*, 15(6), 72–77.

Kuhn, T. S. (1996). *The structure of scientific revolutions* (3rd ed.). University of Chicago Press. 10.7208/chicago/9780226458106.001.0001

Kumar, S., Musharaf, D., Musharaf, S., & Sagar, A. K. (2023). A Comprehensive Review of the Latest Advancements in Large Generative AI Models. In *International Conference on Advanced Communication and Intelligent Systems* (pp. 90-103). Cham: Springer Nature Switzerland. 10.1007/978-3-031-45121-8_9

Kumar, P., Chauhan, S., & Awasthi, L. K. (2023). Artificial intelligence in healthcare: Review, ethics, trust challenges & future research directions. *Engineering Applications of Artificial Intelligence*, 120, 105894. 10.1016/j.engappai.2023.105894

Kumar, P., Kumar, A., & Sankar, J. G. (2020). Service quality of health tourism in India: A structural equation modelling approach. *Solid State Technology*, 63(2), 1187–1191.

Kurni, M., Mohammed, M. S., & Srinivasa, K. G. (2023). Ethics of Artificial Intelligence in Education. In *A Beginner's Guide to Introduce Artificial Intelligence in Teaching and Learning* (pp. 213–229). Springer International Publishing.

Lamsiah, A., & Bentalha, B. (2023). Moroccan jews and economic intelligence: the implicit power of belonging. Le concept de l'intelligence en sciences juridiques, économiques et sociales, pp.71-90, 978-9920-9012-4-6.

Lamsiah, A., Benabderrazik, Y., & Bentalha, B. (2021). The Economic and political components of diplomatic discourse: State actors in Morocco-UK Free Trade Agreement as a case study. *Alternatives Managériales Economiques*, 3(4), 496–517.

Lamsiah, A., & Bentalha, B. (2022a). Dakhla: A Growing Touristic Destination with a Diplomatic Sway. *Alternatives Managériales Economiques*, 1, 94–115.

Lamsiah, A., & Bentalha, B. (2022b). Economic Diplomacy and Economic Intelligence Amalgamation: The Moroccan-Nigerian Economic Exchange as a Case Study. *Alternatives Managériales Economiques*, 4(4), 582–603.

Larsson, S. (2020). On the governance of artificial intelligence through ethics guidelines. *Asian Journal of Law and Society*, 7(3), 437–451. 10.1017/als.2020.19

Lary, D. J., Alavi, A. H., Gandomi, A. H., & Walker, A. L. (2016). Machine learning in geosciences and remote sensing. *Geoscience Frontiers*, 7(1), 3–10. Advance online publication. 10.1016/j.gsf.2015.07.003

Latha, C. J., Sankriti, R., David, A., & Srivel, R. (2020). IoT based water purification process using ultrasonic aquatic sound waves. *Test Engineering & Management, The Mattingley Publishing Co., Inc. ISSN*, 0193-4120.

Lee, T.-K., Park, E. H., & Lee, M. H. (2024). Medical ethics and artificial intelligence in neurosurgery—How should we prepare? *World Neurosurgery*, S1878875024006296, e199–e209. Advance online publication. 10.1016/j.wneu.2024.04.06738641244

Legoux, G. (2023, April 16). *History of the generative AI - Gilles legoux*. Medium. https://medium.com/@glegoux/history-of-the-generative-ai-aa1aa7c63f3c

Leitch, R. (2021). Artificial intelligence in engineering. *Computing & Control Engineering Journal*, 3(4), 152–157. 10.1049/cce:19920042

Lévesque, M., Obschonka, M., & Nambisan, S. (2022). Pursuing Impactful Entrepreneurship Research Using Artificial Intelligence. *Entrepreneurship Theory and Practice*, 46(4), 803–832. 10.1177/1042258720927369

Li, W., & Hsu, C. Y. (2022). GeoAI for Large-Scale Image Analysis and Machine Vision: Recent Progress of Artificial Intelligence in Geography. In *ISPRS International Journal of Geo-Information* (Vol. 11, Issue 7). 10.3390/ijgi11070385

Lian, A. (2023). The Legal Implications of AI-Generated Content in Copyright Law. INDIAai. https://indiaai.gov.in/article/the-legal-implications-of-ai-generated-content-in-copyright-law

Li, B., Feng, Y., Xiong, Z., Yang, W., & Liu, G. (2021). Research on AI security enhanced encryption algorithm of autonomous IoT systems. *Information Sciences*, 575, 379–398. 10.1016/j.ins.2021.06.016

Li, B., Qi, P., Liu, B., Di, S., Liu, J., Pei, J., Yi, J., & Zhou, B. (2023). Trustworthy AI: From Principles to Practices. *ACM Computing Surveys*, 55(9), 1–46. 10.1145/3555803

Liberto, D. (2023, November 3). *Social science: What it is and the 5 major branches*. Investopedia. https://www.investopedia.com/terms/s/social-science.asp

Li, J. S., Liu, I. H., Tsai, C. J., Su, Z. Y., Li, C. F., & Liu, C. G. (2020). Secure content-based image retrieval in the cloud with key confidentiality. *IEEE Access : Practical Innovations, Open Solutions*, 8, 114940–114952. 10.1109/ACCESS.2020.3003928

Lin, L., Yang, H., & Xu, X. (2022). Effects of Water Pollution on Human Health and Disease Heterogeneity: A Review. In *Frontiers in Environmental Science* (Vol. 10). 10.3389/fenvs.2022.880246

Lincoln, Y. S., & Guba, E. (1985). *Naturalistic inquiry* (1st ed.). Sage Publications. 10.1016/0147-1767(85)90062-8

Lin, Y., Wang, J., Sun, X., Ren, K., & Li, C. (2021). Generating adversarial examples for network intrusion detection systems through generative adversarial networks. *IEEE Transactions on Information Forensics and Security*, 16, 3498–3511.

Liu, R., Wei, J., Liu, F., Si, C., Zhang, Y., Rao, J., Zheng, S., Peng, D., Yang, D., Zhou, D., & Dai, A. M. (2024). *Best Practices and Lessons Learned on Synthetic Data for Language Models* (arXiv:2404.07503). arXiv. http://arxiv.org/abs/2404.07503

Liu, P., Yuan, W., Fu, J., Jiang, Z., Hayashi, H., & Graham Neubig, G. (2023). Pre-train, prompt, and predict: A systematic survey of prompting methods in natural language processing. *ACM Computing Surveys*, 55(9), 1–35. 10.1145/3560815

Liu, W., Wang, B., Yang, Y., Mou, N., Zheng, Y., Zhang, L., & Yang, T. (2022). Cluster analysis of microscopic spatio-temporal patterns of tourists' movement behaviors in mountainous scenic areas using open GPS-trajectory data. *Tourism Management*, 93, 104614. Advance online publication. 10.1016/j.tourman.2022.104614

Li, W. (2020). GeoAI: Where machine learning and big data converge in GIScience. *Journal of Spatial Information Science*, 20(20). Advance online publication. 10.5311/JOSIS.2020.20.658

Logan, R., IV, Bala˘zevi'c, I., Wallace, E., Petroni, F., Singh, S., & Riedel, S. (2022) Cutting down on prompts and parameters: simple few-shot learning with language models. Findings of the Association for Computational Linguistics, 2824–2835.

Lomurno, E., Archetti, A., Cazzella, L., Samele, S., Di Perna, L., & Matteucci, M. (2022, September). SGDE: Secure generative data exchange for cross-silo federated learning. In *Proceedings of the 2022 5th International Conference on Artificial Intelligence and Pattern Recognition* (pp. 205-214). 10.1145/3573942.3573974

Loukil, F. (2020). Intelligence territoriale et performance des territoires. *Revue Gouvernance*, 17(1), 32–50.

Loureiro, S. M. C., Guerreiro, J., & Tussyadiah, I. (2021). Artificial intelligence in business: State of the art and future research agenda. *Journal of Business Research, 129*(August), 911–926. 10.1016/j.jbusres.2020.11.001

Lund, B. D., & Wang, T. (2023). Chatting about ChatGPT: How may AI and GPT impact academia and libraries? *Library Hi Tech News*, 40(3), 26–29. 10.1108/LHTN-01-2023-0009

Lund, B. D., Wang, T., Mannuru, N. R., Nie, B., Shimray, S., & Wang, Z. (2023). ChatGPT and a new academic reality: Artificial Intelligence-written research papers and the ethics of the large language models in scholarly publishing. *Journal of the Association for Information Science and Technology*, 74(5), 570–581. 10.1002/asi.24750

Luo, Y., Chen, Y., Li, T., Tan, C., & Dou, H. (2024). Cloud-SMPC: Two-round multilinear maps secure multiparty computation based on LWE assumption. *Journal of Cloud Computing (Heidelberg, Germany)*, 13(1), 22. 10.1186/s13677-023-00586-5

Lv, Z. (2023). Generative artificial intelligence in the metaverse era. *Cognitive Robotics*, 3, 208–217. 10.1016/j.cogr.2023.06.001

Lv, Z., Chen, D., Lou, R., & Wang, Q. (2021). Intelligent edge computing based on machine learning for smart city. *Future Generation Computer Systems*, 115, 90–99. 10.1016/j.future.2020.08.037

Madaan, G., Swapna, H. R., Kumar, A., Singh, A., & David, A. (2021). Enactment of sustainable technovations on healthcare sectors. *Asia Pacific Journal of Health Management*, 16(3), 184–192. 10.24083/apjhm.v16i3.989

Madhavi. (2021). Role of AI in business development. *Open Journal of Social Sciences, 6*(6), 28–33. https://doi.org/10.51397/OAIJSE06.2021.0005

Madry, A., Makelov, A., Schmidt, L., Tsipras, D., & Vladu, A. (2018). Towards deep learning models resistant to adversarial attacks. arXiv preprint arXiv:1706.06083.

Maglogiannis, I., Iliadis, L., Macintyre, J., & Cortez, P. (Eds.). (2023). *Artificial intelligence applications and innovations: 18Th IFIP WG 12.5 international conference, AIAI 2022, hersonissos, Crete, Greece, June 17-20, 2022, proceedings, part II* (1st ed.). Springer International Publishing.

Ma, H., & Zhang, Z. (2020). A new private information encryption method in internet of things under cloud computing environment. *Wireless Communications and Mobile Computing*, 2020, 1–9. 10.1155/2020/8810987

Maisiri, W., Darwish, H., & van Dyk, L. (2019). An investigation of Industry 4.0 skills requirements. *South African Journal of Industrial Engineering*, 30(3), 90–105. 10.7166/30-3-2230

Mai, W. (2023). *Developing an Ethical Framework for Artificial Intelligence in Investment Decision-Making: A Fuzzy Analytic Hierarchy Analysis*. EAI/MSIEID.

Mangalampalli, S., Karri, G. R., Kumar, M., Khalaf, O. I., Romero, C. A. T., & Sahib, G. A. (2024). DRLBTSA: Deep reinforcement learning based task-scheduling algorithm in cloud computing. *Multimedia Tools and Applications*, 83(3), 8359–8387. 10.1007/s11042-023-16008-2

Manning, B. S., Zhu, K., & Horton, J. J. (2024). *Automated social science: Language models as scientist and subjects* (Working Paper 32381). National Bureau of Economic Research. 10.3386/w32381

Mansouri, N., M'zali, B., & Peretti, J. M. (2008). La construction d'une échelle de mesure des problématiques de l'environnement tétranormalisé de l'entreprise: Application du paradigme de Churchill. 5ème Congrès de l'ADERSE: Transversalité de la Responsabilité Sociale de l'Entreprise, Grenoble, 10.

Mateen, H. (2018). Weapons of Math Destruction: How Big Data Increases Inequality and Threatens Democracy. *Berkeley Journal of Employment and Labor Law*, 39(1), 285–292.

Ma, W., Zhou, T., Qin, J., Xiang, X., Tan, Y., & Cai, Z. (2022). A privacy-preserving content-based image retrieval method based on deep learning in cloud computing. *Expert Systems with Applications*, 203, 117508. 10.1016/j.eswa.2022.117508

McKinsey & Company. (2024, April 2). *What is ChatGPT, DALL-E, and generative AI?*https://www.mckinsey.com/featured-insights/mckinsey-explainers/what-is-generative-ai

McMaughan, D. J., Oloruntoba, O., & Smith, M. L. (2020). Socioeconomic Status and Access to Healthcare: Interrelated Drivers for Healthy Aging. In *Frontiers in Public Health* (Vol. 8). 10.3389/fpubh.2020.00231

McStay, A., & Rosner, G. (2021). Emotional artificial intelligence in children's toys and devices: Ethics, governance and practical remedies. *Big Data & Society*, 8(1), 2053951721994877. 10.1177/2053951721994877

Mdaka, Y. (2023, March 29). *Jobs that are most exposed to generative AI, according to a new study*. News24. https://www.news24.com/news24/tech-and-trends/jobs-that-are-most-exposed-to-generative-ai-according-to-new-study-20230329

Mehrabi, N., Morstatter, F., Saxena, N., Lerman, K., & Galstyan, A. (2019). *A Survey on Bias and Fairness in Machine Learning*. 10.48550/ARXIV.1908.09635

Melanson, D., Maia, R., Kim, H. S., Nascimento, A., & De Cock, M. (2023). Secure multi-party computation for personalized human activity recognition. *Neural Processing Letters*, 55(3), 2127–2153. 10.1007/s11063-023-11182-8

Menon, S. P., Shukla, P. K., Sethi, P., Alasiry, A., Marzougui, M., Alouane, M. T. H., & Khan, A. A. (2023). An Intelligent Diabetic Patient Tracking System Based on Machine Learning for E-Health Applications. *Sensors (Basel)*, 23(6), 3004. Advance online publication. 10.3390/s2306300436991714

Meta. (2023, July 18). Meta and Microsoft Introduce the next generation of Llama. *Meta*. https://about.fb.com/news/2023/07/llama-2/

Metta, S., Chang, I., Parker, J., Roman, M. P., & Ehuan, A. F. (2024). Generative AI in Cybersecurity. arXiv preprint arXiv:2405.01674.

Mhlanga, D. (2022). The role of artificial intelligence and machine learning amid the COVID-19 pandemic: What lessons are we learning on 4IR and the sustainable development goals. *International Journal of Environmental Research and Public Health*, 19(3), 1879. 10.3390/ijerph1903187935162901

Miao, J., Thongprayoon, C., Suppadungsuk, S., Garcia Valencia, O. A., & Cheungpasitporn, W. (2024). Integrating Retrieval-Augmented Generation with Large Language Models in Nephrology: Advancing Practical Applications. *Medicina*, 60(3), 445. 10.3390/medicina6003044538541171

Miao, Z. (2020). The Influence Factors of Psychological Understanding and Behavior Choice for Legal Industry Entrepreneurs Based on Artificial Intelligence Technology. *Frontiers in Psychology*, 11(July), 1–10. 10.3389/fpsyg.2020.0161532793042

Michael, K., Abbas, R., & Roussos, G. (2023). AI in Cybersecurity: The Paradox. *IEEE Transactions on Technology and Society*, 4(2), 104–109. 10.1109/TTS.2023.3280109

Michelucci, U. (2019). *Advanced applied deep learning: convolutional neural networks and object detection*. Apress. 10.1007/978-1-4842-4976-5

Milgram, S. (1963). Behavioral study of obedience. *Journal of Abnormal and Social Psychology*, 67(4), 371–378. 10.1037/h004052514049516

Mirski, P., Grosberg, J., Kull, T., Mellov, P., Tõnisalu, G., Väli, V., & Väli, Ü. (2024). Movement of avian predators points to biodiversity hotspots in agricultural landscape. *Royal Society Open Science*, 11(1), 231543. Advance online publication. 10.1098/rsos.23154338204791

Mishra, S., & Tripathi, A. R. (2021). AI business model: An integrative business approach. *Journal of Innovation and Entrepreneurship*, 10(1), 18. Advance online publication. 10.1186/s13731-021-00157-5

Mittelstadt, B. D., Allo, P., Taddeo, M., Wachter, S., & Floridi, L. (2016). The ethics of algorithms: Mapping the debate. *Big Data & Society*, 3(2), 205395171667967. 10.1177/2053951716679679

Mohana, J., Yakkala, B., Vimalnath, S., Benson Mansingh, P. M., Yuvaraj, N., Srihari, K., Sasikala, G., Mahalakshmi, V., Yasir Abdullah, R., & Sundramurthy, V. P. (2022). Application of Internet of Things on the Healthcare Field Using Convolutional Neural Network Processing. *Journal of Healthcare Engineering*, 2022, 1–7. Advance online publication. 10.1155/2022/189212335126905

Molaiepour, S. (2024, February 1). *EU AI Act: What HR teams need to know*. https://www.jobylon.com/blog/eu-ai-act-what-hr-teams-need-to-know

Morales-Forero, A., Bassetto, S., & Coatanea, E. (2023). Toward safe AI. *AI & Society*, 38(2), 685–696. 10.1007/s00146-022-01591-z

Mortaheb, R., & Jankowski, P. (2023). Smart city re-imagined: City planning and GeoAI in the age of big data. *Journal of Urban Management*, 12(1), 4–15. Advance online publication. 10.1016/j.jum.2022.08.001

Moses, M. E., & Gipson Rankin, S. M. (2024). *Medical artificial intelligence should do no harm*. Nature Reviews Electrical Engineering., 10.1038/s44287-024-00049-2

Munnangi, A. K., UdhayaKumar, S., Ravi, V., Sekaran, R., & Kannan, S. (2023). Survival study on deep learning techniques for IoT enabled smart healthcare system. *Health and Technology*, 13(2), 215–228. Advance online publication. 10.1007/s12553-023-00736-436818549

Munyai, O., & Nunu, W. N. (2020). Health effects associated with proximity to waste collection points in Beitbridge Municipality, Zimbabwe. *Waste Management (New York, N.Y.)*, 105, 501–510. Advance online publication. 10.1016/j.wasman.2020.02.04132145684

Murad, A. (2023). *The computers rejecting your job application*. Pocket. https://getpocket.com/explore/item/the-computers-rejecting-your-job-application

Murad, A., & Khashoggi, B. F. (2020). Using GIS for disease mapping and clustering in Jeddah, Saudi Arabia. *ISPRS International Journal of Geo-Information*, 9(5), 328. Advance online publication. 10.3390/ijgi9050328

Murphy, K., Di Ruggiero, E., Upshur, R., Willison, D. J., Malhotra, N., Cai, J. C., Malhotra, N., Lui, V., & Gibson, J. (2021). Artificial intelligence for good health: A scoping review of the ethics literature. *BMC Medical Ethics*, 22(1), 1–17. 10.1186/s12910-021-00577-833588803

Musiol, M. (2024). *Generative AI: Navigating the course to the artificial general intelligence future*. John Wiley & Sons.

Nadjia, M. (2024). The Impact of Artificial Intelligence on Legal Systems: Challenges and Opportunities. *Problems of Legality, 164*. http://plaw.nlu.edu.ua/article/download/289266/293702/695683

Nagai, H., Nakazawa, E., & Akabayashi, A. (2022). The creation of the Belmont Report and its effect on ethical principles: A historical study. *Monash Bioethics Review*, 40(2), 157–170. 10.1007/s40592-022-00165-536357708

Nahra, K. J., Evers, A., Jessani, A. J., Braun, M., Vallery, A., & Benizri, I. (2024, March 14). *The European Parliament adopts the AI Act*. https://www.wilmerhale.com/en/insights/blogs/wilmerhale-privacy-and-cybersecurity-law/20240314-the-european-parliament-adopts-the-ai-act

Naidoo, M. (2021). Artificial intelligence and global governance: How AI ethics and standards should be addressed at the global level. *The iJournal. Student Journal of the Faculty of Information*, 7(1). Advance online publication. 10.33137/ijournal.v7i1.37894

Nain, G., Pattanaik, K. K., & Sharma, G. K. (2022). Towards edge computing in intelligent manufacturing: Past, present and future. *Journal of Manufacturing Systems*, 62, 588–611. 10.1016/j.jmsy.2022.01.010

Nair, M. M., & Tyagi, A. K. (2023). AI, IoT, blockchain, and cloud computing: The necessity of the future. In *Distributed Computing to Blockchain* (pp. 189–206). Academic Press. 10.1016/B978-0-323-96146-2.00001-2

Nasim, S. F., Ali, M. R., & Kulsoom, U. (2022). Artificial intelligence incidents & ethics a narrative review. *International Journal of TechnologyInnovation and Management*, 2(2), 52–64.

Nath, R., & Sahu, V. (2020). The problem of machine ethics in artificial intelligence. *AI & Society*, 35(1), 103–111. 10.1007/s00146-017-0768-6

National Institutes of Health. (n.d.). *Nuremberg Code*. Retrieved May 2, 2024, from https://history.nih.gov/display/history/Nuremberg+Code

Nguyen, T. D., Nguyen, T. D., & Park, M. (2022). Generative Adversarial Networks for Generating Synthetic Network Traffic Data. arXiv preprint arXiv:2205.09352.

Nguyen, A., Ngo, H. N., Hong, Y., Dang, B., & Nguyen, B.-P. T. (2023). Ethical principles for artificial intelligence in education. *Education and Information Technologies*, 28(4), 4221–4241. 10.1007/s10639-022-11316-w36254344

Nguyen, T. T., Nguyen, H. D., & Le, N. G. (2022). AI-based cybersecurity: Opportunities and challenges. *SN Computer Science*, 3(2), 1–21.

Nickerson, C. (2024, February 13). *Emile Durkheim's theory*. https://www.simplypsychology.org/emile-durkheims-theories.html

Nisar, D. E. M., Amin, R., Shah, N. U. H., Ghamdi, M. A. A., Almotiri, S. H., & Alruily, M. (2021). Healthcare Techniques through Deep Learning: Issues, Challenges and Opportunities. *IEEE Access : Practical Innovations, Open Solutions*, 9, 98523–98541. Advance online publication. 10.1109/ACCESS.2021.3095312

Nofil, B. (2024). *The CIA's appalling human experiments with mind control*. The HISTORY Channel. https://www.history.com/mkultra-operation-midnight-climax-cia-lsd-experiments

Novelli, C., Casolari, F., Hacker, P., Spedicato, G., & Floridi, L. (2024). Generative AI in EU Law: Liability, Privacy, Intellectual Property, and Cybersecurity. arXiv preprint arXiv:2401.07348.

Obermeyer, Z., Powers, B., Vogeli, C., & Mullainathan, S. (2019). Dissecting racial bias in an algorithm used to manage the health of populations. *Science*, 366(6464), 447–453. 10.1126/science.aax234231649194

Obschonka, M., & Audretsch, D. B. (2019). Artificial intelligence and big data in entrepreneurship: A new era has begun. *Small Business Economics*, 55(3), 529–539. 10.1007/s11187-019-00202-4

Office for Human Research Protections. (2022, October 17). *The Belmont Report* [Text]. https://www.hhs.gov/ohrp/regulations-and-policy/belmont-report/index.html

Office of Research Integrity. (n.d.). *Misconduct case summaries*. Retrieved March 16, 2024, from https://ori.hhs.gov/content/case_summary

Olabanji, S. O., Olaniyi, O. O., Adigwe, C. S., Okunleye, O. J., & Oladoyinbo, T. O. (2024). AI for Identity and Access Management (IAM) in the cloud: Exploring the potential of artificial intelligence to improve user authentication, authorization, and access control within cloud-based systems. *Authorization, and Access Control within Cloud-Based Systems (January 25, 2024).*

Olawade, D. B., Wada, O. J., David-Olawade, A. C., Kunonga, E., Abaire, O., & Ling, J. (2023). Using artificial intelligence to improve public health: a narrative review. In *Frontiers in Public Health* (Vol. 11). 10.3389/fpubh.2023.1196397

onlinepsychologydegree. (n.d.). 20 most unethical experiments in psychology. *Online Psychology Degree Guide*. Retrieved March 16, 2024, from https://www.onlinepsychologydegree.info/unethical-experiements-psychology/

Open, A. I. (2022). *OpenAI*. https://openai.com/

Originality.ai. (2024). *AI content checker | Accurate on ChatGPT, GPT-4, Bard & Claude*. https://originality.ai

Owe, A., & Baum, S. D. (2021, December). The ethics of sustainability for artificial intelligence. In *Proceedings of the 1st international conference on AI for people: towards sustainable AI (CAIP 2021b)* (pp. 1-17). 10.4108/eai.20-11-2021.2314105

Padmanaban, H. (2024). Quantum Computing and AI in the Cloud. *Journal of Computational Intelligence and Robotics*, 4(1), 14–32.

Palanivelu, V. R., & Vasanthi, B. (2020). Role of artificial intelligence in business transformation. *International Journal of Advanced Science and Technology, 29*(4 Special Issue), 392–400.

Palumbo, G., Carneiro, D., & Alves, V. (2024). Objective metrics for ethical AI: A systematic literature review. *International Journal of Data Science and Analytics*. Advance online publication. 10.1007/s41060-024-00541-w

Park, J. S., Popowski, L., Cai, C., Morris, M. R., Liang, P., & Bernstein, M. S. (2022). Social simulacra: Creating populated prototypes for social computing systems. *Proceedings of the 35th Annual ACM Symposium on User Interface Software and Technology*, 1–18. 10.1145/3526113.3545616

Park, J., Kim, D. S., & Lim, H. (2020). Privacy-preserving reinforcement learning using homomorphic encryption in cloud computing infrastructures. *IEEE Access : Practical Innovations, Open Solutions*, 8, 203564–203579. 10.1109/ACCESS.2020.3036899

Patel, N., & Trivedi, S. (2020). Choosing Optimal Locations for TemporaryHealth Care Facilities During Health Crisis Using Binary Integer Programming. *Journals Sagescience*, 3(2).

Patra, B. G., Sharma, M. M., Vekaria, V., Adekkanattu, P., Patterson, O. V., Glicksberg, B., Lepow, L. A., Ryu, E., Biernacka, J. M., Furmanchuk, A., George, T. J., Hogan, W., Wu, Y., Yang, X., Bian, J., Weissman, M., Wickramaratne, P., Mann, J. J., Olfson, M., . . . Pathak, J. (2021). Extracting social determinants of health from electronic health records using natural language processing: A systematic review. In *Journal of the American Medical Informatics Association* (Vol. 28, Issue 12). 10.1093/jamia/ocab170

Pavaloiu, A., & Kose, U. (2017). *Ethical Artificial Intelligence—An Open Question*. 10.48550/ARXIV.1706.03021

Pecqueur, B. (2005). *Le territoire est mort Vive les territoires! Une (re)fabrication au nom du développement*. IRD Éditions Paris.

Peng, X., Li, Y., Wang, Y., & Xiang, Y. (2022). Generating synthetic data for cyber threat hunting with generative adversarial networks. In *Proceedings of the 2022 ACM SIGSAC Conference on Computer and Communications Security* (pp. 2181-2195).

Penn Today. (2023, June 16). *AI could transform social science research*. Penn Today. https://penntoday.upenn.edu/news/ai-could-transform-social-science-research

Pierdicca, R. (2021). *GeoAI:artificial intelligence for interpretation and processing of complex geomatic data*. EGU General Assembly.

Prabhu Kavin, B., Ganapathy, S., Kanimozhi, U., & Kannan, A. (2020). An enhanced security framework for secured data storage and communications in cloud using ECC, access control and LDSA. *Wireless Personal Communications*, 115(2), 1107–1135. 10.1007/s11277-020-07613-7

Pratheepkumar, P., Sharmila, J. J., & Arokiaraj, D. (2017). Towards mobile opportunistic in cloud computing. *Indian Journal of Scientific Research*, 17(02), 2250–0138.

Price, D. H. (2007). Buying a piece of anthropology part 1: Human ecology and unwitting anthropological research for the CIA. *Anthropology Today*, 23(3), 8–13. 10.1111/j.1467-8322.2007.00510.x

Prieto, I., & Blakely, B. (2023). Proposed Uses of Generative AI in a Cybersecurity-Focused Soar Agent. In *Proceedings of the AAAI Symposium Series* (Vol. 2, No. 1, pp. 386-390).

Psychogyios, K., Velivassaki, T. H., Bourou, S., Voulkidis, A., Skias, D., & Zahariadis, T. (2023). GAN-driven data poisoning attacks and their mitigation in federated learning systems. *Electronics (Basel)*, 12(8), 1805. 10.3390/electronics12081805

Publishers International Linking Association, Inc. (2024). *Crossref* [Website]. Crossref. https://www.crossref.org/

Pukkala, T. (2019). Using ALS raster data in forest planning. *Journal of Forestry Research*, 30(5), 1581–1593. Advance online publication. 10.1007/s11676-019-00937-6

Pu, Q., Yoo, E. H., Rothstein, D. H., Cairo, S., & Malemo, L. (2020). Improving the spatial accessibility of healthcare in North Kivu, Democratic Republic of Congo. *Applied Geography (Sevenoaks, England)*, 121, 102262. Advance online publication. 10.1016/j.apgeog.2020.102262

Qadir, J. (2023). Engineering education in the era of ChatGPT: Promise and pitfalls of generative AI for education. *2023 IEEE Global Engineering Education Conference (EDUCON)*, 1–9. 10.1109/EDUCON54358.2023.10125121

Radford, A., Wu, J., Child, R., Luan, D., Amodei, D., & Sutskever, I. (2019). Language models are unsupervised multitask learners. https://openai.com/index/better-language-models

Radford, A., Wu, J., Child, R., Luan, D., Amodei, D., & Sutskever, I. (2019). Language models are unsupervised multitask learners. OpenAI blog, 1(8), 9.

Radford, A., Kim, J. W., Hallacy, C., Ramesh, A., Goh, G., Agarwal, S., & Sutskever, I. (2022). Learning transferable visual models from natural language supervision. In *International Conference on Machine Learning* (pp. 8748-8763). PMLR.

Radford, A., Wu, J., Child, R., Luan, D., Amodei, D., & Sutskever, I. (2019). Language Models are Unsupervised Multitask Learners. *OpenAI Blog*, 1(8), 9.

Rahman, M. M., & Watanobe, Y. (2023). ChatGPT for education and research: Opportunities, threats, and strategies. *Applied Sciences (Basel, Switzerland)*, 13(9), 9. Advance online publication. 10.3390/app13095783

Rajkomar, A., Hardt, M., Howell, M. D., Corrado, G., & Chin, M. H. (2018). Ensuring Fairness in Machine Learning to Advance Health Equity. *Annals of Internal Medicine*, 169(12), 866. 10.7326/M18-199030508424

Rallet, A., & Rochelandet, F. (2019). La souveraineté numérique, une ambition pour les régions. *Revue d'Économie Régionale et Urbaine*, 2019(3), 447–465.

Ramachandran, S., Agrahari, R., Mudgal, P., Bhilwaria, H., Long, G., & Kumar, A. (2023). Automated log classification using deep learning. *Procedia Computer Science*, 218, 1722–1732. 10.1016/j.procs.2023.01.150

Raman, P. (2023, September 30). *The transformative role of AI in social science research.* https://uniathena.com/role-of-AI-in-social-science-research

Ramesh, A., Pavlov, M., Goh, G., Gray, S., Voss, C., Radford, A., & Sutskever, I. (2021). Zero-Shot Text-to-Image Generation. arXiv preprint arXiv:2102.12092.

Ramirez, M. A., Kim, S. K., Hamadi, H. A., Damiani, E., Byon, Y. J., Kim, T. Y., . . . Yeun, C. Y. (2022). Poisoning attacks and defenses on artificial intelligence: A survey. arXiv preprint arXiv:2202.10276.

Rathi, A., & Asava, T. (2021). The role of artificial intelligence in disinformation. *Data & Policy*, 3(01), 175–179. 10.1017/dap.2021.20

Ravi, G. S., Smith, K. N., Gokhale, P., & Chong, F. T. (2021, November). Quantum computing in the cloud: Analyzing job and machine characteristics. In *2021 IEEE International Symposium on Workload Characterization (IISWC)* (pp. 39-50). IEEE. 10.1109/IISWC53511.2021.00015

Ravi, S., David, A., & Imaduddin, M. (2018). Controlling & calibrating vehicle-related issues using RFID technology. *International Journal of Mechanical and Production Engineering Research and Development*, 8(2), 1125–1132. 10.24247/ijmperdapr2018130

Reim, W., Åström, J., & Eriksson, O. (2020). Implementation of Artificial Intelligence (AI): A Roadmap for Business Model Innovation. *AI*, 1(2), 180–191. 10.3390/ai1020011

Renaud, K., Warkentin, M., & Westerman, G. (2023). From ChatGPT to HackGPT: Meeting the cybersecurity threat of generative AI. *MIT Sloan Management Review*.

Research. (2024). *Merriam-Webster's collegiate dictionary*. https://www.merriam-webster.com/dictionary/research

Resnik, D. B., & Hofweber, F. W. (2023, August 22). *Research ethics timeline.* National Institute of Environmental Health Sciences. https://www.niehs.nih.gov/research/resources/bioethics/timeline

Reyes-Riveros, R., Altamirano, A., De La Barrera, F., Rozas-Vásquez, D., Vieli, L., & Meli, P. (2021). Linking public urban green spaces and human well-being: A systematic review. In *Urban Forestry and Urban Greening* (Vol. 61). 10.1016/j.ufug.2021.127105

Reynolds, G. (2003, March 16). The stuttering doctor's "monster study." *The New York Times*. https://www.nytimes.com/2003/03/16/magazine/the-stuttering-doctor-s-monster-study.html

Richards, D. R., Belcher, R. N., Carrasco, L. R., Edwards, P. J., Fatichi, S., Hamel, P., Masoudi, M., McDonnell, M. J., Peleg, N., & Stanley, M. C. (2022). Global variation in contributions to human well-being from urban vegetation ecosystem services. *One Earth*, 5(5), 522–533. Advance online publication. 10.1016/j.oneear.2022.04.006

Richardson, B., & Gilbert, J. E. (2021). *A Framework for Fairness: A Systematic Review of Existing Fair AI Solutions* (arXiv:2112.05700). arXiv. http://arxiv.org/abs/2112.05700

Risanger, S., Singh, B., Morton, D., & Meyers, L. A. (2021). Selecting pharmacies for COVID-19 testing to ensure access. *Health Care Management Science*, 24(2), 330–338. Advance online publication. 10.1007/s10729-020-09538-w33423180

Roberts, H., Cowls, J., Morley, J., Taddeo, M., Wang, V., & Floridi, L. (2021). The Chinese approach to artificial intelligence: an analysis of policy, ethics, and regulation. *Ethics, governance, and policies in artificial intelligence*, 47-79.

Rodriguez, M. A., & García, R. (2013). First, do no harm: The US sexually transmitted disease experiments in Guatemala. *American Journal of Public Health*, 103(12), 2122–2126. 10.2105/AJPH.2013.30152024134370

Rogers, K. (2024, March 29). *Guatemala syphilis experiment: American medical research project*. https://www.britannica.com/event/Guatemala-syphilis-experiment

Rohlf, M. (2010). Immanuel Kant. *Stanford Encyclopedia of Philosophy*. https://plato.stanford.edu/entries/kant/?rid=903123293s840c38

Rosenberg, A. (1998). *Why a philosophy of social science?* https://faculty.washington.edu/lynnhank/pss.pdf

Roundy, P. T. (2022). Artificial intelligence and entrepreneurial ecosystems: Understanding the implications of algorithmic decision-making for startup communities. *Journal of Ethics in Entrepreneurship and Technology*, 2(1), 23–38. 10.1108/JEET-07-2022-0011

Rovira, J., Domingo, J. L., & Schuhmacher, M. (2020). Air quality, health impacts and burden of disease due to air pollution (PM10, PM2.5, NO2 and O3): Application of AirQ+ model to the Camp de Tarragona County (Catalonia, Spain). *The Science of the Total Environment*, 703, 135538. Advance online publication. 10.1016/j.scitotenv.2019.13553831759725

Roy, M. (2021). An Exploratory study on Origin of AI: Journey through the Ancient Indian Texts & other technological descriptions, its past, present & future. *Turkish Online Journal of Qualitative Inquiry*, 12(7), 10261–10288.

Rudin, C. (2018). Stop Explaining Black Box Machine Learning Models for High Stakes Decisions and Use Interpretable Models Instead. 10.48550/ARXIV.1811.10154

Rueß, H., & Burton, S. (2022). Safe AI — How is this Possible? 10.48550/ARXIV.2201.10436

Rumisha, S. F., Lyimo, E. P., Mremi, I. R., Tungu, P. K., Mwingira, V. S., Mbata, D., Malekia, S. E., Joachim, C., & Mboera, L. E. G. (2020). Data quality of the routine health management information system at the primary healthcare facility and district levels in Tanzania. *BMC Medical Informatics and Decision Making*, 20(1), 340. Advance online publication. 10.1186/s12911-020-01366-w33334323

Ryan, M. (2020). In AI we trust: Ethics, artificial intelligence, and reliability. *Science and Engineering Ethics*, 26(5), 2749–2767. 10.1007/s11948-020-00228-y32524425

Šabić, E., Keeley, D., Henderson, B., & Nannemann, S. (2021). Healthcare and anomaly detection: Using machine learning to predict anomalies in heart rate data. *AI & Society*, 36(1), 149–158. Advance online publication. 10.1007/s00146-020-00985-1

Sadiku, M. N. O., Fagbohungbe, O., & Musa, S. M. (2020). Artificial Intelligence in Business. *International Journal of Engineering Research and Advanced Technology*, 06(07), 62–70. 10.31695/IJERAT.2020.3625

Sahana, K. S., Karthik, C. B., Sree, M. M., Chaithra, M., Abhinandithe, S. K., Snehalatha, B., Sridhar, R., Balasubramanian, S., & Madhu, B. (2023). Geospatial Artificial Intelligence (GeoAI): Applications in Health Care. *International Journal of Health & Allied Sciences*, 11(4). Advance online publication. 10.55691/2278-344X.1044

Saheb, T., Saheb, T., & Carpenter, D. O. (2021). Mapping research strands of ethics of artificial intelligence in healthcare: A bibliometric and content analysis. *Computers in Biology and Medicine*, 135, 104660. 10.1016/j.compbiomed.2021.10466034346319

Saibi, H., Bersi, M., Mia, M. B., Saadi, N. M., Al Bloushi, K. M. S., & Avakian, R. W. (2018). Applications of Remote Sensing in Geoscience. In *Recent Advances and Applications in Remote Sensing*. 10.5772/intechopen.75995

Sai, S., Yashvardhan, U., Chamola, V., & Sikdar, B. (2024). Generative ai for cyber security: Analyzing the potential of chatgpt, dall-e and other models for enhancing the security space. *IEEE Access : Practical Innovations, Open Solutions*, 12, 53497–53516. 10.1109/ACCESS.2024.3385107

Salehi, P., Hassan, S. Z., Lammerse, M., Sabet, S. S., Riiser, I., Røed, R. K., Johnson, M. S., Thambawita, V., Hicks, S. A., Powell, M., Lamb, M. E., Baugerud, G. A., Halvorsen, P., & Riegler, M. A. (2022). Synthesizing a talking child avatar to train interviewers working with maltreated children. *Big Data and Cognitive Computing*, 6(2), 2. Advance online publication. 10.3390/bdcc6020062

Sallam, M. (2023). ChatGPT utility in healthcare education, research, and practice: Systematic review on the promising perspectives and valid concerns. *Health Care*, 11(6), 6. Advance online publication. 10.3390/healthcare1106088736981544

Saluja, S., Kukreja, J., & Sharma, S. (Eds.). (2024). *Building Organizational Resilience with Neuroleadership*. IGI Global. 10.4018/979-8-3693-1785-3

Samunnisa, K., Kumar, G. S. V., & Madhavi, K. (2023). Intrusion detection system in distributed cloud computing: Hybrid clustering and classification methods. *Measurement. Sensors*, 25, 100612. 10.1016/j.measen.2022.100612

Sanders Thompson, V. L. (2013). Making decisions in a complex information environment: Evidential preference and information we trust. *BMC Medical Informatics and Decision Making*, 13(S3, SUPPL.3), S7. Advance online publication. 10.1186/1472-6947-13-S3-S724565305

Sankar, J. G. (2024). AI-Driven Marketing Success Stories: A Case Note of Industry Pioneers. In *AI-Driven Marketing Research and Data Analytics* (pp. 48-66). IGI Global. 10.4018/979-8-3693-2165-2.ch003

Sankar, J. G., & David, A. (2023). Measuring the Service Quality of Artificial Intelligence in the Tourism and Hospitality Industry. In *Handbook of Research on Innovation, Differentiation, and New Technologies in Tourism, Hotels, and Food Service* (pp. 133-155). IGI Global. 10.4018/978-1-6684-6985-9.ch007

Sankar, J. G., & David, A. (2024). A Comprehensive Examination of Mobile Augmented Reality in Tourism (MART) Adoption: Using the UTAUT2 Framework. In *Contemporary Trends in Innovative Marketing Strategies* (pp. 241-262). IGI Global.

Sankar, J. G., & David, A. (2024). Transforming the Travel Landscape: Smart Contracts in Tourism Management. In *Decentralizing the Online Experience With Web3 Technologies* (pp. 246-266). IGI Global.

Sankar, J. G., David, A., & Ramasamy, R. (2023). Assessing Water and Sanitation Service Quality at Pilgrimage Sites After COVID-19: An Empirical Investigation. In *Prospects and Challenges of Global Pilgrimage Tourism and Hospitality* (pp. 160-179). IGI Global.

Sankar, J. G., David, A., & Shrutimeena, G. (2024). From Hesitation to Integration: Understanding Digital Healthcare Adoption. In *Multi-Sector Analysis of the Digital Healthcare Industry* (pp. 1-32). IGI Global.

Sankar, G., & Naveenkumar, K. (2018). *Material Handling Management in Third Party Logistics Warehouse. International Journal for Research in Engineering Application & Management*. IJREAM.

Sankar, J. G. (2020a). Customer perception about innovative safety food delivery during lockdown. *Journal of Contemporary Issues in Business and Government*, 26(2).

Sankar, J. G. (2020b). Innovative celebrity endorsement and consumer purchase. *Journal of Contemporary Issues in Business and Government*, 26(2).

Sankar, J. G. (2020c). Innovative consumer behaviour towards sportswear. *Journal of Contemporary Issues in Business and Government*, 26(2).

Sankar, J. G. (2020d). Service Factors Influence on Customer Satisfaction in Innovative Ecommerce. *Journal of Contemporary Issues in Business and Government*, 26(2), 651–656.

Sankar, J. G. (2020e). Service quality of e-Commerce logistics services. *Journal of Contemporary Issues in Business and Government*, 26(2).

Sankar, J. G., David, A., & Ganesh Kumar, C. (2022). Adaptation of Blockchain Technology In HRM. *Available atSSRN* 4515408.

Sankar, J. G., David, A., & Valan, P. (2023). Examining User Understanding and Perceptions of E-Commerce Data Privacy, Security, and Protection. In *Confronting Security and Privacy Challenges in Digital Marketing* (pp. 159–185). IGI Global. 10.4018/978-1-6684-8958-1.ch008

Sankar, J. G., Rajeswari, M., & Dwarak, M. V. S. (2020). To Measure the Service Quality of Film and Television Technology. *Solid State Technology*, 63(2), 1192–1195.

Sankar, J. G., Valan, P., & Siranjeevi, M. S. (2020). Various Models to Evaluate Quality in the Service Industry. In *Digital Transformation and Innovative Services for Business and Learning* (pp. 181–194). IGI Global.

Sarai, T. (2023, May 15). *Holmesburg Prison's medical experiments are Philadelphia's "lasting shame."* Prism. https://prismreports.org/2023/05/15/philadelphia-holmesburg-prison-experiments/

Sarker, I. H. (2021). Machine learning: Algorithms, real-world applications and research directions. *SN Computer Science*, 2(3), 160. 10.1007/s42979-021-00592-x33778771

Sasikala, J., & Jeganathan, G. S. (2017). A Study on Employee Engagement in Information Technology (IT) Industry. *SSRN*, 1(1), 233–239. 10.2139/ssrn.3536354

Schmälzle, R., & Wilcox, S. (2022). Harnessing Artificial Intelligence for Health Message Generation: The Folic Acid Message Engine. *Journal of Medical Internet Research*, 24(1), e28858. Advance online publication. 10.2196/2885835040800

Schröder, A. K., Fassmer, A. M., Allers, K., & Hoffmann, F. (2020). Needs and availability of medical specialists' and allied health professionals' visits in German nursing homes: A cross-sectional study of nursing home staff. *BMC Health Services Research*, 20(1), 332. Advance online publication. 10.1186/s12913-020-05169-732317028

Schuett, J., Reuel, A.-K., & Carlier, A. (2024). How to design an AI ethics board. *AI and Ethics*. Advance online publication. 10.1007/s43681-023-00409-y

Secretary, P. (2023). A pro-innovation approach to AI regulation. *Open Government Licence, 1*(12).

Seth, B., Dalal, S., Jaglan, V., Le, D. N., Mohan, S., & Srivastava, G. (2022). Integrating encryption techniques for secure data storage in the cloud. *Transactions on Emerging Telecommunications Technologies*, 33(4), e4108. 10.1002/ett.4108

Shafahi, A., Huang, W. R., Najibi, M., Suciu, O., Studer, C., Dumitras, T., & Goldstein, T. (2018). Poison frogs! Targeted clean-label poisoning attacks on neural networks. *Advances in Neural Information Processing Systems*, 31.

Shahriar, M. H., Khalil, A. A., Rahman, M. A., Manshaei, M. H., & Chen, D. (2021, October). iattackgen: Generative synthesis of false data injection attacks in cyber-physical systems. In *2021 IEEE Conference on Communications and Network Security (CNS)* (pp. 200-208). IEEE. 10.1109/CNS53000.2021.9705034

Shamim, R., & Bentalha, B. (2023). Blockchain-Enabled Machine Learning Framework for Demand Forecasting in Supply Chain Management. In Integrating Intelligence and Sustainability in Supply Chains (pp. 28-48). IGI Global. 10.4018/979-8-3693-0225-5.ch002

Sharma, N. (2023, December 26). The computers rejecting your job application. *ISHIR | Software Development India*. https://www.ishir.com/blog/106625/the-computers-rejecting-your-job-application.htm

Shaw, J., Ali, J., Atuire, C. A., Cheah, P. Y., Español, A. G., Gichoya, J. W., Hunt, A., Jjingo, D., Littler, K., Paolotti, D., & Vayena, E. (2024). Research ethics and artificial intelligence for global health: Perspectives from the global forum on bioethics in research. *BMC Medical Ethics*, 25(1), 46. 10.1186/s12910-024-01044-w38637857

Sherubha, P., Sasirekha, S. P., Anguraj, A. D. K., Rani, J. V., Anitha, R., Praveen, S. P., & Krishnan, R. H. (2023). An Efficient Unsupervised Learning Approach for Detecting Anomaly in Cloud. *Computer Systems Science and Engineering*, 45(1), 149–166. 10.32604/csse.2023.024424

Shickel, B., Gillies, R., Suomala, L., & Nickerson, T. (2022). Generative AI models for forecasting cyber intelligence reports. arXiv preprint arXiv:2206.07849.

Shin, D. (2024). *Artificial Misinformation: Exploring Human-Algorithm Interaction Online*. Springer Nature Switzerland., 10.1007/978-3-031-52569-8

Shinde, S. (2024, February 26). Unlocking intelligence: Top 10 open source AI tools shaping the future. *Emeritus Online Courses*. https://emeritus.org/blog/open-source-ai/

Shine, I., & Whiting, K. (2023, May 4). *These are the jobs most likely to be lost – and created – because of AI*. World Economic Forum. https://www.weforum.org/agenda/2023/05/jobs-lost-created-ai-gpt/

Shirazi, Z. A., de Souza, C. P. E., Kashef, R., & Rodrigues, F. F. (2020). Deep learning in the healthcare industry: Theory and Applications. In *Computational Intelligence and Soft Computing Applications in Healthcare Management Science*. 10.4018/978-1-7998-2581-4.ch010

Shokri, R., Stronati, M., Song, C., & Shmatikov, V. (2021). Membership inference attacks against machine learning models. *IEEE Symposium on Security and Privacy (SP)*, 3-18.

Shuford, J. (2024). Quantum Computing and Artificial Intelligence: Synergies and Challenges. *Journal of Artificial Intelligence General science (JAIGS) ISSN: 3006-4023, 1*(1).

Shyr, C., Hu, Y., & Harris, P. A. Xu, &H., (2023). Identifying and extracting rare disease phenotypes with Large language models; ArXiv:2306.12656.

Siddik, M. S. M., Ahmed, T. E., Awad Ahmed, F. R., Mokhtar, R. A., Ali, E. S., & Saeed, R. A. (2023). Development of Health Digital GIS Map for Tuberculosis Disease Distribution Analysis in Sudan. In *Journal of Healthcare Engineering* (Vol. 2023). 10.1155/2023/6479187

Silverman, F. H. (1988). The "monster" study. *Journal of Fluency Disorders*, 13(3), 225–231. 10.1016/0094-730X(88)90049-6

Simitha, S., Mugila, P., & Sankar, J. G. (2020). A Study on Customer Relationship Management in Siemens Healthineers. *Solid State Technology*, 63(2), 1199–1203.

Simon, M. K., & Goes, J. (2018). *Dissertation and scholarly research: Recipes for success*. Dissertation Recipes LLC.

Singh, K. D., & Singh, P. (2024). Fog Cloud Computing and IoT Integration for AI enabled Autonomous Systems in Robotics. *EAI Endorsed Transactions on AI and Robotics, 3*.

Singh, V., Poonia, R. C., Kumar, S., Dass, P., Agarwal, P., Bhatnagar, V., & Raja, L. (2020). Prediction of COVID-19 corona virus pandemic based on time series data using support vector machine. *Journal of Discrete Mathematical Sciences and Cryptography*, 23(8), 1583–1597. Advance online publication. 10.1080/09720529.2020.1784535

Sipahioglu, M. (2024). Empowering Teachers with Generative AI Tools and Support. In *Transforming Education with Generative AI: Prompt Engineering and Synthetic Content Creation* (pp. 214-238). IGI Global. 10.4018/979-8-3693-1351-0.ch011

Smith, M. J., Axler, R., Bean, S., Rudzicz, F., & Shaw, J. (2020). Four equity considerations for the use of artificial intelligence in public health. *Bulletin of the World Health Organization*, 98(4), 290–292. 10.2471/BLT.19.23750332284656

Sobien, D., Yardimci, M. O., Nguyen, M. B. T., Mao, W.-Y., Fordham, V., Rahman, A., Duncan, S., & Batarseh, F. A. (2023). AI for Cyberbiosecurity in Water Systems—A Survey. In Greenbaum, D. (Ed.), *Cyberbiosecurity* (pp. 217–263). Springer International Publishing. 10.1007/978-3-031-26034-6_13

Solanki, P., Grundy, J., & Hussain, W. (2023). Operationalising ethics in artificial intelligence for healthcare: A framework for AI developers. *AI and Ethics*, 3(1), 223–240. 10.1007/s43681-022-00195-z

Song, Z., Jia, X., Bao, J., Yang, Y., Zhu, H., & Shi, X. (2021). Spatio-temporal analysis of influenza-like illness and prediction of incidence in high-risk regions in the united states from 2011 to 2020. *International Journal of Environmental Research and Public Health*, 18(13), 7120. Advance online publication. 10.3390/ijerph1813712034281057

Soni, N., Sharma, E. K., Singh, N., & Kapoor, A. (2020). Artificial Intelligence in Business: From Research and Innovation to Market Deployment. *Procedia Computer Science, 167*(2019), 2200–2210. 10.1016/j.procs.2020.03.272

Soni, N., Sharma, E. K., Singh, N., & Kapoor, A. (2019). Impact of Artificial Intelligence on Businesses: from Research, Innovation, Market Deployment to Future Shifts in Business Models. *Open Journal of Business and Management, 6*(2), 1–38. Retrieved from http://arxiv.org/abs/1905.02092

SP, M. S., & Sankar, J. G. An Overview of Measurement model in Marketing Research.

Srivastava, V., Singh, A. K., David, A., & Rai, N. (2022). Modelling student employability on an academic basis: A supervised machine learning approach with R. In *Handbook of Research on Innovative Management Using AI in Industry 5.0* (pp. 179–191). IGI Global. 10.4018/978-1-7998-8497-2.ch012

Stahl, B. C. (2021). *Artificial intelligence for a better future: an ecosystem perspective on the ethics of AI and emerging digital technologies.* Springer Nature. 10.1007/978-3-030-69978-9

Staines, Z., Hoffstaedter, G., & Binnie, N. (2023). *What are the social sciences?*https://uq.pressbooks.pub/introduction-social-sciences/chapter/what-are-social-sciences/

Stamp, C. (2023, November 13). *What are the top 10 unethical psychology experiments?* Online Psychology Degrees. https://www.online-psychology-degrees.org/study/top-unethical-experiments-psychology/

Stark, L., & Hoey, J. (2021, March). The ethics of emotion in artificial intelligence systems. In *Proceedings of the 2021 ACM conference on fairness, accountability, and transparency* (pp. 782-793). 10.1145/3442188.3445939

Stergiou, C. L., Plageras, A. P., Psannis, K. E., & Gupta, B. B. (2020). Secure machine learning scenario from big data in cloud computing via internet of things network. *Handbook of Computer Networks and Cyber Security: Principles and Paradigms*, 525-554.

Strobel, G., Banh, L., Möller, F., & Schoormann, T. (2024). Exploring Generative Artificial Intelligence: A Taxonomy and Types. *Hawaii International Conference on System Sciences (HICSS)*, (January), 1–10. Retrieved from https://www.researchgate.net/publication/373927156

Strubell, E., Ganesh, A., & McCallum, A. (2019). Energy and policy considerations for deep learning in NLP. arXiv preprint arXiv:1906.02243.

Strubell, E., Ganesh, A., & McCallum, A. (2019). Energy and Policy Considerations for Deep Learning in NLP. *Proceedings of the 57th Annual Meeting of the Association for Computational Linguistics.* 10.18653/v1/P19-1355

Sudhakar, B. D., Kattepogu, N., & David, A. (2017). Marketing assistance and digital branding-an insight for technology up-gradation for MSME's. *International Journal of Management Studies & Research*, 5(1), 2455–1562.

Sun, L., Jiang, X., Ren, H., & Guo, Y. (2020). Edge-cloud computing and artificial intelligence in internet of medical things: Architecture, technology and application. *IEEE Access : Practical Innovations, Open Solutions*, 8, 101079–101092. 10.1109/ACCESS.2020.2997831

Sweeney, S. (2023). Who wrote this? Essay mills and assessment – Considerations regarding contract cheating and AI in higher education. *International Journal of Management Education*, 21(2), 100818. 10.1016/j.ijme.2023.100818

Taddeo, M., McNeish, D., Blanchard, A., & Edgar, E. (2021). Ethical principles for artificial intelligence in national defence. *Philosophy & Technology*, 34(4), 1707–1729. 10.1007/s13347-021-00482-3

Tainio, M., Jovanovic Andersen, Z., Nieuwenhuijsen, M. J., Hu, L., de Nazelle, A., An, R., Garcia, L. M. T., Goenka, S., Zapata-Diomedi, B., Bull, F., & de Sá, T. H. (2021). Air pollution, physical activity and health: A mapping review of the evidence. In *Environment International* (Vol. 147). 10.1016/j.envint.2020.105954

Taiwo, O. J. (2021). Maximal Covering Location Problem (MCLP) for the identification of potential optimal COVID-19 testing facility sites in Nigeria. *African Geographical Review*, 40(4), 395–411. Advance online publication. 10.1080/19376812.2020.1838306

Targett, E. (2023, May 2). *WEF warns on AI, job losses: 83 million roles to vanish in 5 years*. The Stack. https://www.thestack.technology/ai-job-losses-wef-future-of-jobs-report/

Tasneem, S., Gupta, K. D., Roy, A., & Dasgupta, D. (2022, December). Generative Adversarial Networks (GAN) for Cyber Security: Challenges and Opportunities. In *Proceedings of the 2022 IEEE Symposium Series on Computational Intelligence*, Singapore (pp. 4-7).

Tayag, Y. (2015, July 13). *6 immoral studies that led to breakthroughs*. Inverse. https://www.inverse.com/article/4522-6-immoral-studies-that-led-to-breakthroughs

TeamLease EDTECH. (n.d.). *What is causing the skill gap in India?* Retrieved May 16, 2023, from https://www.teamleaseedtech.com/blog/what-is-causing-the-skill-gap-in-india.html

Teller, J. (2021). Urban density and Covid-19: Towards an adaptive approach. *Buildings & Cities*, 2(1), 150–165. Advance online publication. 10.5334/bc.89

Terzidis, K., Fabrocini, F., & Lee, H. (2023). Unintentional intentionality: Art and design in the age of artificial intelligence. *AI & Society*, 38(4), 1715–1724. 10.1007/s00146-021-01378-8

Tew, M. M., Hatah, E., Arif, F., Abdul Wahid, M. A., Makmor-Bakry, M., & Abdul Maulad, K. N. (2021). Geospatial analysis of distribution of community pharmacies and other health care facilities providing minor ailments services in Malaysia. *Journal of Pharmaceutical Policy and Practice*, 14(1), 24. Advance online publication. 10.1186/s40545-021-00308-933627199

Thabit, F., Alhomdy, S., Al-Ahdal, A. H., & Jagtap, S. (2021). A new lightweight cryptographic algorithm for enhancing data security in cloud computing. *Global Transitions Proceedings*, 2(1), 91–99. 10.1016/j.gltp.2021.01.013

Thiebes, S., Lins, S., & Sunyaev, A. (2021). Trustworthy artificial intelligence. *Electronic Markets*, 31(2), 447–464. 10.1007/s12525-020-00441-4

Thummula, E., Yadav, R. K., & David, A. (2019). A cost-effective technique to avoid communication and computation overhead in vehicle insurance database for online record monitoring. *International Journal of Mechanical and Production Engineering Research and Development*, 9(2), 711–722.

Townsend, D. M., & Hunt, R. A. (2019, January). Entrepreneurial action, creativity, & judgment in the age of artificial intelligence. *Journal of Business Venturing Insights*, 11, e00126. 10.1016/j.jbvi.2019.e00126

Trust, T., Whalen, J., & Mouza, C. (2023). Editorial: ChatGPT: Challenges, opportunities, and implications for teacher education. *Contemporary Issues in Technology & Teacher Education*, 23(1), 1–23.

Tsamados, A., Aggarwal, N., Cowls, J., Morley, J., Roberts, H., Taddeo, M., & Floridi, L. (2021). The ethics of algorithms: key problems and solutions. *Ethics, governance, and policies in artificial intelligence*, 97-123.

Tse, K. W., & Hung, K. (2022). Framework for user behavioural biometric identification using a multimodal scheme with keystroke trajectory feature and recurrent neural network on a mobile platform. *IET Biometrics*, 11(2), 157–170. 10.1049/bme2.12065

Tudor, M. (1939). *An experimental study of the effect of evaluative labeling of speech fluency* [Master of Arts, University of Iowa]. 10.17077/etd.9z9lxfgn

Tuli, S., Gill, S. S., Xu, M., Garraghan, P., Bahsoon, R., Dustdar, S., Sakellariou, R., Rana, O., Buyya, R., Casale, G., & Jennings, N. R. (2022). HUNTER: AI based holistic resource management for sustainable cloud computing. *Journal of Systems and Software*, 184, 111124. 10.1016/j.jss.2021.111124

Turkina, E. (2018). The importance of networking to entrepreneurship: Montreal's artificial intelligence cluster and its born-global firm Element AI. *Journal of Small Business and Entrepreneurship*, 30(1), 1–8. 10.1080/08276331.2017.1402154

Turnitin, L. L. C. (2024a). *AI writing detection | AI tools | Turnitin*. https://www.turnitin.com/solutions/topics/ai-writing/

Turnitin, L. L. C. (2024b). *iThenticate | Plagiarism checking for high-stakes writing | Turnitin*. https://www.turnitin.com/products/ithenticate/

Tuskegee University. (2024). *About the USPHS syphilis study*. https://www.tuskegee.edu/about-us/centers-of-excellence/bioethics-center/about-the-usphs-syphilis-study

Tyagi, A. K., & Abraham, A. (2022). Recurrent Neural Networks: Concepts and Applications. In *Recurrent Neural Networks: Concepts and Applications*. 10.1201/9781003307822

Übellacker, T. (2024). AcademiaOS: Automating Grounded Theory Development in Qualitative Research with Large Language Models (arXiv:2403.08844). arXiv. http://arxiv.org/abs/2403.08844

Uddin, M. Z., Hassan, M. M., Alsanad, A., & Savaglio, C. (2020). A body sensor data fusion and deep recurrent neural network-based behavior recognition approach for robust healthcare. *Information Fusion*, 55, 105–115. Advance online publication. 10.1016/j.inffus.2019.08.004

Ughulu, J., & Ph, D. (2022). The importance of AI in starting, automating, and scaling businesses for entrepreneurs Department of Entrepreneurship & Innovation Cornerstone Christian University CCU The role of Artificial intelligence (AI) in Starting, automating and scaling busin. *Open Journal of Business and Management*, 2(8), 1–7. 10.14293/S2199-1006.1.SOR-.PP5ZKWJ.v1

United States Holocaust Memorial Museum. (2006, August 30). *Nazi medical experiments*. https://encyclopedia.ushmm.org/content/en/article/nazi-medical-experiments

United States Holocaust Memorial Museum. (n.d.-a). *Antisemitism*. Retrieved May 2, 2024, from https://encyclopedia.ushmm.org/content/en/article/antisemitism

United States Holocaust Memorial Museum. (n.d.-b). *Holocaust encyclopedia*. Retrieved May 2, 2024, from https://encyclopedia.ushmm.org/en

Université de Montréal. (2017, November 3). *Montreal Declaration for a Responsible Development of Artificial Intelligence*. https://recherche.umontreal.ca/english/strategic-initiatives/montreal-declaration-for-a-responsible-ai/

University of Nevada. Las Vegas. (2012, June 12). *History of research ethics*. https://www.unlv.edu/research/ORI-HSR/history-ethics

UNSESCO. I. (2024). Challenging Systematic Prejudices: An Investigation into Bias Against Women and Girls in Large Language Models. https://unesdoc.unesco.org/ark:/48223/pf0000388971

Vaishya, R., Javaid, M., Khan, I. H., & Haleem, A. (2020). Artificial intelligence (AI) applications for COVID-19 pandemic. *Diabetes & Metabolic Syndrome*, 14(4), 337–339. 10.1016/j.dsx.2020.04.01232305024

van der Zant, T., Kouw, M., & Schomaker, L. (2013). *Generative artificial intelligence*. Springer Berlin Heidelberg.

Vaswani, A., Shazeer, N., Parmar, N., Uszkoreit, J., Jones, L., Gomez, A. N., Kaiser, L., & Polosukhin, I. (2017). Attention is all you need. http://arxiv.org/abs/1706.03762

Vaswani, A., Shazeer, N., Parmar, N., Uszkoreit, J., Jones, L., Gomez, A. N., & Polosukhin, I. (2017). Attention is All You Need. *Advances in Neural Information Processing Systems*, 30, 5998–6008.

Velmurugan, T. A., & Sankar, J. G. (2017). A comparative study on motivation theory with Maslow's hierarchy theory and two factor theory in organization. *Indo-Iranian Journal of Scientific Research*, 1(1), 204–208.

Veltman, C. (2024, August 30). AI is contentious among authors. So why are some feeding it their own writing? *NPR*. https://www.npr.org/2024/04/30/1246686825/authors-using-ai-artificial-intelligence-to-write

Vemuri, N., Thaneeru, N., & Tatikonda, V. M. (2024). Adaptive generative AI for dynamic cybersecurity threat detection in enterprises.

Vincent, J. (2016, March 30). *Microsoft's AI chatbot briefly came back online and spammed everyone*. The Verge. https://www.theverge.com/2016/3/30/11329858/tay-microsoft-ai-chatbot-back-spam

Virvilis, N., & Gritzalis, D. (2013). The big four-what we did wrong in advanced persistent threat detection? In *2013 International Conference on Availability, Reliability and Security* (pp. 248-254). IEEE. 10.1109/ARES.2013.32

Viviani, M., & Pasi, G. (2017). Credibility in social media: opinions, news, and health information—a survey. In *Wiley Interdisciplinary Reviews: Data Mining and Knowledge Discovery* (Vol. 7, Issue 5). 10.1002/widm.1209

Volkmar, G., Fischer, P. M., & Reinecke, S. (2022). Artificial Intelligence and Machine Learning: Exploring drivers, barriers, and future developments in marketing management. *Journal of Business Research*, 149, 599–614. 10.1016/j.jbusres.2022.04.007

Von Solms, R., & Van Niekerk, J. (2013). From information security to cyber security. *Computers & Security*, 38, 97–102. 10.1016/j.cose.2013.04.004

Vrabec, J., Byrtusova, A., & Ronai, M. (2020). Living off the land: Modern trend in malware obfuscation. In 2020 IEEE 15th International Conference on Malicious and Unwanted Software (MALWARE) (pp. 59-68). IEEE.

Vyas, K. (2020, December 30). *11+ most controversial psychological experiments in history*. Interesting Engineering. https://interestingengineering.com/lists/11-most-controversial-psychological-experiments-in-history

Vyas, P. G., & Priya, S. (2023). Social Media and Gen Y at Work: The Uses and Gratifications of Technology. In *5G, Artificial Intelligence, and Next Generation Internet of Things: Digital Innovation for Green and Sustainable Economies* (pp. 123-142). IGI Global.

Wadood, A. (2024). Generative AI From Theory to Model: Unleashing the Creative Power of Artificial Intelligence. In *Deep Learning, Reinforcement Learning, and the Rise of Intelligent Systems* (pp. 77-105). IGI Global.

Wagstaff, A., & Neelsen, S. (2020). A comprehensive assessment of universal health coverage in 111 countries: A retrospective observational study. *The Lancet. Global Health*, 8(1), e39–e49. Advance online publication. 10.1016/S2214-109X(19)30463-231837954

Wang, S., Huang, X., Liu, P., Zhang, M., Biljecki, F., Hu, T., Fu, X., Liu, L., Liu, X., Wang, R., Huang, Y., Yan, J., Jiang, J., Chukwu, M., Reza Naghedi, S., Hemmati, M., Shao, Y., Jia, N., Xiao, Z., . . . Bao, S. (2024). Mapping the landscape and roadmap of geospatial artificial intelligence (GeoAI) in quantitative human geography: An extensive systematic review. In *International Journal of Applied Earth Observation and Geoinformation* (Vol. 128). 10.1016/j.jag.2024.103734

Wang, X., Wei, J., Schuurmans, D., Le, Q., Ed H. Chi. E.H., Narang, S., Chowdhery, A., & Zhou, D., (2023). Self-Consistency Improves Chain of Thought Reasoning In Language Models. *ICLR 2023*

Wang, M. (2024). Generative AI: A New Challenge for Cybersecurity. *Journal of Computer Science and Technology Studies*, 6(2), 13–18. 10.32996/jcsts.2024.6.2.3

Wang, S., Ding, S., & Xiong, L. (2020). A new system for surveillance and digital contact tracing for COVID-19: Spatiotemporal reporting over network and GPS. *JMIR mHealth and uHealth*, 8(6), e19457. Advance online publication. 10.2196/1945732499212

Wang, Y., Chen, L., Wu, G., Yu, K., & Lu, T. (2023). Efficient and secure content-based image retrieval with deep neural networks in the mobile cloud computing. *Computers & Security*, 128, 103163. 10.1016/j.cose.2023.103163

Wang, Y., Willis, E., Yeruva, V. K., Ho, D., & Lee, Y. (2023). A case study of using natural language processing to extract consumer insights from tweets in American cities for public health crises. *BMC Public Health*, 23(1), 935. Advance online publication. 10.1186/s12889-023-15882-737226165

Wang, Z., Zhang, J., Du, H., Zhang, R., Niyato, D., Ai, B., & Letaief, K. B. (2024). Generative AI agent for next-generation MIMO design: Fundamentals, challenges, and vision. http://arxiv.org/abs/2404.08878

Watson, J. B. (1913). Psychology as the behaviorist views it. *Psychological Review*, 20(2), 158–177. 10.1037/h0074428

Watson, J. B. (1928). *Psychological care of infant and child*. Norton.

Watson, J. B., & Rayner, R. (1920). Conditioned emotional reactions. *Journal of Experimental Psychology*, 3(1), 1–14. 10.1037/h0069608

Watts, M. J., Kotsila, P., Mortyn, P. G., Sarto i Monteys, V., & Urzi Brancati, C. (2020). Influence of socio-economic, demographic and climate factors on the regional distribution of dengue in the United States and Mexico. *International Journal of Health Geographics*, 19(1), 44. Advance online publication. 10.1186/s12942-020-00241-133138827

Weber, A. (1949). The philosophy of Immanuel Kant. *History of Philosophy*.

Weber, A. M., Gupta, R., Abdalla, S., Cislaghi, B., Meausoone, V., & Darmstadt, G. L. (2021). Gender-related data missingness, imbalance and bias in global health surveys. *BMJ Global Health*, 6(11), e007405. Advance online publication. 10.1136/bmjgh-2021-00740534836912

Weber, M. (1962). *Basic concepts in sociology*. Citadel Press.

Wessel, M., Adam, M., Benlian, A., & Majchrzak, A. (2024). Journal of Management Information Systems Generative AI and its Transformative Value for Digital Platforms Guest Editors Motivation. *Journal of Management Information Systems*, 1–6.

WHO. (2021). Ethics and governance of artificial intelligence for health: WHO guidance Executive summary. https://iris.who.int/bitstream/handle/10665/350567/9789240037403-eng.pdf

Wolford, B. (2018, November 7). *What is GDPR, the EU's new data protection law?* GDPR.Eu. https://gdpr.eu/what-is-gdpr/

Wu, Y., He, K., & Xu, J. (2019). The impact of artificial intelligence on scientific research. *AI Perspectives*, 1(1), 1–14.

Wu, Y., Wang, X., Susilo, W., Yang, G., Jiang, Z. L., Yiu, S. M., & Wang, H. (2022). Generic server-aided secure multi-party computation in cloud computing. *Computer Standards & Interfaces*, 79, 103552. 10.1016/j.csi.2021.103552

Xue, M., Xiu, G., Saravanan, V., & Montenegro-Marin, C. E. (2021). Cloud computing with AI for banking and e-commerce applications. *The Electronic Library*, 39(4), 539–552.

Xu, H., Li, Y., Balogun, O., Wu, S., Wang, Y., & Cai, Z. (2024). Security Risks Concerns of Generative AI in the IoT. *IEEE Internet of Things Magazine*, 7(3), 62–67. 10.1109/IOTM.001.2400004

Xu, R., Sun, Y., Ren, M., Guo, S., Pan, R., Lin, H., Sun, L., & Han, X. (2024). AI for social science and social science of AI: A survey. *Information Processing & Management*, 61(3), 103665. 10.1016/j.ipm.2024.103665

Yao, S., Zhao, J., Yu, D., Du, N., Shafran, I., Narasimhan, K., & Yuan Cao, Y., (2023). React: Synergizing Reasoning and Acting in Language Models. *ICLR 2023*.

Yigit, Y., Buchanan, W. J., Tehrani, M. G., & Maglaras, L. (2024). Review of Generative AI Methods in Cybersecurity. arXiv preprint arXiv:2403.08701.

Yin, L., Alba, D., & Nicoletti, L. (2024, March 7). OpenAI's GPT Is a recruiter's dream tool. Tests show there's racial bias. *Bloomberg.Com*. https://www.bloomberg.com/graphics/2024-openai-gpt-hiring-racial-discrimination/

Yi, X., Walia, E., & Babyn, P. (2019). Generative adversarial network in medical imaging: A review. *Medical Image Analysis*, 58, 101552. 10.1016/j.media.2019.10155231521965

Yorks, L., & Jester, M. Y. (2024). Applying generative AI ethically in HRD practice. *Human Resource Development International*, 27(3), 1–18. 10.1080/13678868.2024.2337963

Yudono, A., Afrianto, F., & Hariyanto, A. D. (2023). The Evaluation of Geographical Health Facilities Structure in Makassar City, Indonesia. *International Journal of Environmental Research and Public Health*, 20(6), 5210. Advance online publication. 10.3390/ijerph2006521036982119

Yu, P., Mulli, J., Syed, Z. A. S., & Umme, L. (Eds.). (2023). *Facilitating Global Collaboration and Knowledge Sharing in Higher Education with Generative AI*. IGI Global.

Yuvaraj, N., Raja, R. A., Karthikeyan, T., & Kousik, N. V. (2020). Improved privacy preservation framework for cloud-based internet of things. In *Internet of things* (pp. 165–174). CRC Press. 10.1201/9781003032441-11

Zellers, R., Holtzman, A., Bisk, Y., Farhadi, A., & Choi, Y. (2019). HellaSwag: Can a Machine Really Finish Your Sentence

Zhang, B., Anderljung, M., Kahn, L., Dreksler, N., Horowitz, M. C., & Dafoe, A. (2021). Ethics and governance of artificial intelligence: Evidence from a survey of machine learning researchers. *Journal of Artificial Intelligence Research*, 71, 591–666. 10.1613/jair.1.12895

Zhang, J., & Zhang, Z. M. (2023). Ethics and governance of trustworthy medical artificial intelligence. *BMC Medical Informatics and Decision Making*, 23(1), 7. 10.1186/s12911-023-02103-936639799

Zhang, Z., Han, Z., & Deng, H. (2021). AI in Business: Trends and Opportunities. *International Journal of Business Intelligence Research*, 12(2), 30–45.

Zhao, B. (2023). Analysis on the Negative Impact of AI Development on Employment and Its Countermeasures. *SHS Web of Conferences, 154*, 03022. 10.1051/shsconf/202315403022

Zhao, Y., Yin, J., Wei, S., & Tang, Y. (2019). Generating automated generation of phishing email for cognitive security awareness training. In 2019 International Conference on Cyber-Enabled Distributed Computing and Knowledge Discovery (CyberC) (pp. 233-238). IEEE.

Zhao, M., An, B., Gao, W., Zhang, T., Xia, P., Du, X., & Yu, N. (2021). Adversarial attacks and defenses for deep learning-based malware detection. *IEEE Transactions on Information Forensics and Security*, 17, 1063–1077.

Zhao, M., An, B., Shi, Y., Gui, X., & Yu, N. (2022). Adversarial machine learning for cybersecurity: Attacks, defenses, and open issues. *IEEE Transactions on Network Science and Engineering*, 9(5), 3501–3522.

Zhao, Y., Kozey, V., & Miao, R. (2019). Automated generation of phishing emails for security awareness training. In *2019 IEEE International Conference on Artificial Intelligence and Virtual Reality (AIVR)* (pp. 155-159). IEEE.

Zharovskikh, A. (2023, September 12). *ChatGPT large language model explained.* InData Labs. https://indatalabs.com/blog/chatgpt-large-language-model

Zhu, R., Guo, D., Qi, D., Chu, Z., Yu, X., & Li, S. (2024). A Survey of Trustworthy Representation Learning Across Domains. *ACM Transactions on Knowledge Discovery from Data*, 3657301(7), 1–53. Advance online publication. 10.1145/3657301

Zimbardo, P. G. (1973). On the ethics of intervention in human psychological research: With special reference to the Stanford prison experiment. *Cognition*, 2(2), 243–256. 10.1016/0010-0277(72)90014-511662069

Zohny, H., McMillan, J., & King, M. (2023). Ethics of generative AI. *Journal of Medical Ethics*, 49(2), 79–80. 10.1136/jme-2023-10890936693706

Zong, B., Song, Q., Min, M. R., Cheng, W., Lumezanu, C., Cho, D., & Chen, H. (2018). Deep autoencoding gaussian mixture model for unsupervised anomaly detection. In *International Conference on Learning Representations (ICLR)*.

Zu, L., Qi, W., Li, H., Men, X., Lu, Z., Ye, J., & Zhang, L. (2024). UP-SDCG: A Method of Sensitive Data Classification for Collaborative Edge Computing in Financial Cloud Environment. *Future Internet*, 16(3), 102. 10.3390/fi16030102

Zunic, A., Corcoran, P., & Spasic, I. (2020). Sentiment analysis in health and well-being: Systematic review. In *JMIR Medical Informatics* (Vol. 8, Issue 1). 10.2196/16023

About the Contributors

Jeganathan Gomathi Sankar, a distinguished scholar in the field of marketing, currently serves as a faculty member at the BSSS Institute of Advanced Studies. He holds a Ph.D. from Pondicherry University, where his research concentrated on information diffusion, Information and Communication Technology (ICT), marketing technology, artificial intelligence, and data science. His scholarly contributions have been disseminated through publications in esteemed journals indexed in Scopus and the Australian Business Deans Council (ABDC). Sankar's academic approach is characterized by the integration of theoretical insights with practical applications, enabling students to acquire a comprehensive understanding of contemporary marketing trends. Proficient in analytical tools such as SPSS, AMOS, STATA, PowerBI, and Python, Sankar enhances the rigor of his research endeavors. His commitment to academic excellence is evident in his efforts to cultivate an environment that promotes critical thinking and intellectual engagement among students. Renowned for his dynamic teaching style, Sankar continues to mentor future marketing professionals at the BSSS Institute of Advanced Studies. His dedication to advancing knowledge in marketing and technology is underscored by his doctoral research and a robust record of academic and pedagogical achievements.

* * *

Munir Ahmad is a seasoned professional in the realm of Spatial Data Infrastructure (SDI), Geo-Information Productions, Information Systems, and Information Governance, boasting over 25 years of dedicated experience in the field. With a PhD in Computer Science, Dr. Ahmad's expertise spans Spatial Data Production, Management, Processing, Analysis, Visualization, and Quality Control. Throughout his career, Dr. Ahmad has been deeply involved in the development and deployment of SDI systems specially in the context of Pakistan, leveraging his proficiency in Spatial Database Design, Web, Mobile & Desktop GIS, and Geo Web Services Architecture. His contributions to Volunteered Geographic Information (VGI) and Open Source Geoportal & Metadata Portal have significantly enriched the geospatial community. As a trainer and researcher, Dr. Ahmad has authored over 50 publications, advancing the industry's knowledge base and fostering innovation in Geo-Tech, Data Governance, and Information Infrastructure, and Emerging Technologies. His commitment to Research and Development (R&D) is evident in his role as a dedicated educator and mentor in the field.

Badr Bentalha teaches Supply Chain and Operations Management at National School Of Business and Management – Fez, Sidi Mohamed Ben Abdellah University – Morocco. Dr. Bentalha investigates the structural dynamics and control of complex networks, applying his findings to supply chain management, Industry 4.0, risk analysis, and digital supply chains. His work emphasizes the intersection of supply chain management, operations research, industrial engineering, and digital technology. As a professor, he teaches undergraduate, graduate, and, doctoral courses in operations management, supply chain management, logistics, management information systems, and strategic management. Through guest lectures, webinars, and scholarly presentations, he engages students and fosters an active learning environment. Professor Bentalha specializes in supply chain and operations management, operations research, and service management. He is passionate about integrating knowledge across disciplines to solve real-world problems. He has delivered numerous invited plenary talks, keynotes, and panel discussions at conferences and global webinars.

B. Anthony Brown is a Business Strategy and Maritime Consultant specializing in corporate restructuring and change management. His work emphasizes ethical and sustainable organizational transformation, diversity, and inclusion. He earned his Ph.D. in Management With an Emphasis on Leadership and Organizational Change from Walden University in 2020. He has over 30 years in the Maritime Industry, where he served as Captain on passenger and cargo ships, as well as Marine Superintendent, Chief Operations Officer, and Maritime Consultant for land-based maritime corporations.

Ganeshkumar C. is an Associate Professor at the Indian Institute of Foreign Trade IIFT in the Department of Decision Science & Operation Management. He received his PhD and MBA from Pondicherry Central University and cleared UGC-NET in Management in 2010. He has two years of postdoctoral research experience at the IIMB and served as a faculty member at VIT University, Vellore. He has published 60 articles in International Journals listed in ABDC and ABS and indexed in Scopus and Web of Science in the area of Operations and Supply Chain Analytics.

Veena Christy completed her graduation in Commerce from the renowned Madras Christian College, affiliated to University of Madras. Her urge for higher studies led her to complete her MBA with laurels. She was awarded the University rank in her PG program which was also affiliated to University of Madras. Lured by passion for research, she completed her doctoral studies in organisational behaviour and has many Scopus-indexed publications to her credit. With ten years of teaching experience in different institutions of repute and six years of research expertise, she is also the recipient of Innovative Researcher and Dedicated Academician Award conferred by The Innovative Scientific Research Professional Institute, Chennai. She is an Associate member of Madras Management Association (MMA) (Mem No: AM863) and Affiliate member of Association of Behavior Analysis International (Mem No: 102469). Presently, She is serving as Assistant Professor in SRM University, KTR Campus, Chennai.

Keri L. Heitner is a research psychologist, consultant, and contributing faculty in the PhD in Management Program at Walden University. Her work involves applied research, evaluation, and program development about diversity and inclusion; career advancement and re-entry; service delivery research and development in health, mental health, and the government and nonprofit sectors; and entrepreneurship. She is also a writer, editor, methodologist, and curriculum developer."

Mohammad Kashif is a distinguished academician and researcher in the area of finance, economics and international business at the Graphic Era Deemed to be University, Dehradun, India. He has several publications indexed in WoS, Scopus and ABDC. He authored a text book titled Financial Management for undergraduate students. He is the editor in upcoming edited books under Emerald Publishers and Bentham Science Publishers. He is guiding PhD scholars in his area of expertise. Besides, he is a member of several professional bodies at the university level. He has been awarded many academic and research awards by reputed organizations.

Kritika is a post graduate (Master of Technology(M.Tech)) in computer science and engineering and holds the position of an independent researcher, author and peer reviewer of reputed journals indexed in SCOPUS, Web of Science, etc. She is the recipient of Young Engineer Award 2024, Young Researcher Award 2023, Gold Medallist and Silver Medallist in International Olympiad of Mathematics and holds accolades from Government of India for obtaining distinction during high school and senior school. The author is serving as Lifetime Member of International Association of Engineers(IAENG), Member of Women In Cybersecurity(WiCys) India Affiliate and professional member of InSc Institute of Scholars. She has published 2 books, 10+ chapters and 15+ research papers in the interdisciplinary field of cybersecurity. The author has obtained certifications in cyber security and is a top scorer in examinations like NTSE(India). The area of research includes cyber security, digital forensics, neuroscience, and governance.

Gnanadasan M. L., an accomplished academician and researcher, holds a Ph.D. in Management from the University of Madras, supplemented by a UGC-NET qualification in Management. With over two decades of experience in business management, he has held diverse roles including Program Coordinator-MBA at the Directorate of Online Education, SRMIST, where he spearheads content development and oversees student affairs. Previously, as Professor & Head at DMI College of Engineering, he led initiatives in entrepreneurship development and organized international virtual panel discussions on online education. Dr. Gnanadasan's expertise spans various management subjects, from Banking and Insurance to Human Resource Management. His dedication to scholarly pursuits is evidenced by numerous publications in esteemed journals and presentations at national and international conferences. Recognized for his contributions, he has received accolades such as the Global Excellence Award for Achievements in Higher Education Leadership. Committed to fostering knowledge and innovation, Dr. Gnanadasan continues to make significant strides in academia and research.

Geetika Madaan is working as an Assistant Professor at the research center department of Marwadi University, Gujrat, India.

Vijaya Kittu Manda has nearly 13+ years of experience in capital markets, financial planning, and investing. He is a Researcher at PBMEIT. He is an Advocate, a technocrat, an academician, a book writer, and a stock market enthusiast. He has 11 University Postgraduate Degrees and is a Ph.D. in Management / Finance with focus on Mutual Funds and their Market Competition. His thesis won the prestigious NSE-IEA Best Thesis Award in 2023. He is currently pursuing his second Ph.D. in Computer Science with focus on Blockchain. He contributed over 750 articles to various magazines. He is the Chief Editor for a Management Book Series, is a Peer Review, is a Certified Peer Review Supervisor, is a Session Chair and an Advisor for various academic and industrial conferences, writes Research Papers and Case Studies, sits on Editorial Boards of various publishers, and is a guest speaker on various research, management and computer science topics for colleges and universities.

Kashif Mehmood Khan earned his B.S. degree in Computer Science from Hamdard University, Karachi, in 2016, and completed his M.S. in Computer Science from Shaheed Zulfikar Ali Bhutto Institute of Science and Technology, Karachi, where he achieved the Chancellor's Honor Roll for highest CGPA. His research interests encompass Computer Vision, Digital Image Processing, Artificial Intelligence, Data Mining, Natural Language Processing, Deep Learning, Machine Learning, and Expert Systems, focusing on digital twins of computer vision and AI in medical and healthcare systems. Kashif specializes in face detection for security and surveillance systems, and crowd counting and density estimation in real-time scenarios such as Hajj and pilgrimages. His undergraduate work in Image Processing, specifically on URDU OCR, stands as a significant contribution to Urdu literature, demonstrating strong technical skills and a solid understanding of these domains. Kashif is motivated by a mission to apply his skills and expertise towards driving digital transformation and growth in society with Next Generation AI.

Amrita Baid More is an enthusiastic educationalist with over a decade of experience in academia. She specializes in management and communication, holding a Ph.D. in Management with a focus on marketing strategies of equity firms in India. In addition, she has an MBA in Marketing and Finance and a Master's degree in English Literature. Throughout her career, Dr. More has coordinated key academic events, and has also contributed to initiatives like the SANKALP project under the Ministry of Skill Development & Entrepreneurship at IIM Indore. Her research interests include consumer communication and artificial intelligence, with a particular focus on their applications in improving customer service.Beyond her research and teaching, she is actively involved in mentoring students and reviewing academic work for various journals and conferences.Dr. More is passionate about fostering academic excellence and developing management practices that benefit both business and society.

Manas Kumar Yogi is currently working as Assistant Professor in Computer Science and Engineering Department in Pragati Engineering College (Autonomous), Surampalem. He has teaching experience of over 14 years and has published more than 230 Papers in various reputed journals, conferences. In addition, he has published 5 Books, 8 Book chapters with reputed publishers like CRC Press, Wiley, Bentham and IGI Global Inc. He has also published 5 Patents to his credit. His research interest is cyber security, Soft computing, Cyber Physical systems, Machine Learning.

Rida Zahid is a super skilled and hardworking doctor who got her MBBS degree from Capital Medical University in Beijing, China. She boosted her skills with a one-year clinical internship at Beijing Chaoyang Hospital, which is one of the best hospitals around. There, she got loads of practical experience, which let her use what she learned in her books in real life. While studying at Capital Medical University, Rida learned a ton about medical stuff. The school had cool facilities and taught her all about different areas of medicine. She did awesome in her classes because she's focused on being a great doctor. Her internship at Beijing Chaoyang Hospital was intense. She worked with some of the best doctors, saw complicated medical treatments, and helped take care of lots of different patients. This didn't just make her better at medical stuff; it also made her more confident and ready to tackle tough medical problems. Rida loves learning new things in medicine and always tries to stay up to date by going to workshops, seminars, and conferences. She wants to use the newest medical info to help her patients as best as she can. Besides her job, Rida is all about helping people stay healthy and improving healthcare for everyone, especially those who don't get much medical help. She works on health projects, helps out at clinics, and teaches people about staying healthy. She also fights for better healthcare laws to make things better for everyone. Rida Zahid is all about caring, helping, and being excellent in her job as a doctor. She works super hard for her patients, keeps learning new things, and helps her community be healthier. She plans to keep on making a big difference in medicine, helping both people and whole communities get better.

Index

A

O

P

Q

R

S

T

U